MW01640254

Graphis Mission Statement: *Graphis* is committed to presenting exceptional work in international Design, Advertising, Illustration and Photography. Since 1944, we have presented individuals and companies in the visual communications industry who have consistently demonstrated excellence and determination in overcoming economic, cultural and creative hurdles to produce true brilliance.

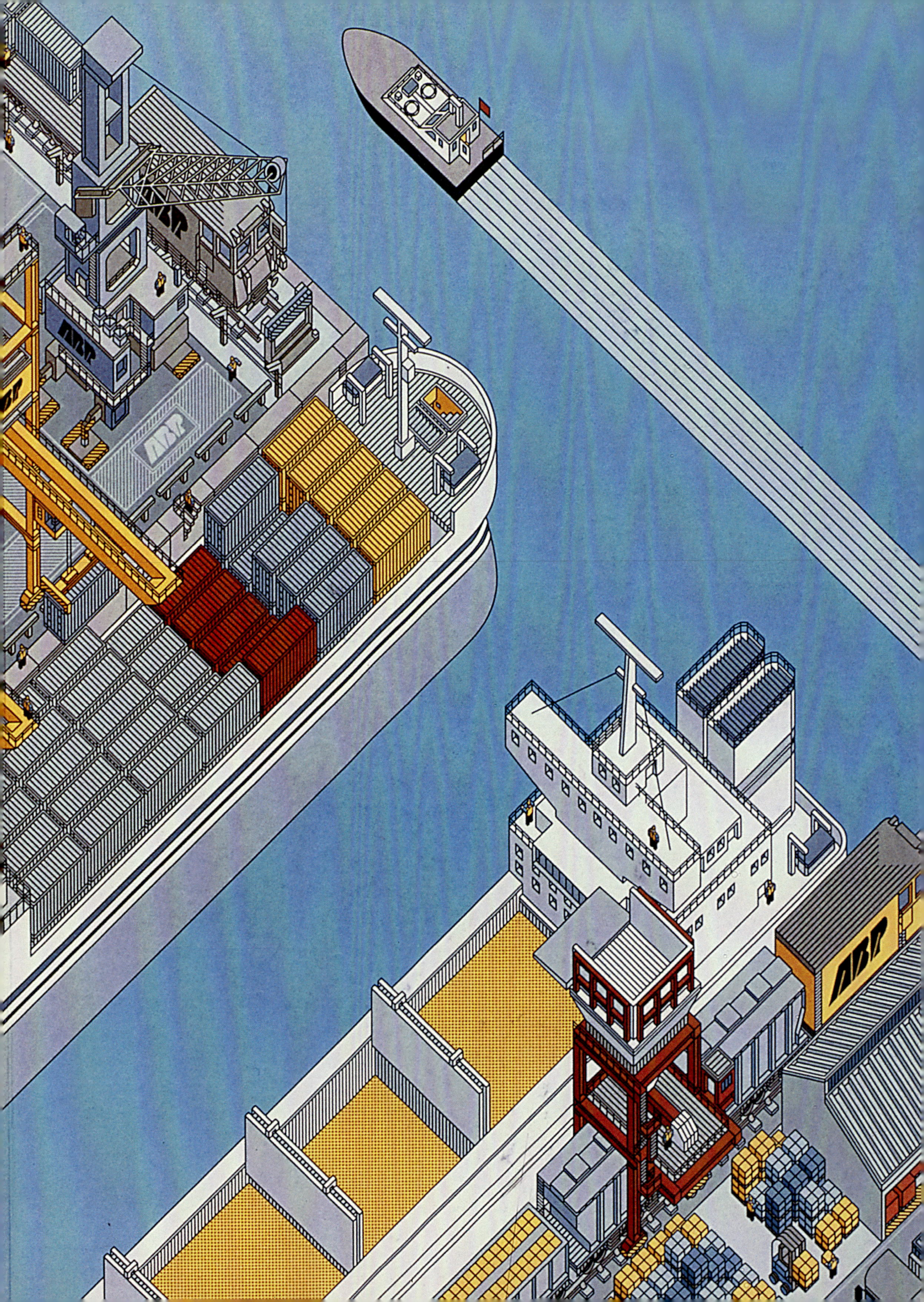
ABP
ABP
ABP
ABP
ABP

AnnualReports2006

CEO & Creative Director: B. Martin Pedersen

Editor: Anna Carnick
Designers: Doug Oliver and Abby Bennett, Douglas Oliver Design Office
Production: Jennah Synnestvedt, Danielle Baker

Published by Graphis Inc.

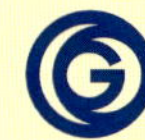

(opposite page) Illustrated by Johnny Kelly (following page) Photography and Artwork by Marin Topic, Domagoj Kunic, Davor Bruketa, Nikola Zinic

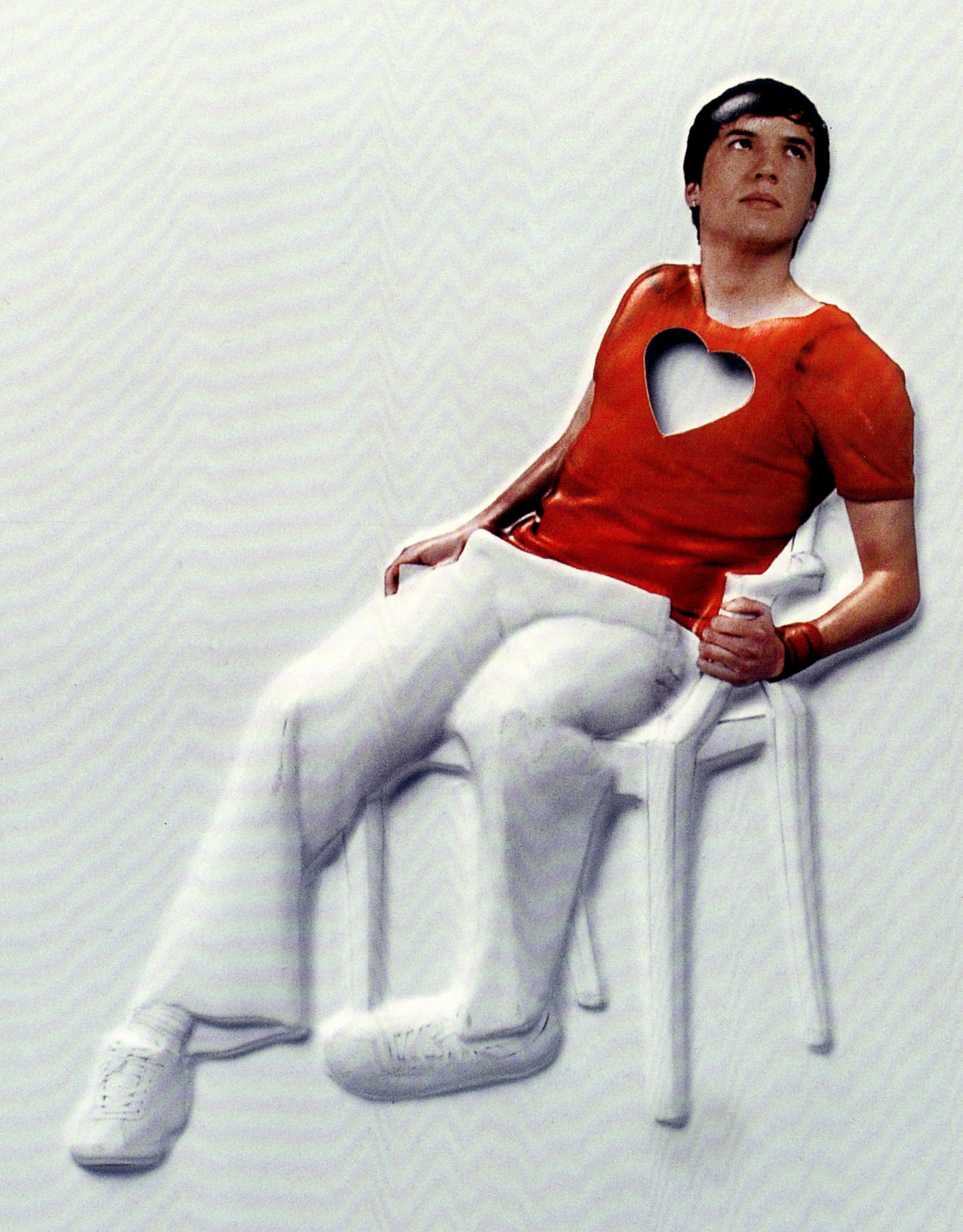

ContentsInhaltSommaire

Remarks: We extend our heartfelt thanks to contributors throughout the world who have made it possible to publish a wide and international spectrum of the best work in this field. Entry instructions for all Graphis Books may be requested from: Graphis Inc., 307 Fifth Avenue, Tenth Floor, New York, New York 10016, or visit our Web site at www.graphis.com.

Anmerkungen: Unser Dank gilt den Einsendern aus aller Welt, die es uns ermöglicht haben, ein breites, internationales. Spektrum der besten Arbeiten zu veröffentlichen. Teilnahmebedingungen für die Graphis-Bücher sind erhältlich bei: Graphis Inc., 307 Fifth Avenue, Tenth Floor, New York, New York 10016. Besuchen Sie uns im World Wide Web, www.graphis.com.

Remerciements: Nous remercions les participants du monde entier qui ont rendu possible la publication de cet ouvrage offrant un panorama complet des meilleurs travaux. Les modalités d'inscription peuvent être obtenues auprès de: Graphis Inc., 307 Fifth Avenue, Tenth Floor, New York, New York 10016. Rendez-nous visite sur notre site web: www.graphis.com.

ISBN: 1-932026-24-X Printed in Korea.

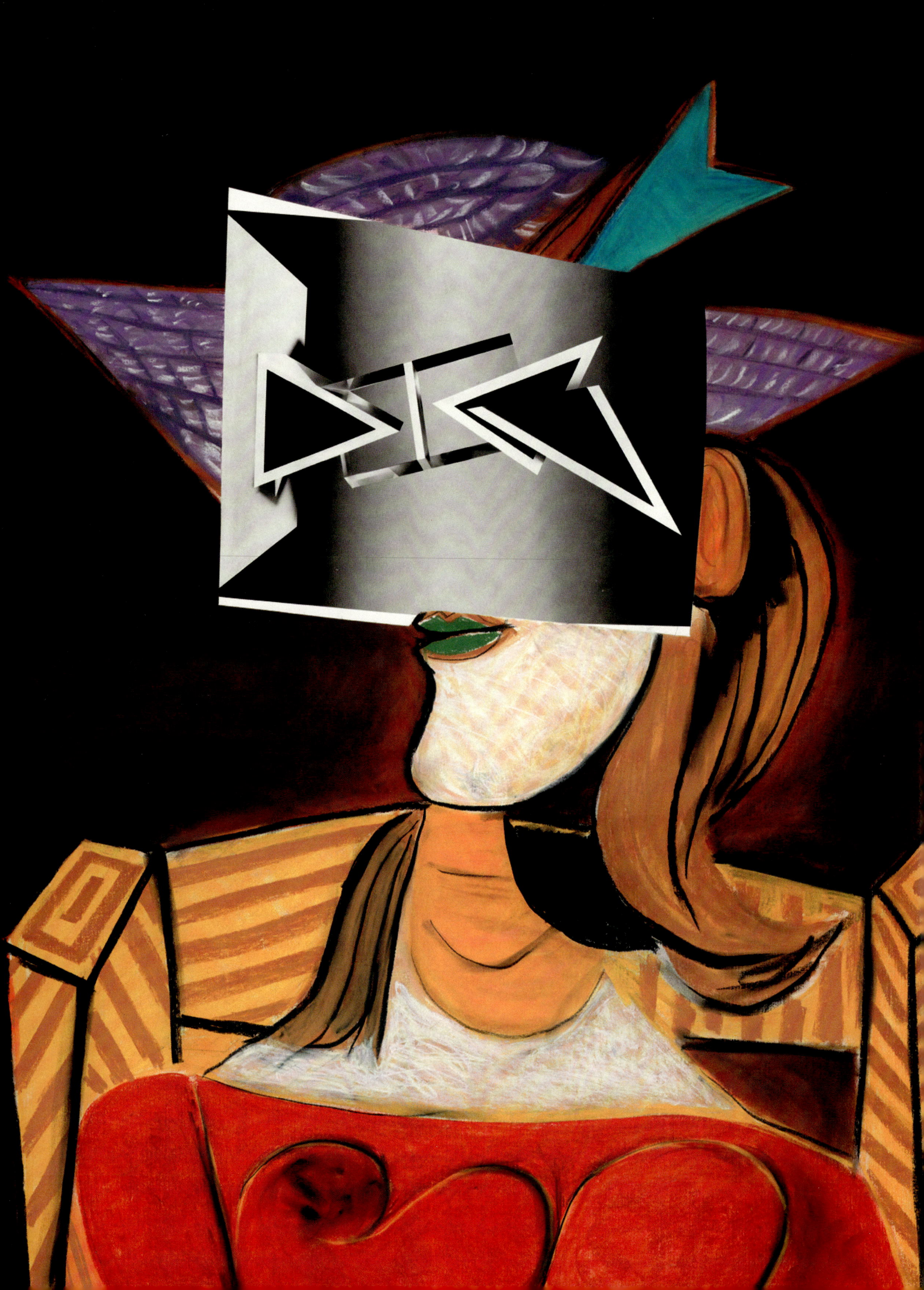

<ART: Jayme Odgers
Woman In Red Dress
1984

Trust in what you see. Trust more in what you feel.

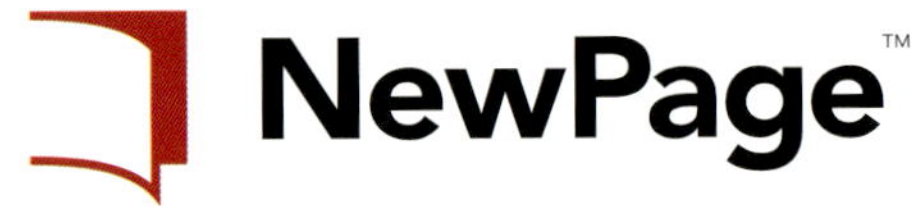
NewPage™

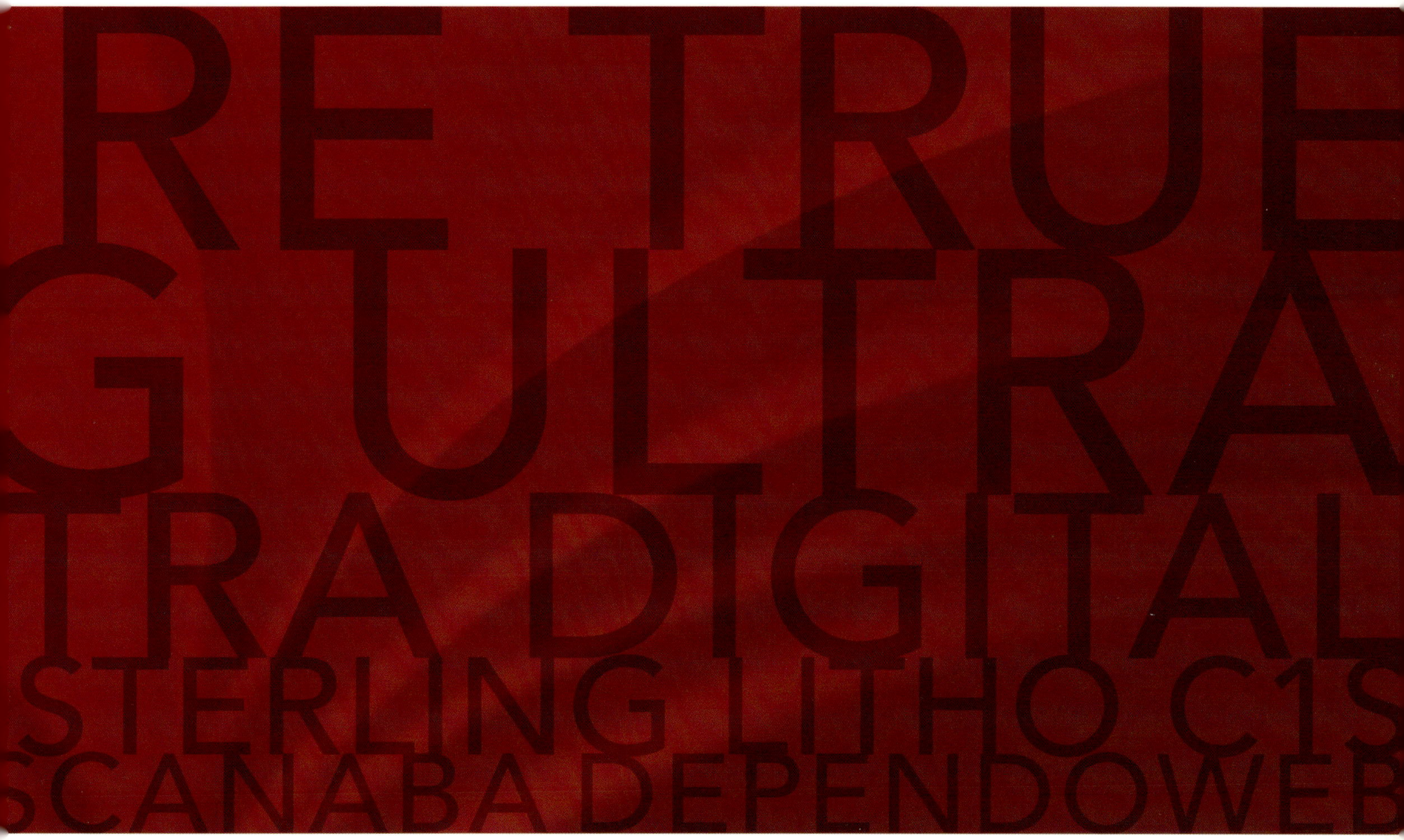

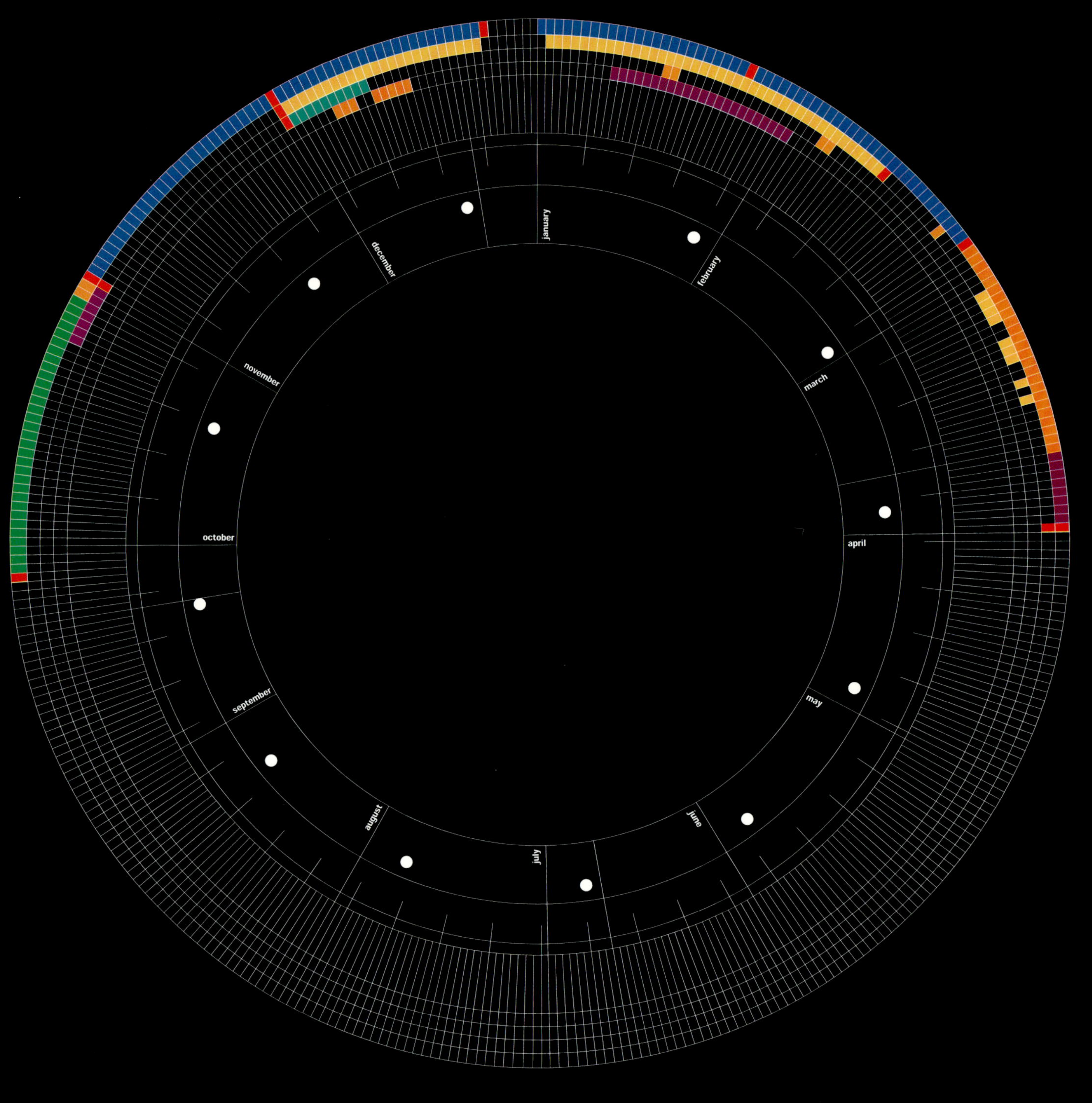

Annual Report Season: Circular Project Calendar by The Douglas Oliver Design Office

with my same name. I once needed an interpreter to make color corrections and have attended press checks in all four US time zones. I recently sat down with a US map and counted 70 US airports that I've flown either into or out of. It has been almost surreal and, almost always, it has been fun.

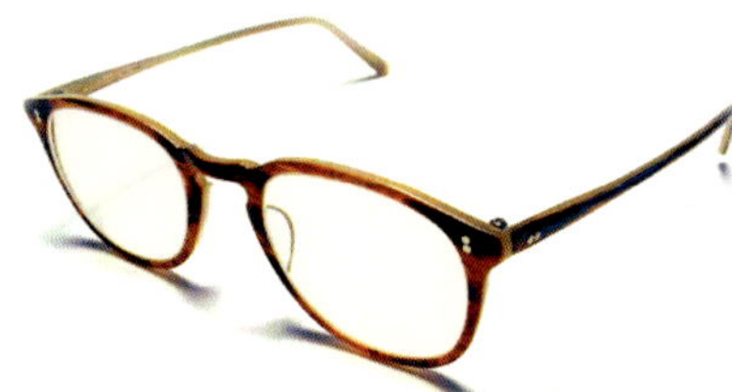

Today, we ask: Is Annual Reporting in decline? It depends on your point of view. Certainly, the events at the beginning of this decade have brought some dramatic changes. Many of the economic or business shocks initially were discouraging, but I think we have adapted. The American economy is improving and some new uses for the Annual Report have restored my optimism. The judging of this Graphis 2006 gave me a close look at the state of the industry and it was boost for my morale. Companies with improving numbers were shedding their paranoia and looking to presenting their performances with targeted messaging or points of view. The international books were particularly bold or even lavish. Chief executives on any continent have recognized that the Annual Report is still an important opportunity to influence and persuade new and old target audiences and project a well-crafted message beyond the bounds of a desktop printer. As long as that view prevails, companies will still seek out the best designers to deliver their message. These designers will be those who can see the client company as it wishes (and needs) to be seen. My view now is that our best work as Annual Report designers is still ahead of us. Other points of view will influence our work.

The View from the Top is usually that of the chairman or the chief executive officer, the person that really runs the company, the decisionmaker. These decision-makers have historically viewed the Annual Report as a personal document. The book is a record of their stewardship and vision for the future. Most will take a very keen interest in the messaging and the self presentation of the company to key audiences. This is not to say we design 'vanity' pieces to massage an ego but rather build a book that speaks for the CEO in his marketplace and to his friends.

The collective image of CEOs has taken some negative hits in the last decade, but in my experience, there are few bad ones. Despite the cultural tendency to stereotype them, over my 30 years, I've found them all different. Robert Miles Runyan, an early pioneer of Annual Report design and a vivid part of my early training, used to insist, "We have to have access to the decision-maker..." This access has always been a fundamental key to the designer's chance for success.

We have a series of questions ready for a first meeting with a new CEO. Some are obvious but some are not because they are intended to spark conversation about the company and the challenges he views as important. While his responses are important, the manner in which he speaks, the expression on his face while he speaks, the words he chooses as he describes his company and even the phrases he uses to describe the competition are the designer's best view into the company. This dialogue opens and closes doors in the design process and offers the deft designer his best chance to returnwith a presentation that is both fresh and familiar but also appropriate to the CEO's needs.

The CEO's personality is often a strength of the company or in fact, the personality of the company. His character and vision are often reflected in the manner in which the company conducts business, and directly affect short and long-term potential for growth. The companies that have strong leadership need to communicate this as a strength, because it will not read as a line item in the financial numbers. It is important to allow that personality to be seen in the design of the book and reseen consistently over a series of books, as long as it remains to be true. The Annual Reports that are intentionally detached or sterile spark little interest and represent, to the discerning eye, a missed opportunity.

The View from the Bottom (line) is not necessarily a look at the company's performance, but rather the effect it has on a designer's success. Recent years have seen a trend toward corporate downsizing, reduced manpower and monies available to the project. Large companies with huge resources have lost the resolve to mount the effort necessary to project their message or leadership in their marketplace.

This has led to corporate downsizing and has meant staff reductions in corporate communications departments. Where there was once an office of eight or 10 busy people in CC, today there are three to four beleaguered people with little time to spend away from their PC's. They are younger, less experienced, working for less, and without a clear understanding of creating image or influencing target audience decisionmaking. All of this accelerated after 2001, after the dot.com collapse, the bursting of the stock market bubble, the Enron debacle that lingers today and, of course, 9/11. After 2001, the CEO was being advised to "not say anything you don't have to..." and a fear factor interjected itself into the annual report process. Enron was particularly debilitating to our industry because the participation of the accounting firm called into question the confidence in any number in any annual report. This confidence is the foundation for our industry. Annual reporting took a giant step backwards. Hence, the 10K wrap, the ultimate "missed opportunity."

And finally, "All this information is available on the Internet..." What it was once our collective curse can now be our salvation. Recent developments concerning the mailing requirements for the printed financial statements will, in fact, help us. The full financials are available online and the printed 10K will be made available only upon request. We can be relieved of the responsibility of conveying all the numbers and free to channel the resources to craft the summary message carefully targeted to a company's target audiences. The traditional "front" of the book will continue to flourish. The "back" will return to circa-1960 summary financials. A broader annual can now be tailored not only to investors but also to customers, venture partners, the media, government agencies, legislators, special interest groups, and employees.

The View from Here is mine, but I was impressed by a talk Marty Neumaier gave at the 1998 Mead Annual Report Conference in New York. He spoke of the the four Ps of printed Annual Reports: Portable, Personal, Precise and Permanent.

Portable– The annual (usually) fits in a briefcase and can be sent ahead or left behind. An Annual Report is the corporate business card and often supplies the first impression to new audiences behind doors closed to a company's representatives. It must speak well for the CEO in his absence and perhaps open new doors for his company.

Personal– How many times have you heard, "Can I keep this?" Of course they can... because then it is working for the company. The reader wants to take it away so he can look it over in his own space, in his own time, and perhaps, even study it. Deft designers are able to layer the presentation, so whether he spends three minutes or three hours, he takes away the core message.

Precise– To the CFO and the accounting firms, precision is the careful presentation of the numbers rendered, not in pencil or in pixels, but in ink. They are numbers they can sign their names to and that the system requires as a foundation for trust. To the designer, precision is the subtlety and finesse that his training and experience allow him to bring to the book. It is the handling of the typography, the visual elements, the paper, the colors, the white space, et cetera, that create the impression. The impression is why Annual Report design exists and allows the reader to remember "that's a good company..." long after he has forgotten the numbers.

Permanent– Those of us who have made a living crafting or even creating the corporate image view this year's Annual Report project as another chapter in corporate history. Although the Annual Report has a reputation for a short shelf life, there is a permanence to an annual report. Each year's book documents and measures a company's performance but also management's attitudes, confidence and vision in any given year. Many times we ask for five or even 10 years of past Annual Reports. A series of books, viewed together, review the ebb and flow that most companies experience and occasionally reveal remarkable continuity. I have in my collection an IBM Annual Report from 1968. The legacy bestowed by Paul Rand is still reassuring today. The strong black and white photographic annuals initiated by James Cross in the late 1960s associated Northrop (later NorthropGrumman) with quality, clarity and strength through to the late 1990s. This clarity of image came from the conviction of Northrop management and four more design firms carried this torch until a management change extinguished the flame.

My view is that pixels are an important tool for us all, but are simply light and change in a blink of an eye. Information viewed today might disappear tomorrow. The Web is built for the transmission of the quick answer but gives little indication of character or competence. It lacks permanence.

The future of the Annual Report? It depends on your point of view. My view is that it is about to be fun again.

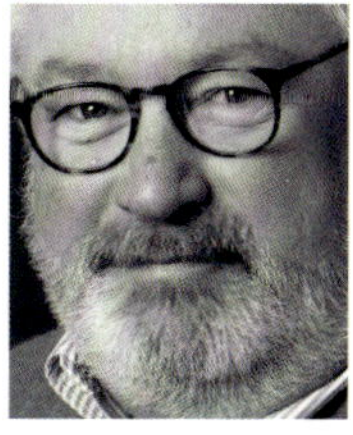

Douglas Oliver is a 30-year veteran of Annual Reports with his own design firm in Santa Monica, California. He served as the chair of this year's judging, charged with both organizing and assembling the panel of judges in New York City. In addition, he is a founding member of the Annual Report Society.

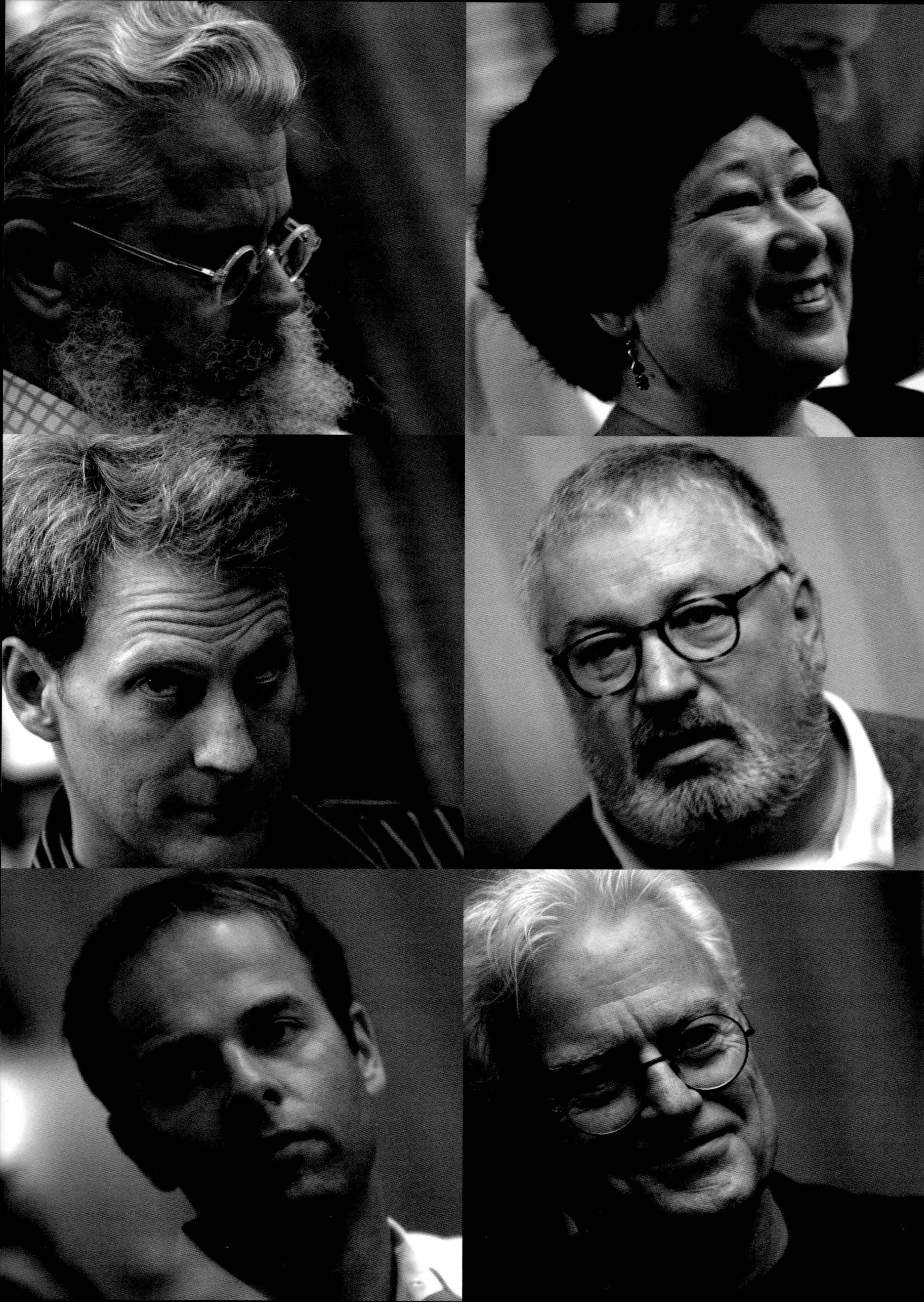

Personally, I've always viewed the Annual Report as a corporate capability communication in addition to a financial document.

Steve Frykholm

However one spins it, companies have renewed appreciation for how printed annuals give them control over their message.

Delphine Hirasuna

Unfortunately, after this year's judging, I kept thinking about mullets. More specifically, mullet Annual Reports.

John Klotnia

Any piece of mail has but a second or two to avoid the landfill. An Annual Report shares this burden.

Doug Oliver

Open any British annual and you'll probably find sans serif, set in three columns, accompanied by imaginative themes such as 'a day in the life' or 'people and kit.'

Gilmar Wendt

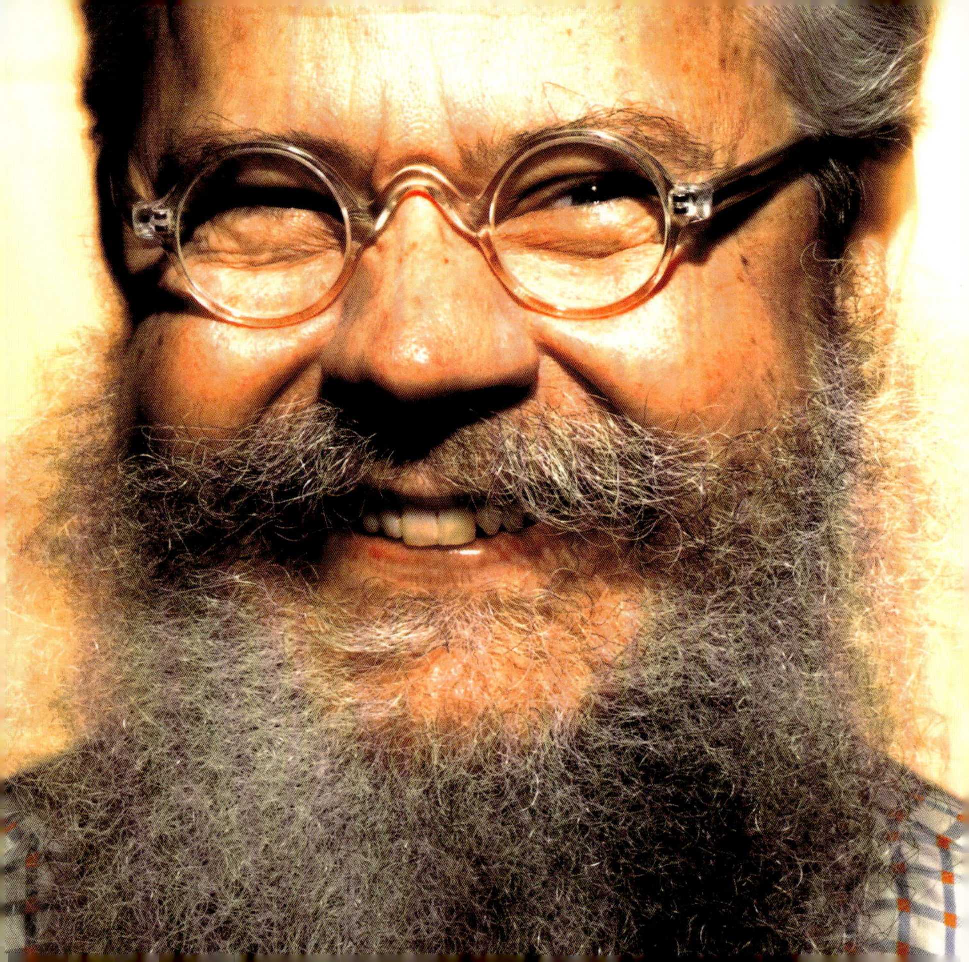

I try to be fresh and original in the design, and our Annual Reports have become a corporate tradition. Annual Report competitions provide feedback on how well we've done, but I like the feedback from employees – it's more helpful. I view the audience as Herman Miller employees, customers, and investors.

Same Old? Not quite.

I've been designing or directing Herman Miller's Annual Report for 29 years. As you can imagine, some have turned out pretty good, and others could have been better. All in all, it's been a good run.

I was hired as Herman Miller's first inside graphic designer in 1970, the same year the company went public. John Massey (of Container Corporation of America and Center for Advanced Design and Research fame) was our communication and graphic design consultant. John, along with the other designers at the Center, designed our Annual Reports from 1970 to 1975. As a young designer, I found the inventiveness John brought to the project inspirational. One year the report was a poster, another it was a newspaper, and another it was a slip-cased catalog of Eames designs from the Museum of Modern Art. Many years later I realized that John had established among senior management the expectation of producing unusual and unique Annual Reports. That expectation allowed me to explore and experiment with many expressions through the years.

When the company asked if I'd like to design the report in 1976, of course I said yes. Because our fiscal year ends in May, I've been filling up my summers with the project ever since.

Some of the greater creative challenges have been telling the company's story on four wheel charts (1979), taking and using the photographs of every employee in the company to celebrate the beginning of our employee ownership program (1985), doing a complete annual report using both sides of a 26 x 40 press sheet during a crummy year (1987), introducing a new CEO with a paperback book of his personal essays (1992), showing the positive feedback from customers and shareholders by faithfully reproducing their letters and notes (1993), creating a 11 x 72 foldout celebrating a banner year (1997), showing how fuzzy innovation can be by using vellum stock throughout the editorial content (2001), putting a plastic rain pon-

2001 Annual Report
Creative Director: Stephen Frykholm (Herman Miller)
Designer: Yang Kim (BBK Studio)
Editorial Writer: Clark Malcolm (Herman Miller)
Printer: Hennegan Company
Production Manager: Marlene Capotosto (Herman Miller)
Cover Paper: 40# Glama Natural Clear,
Text paper: pages (1-48) 21.25# Glama Natural Clear (49-84) 70# Beckett Expressions smooth basil text
Page count: 84
Print run: 32,000
Size: 8 1/4" X 10 3/4"
Number of Images: 5
Photographer: Various
Montage Artist: Michele Chartier (BBK Studio)
Company: Herman Miller is a leader in the design of furniture and services for work environments, homes, learning and healthcare environments.

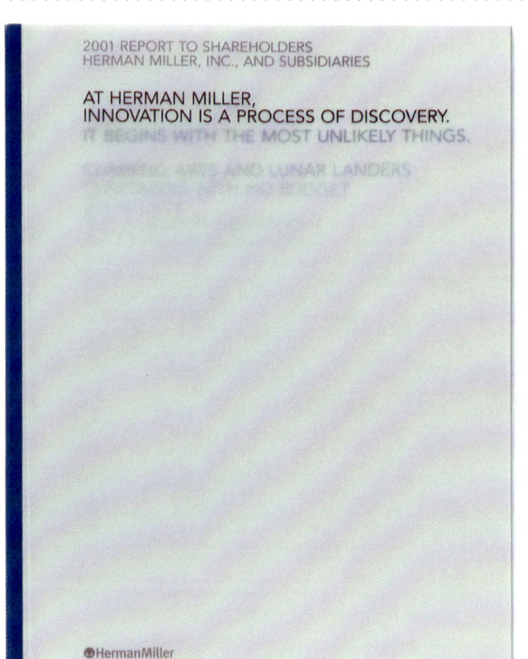

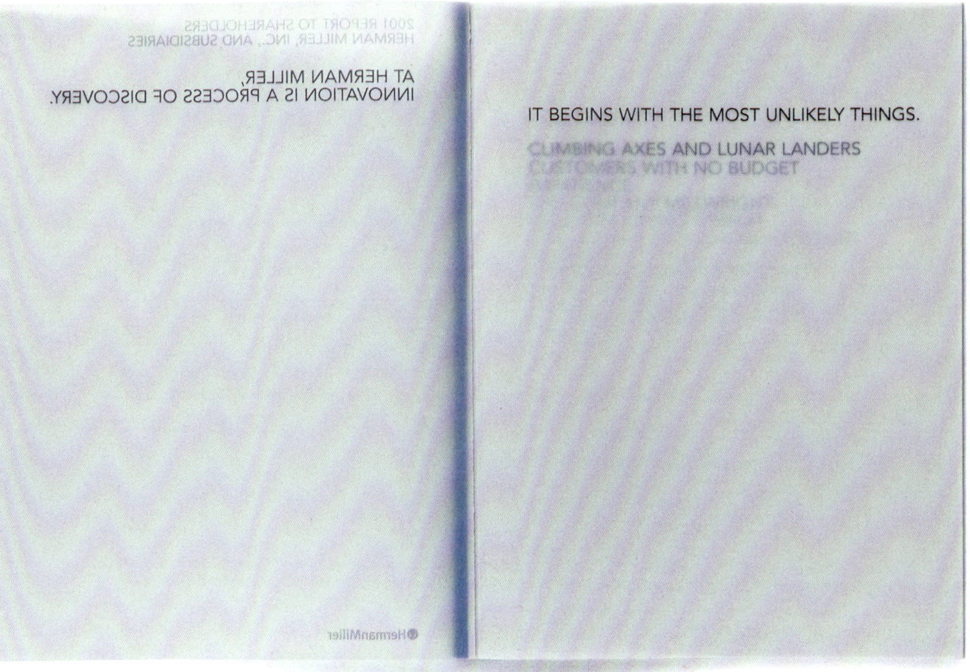

cho on the cover as we weathered the economic storm (2002), and incorporating lick-n-stick stamps portraying employees participating in our customer experience programs (2004).

Of course I've collaborated with others: writers Clark Malcolm, Nancy Green, and Melissa Brown; designers Linda Powell, Gary Cronkhite, Sara Giovanitti, Rob Hugel, Yang Kim, Brian Edlefson, and Andy Dull; photographers Earl Woods, Peter Kiar, Joe Baraban, Bill Lindhout, Nick Merrick, Brad Trent, Terry Vine, Bill Gallery, Bill Sharpe, Jim Powell, and Andy Sacks; illustrators Linda Nelson, Guy Billout, and Jack Unruh.

Over the years I've worked with six CEOs and six CFOs. Page count dedicated to financial reporting has multiplied from 12 to 60. Checkpoints and approvals have become an exercise in corporate patience and caution.

Personally, I've always viewed the Annual Report as a corporate capability communication in addition to a financial document. The reports seem more successful if the theme deals with a specific topic. I try to be fresh and original in the design, and our Annual Reports have become a corporate tradition. Annual Report competitions provide feedback on how well we've done, but I like the feedback from employees – it's more helpful. I view the audience as Herman Miller employees, customers, and investors.

I'm beginning to work on my 30th Annual Report for Herman Miller. I hope that it will carry on the tradition of inventiveness and surprise.

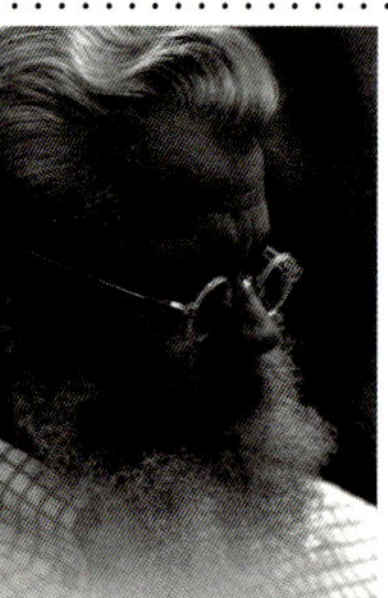

After teaching in Nigeria with the US Peace Corps, Steve attended and graduated from Cranbrook Academy of Art. Furniture icon Herman Miller, Inc. then hired him to be its first internal graphic designer. For 35 years he has been largely responsible for Herman Miller's image and graphic identity, its posters, Annual Reports, and other collateral literature.

Not only has Steve received Herman Miller's highest recognition for an employee, The Carl F. Frost Award, but he has also received recognition from professional peers. His work has been published and exhibited, and he's received Gold and Silver medals, Triad awards, and Certificates of Excellence from AIGA, N.Y. Art Directors Club, American Center for Design, Mead Annual Report Show, Communication Arts, Graphis, Creativity, Print, and ID.

Steve and his wife, Nancy Phillips, an interior architectural designer and equestrian, live in rural Michigan where she rides dressage and he spreads manure and photographs wild flowers.

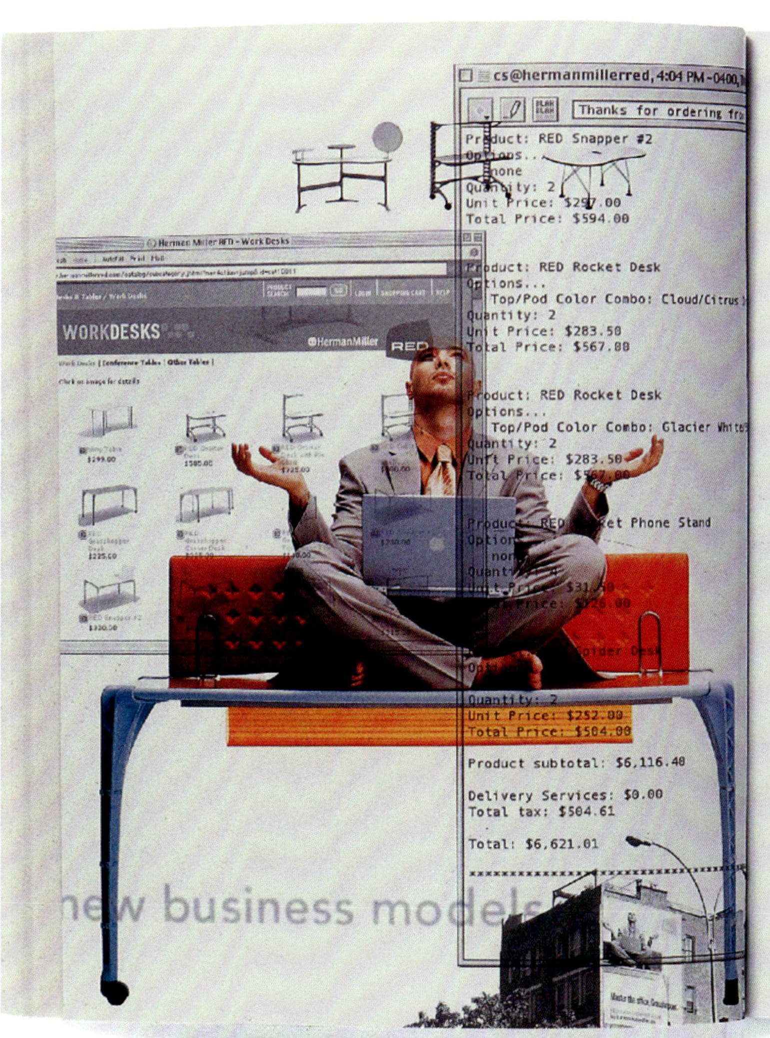

INNOVATIVE BUSINESS MODELS HAVE BEEN THE NORM WITH HERMAN MILLER FROM OUR MOVE INTO "MODERN" FURNITURE IN THE 1930S, TO OUR TRANSFORMATION OF THE OFFICE FURNITURE INDUSTRY IN THE 1970S, TO THE "SIMPLE, QUICK, AND AFFORDABLE" SUCCESSES OF THE 1990S. HERMAN MILLER RED IS NOW INTRODUCING US TO A FRESH SET OF CUSTOMERS WITH NEW CHANNELS TO MARKET, HIP NEW PRODUCTS, AND AN ATTITUDE TO MATCH.

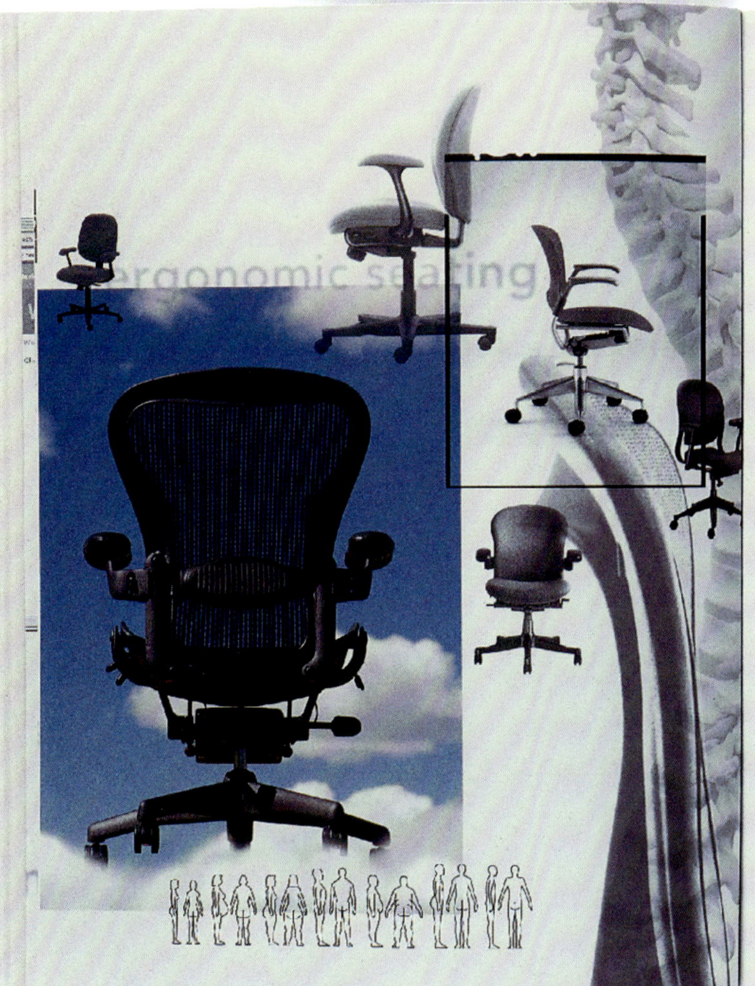

THE SUPERLATIVE AERON CHAIR IS ONLY THE LATEST IN A STRING OF INNOVATIVE, ERGONOMICALLY SUPERIOR WORK CHAIRS. IN FACT, WE INTRODUCED ERGONOMICS TO OUR INDUSTRY WITH BILL STUMPF'S ERGON CHAIR IN 1976. WE CURRENTLY STAND AS LEADER IN SEATING FOR OUR INDUSTRY, AND WE INTEND TO STAY THERE.

2004 Annual Report
Creative Director: Stephen Frykholm (Herman Miller)
Designer: Andy Dull (Herman Miller)
Editorial Writer: Clark Malcolm (Herman Miller)

Printer: SVH
Production Manager: Marlene Capotosto (Herman Miller)
Cover Paper: Stora Enso,80# Productolith gloss cover

Text paper: stamp pages: 60#Tromark Dry Gum, text: 70# Via bright white smooth text
Page count: 74
Print run: 22,000
Size: 8 1/8" X 11 5/8"

Number of Images: 232 portraits; # 36 editorial
Portrait Photographer: Jim Powell
Editorial Photographers: Various

Company: Herman Miller is a leader in the design of furniture and services for work environments, homes, learning and healhcare environments.

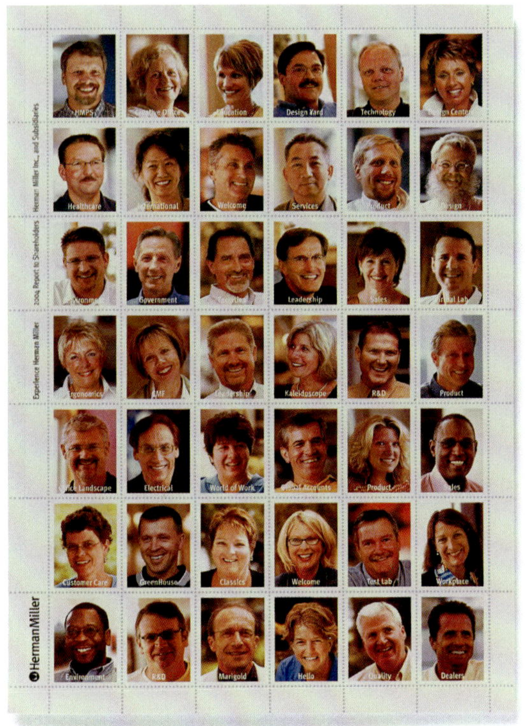

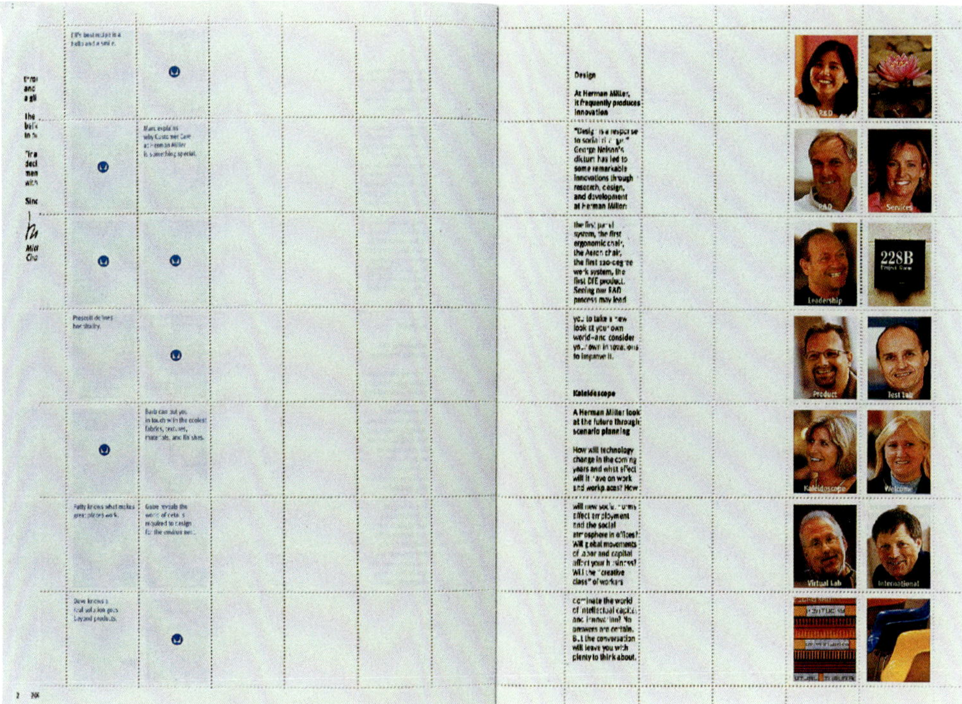

through their words and actions. When prospective customers come to visit us at our West Michigan headquarters and facilities, they not only gain an understanding of what makes a great place to work, or learn, or heal—they get a glimpse of what makes Herman Miller a very special place. And they usually become our customers.

The people of Herman Miller have a renewed energy, the pipeline is bursting with exciting new products, and we believe that we have a business model and strategy well suited to win in the marketplace and to deliver superior value to our customers and to you, our shareholders. Yes, the future looks much brighter!

Finally, we want to acknowledge the great work of the leadership team, who guided us through a difficult period with decisive action and unwavering allegiance to our corporate values. The leadership team is a gifted group of women and men who will encourage and cultivate the momentum at every turn in the days ahead. We consider it an honor to serve with each of them and our employee-owners—and in turn to serve our shareholders, our dealers, and our customers.

Sincerely

Michael A. Volkema
Chairman of the Board

Brian C. Walker
President and Chief Executive Officer

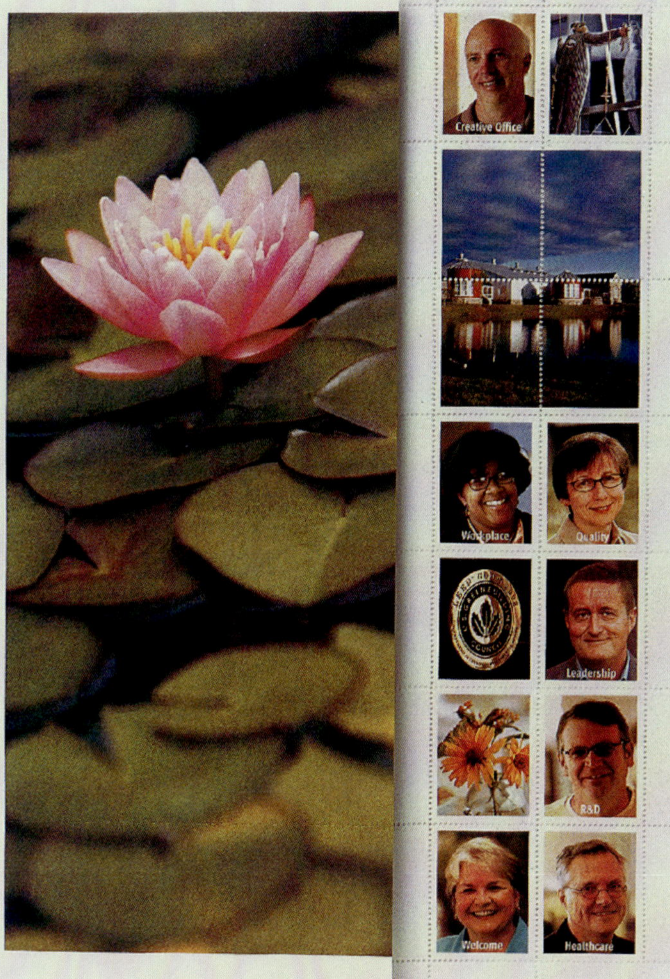

Ray turns the idea of continuous improvement into reality.

Ken keeps our promises.

Mike directs our business with the federal government.

Andy has the best seats in the house.

Barb cares for our many relationships with industrial designers.

Brian, our new CEO, is determined to develop people who inspire our customers.

Willie is our recycling guru.

Alex powers your work environment.

Facilities

Concrete examples of what we believe

Though Herman Miller's facilities have won many awards over the years, they really express in a way you'll never forget the powerful appeal of a well-designed work environment. They comfort the people who work in them and inspire the people who visit. Good architecture, like good office furniture, puts people first.

New Office Landscape

Planning offices for innovation

In a business world where competitive pressures run high and the demand for innovative products and services increases day by day, what kind of workplace will attract and keep the brightest and most creative employees? How can the workplace raise the creative quotient of every person working there and stimulate and capture the creative sparks when people work together? We'd like to talk to you about your own brand of the many new office landscapes that lie ahead.

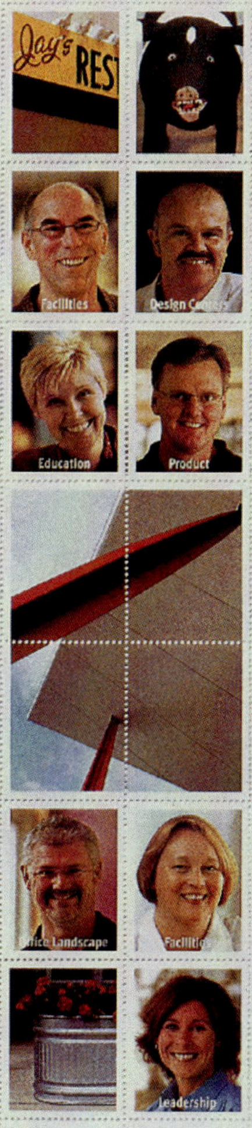

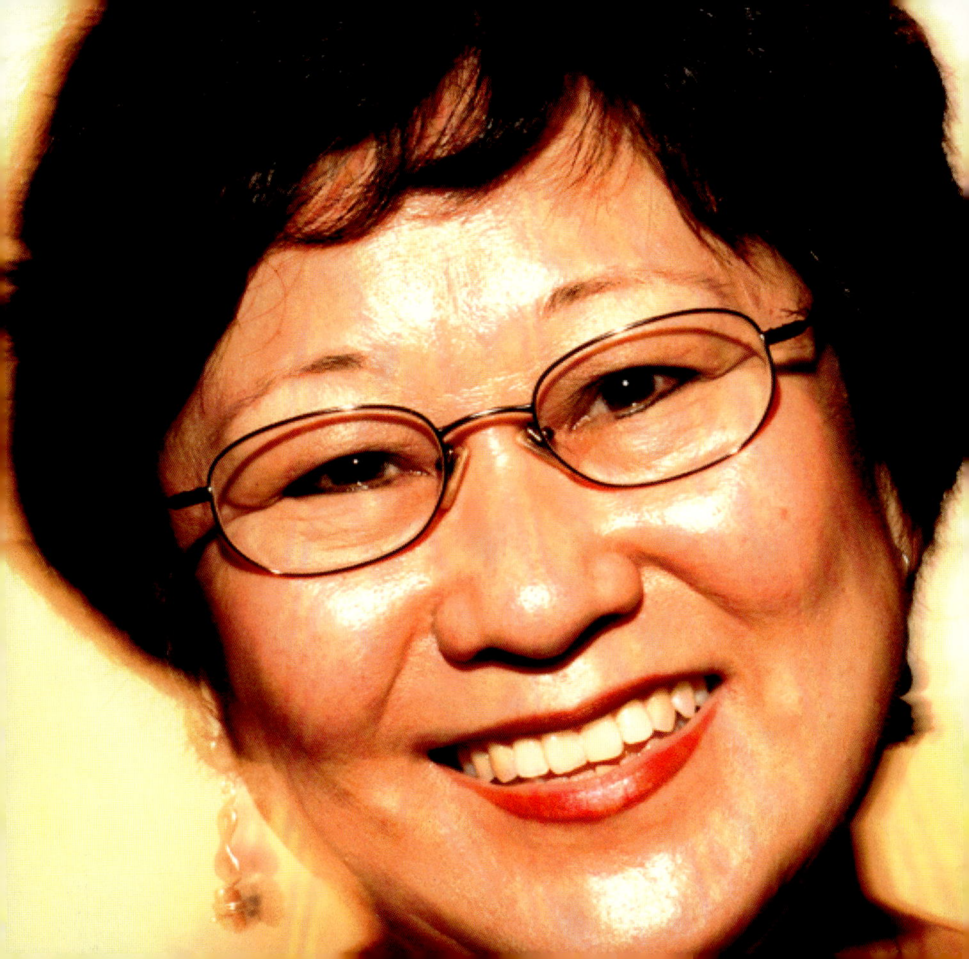

Although critics have charged that Annual Reports are never read cover to cover, they have to admit that shareholders invariably check out the narrative flow and reflect on the approach to the visuals. Even if recipients do nothing more than hold the annual in their hands and fan through the pages, they should come away with a sense of the company's personality.

Reclaiming the Corporate Voice

Judging the 2005 Graphis show reassured me that the traditional Annual Report had not been completely replaced by 10-K wraps, which are typically printed on cheesy paper and devoid of any hint of design. If the Graphis entries are an indication, corporate Annual Reports with thoughtfully conceived theme messages and evocative imagery not only exist, they are better and more sophisticated than ever.

This, I hope, is a sign that the pendulum is swinging away from the frugality of the past few years and that corporate communicators are searching for a "new normal" when it comes to Annual Reports. Certainly, during the euphoric late 1990s, extravagant Annual Reports sent the message "We're so successful or we plan to be so successful (as soon as we have a product) that money is no object." Then the dot.com bubble burst and seemingly invincible giants like Enron collapsed, prompting passage of the Sarbanes-Oxley Act which imposed stricter reporting standards and accountability. Companies sought to avoid the appearance and reality of excess. In a case of reverse one-upmanship, they vied to look more penny-pinching than their competitors. Many companies completely dropped the narrative section of their Annual Reports, providing only the SEC-required financials. Part of the rationale was that their corporate website would fill the communication gap: "If you want to know about, visit our website."

That turned out not to be the case. Corporate communicators are discovering that the immediacy of Web access does not mean that target audiences will look where they want them to. If shareholders

1990 Norcen Annual Report
Theme essay:
Delphine Hirasuna

Design: Kit Hinrichs, Pentagram

Photography: Jeff Corwin

This has remained one of my favorite annuals because it allowed me to write in a "prose" style about the mystery, excitement and romance of exploring for oil.

do visit their website at all, they may dart around, go a few clicks in and leave. They may check out recent news and the stock price, but not bother to look at what they consider "boiler plate" text about the company. Older Web-shy investors will not even do that. Despite their ease of accessibility, most corporate websites have an off-putting sameness – terrible typography, stagnant photographs and distracting clutter. Personally, I yearn for the directorial skill of a good designer to guide me, focus my attention, juxtapose related subjects to improve my understanding, and simply offer some aesthetic relief.

Although critics have charged that Annual Reports are never read cover to cover, they have to admit that shareholders invariably check out the narrative flow and reflect on the approach to the visuals. Even if recipients do nothing more than hold the annual in their hands and fan through the pages, they come away with a sense of a company's personality. The size and format of the book, the feel of the paper, the integration of elements like die-cuts and emboss, the choice of illustration over photography, black-and-white over color – everything communicates both overtly and subliminally. We're bold. Conservative. Warm and fuzzy. Cerebral. Edgy. Stylish. Conversely, when executed badly, the visual message may say we're timid, stodgy and boring as dishwater.

The so-called "front of the book" – as opposed to the legally worded financials which provide a historical picture of performance – is where companies can reveal their philosophy, strategy and hopes for the future, marketing achievements and civic good deeds in an inviting and approachable manner. This is the part of the annual that helps the reader decide whether they like and trust the company, even if the hard numbers tell a less than positive story.

Annual Reports also offer the advantage of being annual – which makes them timely and up-to-date. That is more than could be said of the corporate image brochure, which typically gets updated every three to five years when the supply runs low or an event makes it embarrassingly inaccurate.

Without a comprehensive Annual Report available, many companies of late have discovered that they don't have anything to send out when someone requests information about them. They stuff the envelope with a 10-K, a few product brochures and maybe copies of the CEO's recent speeches – an array of materials that leaves the recipient more bewildered than informed.

Hence, Annual Reports with theme messages are beginning to reappear – albeit in different iterations such as corporate responsibility reports. However one spins it, companies have renewed appreciation for how printed annuals give them control over their message. It gives them a vehicle that they can place directly in their shareholders' hands.

That is not to say that the Web will lose its importance. We are fast approaching the day of multimedia Annual Reports that offer online tours of manufacturing facilities and audio/visual interviews with CEOs. But print will always have its place. The well-designed annual report is not a symbol of corporate ego, but of a sincere effort to communicate the intangible, present a hierarchy of information to help guide the reader to what they consider important, tell a story through design that goes beyond the printed word and captures the vitality and uniqueness of the company. Those qualities are all evident in this year's slate of Graphis winners.

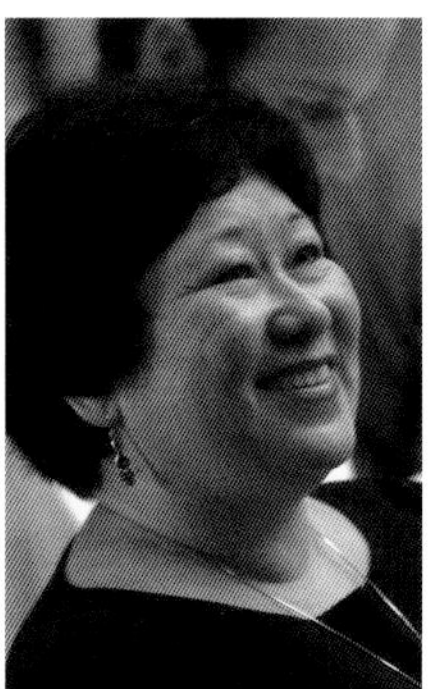

Over the course of her career, Delphine Hirasuna has written more than 100 Annual Reports for industries ranging from forest products and banking to biotechnology and retail. Through Hirasuna Editorial, founded in 1985, she provides editorial supervision and copywriting services to corporations, graphic design firms and advertising agencies throughout the US Delphine is also the editor of the much-acclaimed @Issue magazine, sponsored by Sappi Fine Paper and Lithographix, and had previously served as editor of Fox River's NEO and Apple Media Arts. Her articles and essays on design have appeared in a number of design publications, including Graphis, Communication Arts, Step, and Graphic Design America 3. Over the years, her projects have won dozens of national and international awards. In addition to her corporate consulting work, Delphine has co-authored several books on design and other subjects, including "TypeWise" and "Long May She Wave," with Kit Hinrichs of Pentagram. Her most recent book is "The Art of Gaman," on the arts and crafts of the Japanese American internment camps during World War II. A columnist for the two largest Japanese-American newspapers for many years and the author of a Japanese cookbook, she has been a popular guest lecturer. In 2002, she was named a laureate of the San Francisco Public Library. Prior to starting her own business, Delphine served as corporate publications manager at Potlatch Corporation, where she produced the company's award-winning Annual Report and corporate magazine. Previously, she spent ten years at Transamerica Corporation and its subsidiary, Transamerica Airlines, producing their publications. Her early career began in financial public relations and journalism, working for Ruder & Finn, the San Francisco Chronicle Features Syndicate and the Lodi News-Sentinel.

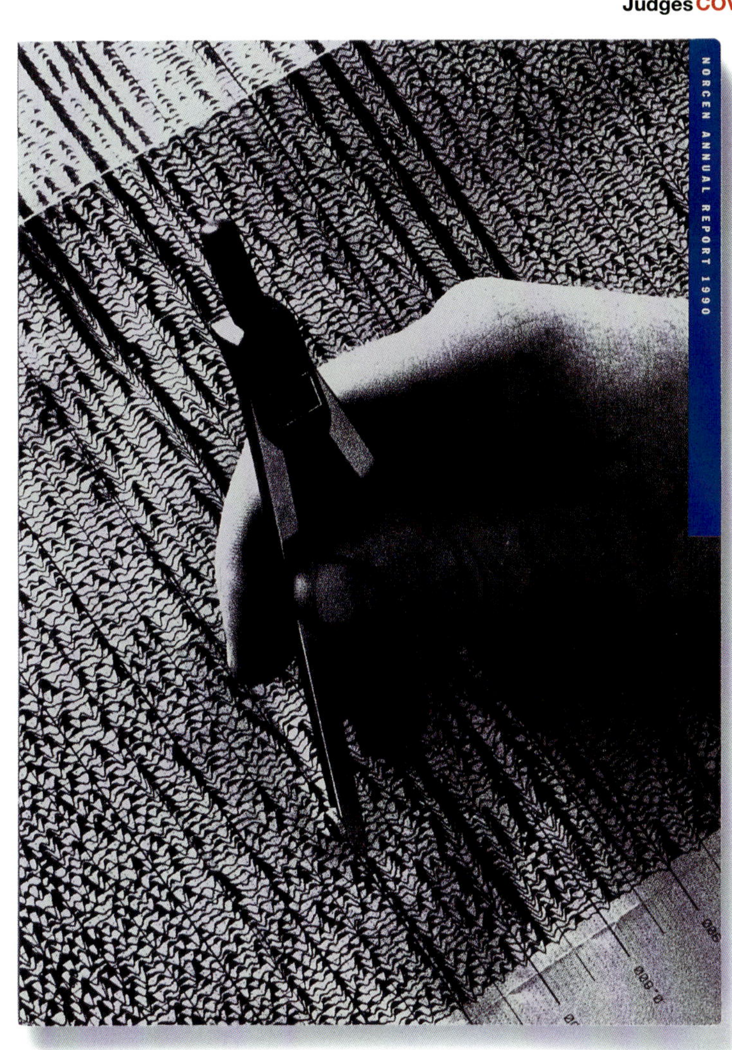
NORCEN ANNUAL REPORT 1990

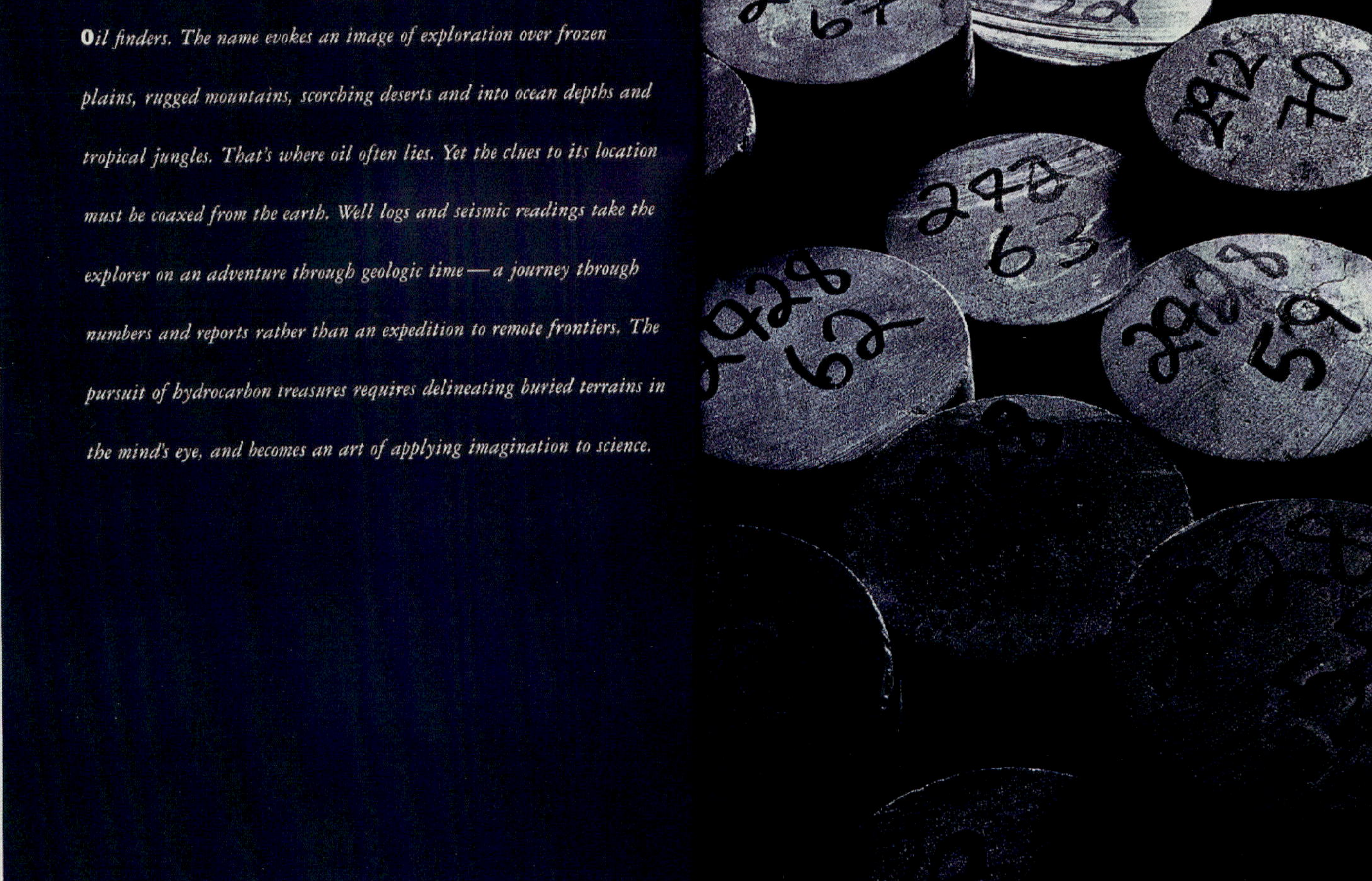
THE OIL FINDERS
Oil finders. The name evokes an image of exploration over frozen plains, rugged mountains, scorching deserts and into ocean depths and tropical jungles. That's where oil often lies. Yet the clues to its location must be coaxed from the earth. Well logs and seismic readings take the explorer on an adventure through geologic time — a journey through numbers and reports rather than an expedition to remote frontiers. The pursuit of hydrocarbon treasures requires delineating buried terrains in the mind's eye, and becomes an art of applying imagination to science.
24
2428 67
2428 52
2428 70
2428 63
2428 62
2428 59

1983 Potlatch Corporation Annual
Project manager/copywriter: Delphine Hirasuna
Design: Kit Hinrichs, Pentagram
Primary photography: Tom Tracy
Illustrations: Justin Carroll, Will Nelson, Colleen Quinn

I served as project manager and writer on the Potlatch Annual Report between 1980 and 2003, working with Kit Hinrichs and Tom Tracy the entire time.

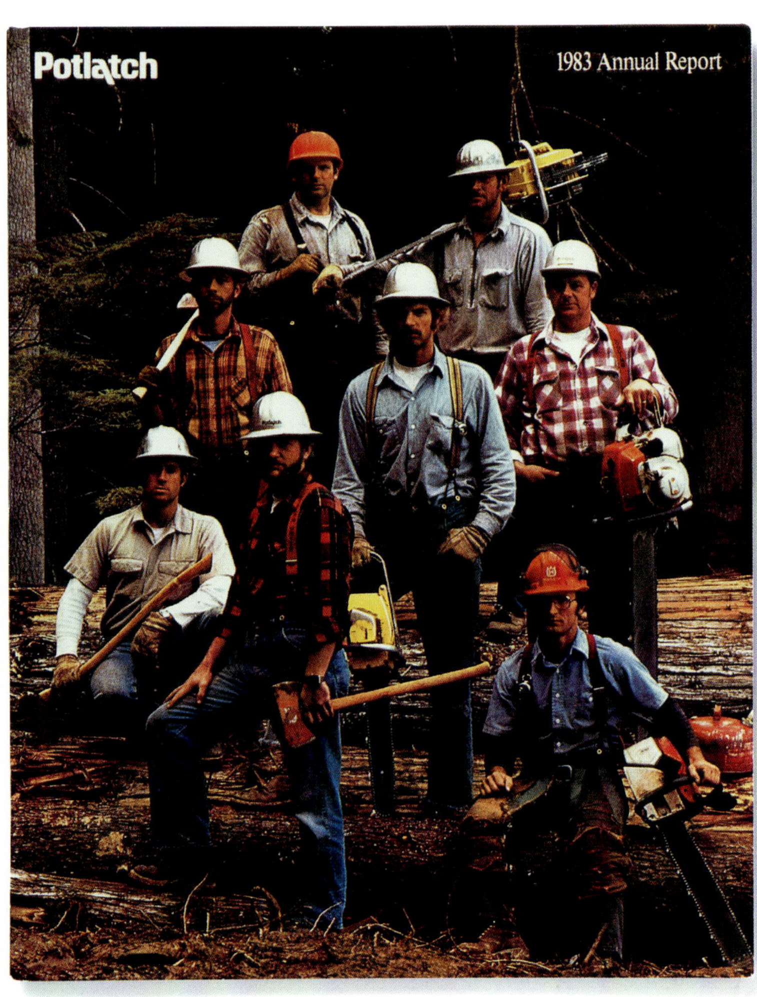

Harvesting Timber

On some Potlatch lands in Idaho, harvest time might come only once a century, since it can take nearly an average person's lifetime for a tree to reach sawlog-size maturity.

Rotation periods can be equally long in northern Minnesota, while lands in southern Arkansas produce sawlogs as often as every 35 years.

Growing and harvesting raw material is a complex task. Even before one tree is cut, woodlands experts devote many hours to studying the ramifications of a harvesting plan on overall forest management. They sometimes need to act as trustees for young stands of trees that will be bequeathed to another generation to harvest. At the same time, supplying sufficient raw materials to meet current demand is essential.

At Potlatch, each mill specifies how much wood fiber it will need to run its manufacturing operations for the year. Specialists trained in logging and forestry analyze these budgets to determine how much wood to cut and in what sizes and species. With this information, they determine harvest sites, equipment mix, and a delivery schedule.

A key consideration in their calculations is the concept of sustained yield/allowable cut. This means that in establishing a harvest plan, managers must balance wood fiber needs, both current and future, with the rate of forest regeneration.

In Arkansas, Idaho and Minnesota–Potlatch's three wood basket regions–the woodlands departments satisfy volume requirements through a combination of logging on company land, buying contracts to log on other ownerships, both public and private, and log purchases.

Economic considerations are basic to any harvest scheme, which also must consider terrain, timber size and conditions, stream and drainage patterns, soil types and wildlife protection.

Incorporated into the plan are a number of forest management options. For instance, some raw material can be secured from commercial thinning–the removal of small diameter logs to give better spacing to young stands. Selective harvesting and overstory removal take out designated trees which block light and rob nutrients and moisture from younger, faster-growing trees. Other areas may call for a clearcut–complete removal of a tract of timber, for economic or environmental reasons.

By implementing varied silvicultural, or "farming," methods, it is possible to achieve specific management objectives, while pulling together the sizes and species required by the mills.

Keeping all these factors in mind, logging managers plot boundaries for stream buffer zones, skidding trails, yarding sites, and road construction that will protect the forest floor and prevent soil erosion.

From there, loggers determine the complement of equipment needed to carry out the operation efficiently and economically.

After the entire harvesting plan has been laid out, the logging crew is ready to move in. As part of the evolution of forest management into a science, logging has become less an occupation of brawn and daring, and more of an exacting skill. Over the years integrated forest products companies have learned to utilize parts and grades of logs that at one time had no market value. As a result, the logger's skill is more critical because it affects total wood fiber recovery and the products that can be made from the log.

In many ways, timber harvesting must be viewed as the essential preparatory step to a new growth cycle, as well as the culmination of the old. After all, timber management involves much more than cutting down trees and moving them out of the woods. The care that we take in managing our timber supply is our legacy to future generations.

Idaho

Of our three timberland regions, Idaho presents the most challenging logging conditions and grows the largest trees. Softwood species proliferate on Idaho's mountainous terrain, yielding logs that sometimes weigh several tons.

However, steep slopes normally require the use of cable systems to lift logs to loading areas.

In Idaho, Potlatch manufactures a variety of wood products, household tissue, and bleached pulp and paperboard.

Minnesota

Northern Minnesota's timber region is characterized by mixed hardwood/softwood stands, small diameter trees, and extreme seasonal temperature swings.

To utilize the local forest's special fiber qualities, Potlatch manufactures fine printing and business papers, oriented strand board and construction lumber in the state.

Since many of Minnesota's forests have small diameter trees and relatively flat terrain, they lend themselves to mechanical harvesting.

Arkansas

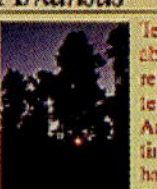

Temperate climate, abundant rainfall and relatively flat, fertile terrain give southern Arkansas productive timber growing and harvesting conditions. Potlatch's Arkansas stands are mostly pine, with a mixture of hardwoods dominating the bottomlands.

While most tree harvesting is still done with chainsaws, mechanical equipment is coming into broader use on small diameter trees.

In Arkansas, Potlatch converts timber to construction lumber, specialty wood products and bleached paperboard.

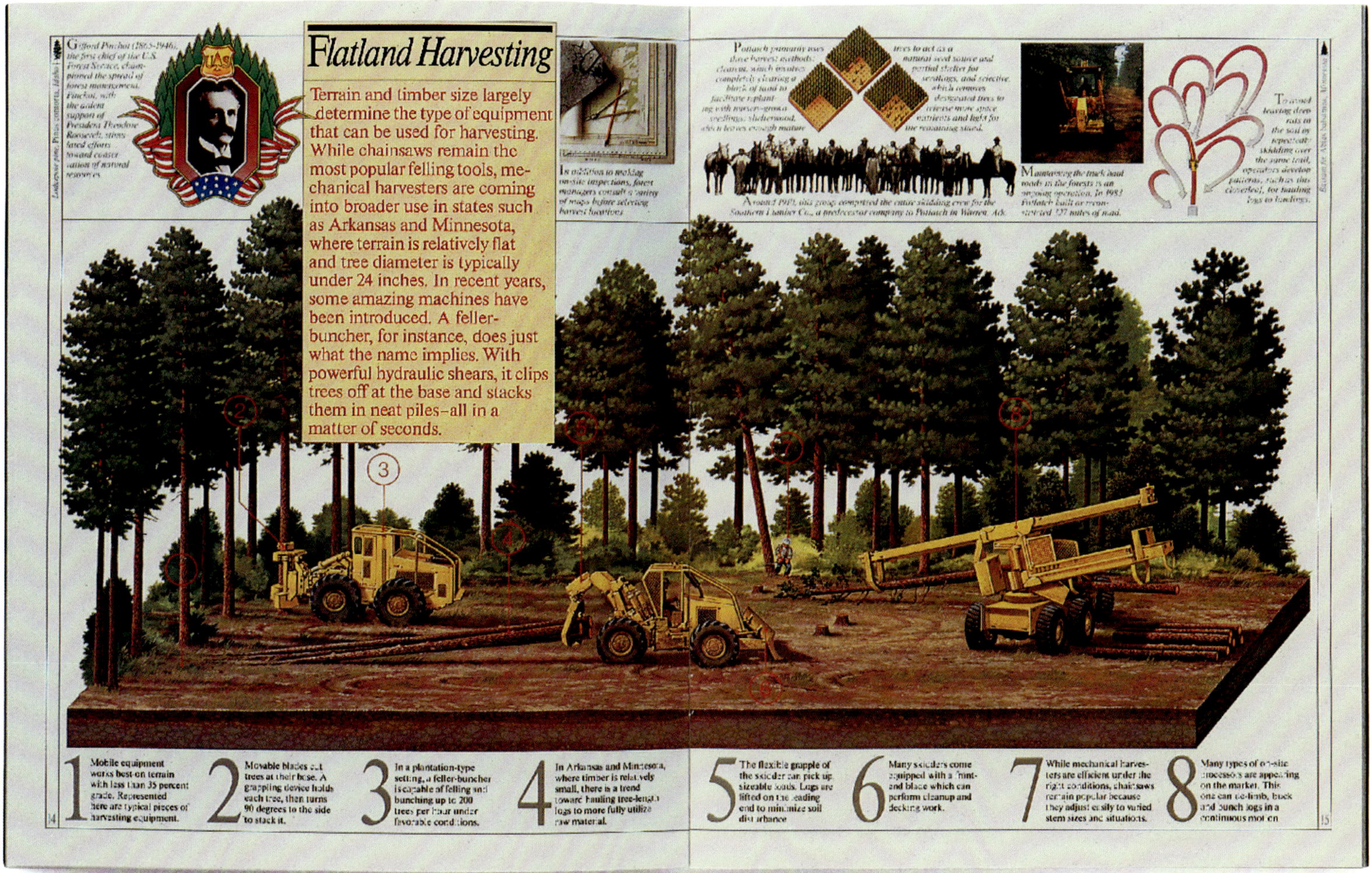

Gifford Pinchot (1865-1946), the first chief of the U.S. Forest Service, championed the spread of forest management. Pinchot, with the ardent support of President Theodore Roosevelt, stressed efforts toward conservation of natural resources.

Flatland Harvesting

Terrain and timber size largely determine the type of equipment that can be used for harvesting. While chainsaws remain the most popular felling tools, mechanical harvesters are coming into broader use in states such as Arkansas and Minnesota, where terrain is relatively flat and tree diameter is typically under 24 inches. In recent years, some amazing machines have been introduced. A feller-buncher, for instance, does just what the name implies. With powerful hydraulic shears, it clips trees off at the base and stacks them in neat piles—all in a matter of seconds.

In addition to making on-site inspections, forest managers consult a variety of maps before selecting harvest locations.

Potlatch primarily uses three harvest methods: clearcut, which involves completely clearing a block of land to facilitate replanting with nursery-grown seedlings; shelterwood, which leaves enough mature trees to act as a natural seed source and partial shelter for seedlings; and selective, which removes designated trees to release more space, nutrients and light for the remaining stand.

Around 1910, this group comprised the entire skidding crew for the Southern Lumber Co., a predecessor company to Potlatch in Warren, Ark.

Maintaining the truck haul roads in the forests is an ongoing operation. In 1983 Potlatch built or reconstructed 127 miles of road.

To avoid leaving deep ruts in the soil by repeatedly skidding over the same trail, operators develop patterns, such as this cloverleaf, for hauling logs to landings.

1 Mobile equipment works best on terrain with less than 35 percent grade. Represented here are typical pieces of harvesting equipment.

2 Movable blades cut trees at their base. A grappling device holds each tree, then turns 90 degrees to the side to stack it.

3 In a plantation-type setting, a feller-buncher is capable of felling and bunching up to 200 trees per hour under favorable conditions.

4 In Arkansas and Minnesota, where timber is relatively small, there is a trend toward hauling tree-length logs to more fully utilize raw material.

5 The flexible grapple of the skidder can pick up sizeable loads. Logs are lifted on the leading end to minimize soil disturbance.

6 Many skidders come equipped with a "front-end blade which can perform cleanup and decking work.

7 While mechanical harvesters are efficient under the right conditions, chainsaws remain popular because they adjust easily to varied stem sizes and situations.

8 Many types of on-site processors are appearing on the market. This one can de-limb, buck and bunch logs in a continuous motion.

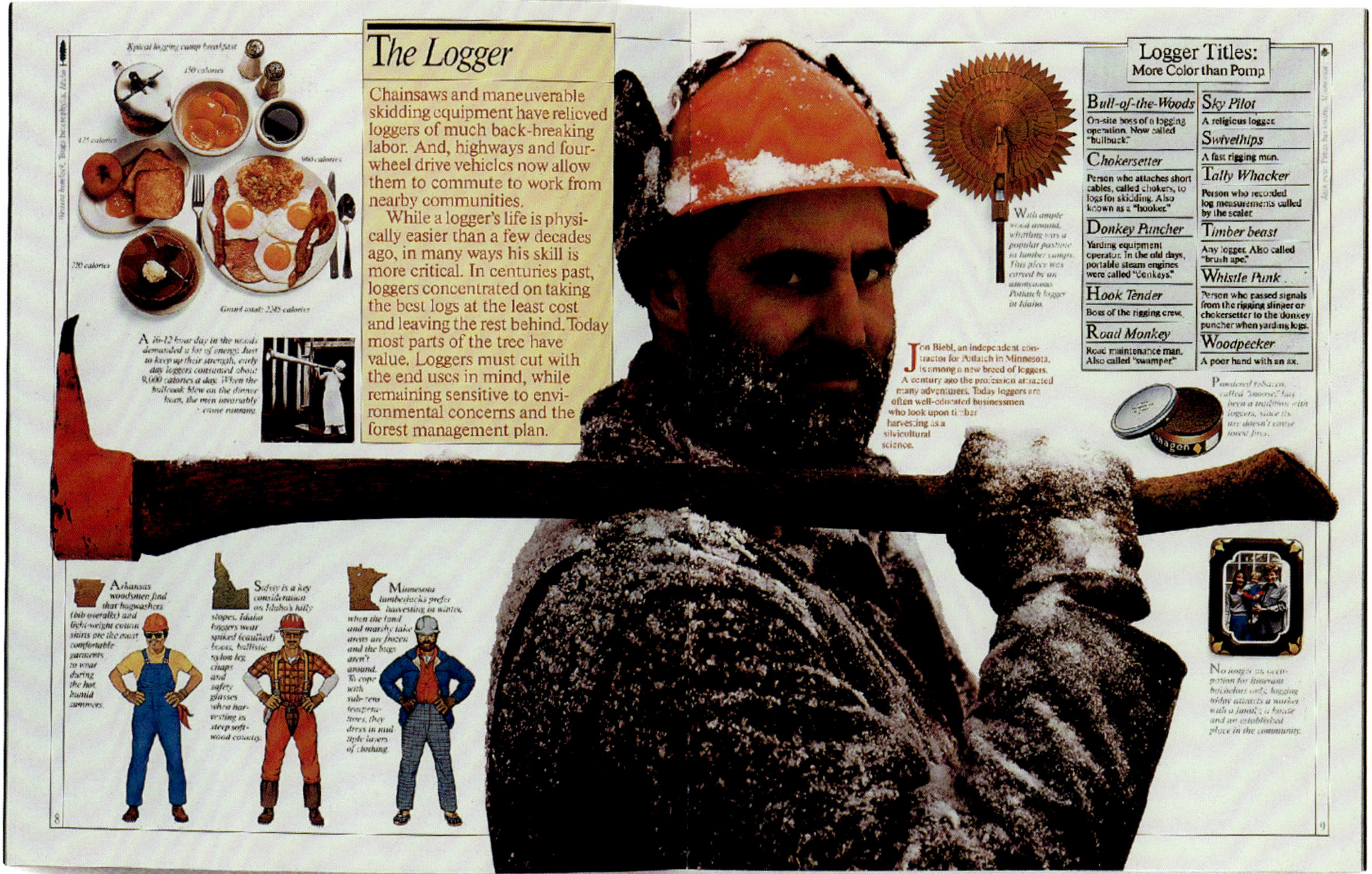

Typical logging camp breakfast

150 calories

425 calories

960 calories

720 calories

Grand total: 2245 calories

A 10-12 hour day in the woods demanded a lot of energy. Just to keep up their strength, early day loggers consumed about 9,000 calories a day. When the bullcook blew on the dinner horn, the men invariably came running.

The Logger

Chainsaws and maneuverable skidding equipment have relieved loggers of much back-breaking labor. And, highways and four-wheel drive vehicles now allow them to commute to work from nearby communities.

While a logger's life is physically easier than a few decades ago, in many ways his skill is more critical. In centuries past, loggers concentrated on taking the best logs at the least cost and leaving the rest behind. Today most parts of the tree have value. Loggers must cut with the end uses in mind, while remaining sensitive to environmental concerns and the forest management plan.

With ample wood around, whittling was a popular pastime in lumber camps. This piece was carved by an anonymous Potlatch logger in Idaho.

Jon Biebl, an independent contractor for Potlatch in Minnesota, is among a new breed of loggers. A century ago the profession attracted many adventurers. Today loggers are often well-educated businessmen who look upon timber harvesting as a silvicultural science.

Logger Titles: More Color than Pomp

Bull-of-the-Woods — On-site boss of a logging operation. Now called "bullbuck."

Chokersetter — Person who attaches short cables, called chokers, to logs for skidding. Also known as a "hooker."

Donkey Puncher — Yarding equipment operator. In the old days, portable steam engines were called "donkeys."

Hook Tender — Boss of the rigging crew.

Road Monkey — Road maintenance man. Also called "swamper."

Sky Pilot — A religious logger.

Swivelhips — A fast rigging man.

Tally Whacker — Person who recorded log measurements called by the scaler.

Timber beast — Any logger. Also called "brush ape."

Whistle Punk — Person who passed signals from the rigging slinger or chokersetter to the donkey puncher when yarding logs.

Woodpecker — A poor hand with an ax.

Powdered tobacco, called "snoose," has been a tradition with loggers, since its use doesn't cause forest fires.

Arkansas woodsmen find that hogwashers (bib overalls) and light-weight cotton shirts are the most comfortable garments to wear during the hot, humid summers.

Safety is a key consideration on Idaho's hilly slopes. Idaho loggers wear spiked (caulked) boots, ballistic nylon leg chaps and safety glasses when harvesting in steep softwood country.

Minnesota lumberjacks prefer harvesting in winter, when the land and marshy lake areas are frozen and the bugs aren't around. To cope with sub-zero temperatures, they dress in multiple layers of clothing.

No longer an occupation for itinerant bachelors only, logging today attracts a worker with a family, a house and an established place in the community.

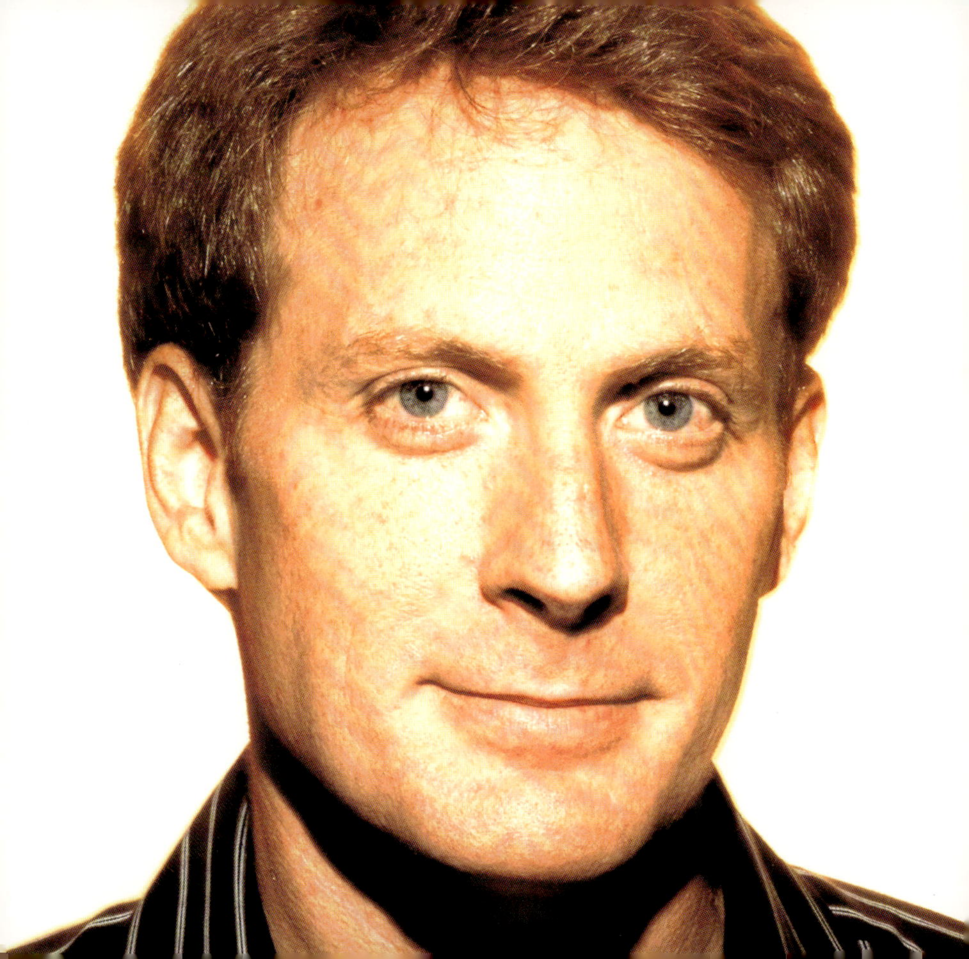

In the world of public companies and Annual Reporting, I wonder which audience does the mullet Annual Report speak to? Even in tough economic times, you have to respect the audience and the venue. If the mullet Annual Report were clothing, we'd all be wearing tuxedo t-shirts to our next formal event. Formal yet economic.

Lament on the 10K Wrap

Doug Oliver, chair of this year's Graphis Annual Report judging, asked me to write about designing Annual Reports for a targeted audience. Unfortunately, after this year's judging, I kept thinking about mullets. More specifically, mullet annual reports. For those who can't recall the mullet hair style of the 1980s, it was popular with the heavy metal crowd – in front, the hair was shorn tight, almost crew-cut in appearance and very conservative looking, and in back, it revealed a surprisingly long mane of locks, cascading down below the shoulders. An odd juxtaposition of styles – or as my senior designer Brad Simon describes it, "A haircut that says business up front with a party out back."

The mullet Annual Report occupies that same disjointed space. Up front, it presents an editorially clever and carefully crafted corporate message designed to promote shareholder confidence in the progress of a given company; out back, a built-in pocket houses the frugal looking, non-designed 10K wrap. The 10K wrap, an antiquated typeset financial format better suited for manual typewriters, appears to have evolved horribly on some island of misfit typesetters. Untouched by the modern fundamentals of legibility and typographic standards, it features a mixture of type weights, alignments, sizes, underlines, tight leading and long measures that seems better designed to camouflage information than to convey it.

In the world of public companies and Annual Reporting, I wonder which audience does the mullet Annual Report speak to? Even in tough economic times, you have to respect the audience and the venue. If the mullet Annual Report were clothing, we'd all be wearing tuxedo t-shirts to our next formal event. Formal yet economic.

And don't get me wrong, I love economy. The 10K wrap paper should be applauded for its use of cost-saving materials, paper near transparent and dictionary-like, feeling as though it could dissolve in your hands or float away. Super cheap too, both to purchase and to mail, and I bet it is recycled and/or recyclable – all great things.

Creative Director: John Klotnia
Art Director: Brad Simon
Designer: Brad Simon, Kelly Atkins, Nancy Caal
Printer: ColorGraphics
Cover Paper: Fibermark Touche Black 27 point
Text paper: Mohawk Superfine Ultrwhite Eggshell 100# text, Mohawk Superfine Softwhite Eggshell 80# text, Utopia ONE X Book Silk 100# text, Clear Polyester Vinyl .004 point
Page count: 54
Print run: 8,500
Size: 11" x 10"
Number of Images: 20
Client: Alexandria Real Estate Equities Inc. 2003 Annual Report

My problem: too many audiences and too many messages. I can almost hear the initial conversation, "Up front, we've gotta send a confident message and it has gotta look good. Out back, let's save a few bucks and have my accounting department set the financials." Either end of this mullet by itself would be fine; I just think if a company wants to send the message of financial responsibility by delivering such a frugal presentation of their financials out back, they ought to employ that same sensibility up front, too. One-color, cheap paper, a bit of typesetting and really direct language.

One audience, one message. This year, Weymouth Design produced a wonderful book for the Courier Corporation, my favorite from the show. At first glance, the beautiful ballpoint sketches on the krafty cover perfectly recall those high-school brown-bag dust jackets we all made to prolong the life of our text book covers. That same brown canvas that required instant personalization by its owner and updating throughout the school year. Courier, being a tradition-rich book packager, recently renewed their focus on the educational marketplace. Their 2004 Annual Report spoke volumes about this potential growth area and their understanding of the industry, spilled over with creativity, vision and the desire to take the appropriate measured risks. As a shareowner, I would feel great confidence in the leadership of this organization. They've got vision and it shows.

Woody Pirtle, an AIGA Medal recipient and an extraordinary designer I had the pleasure to work with for a number of years at Pentagram, is the master of one message and one audience. Woody and I designed Annual Reports for the United Technologies Corporation (UTC). UTC is a great company, and (in 1996) it was comprised of six distinct businesses in five industries. UTC had and has no shortage of terrific things to say about itself. They could fill volumes on their history as an industry creator and innovator in helicopters, aerospace, elevators, air conditioners or their infinite product lines or their worldwide presence or their financial strength. In 1996, UTC wanted to reveal one thing – the unique and intelligent way they went about problem solving. Some problems they addressed were actual and some problems did not yet exist. They developed plans for elevators that sped people through mile-high buildings both horizontally and vertically, they produced jet engines that power-slid through turns while maintaining airspeed and reducing G-forces, incredible ideas meant for an audience of shareowners with a message of innovative thinking. George David, the CEO, held up that Annual Report and said, "Better than a rocket ship."

More recently, I've had the pleasure of working for another great company, Alexandria Real Estate Equities, the premier REIT for the life sciences industry. Each year I meet with the Joel Marcus, Alexandria's CEO, and we discuss his message and intended audience. In 2004, we designed for the message of "strategic clustering" and those elements essential to a successful life sciences cluster. The audience, tenants and future tenants comprised of scientists (Nobel Prize winners among them), venture capitalists, investment partners, government leaders and other decision makers who determine the developer best suited to own and manage their company's property and lab space, were given a compelling presentation of Alexandria's understanding of their needs. Each element of the strategic cluster – Location, Capital, Science and Talent – along with the letter and financial report, clad in a familial cover- all, combined to create a large Alexandria cluster in itself. The interiors of each booklet uniquely reflected their own individual subject matter and presented Alexandria's deep understanding of their customers and their marketplace. One message, strategic clustering, one audience, decision makers.

Annual Reports will be seen by an audience of shareowners, analysts, management, board of directors, customers, employees, potential employees and vendors. If you target this entire group with the hope of speaking to them all, then you miss the opportunity to deliver the message to the one audience who needs to hear it most. Worse yet, you might end up sporting a mullet.

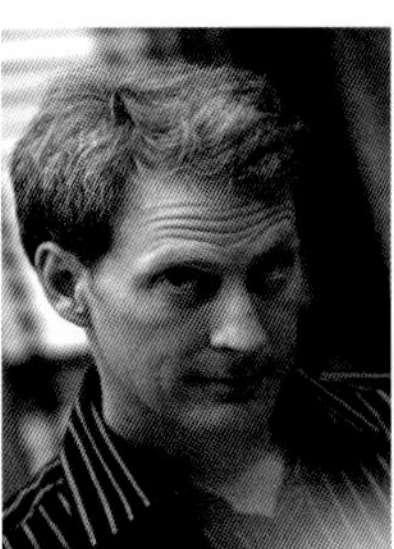

John Klotnia is a co-founder of Opto Design in New York City. Opto specializes in Annual Report design, brand identity, editorial and web development for a variety of clients such as: Alexandria Real Estate Equities, Inc., The New York Times Company, Rizzoli Publishing, BusinessWeek, New York Public Radio, Studio 360, Booz Allen Hamilton and New York University. Born in Homewood, Illinois, John received his BFA in Graphic Design from the University of Illinois, Urbana-Champaign, in 1987. In that same year, he moved to New York and joined Bonnell Design Associates. Then in 1989, John accepted a design position at Pentagram NY, where he quickly rose to become an Associate Partner working with Woody Pirtle. While there, he produced Annual Reports for United Technologies, The Rockefeller Foundation, Texaco and Nine West. In 1999, John, along with his good friend and colleague Ron Louie, a former Pentagram designer himself and design director for New York Times Digital, opened shop in the West Village and formed Opto Design. For his design, John has been recognized by the AIGA, Graphis, Mead Paper, Communication Arts, ASME, AR100 and his work is in the permanent collection of the Library of Congress. John lives in Park Slope with his wife Laura and two sons, Aaron and William.

THERAPEUTIC MONOCLONAL ANTIBODIES: MOVING THROUGH THE HUMAN BODY LIKE A GUIDED MISSILE TARGETING CANCER

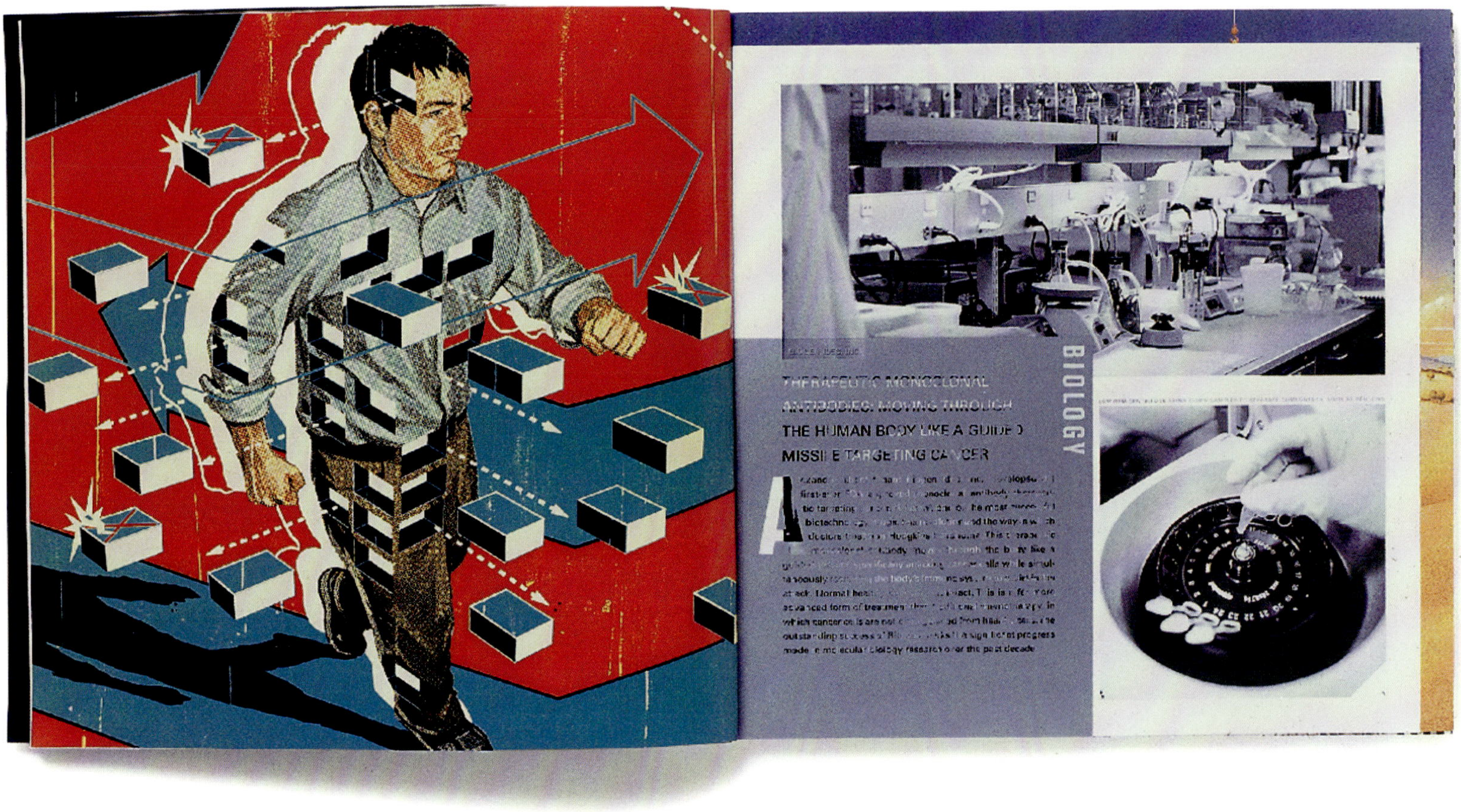

BIOLOGY

Creative Director: John Klotnia
Art Director: Brad Simon
Designer: Brad Simon, Kelly Atkins, Nancy Caal
Printer: ColorGraphics
Cover Paper: Curious Touch Soft Milk 111# cover
Text paper: Book 1: Fox River EverGreen Kraft 70# text, Book 2: Mohawk Superfine Softwhite Eggshell 80# text, Book 3: Kromekote Plus Two Side 100# text, Book 4: Carnival New Black 80# text, Book 5: Curious Translucent Pearl 27# text, Book 6: French Durotone Primer Gold 60#text.
Page count: Book 1: 8+cover, Book 2: 8+cover, Book 3: 12+cover, Book 4: 4+cover, Book 5: 12+cover, Book 6: 44+cover
Print run: 8,500
Size: 6" x 9" per book
Number of Images: 15
Client: Alexandria Real Estate Equities Inc.
2004 Annual Report

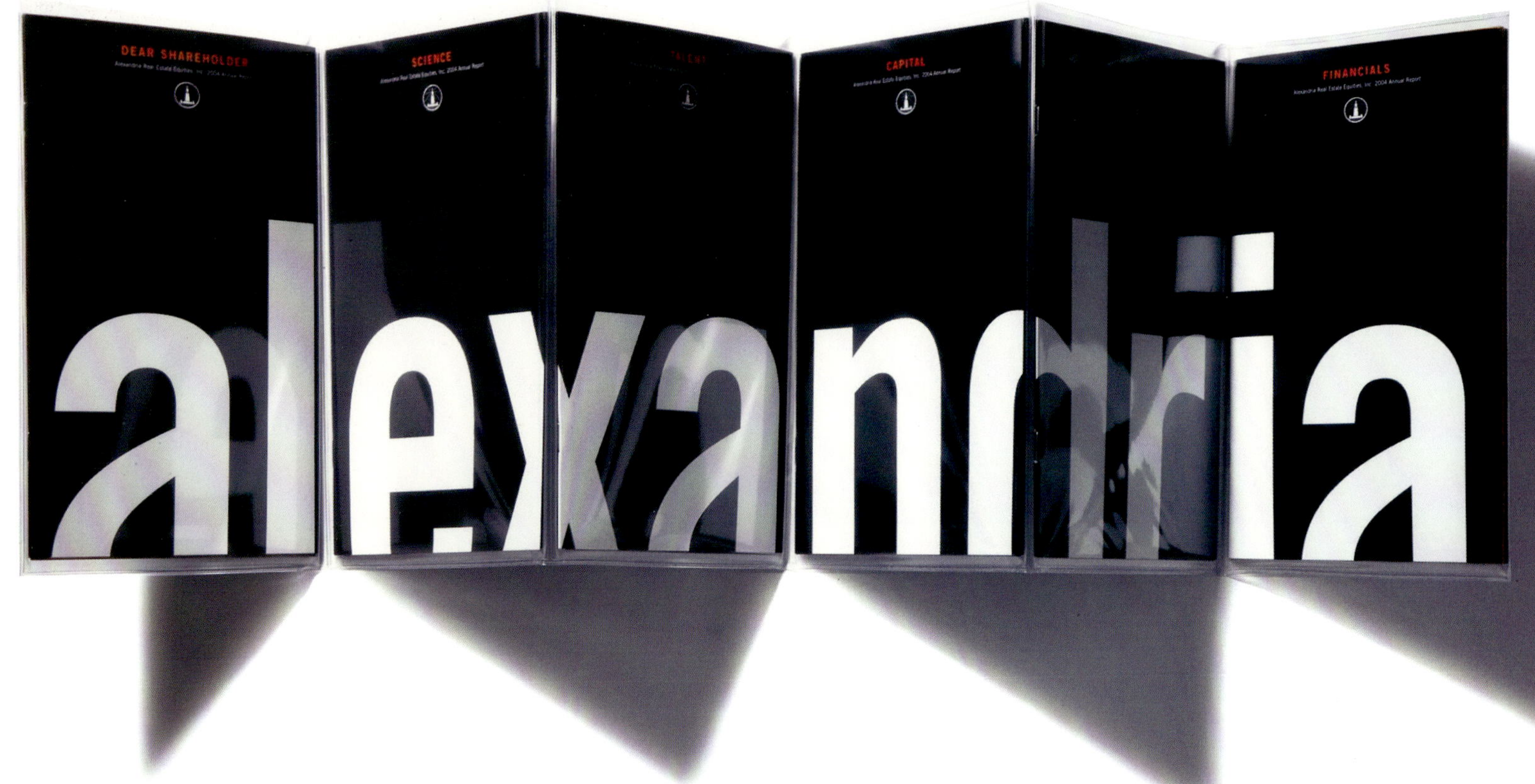

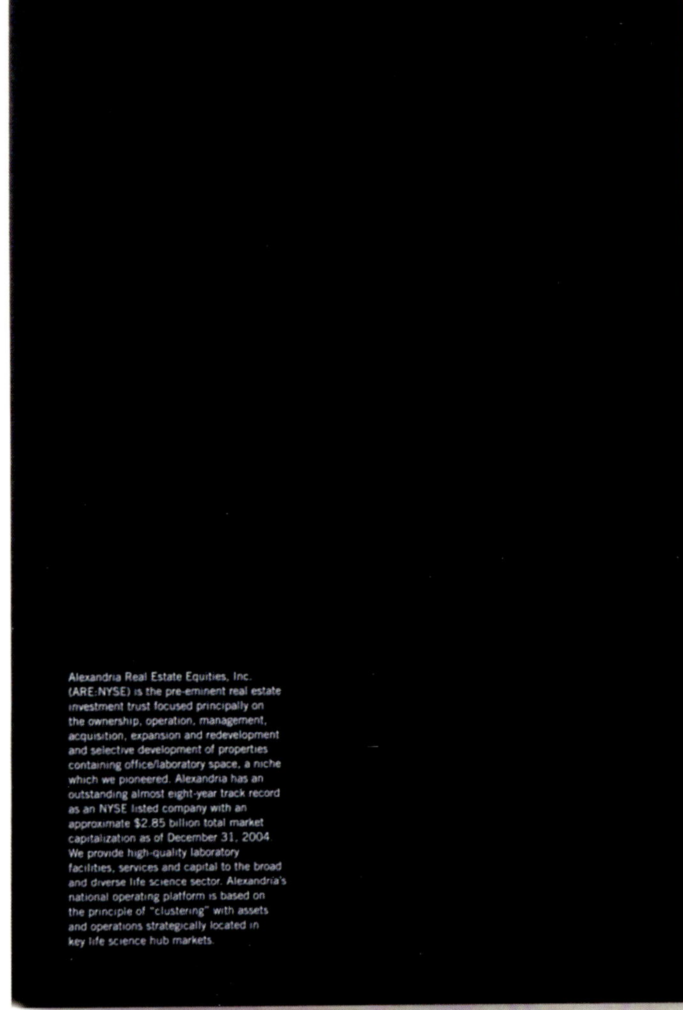

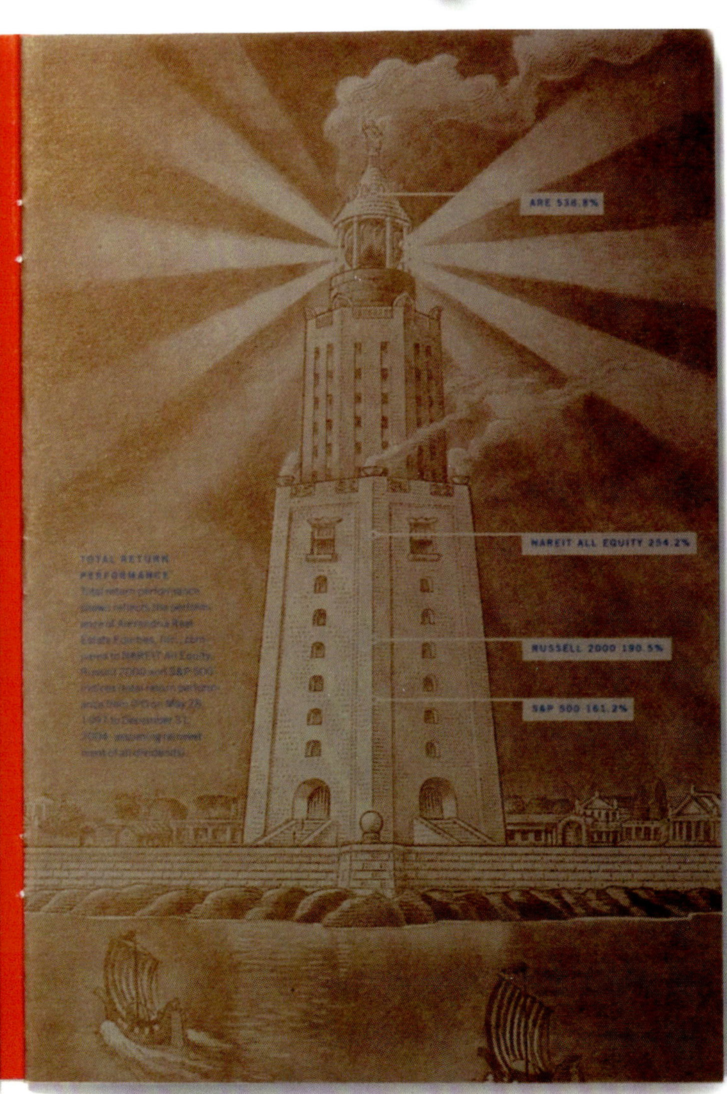

Alexandria Real Estate Equities, Inc. (ARE:NYSE) is the pre-eminent real estate investment trust focused principally on the ownership, operation, management, acquisition, expansion and redevelopment and selective development of properties containing office/laboratory space, a niche which we pioneered. Alexandria has an outstanding almost eight-year track record as an NYSE listed company with an approximate $2.85 billion total market capitalization as of December 31, 2004. We provide high-quality laboratory facilities, services and capital to the broad and diverse life science sector. Alexandria's national operating platform is based on the principle of "clustering" with assets and operations strategically located in key life science hub markets.

SCIENCE The critical mission driving the creation of life science clusters is to foster collaboration and the translation of life science discoveries into commercialized technologies beneficial to human healthcare. Over 500,000 people worldwide lose their vision annually from a disease called wet age-related macular degeneration ("AMD"). Wet AMD is the leading cause of blindness in people over the age of fifty. More than 1.6 million people are affected by the disease in the United States alone. With increasing senior populations in many countries, there is an urgent, growing need for a cure for Wet AMD. In December 2004, the U.S. Food & Drug Administration approved a new drug called Macugen® for the treatment of all types of Wet AMD. Alexandria's client tenant Eyetech Pharmaceuticals, Inc., launched the drug in collaboration with international pharmaceutical giant, Pfizer, Inc., successfully delivering Macugen® from the laboratory to the patient.

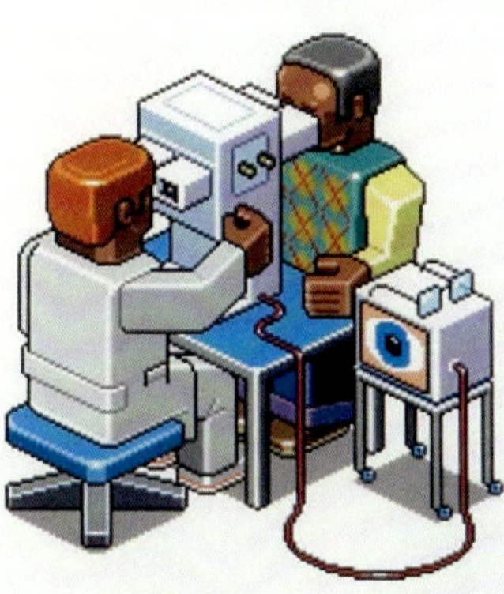

1 A patient visits a medical clinic demonstrating symptoms of disease.

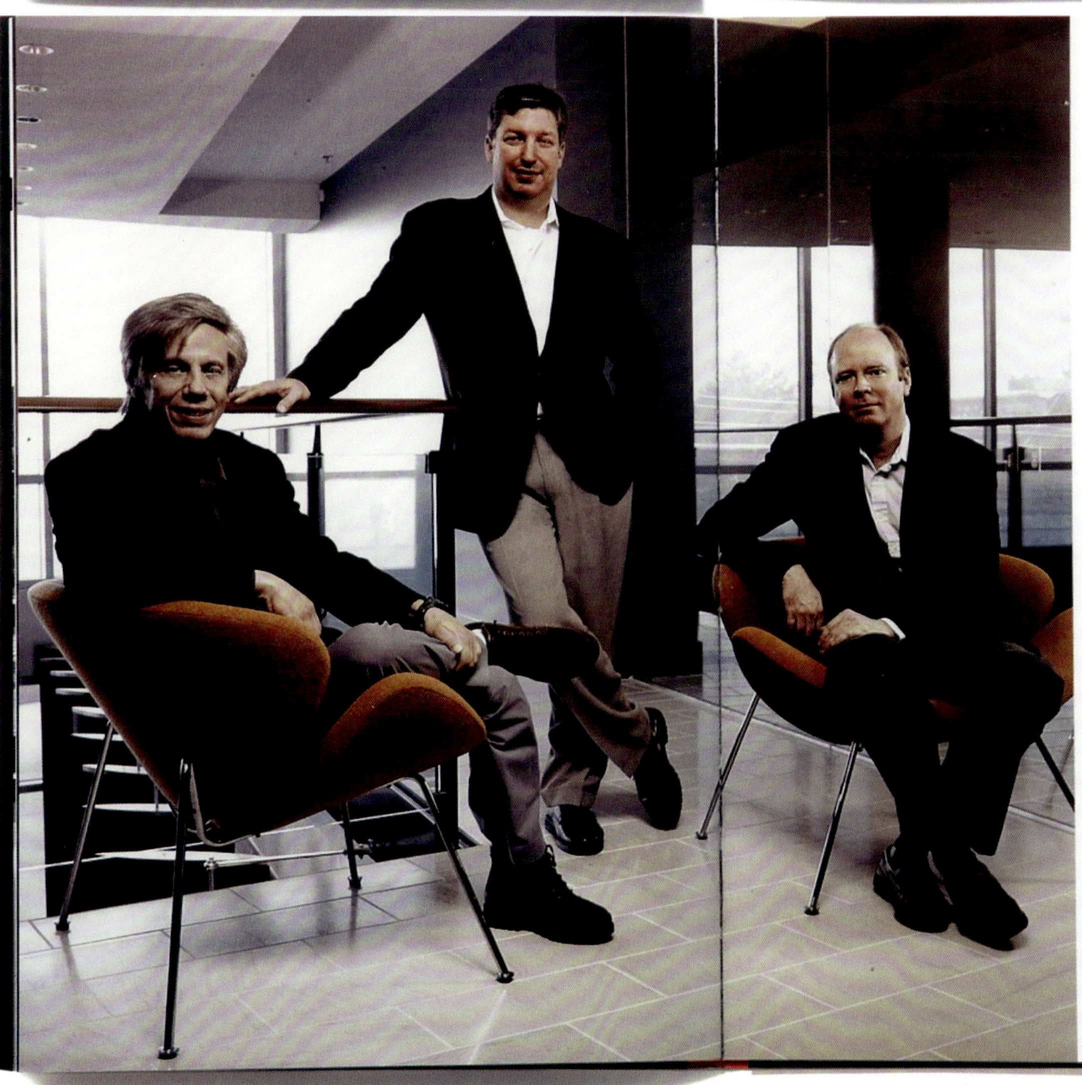

CRAIG A. SMITH, Ph.D. (left)
Chief Scientific Officer
VLST Corp.

CARL WEISSMAN (center)
President & CEO
Accelerator Corp.

STEVEN R. WILEY, Ph.D. (right)
Chief Technology Officer
VLST Corp.

The scientific team of Drs. Craig Smith and Steven Wiley, invented the arthritis drug Enbrel®, which is now a multibillion dollar biotechnology product, and are co-founders of an emerging biotechnology company dedicated to the development of next-generation monoclonal antibody therapeutics. This company was founded, in part, by Accelerator Corp., led by President and CEO Carl Weissman. Accelerator Corp., an innovative and creative vehicle designed to foster promising start-ups, is anchored by The Institute for Systems Biology, together with Alexandria and several prominent venture capital firms.

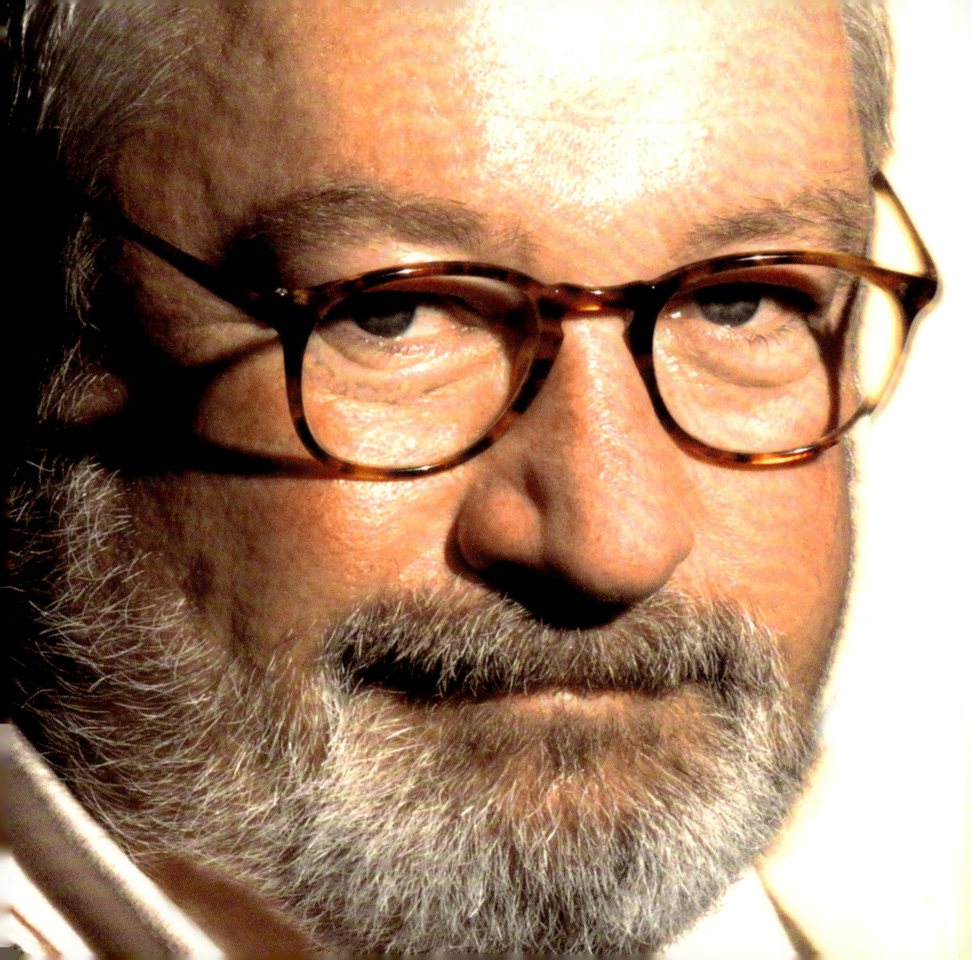

If fifteen seconds burns by and I don't understand the company's business, a switch is then triggered in my head. I put the book down and move on.

Fifteen Seconds

The judging for this year's book went very well. The chemistry among the judges was excellent and the atmosphere was relaxed. A major contributor to the mood was Martin Pederson's suggestion that the judges' entries be removed from consideration. He offered instead a new section in this book, which would show each judge's past Annual Report history and samples of their work. Thus the anxiety of witnessing your own work being weighed was removed, and the task became more interesting and businesslike (15 seconds is up). We were free to build Graphis the best possible show.

The task before us then became to wade through all the hundreds of entries to cut the books down to a manageable number. This meant the first voting needed to be finished by the noon break. It also meant that as we went around the table, the average judge's review of any particular book was about fifteen seconds.

Fifteen seconds probably doesn't sound very fair, but actually, a large part of the judging needs to be based on the immediate first impression. That is the world an Annual Report lives in and why our Annual Report design industry exists: to craft that impression on behalf of the client's company.

Like most people, I imagine you open your mail near a waste bin. Any piece of mail has but a second or two to avoid the landfill. An Annual Report shares this burden. The cover needs to hook you and draw you in. The inside information needs to be interesting but also easily accessible and presented with a system of visual clues to lead the reader through the book. If fifteen seconds burns by and I don't understand the company's business, a switch is then triggered in my head. I put the book down and move on. Fifteen seconds isn't so short if a book has an apparent flaw or two.

After the initial vote, the top vote recipients, still too many, entered the discussion phase. The judges pointed out each book's relative strengths and weaknesses. More time was spent with each book and the subtleties and consistencies emerged to add to the first impression. Taste, materials and a command of the visuals and production process helped sway opinions and win votes.

National Golf Properties, Inc.
Creative Director: Doug Oliver

Designer: Doug Oliver
Photographer: Rik Besser
Copywriter: Neil Miller

Printer: Lithographix
Print Run: 20,000
Size: 8x11

Company: National Golf Properties was a real estate investment trust and owned over 120 golf courses nationwide.

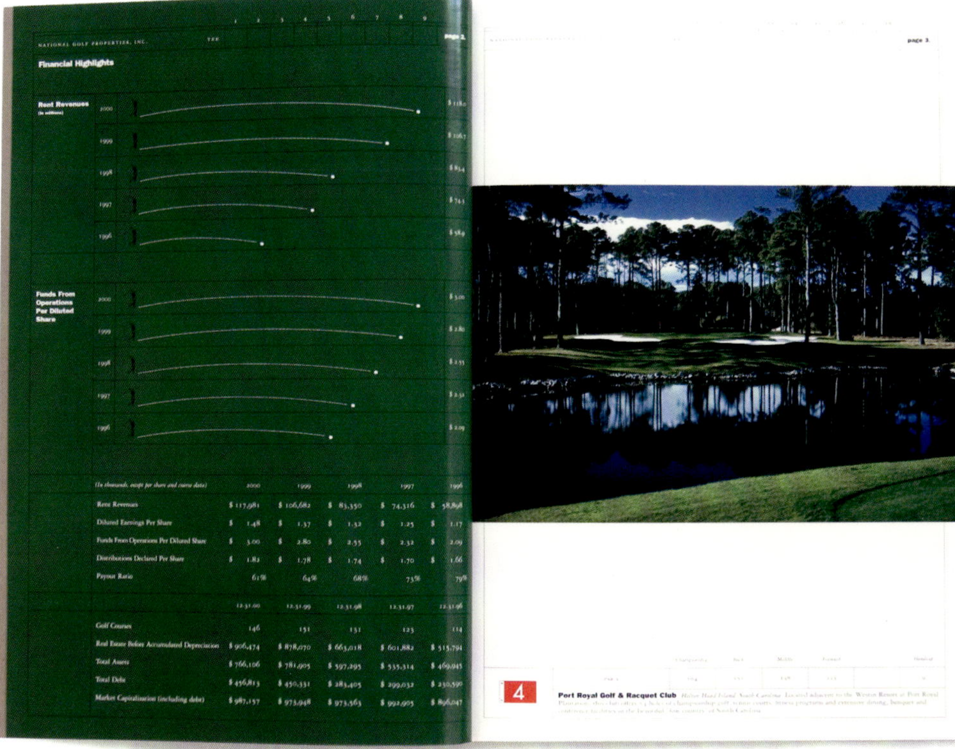

The discussion phase concluded with the review of several books vying for the "last one in" spot in the show. The conversation became more animated as one judge championed an entry while another judge felt strongly about another. In the end, bargains were struck and alliances were made and the "in or out?" process came to a close. Then the day came to an end and the winning books were put aside for the night. After dinner, the judges slept on their decisions and met again for a morning session to review the overall balance of the show. The winners were discussed again and affirmed as winners. Few, if any, swaps were made and by midmorning the show was locked down and handed over to Graphis.

I found the judging experience to be both an honor and privilege. I made new friends and renewed some old ones. As judges, we were aware of the gratification that the winners draw from our selections and in sympathy with those books that just missed. We chose 34 annuals for this show but admit the selection was difficult inside the last 100. Finally, we owe a debt to Graphis for picking up the torch of the fallen Mead Annual Report Show, which ended in 2001 after 45 years. With Graphis Annual Reports, designers have a new benchmark to measure their Annual efforts and shine.

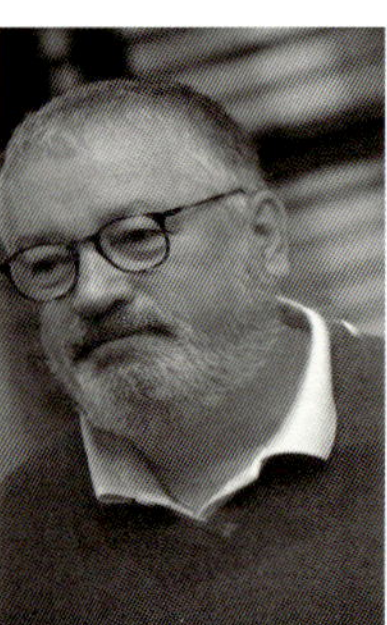

Douglas J. Oliver is President and Chief Creative Officer of Douglas Oliver Design Office, located in Santa Monica, California.His work has been recognized by all of the major design institutions, garnering awards from the Communication Arts Design Annual, Graphis Annual Reports, The AR 100, Critique magazine's "The Big Crit," American Institute of Graphic Arts, New York Art Director's Club, The Los Angeles Art Director's Club, and The Western Art Director's Club. His work is also part of the Permanent Design Collection of the Library of Congress.

The consistent excellence of Doug's design of Annual Reports also made him a perenial favorite in the prestigious Mead Annual Report Show. His annuals were chosen among the best for 15 consecutive years, until the Mead Show came to an end in 2001.

He began his professional career in Los Angeles, working with the legendary James Cross and the late Robert Miles Runyan, who is often called the "father of the modern annual report." In 1983, Doug opened his own studio to design for Fortune 500 companies, major universities, institutions and foundations across the US, Europe and Japan.

Over the years, Doug has remained active in the larger design community. In 1998, he served as Chair of The Annual Report Design Conference held at the World Trade Center in New York City. More recently, he returned to his alma mater, the University of Kansas, as a Hallmark Symposium speaker. He has also maintained close ties with Art Center, serving as an alumni board member, teacher, guest speaker and consultant. In 2004, Doug was one of a handful of graphic designers included in Art Center's "Design Impact," which detailed the contributions of Art Center alumni over the past 75 years.

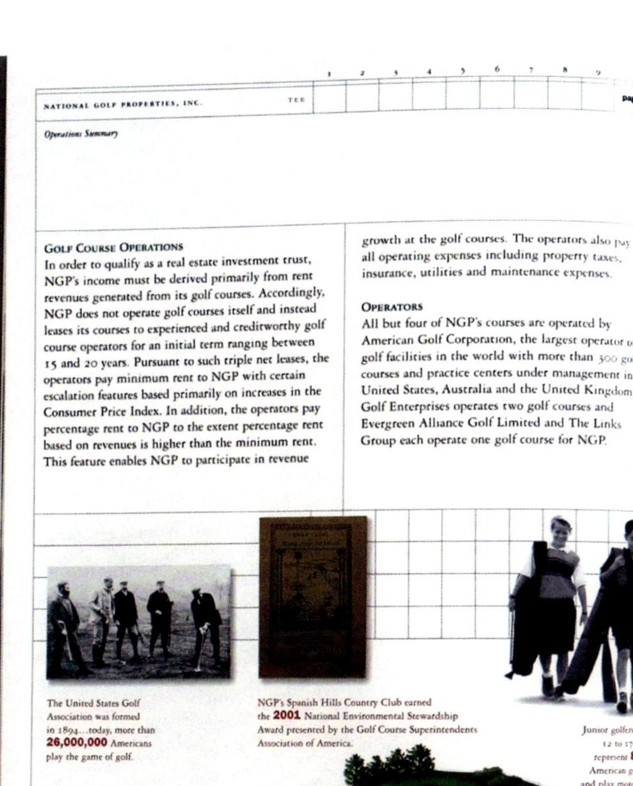
NATIONAL GOLF PROPERTIES, INC. TEE 1 2 3 4 5 6 7 8 9 page 12

Operations Summary

Golf Course Operations

In order to qualify as a real estate investment trust, NGP's income must be derived primarily from rent revenues generated from its golf courses. Accordingly, NGP does not operate golf courses itself and instead leases its courses to experienced and creditworthy golf course operators for an initial term ranging between 15 and 20 years. Pursuant to such triple net leases, the operators pay minimum rent to NGP with certain escalation features based primarily on increases in the Consumer Price Index. In addition, the operators pay percentage rent to NGP to the extent percentage rent based on revenues is higher than the minimum rent. This feature enables NGP to participate in revenue growth at the golf courses. The operators also pay all operating expenses including property taxes, insurance, utilities and maintenance expenses.

Operators

All but four of NGP's courses are operated by American Golf Corporation, the largest operator of golf facilities in the world with more than 300 golf courses and practice centers under management in the United States, Australia and the United Kingdom. Golf Enterprises operates two golf courses and Evergreen Alliance Golf Limited and The Links Group each operate one golf course for NGP.

The United States Golf Association was formed in 1894…today, more than **26,000,000** Americans play the game of golf.

NGP's Spanish Hills Country Club earned the **2001** National Environmental Stewardship Award presented by the Golf Course Superintendents Association of America.

Junior golfers aged 12 to 17 years represent **8%** of American golfers and play more than 30 million rounds of golf per year

The **10th** hole at NGP's Witch Hollow Course at Pumpkin Ridge Golf Club where Tiger Woods secured his 3rd consecutive United States Amateur Championship in 1996.

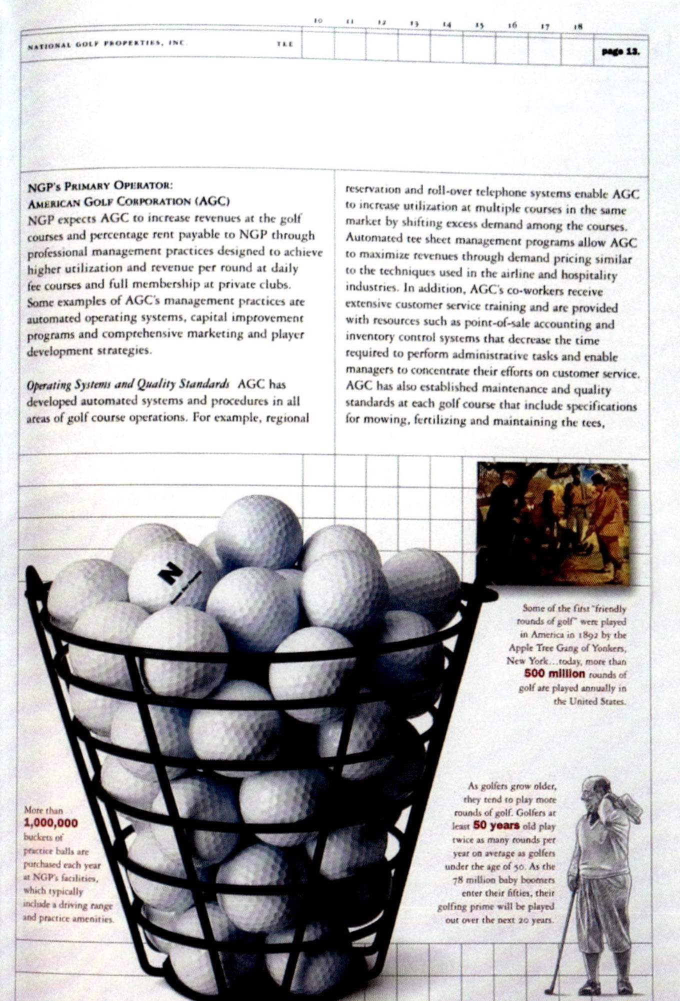
NATIONAL GOLF PROPERTIES, INC. TEE 10 11 12 13 14 15 16 17 18 page 13.

NGP's Primary Operator: American Golf Corporation (AGC)

NGP expects AGC to increase revenues at the golf courses and percentage rent payable to NGP through professional management practices designed to achieve higher utilization and revenue per round at daily fee courses and full membership at private clubs. Some examples of AGC's management practices are automated operating systems, capital improvement programs and comprehensive marketing and player development strategies.

Operating Systems and Quality Standards AGC has developed automated systems and procedures in all areas of golf course operations. For example, regional reservation and roll-over telephone systems enable AGC to increase utilization at multiple courses in the same market by shifting excess demand among the courses. Automated tee sheet management programs allow AGC to maximize revenues through demand pricing similar to the techniques used in the airline and hospitality industries. In addition, AGC's co-workers receive extensive customer service training and are provided with resources such as point-of-sale accounting and inventory control systems that decrease the time required to perform administrative tasks and enable managers to concentrate their efforts on customer service. AGC has also established maintenance and quality standards at each golf course that include specifications for mowing, fertilizing and maintaining the tees,

Some of the first "friendly rounds of golf" were played in America in 1892 by the Apple Tree Gang of Yonkers, New York…today, more than **500 million** rounds of golf are played annually in the United States.

More than **1,000,000** buckets of practice balls are purchased each year at NGP's facilities, which typically include a driving range and practice amenities.

As golfers grow older, they tend to play more rounds of golf. Golfers at least **50 years** old play twice as many rounds per year on average as golfers under the age of 50. As the 78 million baby boomers enter their fifties, their golfing prime will be played out over the next 20 years.

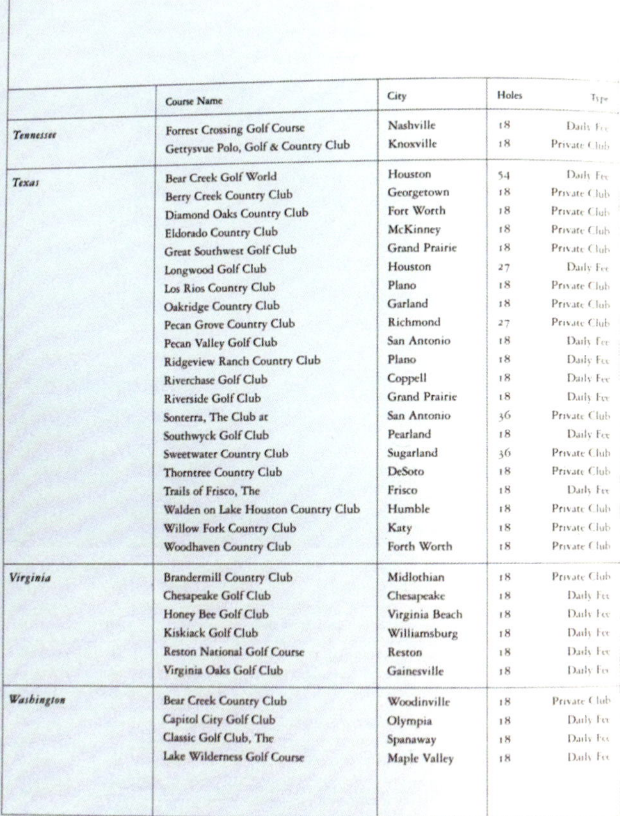
NATIONAL GOLF PROPERTIES, INC. TEE 1 2 3 4 5 6 7 8 9 page 26

Portfolio of Golf Courses

	Course Name	City	Holes	Type
Tennessee	Forrest Crossing Golf Course	Nashville	18	Daily Fee
	Gettysvue Polo, Golf & Country Club	Knoxville	18	Private Club
Texas	Bear Creek Golf World	Houston	54	Daily Fee
	Berry Creek Country Club	Georgetown	18	Private Club
	Diamond Oaks Country Club	Fort Worth	18	Private Club
	Eldorado Country Club	McKinney	18	Private Club
	Great Southwest Golf Club	Grand Prairie	18	Private Club
	Longwood Golf Club	Houston	27	Daily Fee
	Los Rios Country Club	Plano	18	Private Club
	Oakridge Country Club	Garland	18	Private Club
	Pecan Grove Country Club	Richmond	27	Private Club
	Pecan Valley Golf Club	San Antonio	18	Daily Fee
	Ridgeview Ranch Country Club	Plano	18	Daily Fee
	Riverchase Golf Club	Coppell	18	Daily Fee
	Riverside Golf Club	Grand Prairie	18	Daily Fee
	Sonterra, The Club at	San Antonio	36	Private Club
	Southwyck Golf Club	Pearland	18	Daily Fee
	Sweetwater Country Club	Sugarland	36	Private Club
	Thorntree Country Club	DeSoto	18	Private Club
	Trails of Frisco, The	Frisco	18	Daily Fee
	Walden on Lake Houston Country Club	Humble	18	Private Club
	Willow Fork Country Club	Katy	18	Private Club
	Woodhaven Country Club	Forth Worth	18	Private Club
Virginia	Brandermill Country Club	Midlothian	18	Private Club
	Chesapeake Golf Club	Chesapeake	18	Daily Fee
	Honey Bee Golf Club	Virginia Beach	18	Daily Fee
	Kiskiack Golf Club	Williamsburg	18	Daily Fee
	Reston National Golf Course	Reston	18	Daily Fee
	Virginia Oaks Golf Club	Gainesville	18	Daily Fee
Washington	Bear Creek Country Club	Woodinville	18	Private Club
	Capitol City Golf Club	Olympia	18	Daily Fee
	Classic Golf Club, The	Spanaway	18	Daily Fee
	Lake Wilderness Golf Course	Maple Valley	18	Daily Fee

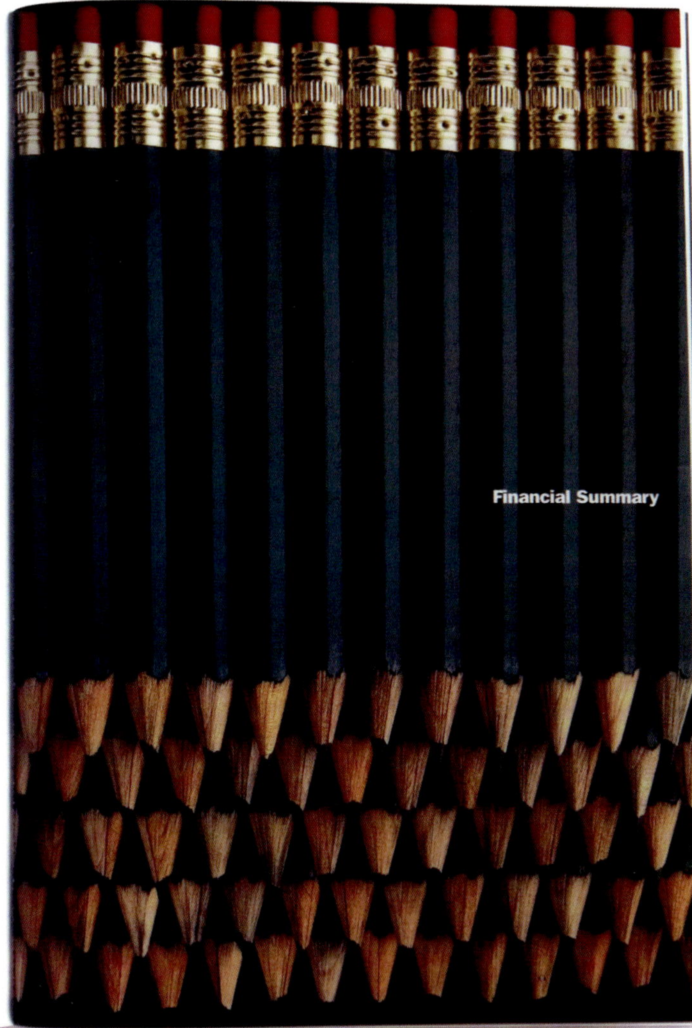

Northrop Grumman Corporation	Creative Director: Doug Oliver Designer: Doug Oliver	Printer: Lithographix Photography: Bill Varie, John Amrhein	Copy: Guy Hicks, Cynthia Crothers Company: Northrop	Grumman is a leading Aerospace and Defense Contractor.

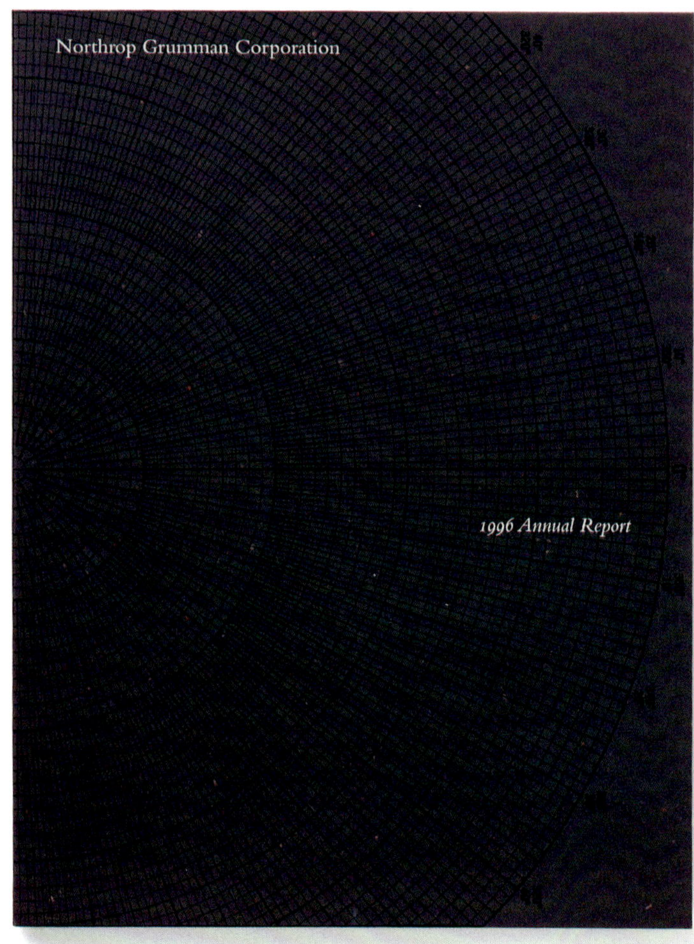

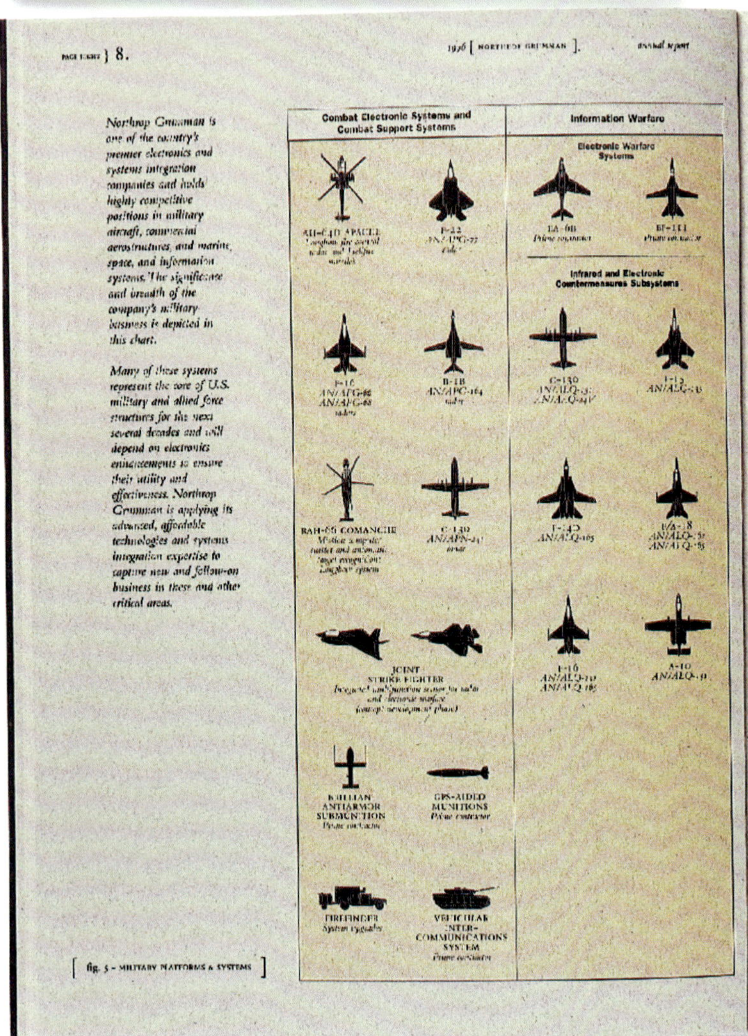

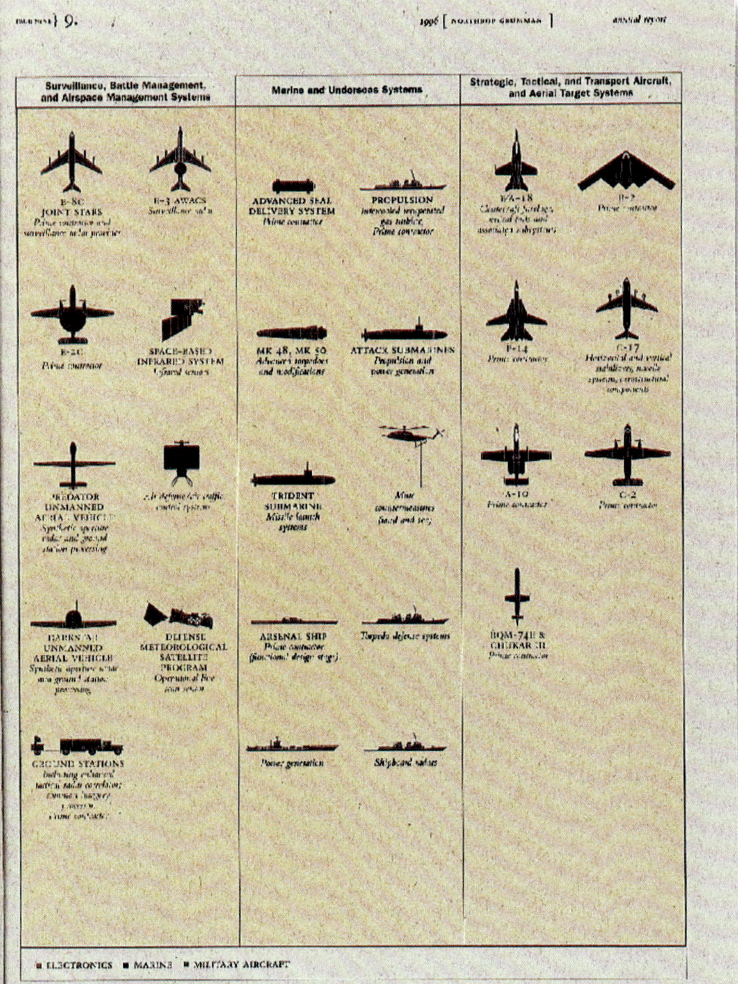

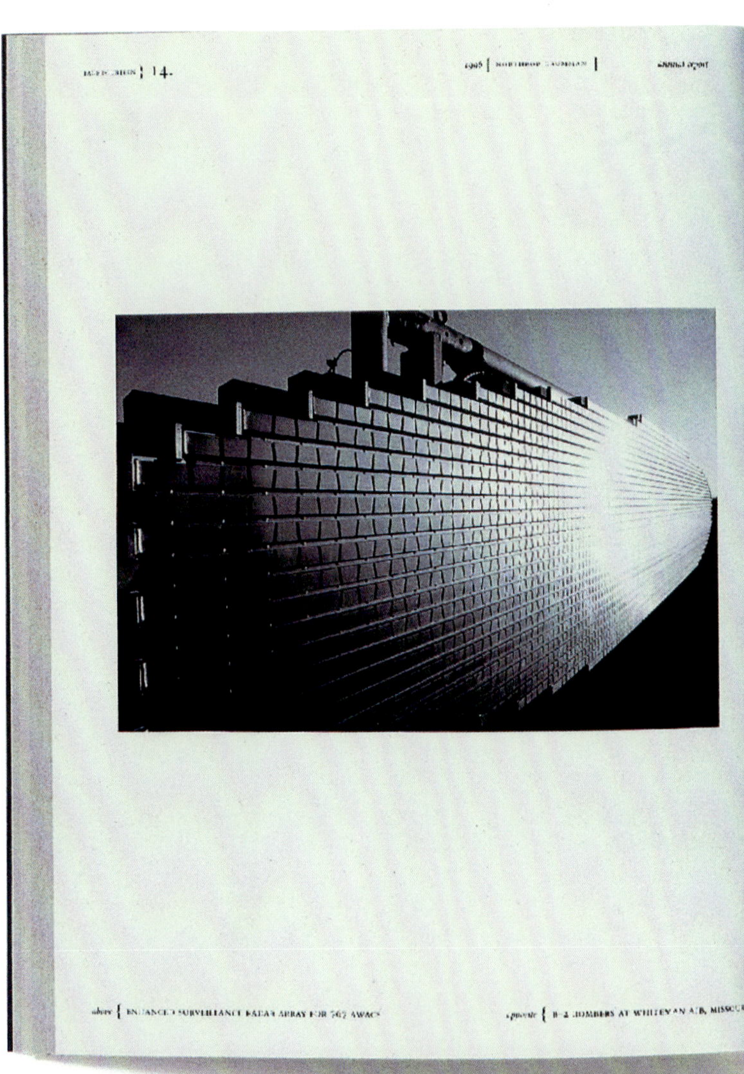

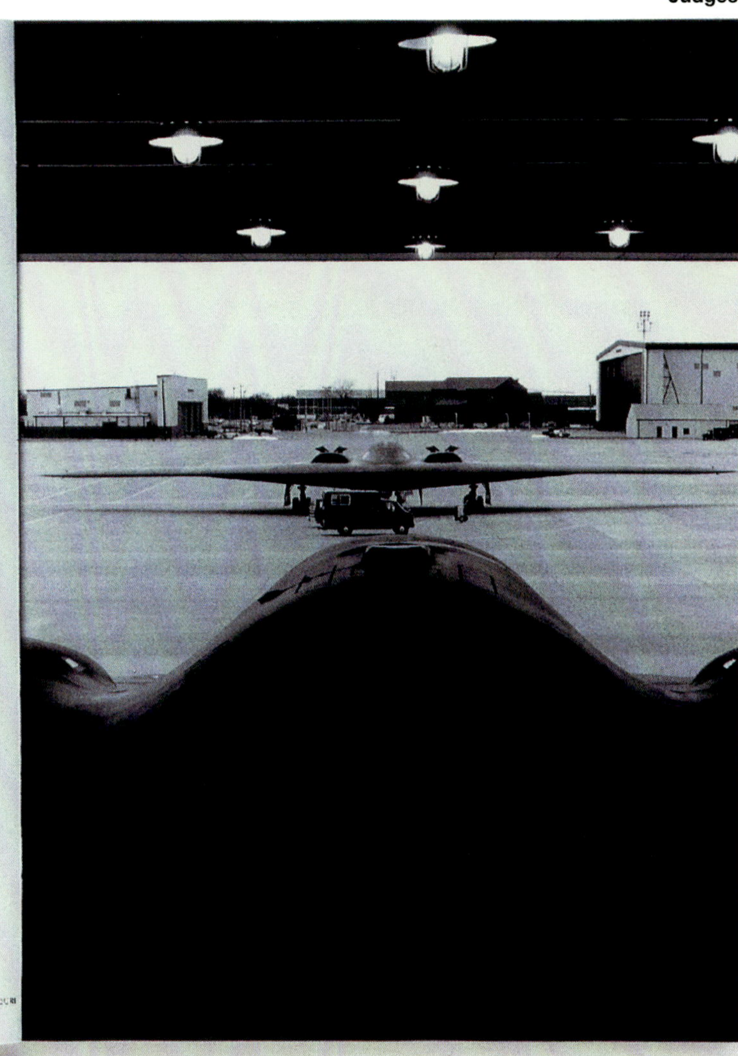

above { ENHANCED SURVEILLANCE RADAR ARRAY FOR 767 AWACS

opposite { B-2 BOMBERS AT WHITEMAN AFB, MISSOURI

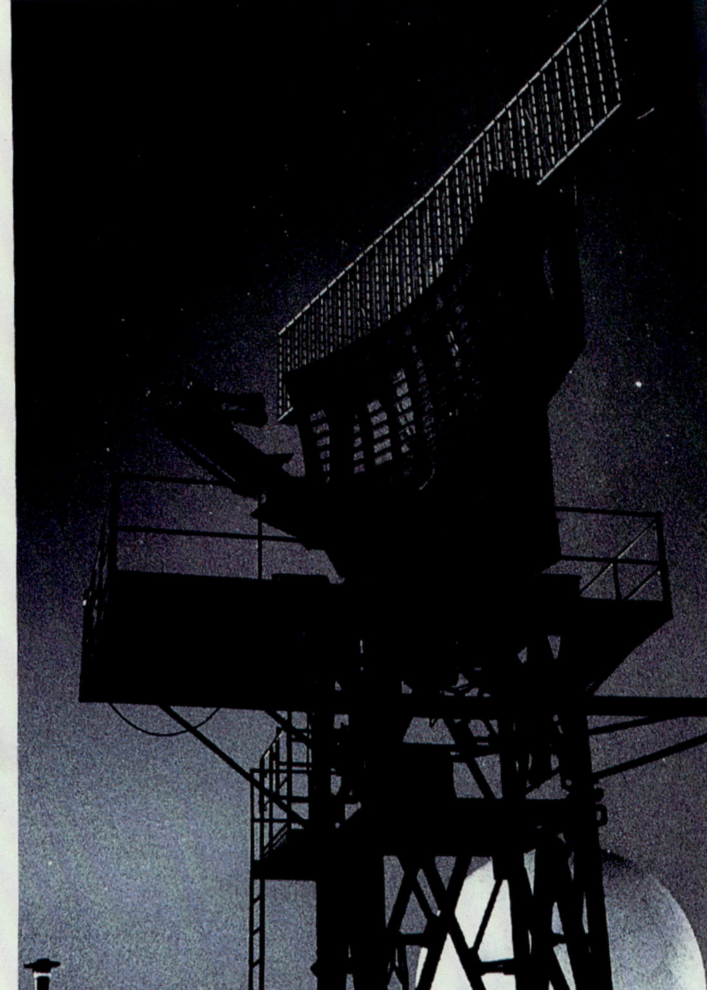

Operations Review

Northrop Grumman participates on many key military and commercial programs within its primary business areas. These systems will remain operational for several decades, and the company's incumbent position creates a competitive advantage in capturing new and follow-on business. As reflected in its 1996 operations, Northrop Grumman is developing and applying affordable, advanced technology solutions to strengthen its market position and meet new customer requirements.

Electronics One clear characteristic of military forces in the future will be their reliance on electronics. Although the Administration's defense budget is essentially flat over the next five years, various studies indicate that the electronics segment will increase as a percentage of the total budget. Faced with budget realities, defense leaders are analyzing the fit between national security strategy and future missions. As the military services continue to look for ways to achieve greater precision, flexibility, and survivability, defense electronic systems become increasingly important. Experience in large-scale systems integration of surveillance, battle management, and strike platforms—including the electronic linkages among these systems—positions companies such as Northrop Grumman to meet emerging military requirements.

Surveillance and Battle Management
Collecting, organizing, and delivering key tactical and strategic information to decision makers and operational forces on a near-real-time basis are among the principal challenges of future military operations. Airborne platforms, including the E-8 Joint STARS surveillance and battle management system, the E-2C airborne early warning and control (AEW&C) system, and the E-3 Airborne Warning And Control System (AWACS), will fill many of the needs of domestic and foreign customers — including warfighting requirements, peace enforcement, treaty verification, and crisis management. As prime contractor for the E-8 and E-2C and major sensor provider for the E-3, Northrop Grumman is working with its customers to combine and enhance existing platforms and to improve data processing techniques, thus enabling systems to distribute information more quickly to combat elements that immediately affect the battle.

{ JOINT STARS }

fig. 8
E-8C
JOINT SURVEILLANCE TARGET ATTACK RADAR SYSTEM
[JOINT STARS]

Description: Detects, locates, classifies, and tracks fixed and moving ground forces, including jeeps and armored vehicles, as well as patrol boats and slow-flying rotary and fixed-winged aircraft, day or night, in all weather conditions.

Company Role: Prime contractor and radar sensor provider.

Customer: U.S. Air Force, U.S. Army.

Revenue: 1996 sales $606 million; potential revenue $6 billion through 2003.

In ground surveillance, Joint STARS proved to be an essential surveillance and battle management asset during 1996 NATO peacekeeping operations in Bosnia-Herzegovina, offering allied commanders an unprecedented view of fixed and moving ground forces, greatly increasing situational awareness. Northrop Grumman's Electronics and Systems Integration Division (ESID) is prime contractor for Joint STARS, and the system's radar sensor is produced by the company's Electronic Sensors and Systems Division (ESSD).

The company is leading a team that is offering Joint STARS to NATO to meet its airborne ground surveillance requirements. Team members include some of the largest European

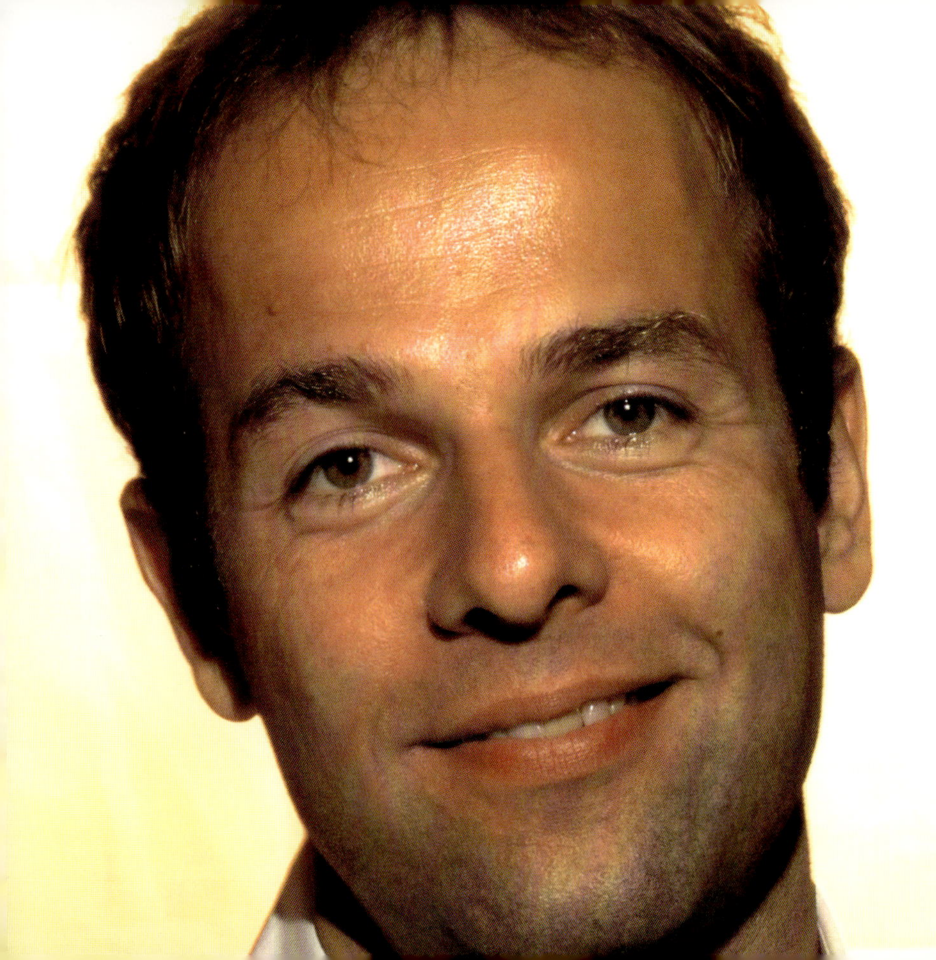

Shareholders are asking for better information and new legislation is forcing companies to think harder about their messages. A bright future for Annual Report designers? Potentially – if we keep our audiences in mind and think about content. Our job isn't just about pretty graphics anymore. We must help our clients identify their key messages before finding appropriate and imaginative ways to present them.

Why should I invest in you? – Annual Reports in the UK and Europe

The average reader spends precious few minutes with an Annual Report. Yet for many companies it is the biggest single (and by far the most expensive) means of communication to shareholders. Do companies make the most of their reader's short attention?

Statutory financial reports aside, companies usually take one of two approaches for their summary statements. US companies regard it as a marketing tool and use it to promote company messages. In the UK, companies usually comment on last year's business performance.

The main reason for the latter is that, in the UK, the Annual Report is often owned by the finance department. It's unfortunate for us designers, because it means that the success of the report is measured on project process and delivery, not on message and audience feedback.

Given these circumstances it is perhaps not surprising that few British reports break the conventions. The blame, though, has to be put on the designers too. Open any British annual and you'll probably find sans serif, set in three columns, accompanied by imaginative themes such as "a day in the life" or "people and kit."

European annual report designs are too varied and too different to write about in two paragraphs without falling into cliches. However, there are three trends I find worth noting. First, in Germany, designing Annual Reports has become fashionable again. There is a great emphasis on typographic craft and production values and many reports are beautiful, although some clearly put beauty before meaning. It is disappointing to spend 15 minutes deciphering a graphic when all it says in the end is "we deliver growth." Well, who doesn't?

Trend number two: our Eastern European neighbors are adding a new spirit to Annual Report design. This year's show features a few of them. Some reports use only two colors but feel fresh and vibrant; others are lavishly produced books, perhaps trying to gain credibility through scale. Some of these reports are very playful. I haven't come

MFI
Creative Director: David Stocks, Gilmar Wendt

Designer: Andy Spencer
Printer: Fulmar Colour Ltd
Paper: ZEN from GF Smith

Page count: 76 + 8 page + cover
Print run: 25,000

Size: 18.5cm x 27cm
Number of Images: 0

Client: MFI is a furniture company.

MFI Annual Report 2004

How far
have we come
in the last five years?

Contents

Five years ago
MFI was very different from today.
A retail kitchen and bedroom business
selling in the UK and in France.
We carried high debt
and a weak balance sheet.
The outlook was not good.

The business needed to change.

In purely financial terms
we have grown our total sales
from under £800 million
to over £1.5 billion.

across many boards of directors shown as birds on pylons.

Lastly, and this affects all annuals, companies are waking up to the fact that they have to communicate more. Shareholders are asking for better information and new legislation is forcing companies to think harder about their messages. A bright future for Annual Report designers? Potentially – if we keep our audiences in mind and think about content. Our job isn't just about pretty graphics anymore. We must help our clients identify their key messages before finding appropriate and imaginative ways to present them.

At SAS, we see the Annual Report as a presentation of the investment case to the reader. What are the company's achievements, opportunities, risks and strategy? Figures may well speak for themselves. But they require knowledge and time, something not all of us investors have. That's why we need a clear argument for why we should invest. Presenting that argument in an inspiring and memorable way is what it's all about.

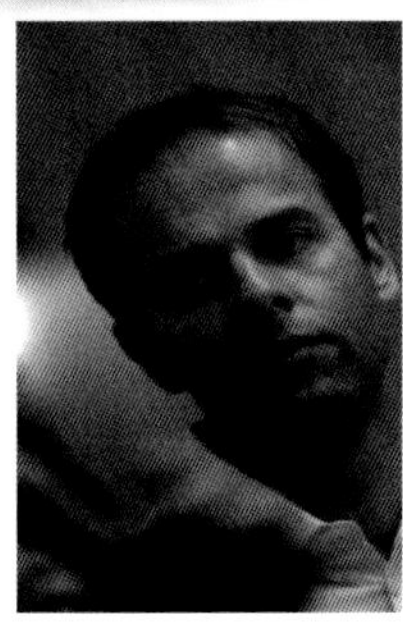

Born in Berlin to an East-German father and a West-German mother, Gilmar Wendt studied graphic design with Hans Peter Willberg and Olaf Leu in Mainz, Germany, before joining Groothuis+Malsy in Bremen. At G+M he designed over 100 books and jackets, and was responsible for the multi award-winning books of the DuMont Literatur Publishing House. He quickly progressed from designer to Art Director as G+M became one of the top ten creative agencies in Germany.

In 1999 he followed his girlfriend Christine, to London and joined SAS. SAS has been going for 16 years, helping its various blue-chip clients communicate more effectively with their investors, business customers and employees. Gilmar became SAS's creative director in 2003, Christine's husband in 2004, and a shareholding partner in 2005.

His Annual Report clients include Ericsson, MFI furniture Group, BBA, Lonmin, Scottish-Power and Sainsbury's. Gilmar has won numerous industry awards. Some of them are TDC, ADC New York and Germany, Graphis Annual Reports, The Black Book, British Design and Art Direction (D&AD), Design Week, Red-Dot and Best German Books.

Gilmar regularly gives workshops and lectures at colleges. He is a Fellow and council member of the International Society of Typographic Designers and a member of D&AD.

We now have
a stronger balance sheet and lower debt
giving us a far greater ability
to make choices about the investments
with which we need to build
long-term strength in our business.

Our retail stores are being transformed
into fresher modern environments.
Our customers tell us
they enjoy the experience far more.

We are no longer reliant
on a single route to market.

Howdens is a remarkable success
and continues to grow strongly.

It complements our consumer business
and reduces risk.

Through seedcorn investments
we expect other ways to emerge
that will enable us
to spread risk in the future.

Corporate and social responsibility

Introduction

Last year the Group included a corporate and social responsibility statement for the first time and we intend to continue to report our progress in this area. The Group continues to recognise its actual and potential corporate and social responsibilities to society and acts in a strategic way to implement them. Relevant laws and regulations are considered a starting point from which responsible behaviour can build. This year we will be launching a link from our corporate website to a new CSR website to give more detailed information on the subjects covered in this section.

Our areas of responsibility are organised and described under four headings:

- Marketplace
- Environment
- Workplace
- Community

i) Marketplace

Customers

Our aim is to help people live better lives in their own homes by striving to deliver quality merchandise on time and in full, notwithstanding the challenges in delivering the hundreds of individual components required in our products. We are a member of Qualitas, the independent arbitrator, and also participate in an Office of Fair Trading (OFT) payment protection scheme.

Supply chain

It is important for the Group to manage both its own internal supply chain as well as the relationships with our many external suppliers. Our new global sourcing questionnaire continues to assess the corporate and social responsibility performance of external suppliers on the basis of labour standards, human rights and the environment. We will be using the new questionnaire for all new suppliers of goods and services with appropriate follow up and audit, as we deem necessary. We used new suppliers in the development of our new questionnaire to utilise their own experiences in this area. Existing suppliers will be requested to use the new questionnaire when contracts are reviewed or new products purchased.

The Group's purchasing is governed by an Ethical Sourcing Policy when making purchasing decisions. This policy was reviewed to account for changes and expansion into overseas markets, as we recognised the need for greater vigilance of social and environmental issues within our supply chain.

Distribution

The Group has a complex distribution system. We endeavour to operate our 154 HGVs and 400 vans and assorted vehicles as efficiently as possible. We are planning on replacing 30 of the HGVs this coming year with new Euro 4 engines to increase efficiency and reduce emissions. We will also be replacing 60 of our primary trailers with a new ergonomically designed flexible 'step frame trailer' which can increase capacity by 30%, be more versatile for bulky goods and encourage less damage to products. The additional benefits will be less vehicle movements and hence less CO_2 emissions.

Wood

Approximately 80% of the Group's raw materials are wood or wood fibres. In 2004 we used 402,500 cubic metres of wood in the form of chipboard (351,100 cubic metres), MDF (49,200 cubic metres) and solid wood (2,200 cubic metres). We also used 7,800 tonnes of cardboard packaging for our manufactured products.

To ensure a sustainable future for the business it is important that we source our wood in an environmentally and socially sustainable manner. Wherever possible we specify the Forest Stewardship Council (FSC) or the Programme for the Endorsement of Forest Certification (PEFC) schemes as the preferred options. The wood products used were 68.5% FSC and 31% PEFC accredited. The cardboard packaging was 100% FSC accredited.

Within the ethical sourcing policy we reserve the right to audit suppliers and this is especially so for the chain of custody for wood and wood products.

ii) Environment

We are committed to preserving the natural environment and our key objectives in this regard are to:

- reduce consumption;
- re-use or re-cycle wherever possible;
- measure progress by setting key performance indicators;

Corporate and social responsibility

continued

- continue working towards re-accreditation of the environmental management systems (ISO 14001) in our manufacturing division;
- work closely with our suppliers to ensure that items we purchase come from sustainable renewable resources and are produced in a socially responsible way;
- ensure that our policy is up to date and relevant to our business and is used throughout the organisation in training and general business undertakings; and
- ensure that a support structure is in place to enable our objectives to be fulfilled.

Energy

We have been active in measuring and reducing our energy use. Our retail stores in the UK and our manufacturing sites have been awarded the Institute of Energy's prestigious Energy Efficiency Accreditation, having first been accredited in 1996 and again in 1999 and 2002.

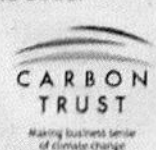

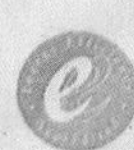

We are continuing to install building energy management systems in all new stores and are monitoring energy performance in all stores. Our framework agreement with the Carbon Trust has allowed us to take advantage of their services and five locations have recently been surveyed to identify CO_2 emissions savings that can be implemented across the retail network.

Energy use (kWh per £1,000 turnover)

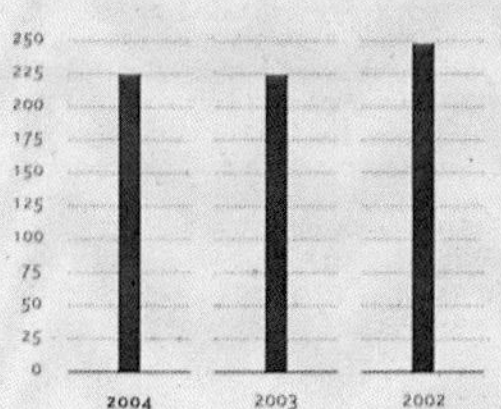

Electricity, gas and fuel consumption result in the emission of CO_2, a greenhouse gas that research indicates contributes to climate change. CO_2 emissions in 2004 totalled 145,705 tonnes representing a decrease per million pound turnover of 3.8 tonnes over the last 12 months. The principal source of emissions is from the use of electricity.

CO_2 emissions (Tonnes per £1m turnover)

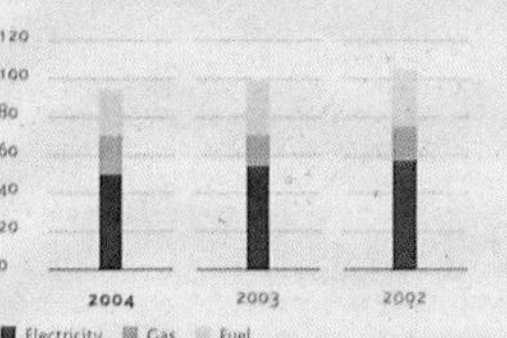

The Group has made considerable efforts to reduce energy consumption over the past ten years, an effort that has been recognised by the Carbon Trust in publicity throughout 2003 and 2004. In addition, 35 stores last year purchased electricity from renewable sources. We will continue to use such sources where available and commercially viable.

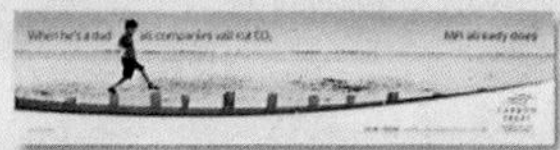

Waste

This year we introduced a total waste management service into the distribution area of the business, which has resulted in an annualised reduction in 1,000 vehicle movements and an efficiency saving of approximately £40,000. This service is to be rolled out to the manufacturing and retail division early in 2005. To help with the promotion of this service and our environmental 3R (reduce, re-use, re-cycle) policy, a Group waste management co-ordinator has been introduced to facilitate the project.

MFI
Creative Director: David Stocks, Gilmar Wendt
Designer: Mike Hall
Printer: Westerham
Paper: Medley Pure, Ikono silk from Zanders
Page count: 88 + page cover
Print run: 16,000
Size: 21cm x 25cm
Number of Images: 14
Client: BBA Group owns businesses in the fields of aviation and non-woven fabrics

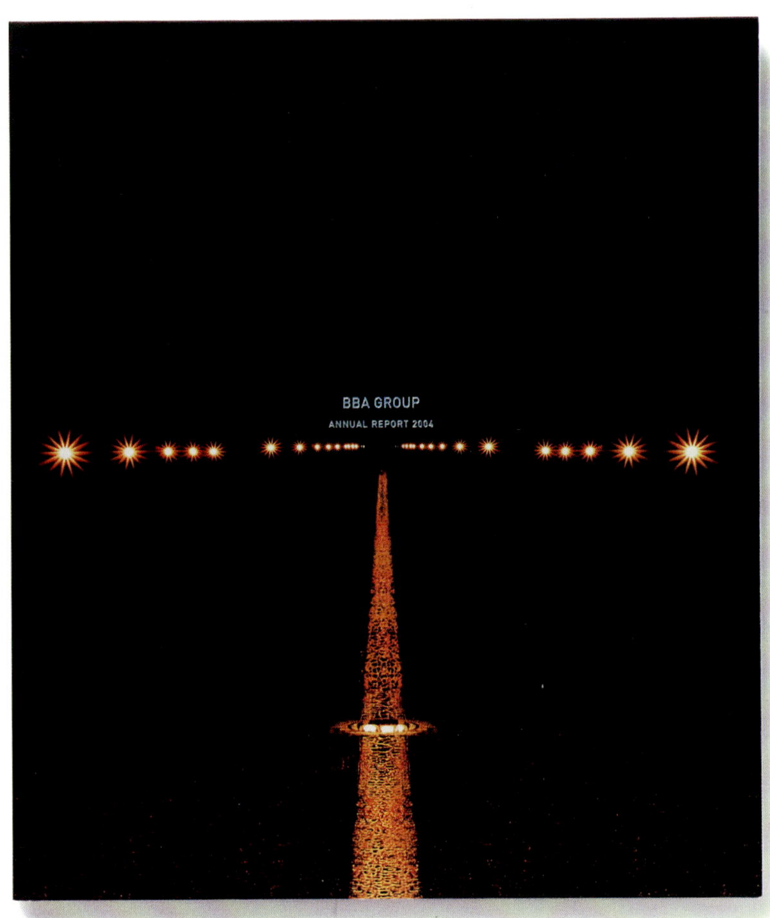

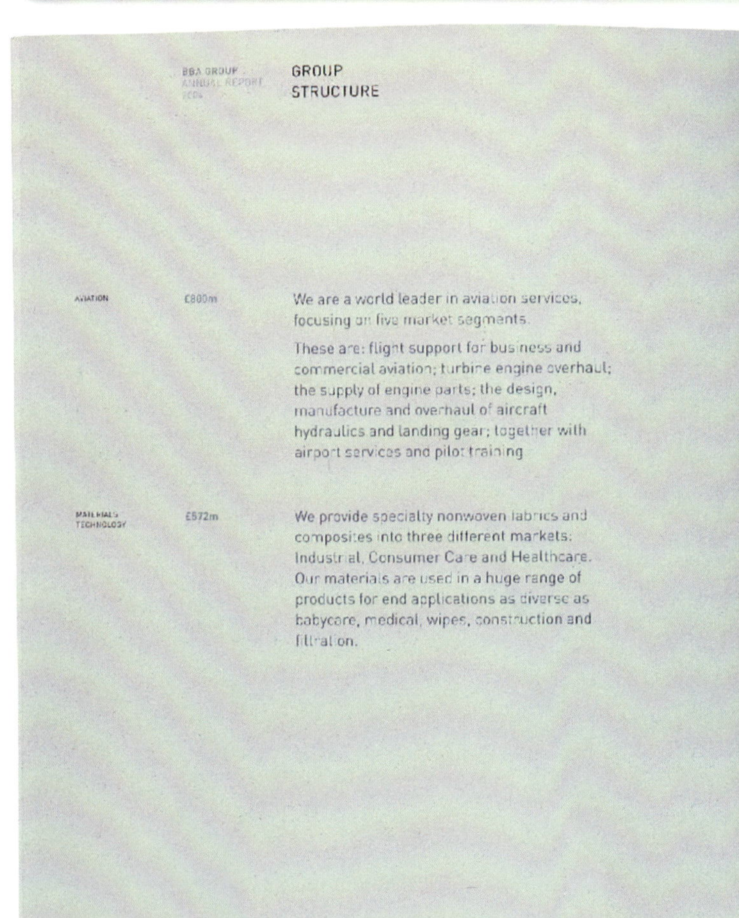

GROUP
STRUCTURE

AVIATION	£800m	We are a world leader in aviation services, focusing on five market segments. These are: flight support for business and commercial aviation; turbine engine overhaul; the supply of engine parts; the design, manufacture and overhaul of aircraft hydraulics and landing gear; together with airport services and pilot training.
MATERIALS TECHNOLOGY	£572m	We provide specialty nonwoven fabrics and composites into three different markets: Industrial, Consumer Care and Healthcare. Our materials are used in a huge range of products for end applications as diverse as babycare, medical, wipes, construction and filtration.

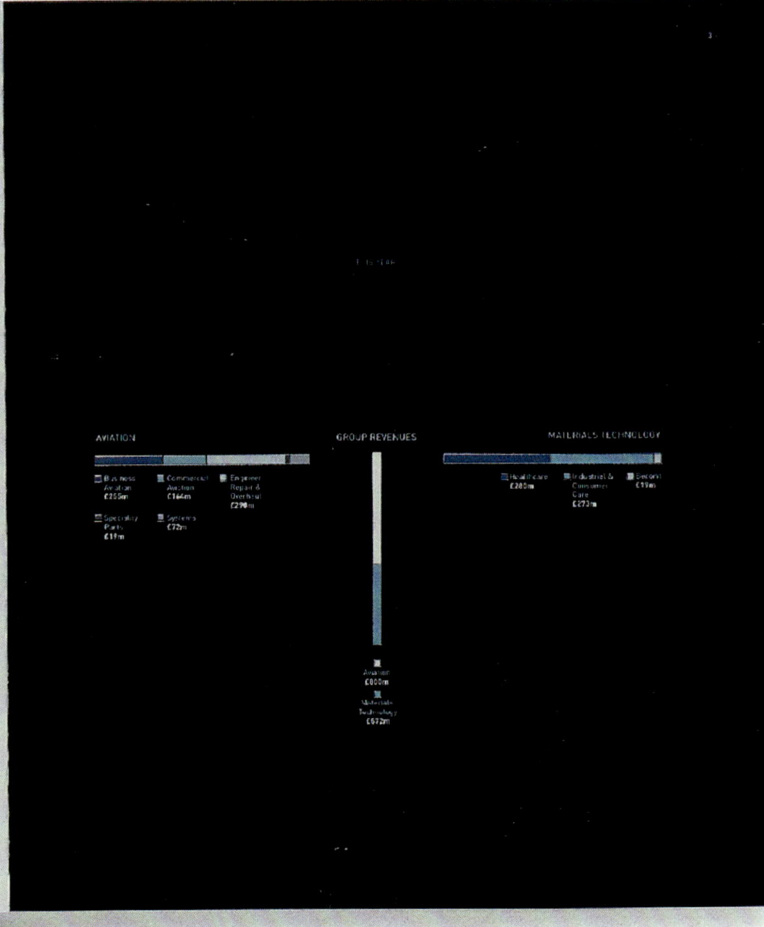

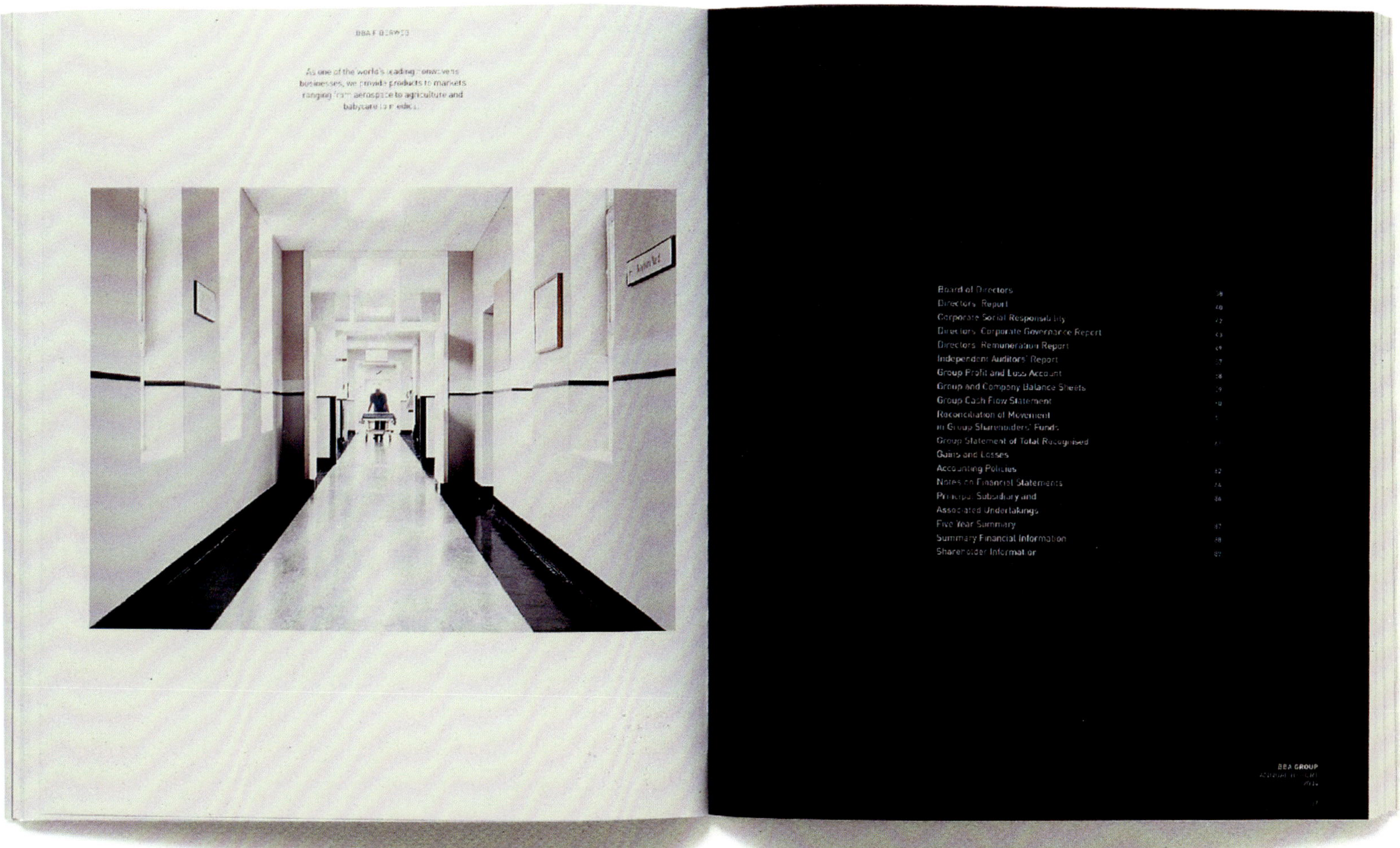

BBA FIBERWEB

As one of the world's leading nonwovens businesses, we provide products to markets ranging from aerospace to agriculture and babycare to medical.

BBA GROUP

ASIG

ASIG operates in 46 of the world's top 100 airports offering a full range of ground handling, fuelling, cargo and ancillary services in 77 cities throughout North America, Europe and Asia.

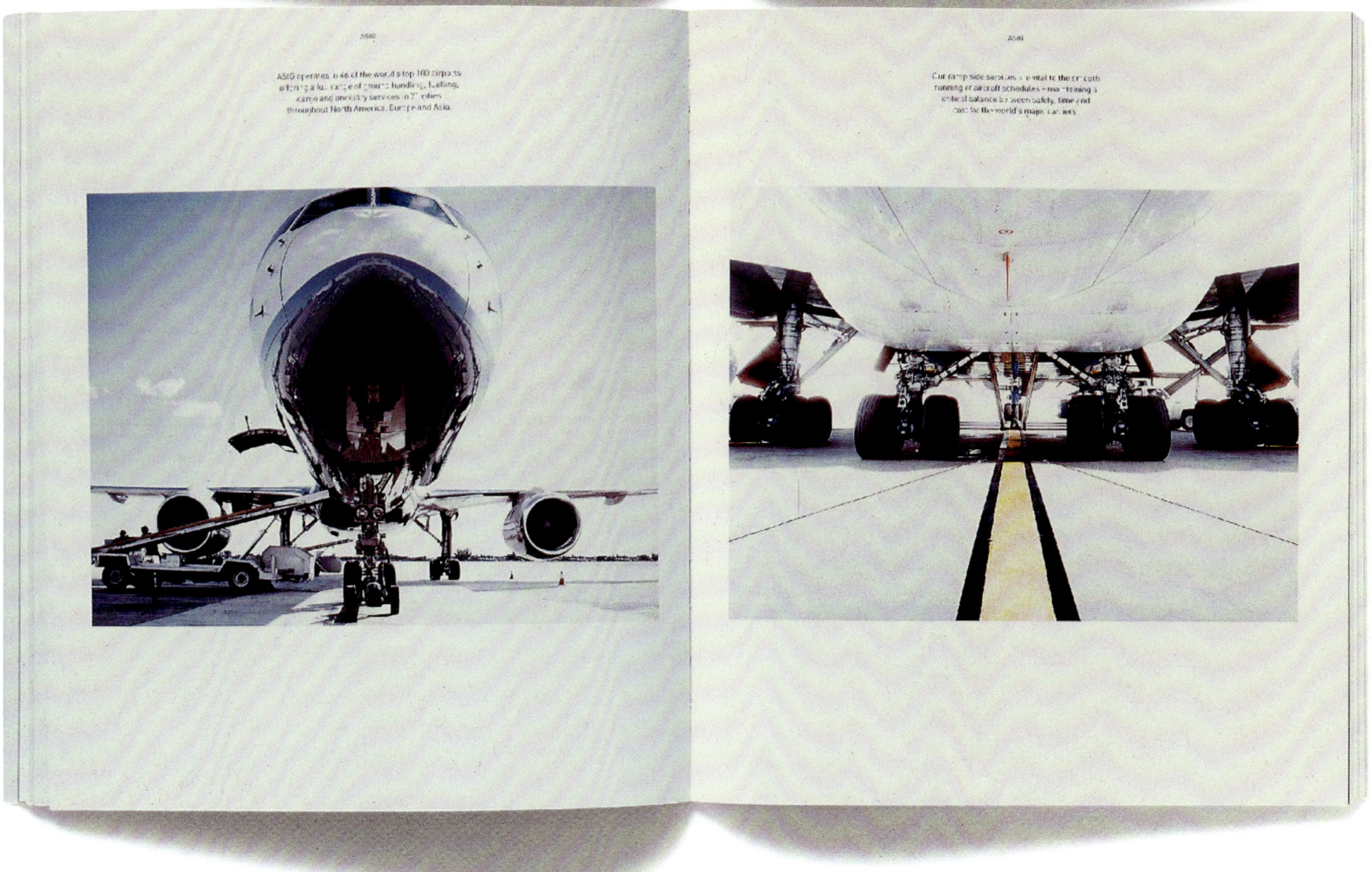

ASIG

Our ramp side services are vital to the smooth running of aircraft schedules – maintaining a critical balance between safety, time and cost for the world's major carriers.

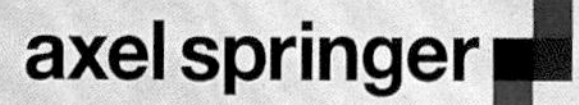

04

Annual Report
2004

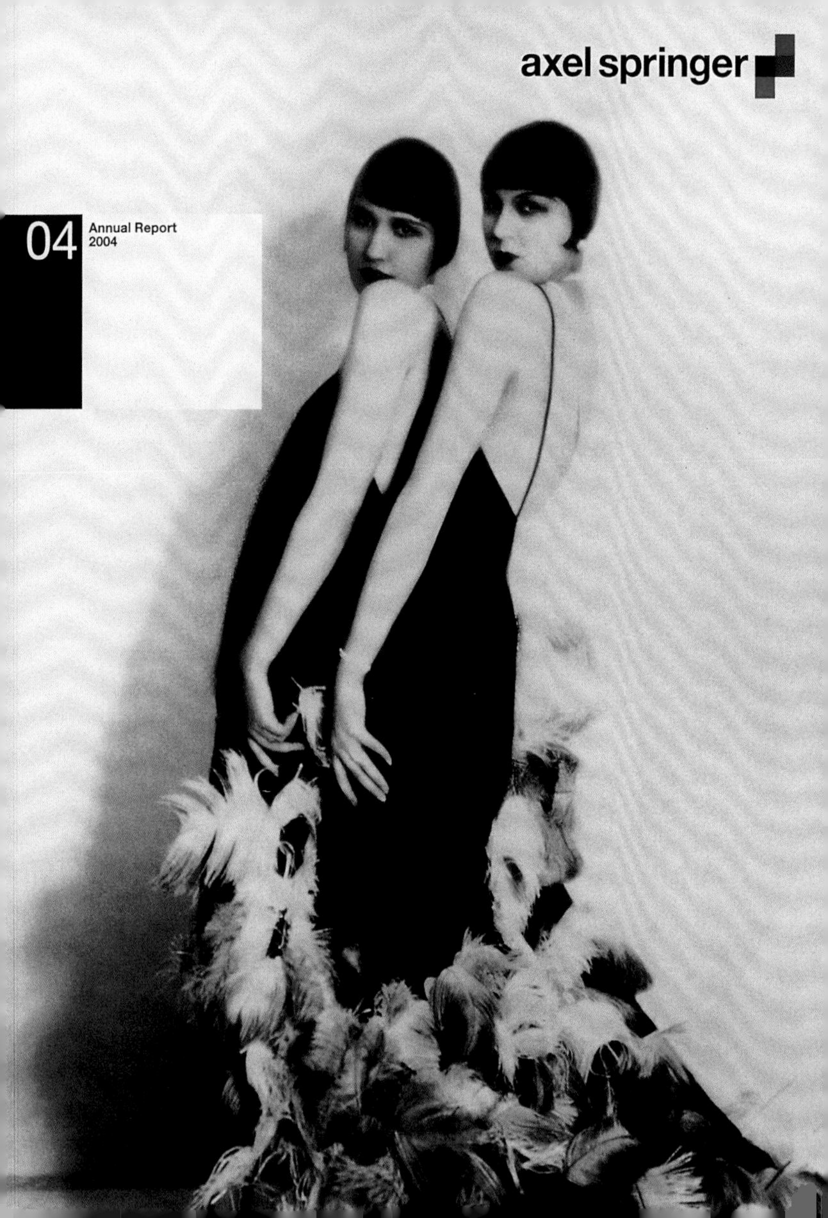

Art Director, Designer: Patrick Märki, Kunt Maierhofer
Project Management: Sandra Ehm
Production: Christina Baur, Kunt Maierhofer
Printer: Graphische Betriebe Biering, Munich
Paper: Galaxy Supermatt, Papier Union, cover 300 g/qm, content 135 g/qm
Page count: 4 +88 (cover + content)
Print run: 5,500 German, 1,500 English
Size: 233 x 316 mm
Number of images: 19 +six management portraits
Client: Axel Springer, newspaper publisher

8 | 2004 / Annual Report // Axel Springer AG

ullstein bild

Life in an optically dominated world demands an appropriate visual memory.

Photography Classics

Cover Photo: The Cold Shoulder...
...is not exactly what the dancers in this cover photo intend to give readers. Erni Kaiser and Kitty Lorenz are simply looking too deeply into their eyes. Also deep is the plunging backline of the dresses molded to their bodies by costume designer Ladislaus Czettel. Erni and Kitty made their stage debut on August 7, 1926, at the "Theater of the West" in the Willi Kollo Revue "The Way West." The photo was taken in Atelier Balázs in Berlin and is one of the ullstein bild agency treasures.

ullstein bild | 9

The agency ullstein bild is such a photo depository. The agency, which has been owned by Axel Springer for over a half-century, boasts a collection of over twelve million photos.
From the beginning of photographic time through the present day.
By Franz Hanfstaengl, Erich Salomon and Fritz Eschen; and by Lotte Jacobi, Sven Simon, Martin Munkacsi and Willy Römer.
All renowned photographers who contributed to a unique collection of precious photo documents.

Q&A with KMS Team

What was the client's directive?
Our client's directive was to be presented as a publishing house with very successful products. The Annual Report is used to communicate the company's major role as a generator of public opinion within Germany and its growing importance in international markets.
How did you define the problem?
The Axel Springer AG became Germany's market leading publishing house. So the central problem we had was how to visualize the company's role in an adequate way and to illustrate its economic impact to the public, and especially to the shareholders.
What was the approach?
The design takes the contemporary historical dimension of journalism as its starting point. We mapped a series of photographs from the archive of *ullstein bild*, an institution that has been a part of the Axel Springer company for over half a century. The archive provides an example of a type of journalism that has the documentation of contemporary history as its main concern. With this we refer to the riches of the archive, provide an indication of the aura of this collection of photographic milestones and thus visualize the journalistic dimensions of the work of Axel Springer.
Which disciplines or people helped you with the project?
The following people were involved in this project:
Creative Director: Knut Maierhofer, Art Director: Patrick Märki, Project Management: Sandra Ehm, Concept: Alexandra Schneiderhan, Production: Christina Baur, Fair Drafting: Christian Ring
Were you happy with the result? What could have been better?
Generally we were very happy with the result of this work. In our opinion the look could have been a little bit more magazine-like, with even more pictures of products and little excursions into the world of journalism.

An Annual Report should not only present the company's financial results, it should reflect the company's spirit.

What was the client's response?

We had a great collaboration in partnership during the working process. It was characterized by an effective and creative exchange that our client appreciated, which led to a very satisfying result for everybody who was involved.

How involved was the CEO in your meetings and presentations?

The CEO of Axel Springer AG, Dr. Mathias Döpfner, took a very vivid interest in the creation of the Annual Report. He contributed actively to the concept, i.e. the integration of *ullstein bild.*

Do you feel that designers are becoming more involved in copywriting?

Our designers take an active part when working out a concept for an Annual Report or other projects. Texts and contents however are provided by our editorial and/or sales strategy department.

How do you define success in Annual Report design?

Success in AR design means to visualize the company's identity. An Annual Report should achieve more than merely reporting the financial situation of a company; it should transport the company's spirit. In our view a well-designed Annual Report is one of the most effective marketing instruments.

How important are awards to your client?

Awards for Annual Reports are not the top priority for our client; business results are.

2 | 2004 / Annual Report // Axel Springer AG

Foreword

Dear Shareholders!

At the beginning of 2004 I personally witnessed the catastrophe of Sharm el Sheik from my hotel room while vacationing in Egypt. A passenger plane crashed directly onto the Egyptian coastline killing 150 people. At the end of last year I witnessed the catastrophic floods in Asia, which claimed the lives of more than 200,000 people, from a safe distance in central Europe as a newspaper reader and TV viewer. In both cases I was helpless and powerless, in both cases I had to depend on information and explanations provided by the media. Fortunately, Axel Springer AG was able to raise over € 40 million for the survivors of the floods through the BILD relief organization "Ein Herz für Kinder" at a gala event in cooperation with ZDF. The year 2004 however, which was clouded by many tragic events, was an extraordinarily successful one for the company Axel Springer.

Group Headquarters Moves to Berlin

What stands out among our activities over the last twelve months? The move of our headquarters from Hamburg to Berlin to be sure. The decision to transfer our headquarters and all administrative operations to Berlin was not simply based on Axel Springer's vision of the city as an intellectual center with tremendous future significance. We are also convinced that by moving our headquarters to the German capital we will also enjoy a long-term location advantage for our publishing and business activities with even better prospects for future success. The move also makes good business sense, because it provided us with an opportunity to streamline operations and improve the efficiency of our central departments.

The list of accomplishments during the past year is long; the successes are extraordinary; and the results speak for themselves: our share price rose from € 70 to € 86, earnings per share from € 3.26 to € 4.66, revenues from € 2.3 billion to € 2.4 billion, net income climbed from € 112 million to € 148 million, and our EBITA after adjustment for non-recurring items of € 336 million is the highest in company history.

Highest Earnings in Company History

How did we succeed in achieving the highest earnings in the history of our publishing house at the height of an ongoing economic crisis, and when our industry is struggling with a structural crisis of its own? And how did we manage to do this despite massive investments aimed at generating new business?

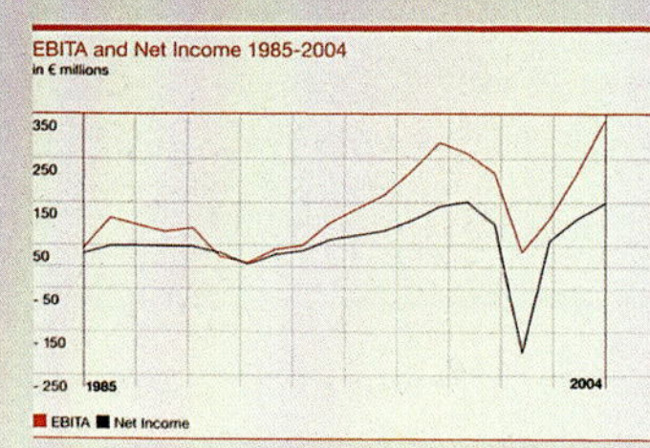

First of all, much of the credit for our success goes to our highly motivated employees, who possess a high degree of expertise and are willing to make courageous decisions in the face of the crisis. Our success is also due to the far-reaching restructuring program carried out quickly and thoroughly during 2002 and 2003. It was also because were able to go against the grain of the economy as a whole and make investments in the future while many of our competitors were struggling to overcome their own internal problems. And it was because we saved money like misers. And because we launched the right concepts in the right market gaps at the right time.

The basis for all of this is the success of our core business, the success of our editorial staffs, the advertising revenues generated by BILD and BILD am SONNTAG, the modernization of the content and design of DIE WELT and WELT am SONNTAG, the stabilization of our regional newspapers, and the anticyclical performance of some of our newspapers. We were successful – at least in some segments – in overcoming the three biggest challenges facing our industry: declining circulation, the aging of society and the increasing availability of free publications. These major challenges will continue to confront us in the years to come. And I am convinced that we will be more than ready to meet them.

Successful Launches Continue

The success rate of our 24 new publication launches during the last two years is unusually high. But we must not allow this series of successes to lead us down the path of unrealistic expectations in the future.

We launched newspapers. In Hungary we introduced REGGEL, a regional newspaper for the greater Budapest area modeled after HAMBURGER ABENDBLATT. In Germany we created WELT KOMPAKT, a smaller, lower-priced and more current version of DIE WELT catering to new, younger target groups. And FAKT, the Polish daily introduced only one year ago, has seen its circulation grow to some 500,000 copies, thereby making it not only Poland's largest tabloid but also the country's largest newspaper overall.

And we launched magazines. In Germany Axel Springer AG occupies the top four places among the ten most successful newly established magazines. Two new innovative publications especially stand out. AUDIO VIDEO FOTO BILD, devoted to the field of consumer electronics, has achieved success in a former niche market that has now developed into a mass segment. And TV DIGITAL, with a circulation of 1.3 million copies by the end of the year, virtually invented the segment for TV guides that cater to the new television generation of digital TV.

Successful Acquisition Strategy

And we did not stop at successful launches; we also made successful purchases. The acquisition of a stake of 14.5 % in Westfalen-Blatt-Verlag is a move that will successively strengthen our position in a segment we know quite well – the regional newspaper market. We also acquired 30 % of PIN AG, Germany's second-largest mail handler. This not only opens the door to important logistical options but gives us a foothold in the lucrative market of mail distribution. And we acquired 49.9 % of StepStone, the second-largest German Internet platform for jobs classified advertising. Together with real estate and cars, we have now gained access to the three large markets for online classified advertising. This move clearly strengthens our strategic position in the world of digital classified advertising.

Foreword / Management Board / Report of the Supervisory Board / Supervisory Board / Strategy / Highlights / Management Report / Divisions / Further Information / | 3

The establishment of publishing operations in China and Russia opens the door to two of the world's important growth markets. Our rotogravure joint venture with Arvato and Gruner + Jahr – if approved by the European anti-cartel authorities – will create a European market leader that can play an active role in the consolidation process. As a result of a settlement reached during the insolvency proceedings of the Kirch Group, we saw our stake in ProSiebenSat.1 Media AG grow by 1.7 % without further financial investment, we received a cash payment of € 60.3 million, and a receivable of € 325 million was acknowledged. The latter will be partially reimbursed in the coming years from the insolvency volume.

Capital Market Communication Improved

Whereas shorter reporting periods were put into effect in 2003, we introduced quarterly reports at the beginning of 2004. The preparation of this annual report in accordance with IFRS one year earlier than is legally required is a step toward improving communication with the capital market.

Stringent Cost Management

After having presented examples of our launches and purchases in 2004, in closing I would like to offer you an example of what we have not done – and what we have learned from it. Because sometimes what a company has not done is more revealing than what a company has done.

We did not buy the "Daily Telegraph" group in England, which changed hands for the price of € 986 million. It would have been a good deal at a lower price, because it is a wonderful newspaper and an excellent brand. It has great potential, but there are also some risks involved. The asking price, for which the newspaper was ultimately sold, appeared unreasonably high to us.

No deal is better than a deal that is too expensive. This is a principle that we will also adhere to during the current financial year. For us, generating large sales increases through acquisitions is not an end in itself. Growth must make good business sense. But if an attractive deal comes along, we are in a position to take advantage of the opportunity. The general economic outlook for 2005 is subdued. There is no substantial economic turnaround in sight. But we are confident that our sales and EBITA (before the one-time proceeds from the Kirch settlement) will increase slightly. We plan to achieve this through tight cost controls and by gradually increasing the profitability of our new endeavors.

At our management meeting last summer I recommended – to the astonishment of some of my colleagues – that our managers take a lesson from the piranha. These fish unfortunately have been given a bad rap. Piranhas are predators to be sure. But more importantly, piranhas know exactly what their limits are and they treat their resources prudently. If the temptation is too great or there are too many fish to eat at one time, they exercise restraint. Because piranhas know that if they eat too much, they will become sluggish and unable to flee or defend themselves, and one day they could be eaten themselves.

The piranha exemplifies what every manager should know: achieving success is sometimes easier than dealing with it. This does not mean that we should curb our own ambitions. Piranhas hunt in packs. And as a group they are able to recognize their limits and resist the temptation to bite off more than they can chew. They know that they will able to digest even the largest catch at the right time.

Yours,

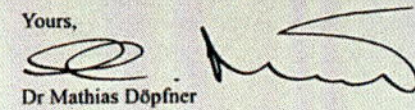

Dr Mathias Döpfner

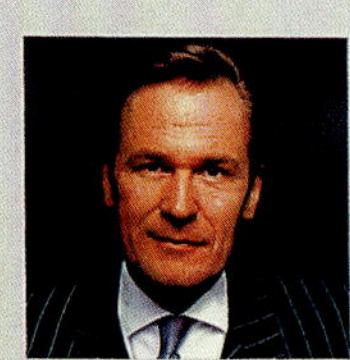

Dr Mathias Döpfner
Chief Executive Officer

Successful Launches
High success rate with new launches / Places 1-4 among the top ten newspaper launches / WELT KOMPAKT launched as compact version of DIE WELT / AUDIO VIDEO FOTO BILD becomes market leader / TV DIGITAL – new TV guide for digital television

Internationalization
Eastern Europe as focal point of new newspaper and magazine launches / FAKT is Poland's largest daily newspaper / Regional newspaper REGGEL for greater Budapest area launched / Global licensing business expanded / Market entry in Russia with new magazines / Representative Office in China opened

Record Earnings
Share price from € 70 to € 86 / Earnings per share from € 3.26 to € 4.66 / Revenues from € 2.3 to € 2.4 billion / Net income from € 112 to € 148 million / Record-high EBITA of € 336 million

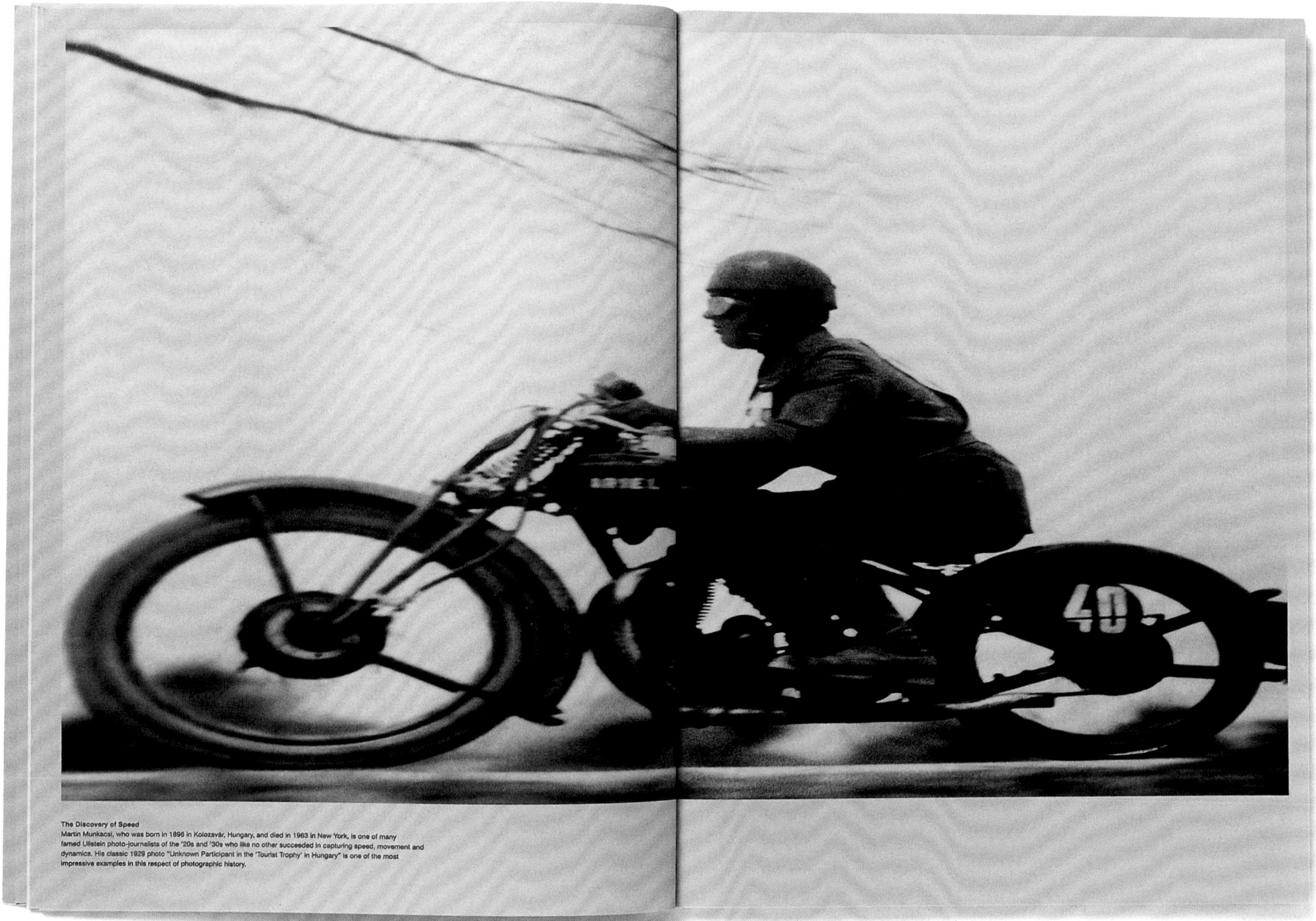

The Discovery of Speed
Martin Munkacsi, who was born in 1896 in Kolozsvár, Hungary, and died in 1963 in New York, is one of many famed Ullstein photo-journalists of the '20s and '30s who like no other succeeded in capturing speed, movement and dynamics. His classic 1929 photo "Unknown Participant in the 'Tourist Trophy' in Hungary" is one of the most impressive examples in this respect of photographic history.

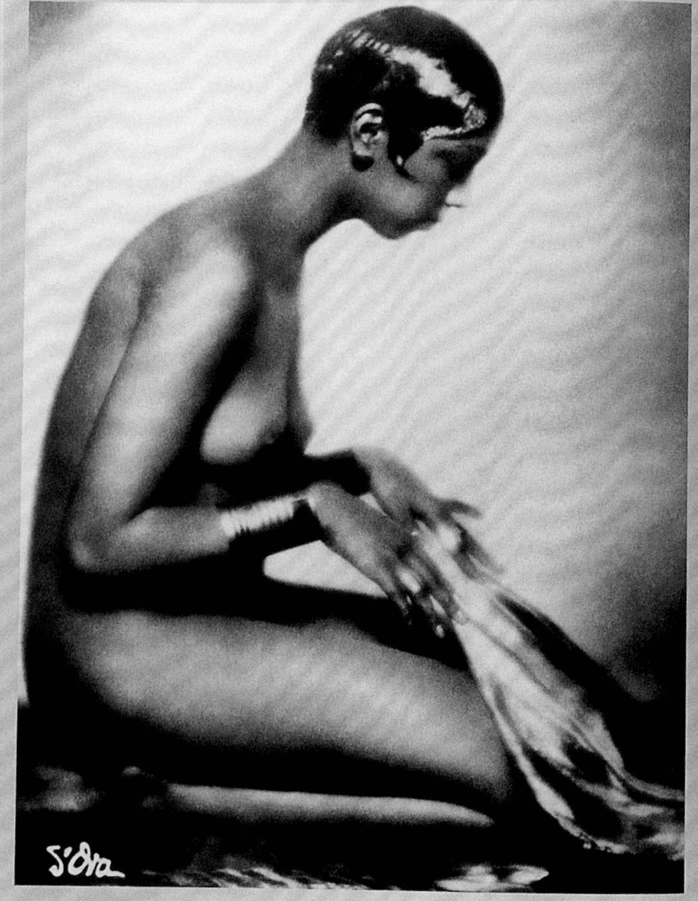

"Black Venus" — a Vintage Print from 1928
Perscheid student Dora Kallmus (1881-1965) opened her first photo atelier in Vienna in 1907 as "Madame d'Ora". But her most important photos were taken during her Paris years in the '20s and '30s. Here she captured both the erotic and the demure in 22-year-old Follies Bergère dancer Josephine Baker, who was then Europe's highest-paid revue star.

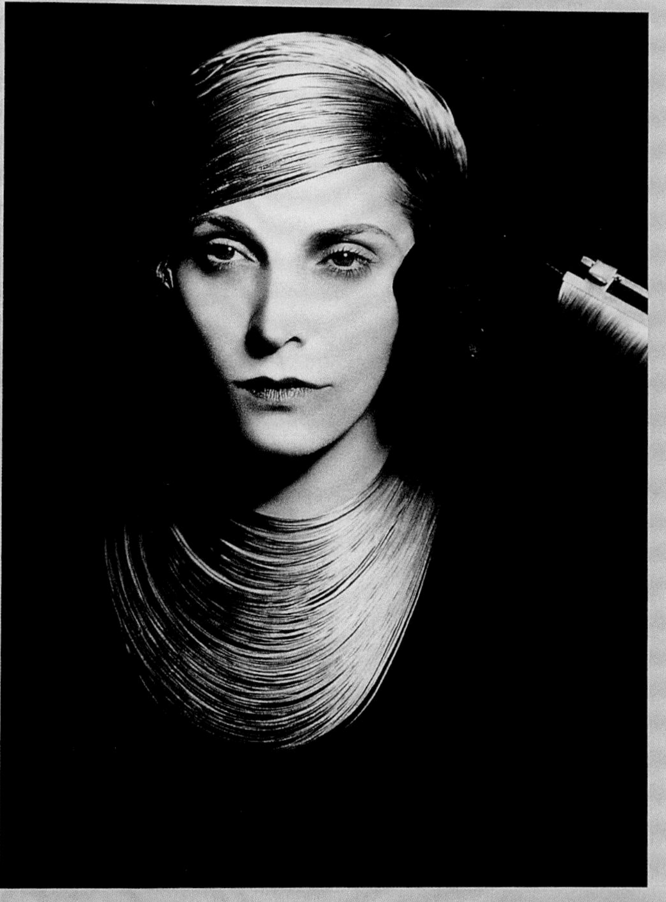

The Cool Factuality of "Die Dame"
"Die Dame" — by far Ullstein's most sophisticated magazine - combined the mundane with a touch of snobbishness. It featured expensive cars, grandiose villas, white sports and elegant attire.
The photo shows a Mrs. Karton with turban and a necklace and bracelet made of platinum-gold stands created by Suzanne Farnier of Paris. Published on the cover of the third December issue in 1933, this was one of the last photos taken by Jewish photographer "Madame d'Ora" that she was able to publish under her own name in Germany.

Two Squaws Named Ida and Evelyne
A perfectly orchestrated photo from the era when Berlin was still considered the German capital of varieté. The most famous venues were the "Plaza" and the "Wintergarten", located at Dorotheenstraße 16. It was at the latter venue that the September 1930 program featured two "delightful representatives of the graceful art" – as the Berliner Morgenpost wrote – the dancing duo of Ida and Evelyne Duffek. The PR photo was taken in Atelier Hilbinger & Co in Munich.

Big City Elegance during the Late '20s
London 1929. Head-hugging felt hats, knee-length summer dresses and matching coats with plush fur trim. The confident posture and casual foot on the taxi running board document the newly acquired self-consciousness of young, sophisticated women of the day. The London News Agency photo, seen here in the original, was published for the first time in Germany in "Uhu" no. 11, August 1929. The caption to the masterful photo reads: "How much is it ...?" The magazine published the photo in "left-right reversed" format for German readers who were not familiar with English left-hand traffic.

Operating Results – Group

Market Environment: Print Circulation Still Down, Advertising Market Slightly Relaxed Due to the persistent weakness in consumer spending, sales volume and revenue figures in the print circulation market decreased further. Total circulation sold for newspapers and magazines effectively dropped by 2.5 %. For the entire market, circulation revenues fell by 1.0 %. Gross revenues from the print media advertising business (excluding classified advertising) experienced growth of 7.1 % to € 8.86 billion. However, the net development, which is the deciding factor economically, was much less favorable as a result of ongoing price pressures. The classified advertising business, a central source of revenues for subscription newspapers, also showed further declines in the job, personals and travel markets.

Revenues
in € millions

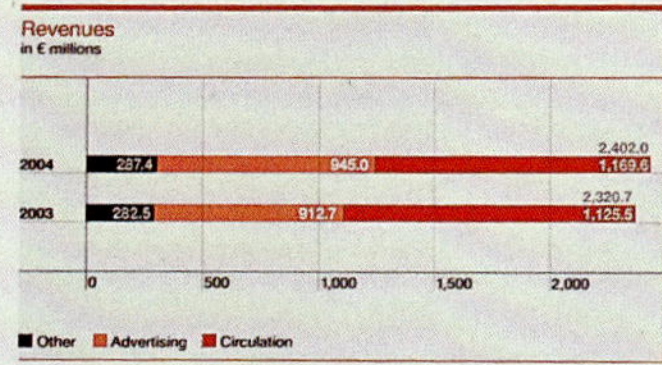

Axel Springer: Circulation and Advertising Revenues Increased In this market environment, Axel Springer increased total revenues for 2004 by € 81.3 million (+ 3.5 %) to € 2,402.0 million. Circulation revenues grew by € 44.1 million (+ 3.9 %) to € 1,169.6 million, representing 48.7 % of total revenues. The increase is mainly a result of the positive development of the newly launched domestic and foreign titles. Advertising revenues grew by € 32.3 million (+ 3.5 %) to € 945.0 million and represented 39.3 % of total revenues. Particularly the newspaper division and the expansion of the international activities contributed to the growth in revenues. Other revenues rose by € 4.9 million (+ 1.7 %) to € 287.4 million.

Foreign Revenues
in € millions

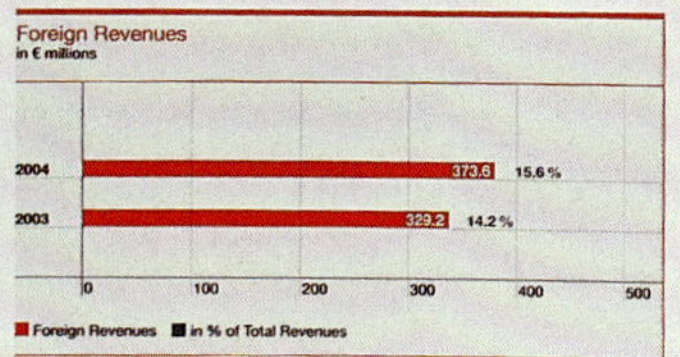

Revenue Growth in Foreign Markets Foreign revenues, at € 373.6 million, were € 44.4 (+ 13.5 %) above the prior year level, thus representing 15.6 % of total revenues (PY: 14.2 %). The main contributing factors here were the increase in the circulation and advertising performance generated by the daily newspaper FAKT, launched in Poland in October 2003, as well as an increase in circulation revenues in Spain and the entry into the Russian market. These positive effects were able to more than offset the decrease in circulation revenues in France, which were the result of stronger competition among TV guides.

Total Expenses Grew Less than Revenues Growing slightly less than revenues, total expenses included in EBITA rose by € 59.3 million (+ 2.7 %) to € 2,281.0 million. At € 745.3 million, purchased goods and services were € 40.3 million (+ 5.7 %) above the prior year level due to the higher external services and professional fees incurred in connection with the expansion process. Personnel expenses fell by € 47.3 million (- 6.1 %) to € 722.0 million due to the lower staffing levels. Other operating expenses increased by € 44.1 million (+ 6.6 %) to € 716.7 million due to the launch of new publications. Depreciation, amortization and impairments (excluding goodwill impairment charges) increased by € 22.3 million (+ 29.9 %) to € 97.0 million due to the completion of construction on the new building in Berlin, the commencement of operations for new equipment and impairment charges on title rights.

EBITA, EBITA Margin
in € millions

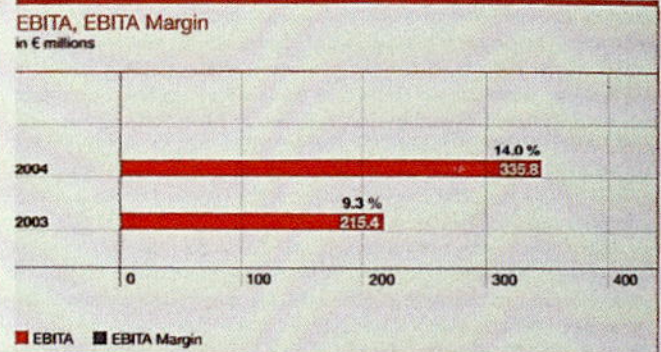

EBITA at a Historic High In 2004 Axel Springer increased EBITA before non-recurring items by € 120.4 million (+ 55.9 %) to € 335.8 million. The conclusion of the settlement agreement as part of the insolvency proceedings of Taurus TV GmbH i.I. (Kirch settlement) contributed € 92.6 million to EBITA. Excluding the income effect of the Kirch settlement, an increase in EBITA from € 215.4 million to € 243.2 million was achieved despite the start-up costs of the expansion process. This growth can be attributed to the higher revenues generated and the continued cost management. The EBITA margin grew from 9.3 % to 14.0 %, and to 10.1 % without the income impact of the Kirch settlement.

Income from Continuing Operations Doubled, Net Income Increased Significantly Income from continuing operations increased by € 84.3 million (+ 121.6 %) to € 153.6 million, consolidated net income by € 35.9 million (+ 32.2 %) to € 147.5 million. The Kirch settlement contributed € 62.3 million to the increase, although its effect on consolidated net income is mostly offset by the reduction in income from discontinued operations.

Net Income
in € millions

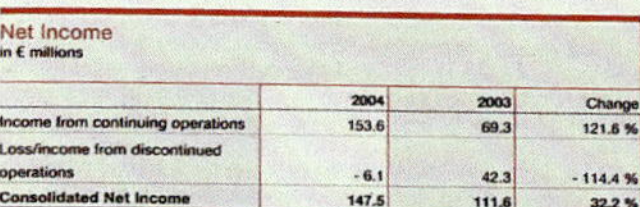

	2004	2003	Change
Income from continuing operations	153.6	69.3	121.6 %
Loss/income from discontinued operations	- 6.1	42.3	- 114.4 %
Consolidated Net Income	147.5	111.6	32.2 %

Income from continuing operations and consolidated net income include a rise in income tax expense by € 46.0 million to € 142.1 million, which is due to improved operating results and to the tax audits for the years 1991 to 1999 being almost completed. Interest charges on the subsequent tax payments explain the increase in net financial expenses from € - 24.4 million to € - 34.3 million. Goodwill impairments amounted to € 20.2 million (PY: € 21.5 million), mainly due to impairment charges resulting from the change in competition in the French TV guide market.

Earnings per Share Improved Significantly The increase in earnings per share from € 3.26 to € 4.66 is largely due to the significant improvement in net income. In addition, the weighted average number of shares outstanding fell from 33,627,000 to 30,623,000 due to the treasury shares purchased in November 2003. Diluted earnings per share for 2004 were € 4.65 (PY: € 3.26). The dilutive effect of the share options purchased under the Management Participation Plan was included in the calculation of this figure.

Earnings per Share

	2004	2003	Change
Net Income after Minority Interests (in € millions)	142.9	109.5	30.5 %
Weighted average shares outstanding (in thousands)	30,623	33,627	- 8.9 %
Basic Earnings per Share (in €)	4.66	3.26	42.9 %
Weighted average shares diluted (in thousands)	30,703	33,627	- 8.7 %
Diluted Earnings per Share (in €)	4.65	3.26	42.6 %

Operating Results – Segments

Newspapers

Market Environment: Further Decrease in Circulation, Advertising Business Slightly Improved In Germany, total paid circulation of the 380 daily and Sunday newspapers reported on by IVW reached an average of 26.1 million per publication day. This represents a decrease of 2.3 % compared to 2003. Newly launched low-priced titles in tabloid format established a new direction in the newspaper market. As in other markets, the inclusion of free promotional items such as CD-ROMs, audio books or novels, sometimes in connection with a higher price, has become established practice in the newspaper market in 2004. Gross advertising volume for newspapers (excluding classified advertisements) saw an increase of 10.7 % to € 4.54 billion, mainly driven by the continued strong advertising efforts of the discounters. However, regional newspapers' advertising volume including classified advertisements was flat compared to the prior year.

Revenues 2004:
€ 2,402.0 million
in %

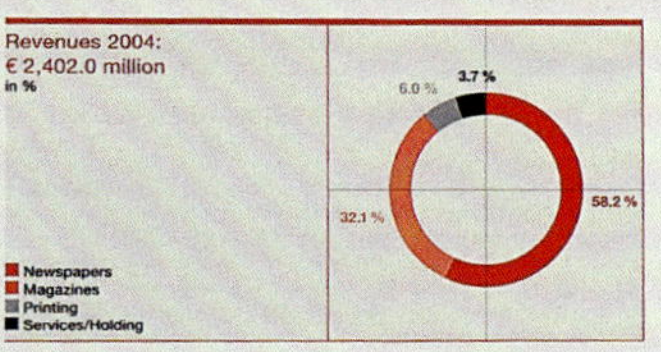

Axel Springer: Newspaper Circulation and Advertising Revenues Increased In this environment, Axel Springer increased newspaper revenues by € 44.8 million (+ 3.3 %) to a total of € 1,398.4 million for the year. At 58.2 %, newspapers were again the Group's largest revenue generator. Circulation revenues rose from € 22.1 million (+ 3.4 %) to € 678.3 million, particularly because of the sales successes of FAKT in Poland and the effects of the price increases implemented at BILD and HAMBURGER ABENDBLATT in mid-2003. Newspaper advertising revenues grew by € 34.7 million (+ 5.3 %), totaling € 684.7 million. BILD and BILD am SONNTAG were the main contributors here.

Key Figures – Newspapers
in € millions

	2004	2003	Change
External Revenues	1,398.4	1,353.6	3.3 %
in % of consolidated revenues	58.2 %	58.3 %	
Circulation revenues	678.3	656.2	3.4 %
in % of revenues	48.5 %	48.5 %	
Advertising revenues	684.7	650.0	5.3 %
in % of revenues	49.0 %	48.0 %	
Other revenues	35.4	47.4	
in % of revenues	2.5 %	3.5 %	
EBITA	250.7	182.1	37.7 %
EBITA margin	17.9 %	13.5 %	

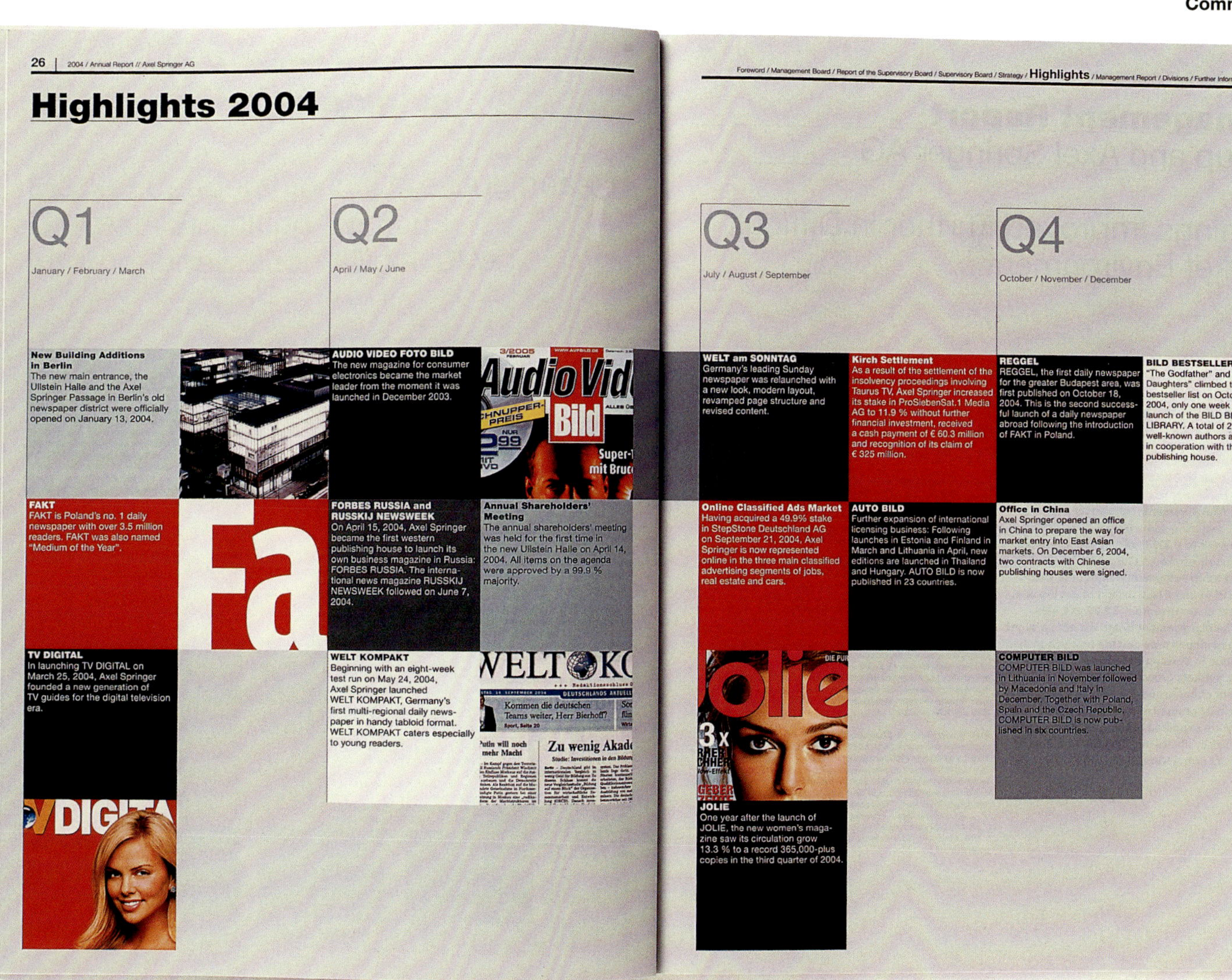

26 | 2004 / Annual Report // Axel Springer AG

Foreword / Management Board / Report of the Supervisory Board / Supervisory Board / Strategy / **Highlights** / Management Report / Divisions / Further Information / | 27

Highlights 2004

Q1
January / February / March

New Building Additions in Berlin
The new main entrance, the Ullstein Halle and the Axel Springer Passage in Berlin's old newspaper district were officially opened on January 13, 2004.

FAKT
FAKT is Poland's no. 1 daily newspaper with over 3.5 million readers. FAKT was also named "Medium of the Year".

TV DIGITAL
In launching TV DIGITAL on March 25, 2004, Axel Springer founded a new generation of TV guides for the digital television era.

Q2
April / May / June

AUDIO VIDEO FOTO BILD
The new magazine for consumer electronics became the market leader from the moment it was launched in December 2003.

FORBES RUSSIA and RUSSKIJ NEWSWEEK
On April 15, 2004, Axel Springer became the first western publishing house to launch its own business magazine in Russia: FORBES RUSSIA. The international news magazine RUSSKIJ NEWSWEEK followed on June 7, 2004.

Annual Shareholders' Meeting
The annual shareholders' meeting was held for the first time in the new Ullstein Halle on April 14, 2004. All items on the agenda were approved by a 99.9 % majority.

WELT KOMPAKT
Beginning with an eight-week test run on May 24, 2004, Axel Springer launched WELT KOMPAKT, Germany's first multi-regional daily newspaper in handy tabloid format. WELT KOMPAKT caters especially to young readers.

Q3
July / August / September

WELT am SONNTAG
Germany's leading Sunday newspaper was relaunched with a new look, modern layout, revamped page structure and revised content.

Kirch Settlement
As a result of the settlement of the insolvency proceedings involving Taurus TV, Axel Springer increased its stake in ProSiebenSat.1 Media AG to 11.9 % without further financial investment, received a cash payment of € 60.3 million and recognition of its claim of € 325 million.

Online Classified Ads Market
Having acquired a 49.9% stake in StepStone Deutschland AG on September 21, 2004, Axel Springer is now represented online in the three main classified advertising segments of jobs, real estate and cars.

AUTO BILD
Further expansion of international licensing business: Following launches in Estonia and Finland in March and Lithuania in April, new editions are launched in Thailand and Hungary. AUTO BILD is now published in 23 countries.

JOLIE
One year after the launch of JOLIE, the new women's magazine saw its circulation grow 13.3 % to a record 365,000-plus copies in the third quarter of 2004.

Q4
October / November / December

REGGEL
REGGEL, the first daily newspaper for the greater Budapest area, was first published on October 18, 2004. This is the second successful launch of a daily newspaper abroad following the introduction of FAKT in Poland.

BILD BESTSELLER LIBRARY
"The Godfather" and "Hanna's Daughters" climbed to the top the bestseller list on October 26, 2004, only one week after the launch of the BILD BESTSELLER LIBRARY. A total of 25 works from well-known authors are published in cooperation with the WELTBILD publishing house.

Office in China
Axel Springer opened an office in China to prepare the way for market entry into East Asian markets. On December 6, 2004, two contracts with Chinese publishing houses were signed.

COMPUTER BILD
COMPUTER BILD was launched in Lithuania in November followed by Macedonia and Italy in December. Together with Poland, Spain and the Czech Republic, COMPUTER BILD is now published in six countries.

60 | 2004 / Annual Report // Axel Springer AG

Consolidated Income Statement

Consolidated Income Statement
EUR thousands

	Note	2004	2003
Revenues	(22)	2,402,035	2,320,685
Other operating income	(23)	186,668	80,021
Change in inventories and internal costs capitalized		2,410	3,626
Purchased goods and services	(24)	- 745,272	- 704,984
Gross Profit		1,845,841	1,699,348
Personnel expenses	(25)	- 721,990	- 769,333
Depreciation, amortization and impairments	(26)	- 117,262	- 96,199
Other operating expenses	(27)	- 716,693	- 672,611
Income from investments	(28)	40,169	28,597
Equity income from associated companies and joint ventures		18,696	17,494
Other investment income		21,473	11,103
Net financial expenses	(29)	- 34,319	- 24,370
Income taxes	(30)	- 142,124	- 96,131
Income from Continuing Operations		153,622	69,301
Loss/Income from Discontinued Operations	(2)	- 6,075	42,257
Consolidated Net Income		147,547	111,558
Consolidated net income attributable to Group shareholders		142,872	109,505
Consolidated net income attributable to minority interests		4,675	2,053
Basic Earnings per Share from Continuing Operations (in EUR)	(31)	4.86	2.00
Diluted Earnings per Share from Continuing Operations (in EUR)	(31)	4.85	2.00
Basic Earnings per Share (in EUR)	(31)	4.66	3.26
Diluted Earnings per Share (in EUR)	(31)	4.65	3.26
Reconciliation to EBIT, EBITA, EBITDA			
Income from continuing operations		153,622	69,301
Net financial expenses		34,319	24,370
Income taxes		142,124	96,131
EBIT before Adjustments for Non-Recurring Items		330,065	189,802
Non-recurring items	(35)	- 14,529	4,084
EBIT — Adjusted for Non-Recurring Items		315,536	193,886
Impairment losses on goodwill		20,218	21,471
EBITA – Adjusted for Non-Recurring Items		335,754	215,357
Depreciation, amortization and impairments on fixed assets (excl. goodwill)		97,044	74,728
EBITDA — Adjusted for Non-Recurring Items		432,798	290,085

/ Report of the Supervisory Board / Supervisory Board / Strategy / Highlights / Management Report / Divisions / Further Information / **Financial Statements** | 61

Consolidated Cash Flow Statement

Consolidated Cash Flow Statement
EUR thousands

	Note	2004	2003
Consolidated net income		147,547	111,558
Depreciation, amortization, impairments on and increases in value of fixed assets		118,055	100,324
Equity income from associated companies and joint ventures		- 18,696	- 17,494
Dividends received from associated companies and joint ventures accounted for under the equity method		15,493	9,825
Gains on disposals of fixed assets		- 2,566	-837
Income(-)/losses(+) from discontinued operations		6,075	- 42,257
Increase/decrease in non-current provisions		- 12,993	16,574
Change in deferred taxes		11,222	32,874
Other non-cash income and expenses		- 30,820	0
Increase/decrease in inventories		- 2,195	5,558
Increase/decrease in trade receivables		366	- 4,974
Increase/decrease in other assets		- 6,310	20,402
Decrease/increase in current provisions		2,129	28,487
Decrease/increase in trade payables		- 15,358	27,327
Increase/decrease in receivables due from and liabilities due to related parties		- 6,107	- 4,298
Decrease/increase in other liabilities		99,162	34,361
Cash Flow from Operating Activities	(33)	305,004	317,430
Proceeds from disposals of intangible assets and property, plant and equipment		1,291	12,547
Proceeds from disposals of consolidated affiliated companies		20,000	148,172
Proceeds from disposals of other non-current financial assets		0	9,719
Net cash inflow on initial consolidation		14,383	0
Purchases of intangible assets, property, plant and equipment and investment property		- 110,736	- 150,129
Purchases of other non-current financial assets		- 20,236	- 8,634
Cash Flow from Investing Activities		- 95,298	11,675
Dividends paid			
Dividends paid to shareholders of Axel Springer AG		- 36,720	- 22,100
Dividends paid to minority shareholders		- 4,685	- 5,255
Capital contributions received		3,382	3,024
Purchase of treasury shares		0	- 184,585
Repayments of finance lease obligations		- 4,349	- 4,118
Additions to other financial liabilities		4,588	120,000
Repayments of other financial liabilities		- 13,311	- 18,443
Cash Flow from Financing Activities		- 51,095	- 111,477
Cash Flow-Related Changes in Cash and Cash Equivalents		158,611	217,628
Effects of exchange rate changes on cash and cash equivalents		497	- 1,407
Cash and cash equivalents at beginning of period	(32)	295,438	79,217
Cash and Cash Equivalents at End of Period	(32)	454,546	295,438

Accident Compensation Corporation

Design Firm: Clemenger BBDO
Creative Directors: Josh Twaddle, Rod Schofield, Bruce Hamilton

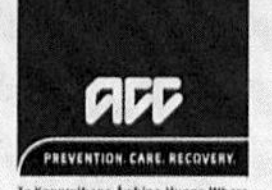

AGE years | AGE years

100 90 80 70 60 50 40 30 20 10 0

1.0 0.5 % 0.5 1.0

ACCIDENT COMPENSATION CORPORATION ANNUAL REPORT 2005

Constantly changing, changing constantly

Art Directors, Designers: Josh Twaddle, Dianne Fuller
Illustrator: Stephen Fuller
Act Director: Odele Rodgers
Mac Artist: Steve Jaycock
Illustrator: Stephen Fuller
Copywriter: James Francis
Print Broker: Craig Jenkins
Writer: Roger Joyce
Printer: Art to print, Print link
Paper: cover, via Pure White Ultra Smooth 216gsm, text, via Pure White Ultra Smooth 118gsm
Page count: 128 +cover
Print run: 3,000; Size: A4
Number of images: 13 Illustrations, 5 photos
Client: Accident Compensation Corp, New Zealand

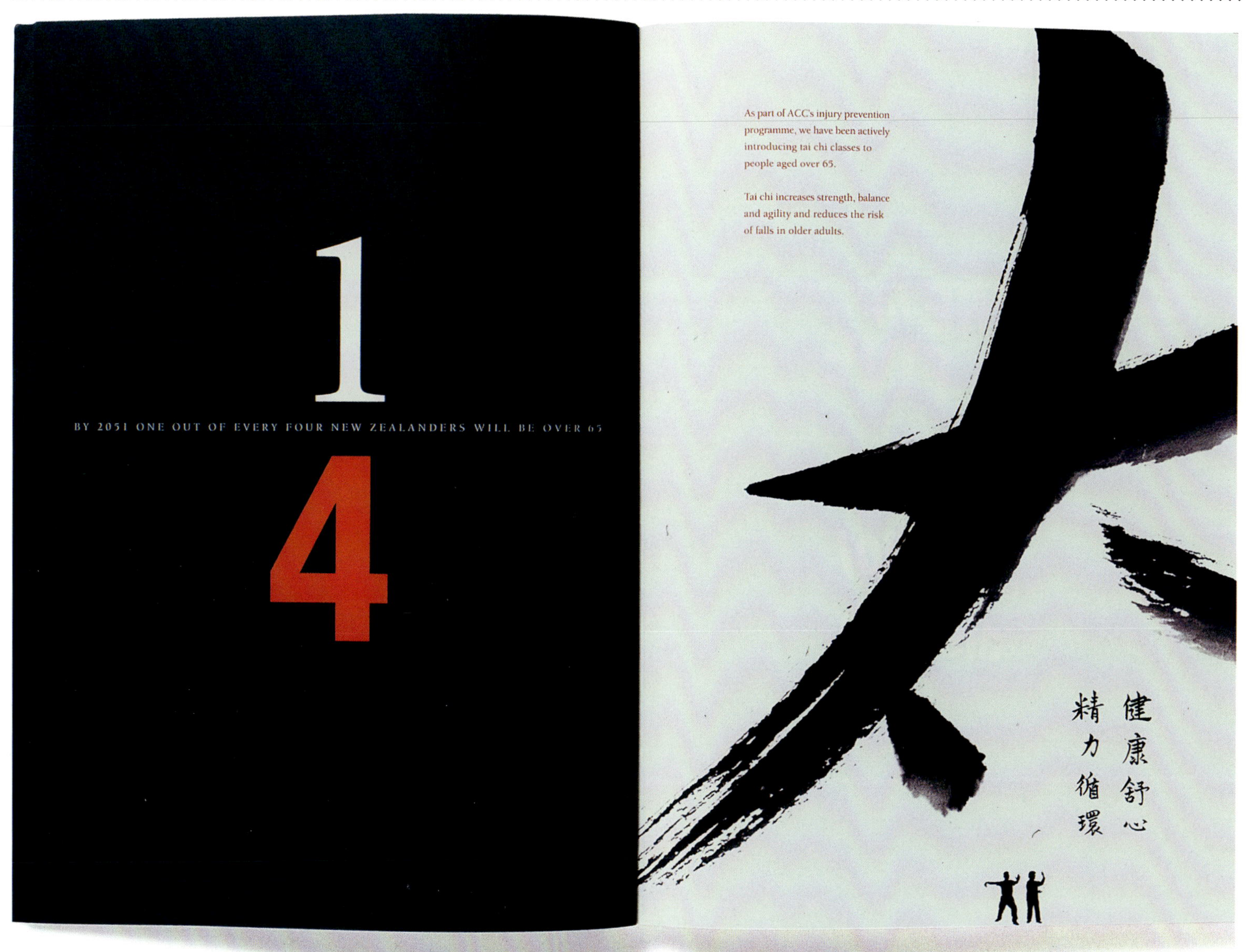

Q&A with Clemenger BBDO

What was the client's directive?

Provide a report that covers the financial performance and the five drivers - Injury Prevention, Rehabilitation, Claimant and Other Stakeholder Satisfaction, Staff Satisfaction and Fair Levies covering the previous year - but also position the Accident Compensation Corporation (ACC) positively and communicate to the New Zealand community about the scheme in general, to enhance knowledge about ACC's role and services and to improve public perceptions around the corporation. Demonstrate that ACC is not resting on its laurels and that it is constantly looking to the future with an eye for improvement.

How did you define the problem?

We had a couple of key insights about the target audience that defined the problem. The vast majority of people who come into contact with the scheme are satisfied with ACC's performance. The rest have their perception formed not by the organization but by the media and ACC claimant "cause champions."

ACC is a low interest subject for most people. The wider community generally relates to ACC through claims experience. Increased awareness would assist greatly in providing context for many of ACC's activities and its obligations.

The problem, therefore, was simple: provide relevance and context to key areas ACC is working in within the New Zealand environment, and support these areas with real life claimant experiences.

What was the approach?

The aim of the 2005 ACC Annual Report was to highlight the steps they were taking to ensure they kept pace with a changing New Zealand society/environment. We used statistics to project upcoming scenarios and then highlighted these scenarios by showing the steps ACC has taken. Real case studies were used to help emphasise how they are keeping up with the changing population. A strong use of typography was used to convey the message and ensure they stood out in the document, and ensure the facts were communicated clearly.

Were you happy with the result? What could have been better?

Yes, we were happy with the end result. It would have been better if we had commissioned the photography of key people instead of those supplied by the client.

What was the client's response?

The client was rapt with the final result and enjoyed the journey.

How involved was the CEO in your meetings and presentations?

The CEO was involved and available throughout the process.

Do you feel that designers are becoming more involved in copywriting?

Yes, especially so since the designer is coming up with the core idea and often has a vision of the way he or she wants it expressed through words. The words form such a strong connection back to the idea the designer is communicating; the words and the designer are intrinsically linked and need to be worked through with a writer in parallel with one another.

How do you define success in Annual Report design?

A simple but strong IDEA that creatively expresses succinctly what your client's business is about and what they have achieved over the past financial year, or what they are looking to achieve in the future. An idea that makes you look at a company from an angle you may not have perceived about their business before reading the report. Plus…a great client who appreciates creativity, a great brief with strategic direction and focus, a great timeline, and a great budget for both design and production.

How important are awards to your client?

Design awards are not important to ACC, but it does confirm that they are getting a great job from their design company.

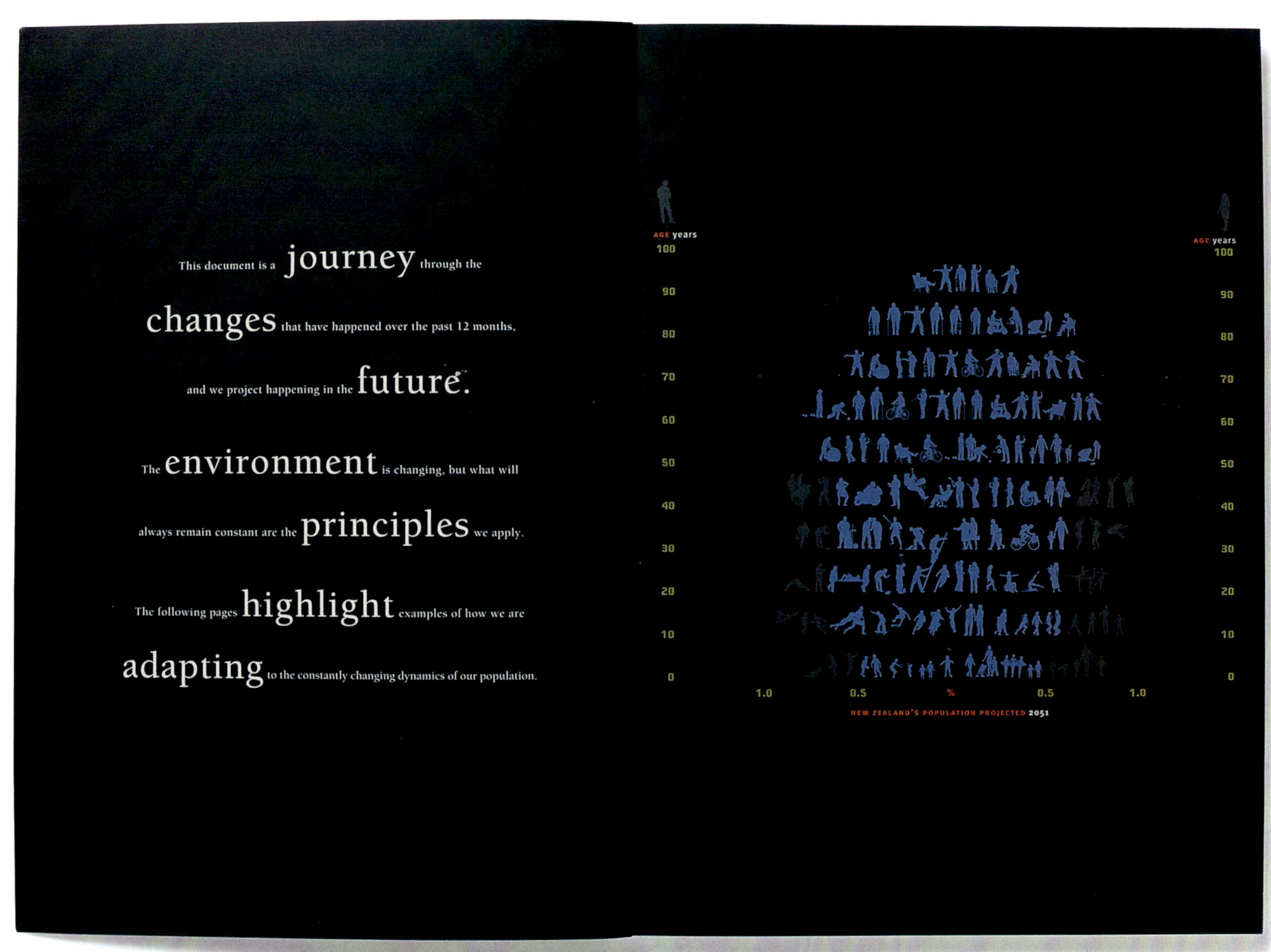

A successful AR should have a simple but strong idea that expresses succinctly what your client's business is about, what they have achieved over the past year, and what they are looking to achieve in the future.

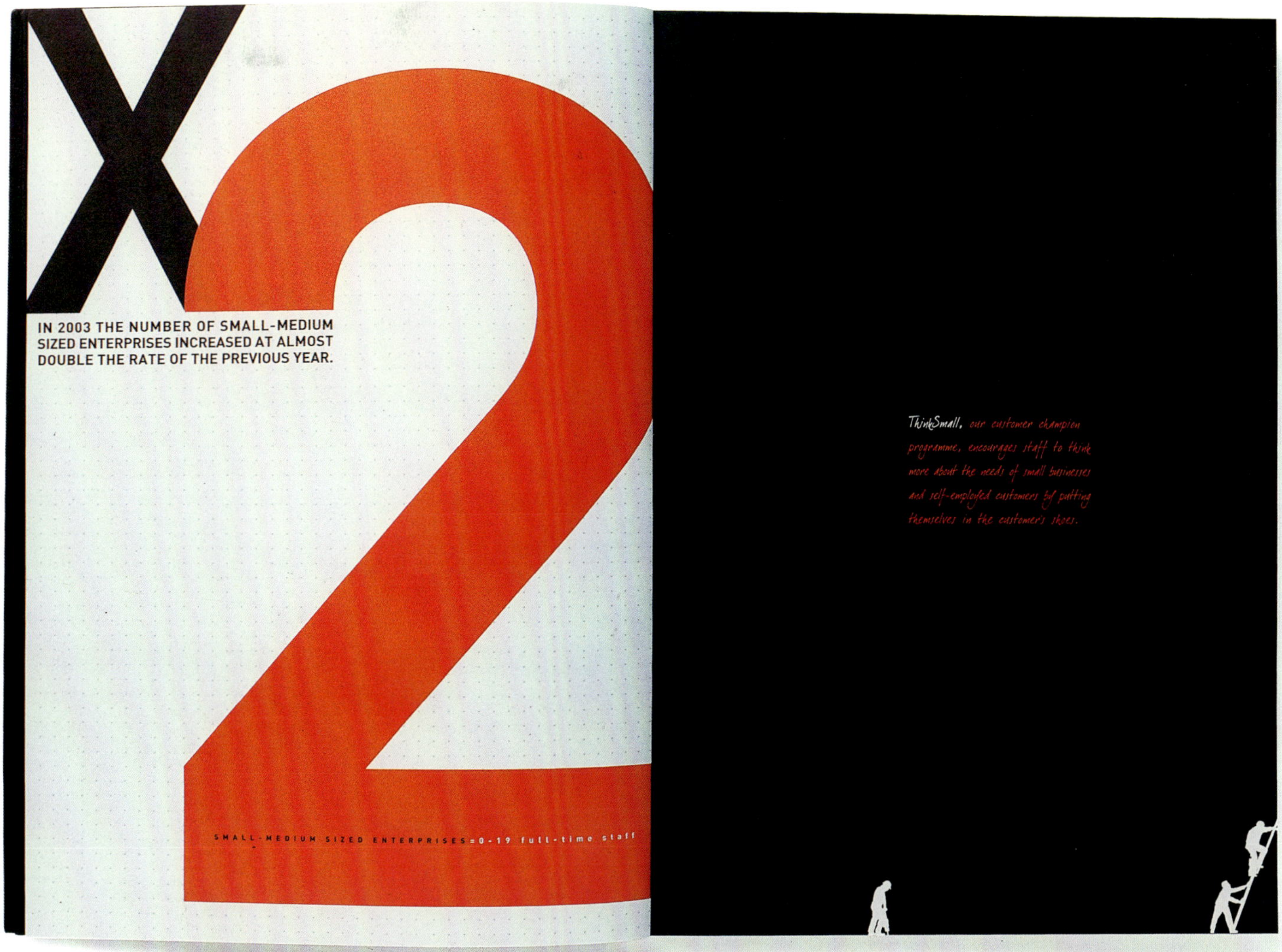

X2

IN 2003 THE NUMBER OF SMALL-MEDIUM SIZED ENTERPRISES INCREASED AT ALMOST DOUBLE THE RATE OF THE PREVIOUS YEAR.

SMALL-MEDIUM SIZED ENTERPRISES=0-19 full-time staff

ThinkSmall, our customer champion programme, encourages staff to think more about the needs of small businesses and self-employed customers by putting themselves in the customer's shoes.

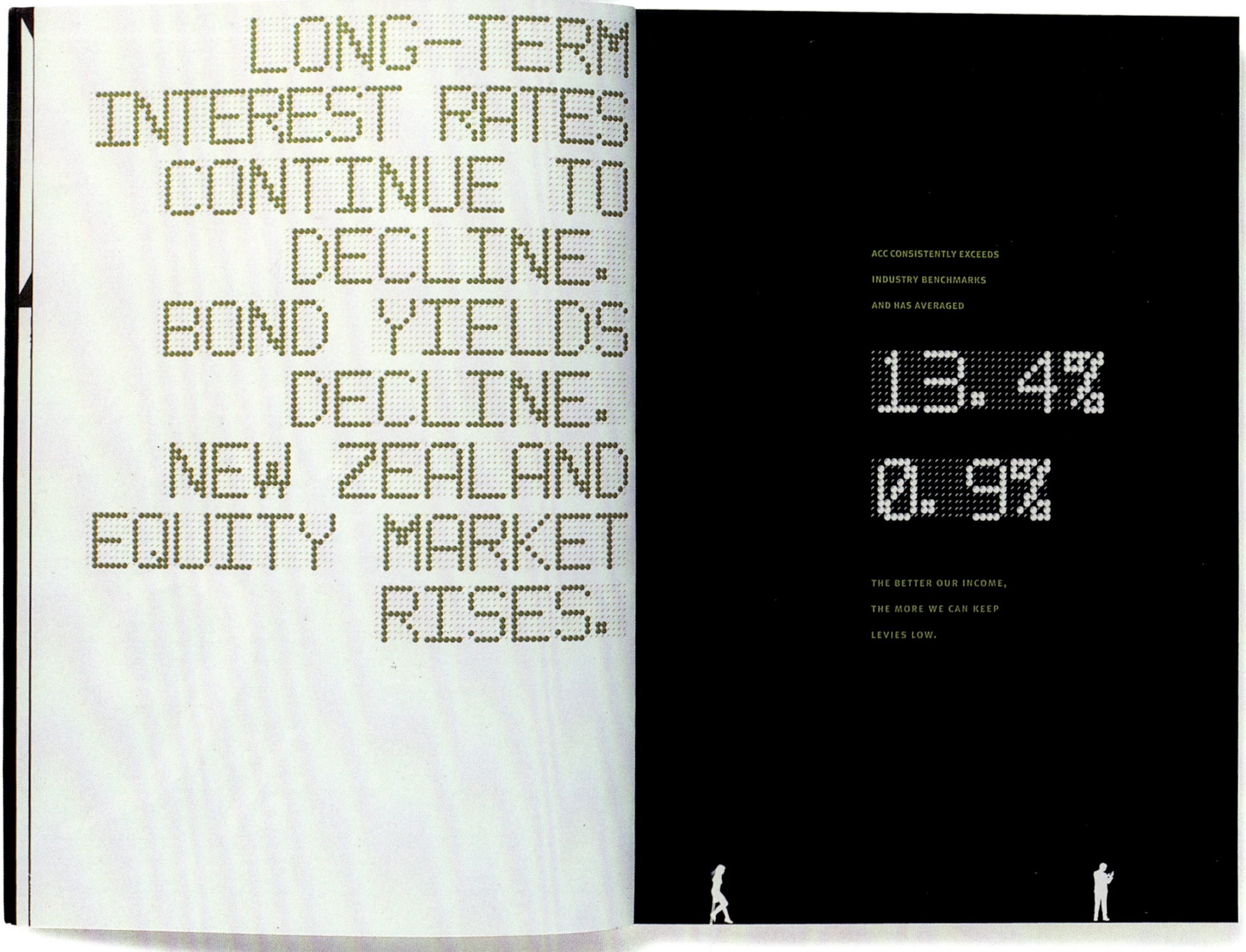

LONG-TERM INTEREST RATES CONTINUE TO DECLINE. BOND YIELDS DECLINE. NEW ZEALAND EQUITY MARKET RISES.

ACC CONSISTENTLY EXCEEDS INDUSTRY BENCHMARKS AND HAS AVERAGED

13.4%

0.9%

THE BETTER OUR INCOME, THE MORE WE CAN KEEP LEVIES LOW.

positive thoughts

Art Director, Illustrator & Designer: Maja Bagic	Printer: Stega tisak Paper: Munken Print Extra	Print Run: 1,000 Page Count: 76	Size: 230 x 340 mm Number of images: 5 ill.	Client: Adris Group, Positive Thoughts

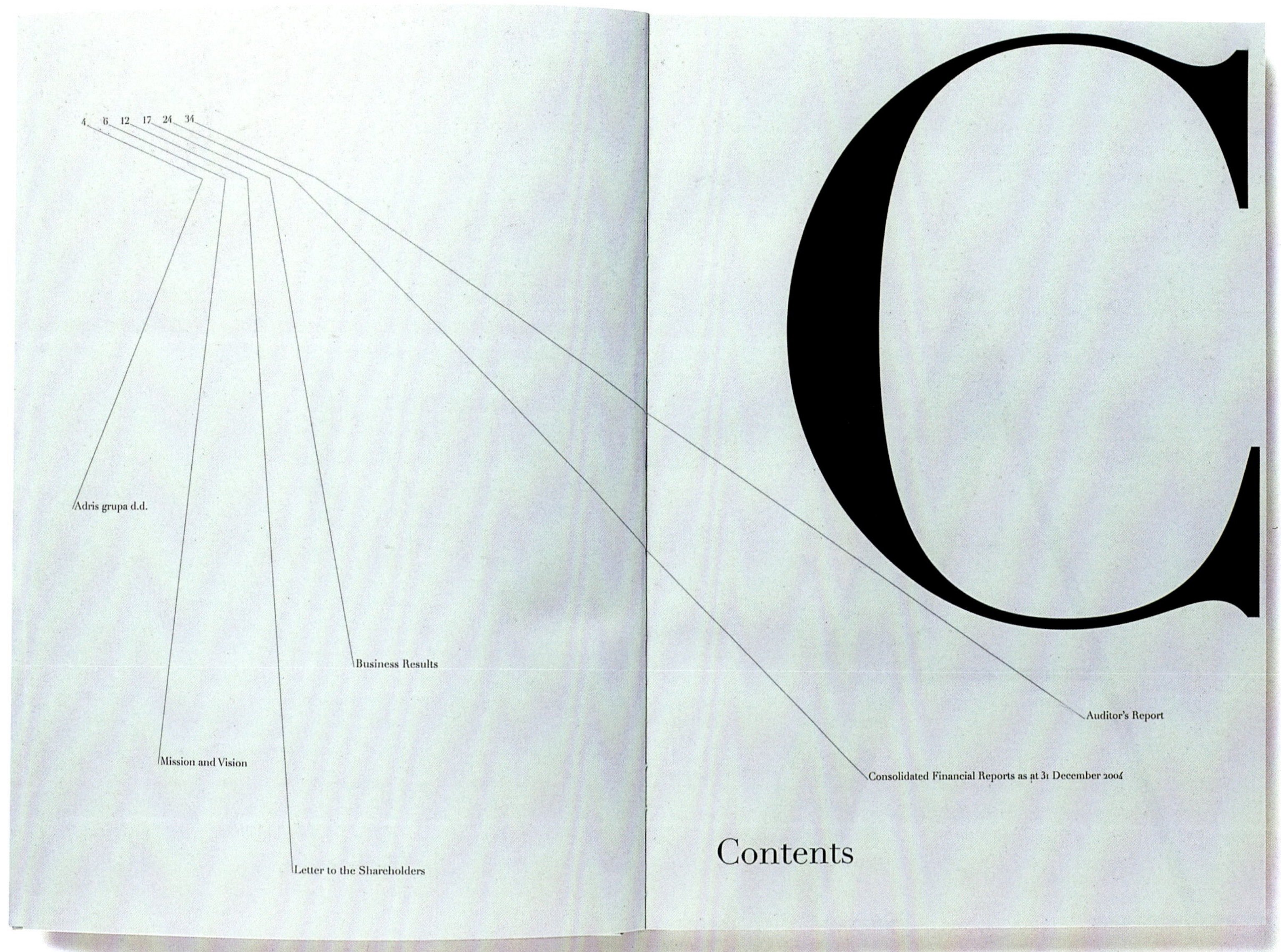

Q&A with Bruketa&Zinic

What was the client's directive?
To create an Annual Report that would reflect Adris Group as one of the largest companies in Croatia.
How did you define the problem? To make a report that would satisfy all of the functional demands, and at the same time communicate the company's values in a creative way.
What was the approach?
The basic concept of the visual identity was typography. The idea came about from the company's logo, serif letter A in the Didot font, which tells us it is a powerful umbrella company. The report was, therefore, executed using typography. The introductory pages to different sections consist of letters extracted from the titles and form separate typographic units. Besides the titles based on typography, the report consists of simple illustrations based on the idea of *Positive Thoughts*. The motifs therefore are thoughts like idea (bridge), creativity (pencil), entrepreneurship (briefcase) and future (binoculars).
Were you happy with the result? What could have been better?
Yes, we were happy with it, but the binding could have been better.
What was the client's response?
The client is happy with it.
How involved was the CEO in your meetings and presentations?
He attended all the key meetings, and gave us his full support.
Do you feel that designers are becoming more involved in copywriting?
Absolutely.
How do you define success in Annual Report design?
When they hire you to do their next Annual Report, and of course, when you win a lot of awards for your work.
How important are awards to your client?
They are very proud of them.

Success is when they hire you to do their next Annual Report. And, of course, when you win awards for your work.

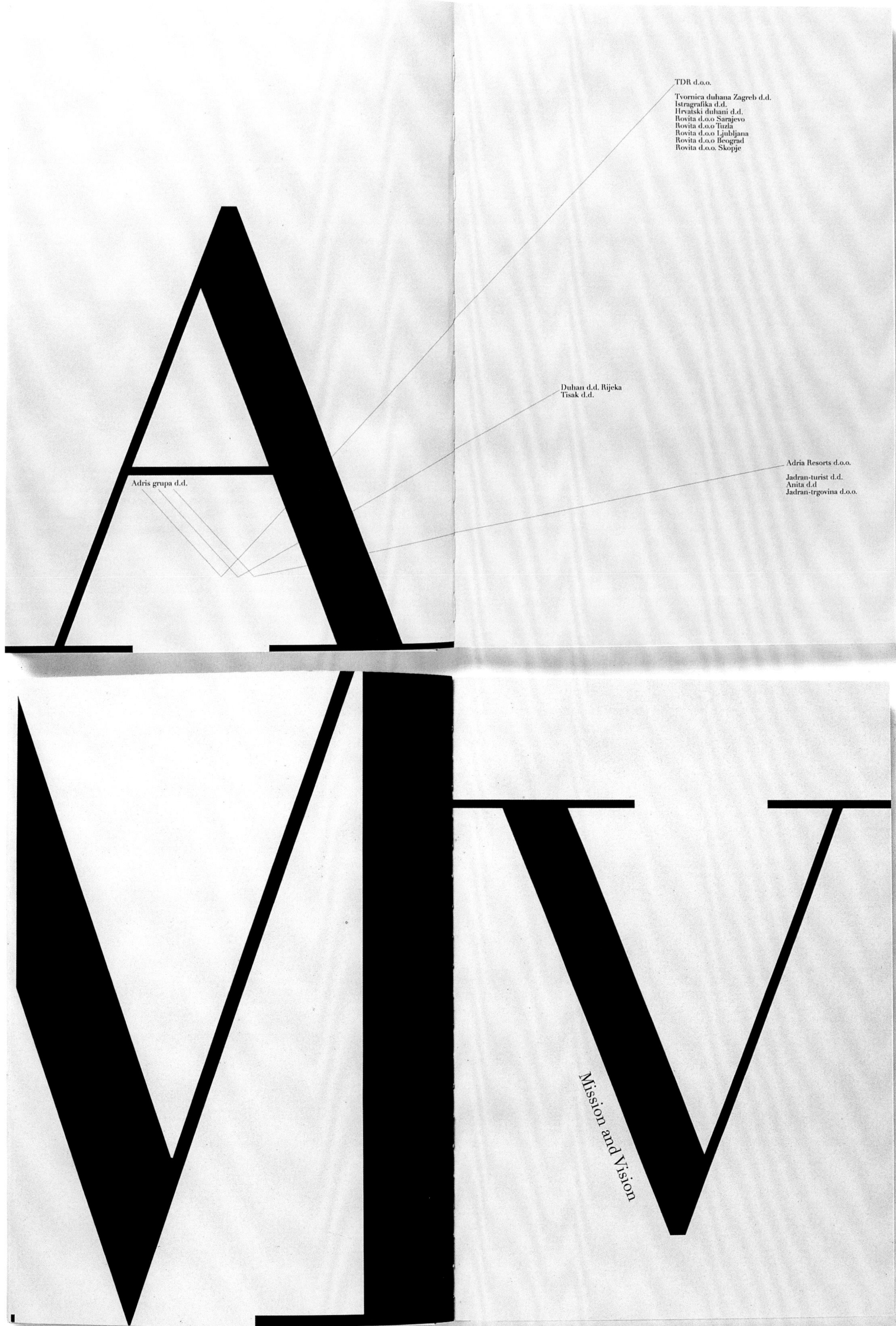
TDR d.o.o.
Tvornica duhana Zagreb d.d.
Istragrafika d.d.
Hrvatski duhani d.d.
Rovita d.o.o Sarajevo
Rovita d.o.o Tuzla
Rovita d.o.o Ljubljana
Rovita d.o.o Beograd
Rovita d.o.o. Skopje
Duhan d.d. Rijeka
Tisak d.d.
Adria Resorts d.o.o.
Jadran-turist d.d.
Anita d.d
Jadran-trgovina d.o.o.
Adris grupa d.d.
Mission and Vision

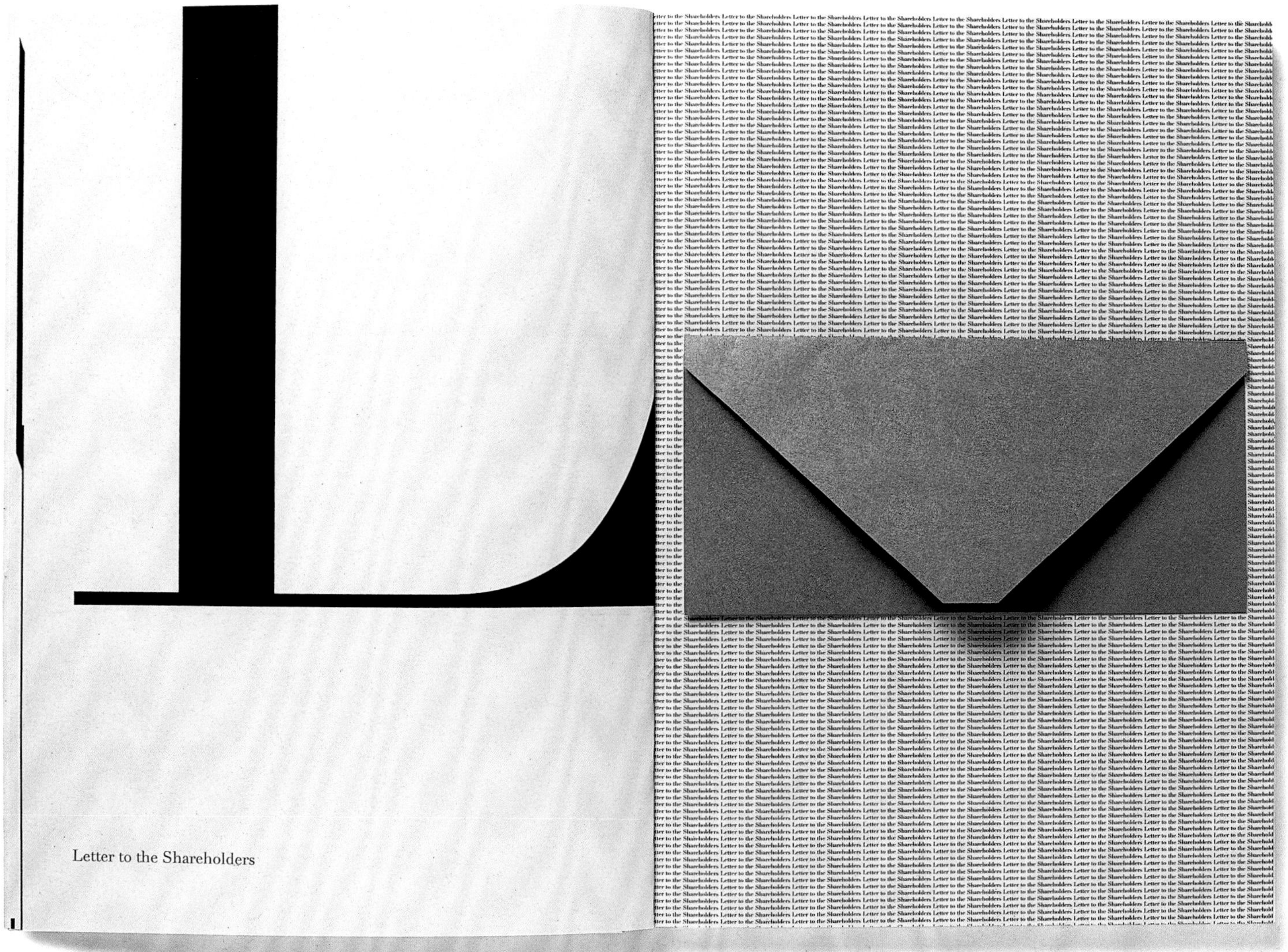

Letter to the Shareholders

Letter to the Shareholders Letter to the Shareholders Letter to the Shareholders Letter to the Shareholders Letter to the Shareholders Letter to the Shareholders Letter to the Shareholders Letter to the Shareholders

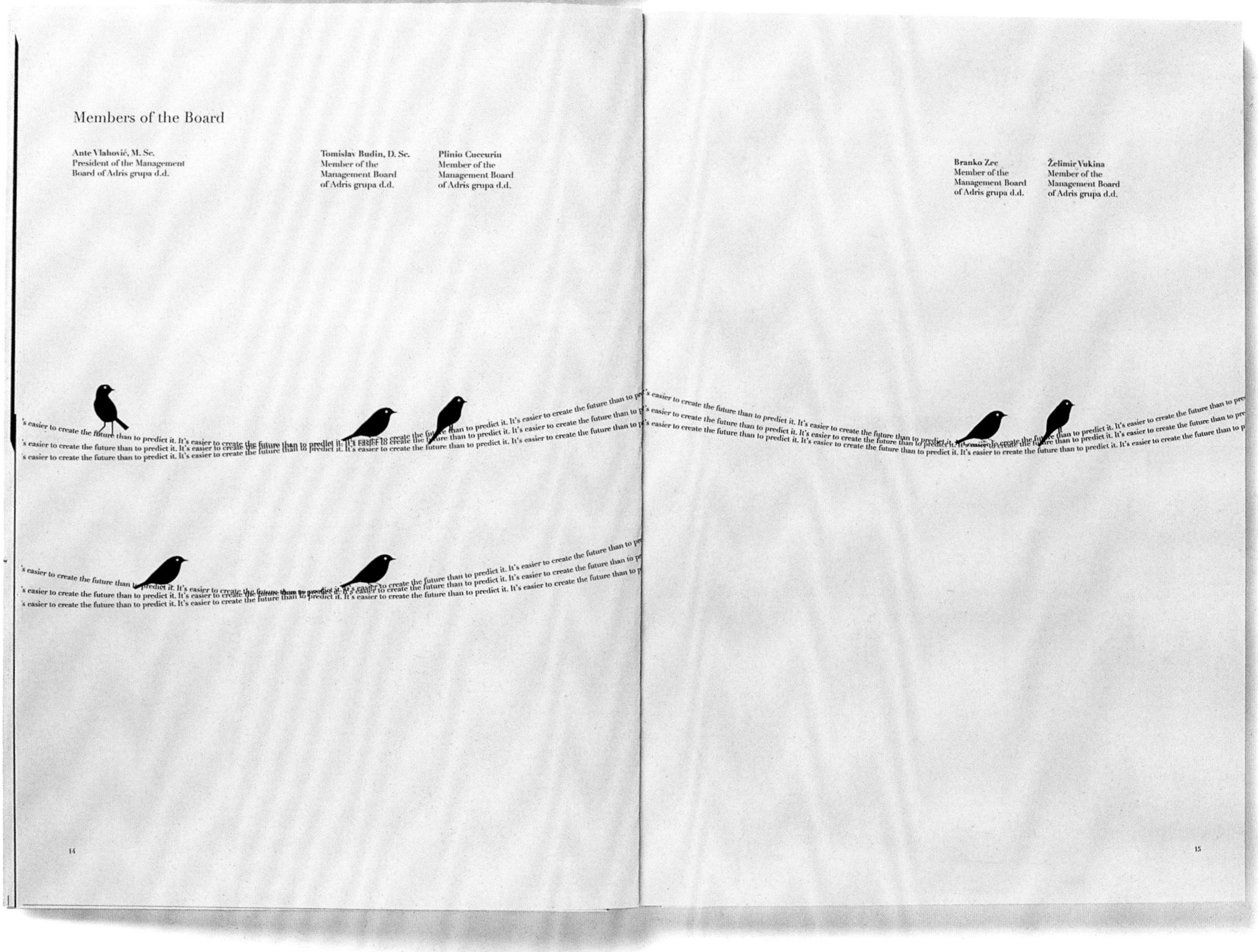

Members of the Board

Ante Vlahović, M. Sc.
President of the Management
Board of Adris grupa d.d.

Tomislav Budin, D. Sc.
Member of the
Management Board
of Adris grupa d.d.

Plinio Cuccurin
Member of the
Management Board
of Adris grupa d.d.

Branko Zec
Member of the
Management Board
of Adris grupa d.d.

Želimir Vukina
Member of the
Management Board
of Adris grupa d.d.

's easier to create the future than to predict it. It's easier to create the future than to predict it. It's easier to create the future than to predict it. It's easier to create the future than to predict it.

14

15

2004 Business Results and Comparison with 2003

Operations of Adris grupa d.d. during 2004 are marked by increases in total revenues, further growth in exports and higher operating profits from sales of goods and services. Continued orientation toward excellence in business operations requires constant improvements in business processes. One could therefore say that the Group's restructuring is a continuous rather then a once-only process. Restructuring costs in 2004 burdened the Group's current results, but optimization of business processes will contribute to higher efficiency in the years to come. The Group's total revenues reached 2.82 billion kunas which represents further growth of 0.7%. Operating revenues are almost at the last year's level, whereas revenues from sales of goods and services raised by 5.1%. 2004 exports showed a 3% increase and amounted to 1.12 billion kunas. Declared operating profit amounted to 863.6 million kunas. Net revenue from financial activities in the reported period shows a positive result of 100 million kunas. Management of currency risk produced positive effects on financial activities result in the amount of 21 million kunas. Interest revenues are 43% higher than in 2003 and amounted to 84,8 million kunas. Profit before taxation amounting to 964,2 million kunas is 5,3 % lower than a year before. Effective tax rate is 20.3% which is higher in comparison with the last year's 18.57%. Declared loss, resulting mainly from high restructuring costs, of the company Hrvatski duhani d.d. (Croatian Tobaccos) together with partially restricted possibilities of using tax losses from the previous years in the Group's tourism division had an impact on effective tax rate growth. Declared net profit of the Group is 768.4 million kunas.

Consolidated Income Statement

in HRK 000's for the Financial Year Jan 1 to Dec 31	2002	2003	2004
Net domestic sales	1,268,507	1,394,964	1,488,058
Net foreign sales	1,048,927	1,088,813	1,122,073
Other operating revenues	65,396	151,143	56,317
Total operating revenues	2,382,830	2,634,920	2,666,448
Cost of material and services	974,185	1,036,119	1,113,103
Employee and related costs	365,372	404,952	407,416
Depreciation	171,252	114,141	102,767
Other operating expenses	113,366	150,941	179,570
Operating profit	758,655	928,767	863,592
Net financial income	101,288	89,567	100,569
Profit before taxation	859,943	1,018,334	964,161
Income tax expense	162,078	189,054	195,732
Net profit for the year	697,865	829,280	768,429
Minority interest	-17,954	-20,301	-15,781
Net profit	679,911	808,979	752,648

Items Affecting Comparability

The restructuring process within the Group continued in 2004 which had some effect on the growth of business expenses in the amount of 33.2 million kunas. In 2003 the binding assessment of long term assets by chartered experts was conducted to include such assets into the capital of newly established company TDR d.o.o. The mentioned activity had positive effects on increase of operating profits by 70.7 million kunas and also affects comparability of figures in the reported periods. Overall, in case of eliminating nonrecurring incomes and charges in the comparable report periods, operating business results show that:

- 2004 operating profit would be 897 million kunas or 4.4% higher than operating profit produced in 2003;
- 2004 profit before taxation would be 997.4 million kunas or 5.2% higher than in the previous report period.

Strategic Business Units

According to the Group's new organization which took place in 2003, its operations have been divided into two strategic business units (SBU): Tobacco and Tourism. 2004 operations have shown that establishment of these strategic business units is reasonable: high decentralization allows for autonomy and flexibility, together with simultaneous use of synergistic effect in respect of sharing management knowledge, skills and financial resources.

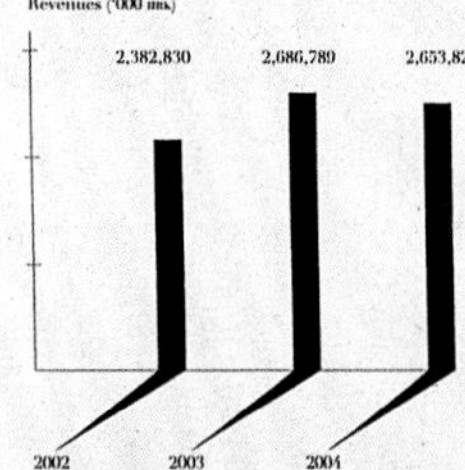

for the Financial Year Jan 1 to Dec 31

Turnover* ('000 HRK)
5,596,170
5,783,366
5,889,226
2002
2003
2004

for the Financial Year Jan 1 to Dec 31
* including Excise Duty and VAT

Assets ('000 HRK)
3,391,471
4,175,038
4,867,513
2002
2003
2004

for the Financial Year Jan 1 to Dec 31

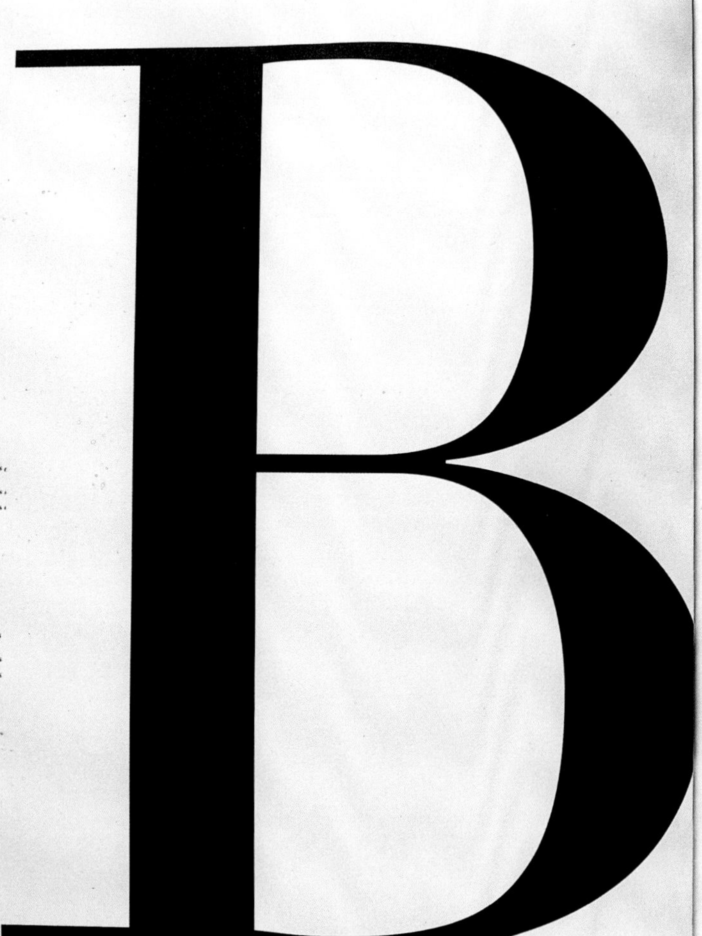

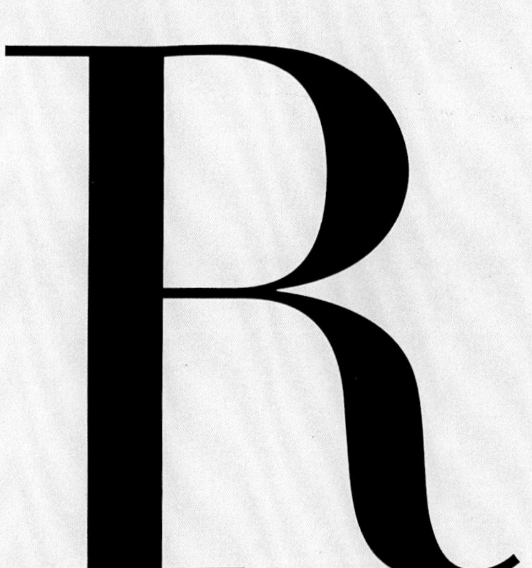

Business Results

Consolidated
Financial
Reports as at
31 December
2004

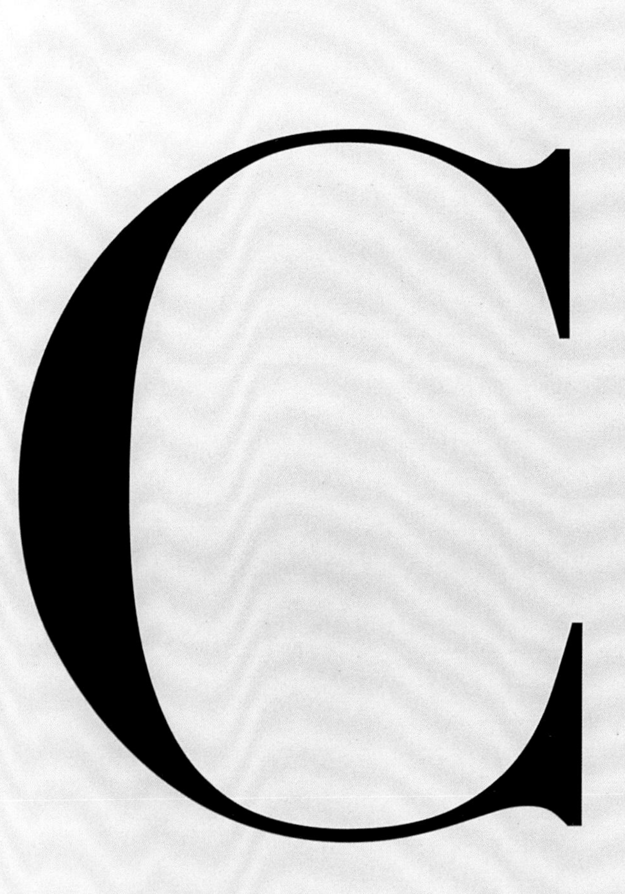

Consolidated Balance Sheet -
31 December 2004

Assets

in HRK 000's for the Financial Year Jan 1 to Dec 31	2002	2003	2004
Non-current assets			
Intangible assets	15,171	27,236	32,045
Tangible assets	1,356,012	1,417,310	1,519,870
Investments	88,244	89,668	156,045
Non-current receivables	533,151	135,877	502,638
Total non-current assets	1,992,578	1,670,091	2,210,598
Current assets			
Cash and cash equivalents	72,962	76,651	44,749
Trade debtors	153,689	173,281	231,046
Inventories	489,346	494,328	503,972
Other current assets	682,896	1,760,687	1,877,148
Total current assets	1,398,893	2,504,947	2,656,915
Total assets	3,391,471	4,175,038	4,867,513

26

Equity and Liabilities

in HRK 000's for the Financial Year Jan 1 to Dec 31	2002	2003	2004
Capital and reserves			
Share capital	164,000	164,000	164,000
Reserves	1,563,708	1,852,614	2,652,975
Retained profit	780,272	1,246,447	1,122,007
Total capital and reserves	2,507,980	3,263,061	3,938,982
Minority interest	300,532	300,726	312,964
Long term provisions	56,078	23,289	35,383
Long term debt	12,753	1,764	1,566
Current liabilities	514,128	586,198	578,618
Total equity and liabilities	3,391,471	4,175,038	4,867,513

27

P22 Type Foundry

Design Firm: P22 type foundry
Creative Director: Richard Kegler

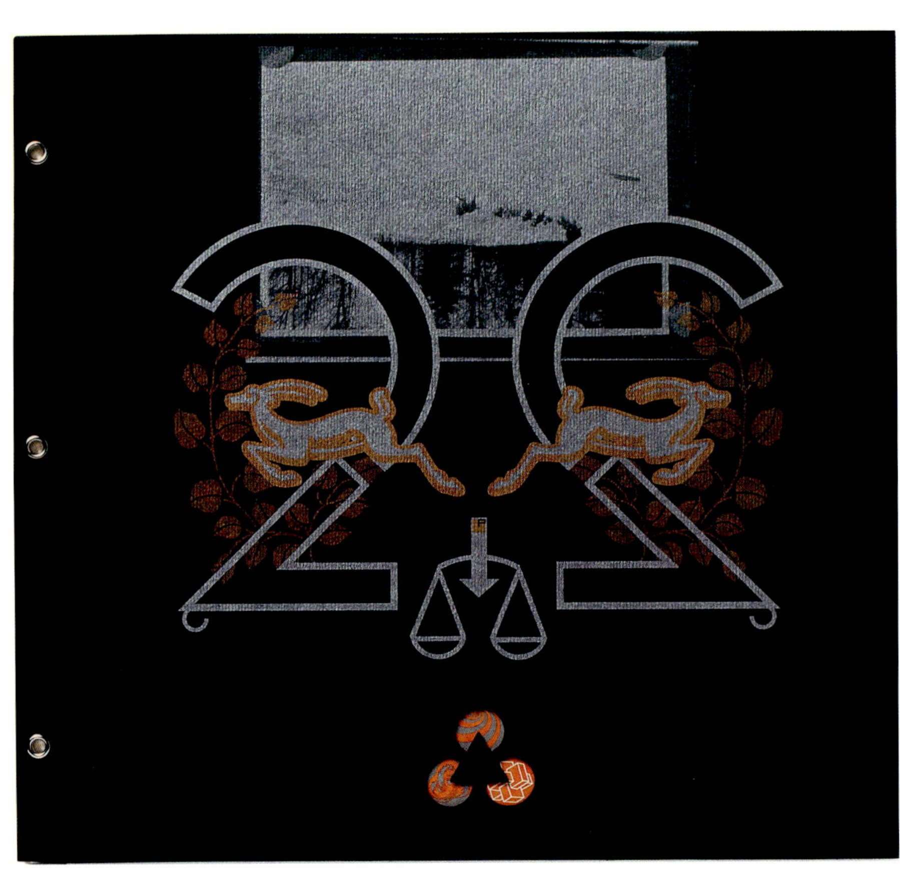

Art Director: Alan Kegler
Designer: Colin Kahn
Photographer: Eric Frick
Writers: Richard Kegler and Blair Boone
Printer: Petit Printing, Buffalo, New York
Paper: Mohawk Ultrafelt Black 80lb cover, Mohawk 50/10 Ultra Soft White smooth 100lb text, Mohawk Superfine Ultra White smooth 100lb text, Mohawk 50/10 Bright White Gloss 100lb text, Mohawk Superfine Soft White smooth 60lb text, Chartham translucent natural white 24lb
Page count: 33
Print Run: 2,500
Size: 9.75"h x 10.25"w
Number of Images: 64
Client: P22 type foundry

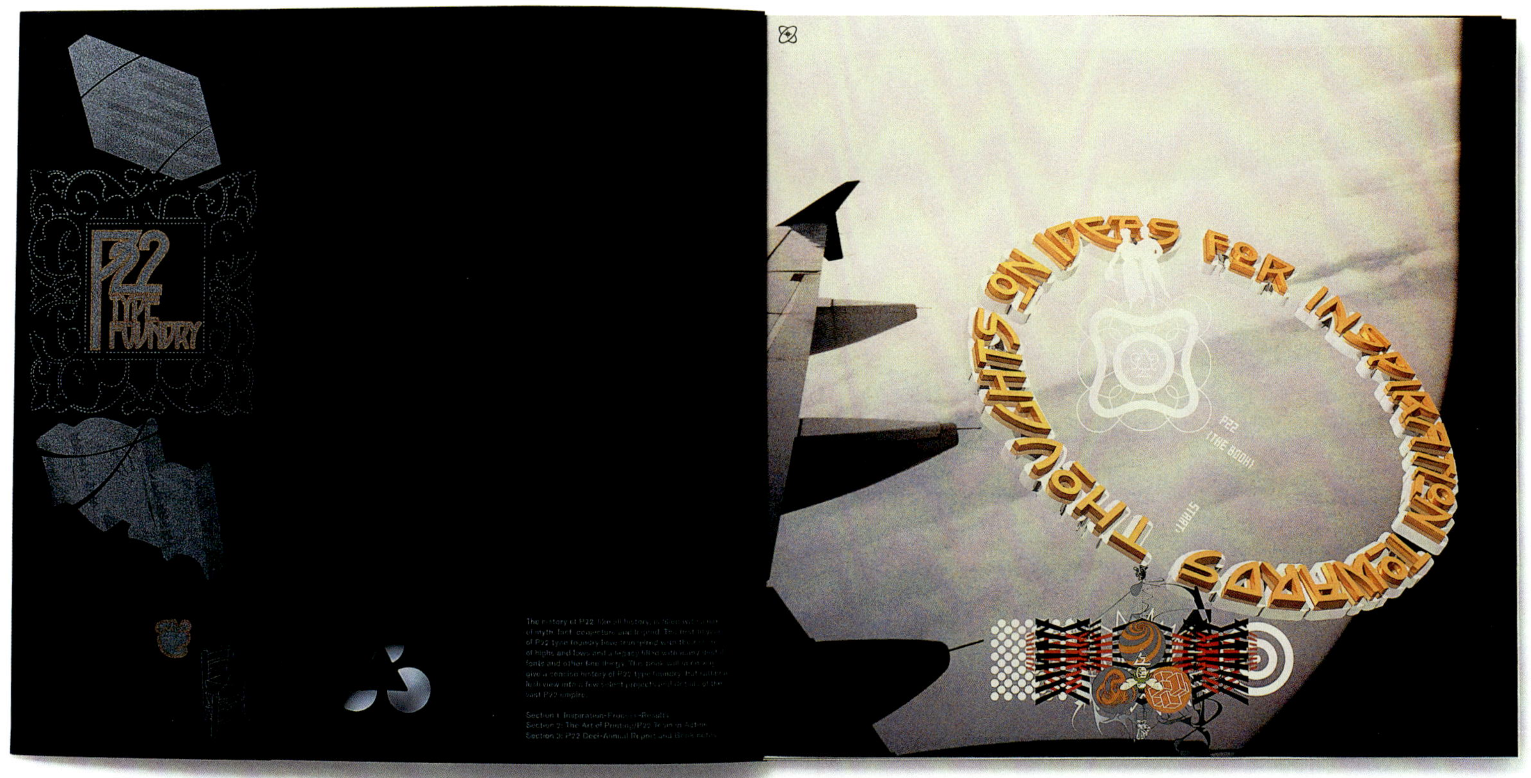

Q&A with P22

What was the client's directive?
Since P22 was the client and design firm, the directive was exuberant self-indulgence.

How did you define the problem?
The problem was to summarize the first 10 years of P22 in a light and informative way, but not to make it a type specimen book.

What was the approach?
To display a visual overload of imagery to be followed and explained in the "Deci-Annual Report," which would be text only.

Which disciplines or people helped you with the project?
The project was art directed by Alan Kegler, who is associate director and senior art director at University Creative Services at the University of NY at Buffalo. P22 designer Colin Kahn was given free reign within the physical constraints of the concept. Photographer Eric Frick worked with the art and project director to conceive surreal environmental portraits of the employees, paired with the dreamy micro shots of the printing and binding machines that produced the book. My background as a book artist may have made such a large run a bit of a physical challenge to the bindery with the various page sizes and single page grommet binding (Richard Kegler).

Were you happy with the result, and what could have been better?
Overall very happy. There was a disproportionate amount of technical problems amongst the printer, die cutter and bindery that makes a reprint of this exact project impossible.

What was the client's response?
Again, as client as well as design firm, we are relieved to have it finished. It took 18 months from start to finish, so it is hard to really step back and be fully objective about it yet.

How involved was the CEO in your meetings and presentations?
As the Project Director and CEO, (Richard Kegler) I had a unique position of dealing with many technical nightmares, and I was therefore a very sympathetic CEO.

Do you feel that designers are becoming more involved in copywriting?
Somewhat. It seems there are many disciplines that cross over. How many people are strictly Typographers today? A designer has to deal with many functions that were formally specialized, so adding copywriting is not that uncommon. Copy proofing is another matter.

How do you define success in Annual Report design?
The longer someone spends looking through it, the more successful it is. Indifference is failure.

How important are awards to your client?
Speaking as the design firm, the client is happy to receive awards and only enters occasional entries. As the client, we like awards just fine, but can't approach a job with the primary goal just to get awards (with the exception of this one of course).

Since P22 was the client and design firm, the directive was exuberant self-indulgence.

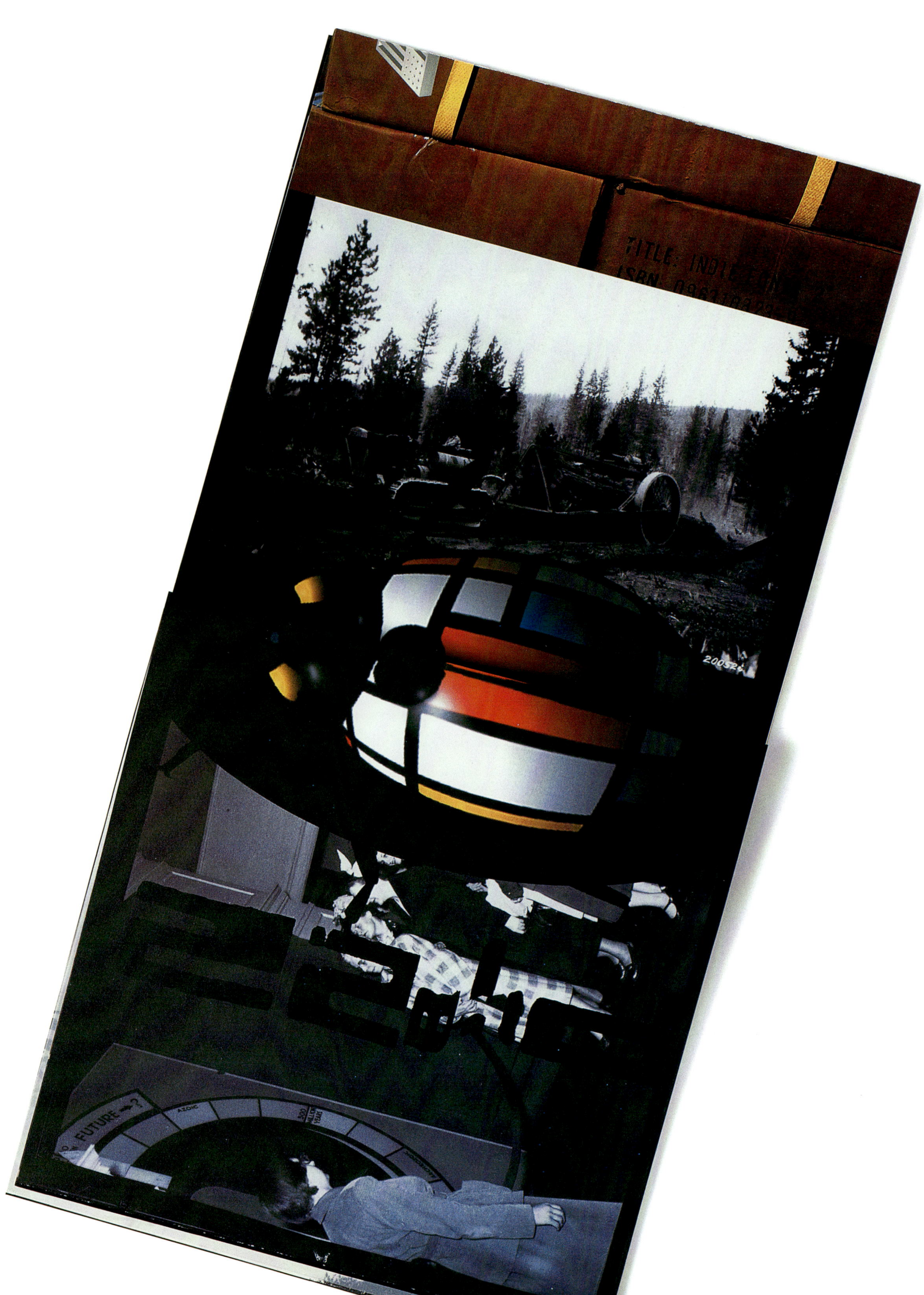
FUTURE →?
AZOIC

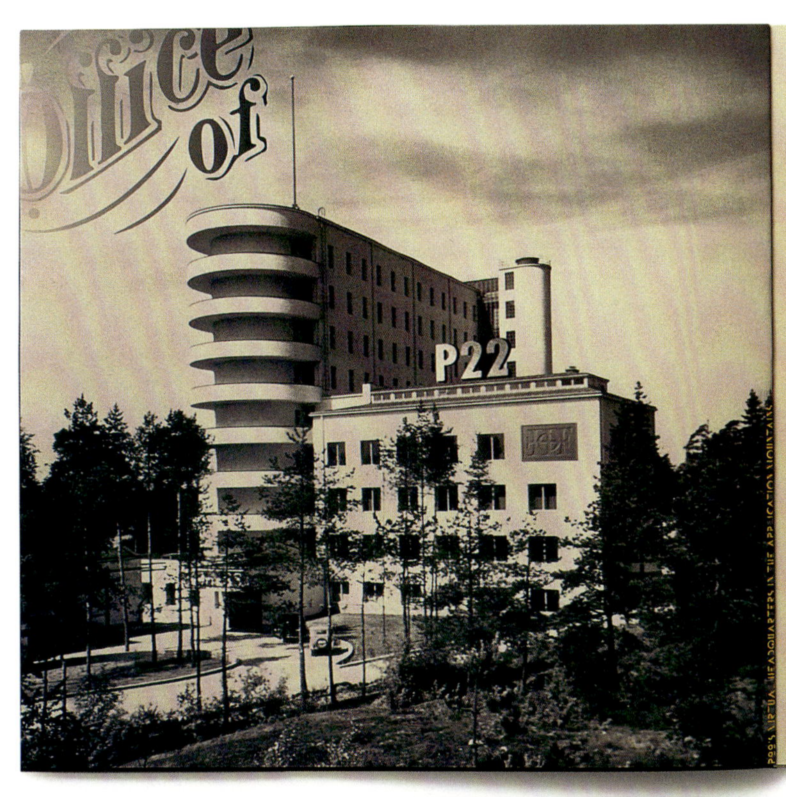

BOLD ADVANCES IN TYPOGRAPHIC INNOVATION. DISCOVERING AND RESURRECTING LOST ARTIFACTS FOR MODERN AUDIENCES. SURPRISING CLASSICS IN ART & DESIGN HISTORY. OCCASIONALLY OBSCURE & LIMITED IN USEFULNESS. RECONTEXTUALIZED MISFIT OFFERINGS OF THE PAST ALONGSIDE INDUSTRIAL PASTICHE & DIGITAL COLLECTIBLES. HYPERBOLIC ENLIGHTENMENT WHIZZING PAST PAGES HENCE. NOT YOUR TYPICAL TYPE.

BOLD ADVANCES IN TYPOGRAPHIC INNOVATION DISCOVERING AND RESURRECTING LOST ARTIFACTS FOR MODERN AUDIENCES SURPRISING CLASSICS IN ART & DESIGN HISTORY OCCASIONALLY OBSCURE & LIMITED IN USEFULNESS RECONTEXTUALIZED MISFIT OFFERINGS OF THE PAST ALONGSIDE INDUSTRIAL PASTICHE & DIGITAL COLLECTIBLES HYPERBOLIC ENLIGHTENMENT WHIZZING PAST PAGES HENCE NOT YOUR TYPICAL TYPE

Indifference to the design of the Annual Report is failure.

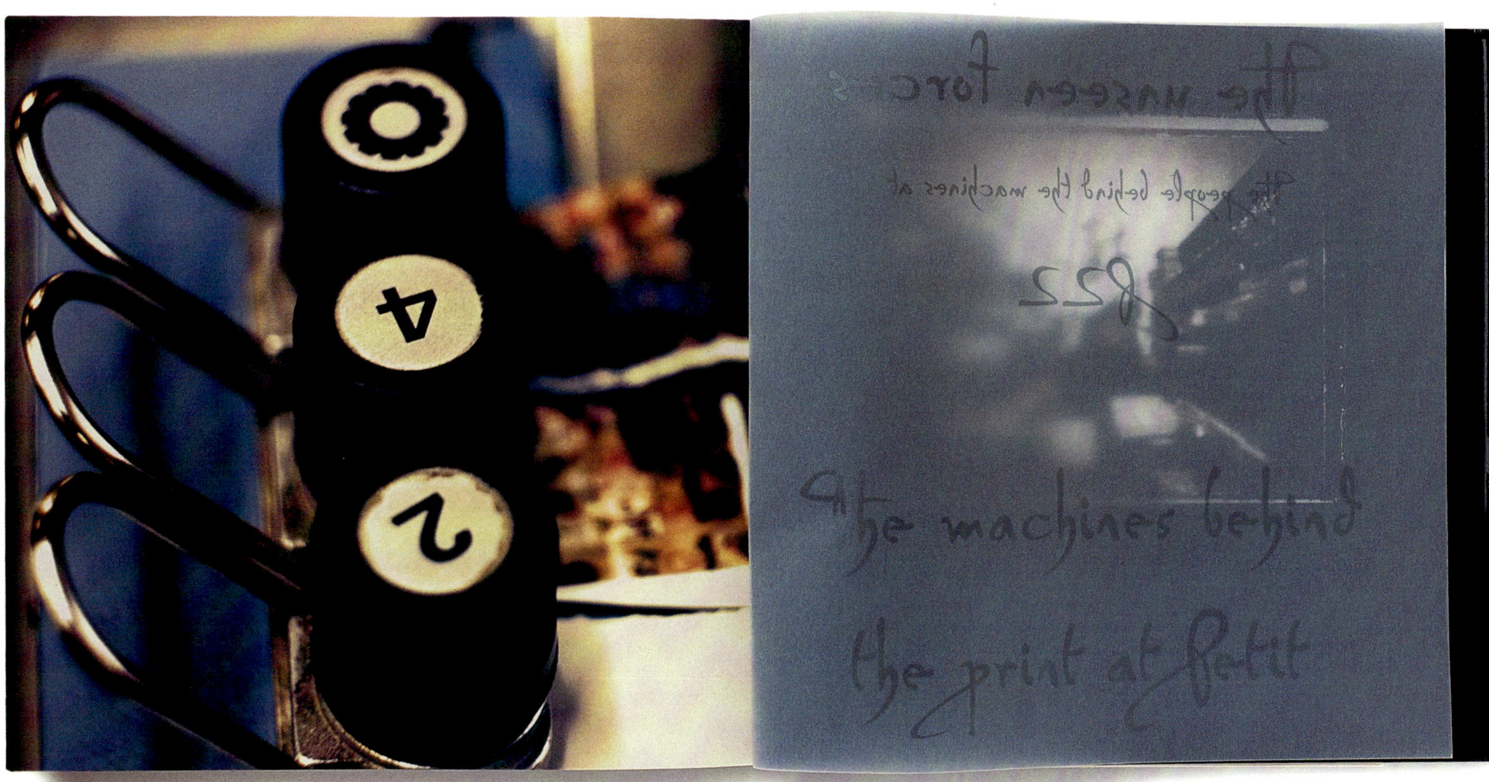
the machines behind
the print at Petit

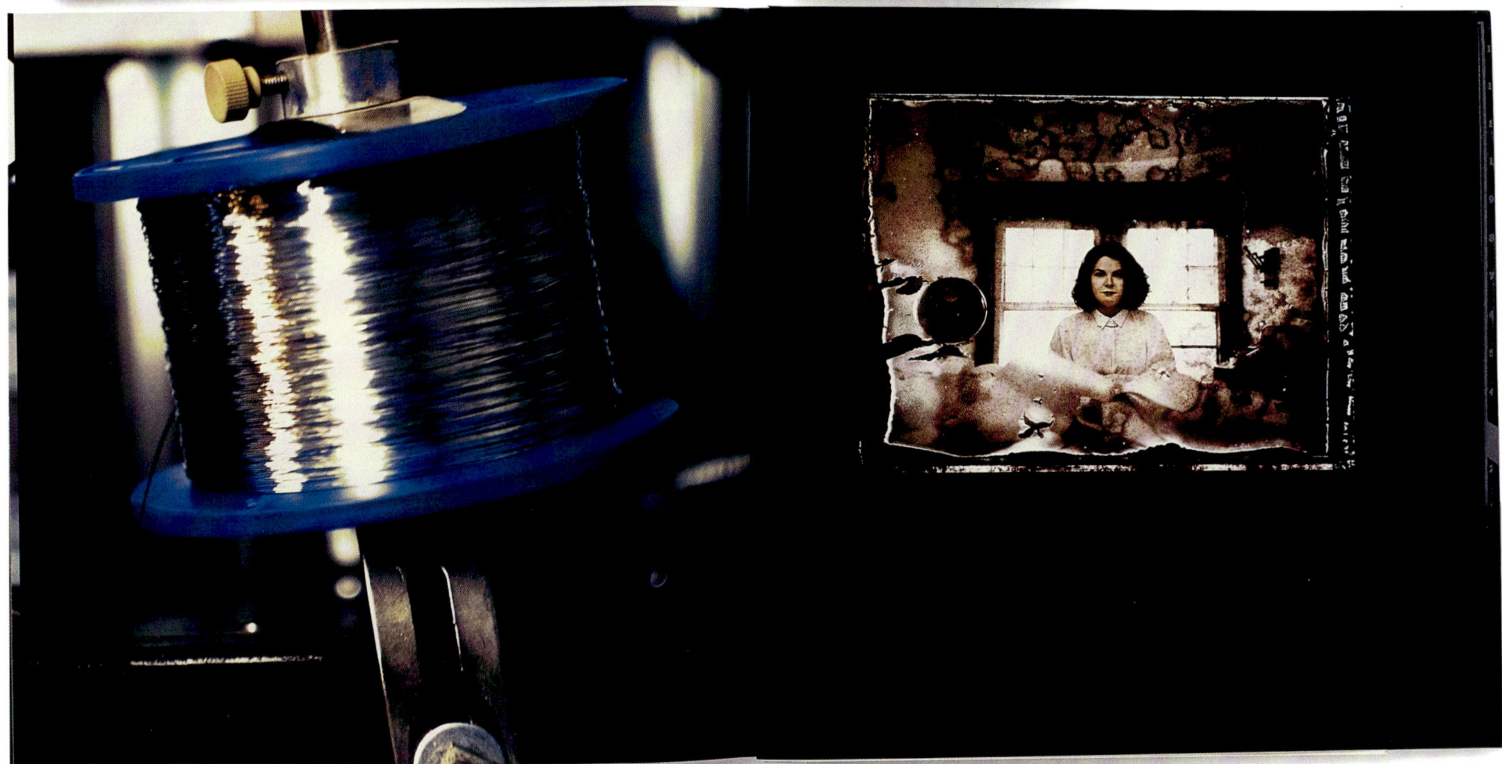

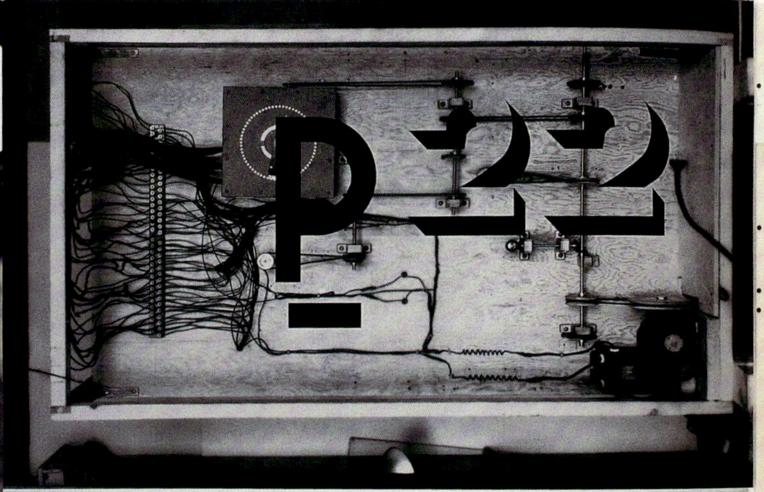

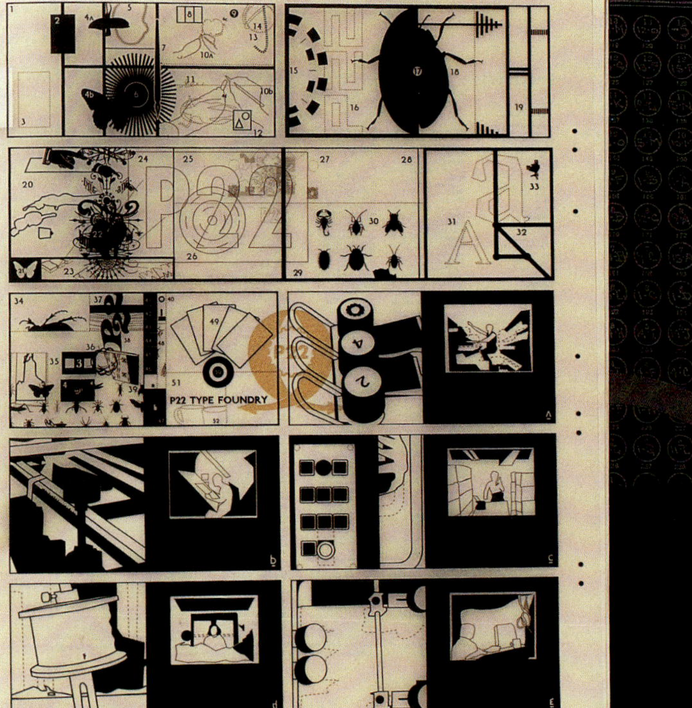
P22 TYPE FOUNDRY

[P22] SCHEMATIC DIAGRAMS
REFERENCE CHART

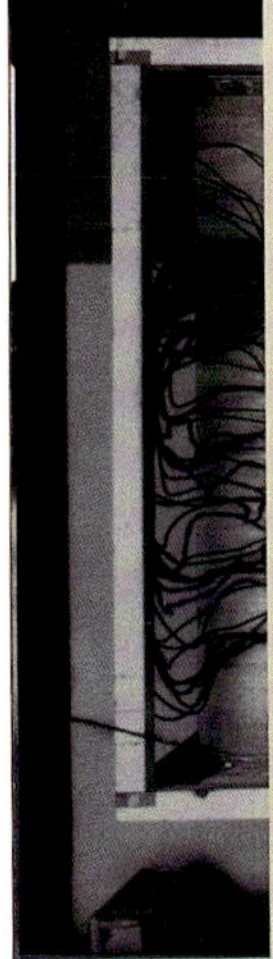

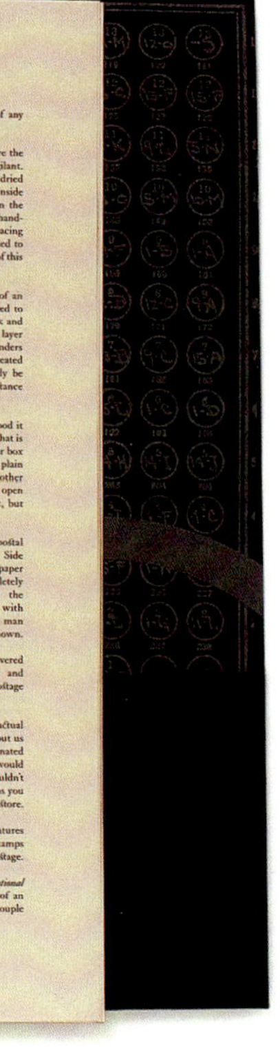
P22 Deci-Annual Report and Book Notes
Introduction
P22 Mail Art
Pre-22

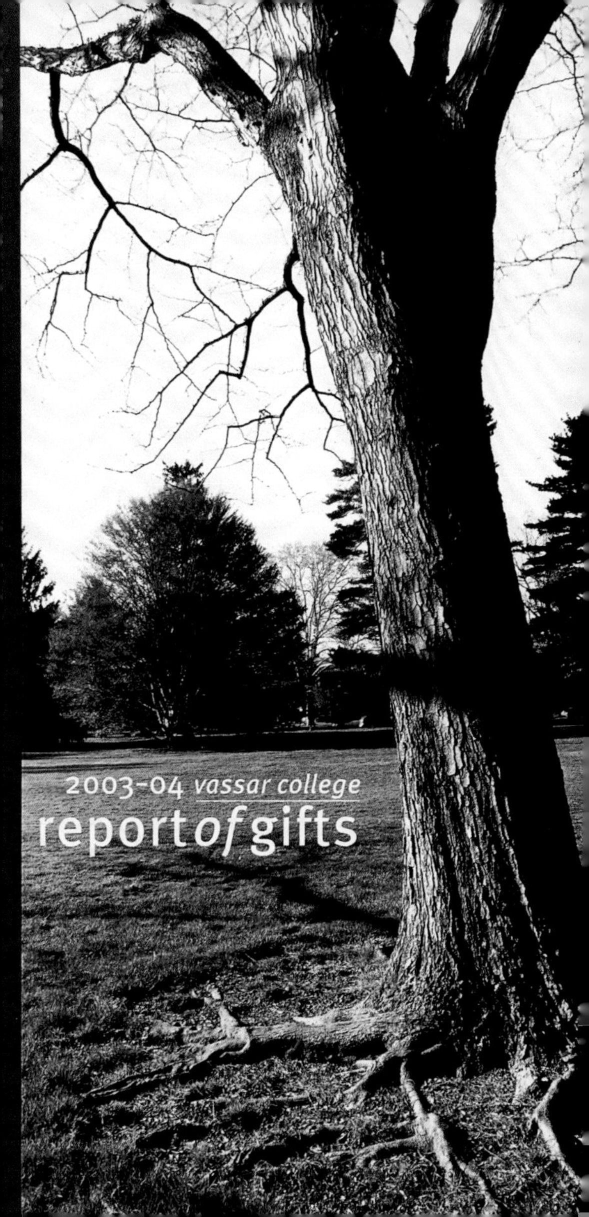
2003-04 vassar college
report of gifts

Designer: Stacie Ross
Photographer: Lois Conner
Writer: Lance Ringel

Printer: Meridian Printing
Paper: Schueflin Parilux silk 92.5# cover, scheuflin Parilux Silk 100# text, Finch Opaque Vellum Vanilla 60# text

Page count: 108 +cover
Print Run: 37,000
Size: 6.25" x 13"

Number of Images: 25
Client: Vassar College

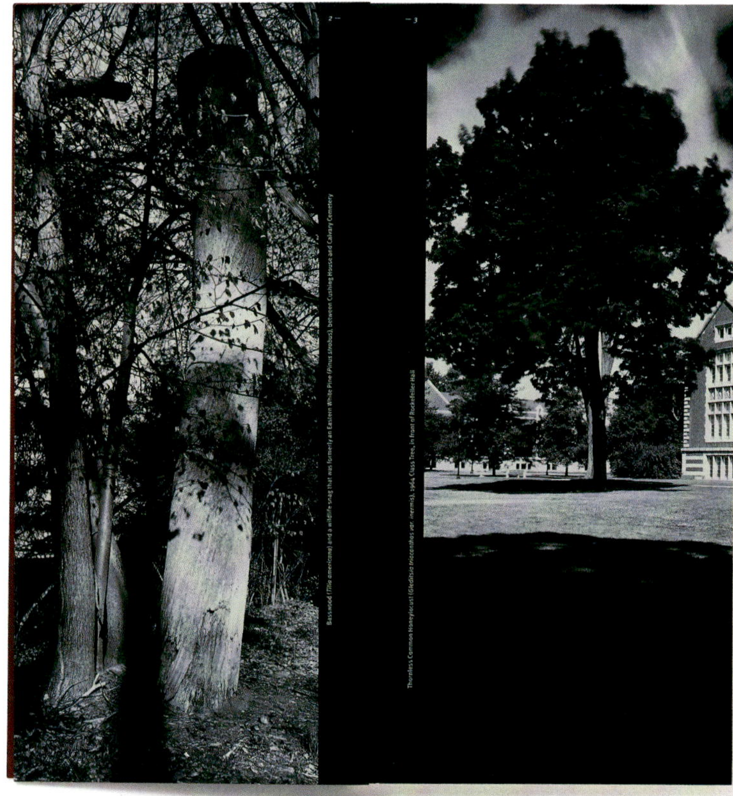

Q&A with Nesnadny+Schwartz

What was the client's directive?

Vassar College has a very strong alumnae constituency and requires an equally strong forum for communicating the support they receive. The Report of Gifts in the annual publication is there to thank all of the supporters of the college for their financial contributions.

How did you define the problem?

We felt the physical environment of Vassar's campus was the common link that all alumnae/alumnai share. Reconnecting them with the campus in a way that appealed to the 25 and 80 year old was our challenge.

What was the approach?

Vassar is a national arboretum with more than 200 species of trees and has a long-standing tradition of each graduating class planting a class tree. The planting and growing of trees also serves as a perfect metaphor for how financial gifts help the college grow and ultimately help young minds grow. These trees, therefore, were the perfect imagery for the Report of Gifts.

Which disciplines or people helped you with the project?

Nesnadny + Schwartz has a long-standing devotion to incorporating fine arts with corporate and institutional communications. With the incredible imagery of a beautiful campus and the vast species of trees that reside there, a black and white fine arts photographer seemed the perfect choice. Lois Conner is an award-winning photographer who often works in a unique 7x17 format, which served as an expressive way to photograph portraits of trees in their environment.

Were you happy with the result?

What could have been better?

We felt the result served all of the purposes of the book perfectly. The photography and reproductions were truly beautiful, and the book became a keepsake for the people it strove to thank.

What was the client's response?

Vassar was very thrilled with the result and received many requests for extra copies of the book.

How involved was the CEO in your meetings and presentations?

The president of the college was very supportive of the project. However, her function was to give final approval rather than to participate in conceptual development.

Do you feel that designers are becoming more involved in copywriting?

Designers have to be involved in the content development for communications to truly be successful. It is only when the graphic design, imagery and words work together perfectly that a piece has a strong holistic message.

How do you define success in Annual Report design?

When a piece is effective in reaching the target audience and communicating something to them that they did not expect.

How important are awards to your client?

Awards serve as confirmation that a piece is an interesting and engaging communication tool but should never be the goal.

When the design, imagery, and words work together harmoniously, the piece then has a strong holistic message.

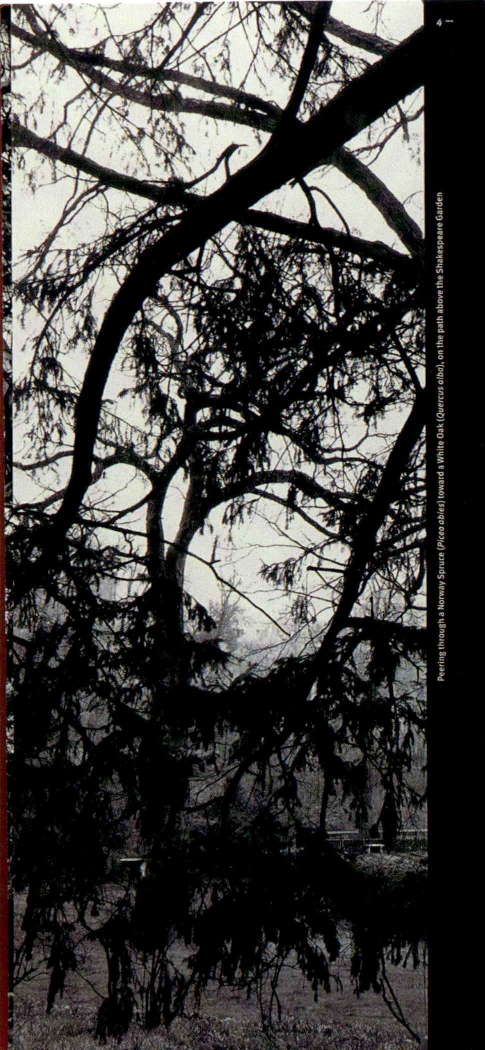

Peering through a Norway Spruce (*Picea abies*) toward a White Oak (*Quercus alba*), on the path above the Shakespeare Garden

contents

the impact of your gifts

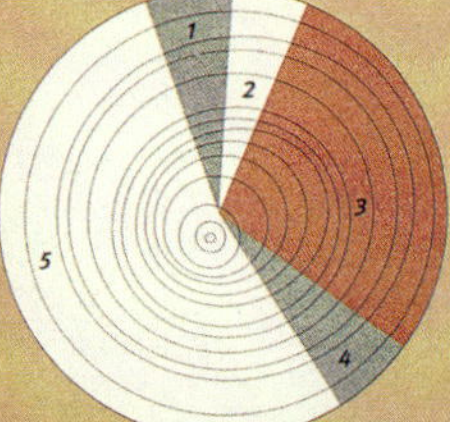

1. Annual Fund 7%
2. Restricted Gifts & Grants 5%
3. Endowment Income 28%
4. Business Services 6%
5. Tuition, Room & Board 54% (Net of Financial Aid)

Why Your Gift is So Important During fiscal year 2003–2004, gifts for current use, including gifts to Vassar through the Annual Fund as well as restricted gifts, accounted for one in every eight dollars available for the College to meet its immediate needs. The importance of giving was further underscored by the fact that income from the College's endowment, which is supported over time by gifts, comprised more than a quarter of the revenue available for Vassar's current use. In any given year tuition, room and board account for only about half of all revenue for Vassar's operating budget.

Three Pillars of Support The present and future of Vassar depend on strong support in each of three categories of giving. Gifts for current use are the College's lifeblood, providing a fundamental source of revenue that ensures the continuation of the Vassar tradition of excellence each and every day. Gifts for endowment help to guarantee Vassar's future while also helping to sustain current operations. Gifts for capital building projects are essential to the College's ongoing plan to retain its architectural heritage while meeting the needs of education in the 21st century. During fiscal year 2003–2004, donors continued to give generously to Vassar in all three of these categories. More than a third of all gifts were directed by donors for current use to help the College meet its immediate needs, either through gifts to the Annual Fund or through restricted academic student program support. Another 30 percent of gifts were directed to capital building projects (which are separate from the current operating budget), and yet another 30 percent were directed to Vassar's endowment. A significant share of the figure for endowment derives from planned gifts, including documented bequest intentions — true votes of confidence in the College's future.

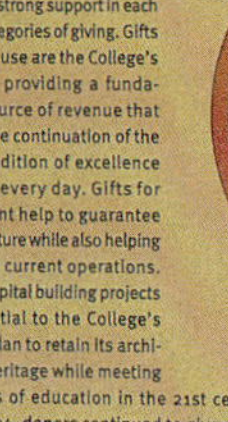

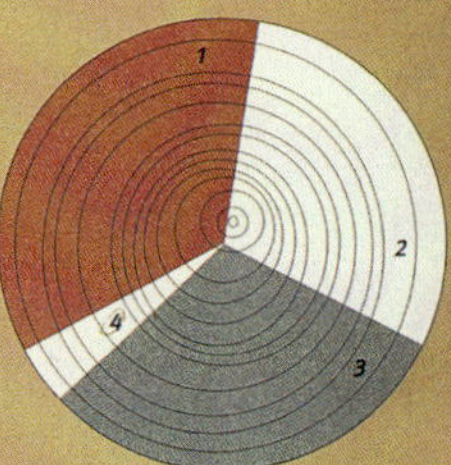

1. Gifts for Current Use 36% (Including Annual Fund & Restricted Gifts)
2. Endowment 30% (Including Planned Gifts)
3. Capital Building Projects 30%
4. Other 4% (Including Gifts in Kind)

1. Alumnae/i 64%
2. Parents 2%
3. Friends 3%
4. Other Organizations 1%
5. Government 2%
6. Corporations 2%
7. Foundations 25%

Who Gives to Vassar From the College's earliest days, gifts from Vassar's own graduates have served as a bulwark of support for its educational mission. During fiscal year 2003–2004, in keeping with recent years, alumnae/i accounted directly for nearly two-thirds of all gifts received by the College. In addition, many of the gifts Vassar received from foundations came from donor-advised funds or family foundations that made a gift to the College at the suggestion of an alumna/us.

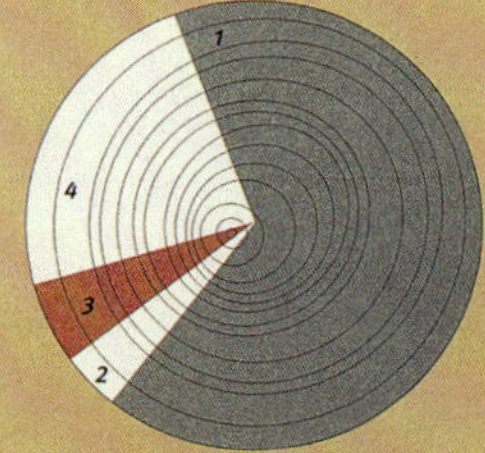

1. Compensation 66%
2. Plant Renewal 4%
3. Other 6%
4. Operating Expenses 24%

Where Your Dollars to Vassar Go Vassar's operating expenses are very much concentrated on *people*, with compensation (including wages and benefits) accounting for nearly two-thirds of all expenditures for current use during fiscal year 2003–2004. A relatively small but crucial 4 percent is allocated toward the constant renewal of the College's technological, architectural and landscape resources, including its venerable academic and residential buildings and the uncommonly beautiful landscape that make the Vassar campus such a uniquely hospitable setting for a learning community.

Dollars in millions
800
700
600
500
400
300
200
100
0
Nominal market value (with gifts)
Nominal market value (less gifts & return)
84 85 86 87 88 89 90 91 92 93 94 95 96 97 98 99 00 01 02 03 04

How Your Gift Can Help the Endowment Grow Over the past two decades, gifts to Vassar's endowment, combined with careful management, have increased the endowment's value by 42 percent. All gifts to the College for endowment have a trifold positive effect: they increase the principle of the endowment, in turn allowing the endowment to increase its return on investment — thereby increasing the amount available for current operating expenses. This helps Vassar's endowment to grow, even as the endowment plays a central role in funding current operating expenses. Thus, a gift to Vassar's endowment helps the College today *and* in the future.

landmark reunion gifts

Class	Landmark Reunion	Annual Fund	Designated Gifts	Total	Participation
1954	Fiftieth	$1,018,183	$1,394,064	$2,412,247	95%
1964	Fortieth	$671,183	$467,073	$1,138,256	88%
1979	Twenty-fifth	$1,005,622	$456,183	$1,461,805	51%
1994	Tenth	$53,233	$14,305	$67,538	33%

top class participation does not include landmark reunion classes

Class	Participation	Class	Participation
1944	82%	1953	69%
1951	78%	1940	68%
1932	72%	1942	68%
1945·4	71%	1939	67%
1949	69%	1947	66%

gifts by class

Class	2003/04 Class Fund or Reunion Gift Chair(s)	Participation	Class Total $ Annual Fund	Class Total $ Designated Gift	2003/04 Total Class Gift
1927		58%	$3,210	$4,185	$7,395
1928		47%	$1,425	$1,100	$2,525
1929 R		55%	$3,975	$862	$4,837
1930		54%	$8,750	$158,252	$167,002
1931		39%	$10,522	$5,120	$15,642
1932	Mary Riepma Ross	72%	$43,388	$162,719	$206,107
1933		39%	$18,284	$2,340	$20,624
1934 R	Brunhilde Reich Knapp	50%	$34,673	$38,050	$72,723
1935		58%	$10,555	$292,041	$302,596
1936	Mary Swissler Oldberg	64%	$40,991	$359,598	$400,589
1937	Ruth Albro Holmes	57%	$20,735	$511,793	$532,528
1938		53%	$34,154	$49,576	$83,730
1939 R	Barbara Drisler Reimers	67%	$52,602	$2,025	$54,627
1940	Susanne Froelicher Holcombe Comfort Cary Richardson	68%	$50,101	$128,710	$178,811
1941	Eleanor Morss English	62%	$47,503	$4,335	$51,838
1942	Frances Prindle Taft	68%	$45,105	$7,270	$52,375
1943	Allison Evans Johnson	63%	$65,365	$253,513	$318,879
1944 R	Priscilla Wright Allen Edith Reynolds White	82%	$103,041	$1,479,370	$1,582,412
1945-4	Ruth Schuster Manos	71%	$181,690	$925,793	$1,107,483
1945	Mary Wetzel Klingensmith	63%	$63,234	$30,590	$93,824
1946	Sylvia Babcock Weaver	61%	$315,683	$2,232,125	$2,547,808
1947	Johanna Seaver Hood	66%	$91,454	$1,817,811	$1,909,264
1948 R	E. Jane Arnold Spanel	53%	$43,252	$41,327	$84,579
1949 R	Barbara Batt Brick	69%	$58,086	$67,698	$125,784
1950	Elisabeth Petschek de Picciotto	56%	$112,925	$38,499	$151,424
1951	Joan Clark Gunn Dorothy Kittell Hesselman	78%	$308,638	$1,612,919	$1,921,557
1952	Margaret Quackenbush Hager Hart	62%	$118,646	$152,827	$271,473
1953	Denise Taft Davidoff	69%	$195,552	$448,198	$643,750
1954 R ✓	Edith McBride Bass Elinor Kenney Farquhar	95%	$1,018,183	$1,394,064	$2,412,247
1955	Frances White Cohen-Knoerdel	57%	$135,531	$543,846	$679,377
1956	Emily Tribble Hart Hope Christopoulos Mihlap	46%	$338,172	$631,741	$969,913
1957	Louise McCarthy Conley Madeleine Perrault Muñoz	57%	$172,523	$4,021,529	$4,194,053
1958	Babs Bullard McKelway Eleanor Pavlo Vale	56%	$120,642	$646,425	$767,067
1959 R	Roberta Dance Steiner	62%	$85,501	$892,574	$978,075
1960		45%	$72,433	$225,941	$298,374
1961	Betsy Shack Barbanell	56%	$102,567	$42,588	$145,154

gifts by class continued

Class	2003/04 Class Fund or Reunion Gift Chair(s)	Participation	Class Total $ Annual Fund	Class Total $ Designated Gift	2003/04 Total Class Gift
1962	Nancy Ann Dunston Dorris	51%	$122,682	$892,466	$1,015,147
1963	Nancy Kerber MacRae	44%	$139,669	$154,195	$293,865
1964 R ✓	Teddi Zopko Wei	88%	$671,183	$467,073	$1,138,256
1965	Caroline Morris Margaret Milner Richardson	33%	$117,110	$21,777	$138,887
1966	Karen McAndrew Allen	39%	$214,032	$364,920	$578,952
1967		44%	$41,228	$10,150	$51,378
1968	Carla L. Engelman	42%	$72,621	$22,885	$95,506
1969 R	Sandra L. Bourgeois	[illegible]	[illegible]	[illegible]	[illegible]
1970	Karen Mary Spencer	43%	$77,400	$54,111	$131,511
1971	Mary Barber Mary Price Joyce Rubin Schwartz	50%	$115,740	$54,933	$170,673
1972	Sandra Kaufmann Battaglia	45%	$124,387	$11,750	$136,137
1973		38%	$142,221	$501,015	$643,236
1974 R	Janet Hafner Harris	42%	$345,968	$728,437	$1,074,405
1975		36%	$92,181	$152,429	$244,611
1976	Diana E. Walsh	36%	$110,926	$220,720	$331,646
1977	Yasmin Attar	30%	$253,713	$524,450	$778,163
1978	Roberta Schuman Kline Scott B. Schaffer	28%	$175,515	$55,549	$231,064
1979 R ✓	Lurita Alexis Doan	51%	$1,005,622	$456,183	$1,461,805
1980	Karen L. Cox	33%	$92,426	$31,838	$124,264
1981	Christopher B. Steward	33%	$98,042	$28,776	$126,818
1982	Frank H. Dearden III C. Forbes Sargent III	29%	$59,174	$8,450	$67,624
1983	Justina Fugh Frenzel	19%	$36,044	$10,980	$47,024
1984 R	Diana B. Altegoer	38%	$150,821	$157,055	$307,876
1985	Heather Hyde	29%	$70,049	$12,325	$82,374
1986	Anne Latimer Barker Brian J. Litten	28%	$41,301	$4,830	$46,131
1987	Ciaran H. Bossom	25%	$27,355	$4,833	$32,188
1988	Carla Van de Walle	21%	$33,489	$1,735	$35,224
1989 R	Lucy Minturn	27%	$30,034	$1,590	$31,624
1990		18%	$27,640	$3,650	$31,290
1991	Christopher Cecil Paul J. Devine	19%	$19,784	$3,500	$23,284
1992	Erin Howarth Bardsley	19%	$14,276	$1,030	$15,306
1993	Kristen Gallagher	16%	$9,083	$200	$9,283
1994 R ✓	Ernest Ceberio	33%	$53,233	$14,305	$67,538
1995	JT Griffith	17%	$2,746	$40,402	$43,148
1996	Justin Manning	20%	$10,402	$615	$11,017
1997	Rachel Weimerskirch Stack	18%	$6,467	$165	$6,632
1998	Jane D. Rudolph	23%	$5,703	$1,205	$6,908
1999 R	Carolyn K. Brooks Annie M. Thottam	36%	$17,298	$565	$17,863
2000	Alison Albeck Lindland	21%	$6,367	$7,030	$13,397
2001	Marissa Ceglian Meghann Hardesty	20%	$3,988	$90	$4,078
2002	Juan S. Acosta Jennifer E. Lee	23%	$4,532	$726	$5,258
2003	Katie Hayman Anna Murphy	21%	$4,210	$291	$4,501
Senior Class Gift					
2004	Stefanie Z. Ackerman Melissa S. Riebe	60%	$12,853	$16,339	$29,192
Alumnae/i Subtotals			$7,161,956	$24,335,510	$31,497,466
Parents and Friends					
	Ann and Doug Logan		$563,640		
Dollar Totals					
Represents cash and pledges			$7,738,449	$24,335,510	$32,073,959

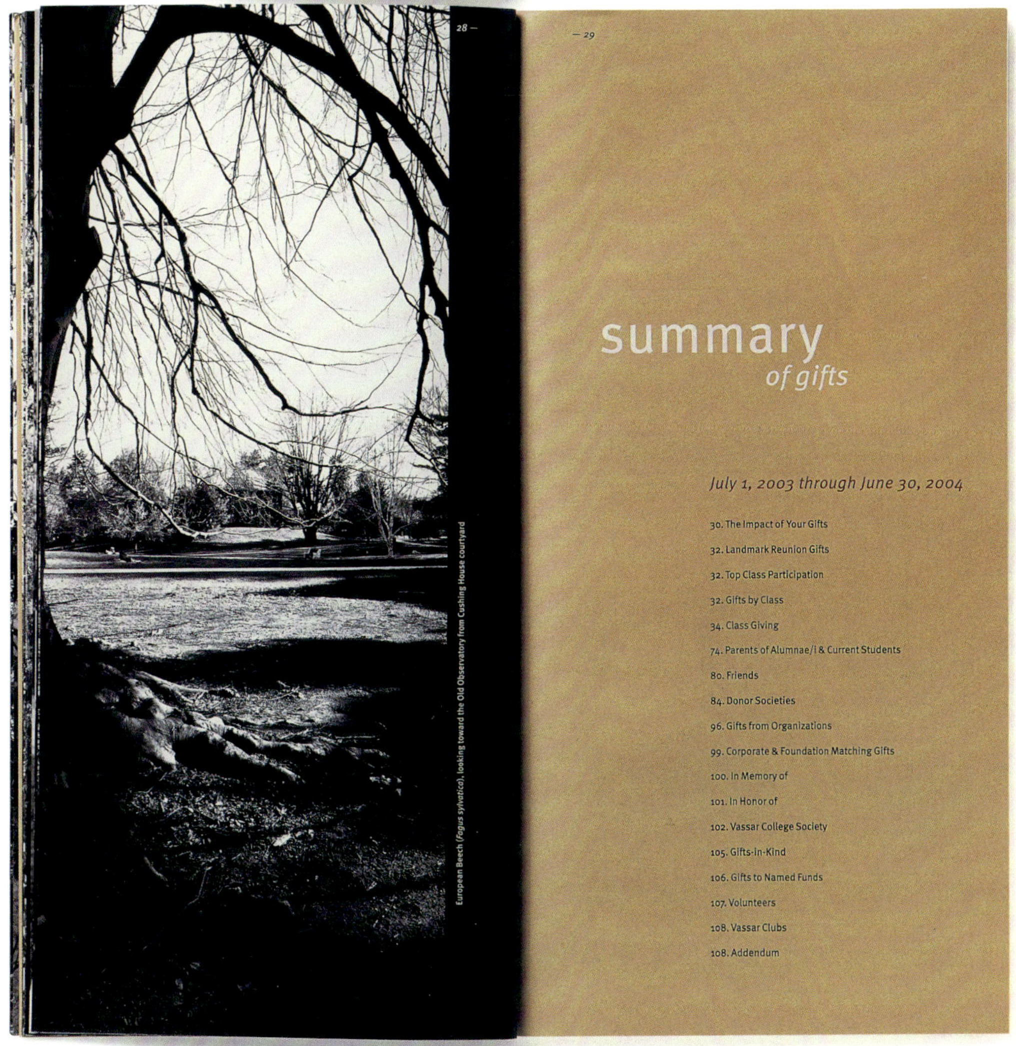

European Beech (*Fagus sylvatica*), looking toward the Old Observatory from Cushing House courtyard

summary *of gifts*

July 1, 2003 through June 30, 2004

ANNUAL REPORT 2003–04

Anatomy

of Northwestern University's
Feinberg School of Medicine

Art Director: Brock Haldeman
Designers: Jill Misawa, Don Emery, Liz Haldeman
Photographer: Jim Ziv

Printer: Quantum Color Graphics
Paper: cover, Cougar Opaque, Smooth White cover, 100#; body, Cougar Opaque, Smooth White text, 100# Transparent: Transvy Gloss Rigid Vinyl, 0.005 mil

Page count: 66 +4 (cover)
Print Run: 8,500
Size: 7" x 10"
Number of Images: 50

Client: Feinberg School of Medicine at Northwestern University

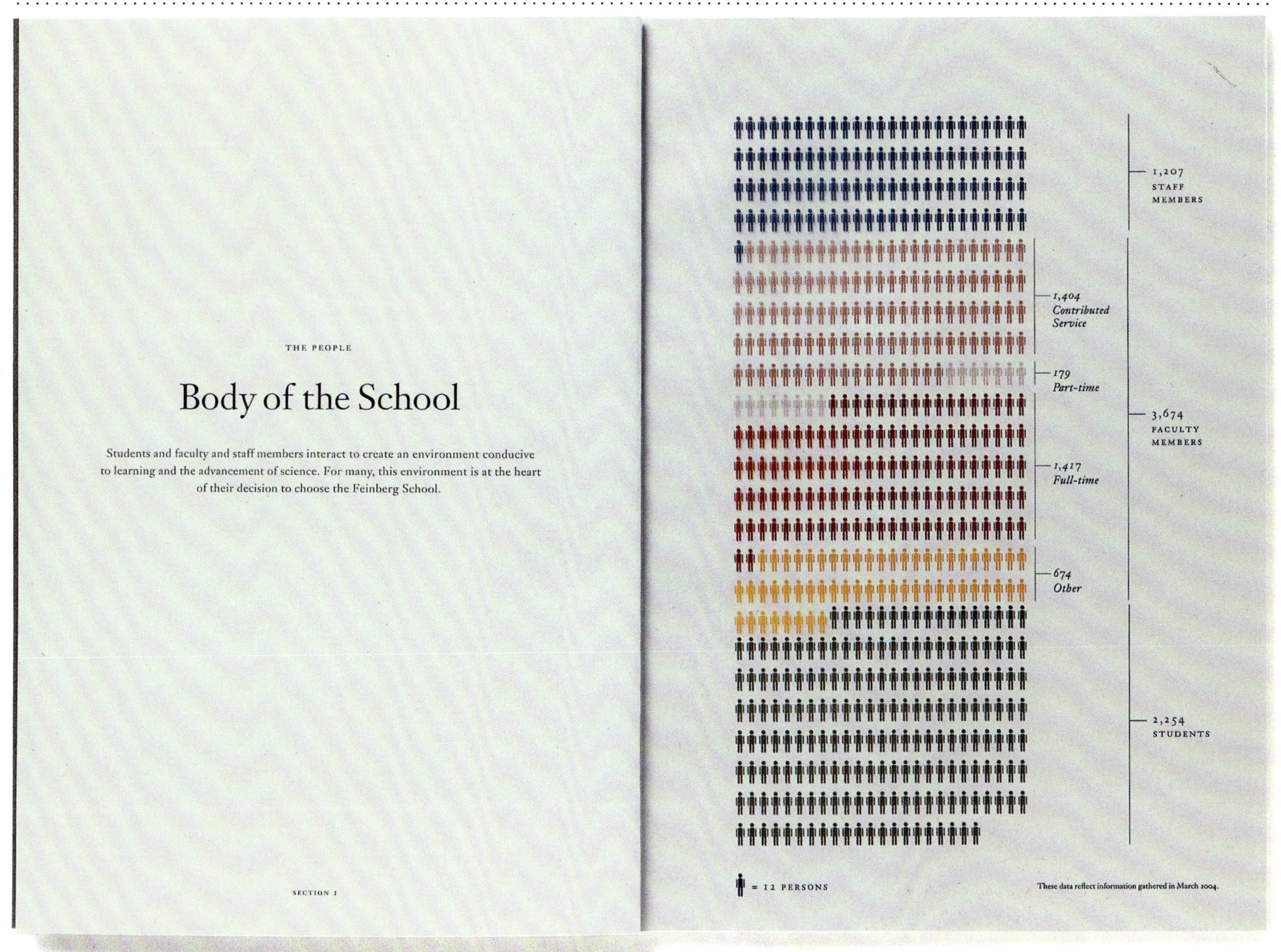

Q&A with Pivot Design

What was the client's directive?

The client's directive was for us to create an Annual Report that accurately reflected this medical school while serving to spur and encourage continued interest, investment and growth.

What was the approach?

The concept "Anatomy" uses the medical metaphor to reflect the many parts of the institution. Visually presented using an academic, anatomical book approach—complete with layered transparent diagrams—this report creatively informs audiences of the year's highlights in an apt way that directly reflects the institution.

Which disciplines or people helped you with the project?

Copywriters, photographer and printer. The printer's knowledge on plastic printing was integral at early stages so we could plan appropriately for image/color adjustments, opacity vs. transparency concerns and binding.

Were you happy with the result? What could have been better?

We were pleased with the finished product and very much appreciate having a client that is willing to support creative solutions that break

A successful solution is one that meets the project's stated objectives and accurately reflects the organization's brand.

with tradition. There are probably minor things we might change, but we believe that's good. As soon as you think a piece can't be improved, we believe you are failing to look at your own work critically.

What was the client's response?

The client measures success, in part, by the response an Annual Report generates from varied recipients. It garnered more positive feedback than any to date, and, needless to say, the client was thrilled.

How involved was the CEO in your meetings and presentations?

The COO delegated responsibility to departments responsible for producing the Annual Report. The COO was actively involved in the concept presentation and review process.

Do you feel that designers are becoming more involved in copywriting?

Yes, we believe that there is increasing cross-over in many of the creative disciplines. As visual communicators, copywriting has always been important, but as the marketplace has become more competitive the tight integration of copy and concept has become critical.

How do you define success in Annual Report design?

We define success in Annual Report design the same way we define success in the design of anything: a successful solution is one that meets the project's stated objectives and accurately reflects the organization's brand.

How important are awards to your client?

While awards are not a motive by any means, they help to validate (or counter) feedback received from the marketplace.

ANNUAL REPORT 2003–04

Anatomy

Like the human body, the Feinberg School of Medicine is composed of finely tuned parts that interconnect to maintain strength, nurture growth, and enable movement.

Education is our primary mission and the lifeblood of our institution—in constant circulation and regeneration as each student and faculty member shares his or her unique knowledge and gains knowledge through new experiences. Research is the muscle that moves us forward, growing larger and stronger with each reach into unknown territory. Clinical service is at the backbone of what we do—medical education and research exist to improve the health and well-being of patients.

Community service is the pathway through which our students and faculty members lend a hand to the underserved. By volunteering for community service programs across the country and around the globe, they breathe life into entire populations.

Here we dissect the anatomy of the Feinberg School of Medicine to reveal how all its parts contribute to the whole.

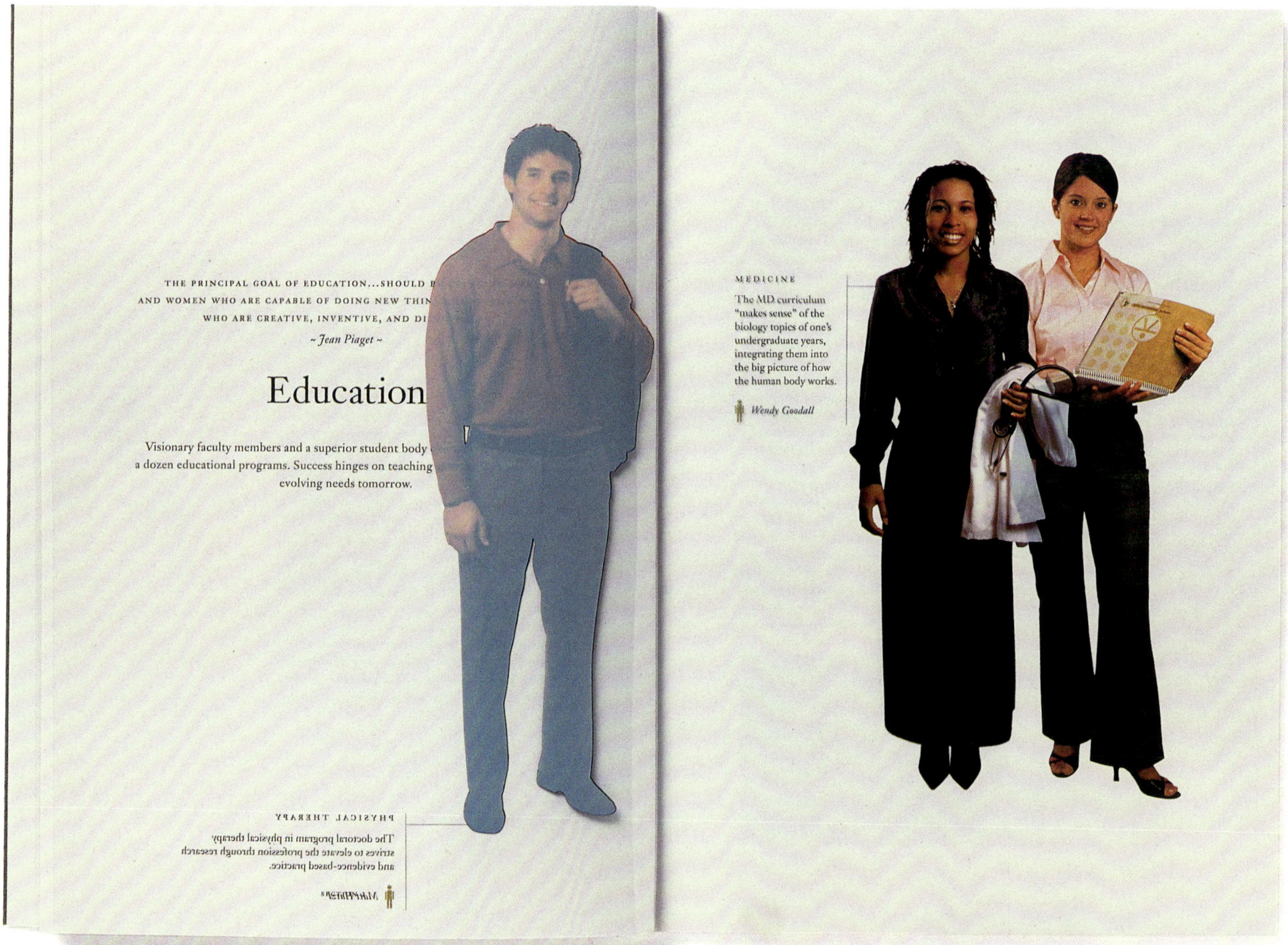

THE PRINCIPAL GOAL OF EDUCATION...SHOULD B
AND WOMEN WHO ARE CAPABLE OF DOING NEW THIN
WHO ARE CREATIVE, INVENTIVE, AND DI

~ *Jean Piaget* ~

Education

Visionary faculty members and a superior student body
a dozen educational programs. Success hinges on teaching
evolving needs tomorrow.

PHYSICAL THERAPY

The doctoral program in physical therapy strives to elevate the profession through research and evidence-based practice.

MEDICINE

The MD curriculum "makes sense" of the biology topics of one's undergraduate years, integrating them into the big picture of how the human body works.

Wendy Goodall

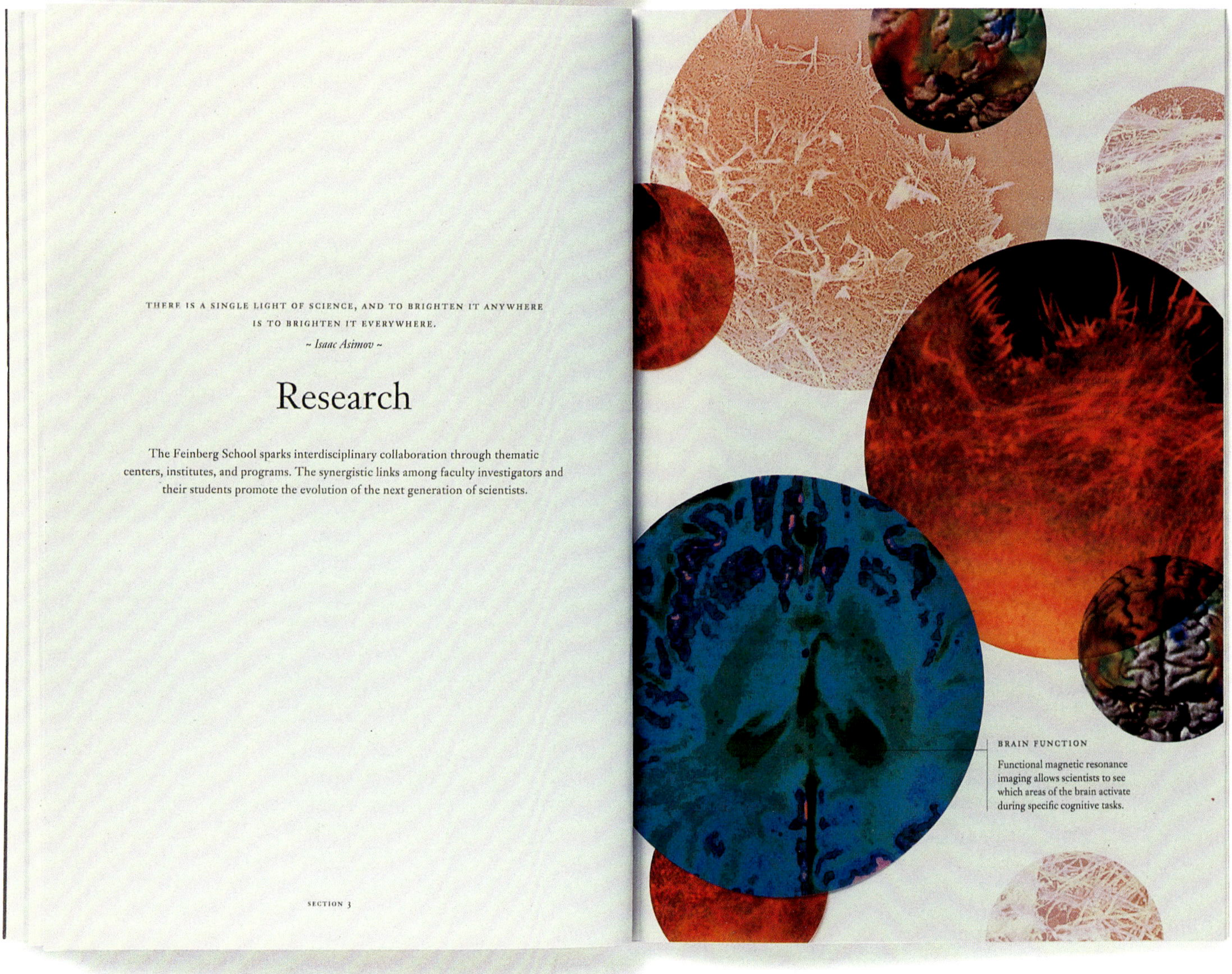

THERE IS A SINGLE LIGHT OF SCIENCE, AND TO BRIGHTEN IT ANYWHERE IS TO BRIGHTEN IT EVERYWHERE.

~ *Isaac Asimov* ~

Research

The Feinberg School sparks interdisciplinary collaboration through thematic centers, institutes, and programs. The synergistic links among faculty investigators and their students promote the evolution of the next generation of scientists.

SECTION 3

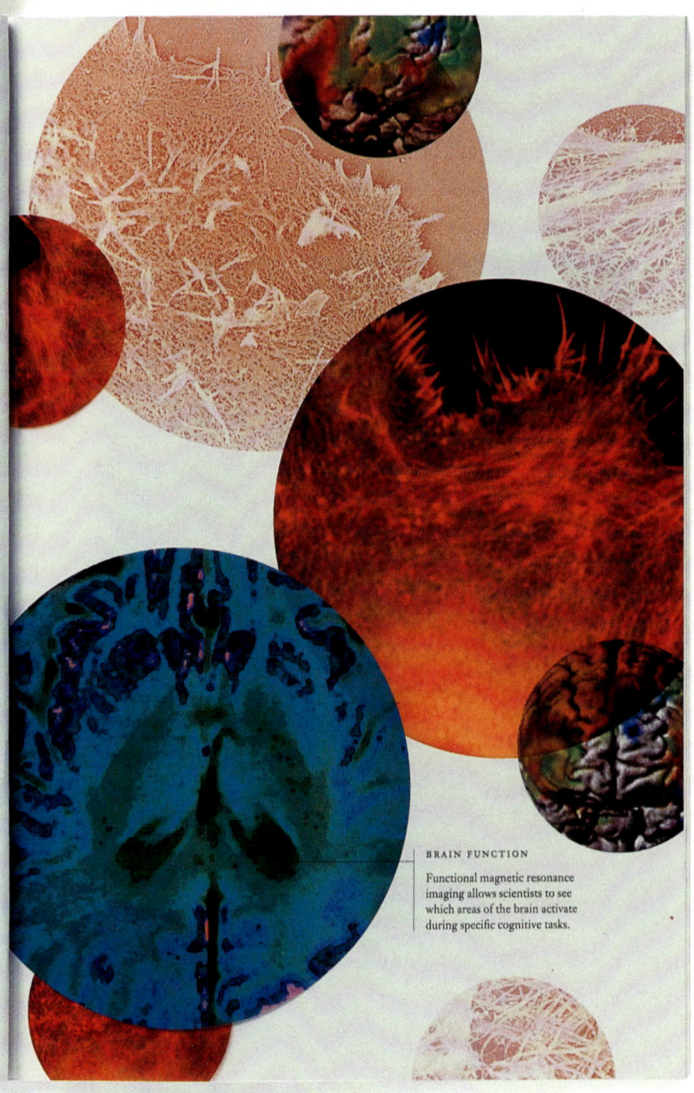

BRAIN FUNCTION

Functional magnetic resonance imaging allows scientists to see which areas of the brain activate during specific cognitive tasks.

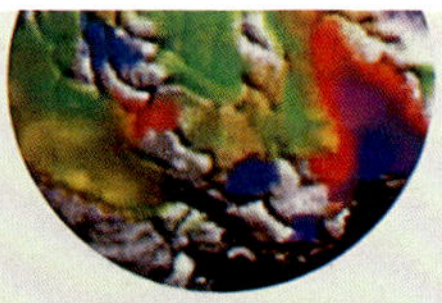

THERE IS A SINGLE LIGHT OF SCIENCE, AND TO BRIGHTEN IT ANYWHERE IS TO BRIGHTEN IT EVERYWHERE.

~ Isaac Asimov ~

Research

The Feinberg School sparks interdisciplinary collaboration through thematic centers, institutes, and programs. The synergistic links among faculty investigators and their students promote the evolution of the next gene…

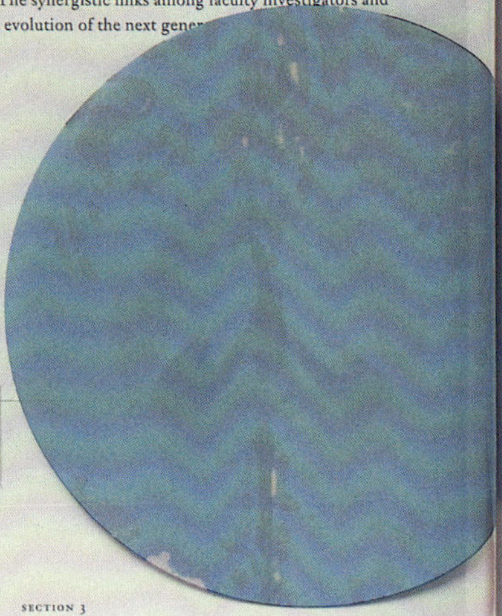

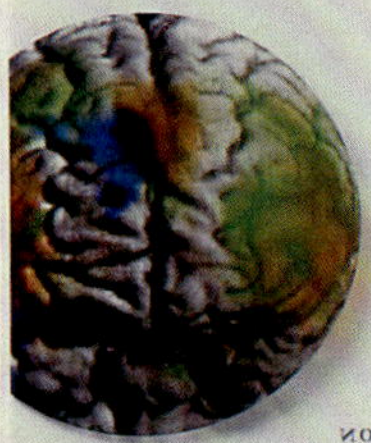

BRAIN FUNCTION

Functional magnetic resonance imaging allows scientists to see which areas of the brain activate during specific cognitive tasks.

SECTION 3

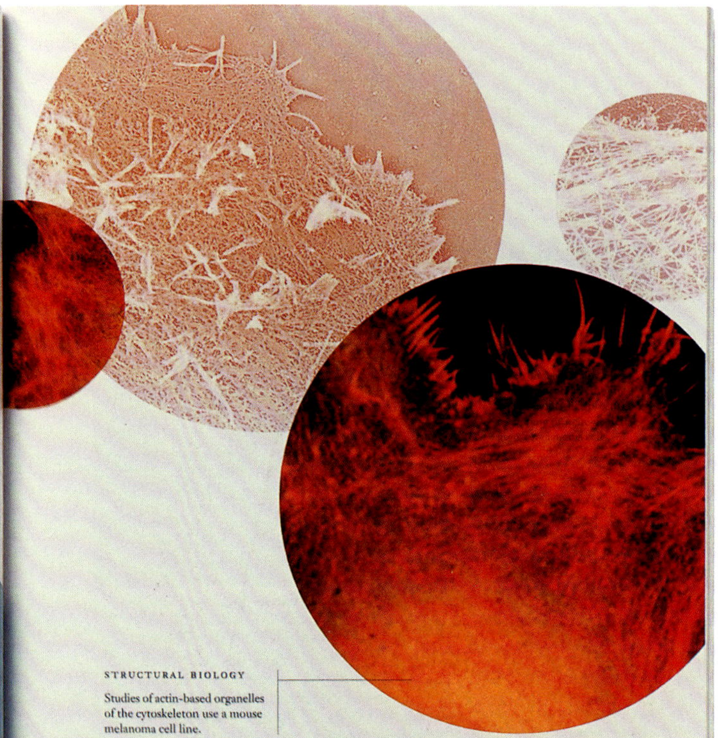

STRUCTURAL BIOLOGY

Studies of actin-based organelles of the cytoskeleton use a mouse melanoma cell line.

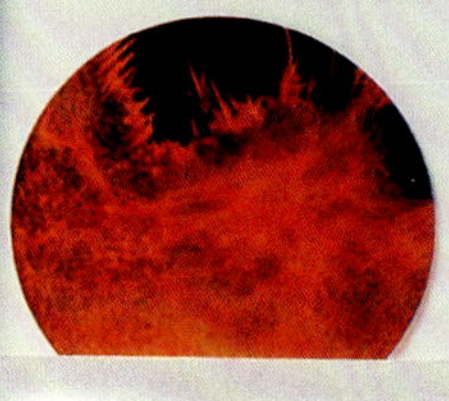

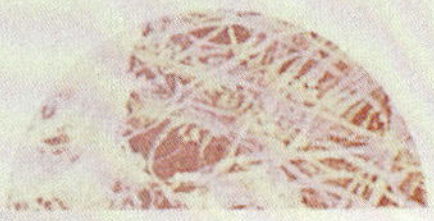

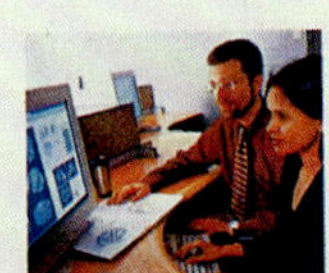

FIG. 1 *Dr. Darren Gitelman and Siri Sonty use functional magnetic resonance imaging to reveal brain activation.*

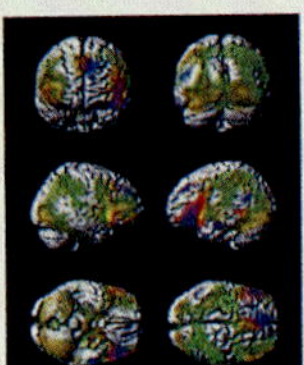

FIG. 2 *Deciding whether two letter strings are identical activates the green areas, and deciding whether two words are synonymous activates the yellow areas.*

MEDICAL SCIENTIST TRAINING PROGRAM › Siri Sonty entered the Feinberg School through the Honors Program in Medical Education. Biomedical research piqued her interest. "I was interested in cognition and how it breaks down in dementia," she says. › She sought out M.-Marsel Mesulam, MD, Evelyn and Ruth Dunbar Professor of Psychiatry and Behavioral Sciences and director of the Cognitive Neurology and Alzheimer's Disease Center, and Darren R. Gitelman, MD, associate professor of neurology, for a Feinberg School-sponsored summer fellowship. "They were using functional magnetic resonance imaging [fMRI] of the brain to study how aging preferentially affects various cognitive domains, such as spatial attention, working memory, and language." › Sonty collected data on patients with primary progressive aphasia (PPA), which affects language function but leaves other cognitive domains relatively unscathed. Subsequently Sonty won a year-long Howard Hughes Medical Institute fellowship. "I continued learning the fMRI technique, data analysis, and experimental design as well as observing the patients' neuropsychological examinations." › She decided to pursue a PhD degree and was accepted to the school's Medical Scientist Training Program, enabling her to earn both MD and PhD degrees in seven to eight years. Her first paper on PPA and the language network was published in January 2003, and those findings will contribute to her PhD thesis project. "Having both degrees will help me contribute to the understanding of these diseases and improve their treatments," she says.

INTEGRATED GRADUATE PROGRAM IN THE LIFE SCIENCES › "The enthusiasm of the researchers I met drew me to Northwestern," says third-year Integrated Graduate Program in the Life Sciences student Derek Applewhite. As a first-year student, he rotated through three laboratories. › He chose the lab led by Gary Borisy, PhD, Leslie B. Arey Professor of Cell, Molecular, and Anatomical Sciences, where he studies actin-based organelles assembled on the cell's cytoskeleton

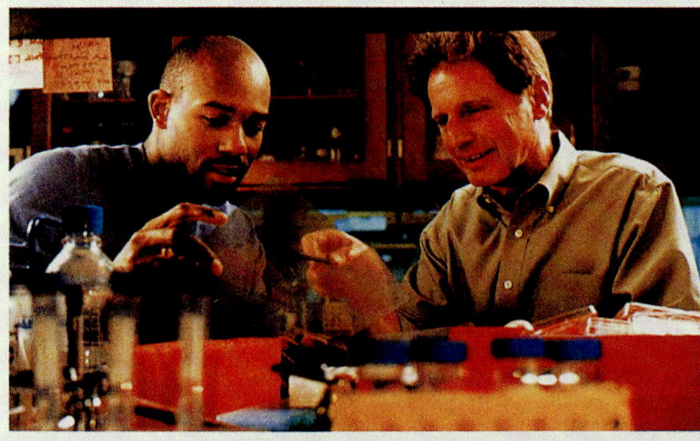

FIG. 3 *Derek Applewhite (left) and Dr. Gary Borisy examine the assembly of actin-based organelles vital to cell motility.*

that facilitate movement. Cell motility drives vital biological processes, including embryonic development. "In cancer," adds Applewhite, "cells use forms of lamellipodia and filopodia to facilitate metastasis." › He was co-author of a published paper that showed the key role of "capping protein" in the assembly or nonassembly of lamellipodia and filopodia. "The technology we're using is just amazing," he says, noting a small-interfering RNA vector developed in the lab that selectively blocks the capping protein and a new total internal reflection microscope (TIRF) system. › "The TIRF laser's evanescent wave deteriorates quickly in space," explains Applewhite. "Consquently, the excitation is limited to 200 nanometers, so we see clearly the plane of the cytoskeleton where these actin structures form. › Applewhite considers Dr. Borisy a "forward thinker" who likes to be on the cutting edge of technology. "His students and postdocs have a wide range of expertise and perspectives," he says.

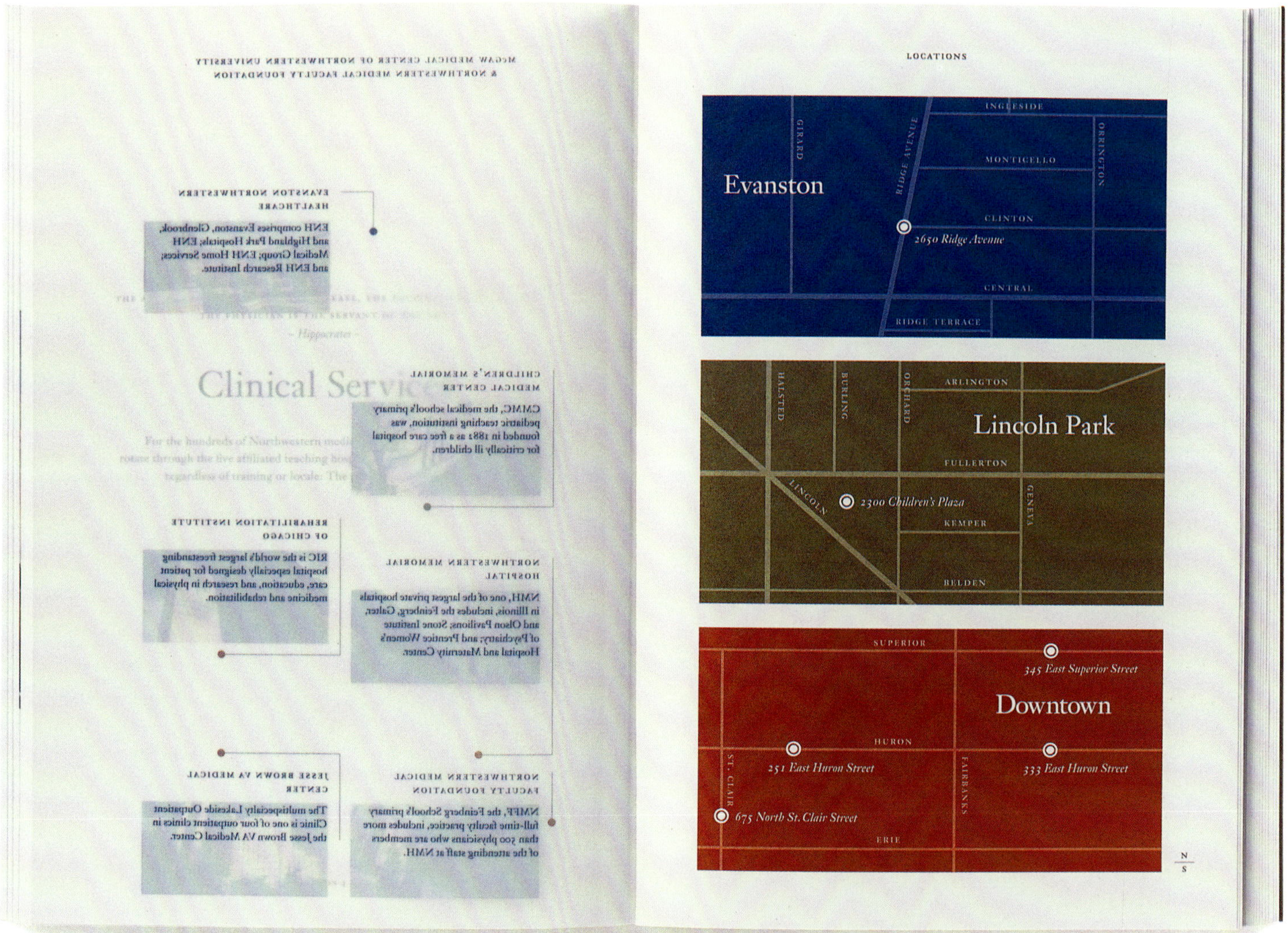

Clinical Serv…

~ Hippocrates ~

LOCATIONS

Evanston

INGLESIDE
MONTICELLO
CLINTON
CENTRAL
RIDGE TERRACE
GIRARD
RIDGE AVENUE
ORRINGTON
2650 Ridge Avenue

Lincoln Park

ARLINGTON
FULLERTON
KEMPER
BELDEN
HALSTED
BURLING
ORCHARD
LINCOLN
GENEVA
2300 Children's Plaza

Downtown

SUPERIOR
HURON
ERIE
ST. CLAIR
FAIRBANKS
345 East Superior Street
251 East Huron Street
333 East Huron Street
675 North St. Clair Street

N
S

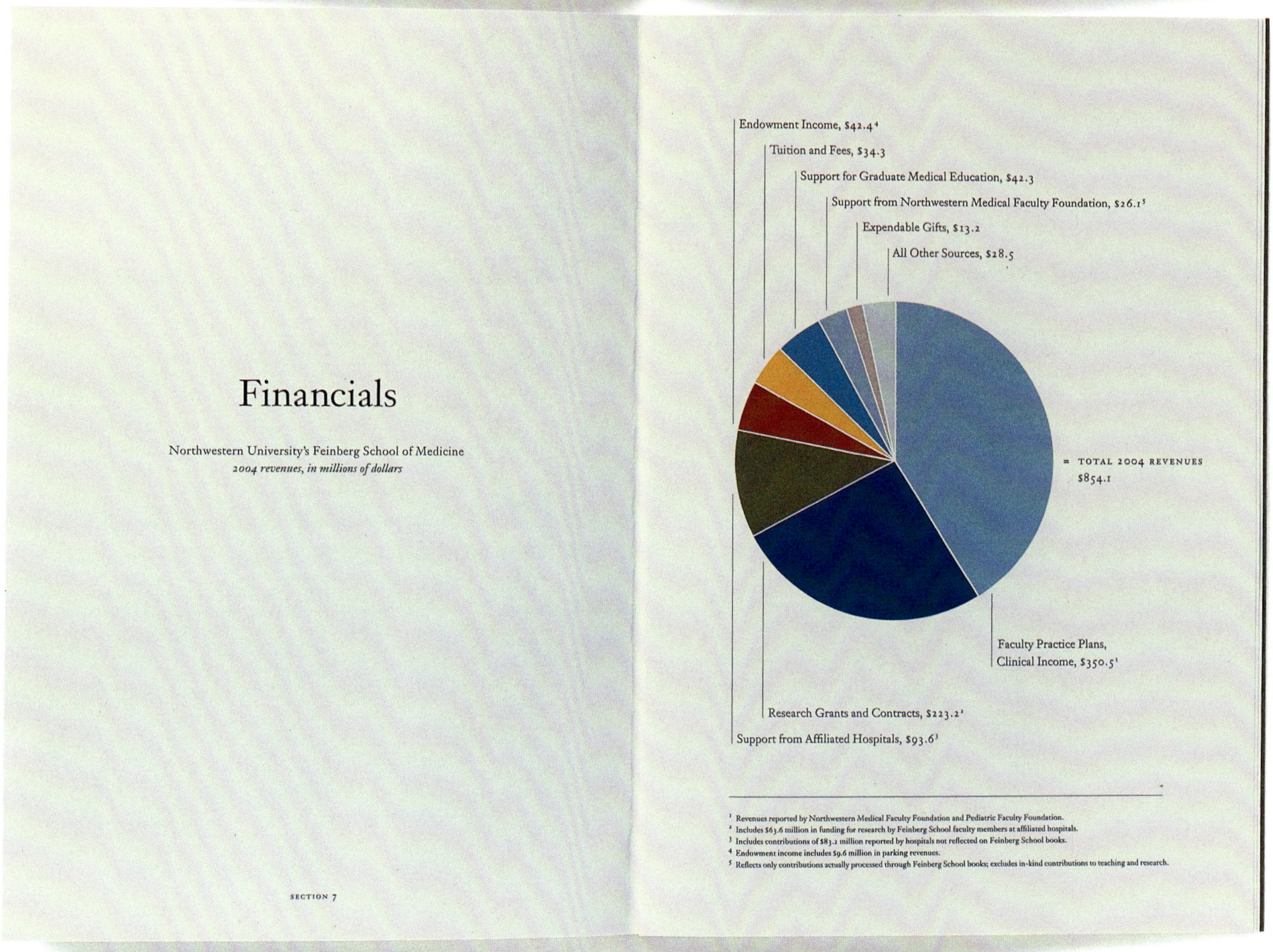

Financials

Northwestern University's Feinberg School of Medicine
2004 revenues, in millions of dollars

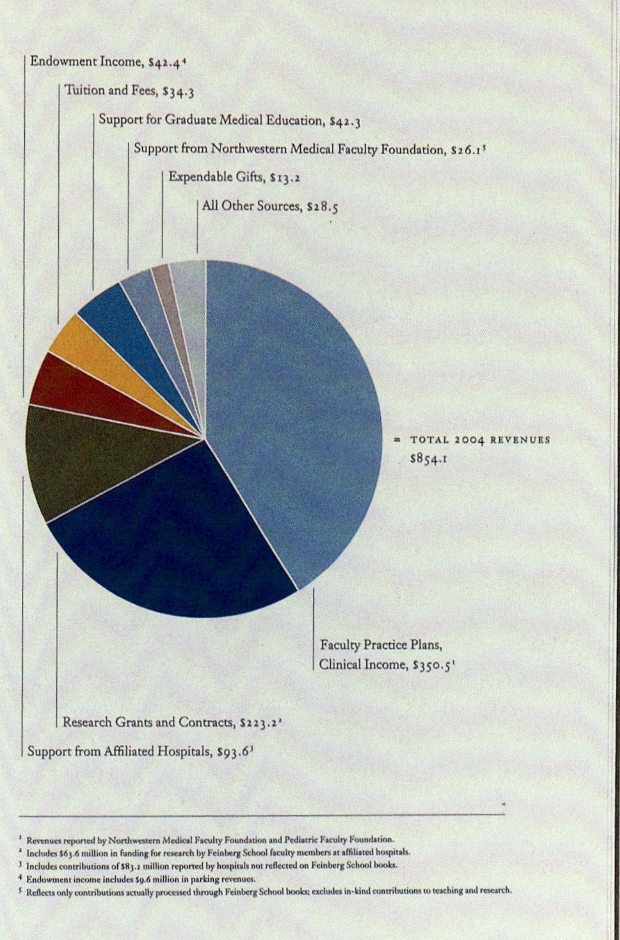

[1] Revenues reported by Northwestern Medical Faculty Foundation and Pediatric Faculty Foundation.
[2] Includes $63.6 million in funding for research by Feinberg School faculty members at affiliated hospitals.
[3] Includes contributions of $83.2 million reported by hospitals not reflected on Feinberg School books.
[4] Endowment income includes $9.6 million in parking revenues.
[5] Reflects only contributions actually processed through Feinberg School books; excludes in-kind contributions to teaching and research.

Ameristar Casinos

Design Firm: Eleven Inc.
Creative Director: Paul Curtin

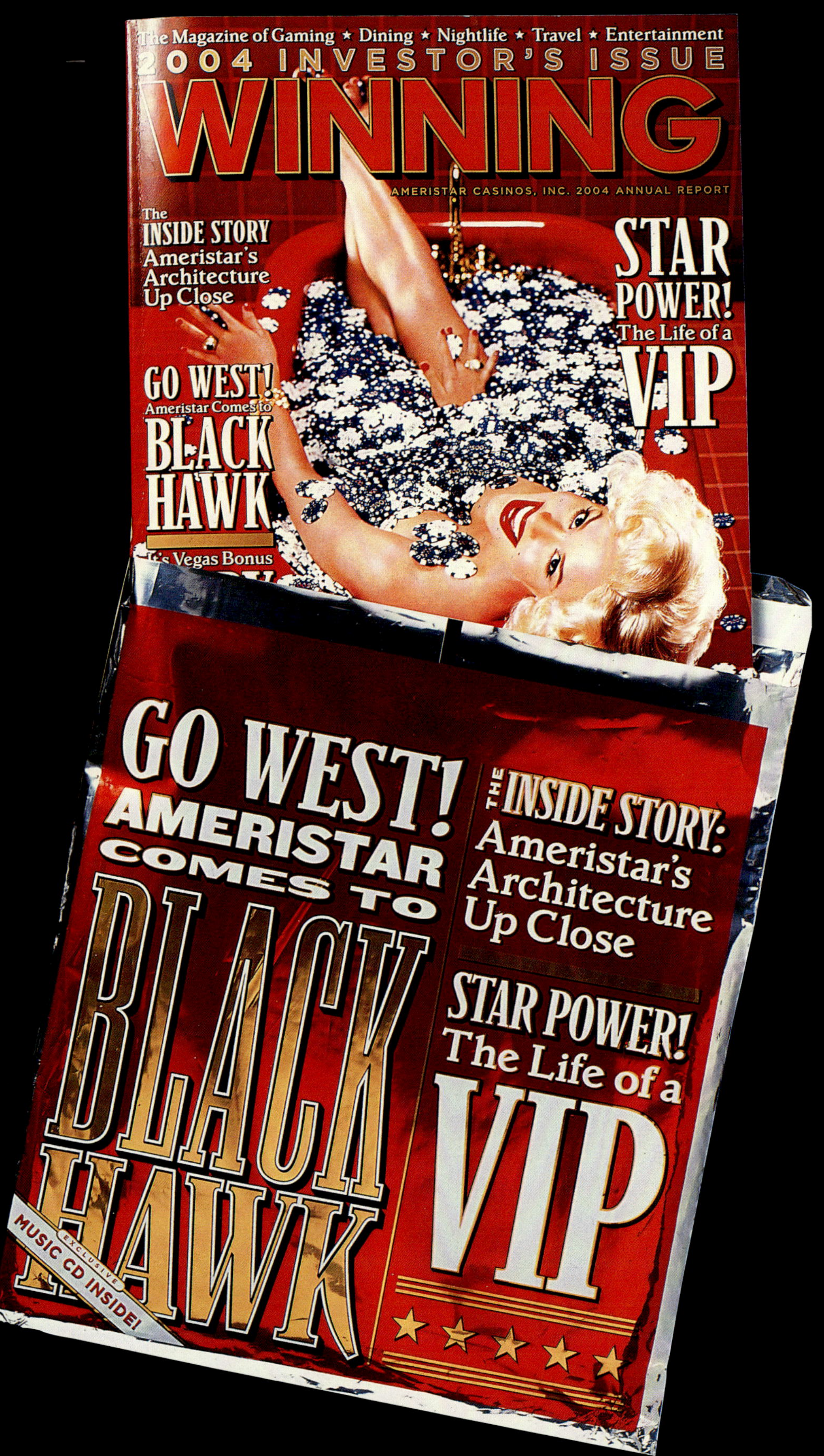

Art Director: Josh Baker, Paul Curtin
Designer: Goldy Van De Water
Illustrators: Terry Allen, Dan Cosgrove, Richard Draper, Edwin Fotheringham, PJ Loughran, John Mattos, Mikohn Gaming, Paul Rogers, Mark Summers
Photographers: Moshe Brakha, Angie Norwood Brown, Bob Delevante, Paul Fusco, Gregg Goldman, Jack Huynh, Gene Hwang, Stephan Swalwell, Alex Webb
Printer: Williamson Printing
Paper: Utopia Two Dull 100#C Ink: 8/5 = 4CP +touch plate +2 PMS +UV coating/ 4CP +varnish (cover), Utopia Two Dull 70#T Ink: 6/6 = 4CP +PMS +varnish over same (text)
Page count: 170 (narrative: 122,financials: 48, gatefolds: (2) 8 pager; (2) 6-pager, inserts: 4)
Number of images: 122
Print run: 20,000
Size: 10" x 12"
Client: Ameristar Casinos

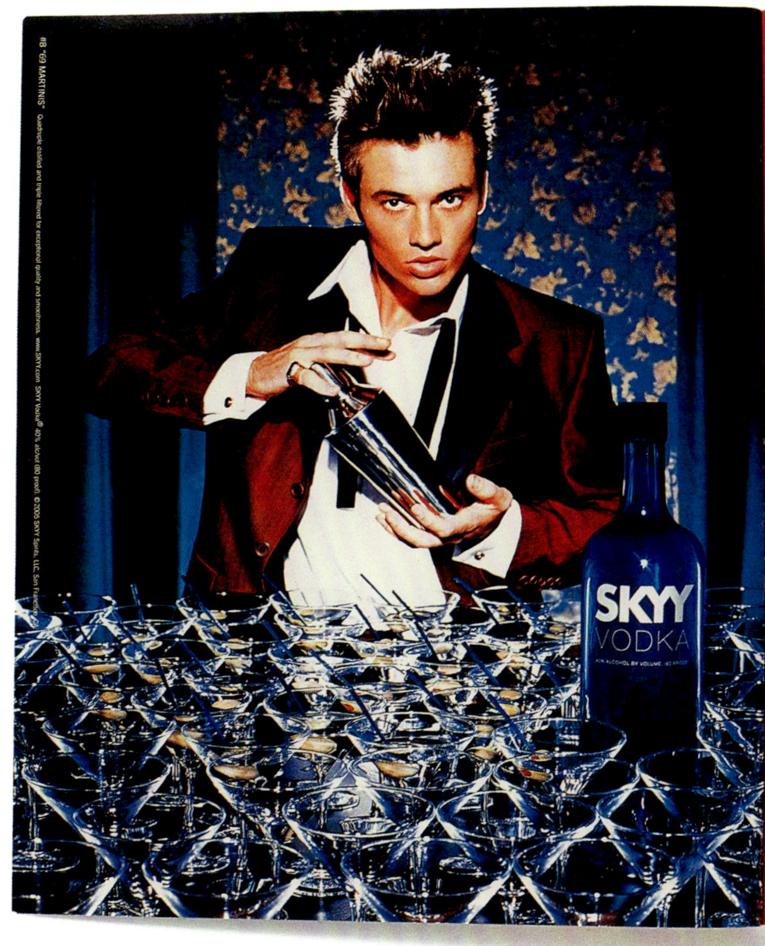

WE HAVE ONE opportunity every year to speak at length to our shareholders, report on our accomplishments and share our exciting plans for the future. And, certainly, a traditional annual report would do the job. *But at Ameristar we've never been about just getting the job done.* That's why for 2004 we created an annual report that reflects not just our numbers and successes but what we are at heart—an entertainment company. *We hope you enjoy it.*

Q&A with Eleven Inc.

What was the client's directive?

Ameristar is in the casino business, but they understand a larger truth—that they're really in the entertainment business.

How did you define the problem?

The way we chose to position Ameristar as a first-rate entertainment company was to create a fictional entertainment magazine as a platform for their 2004 Annual Report.

What was the approach?

Entertainment is, of course, a very sensory thing - color, music, taste, emotion and action, all delivered with a lot of flair. That's what drove us to pack as many sensory experiences as possible into the annual: a pull-out poster, tipped-in music CD, removeable recipe cards, mylar wrapper, and so on. We felt that to keep true to the concept of a magazine, this should carry ads. But not Ameristar ads - that would have been too obvious. Instead, we selected some brands that we respect (Absolut, Pepsi, Converse, Joseph Abboud, Budweiser, Napster, Skyy, Adidas, etc.), and invited them to run an ad in Ameristar's annual free-of-charge. As far as we know, it's the first time this has been done in an Annual Report.

Which disciplines or people helped you with the project?

You name it. For most of us, this was by far the biggest annual any of us had ever worked on. The whole team (account/creative/production) really pulled together to make it happen.

Were you happy with the result? What could have been better?

Definitely. As with most designers, given more time/money/etc. there are things we'd all like to have improved, but overall it's a piece we're extremely proud of.

What was the client's response?

The team at Ameristar loves this annual – it has quickly become the new benchmark by which future reports will be measured.

How involved was the CEO in your meetings, presentations, etc.?

Ameristar's CEO was involved in making the decisions for each and every section.

How important are awards to your client?

Ameristar's attention to detail, combined with a desire to constantly do things differently, makes award winning work an expectation.

This annual for Ameristar quickly became the new benchmark by which their future reports will be measured.

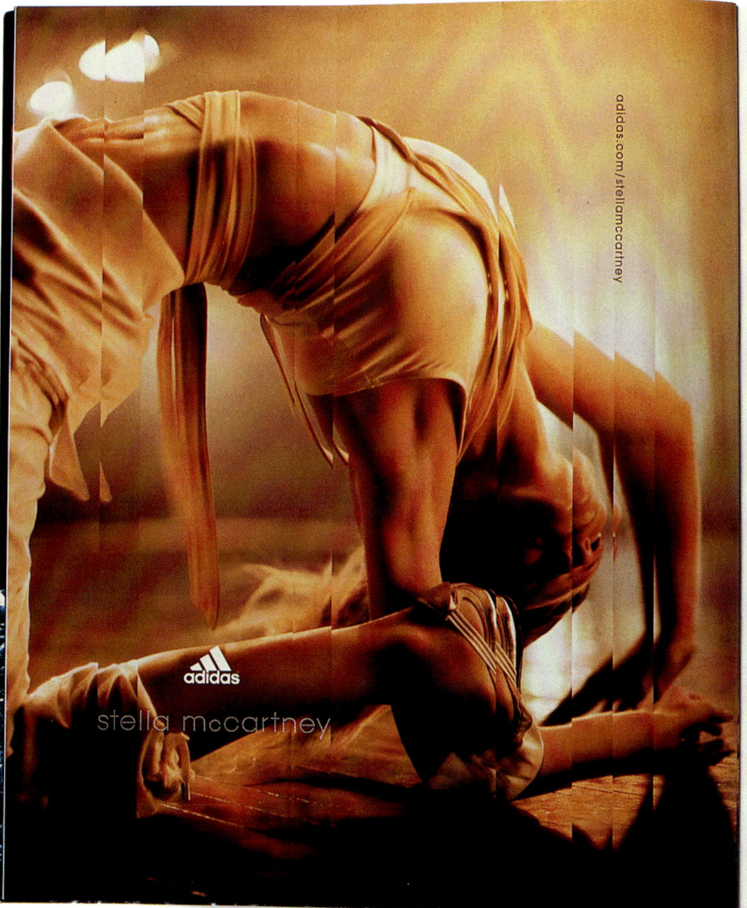

THE NUMBERS GAME

Number of "Best of" gaming awards won by Ameristar in 2004: 133
Total number of table games at Ameristar: 322
Total number of slot machines operated by Ameristar: 11,440
Number of 18-hole golf courses: 1
Percentage of slot machines at our Ameristar-branded properties that are ticket-enabled: 97
Number of years since our original properties, The Horseshu and Cactus Petes, first opened their doors: 49
Number of consecutive years all of our Ameristar-branded properties have held the top position in their markets: 3
Number of consecutive years all of these properties have grown their market share: 4
Total number of Ameristar restaurants and bars: 60
Number serving rattlesnake: 1
Number of pounds of crab served at Ameristar in 2004: 742,440
Number of different martinis on the menu at the King Cat Club, St. Charles: 40
Percentage of pro-football games shown on the 41 screens at Amerisports Brew Pub, Kansas City: 100
Number of consecutive years Council Bluffs has won a Four-Diamond rating from AAA: 7
Number of consecutive years Cactus Petes has won that same rating: 12
Number of bottles of Pepsi given away during our 2004 Instant-Win promotion: 28,832
Number of ounces of soft drinks served at Ameristar in 2004: 130,381,056
Total number of cars won by our guests in 2004: 39
Total number of parking spaces available for guests: 18,430
Number of full-service spaces available at Cactus Petes RV Park: 90
Number of live performances at Ameristar in 2004: 873
Number of concert tickets sold: 121,003
Number of Grammy Awards won by artists who appeared on our stages in 2004: 67
Feet of neon tubing used in our new Vicksburg marquee: 2,500
Number of compact fluorescent bulbs: 5,270
Number of tractor-trailer trucks required to transport the sign from Las Vegas: 4
Number of coupons we sent to our Star Awards players in 2004: 29,753,100
Percentage increase in rated-play revenue in 2004: 21
Number of people who could fit under the porte cochere at Ameristar St. Charles: 20,000
Ranking of Ameristar St. Charles among tourist attractions in the greater St. Louis area: 1
Black Hawk's elevation above sea level, in feet: 8,042
Lowest recorded temperature there, in degrees Fahrenheit: -30
Vicksburg's elevation above sea level, in feet: 119
Highest recorded temperature there, in degrees Fahrenheit: 102
Total gaming revenue generated in 2004 by markets with Ameristar-branded properties (in dollars): 2,263,218,565
Average market share we held in these markets: 36
Percentage increase in our gaming revenue from these markets over the last five years: 81
Percentage increase in Ameristar's stock price over the last five years: 1,035
Percentage decrease in the NASDAQ over that same period: -47
Number of individual pieces in the stained-glass ceiling at Ameristar St. Charles: 148,000
Number of stained-glass installations in the state of Missouri that are larger than this one: 0
Total dollars raised by our Ameristar Cares program in 2004: 1,553,275
Total number of team members that participated: 3,737
Percentage of team members that figure represents: 51
Total number of plasma screens in our casinos: 217
Number of movie theaters at Ameristar Kansas City: 18
Number of Hollywood films shot at Ameristar Vicksburg: 1*

Figures cited are the latest available as of February 2005. *The Ladykillers, starring Tom Hanks.

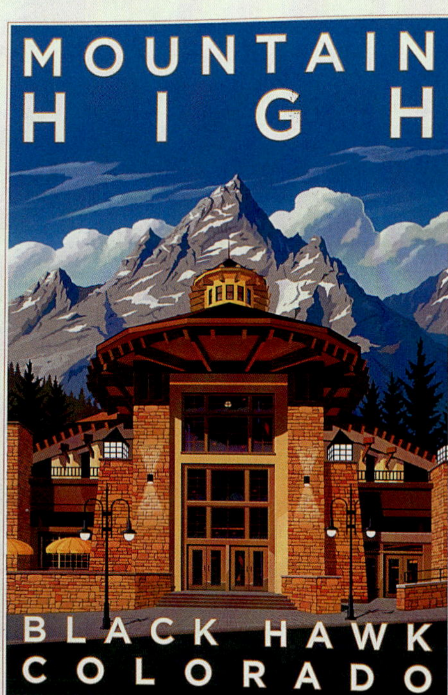

RECORD RETURNS, strong cash flow, *reduced debt,* our first dividends *and a new acquisition*

THE YEAR IN REVIEW

Illustrations by Dan Cosgrove, John Mattos and Paul Rogers

stations, featuring pasta made-to-order, stir-fry and a broiler. We will also increase capacity to 340 guests. Once the project is finished (in the second quarter of 2005), the restaurant will be rebranded as the Heritage Buffet.

We plan to expand the gaming space to accommodate an additional 300 slot machines, a 32-seat deli and a spacious, well-appointed poker room. These upgrades should be completed by the second quarter of 2006.

VICKSBURG
Mississippi

We continued to see notable increases in net revenues and market share in Vicksburg during 2004. Net revenues jumped 13.0% to $107.4 million, and market share grew by an astonishing five percentage points, hitting 45.4%.

In December 2003 we completed a $7.0 million renovation of the Heritage Buffet, including the construction of seven display cooking stations. The net result: during its first full year of operation, the buffet served 35.6% more guests than in 2003, resulting in an equally remarkable 55.5% increase in cash revenue.

Right now we're working on plans to reconfigure and add square footage to the gaming floor; it will house more than 200 additional slot machines and a poker room. We will also expand the Star Club, add a gift shop and build a 1,000-space parking garage with direct access to the casino.

JACKPOT
Nevada

Our Jackpot properties, Cactus Petes and The Horseshu, saw EBITDA increase by 7.5% and net revenues climb 2.3% to an historic $60.2 million.

CACTUS PETES
JACKPOT NEVADA

To keep our dining outlets fresh and exciting, we opened Pancho Villa's Mexican Grill during the first quarter of 2005. Located at The Horseshu, Pancho Villa's provides a new casual-dining option for the market, serving traditional Mexican favorites and specialty dishes.

At Cactus Petes we completed an air-quality improvement project and an upgrade of the heating and cooling systems. We are currently developing designs to renovate the hotel rooms, hospitality suites and poker room.

BLACK HAWK
Colorado

The recent acquisition of Mountain High Casino in Black Hawk, Colorado, gives us a strong presence in yet another gaming market, increasing our geographic diversification. The purchase price of the property was approximately $120.0 million.

Our plans for Mountain High include a major expansion of the gaming floor and the addition of what will be Black Hawk's first Four-Diamond-quality hotel. We will also build additional covered parking, upgrade the food and beverage outlets and add a casual-dining restaurant. You can read more about these projects in our special report on Ameristar Black Hawk following page 54.

HORSESHU
JACKPOT NEVADA

Future Growth

We are always looking for solid development opportunities and potential acquisitions as both provide excellent ways to build on our existing model. Mountain High Casino was one such opportunity. Now we are optimistic about another one.

Pennsylvania recently adopted a gaming law that allows racetracks and other locations to obtain slot machine licenses. Two non-track licenses will be issued for Philadelphia.

We are pleased to report that Ameristar holds an option on a 46-acre development site right off Interstate 95 and within view of the city center. If we are able to obtain one of the non-track gaming licenses, we intend to exercise this option and develop a premier casino and entertainment facility, comparable to our other market-leading properties.

We plan to file our license application as soon as Pennsylvania's Gaming Commission starts accepting them.

A Very Good Year Indeed

By any measure 2004 was an extraordinary year for Ameristar. We could hardly ask for a more resounding affirmation of our core strategies—or of the investments we've made in pursuit of those strategies.

We are extremely confident that the initiatives we'll take on in 2005 will prove every bit as rewarding.

On behalf of all our Ameristar team members, I thank you for your continued support.

Sincerely yours,

Craig H. Neilsen

CRAIG H. NEILSEN
Chairman and CEO, March 2005

WINNING • *The Year in Review* 14

15 AMERISTAR CASINOS, INC. • 2004 ANNUAL REPORT

AT-A-GLANCE

A Pull-Out Guide to the Ameristar Properties

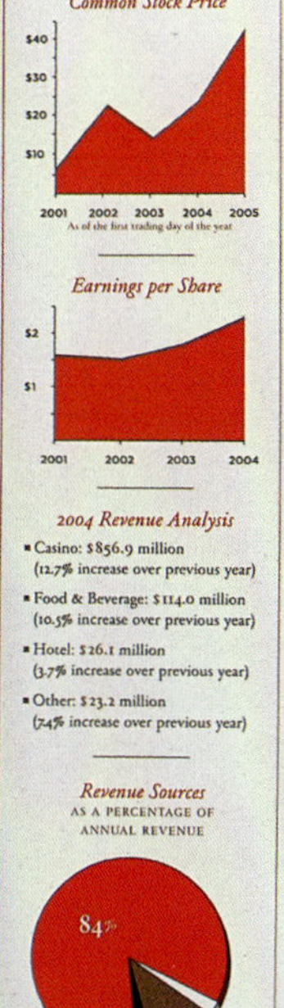

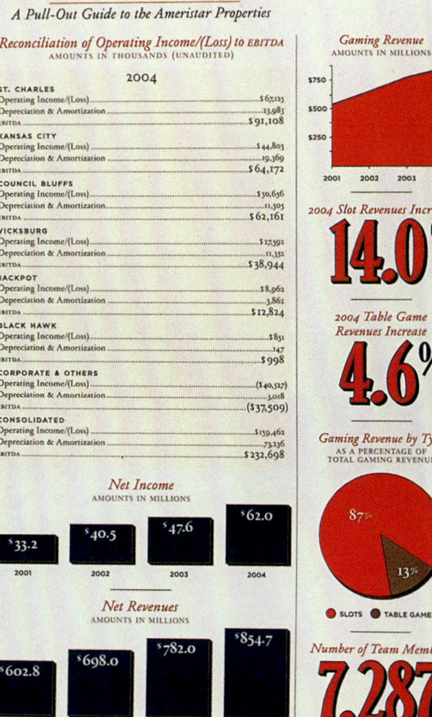

Reconciliation of Operating Income/(Loss) to EBITDA
AMOUNTS IN THOUSANDS (UNAUDITED)

2004	
ST. CHARLES	
Operating Income/(Loss)	$67,125
Depreciation & Amortization	23,983
EBITDA	$91,108
KANSAS CITY	
Operating Income/(Loss)	$44,803
Depreciation & Amortization	19,369
EBITDA	$64,172
COUNCIL BLUFFS	
Operating Income/(Loss)	$50,656
Depreciation & Amortization	11,505
EBITDA	$62,161
VICKSBURG	
Operating Income/(Loss)	$27,592
Depreciation & Amortization	11,352
EBITDA	$38,944
JACKPOT	
Operating Income/(Loss)	$8,962
Depreciation & Amortization	3,862
EBITDA	$12,824
BLACK HAWK	
Operating Income/(Loss)	$851
Depreciation & Amortization	147
EBITDA	$998
CORPORATE & OTHERS	
Operating Income/(Loss)	($40,527)
Depreciation & Amortization	3,018
EBITDA	($37,509)
CONSOLIDATED	
Operating Income/(Loss)	$159,462
Depreciation & Amortization	73,236
EBITDA	$232,698

Gaming Revenue
AMOUNTS IN MILLIONS
$750
$500
$250
2001 2002 2003 2004

2004 Slot Revenues Increase
14.0%

2004 Table Game Revenues Increase
4.6%

Gaming Revenue by Type
AS A PERCENTAGE OF TOTAL GAMING REVENUE
87%
13%
SLOTS TABLE GAMES

Number of Team Members
7,287

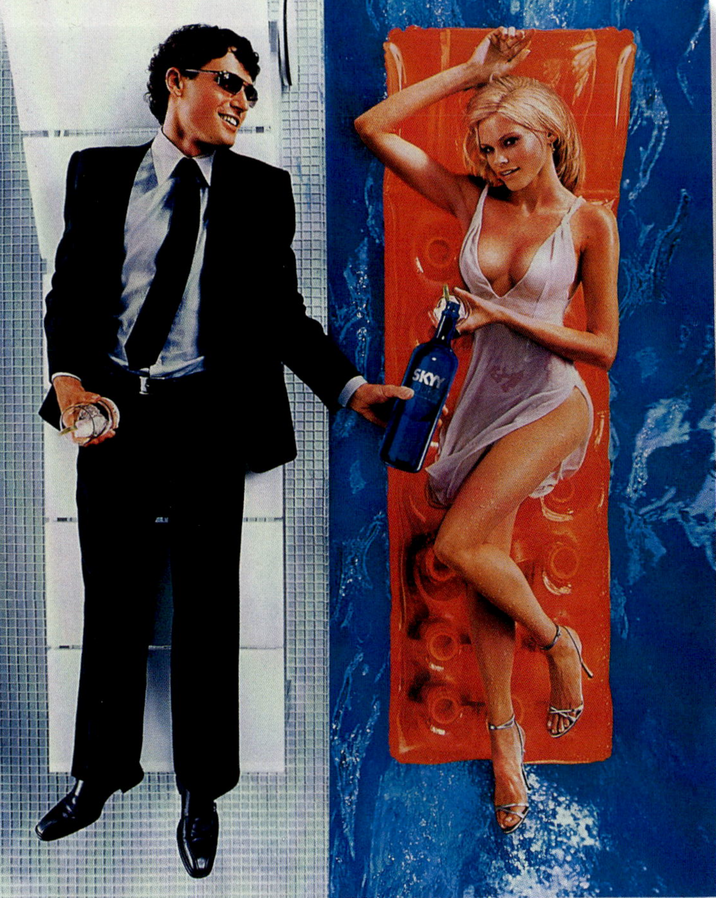

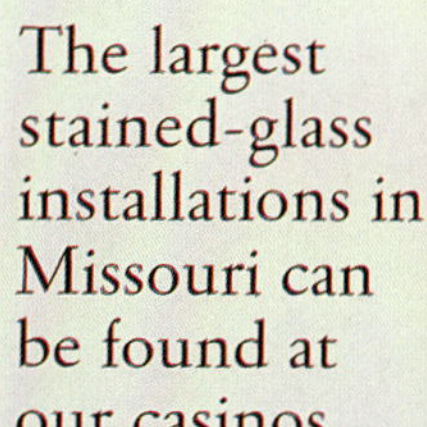

The largest stained-glass installations in Missouri can be found at our casinos.

OUR MISSOURI CASINOS evoke the spirit of the majestic theaters and hotels built during the Victorian era. Period and neoclassical elements like Corinthian columns and ornate metal railings and trusses make guests feel that they have arrived at a truly grand destination. And the most dazzling of these architectural features are the massive stained-glass windows that adorn the ceilings. Breathtaking in both their scale and artistry, they are a sight that guests don't soon forget.

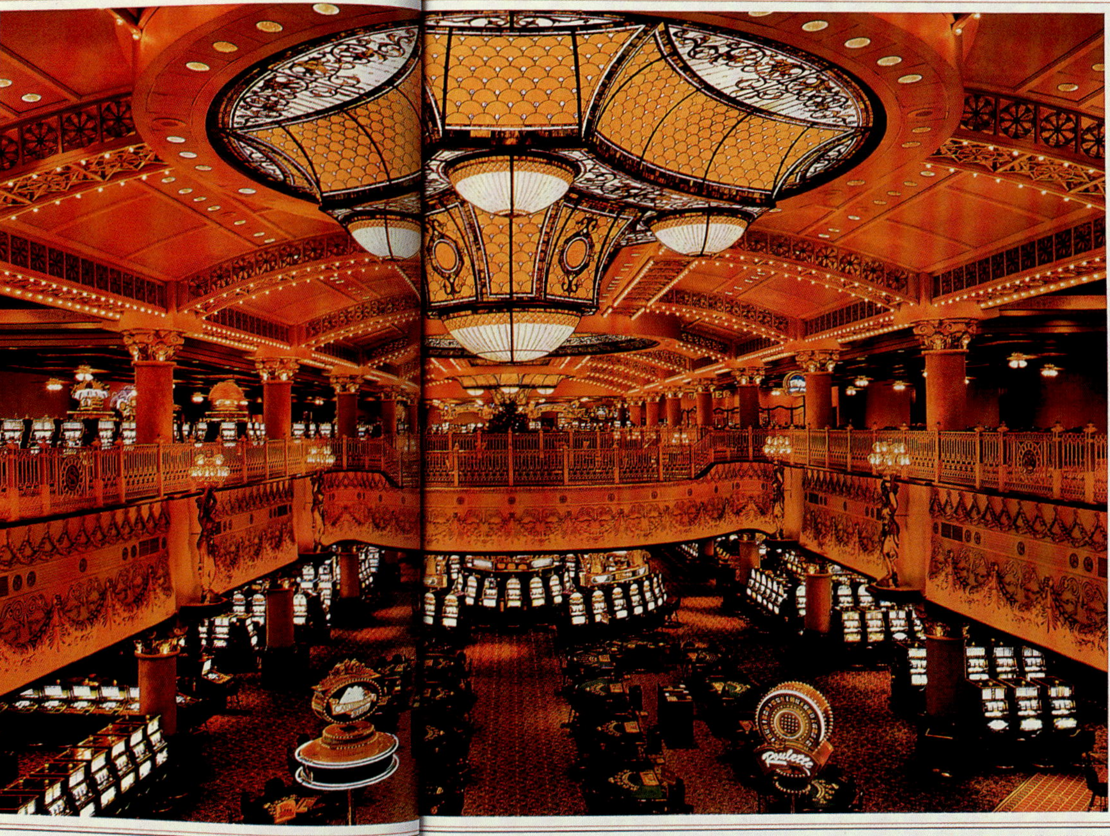

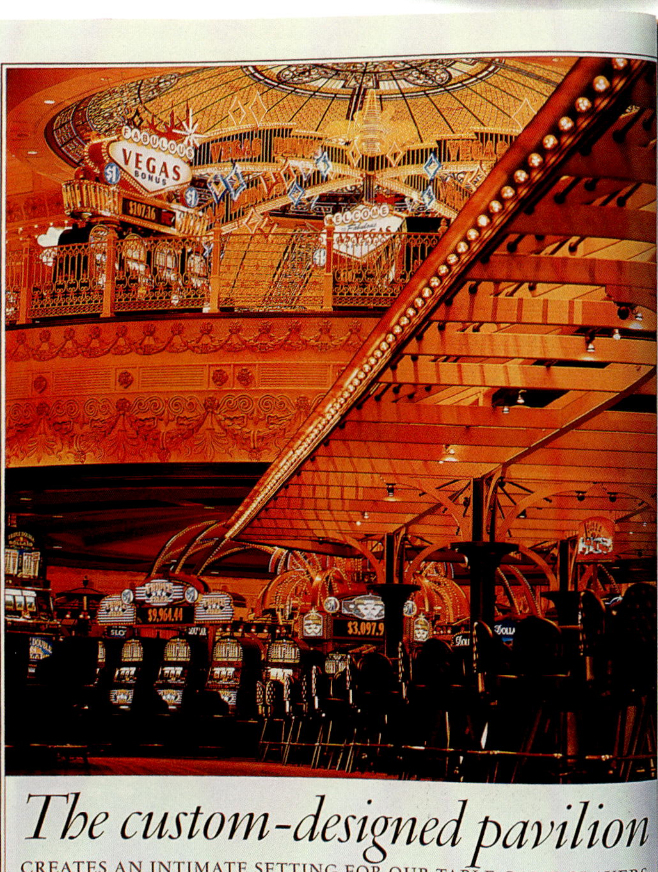

The custom-designed pavilion

CREATES AN INTIMATE SETTING FOR OUR TABLE GAME PLAYERS.

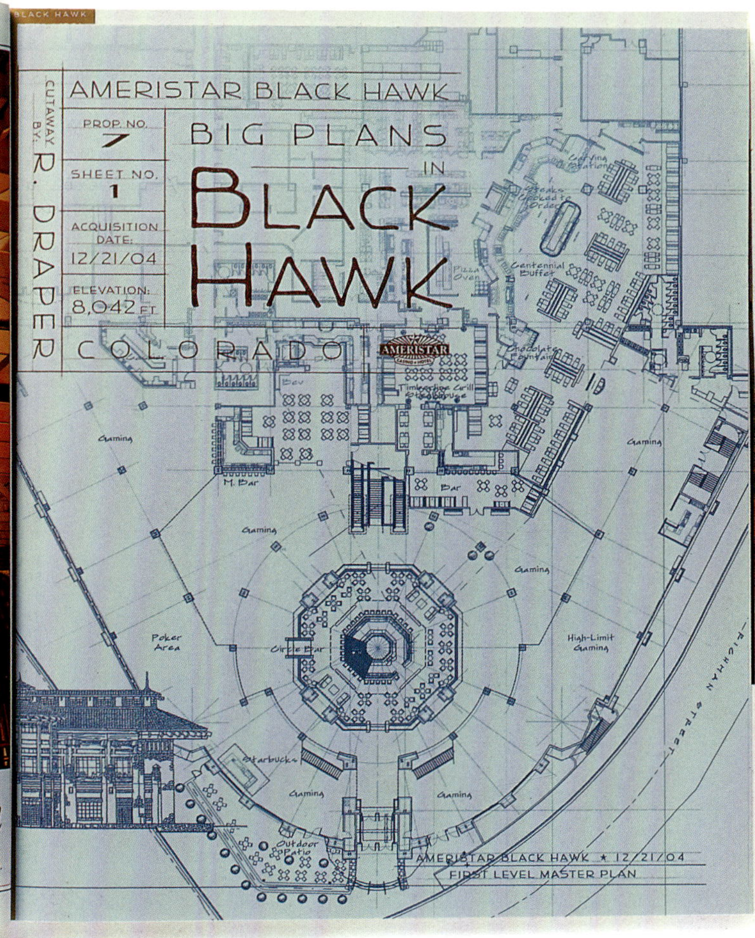

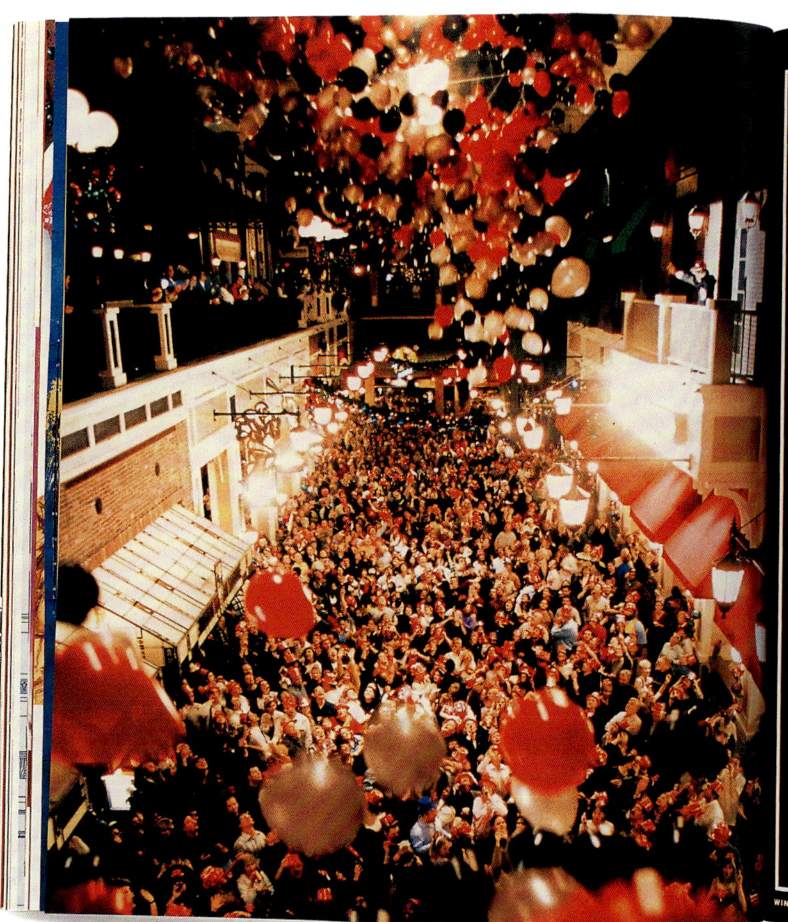

The BIGGEST BASH *in* TOWN

Inside 2004's New Year's Eve Parties

THE WAY WE LOOK AT IT, every night at Ameristar is a party. But New Year's Eve is another thing altogether. It's our single most profitable night of the year, and we pull out all the stops to make the most of it.

Our executive chefs prepare elaborate holiday menus for all our restaurants. We host a spectacular indoor fireworks display. At just the right moment, we drop thousands of balloons from the ceiling. And all night long, top-notch bands and big-name entertainers keep the energy high and the casinos crowded.

Of course our VIP players enjoy all this and more at invitation-only parties, where elegant hors d'oeuvres appear at every turn. A traditional champagne toast is made at the stroke of midnight. And, at the end of the evening, we give out gifts so our best players start the New Year with a wonderful surprise.

On the night of December 31, 2004, we dispatched photographers to all of our Ameristar-branded casinos. Their assignment was to capture the action, and we certainly think they succeeded. ★

Photography by Magnum and Orange

WINNING • *The Biggest Bash in Town* 89 AMERISTAR CASINOS, INC. • 2004 ANNUAL REPORT

the

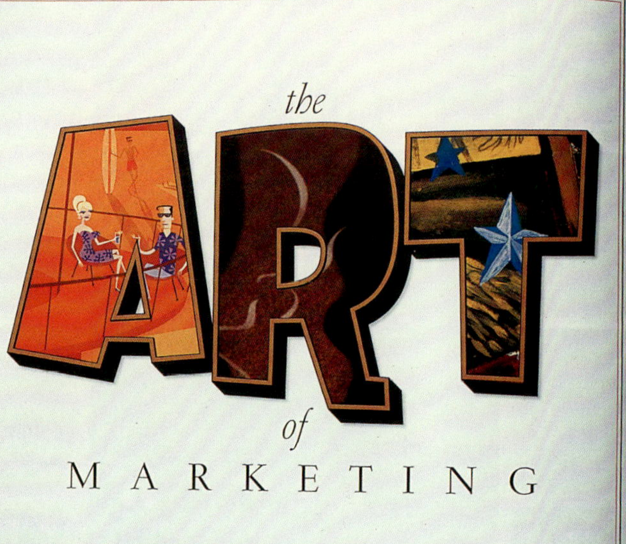

of

the ART *of* MARKETING

MARKETING CAMPAIGNS are traditionally all about consistency—a series of ads that look the same, more or less. But a single glance at the body of work created by Ameristar makes it abundantly clear that tradition has little to do with our approach to marketing.

This "intentional inconsistency" was a purely strategic decision. It gives stopping power to each of our ads. It keeps our image fresh and lively. And it perfectly reinforces one of Ameristar's key brand messages: fun.

Of course, another of Ameristar's brand messages is quality, and this campaign delivers on that, too.

We've commissioned literally dozens of the top commercial artists in the U.S. (not to mention a few outside the country). The illustrations they've created for us have won stacks of the advertising industry's most prestigious awards.

Of course, the real measure of marketing success is not awards, but results. And the results of Ameristar's marketing—steady growth in guest traffic, revenues and market share—are as beautiful to behold as the ads themselves.

Open these pages, and take a look at one of the most original and successful campaigns in gaming today.

Illustrations by the Best in the Business

WINNING • *The Art of Marketing* 106 AMERISTAR CASINOS, INC. • 2004 ANNUAL REPORT

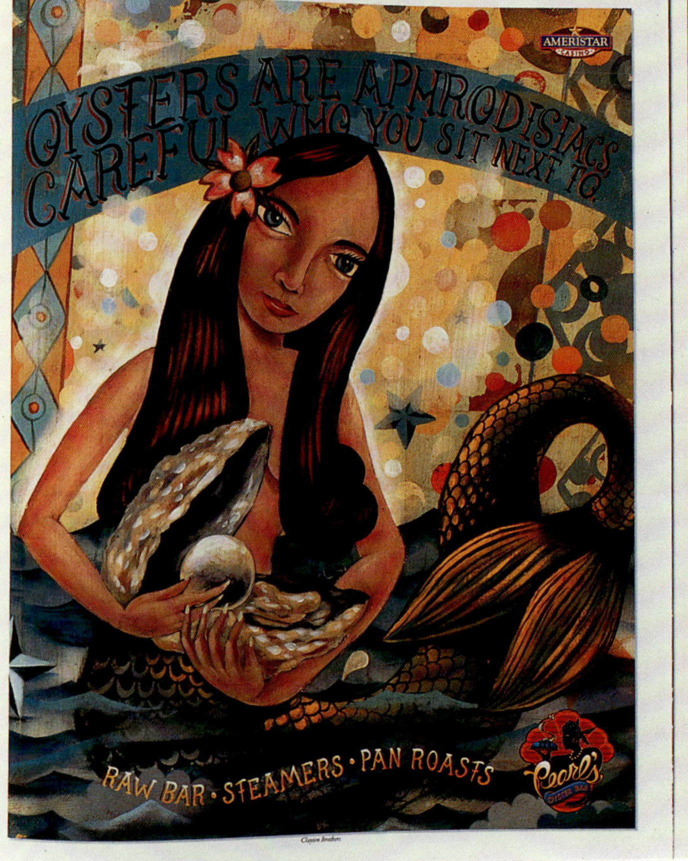

Clayton Brothers

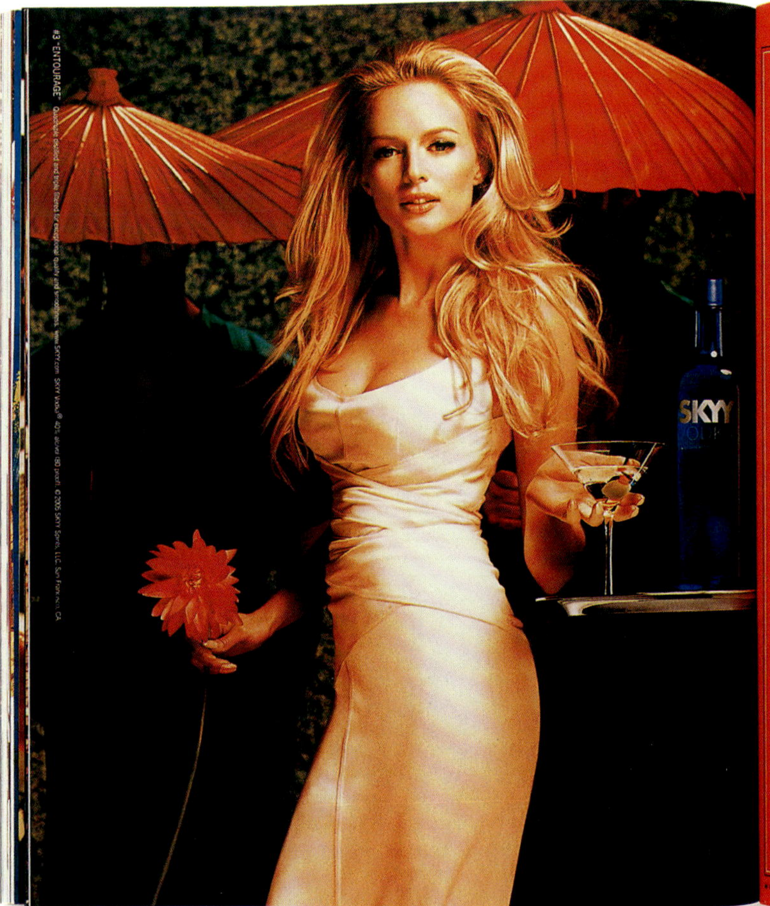

ANOTHER ONE
for the
Record Books

Our 2004
FINANCIAL REVIEW

Table of
CONTENTS

Cautionary Information Regarding
FORWARD-LOOKING STATEMENTS

Unless the context indicates otherwise, all references in this Annual Report to "Ameristar" or "ACI" refer to Ameristar Casinos, Inc., and all references to the "Company," "we," "our," "ours" or "us" refer to Ameristar and its consolidated subsidiaries. This Annual Report contains certain forward-looking statements, including management's plans and objectives for our business, operations and financial performance. These forward-looking statements generally can be identified by the context of the statement or the use of forward-looking terminology, such as "believes," "estimates," "anticipates," "intends," "expects," "plans," "is confident that" or words of similar meaning, with reference to us or our management. Similarly, statements that describe our future plans, objectives, strategies, financial results, financial position, operational expectations or goals are forward-looking statements. Although management believes that the assumptions underlying the forward-looking statements are reasonable, these assumptions and the forward-looking statements are subject to various factors, risks and uncertainties, many of which are beyond our control. Accordingly, actual results could differ materially from those contemplated by any forward-looking statements. In addition to the other cautionary statements relating to certain forward-looking statements throughout this Annual Report, attention is directed to "Business—Risk Factors" and "Management's Discussion and Analysis of Financial Condition and Results of Operations" in our Annual Report on Form 10-K for the year ended December 31, 2004, for a discussion of some of the factors, risks and uncertainties that could materially affect the outcome of future results contemplated by forward-looking statements.

You should also be aware that while we communicate from time to time with securities analysts, we do not disclose to them any material nonpublic information, internal forecasts or other confidential business information. Therefore, you should not assume that we agree with any statement or report issued by any analyst, irrespective of the content of the statement or report. To the extent that reports issued by securities analysts contain projections, forecasts or opinions, those reports are not our responsibility.

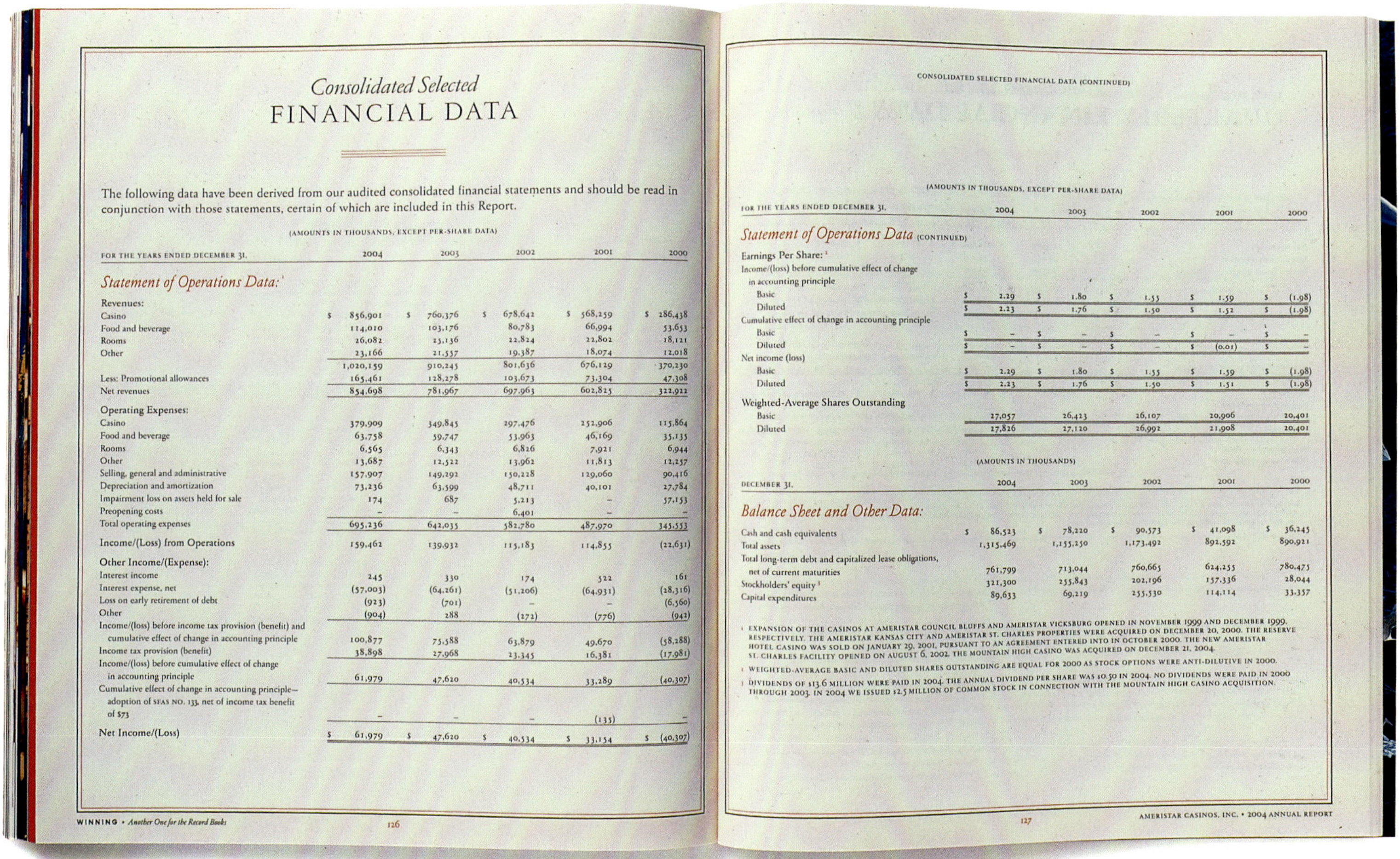

Consolidated Selected FINANCIAL DATA

The following data have been derived from our audited consolidated financial statements and should be read in conjunction with those statements, certain of which are included in this Report.

(AMOUNTS IN THOUSANDS, EXCEPT PER-SHARE DATA)

FOR THE YEARS ENDED DECEMBER 31,	2004	2003	2002	2001	2000
Statement of Operations Data:[1]					
Revenues:					
Casino	$ 856,901	$ 760,376	$ 678,642	$ 568,259	$ 286,438
Food and beverage	114,010	103,176	80,783	66,994	53,653
Rooms	26,082	25,136	22,824	22,802	18,121
Other	23,166	21,557	19,387	18,074	12,018
	1,020,159	910,245	801,636	676,129	370,230
Less: Promotional allowances	165,461	128,278	103,673	73,304	47,308
Net revenues	854,698	781,967	697,963	602,825	322,922
Operating Expenses:					
Casino	379,909	349,845	297,476	252,906	115,864
Food and beverage	63,758	59,747	53,963	46,169	35,135
Rooms	6,565	6,343	6,826	7,921	6,944
Other	13,687	12,522	13,962	11,813	12,257
Selling, general and administrative	157,907	149,292	150,228	129,060	90,416
Depreciation and amortization	73,236	63,599	48,711	40,101	27,784
Impairment loss on assets held for sale	174	687	5,213	–	57,153
Preopening costs	–	–	6,401	–	–
Total operating expenses	695,236	642,035	582,780	487,970	345,553
Income/(Loss) from Operations	159,462	139,932	115,183	114,855	(22,631)
Other Income/(Expense):					
Interest income	245	330	174	522	161
Interest expense, net	(57,003)	(64,261)	(51,206)	(64,931)	(28,316)
Loss on early retirement of debt	(923)	(701)	–	–	(6,560)
Other	(904)	288	(272)	(776)	(942)
Income/(loss) before income tax provision (benefit) and cumulative effect of change in accounting principle	100,877	75,588	63,879	49,670	(58,288)
Income tax provision (benefit)	38,898	27,968	23,345	16,381	(17,981)
Income/(loss) before cumulative effect of change in accounting principle	61,979	47,620	40,534	33,289	(40,307)
Cumulative effect of change in accounting principle—adoption of SFAS NO. 133, net of income tax benefit of $73	–	–	–	(135)	–
Net Income/(Loss)	$ 61,979	$ 47,620	$ 40,534	$ 33,154	$ (40,307)

CONSOLIDATED SELECTED FINANCIAL DATA (CONTINUED)

(AMOUNTS IN THOUSANDS, EXCEPT PER-SHARE DATA)

FOR THE YEARS ENDED DECEMBER 31,	2004	2003	2002	2001	2000
Statement of Operations Data (CONTINUED)					
Earnings Per Share:[2]					
Income/(loss) before cumulative effect of change in accounting principle					
Basic	$ 2.29	$ 1.80	$ 1.55	$ 1.59	$ (1.98)
Diluted	$ 2.23	$ 1.76	$ 1.50	$ 1.52	$ (1.98)
Cumulative effect of change in accounting principle					
Basic	$ –	$ –	$ –	$ –	$ –
Diluted	$ –	$ –	$ –	$ (0.01)	$ –
Net income (loss)					
Basic	$ 2.29	$ 1.80	$ 1.55	$ 1.59	$ (1.98)
Diluted	$ 2.23	$ 1.76	$ 1.50	$ 1.51	$ (1.98)
Weighted-Average Shares Outstanding					
Basic	27,057	26,423	26,107	20,906	20,401
Diluted	27,826	27,120	26,992	21,908	20,401

(AMOUNTS IN THOUSANDS)

DECEMBER 31,	2004	2003	2002	2001	2000
Balance Sheet and Other Data:					
Cash and cash equivalents	$ 86,523	$ 78,220	$ 90,573	$ 41,098	$ 36,245
Total assets	1,315,469	1,155,250	1,173,492	892,592	890,921
Total long-term debt and capitalized lease obligations, net of current maturities	761,799	713,044	760,665	624,255	780,475
Stockholders' equity[3]	321,300	255,843	202,196	157,336	28,044
Capital expenditures	89,633	69,219	255,530	114,114	33,357

1 EXPANSION OF THE CASINOS AT AMERISTAR COUNCIL BLUFFS AND AMERISTAR VICKSBURG OPENED IN NOVEMBER 1999 AND DECEMBER 1999, RESPECTIVELY. THE AMERISTAR KANSAS CITY AND AMERISTAR ST. CHARLES PROPERTIES WERE ACQUIRED ON DECEMBER 20, 2000. THE RESERVE HOTEL CASINO WAS SOLD ON JANUARY 29, 2001, PURSUANT TO AN AGREEMENT ENTERED INTO IN OCTOBER 2000. THE NEW AMERISTAR ST. CHARLES FACILITY OPENED ON AUGUST 6, 2002. THE MOUNTAIN HIGH CASINO WAS ACQUIRED ON DECEMBER 21, 2004.

2 WEIGHTED-AVERAGE BASIC AND DILUTED SHARES OUTSTANDING ARE EQUAL FOR 2000 AS STOCK OPTIONS WERE ANTI-DILUTIVE IN 2000.

3 DIVIDENDS OF $13.6 MILLION WERE PAID IN 2004. THE ANNUAL DIVIDEND PER SHARE WAS $0.50 IN 2004. NO DIVIDENDS WERE PAID IN 2000 THROUGH 2003. IN 2004 WE ISSUED $2.5 MILLION OF COMMON STOCK IN CONNECTION WITH THE MOUNTAIN HIGH CASINO ACQUISITION.

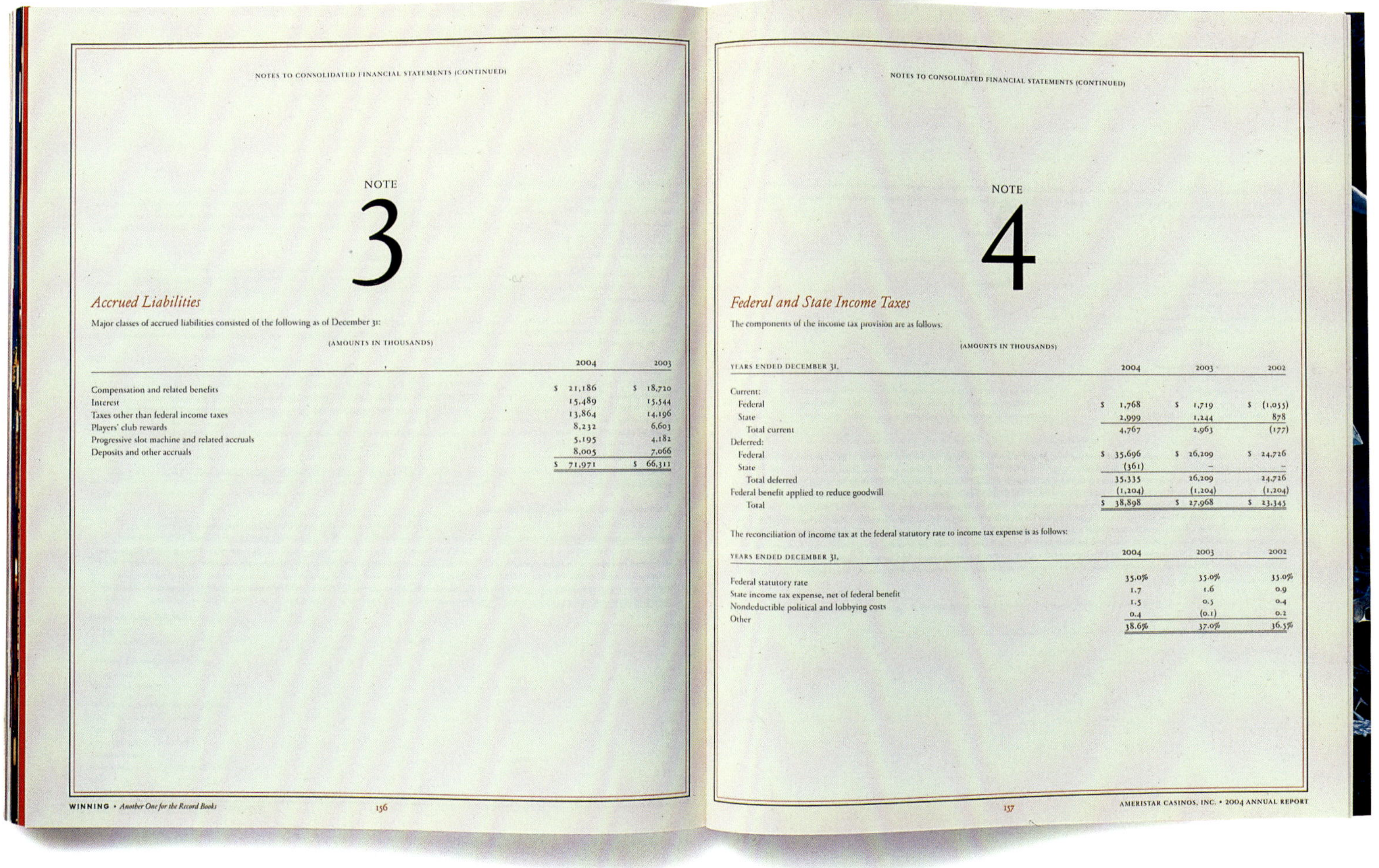

NOTES TO CONSOLIDATED FINANCIAL STATEMENTS (CONTINUED)

NOTE

3

Accrued Liabilities

Major classes of accrued liabilities consisted of the following as of December 31:

(AMOUNTS IN THOUSANDS)

	2004	2003
Compensation and related benefits	$ 21,186	$ 18,720
Interest	15,489	15,544
Taxes other than federal income taxes	13,864	14,196
Players' club rewards	8,232	6,603
Progressive slot machine and related accruals	5,195	4,182
Deposits and other accruals	8,005	7,066
	$ 71,971	$ 66,311

NOTES TO CONSOLIDATED FINANCIAL STATEMENTS (CONTINUED)

NOTE

4

Federal and State Income Taxes

The components of the income tax provision are as follows:

(AMOUNTS IN THOUSANDS)

YEARS ENDED DECEMBER 31,	2004	2003	2002
Current:			
Federal	$ 1,768	$ 1,719	$ (1,055)
State	2,999	1,244	878
Total current	4,767	2,963	(177)
Deferred:			
Federal	$ 35,696	$ 26,209	$ 24,726
State	(361)	–	–
Total deferred	35,335	26,209	24,726
Federal benefit applied to reduce goodwill	(1,204)	(1,204)	(1,204)
Total	$ 38,898	$ 27,968	$ 23,345

The reconciliation of income tax at the federal statutory rate to income tax expense is as follows:

YEARS ENDED DECEMBER 31,	2004	2003	2002
Federal statutory rate	35.0%	35.0%	35.0%
State income tax expense, net of federal benefit	1.7	1.6	0.9
Nondeductible political and lobbying costs	1.5	0.5	0.4
Other	0.4	(0.1)	0.2
	38.6%	37.0%	36.5%

Station Casinos, Inc.

Design Firm: Kuhlmann Leavitt, Inc
Creative Director: Deanna Kuhlmann-Leavitt

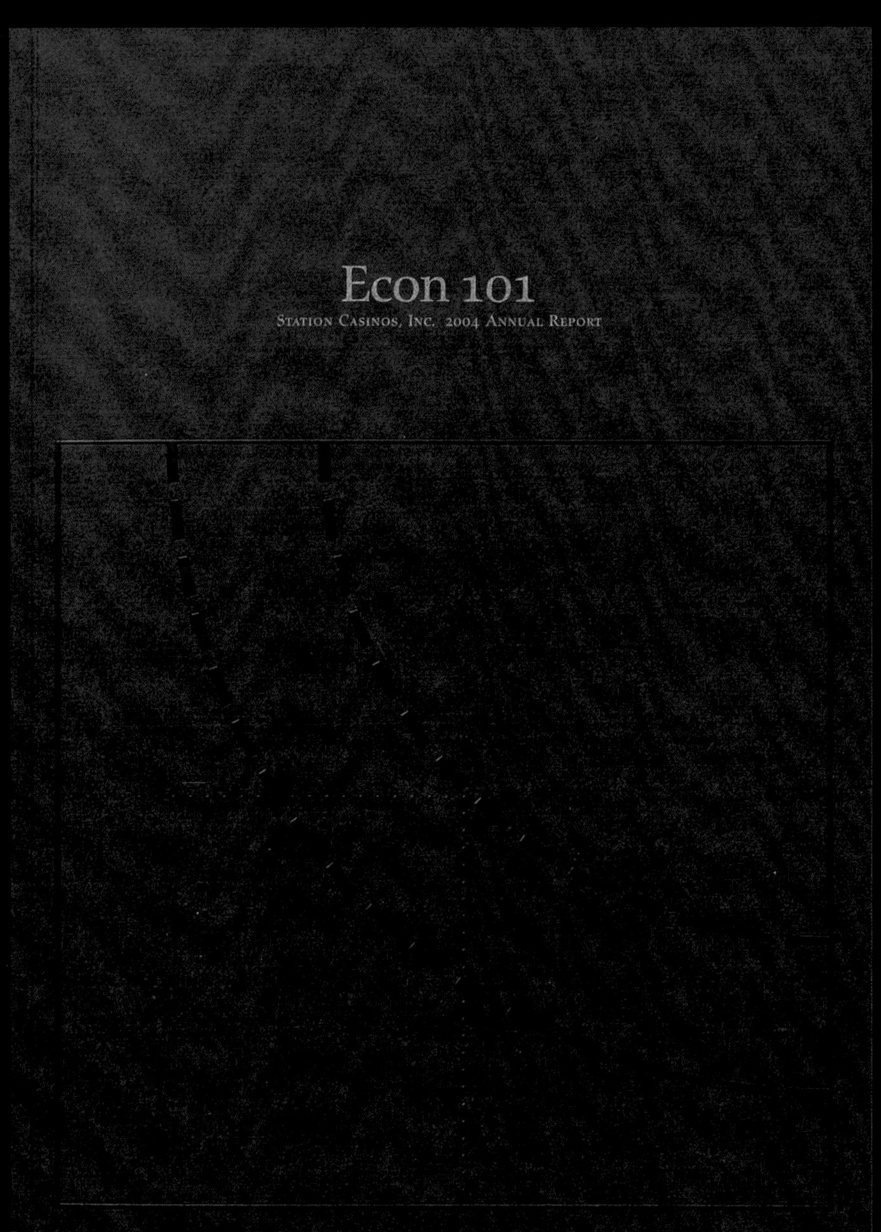

Art Director: Deanna Kuhlmann-Leavitt
Designer: Kerry Layton
Writer: Station Casinos, Inc.
Photographer: Gregg Goldmann
Printer: Hennegan Company
Paper: Carnival® Vellum Coco 80lb cover from SMART Papers Narrative Cast Coated: Kromekote® Plus 6pt/112pt text from SMART Papers Narrative Uncoated: Carnival® Stellar White 80lb text from SMART Papers, Benefit® Vellum Creme Puff 80lb text from SMART Papers, Carnival® Vellum Black 70lb text from SMART Papers Financials Carnival® Vellum Water 70 lb text from SMART Papers
Page count: 144
Print Run: 25,000
Size: 7"x10"
Number of Images: 72
Client: Station Casinos, Inc.

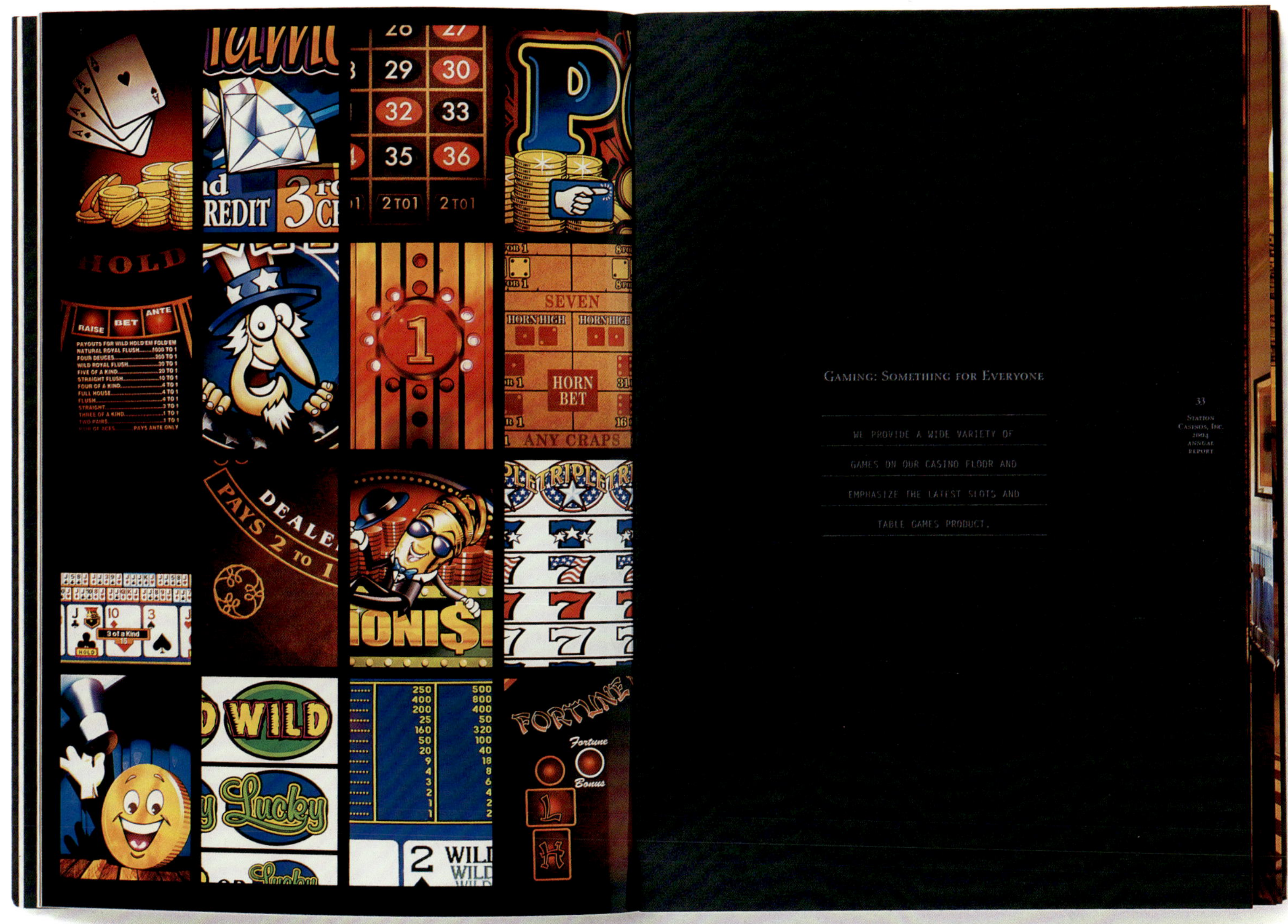

Q&A with Kuhlmann Leavitt Inc.

What was the client's directive?

To clearly explain their strategy using the basic economic principle of supply and demand.

How did you define the problem?

Communicate an Econ 101 story in a way that would keep the reader awake and engaged.

What was the approach?

We used classic textbook typography in the main text, charts and graphs, and then added full-bleed solids, outdoor construction photography, indoor architecture photography, and several types of paper including rich browns and blacks, soothing pale creams and soft blues, bright white uncoated and super glossy coated. The net result is a real page turner designed to educate, entertain and engage the viewer.

Which disciplines or people helped you with the project?

Station's CFO and upper management wrote the text and provided great content and theme direction in a truly collaborative way. We worked closely with Gregg Goldman Photography to arrive at the vast collection of shots made specifically for this book, and the Hennegan Company worked with KLI to get the most out of the presses, the paper and the finisher.

Were you happy with the result? What could have been better?

Delighted. I am not sure that we would change anything.

What was the client's response?

They are quite pleased.

How involved was the CEO in your meetings, presentations, etc.?

The Chairman and CEO, the Vice Chairman and President and the Executive VP and CFO are very involved in the development of the Annual Report. They are strategy experts, respect design and are visually sophisticated.

How do you define success in Annual Report design?

You know you are on your way when you find smart clients that allow you to do great work so that at the end of the day everyone is satisfied and proud of the effort.

How important are awards to your client?

They are happy when we tell them that we won, but they are not necessarily asking us to enter design competitions (except for their industry contests).

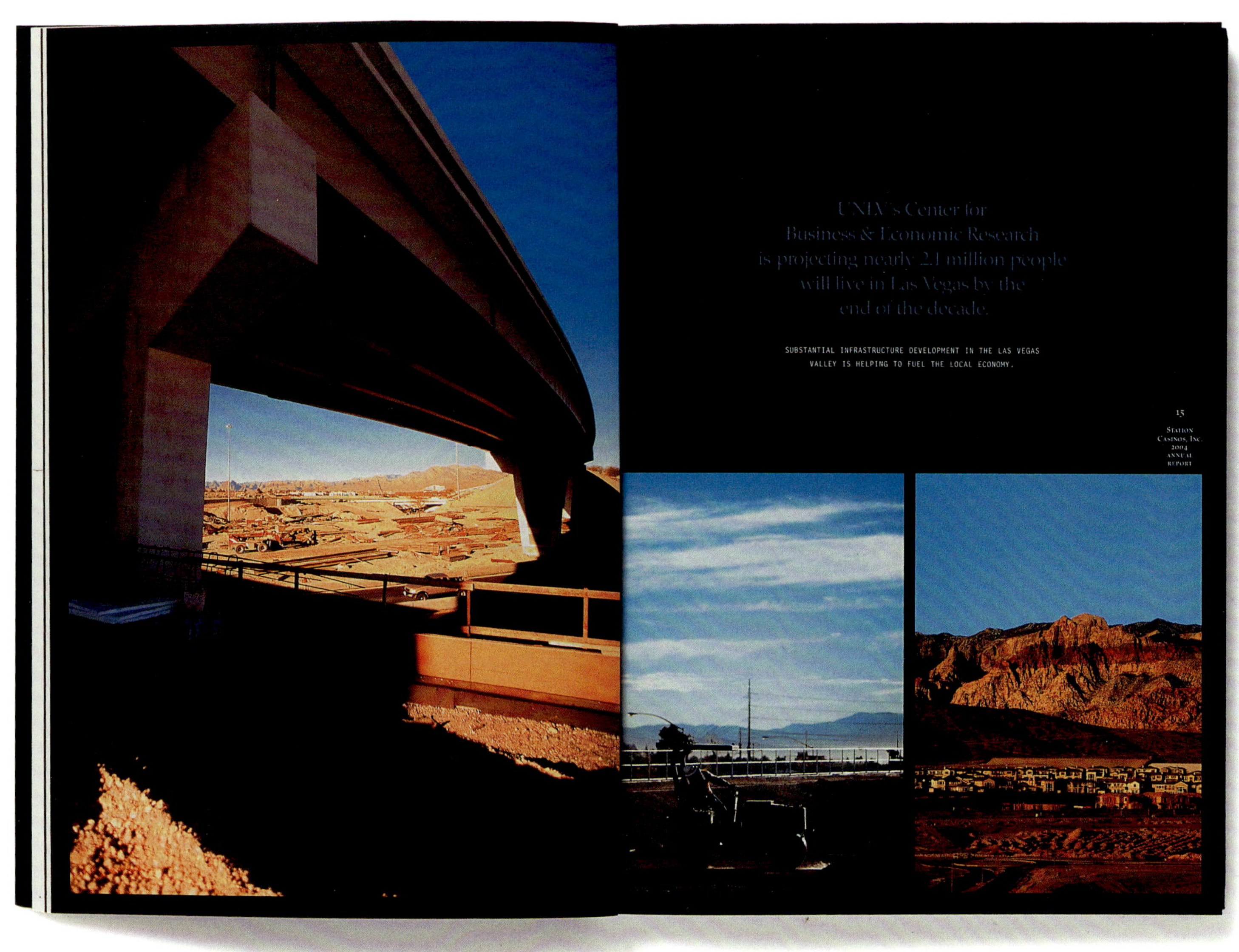

You know you are on your way when you find smart clients that allow you to do great work so that at the end of the day everyone is satisfied and proud of the effort.

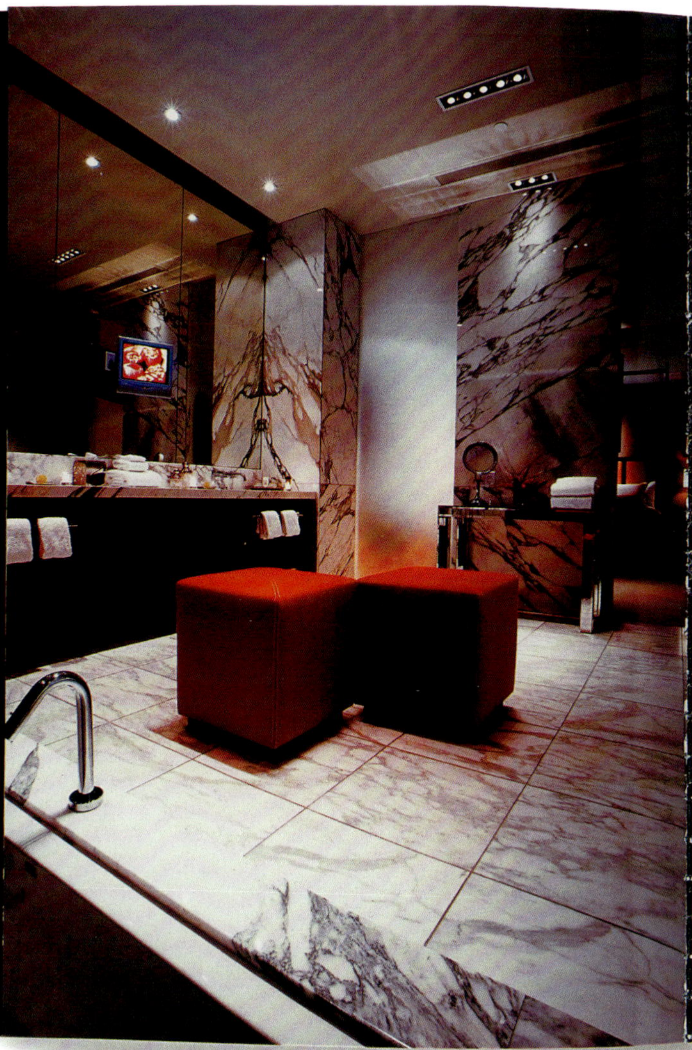

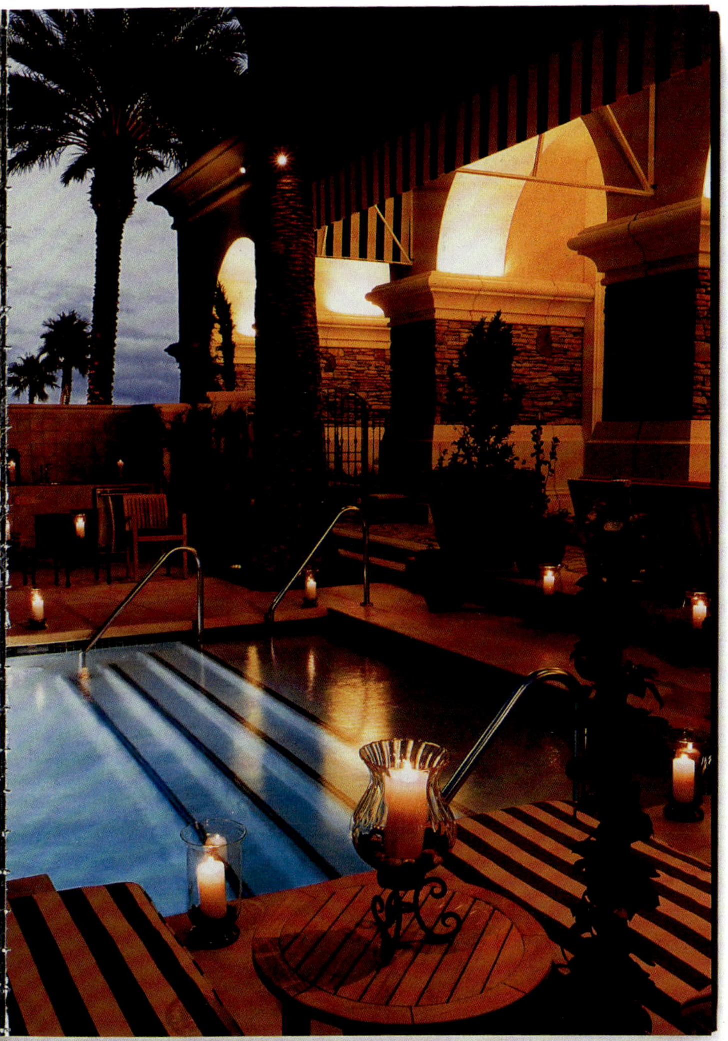

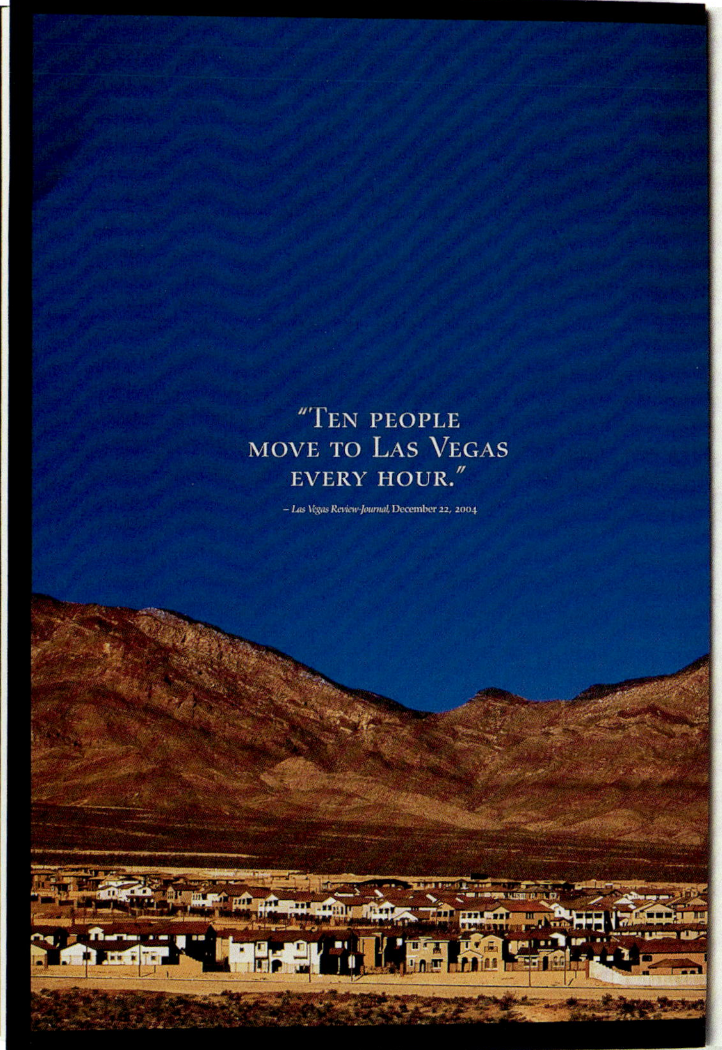

Demand Driver: Population Growth

For the eighteenth year in a row, Nevada has led the country as the fastest growing state, in large measure due to the rapid growth in Southern Nevada. In 2004, the population in the Las Vegas area grew by 95,000 people. Roughly 5,000-8,000 people per month move to Las Vegas due to the availability of good jobs, the fact that there are no state, personal or corporate income taxes, the great year round climate, the relatively low cost of living compared to surrounding states and a variety of entertainment options which are especially appealing to seniors. Clark County has been the fastest growing county in the country for some time, and now North Las Vegas is the second fastest growing city in the country growing 25% over the last three years. The city of Henderson is now the third fastest growing city in the country with 23% growth over the last three years and recently surpassed Reno to become the second largest city in Nevada.

17
Station Casinos, Inc. 2004 Annual Report

Clark County Population
(in thousands)

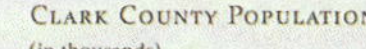

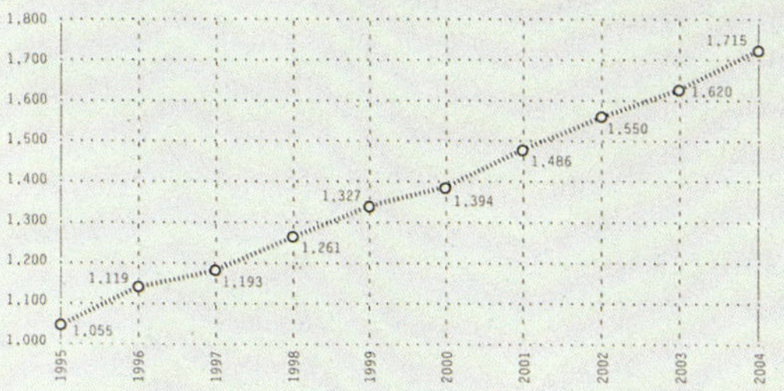

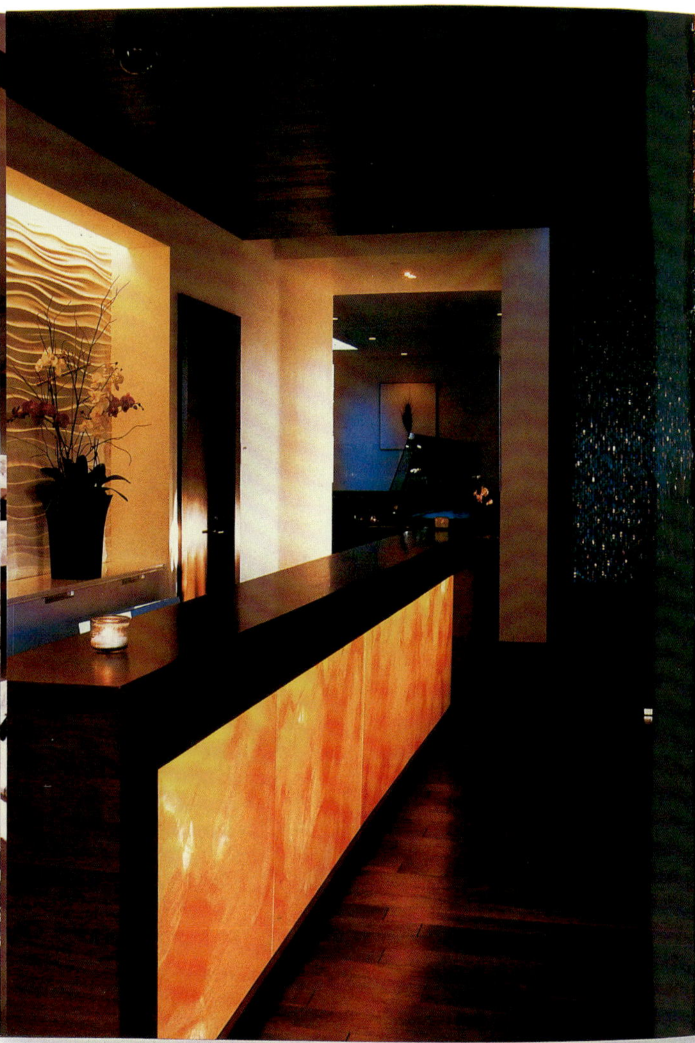

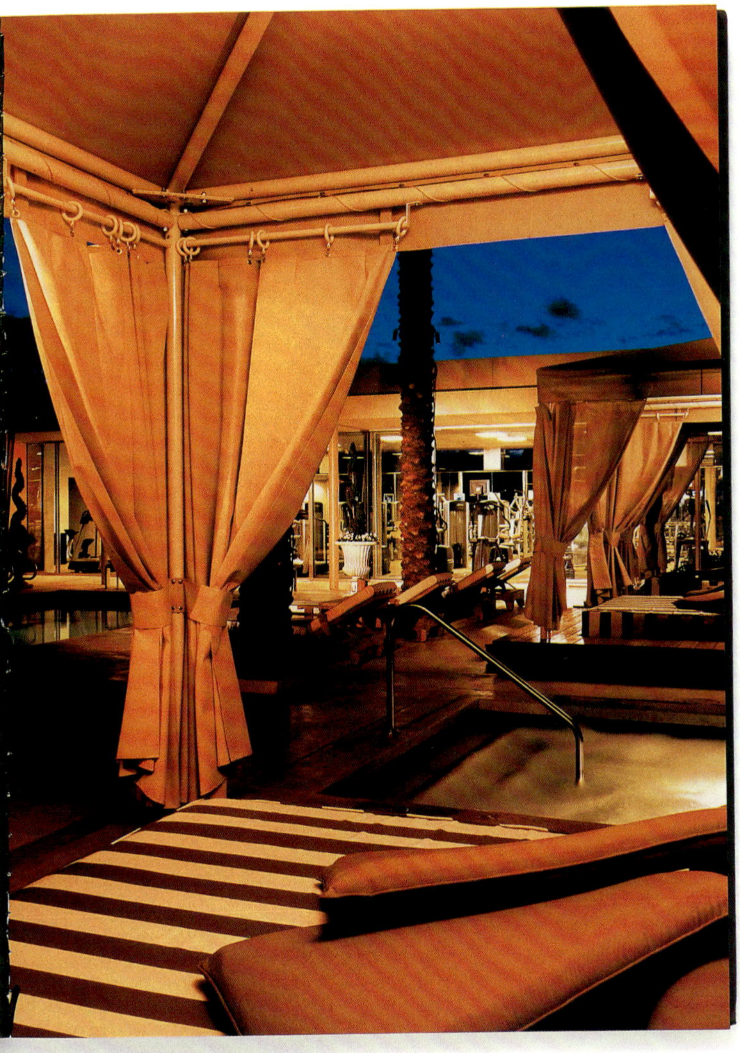

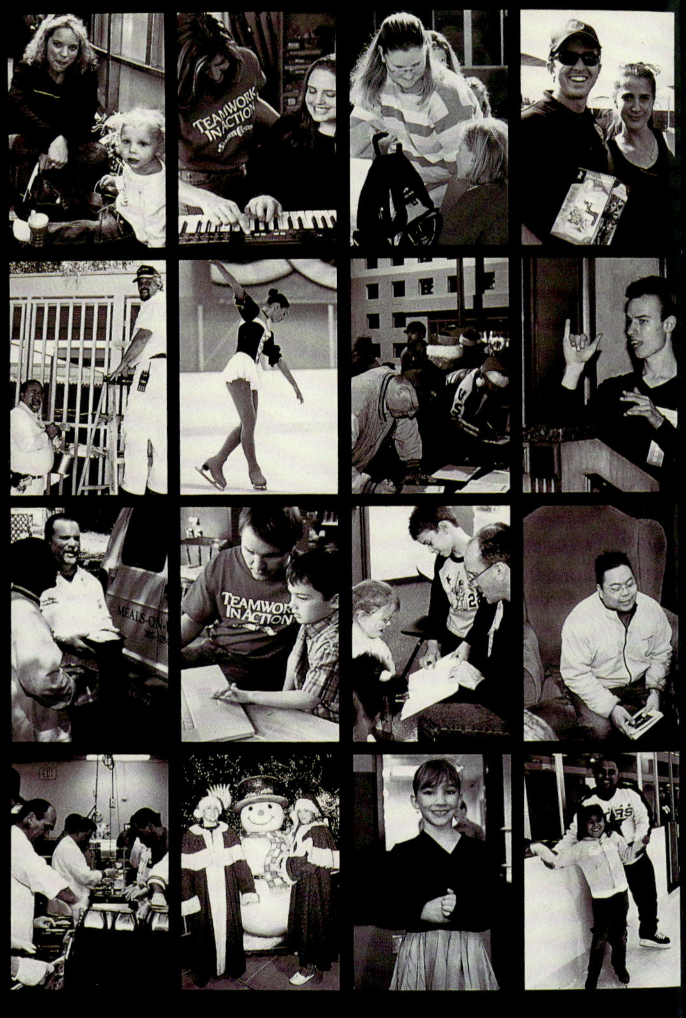

TEAMWORK IN ACTION

TEAMWORK IN ACTION

2004 Areas of Giving

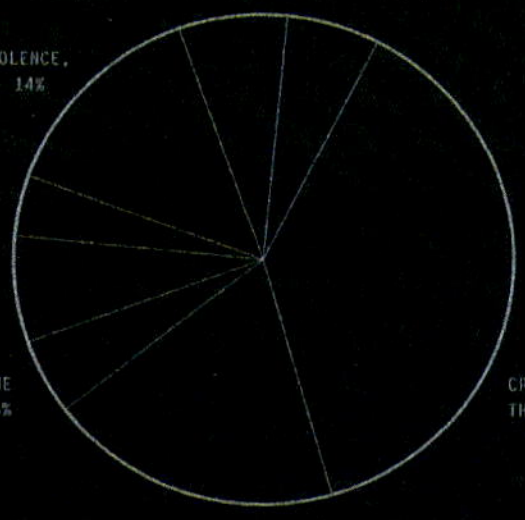

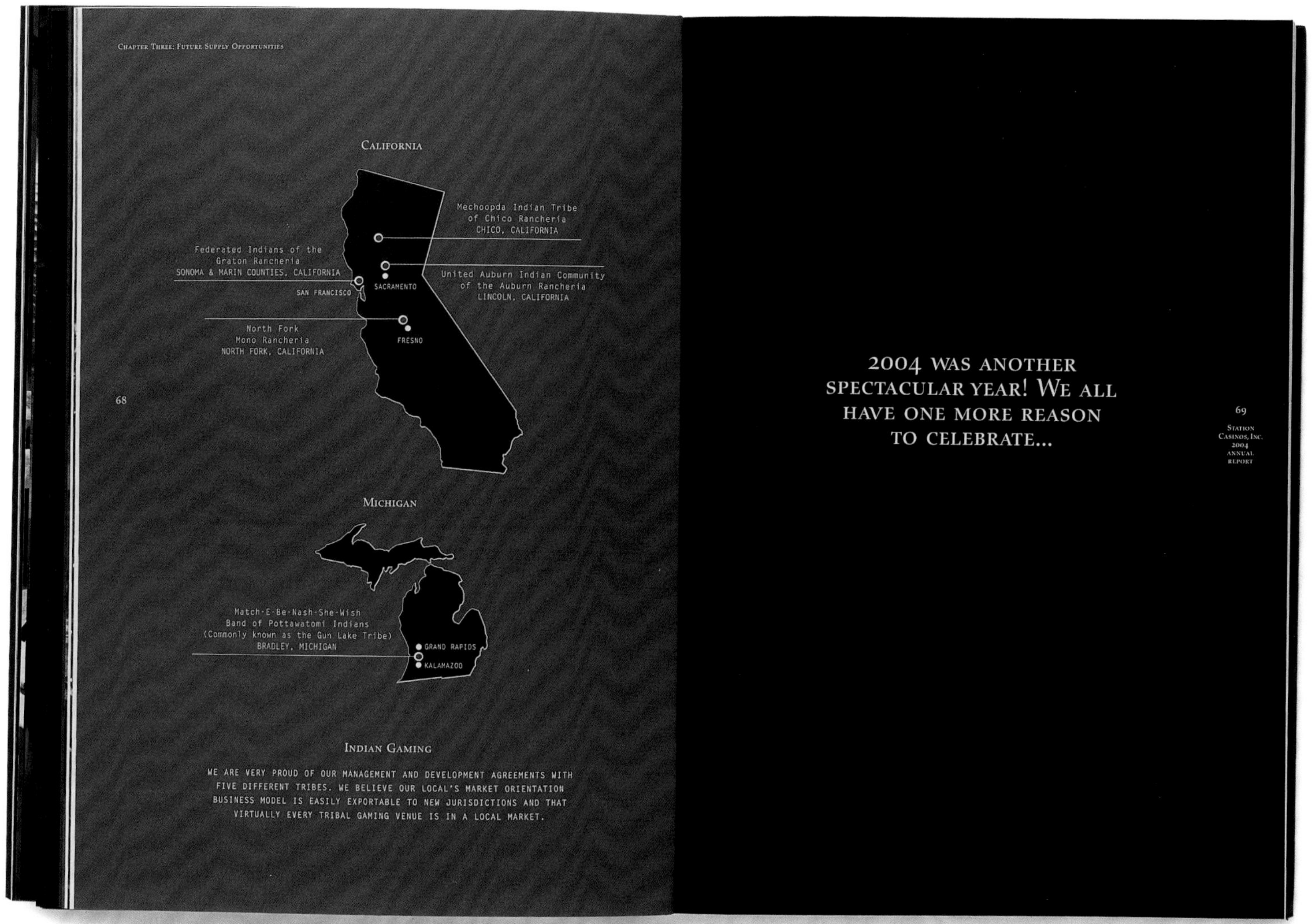

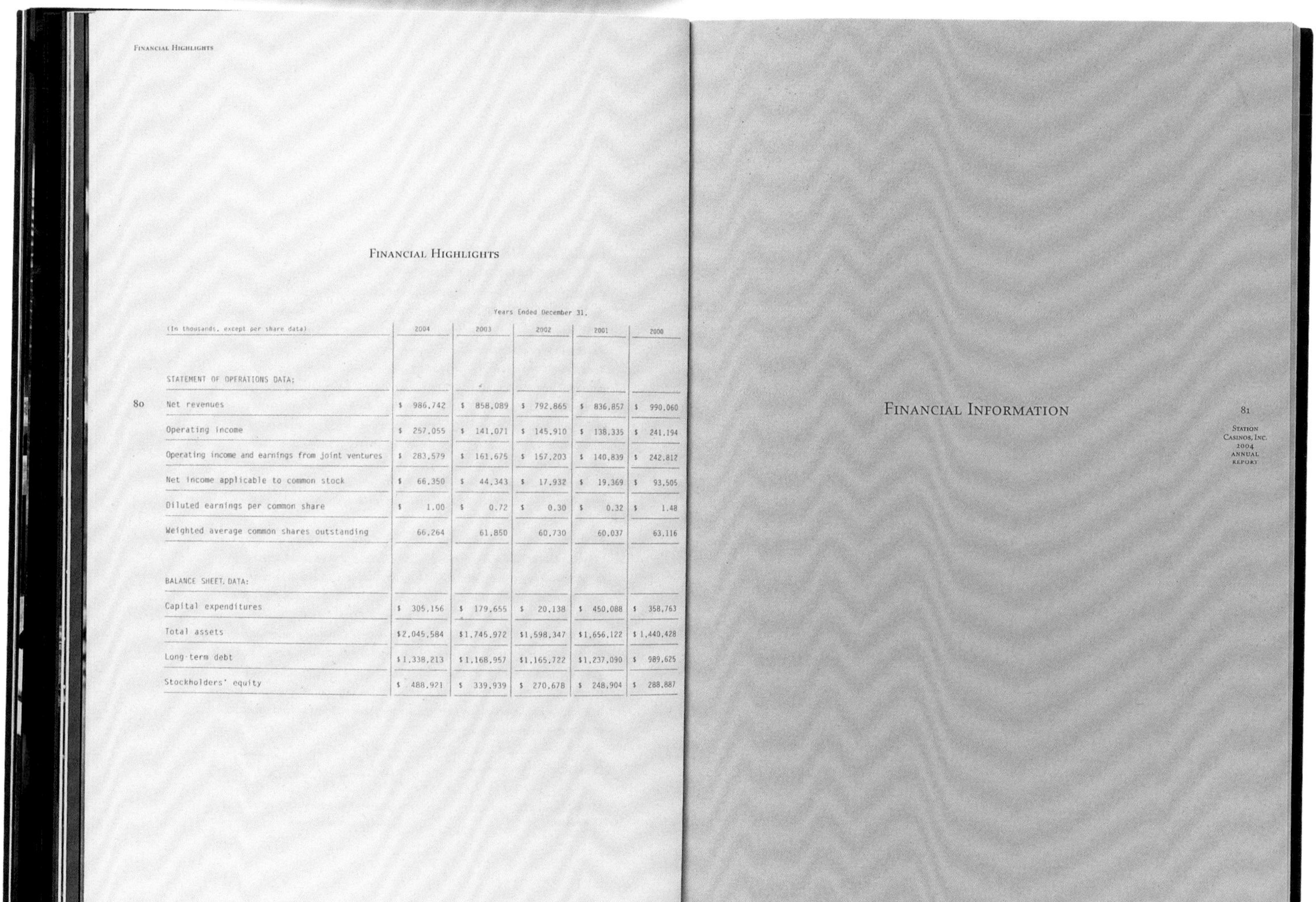

California

Mechoopda Indian Tribe
of Chico Rancheria
CHICO, CALIFORNIA

Federated Indians of the
Graton Rancheria
SONOMA & MARIN COUNTIES, CALIFORNIA

United Auburn Indian Community
of the Auburn Rancheria
LINCOLN, CALIFORNIA

SACRAMENTO

SAN FRANCISCO

North Fork
Mono Rancheria
NORTH FORK, CALIFORNIA

FRESNO

Michigan

Match-E-Be-Nash-She-Wish
Band of Pottawatomi Indians
(Commonly known as the Gun Lake Tribe)
BRADLEY, MICHIGAN

GRAND RAPIDS

KALAMAZOO

Indian Gaming

WE ARE VERY PROUD OF OUR MANAGEMENT AND DEVELOPMENT AGREEMENTS WITH FIVE DIFFERENT TRIBES. WE BELIEVE OUR LOCAL'S MARKET ORIENTATION BUSINESS MODEL IS EASILY EXPORTABLE TO NEW JURISDICTIONS AND THAT VIRTUALLY EVERY TRIBAL GAMING VENUE IS IN A LOCAL MARKET.

2004 WAS ANOTHER SPECTACULAR YEAR! WE ALL HAVE ONE MORE REASON TO CELEBRATE...

Financial Highlights

Years Ended December 31,

(In thousands, except per share data)	2004	2003	2002	2001	2000
STATEMENT OF OPERATIONS DATA:					
Net revenues	$ 986,742	$ 858,089	$ 792,865	$ 836,857	$ 990,060
Operating income	$ 257,055	$ 141,071	$ 145,910	$ 138,335	$ 241,194
Operating income and earnings from joint ventures	$ 283,579	$ 161,675	$ 157,203	$ 140,839	$ 242,812
Net income applicable to common stock	$ 66,350	$ 44,343	$ 17,932	$ 19,369	$ 93,505
Diluted earnings per common share	$ 1.00	$ 0.72	$ 0.30	$ 0.32	$ 1.48
Weighted average common shares outstanding	66,264	61,850	60,730	60,037	63,116
BALANCE SHEET DATA:					
Capital expenditures	$ 305,156	$ 179,655	$ 20,138	$ 450,088	$ 358,763
Total assets	$2,045,584	$1,745,972	$1,598,347	$1,656,122	$1,440,428
Long-term debt	$1,338,213	$1,168,957	$1,165,722	$1,237,090	$ 989,625
Stockholders' equity	$ 488,921	$ 339,939	$ 270,678	$ 248,904	$ 288,887

Financial Information

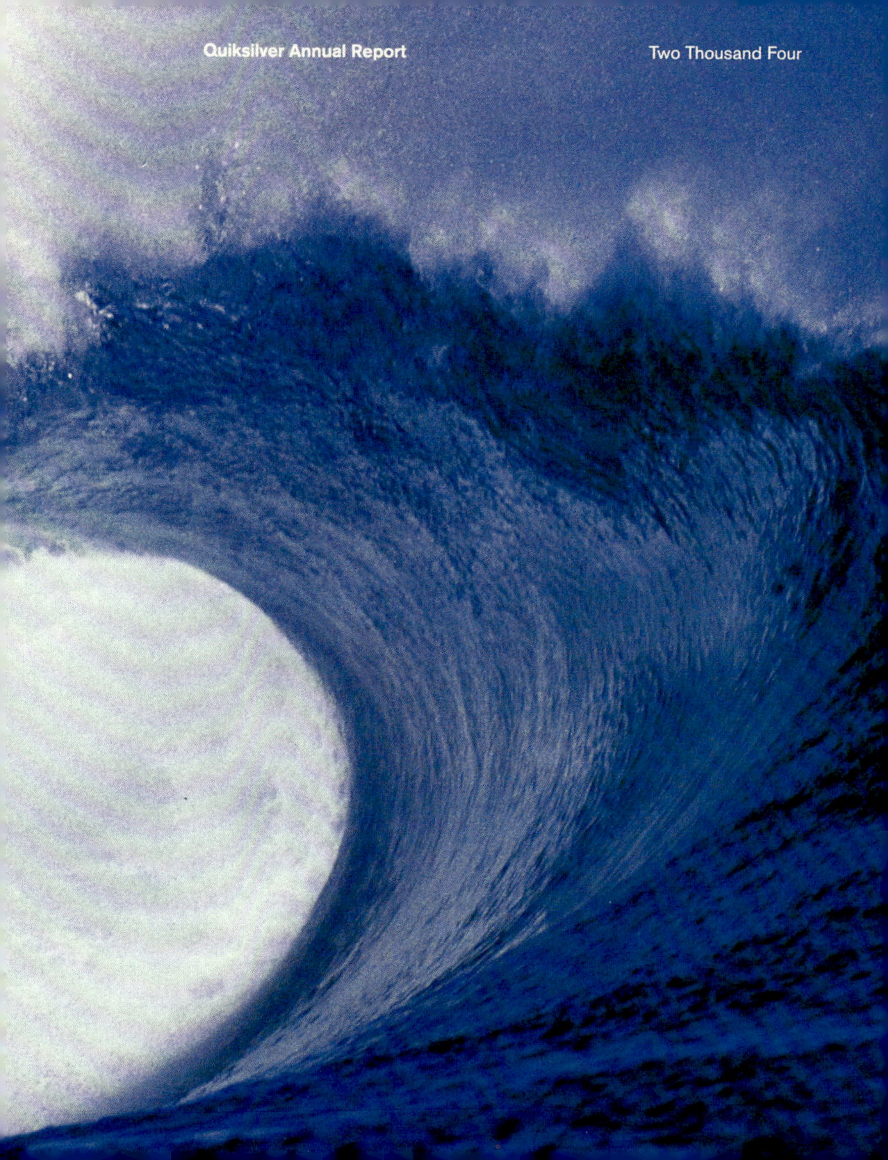
Quiksilver Annual Report
Two Thousand Four

Art Director: David Stoyan Wooters
Designer: Juan Valadez

Printer: ColorGraphics
Paper: cover paper: 27 pt Fibermark, Touche, Black

text paper: Sappi, Patina, Matte, Book, 80lb
Page count: 130 +cover

Print run: 17,000
Size: 8.5" x 11"
Number of Images: 100+

Client: Quiksilver is a leading global youth apparel company.

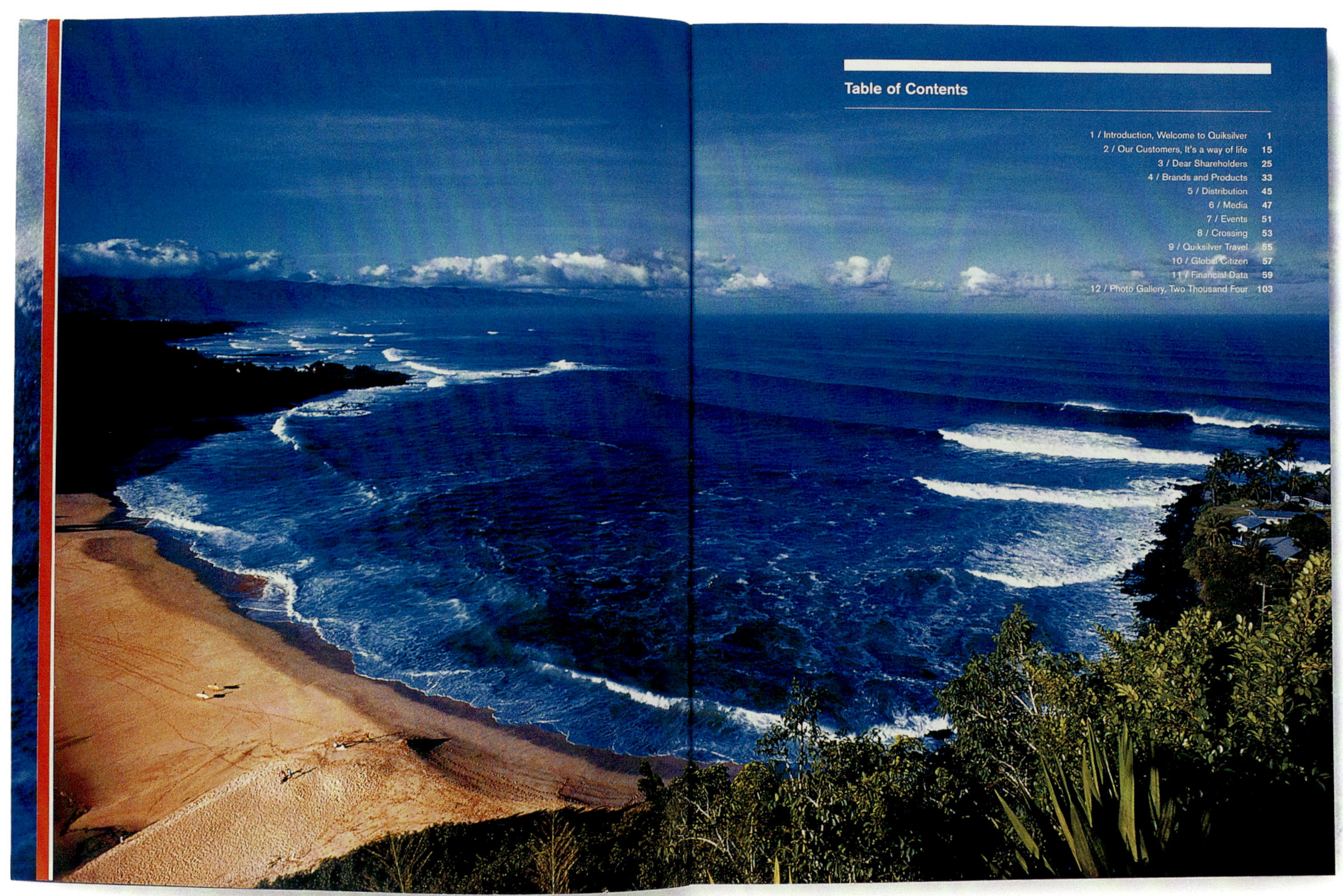

Q&A with Stoyan Design

What was the client's directive?

To produce an Annual Report that reflects the company's brand, a multi-national apparel company grounded in the philosophy of youth with yearly revenues of over a billion dollars.

What was the approach?

We wanted to create a report that was an in depth look at the company. In essence a report that took on the look and feel of a comprehensive book on the subject of Quiksilver.

Were you happy with the results?

We were very happy with the result and so was the client.

How involved was the CEO in your meetings, presentations, etc.?

The CEO is involved throughout the project. He has a strong sense of the culture of the company and gives us great input at every stage.

Do you feel that designers are becoming more involved in copywriting?

The better the writer the better the designer.

How do you define success in Annual Report design?

A report that is well received and understood by all types of people is the one I consider most successful.

How important are awards to your client?

Very few of my clients care about awards. They want to know we are concerned with getting the appropriate message out rather than trying to win an award.

Most clients are more concerned with messages than awards.

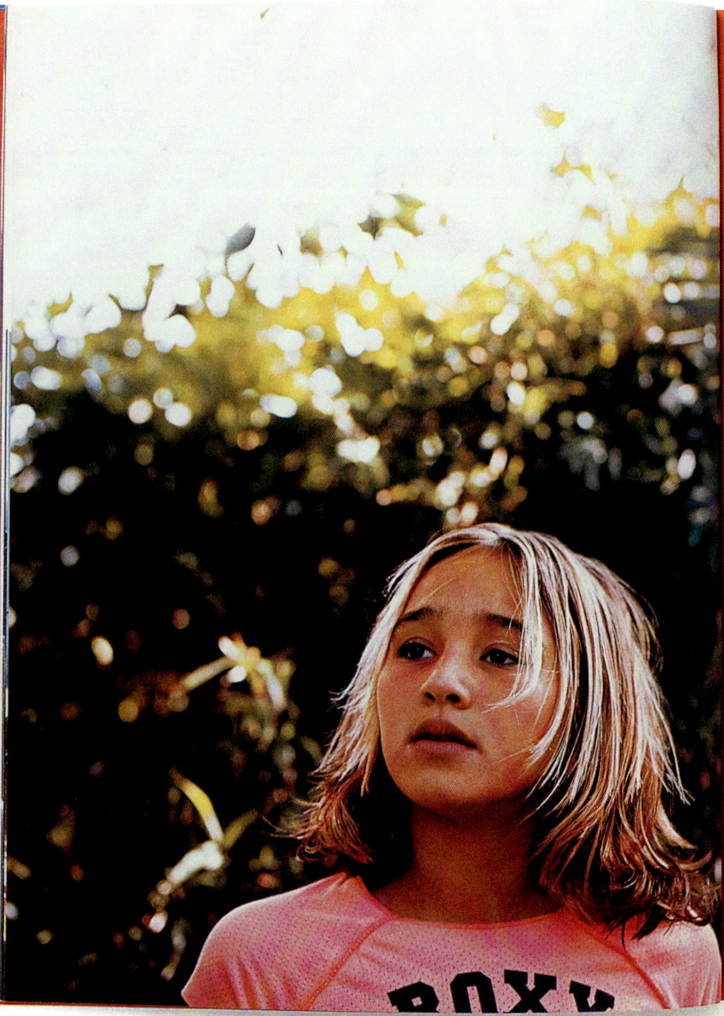

Our Customers

Chapter 2

15

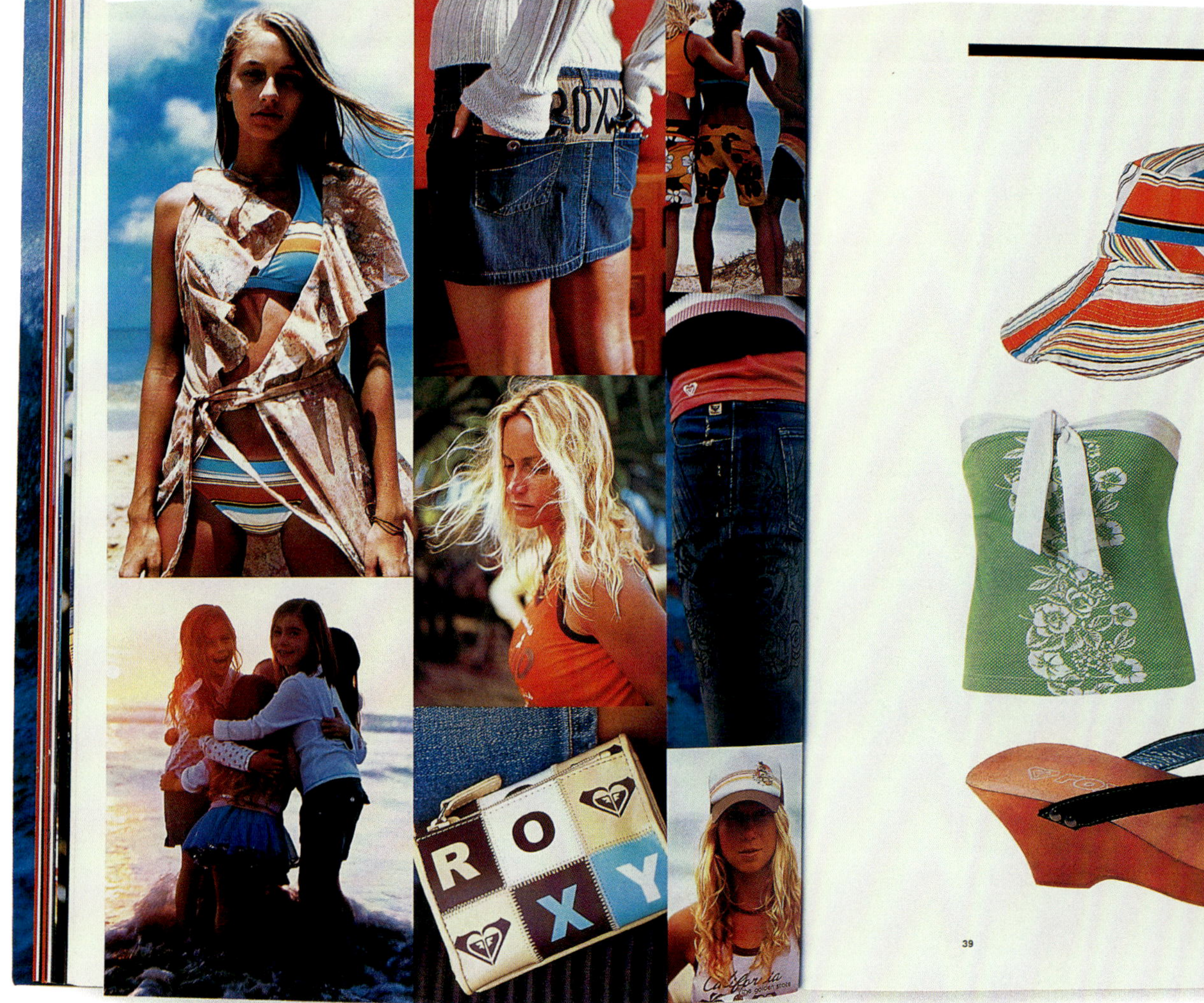

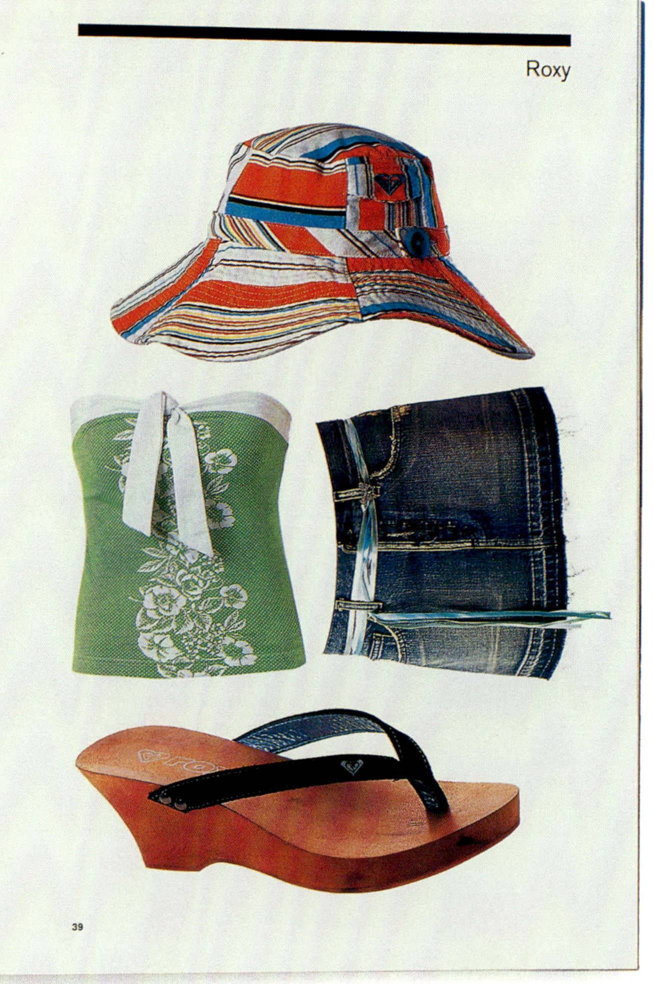

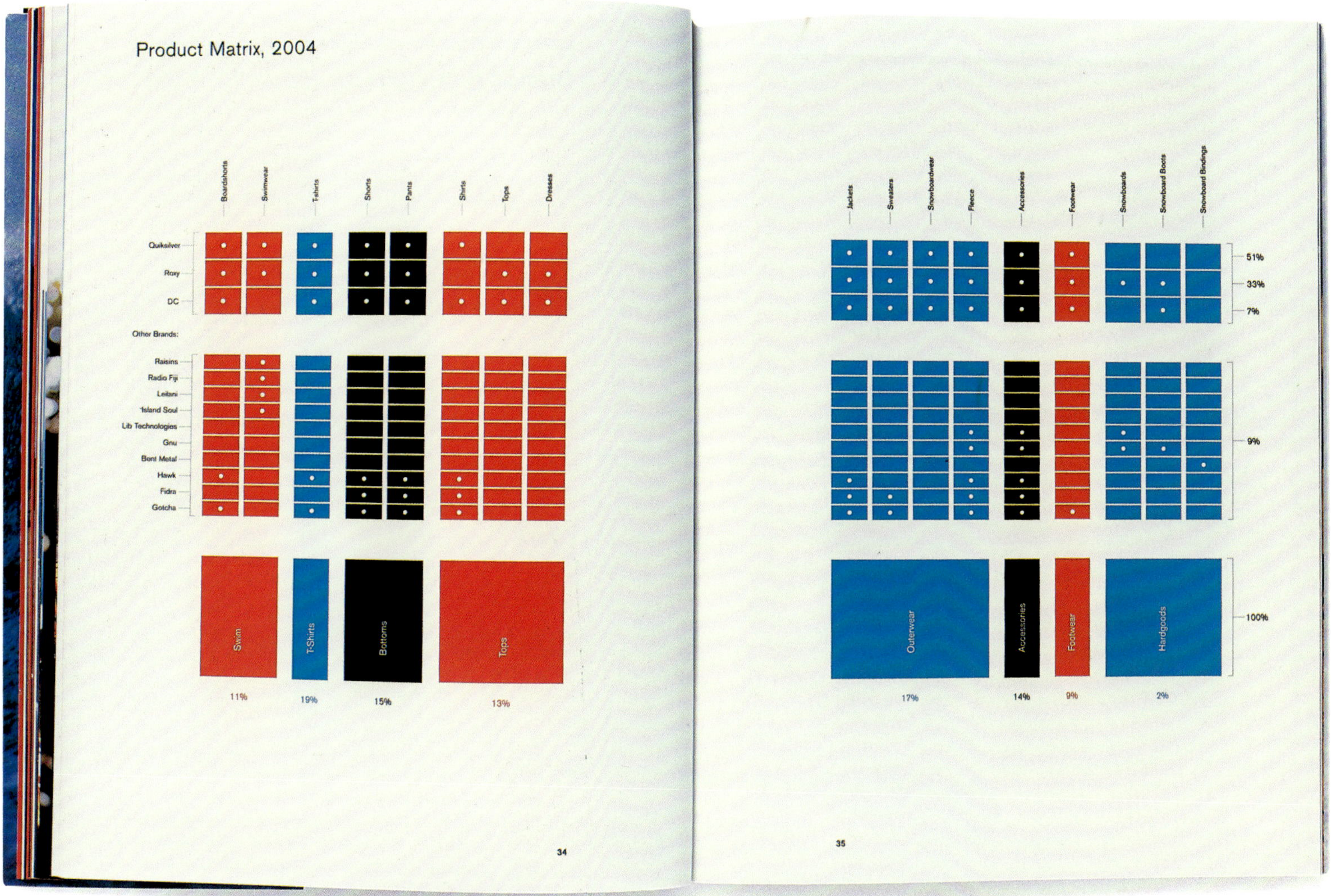

Product Matrix, 2004

Boardshorts
Swimwear
T-shirts
Shorts
Pants
Shirts
Tops
Dresses

Quiksilver
Roxy
DC

Other Brands:

Raisins
Radio Fiji
Leilani
Island Soul
Lib Technologies
Gnu
Bent Metal
Hawk
Fidra
Gotcha

Swim
T-Shirts
Bottoms
Tops

11%
19%
15%
13%

Jackets
Sweaters
Snowboardwear
Fleece
Accessories
Footwear
Snowboards
Snowboard Boots
Snowboard Bindings

51%
33%
7%
9%
100%

Outerwear
Accessories
Footwear
Hardgoods

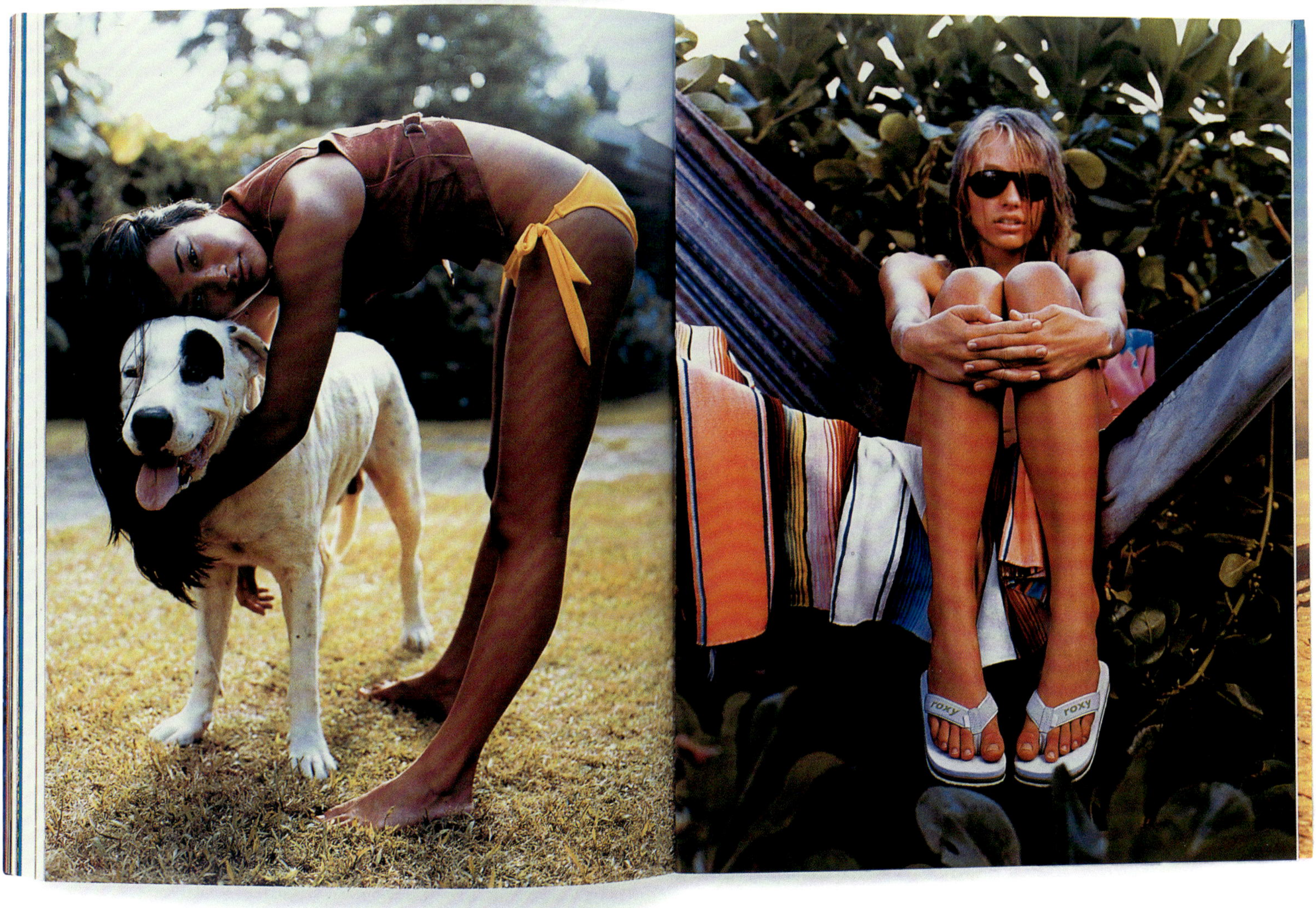

17%
14%
9%
2%

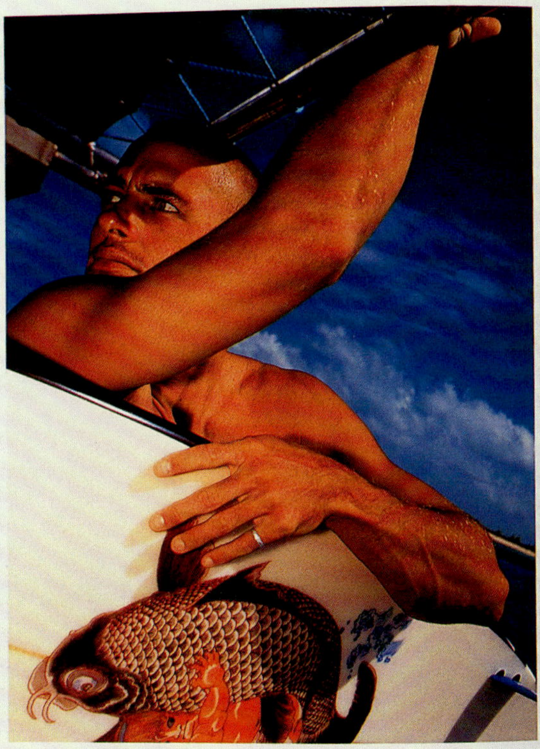

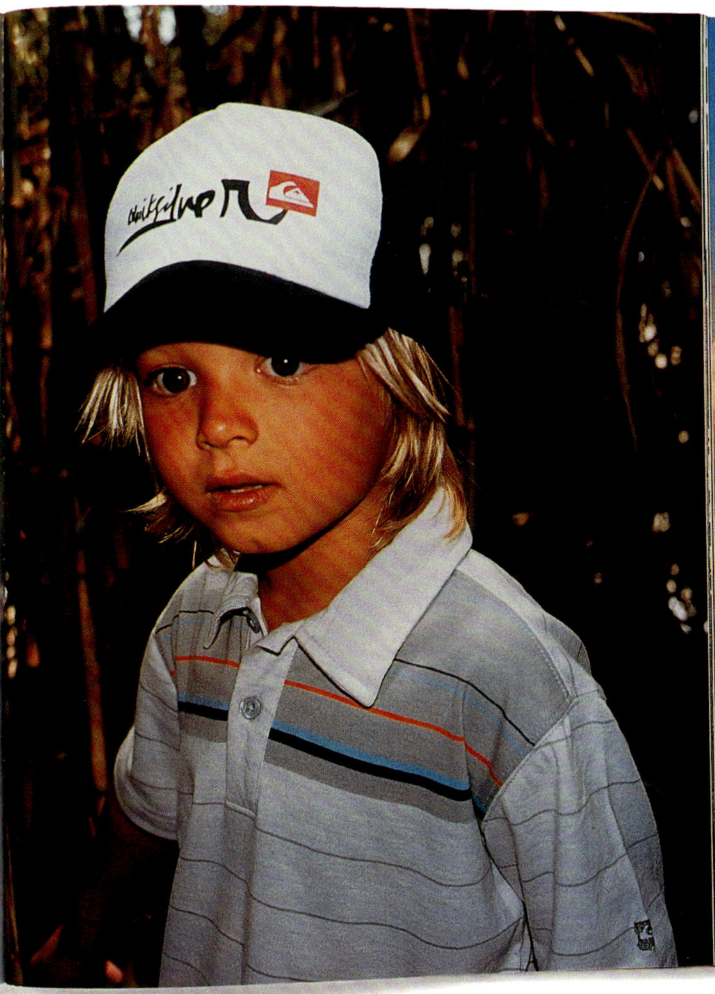

5 Photo: Joliphotos.com
Waimea Bay, Hawaii, USA
2004
The Quiksilver in Memory of Eddie Aikau
Big Wave Invitational - Twenty Year
Anniversary

6 Photo: Jeff Hornbaker
Caribbean
2004
The Quiksilver Crossing
Kelly Slater

7 Photo: Stephen Zeigler
Laguna Beach, California, USA
2004
Jack Genova

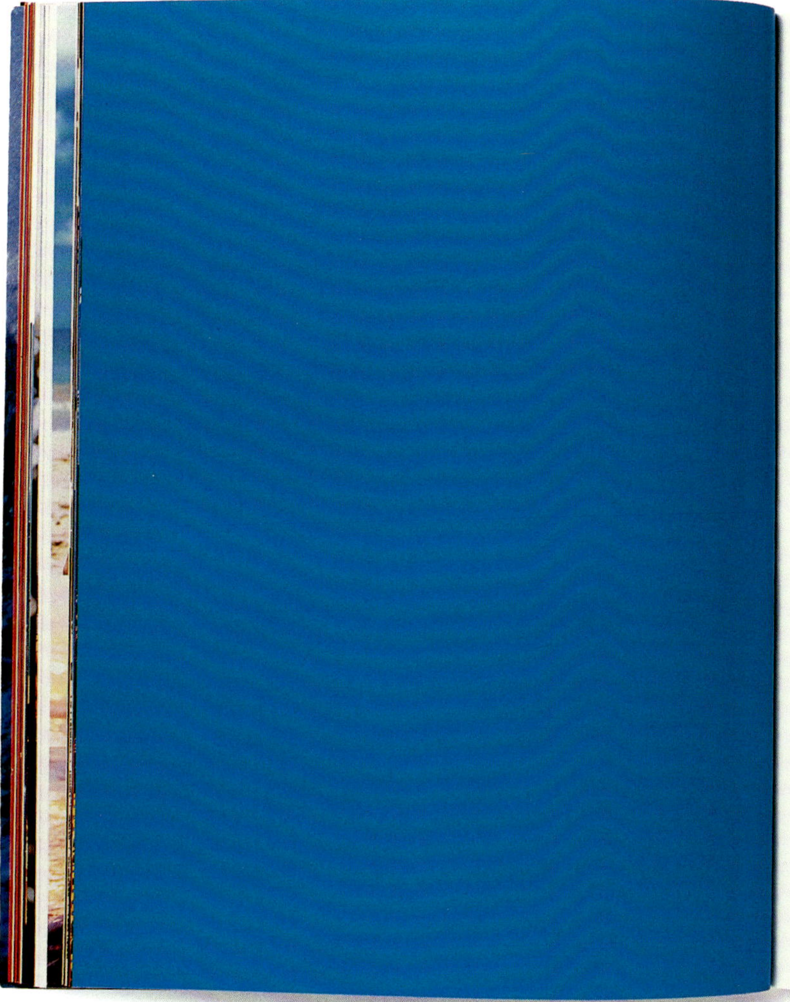

Financial Data

Chapter 11

Notes to Consolidated Financial Statements

Note 15. Segment and Geographic Information

Operating segments are defined as components of an enterprise about which separate financial information is available that is evaluated regularly by the Company's management in deciding how to allocate resources and in assessing performance. The Company operates exclusively in the consumer products industry in which the Company designs, produces and distributes clothing, accessories and related products. Operating results of the Company's various product lines have been aggregated because of their common economic and operating characteristics and their reliance on shared operating functions. Within the consumer products industry, the Company has historically operated in the Americas (primarily the U.S.) and Europe. Effective with its acquisition of Quiksilver Asia/Pacific on December 1, 2002, the Company has added operations in Australia, Japan, New Zealand and other Southeast Asian countries and territories. Accordingly, the Company revised its geographic segments to include Asia/Pacific and corporate operations. Costs that support all three geographic segments, including trademark protection, trademark maintenance and licensing functions are part of corporate operations. Corporate operations also includes sourcing income and gross profit earned from the Company's licensees. No single customer accounts for more than 10% of the Company's revenues.

Although the Company operates in one industry segment, it produces different product lines within the segment. The percentages of revenues attributable to each product line are as follows:

	Percentage of Revenues		
	2004	2003	2002
T-Shirts	19%	20%	20%
Accessories	14	14	12
Jackets, sweaters and snowboardwear	12	12	12
Pants	10	11	11
Shirts	9	10	11
Footwear	9	5	4
Swimwear, excluding boardshorts	7	8	9
Fleece	5	6	7
Shorts	5	6	6
Boardshorts	4	4	3
Tops and dresses	4	3	3
Snowboards, snowboard boots, bindings and accessories	2	1	2
	100%	100%	100%

96

Information related to the Company's geographical segments is as follows:

Years Ended October 31, (in thousands)	2004	2003	2002
Revenues:			
Americas	$ 616,818	$492,442	$418,008
Europe	496,276	386,226	282,684
Asia/Pacific	148,733	94,187	–
Corporate operations	5,112	2,150	4,792
Consolidated	$1,266,939	$975,005	$705,484
Gross profit:			
Americas	$ 251,357	$197,434	$153,561
Europe	251,692	189,462	127,976
Asia/Pacific	73,152	44,206	–
Corporation operations	1,958	2,150	4,792
Consolidated	$ 578,159	$433,252	$286,329
Operating income:			
Americas	$ 63,811	$ 45,734	$ 35,377
Europe	73,517	61,941	41,327
Asia/Pacific	21,164	12,168	–
Corporate operations	(26,554)	(18,778)	(7,000)
Consolidated	$ 131,938	$101,065	$ 69,704
Identifiable assets:			
Americas	$ 443,028	$300,464	$226,715
Europe	413,454	299,977	204,759
Asia/Pacific	118,918	95,835	–
Corporate operations	15,590	11,694	19,115
Consolidated	$ 990,990	$707,970	$450,589
Goodwill:			
Americas	$ 86,382	$ 50,670	$ 15,686
Europe	70,057	41,592	11,292
Asia/Pacific	13,346	6,571	–
Consolidated	$ 169,785	$ 98,833	$ 26,978

Goodwill increased in the Americas, Europe and Asia/Pacific during the fiscal year ended October 31, 2004 as a result of the DC acquisition and a contingent payment related to the acquisition of Quiksilver International. Goodwill increased in the Americas, Europe and Asia/Pacific during the fiscal year ended October 31, 2003 as a result of the Company's acquisitions of its U.S. eyewear licensee, its European licensee for eyewear and wetsuits and its licensees in Australia and Japan. See Note 2 to these consolidated financial statements. Goodwill related to the acquisition of Quiksilver Asia/Pacific and the trademark value was allocated to each respective geographic segment based on where the benefits from these intangibles were estimated to be realized.

97

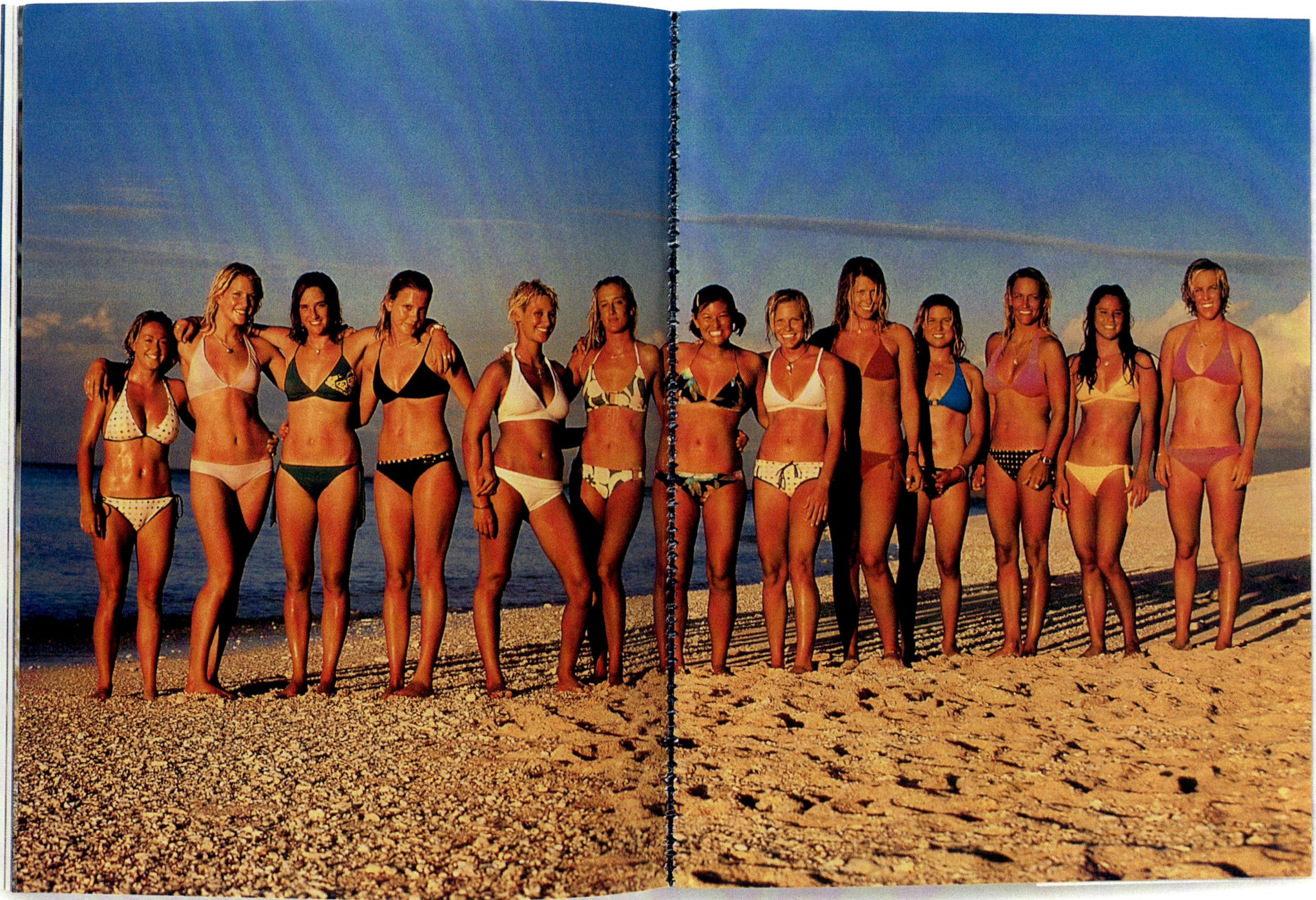

Westpac

Design Firm: DesignworksEnterpriseIG
Creative Director: Olivia Swinn

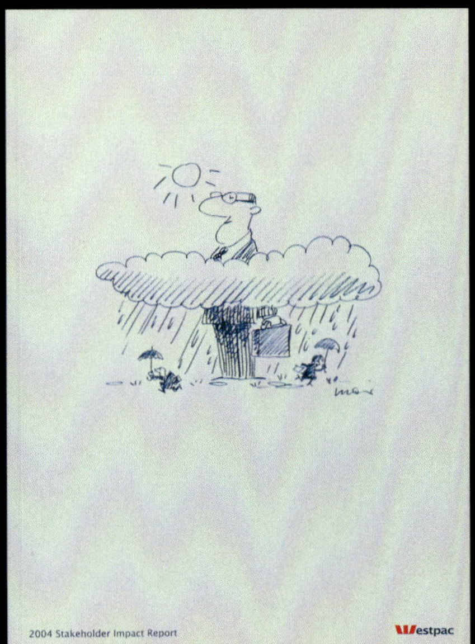

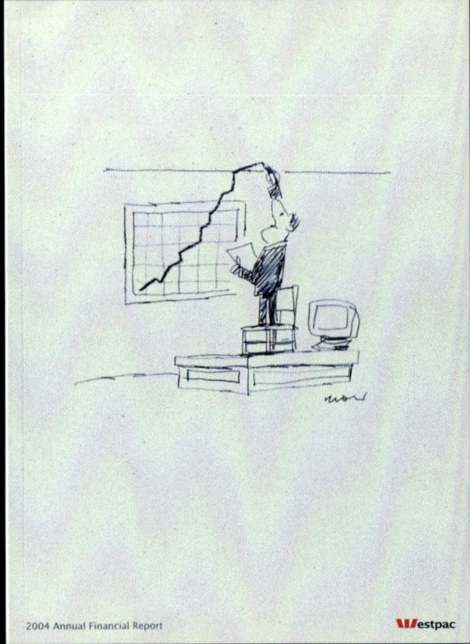

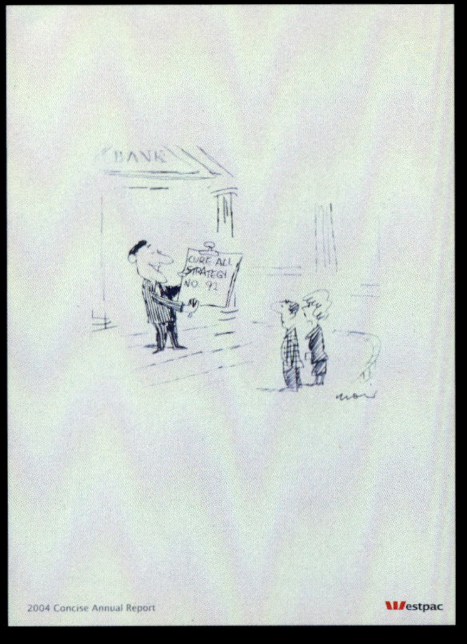

Creative Director: Olivia Swinn	Michael Pennington	Printer: Palms Consortium	84 +cover Print run: 160,000	Number of Images: 30
Designer: Sabine Steiner	Illustrator: Alan Moir	Paper: Monza Page count:	Size: 8.2677" x 11.6929"	Client: Westpac, banking corp.

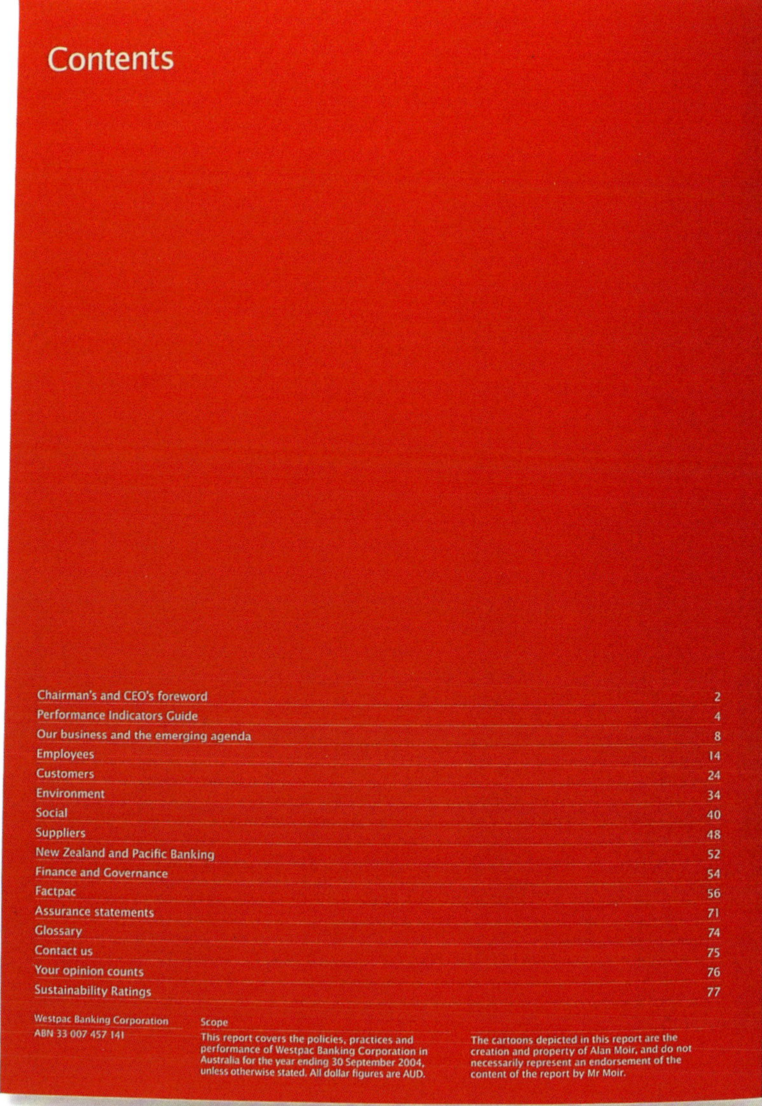

Contents

Westpac Banking Corporation
ABN 33 007 457 141

Scope

This report covers the policies, practices and performance of Westpac Banking Corporation in Australia for the year ending 30 September 2004, unless otherwise stated. All dollar figures are AUD.

The cartoons depicted in this report are the creation and property of Alan Moir, and do not necessarily represent an endorsement of the content of the report by Mr Moir.

Just who is prospering?

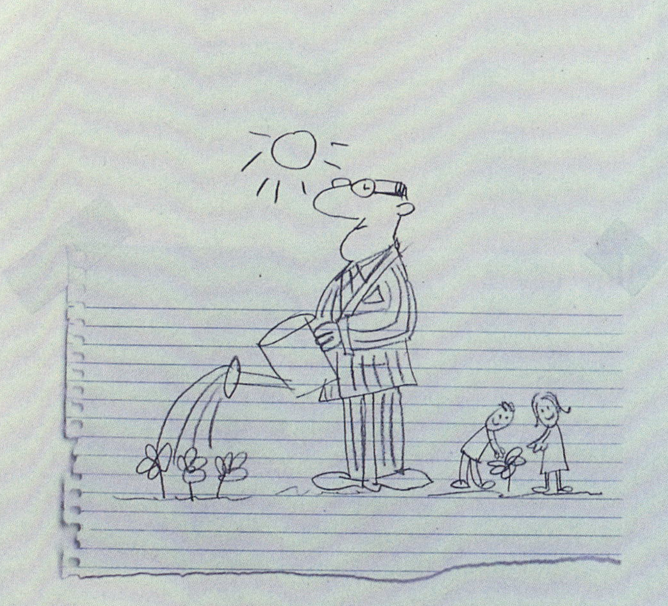

Banks and big companies are often accused of being out of touch and not aware of their impacts in society. Because we know that a prosperous business goes hand-in-hand with a prosperous society, our social, environmental and economic performance is central to the way we operate.

1

Q&A with DesignworksEnterpriseIG

What was the client's directive?

To design an Annual Report which reflected that, unlike most banks, Westpac has been able to create a strong strategic plan for their future and truly stick to it.

How did you define the problem?

We were concerned that such a positive spin on their company would ultimately look like gratuitous PR, so we needed a vehicle to ensure that readers understood that Westpac had a true grasp of public opinion on banks in general.

What was the approach?

We created a report which delivered the common public perceptions of certain banking issues, for example, queueing via an unbiased humorous cartoon which Westpac was then able to refute, explain or give more information on.

Were you happy with the result? What could have been better?

We have done the Westpac report for many years and look for it to be a continued provocative and honest statement about the banking world and where they sit in it.

How involved was the CEO in your meetings, presentations, etc.?

The CEO was involved in the initial concept meeting and then again with the board for direction and visual sign off.

Do you feel that designers are becoming more involved in copywriting?

We believe very strongly that design is empty without great writing. Gone are the days when designers put lorem ipsom in as headlines. We employ 2 full time writers in our NZ offices who are intensely involved in all projects. In Sydney we are still looking to recruit a full time writer, however as designers we find it critical to good work to either work on our own copy or to have a freelance writer.

How do you define success in Annual Report design?

We would define the success of an Annual Report as one that is a true brand touchstone.

How important are awards to your client?

Awards are a very good tool for us with our clients in that they create a lot of kudos for them within their organization. I don't think they would slavishly do something that went against their brand to win an award, but winning prestigious or renowned awards means that they are competing on a world stage with some of the best companies in the world, and for down under clients that is desirable. For us as designers the recognition and enthusiasm for awards means that often we can push more lateral and engaging solutions.

Westpac's plan is not new or complicated.

We want to be a simpler bank for customers to deal with – and a more efficient one in the way we are organised.

This requires an unswerving commitment to doing the right thing and doing things well, and we will not be distracted from this path.

In this report we take a closer look at how we are sticking to our plan and the way our strategy is increasing value at all levels of our business.

Westpac Banking Corporation
ABN 33 007 457 141

Information contained in or otherwise accessible through the websites mentioned in this concise annual report does not form part of the report.

Additionally, all references in this report to websites are inactive textual references and are for information only.

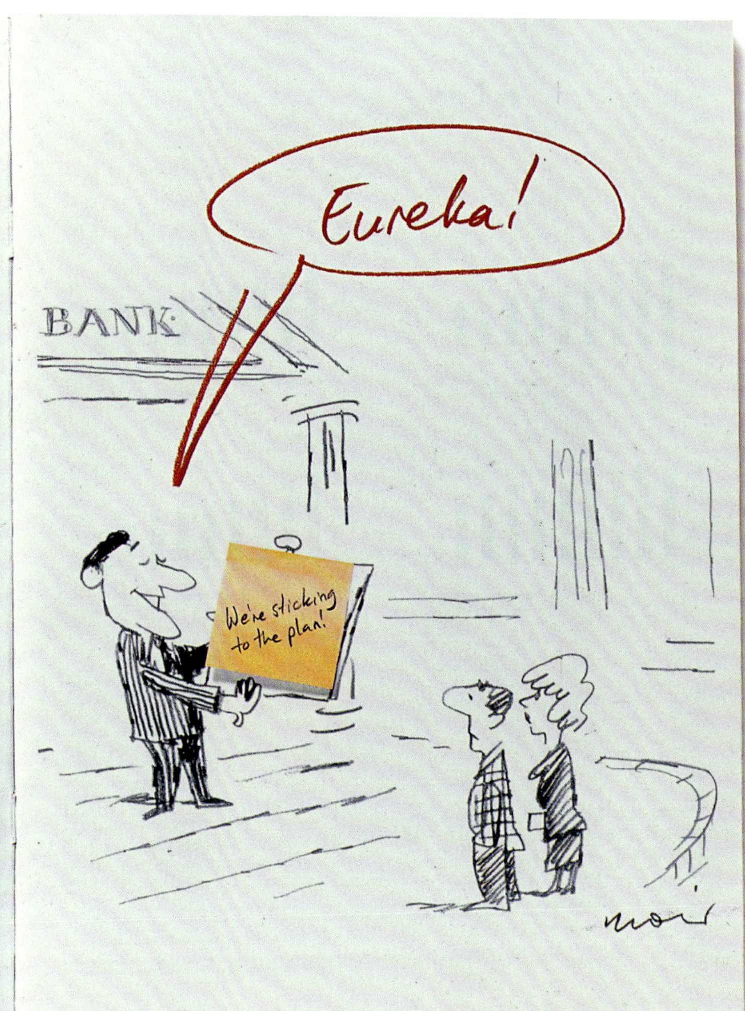

Because this process affects all of our people, we also believe that it is very important that everyone has the opportunity to get involved in the EDA process and have their say about the proposed changes which may affect them.

To date, we have completed several stages of the EDA process, including having developed the main themes for discussion with business leaders, two rounds of consultation with our people, and all the subsequent amendments to the proposed EDA as a result of employee feedback. We have also fully communicated the bargaining proposal internally to ensure everyone is aware of what is being put forward. We are now in formal discussions with the FSU.

Next steps include the employee vote on the final EDA proposal and, once it has the genuine approval of the majority of employees who would be covered by it (50% of employees plus one), it then goes to the Australian Industrial Relations Commission for certification. We will be in a better position to outline some of the key initiatives to emerge from this process in our next report.

Occupational health and safety (OHS)

We review our OHS performance against a number of interlinked performance measures. This helps us to understand the full range of issues affecting our people, and to better ensure their physical and emotional well-being.

Our Critical Incident Management Program provides assistance to employees requiring counselling after a traumatic event. We define a critical incident as any event that exposes our people to a life threatening situation or severe victimisation. This can include hold-ups, personal threats in the workplace, assaults or even significant external events where they impact on our staff such as floods or bushfires. From September 2003 to August 2004, the number of employees affected by a trauma and requiring debriefing dropped from approximately 1.7% in 2003 to 1.3%.

Significant events which occurred throughout the year in addition to armed hold-ups, included the accidental disturbance of asbestos in a couple of branches and offensive behaviour from a member of the public in a branch in Sydney.

While over the period, more of our people have been affected by incidents that are not related to hold-ups, our OHS team in Australia is nonetheless working with Physical Security Services to review the risk assessment procedures for branches to further reduce the likelihood of hold-ups in our branches.

During the period, the Lost Time Injury Frequency Rate (LTIFR) has risen from 6.54 to 7.07. The three most common causes for lost time injuries included body stressing, mental stress and slips and trips in the workplace. In response, we are investigating the causes of these issues in the workplace.

In particular, we will complete a National Workers' Compensation and OHS database in October 2004. This will enable us to conduct a more detailed analysis of trends for workplace incidents, injuries and hazards, and implement more effective preventative measures. The database will also facilitate an improved reporting framework on OHS performance, including quarterly reporting to the Board Social Responsibility Committee.

Our Employee Assistance Program (EAP) provides confidential counseling services for our people and their immediate families. The number of people utilising the program rose from 6.7% last year to 7.1% in 2004. Of those people who chose to access the service, around 25% were associated with work-related concerns, well within industry norms.

Employee satisfaction that OHS issues were effectively managed rose from 78% to 80% in the 2004 Staff Perspectives Survey.

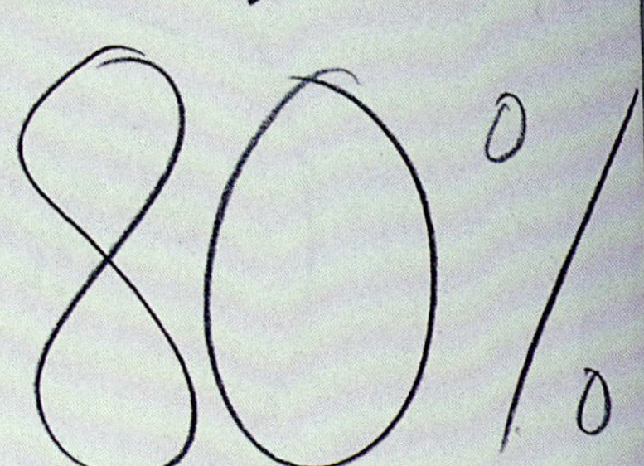

We will complete a National Workers' Compensation and OHS database in October 2004. This will enable us to conduct a more detailed analysis of trends for workplace incidents, injuries and hazards, and implement more effective preventative measures.

From September 2003 to August 2004, the number of employees affected by a trauma and requiring debriefing dropped from approximately 1.7% in 2003 to 1.3%.

To do – 2005

OBJECTIVES

- Recruit up to 900 mature age workers by 2005.
- Respond to key findings from the diversity component of the 2004 Staff Perspectives Survey.
- Implement phase one of eLearning.
- Reduce the average time away from work due to a compensable work-related injury or disease by 5%.

ASPIRATION TARGET

- Increase employee commitment by a further 3%.

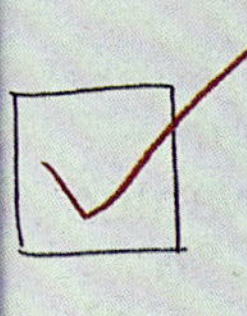

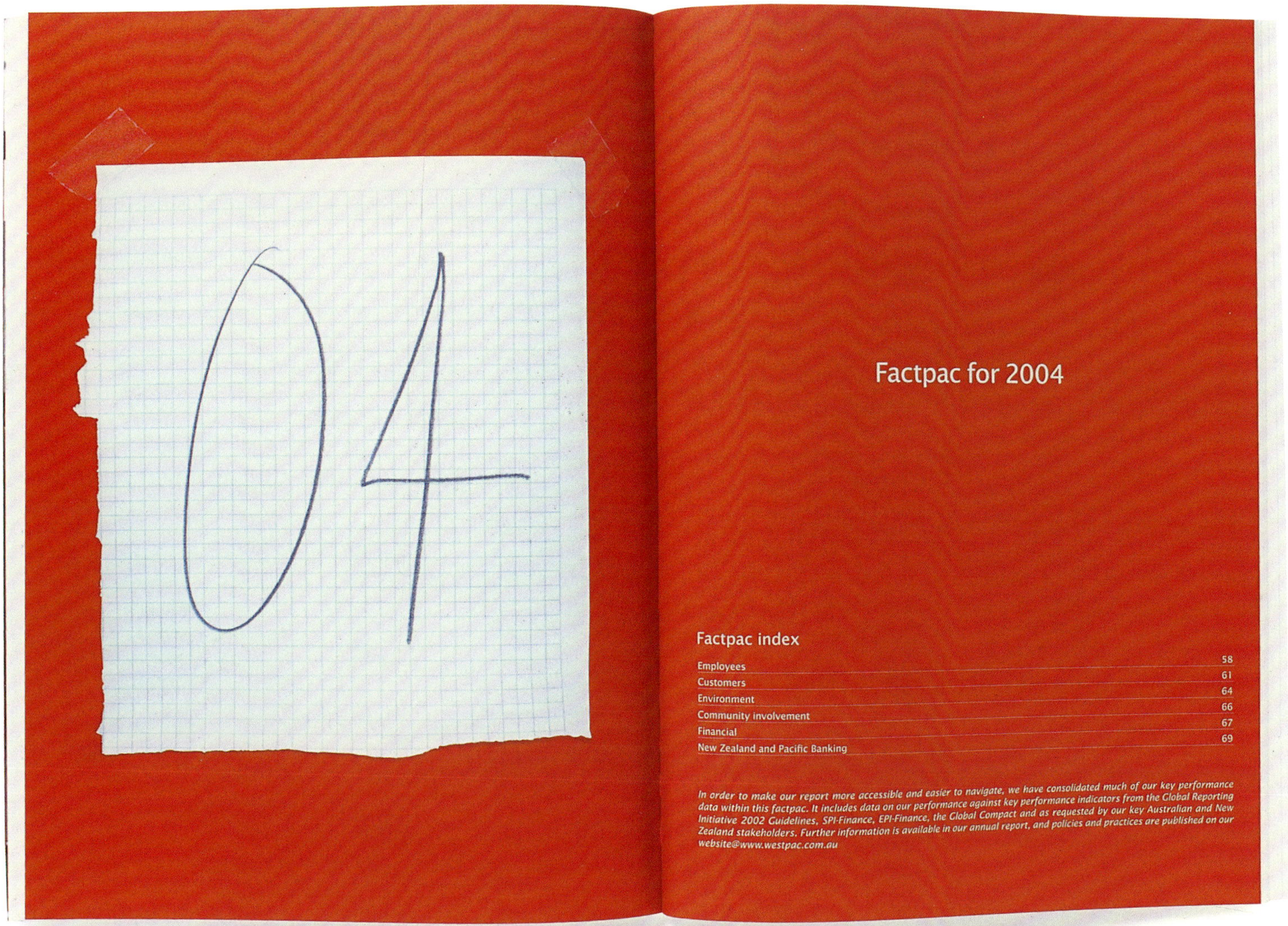

Factpac for 2004

Factpac index

In order to make our report more accessible and easier to navigate, we have consolidated much of our key performance data within this factpac. It includes data on our performance against key performance indicators from the Global Reporting Initiative 2002 Guidelines, SPI-Finance, EPI-Finance, the Global Compact and as requested by our key Australian and New Zealand stakeholders. Further information is available in our annual report, and policies and practices are published on our website@www.westpac.com.au

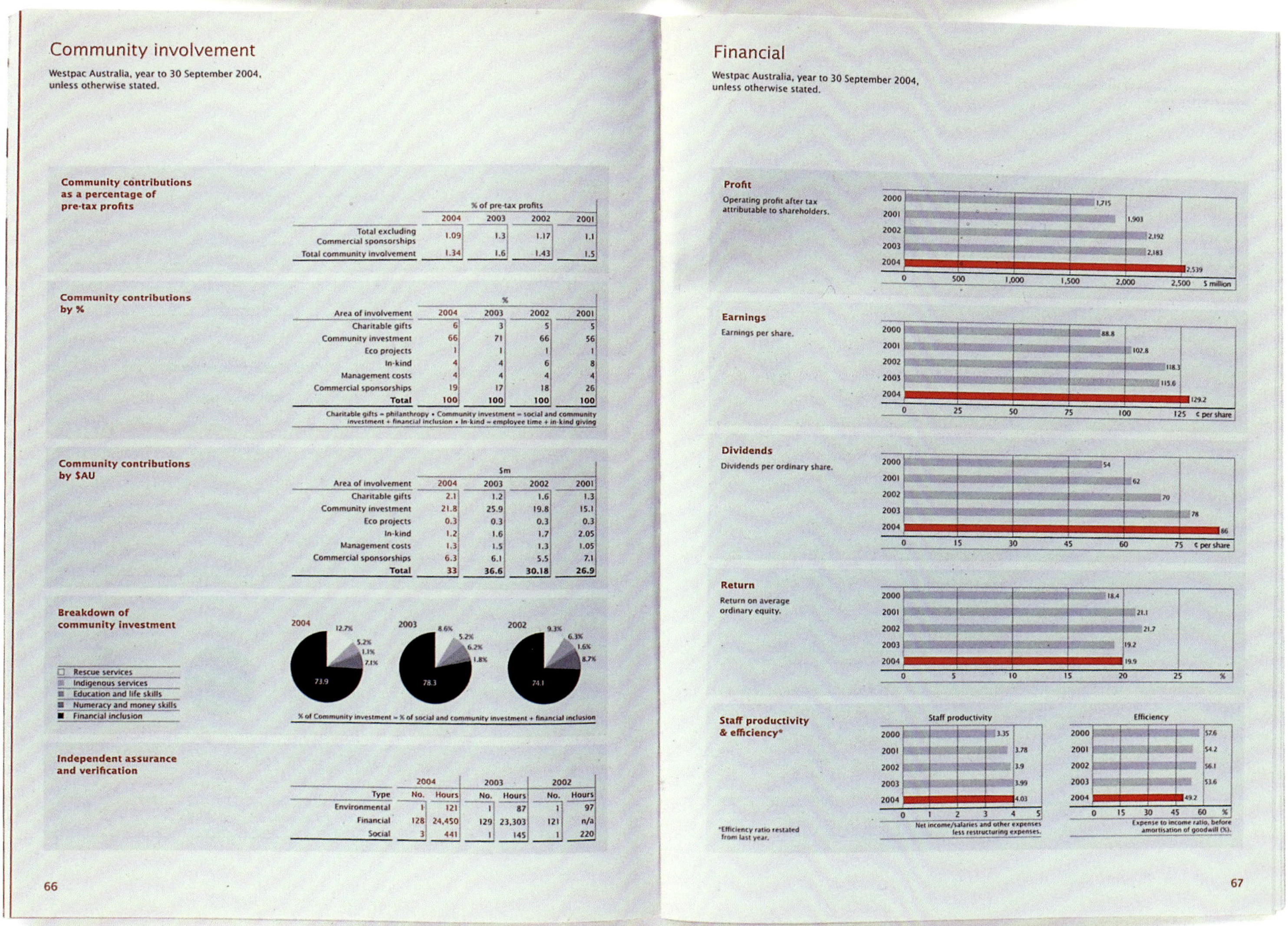

Community involvement

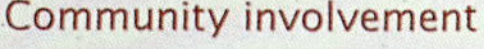

Westpac Australia, year to 30 September 2004, unless otherwise stated.

Community contributions as a percentage of pre-tax profits

	% of pre-tax profits			
	2004	2003	2002	2001
Total excluding Commercial sponsorships	1.09	1.3	1.17	1.1
Total community involvement	1.34	1.6	1.43	1.5

Community contributions by %

	%			
Area of involvement	2004	2003	2002	2001
Charitable gifts	6	3	5	5
Community investment	66	71	66	56
Eco projects	1	1	1	1
In-kind	4	4	6	8
Management costs	4	4	4	4
Commercial sponsorships	19	17	18	26
Total	**100**	**100**	**100**	**100**

Charitable gifts = philanthropy • Community investment = social and community investment + financial inclusion • In-kind = employee time + in-kind giving

Community contributions by $AU

	$m			
Area of involvement	2004	2003	2002	2001
Charitable gifts	2.1	1.2	1.6	1.3
Community investment	21.8	25.9	19.8	15.1
Eco projects	0.3	0.3	0.3	0.3
In-kind	1.2	1.6	1.7	2.05
Management costs	1.3	1.5	1.3	1.05
Commercial sponsorships	6.3	6.1	5.5	7.1
Total	**33**	**36.6**	**30.18**	**26.9**

Breakdown of community investment

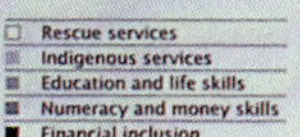

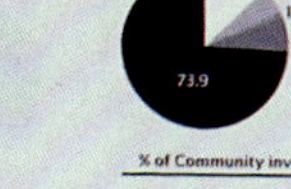

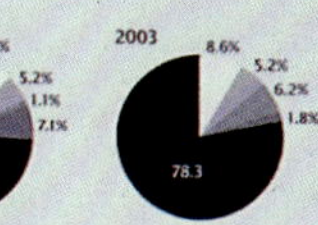

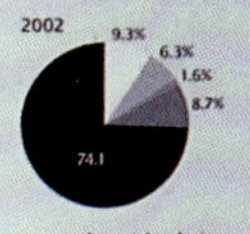

% of Community investment = % of social and community investment + financial inclusion

Independent assurance and verification

	2004		2003		2002	
Type	No.	Hours	No.	Hours	No.	Hours
Environmental	1	121	1	87	1	97
Financial	128	24,450	129	23,303	121	n/a
Social	3	441	1	145	1	220

Financial

Westpac Australia, year to 30 September 2004, unless otherwise stated.

Profit

Operating profit after tax attributable to shareholders.

2000 1,715
2001 1,903
2002 2,192
2003 2,183
2004 2,539
0 500 1,000 1,500 2,000 2,500 $ million

Earnings

Earnings per share.

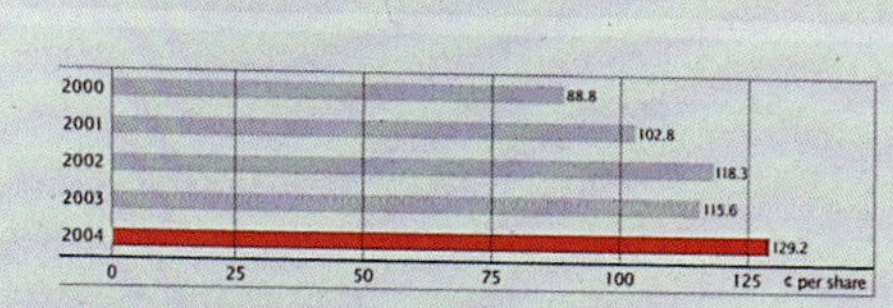

Dividends

Dividends per ordinary share.

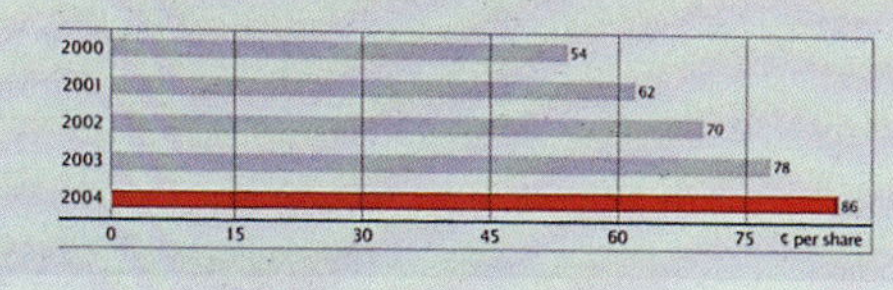

Return

Return on average ordinary equity.

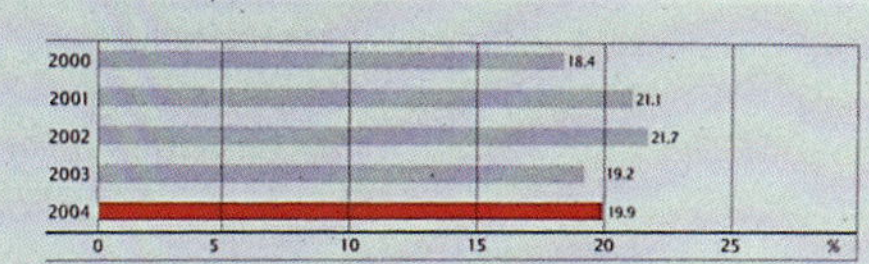

Staff productivity & efficiency*

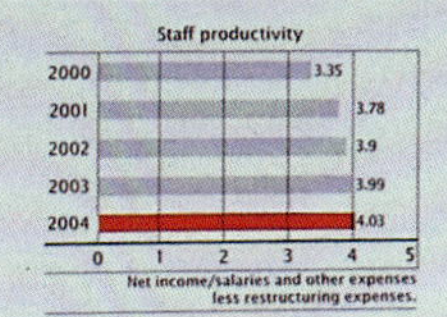

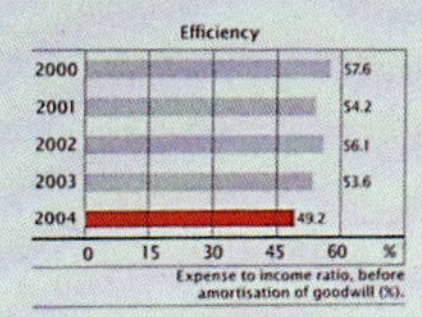

*Efficiency ratio restated from last year.

ÅRSRAPPORT 2004

Art Director: Håvard Dybvig and Kåre Mongstad
Designer & Ill: Trond Fernblad

Photographer: Geir Egil Bergjord
Writer: Håvard Dybvig

Printer: Spesialtrykk
Paper: Highland, (cover) 250gsm, other: 120gsm

Size: 180 x 270 mm
Page count: 80
Number of images: 10 illustrations, 17 photographs
Print run: 5,000
Client: Sandnes Sparebank

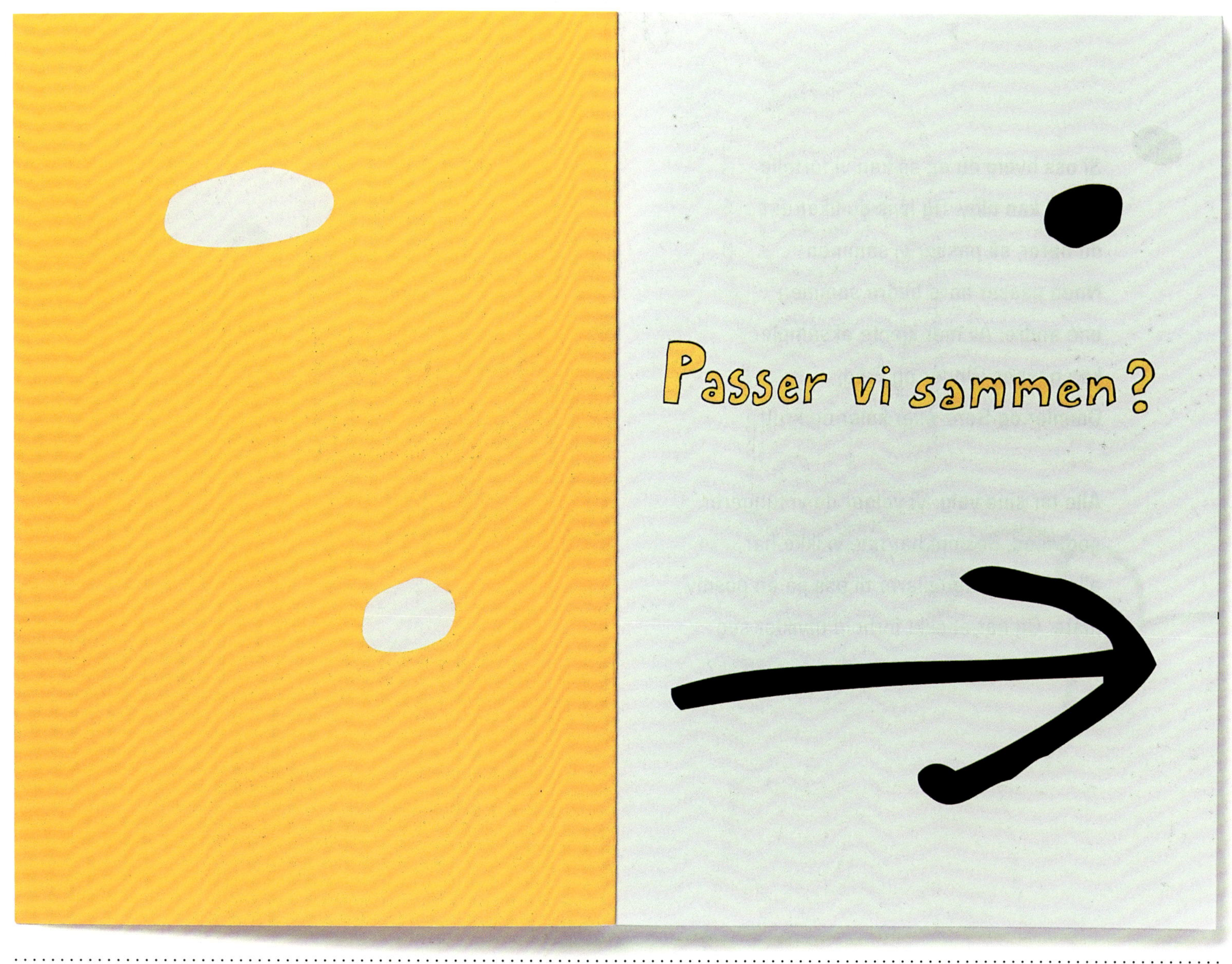

Q&A with Fasett as

What was the client's directive?
To design an Annual Report that reflects the soul of the brand. This is a quite unique bank with exeptionally high customer loyalty and profit. Much thanks to their "just the way you want it" approach.
How did you define the problem?
The challenge was, as always with this client, to make a new approach based on their uniqueness but without repeating last year...
What was the approach?
The 2003 approach was happiness and togetherness...
2004 was focus on cooperation and the importance of working together and build lasting relationships.
Which disciplines or people helped you with the project?
All disciplines within the agency.
Were you happy with the result? What could have been better?
Within the relative small budget limitations we were very happy.
What was the client's response? They applauded both years!
How involved was the CEO in your meetings, presentations, etc.?
The CEO is the "owner" of the AR and he gave us the freedom needed without focusing on details. Trust is the word. The CEO guided the process. An excellent process based on trust and respect.
Do you feel that designers are becoming more involved in copywriting?
NO (strange question).
How do you define success in Annual Report design?
Success with an Annual Report is when we manage to make a document/publication that makes the client proud, that reflects the soul of the brand, and last but not least gains positive response in the target market/groups.
How important are awards to your client?
We have won several national design awards the last five years for Sandnes Sparebank. They appreciate the PR effect and it makes them proud of their company. It also makes the client-agency relation better.

The CEO, as the owner of the report, gave us freedom, trust and respect.

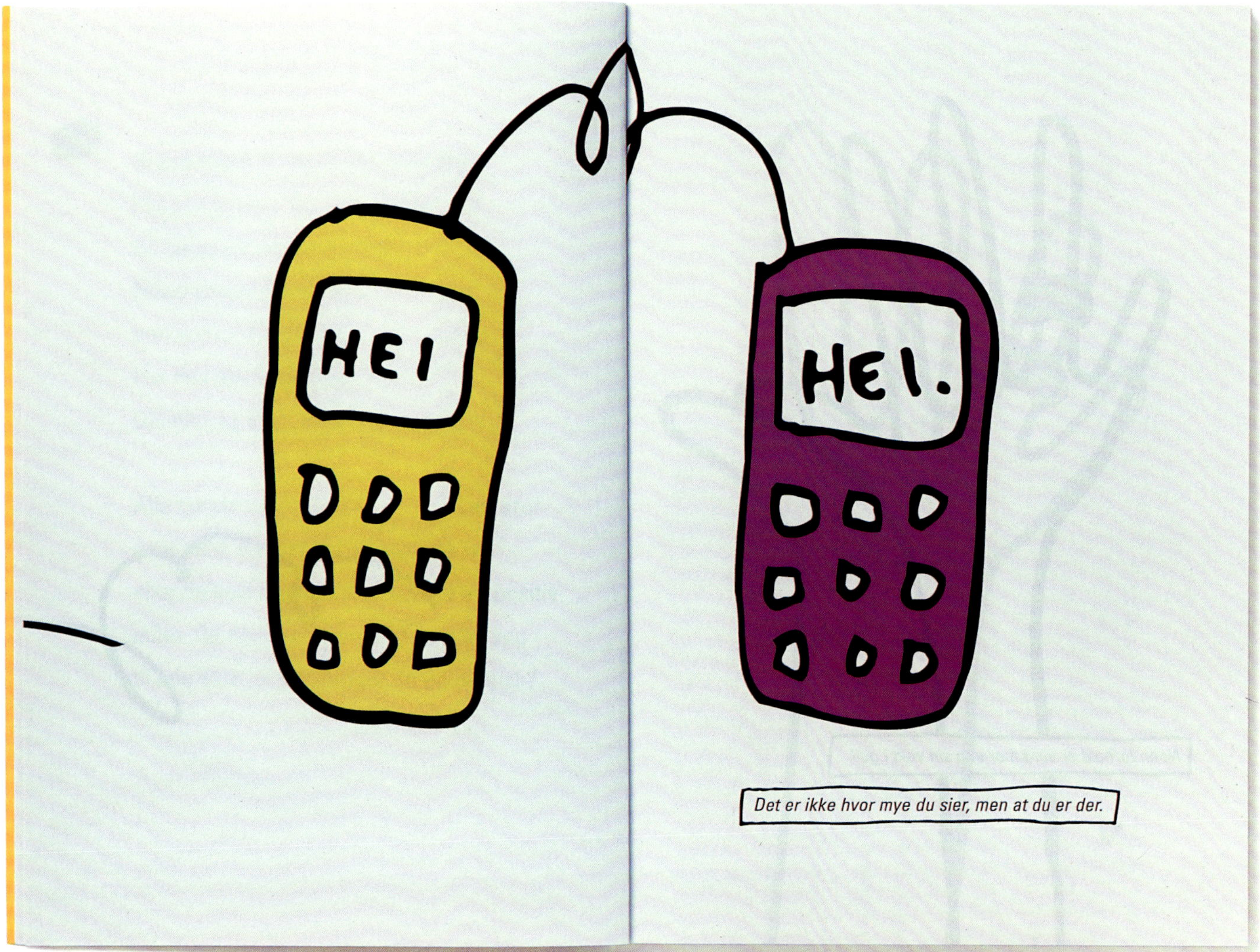

HEI

HEI.

Det er ikke hvor mye du sier, men at du er der.

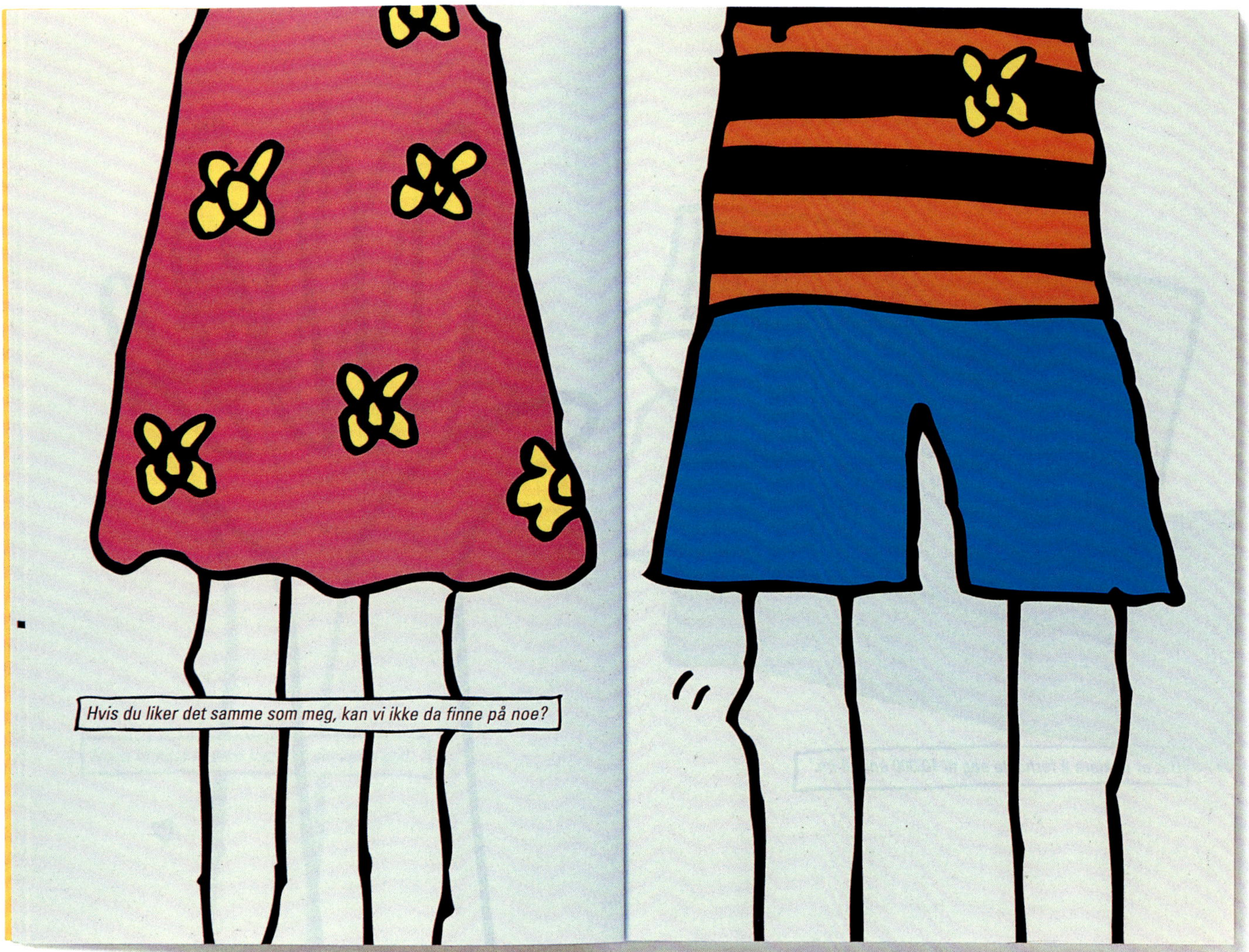

Hvis du liker det samme som meg, kan vi ikke da finne på noe?

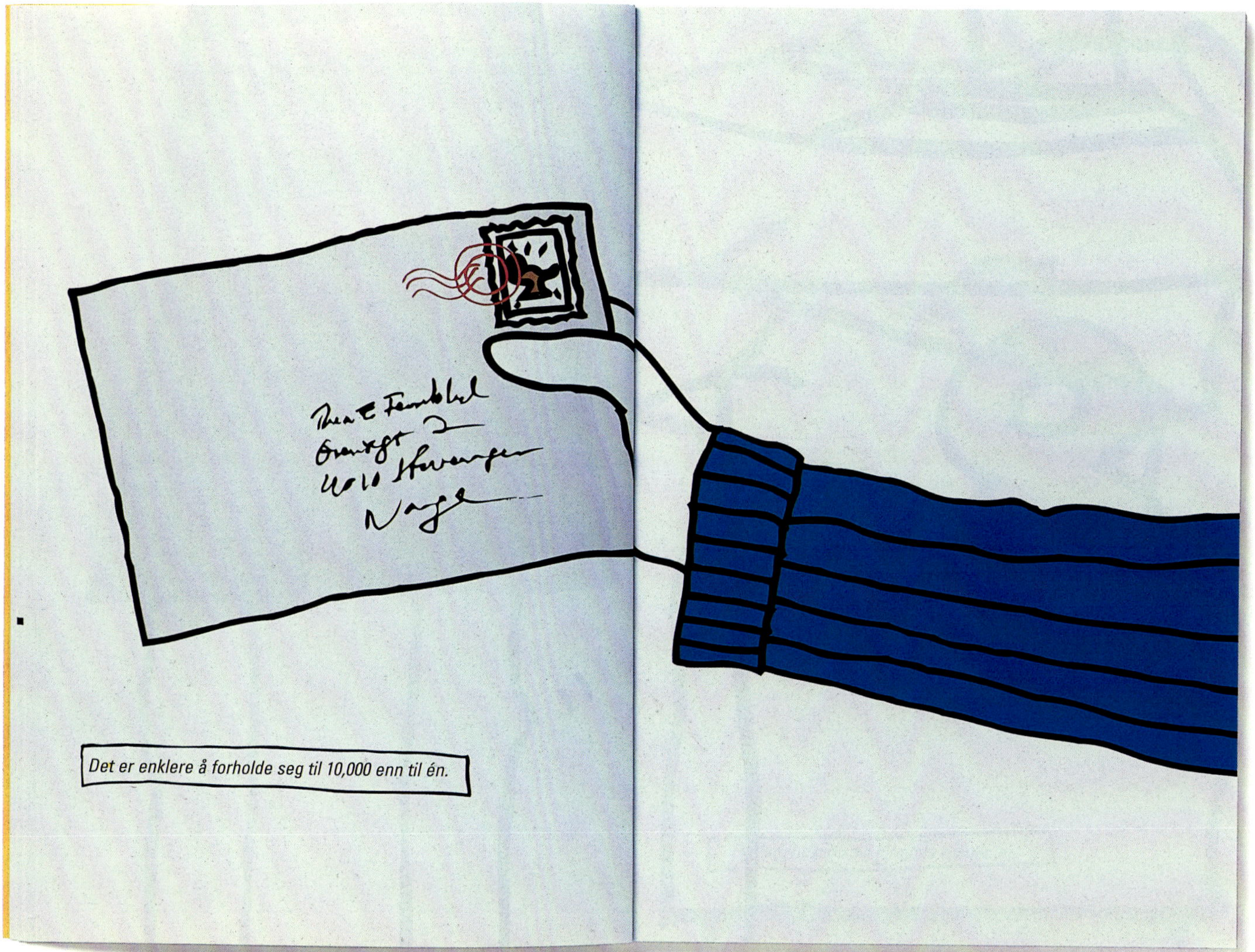

Det er enklere å forholde seg til 10,000 enn til én.

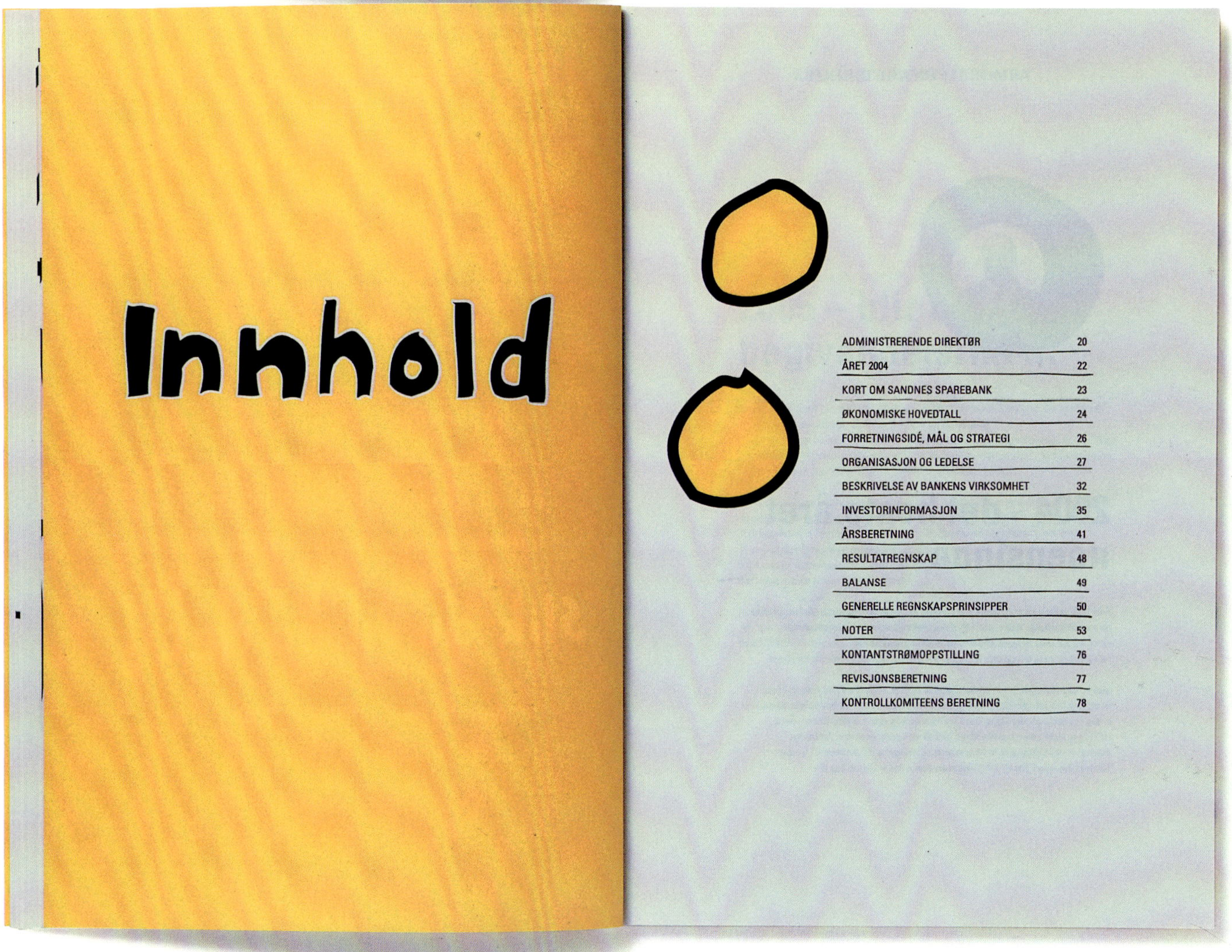

Innhold

Følgende ligningskurser og RISK-beløp er i henhold til vedtatte ligninger frem til og med 2003. Endrede skatteregler gjeldende fra 2003 setter ligningskursen for grunnfondsbevis til 65% av markedsverdi. Ligningskurs for 2004 er derfor satt til 105,625 kroner for SADG.

År	Ligningskurs	Riskbeløp
2004	105,625	
2003	99,45	0,09
2002	118,00	- 0,32
2001	130,00	0,89
2000	160,00	9,29

År	Ligningskurs	Riskbeløp
1999	151,00	9,89
1998	130,00	8,83
1997	131,25	18,08
1996	112,13	15,24
1995	84,75	

Informasjon til markedet

Banken ønsker å føre en åpen informasjonspolitikk med det formål å gi grunnfondsbeviseierne og verdipapirmarkedet korrekt og relevant informasjon om bankens økonomiske utvikling. Banken utarbeider kvartalsvise delårsrapporter. Alle presse- og børsmeldinger er tilgjengelig på bankens hjemmesider www.sandnes-sparebank.no. Alternativt finnes informasjon vedrørende kapitalforhold på hjemmesiden til Oslo Børs www.ose.no. Tickerkoden for grunnfondsbeviset til Sandnes Sparebank på Oslo Børs er SADG.

Finanskalender 2005

Ex-utbyttedato:	1. mars	**1. kvartal:**	21. april
Utbetaling av utbytte:	15. mars	**2. kvartal:**	15. august

3. kvartal vil bli offentliggjort i oktober 2005. Foreløpig regnskap for 2005 vil bli offentliggjort i februar 2006.

Obligasjonsgjeld

Banken baserer en stor del av sin fremmedfinansiering på å utstede obligasjoner i det norske verdipapirmarkedet. I tillegg strukturerer banken en del av sine spareprodukter som obligasjoner med aksjeavkastning. Følgende figurer viser sammensetningen av bankens passivaside og forfallstrukturen på innlån fra fremmedkapitalmarkedet.

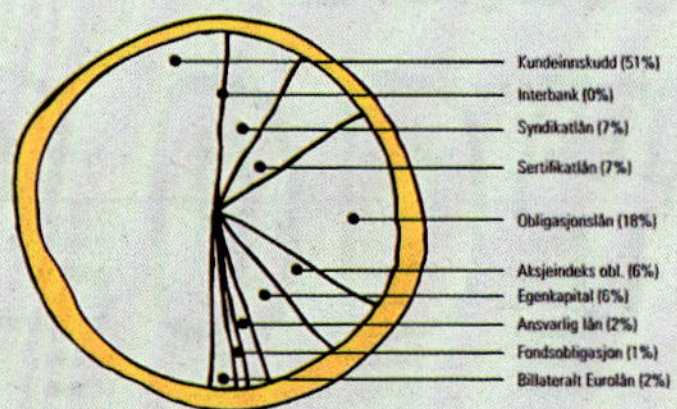

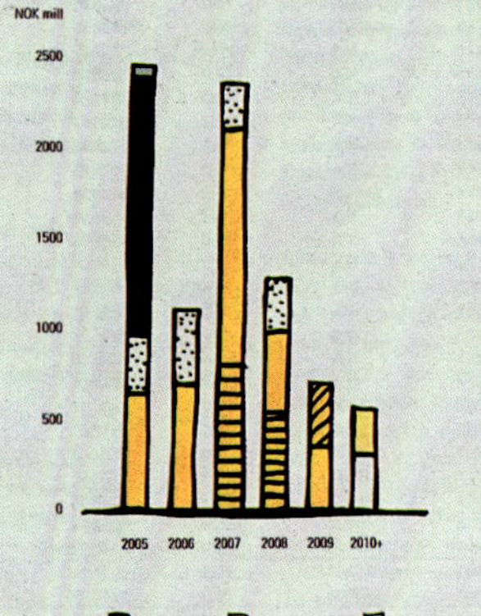

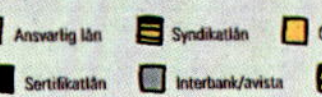

RESULTATREGNSKAP

		2004		2003		2002	
Beløp i hele tusen kroner, % av forvaltningskapital	Note	Beløp	i %	Beløp	i %	Beløp	i %
Renteinntekter og lignende inntekter	1	694 104	4,15	831 443	5,89	909 024	7,99
Rentekostnader og lignende kostnader	1	428 173	2,56	591 035	4,05	681 517	5,99
Netto rente- og kredittprovisjonsinntekter		265 931	1,59	240 408	1,65	227 507	2,00
Utbytte og andre inntekter av verdipapirer med variabel avkastning	2	3 058	0,02	3 211	0,02	1 740	0,02
Provisjonsinntekter og inntekter fra banktjenester	3	65 336	0,39	55 887	0,38	47 206	0,41
Provisjonskostnader og kostnader ved banktjenester		-13 091	-0,08	-13 360	-0,09	-11 572	-0,10
Netto verdiendring og gevinst/tap på valuta og verdipapirer som er omløpsmidler	4	26 572	0,16	32 491	0,22	-10 046	-0,09
Andre driftsinntekter		12	0,00	12	0,00	23	0,00
Sum andre driftsinntekter		81 887	0,49	78 241	0,54	27 351	0,24
Lønn og generelle administrasjonskostnader	5,6	137 729	0,82	126 087	0,86	95 217	0,84
Avskrivninger m.v. av varige driftsmidler og immaterielle eiendeler	16	14 060	0,08	13 350	0,09	7 211	0,06
Andre driftskostnader	7	29 475	0,18	28 557	0,20	20 263	0,18
Sum andre driftskostnader		181 264	1,08	167 994	1,15	122 691	1,08
Tap på utlån og garantier m.v.	8,11	15 001	0,09	37 752	0,26	27 229	0,24
Nedskriving/reversering av nedskriving og gevinst/tap på verdipapirer som er anleggsmidler		0	0,00	760			
Resultat av ordinær drift før skatt		151 553	0,91	113 663	0,78	104 938	0,92
Skatt på ordinært resultat	9	38 432	0,23	12 126	0,08	29 892	0,26
Resultatet for regnskapsåret		113 121	0,68	101 537	0,70	75 046	0,66

Fond for vurderingsforskjeller	201	
Utbytte på grunnfondsbevis	65 000	
Overført til utbyttereguleringsfond	-884	
Overført til sparebankens fond	47 804	
Overført til gaver	1 000	
Disponeringer	113 121	
Fortjeneste per grunnfondsbevis	12,4 kr	13,5 kr
Utvannet resultat per grunnfondsbevis	12,4 kr	13,6 kr

BALANSE

		31.12.2004		31.12.2003	
Beløp i hele tusen kroner, % av forvaltningskapital	Note	Beløp	i %	Beløp	i %
Kontanter og fordringer på sentralbanker		465 252	2	333 705	2
Utlån til og fordringer på kredittinstitusjoner	10	37 409	0	44 210	0
Utlån før spesifiserte og uspesifiserte tapsavsetninger	10	17 572 197	90	14 060 102	92
Spesifiserte tapsavsetninger	11,12	16 188	0	22 547	0
Uspesifiserte tapsavsetninger	11,12	66 686	0	60 686	0
Netto utlån og fordringer på kunder		17 489 323	90	13 976 869	92
Sertifikater, obligasjoner og andre rentebærende verdipapirer med fast avkastning	13	950 991	5	545 116	4
Aksjer, andeler og andre verdipapir med variabel avkastning	14	85 323	0	79 183	1
Eierinteresser i tilknyttet selskap	15	2 092	0	1 891	0
Immaterielle eiendeler	16	36 856	0	69 807	0
Varige driftsmidler	16	17 457	0	18 813	0
Andre eiendeler	17	721		1 211	
Forskuddsbetalte ikke påløpte kostnader og opptjente ikke mottatte inntekter	17	379 978	2	171 698	1
Sum eiendeler		19 465 402		15 242 503	
Gjeld til kredittinstitusjoner	18	1 713 968	9	1 465 179	10
Innskudd fra og gjeld til kunder	19	9 938 649	51	6 870 299	45
Gjeld stiftet ved utstedelse av verdipapirer	20	6 006 977	31	5 320 459	35
Annen gjeld	21	106 544	1	105 125	1
Påløpte kostnader og mottatte ikke opptjente inntekter		82 373	0	102 046	1
Avsetning til påløpte kostnader og forpliktelser	22	6 436	0	4 438	0
Ansvarlig lånekapital	23	509 823	3	321 451	2
Sum gjeld		18 364 770	94	14 188 997	93
Innskutt egenkapital					
Grunnfond	24 ,25	520 000	3	520 000	3
Overkurs ved emisjon	24 ,25	71 968	0	71 968	1
Sum innskutt egenkapital:		591 968	3	591 968	4
Opptjent egenkapital					
Utbyttereguleringsfond	24 ,25	4 730	0	5 615	0
Fond for vurderingsforskjeller	24	1 211	0	1 009	0
Sparebankens fond	24	502 724	3	454 920	3
Sum opptjent egenkapital:		508 665	3	461 544	3
Sum egenkapital	24 ,25	1 100 633	6	1 053 512	7
Sum gjeld og egenkapital		19 465 402		15 242 503	
Poster utenom balansen					
Betingede forpliktelser					
Garantiansvar	26	594 069		616 953	
Bokført verdi av pantestillelser	27	783 800		449 200	

GENERELLE REGNSKAPSPRINSIPPER

OBLIGASJONER OG SERTIFIKATER/OMLØPSMIDLER

Obligasjoner og sertifikater vurderes etter porteføljeprinsippet og er definert som omløpsmidler tilgjengelig for salg, og verdsatt til laveste verdi av anskaffelseskost og markedsverdi.

AKSJER, HEDGE- OG AKSJEFOND/OMLØPSMIDLER

Aksjer, hedge- og aksjefond er inndelt i to porteføljer; handelsportefølje og andre anleggsaksjer. Aksjene som er bestemt for varig eie, klassifiseres som anleggsaksjer. Øvrige finansielle instrumenter som inngås som ledd i egenhandel for å oppnå fortjeneste ved prisforskjeller og prisendringer klassifiseres som handelsportefølje. Bankens definisjon av handelsportefølje er:

- Posisjoner i finansielle instrumenter som banken innehar for egen regning med henblikk på videresalg og/eller banken har ervervet for på kort sikt å dra fordel av reelle og/eller for ventede forskjeller mellom kjøps- og salgspris eller andre pris og rente variasjoner.

Beholdningen av omløpsaksjer vurderes som handelsportefølje og er verdsatt til markedsverdi, som tilsvarer børskurs eller andre observerbare markedsverdier

ANLEGGSAKSJER

Aksjer som er bestemt for varig eie er klassifisert som langsiktig plassering og vurdert til anskaffelseskost. Aksjene blir likevel nedskrevet dersom virkelig verdi er vesentlig lavere enn bokført verdi, og verdinedgangen skyldes forhold som ikke er av forbigående art. Nedskrivningen reverseres i den utstrekning grunnlaget for nedskrivningen ikke lenger er tilstede.

TILKNYTTEDE SELSKAPER

Aksjer i tilknyttede selskaper er vurdert etter egenkapitalmetoden. I resultatregnskapet er resultatandelen vist under utbytte og andre inntekter av verdipapirer med variabel avkastning, mens eierandeler i balansen er vist under eierinteresser i tilknyttede selskaper.

DRIFTSMIDLER OG IMMATERIELLE EIENDELER

Faste eiendommer, andre varige driftsmidler og immaterielle eiendeler blir ført i balansen til anskaffelseskost, fratrukket akkumulerte ordinære avskrivninger. Ordinære avskrivninger er basert på kostpris, og avskrivningene er fordelt lineært over forventet økonomisk levetid. Er virkelig verdi av et driftsmiddel/immateriell eiendel vesentlig lavere enn bokført verdi, og verdinedgangen ikke forventes å være av forbigående art, blir det foretatt nedskrivning til virkelig verdi.

GJELD

Gjeld balanseføres til nominelt mottatt beløp på etableringstidspunktet.

Obligasjonslån er bokført til nominelt beløp med fradrag av underkurs. Underkursen periodiseres over lånets løpetid.

Gjeld oppskrives ikke til virkelig verdi som følge av renteendring.

PENSJONER

Ved regnskapsføring av pensjon er lineær opptjeningsprofil og forventet sluttlønn som opptjeningsgrunnlag lagt til grunn.

Pensjonsforpliktelsen beregnes som nåverdien av fremtidige, sannsynlige pensjonsutbetalinger. Beregningen bygger på aktuarmessige forutsetninger om levealder, lønnsvekst, førtidspensjonering og andre endringer i bestanden av pensjonsberettigede. Forutsetningene som ligger til grunn for beregning av pensjonsforpliktelsene vurderes årlig og kan endres over tid. Slike endringer kan være:

- endringer i pensjonsplaner
- endringer i økonomiske forutsetninger
- endringer i aktuarmessige forutsetninger
- avvik mellom forventet og faktisk avkastning på pensjonsmidler

Estimatavvik og planendringer amortiseres over forventet gjenværende opptjeningstid i den grad de overstiger 10% av den største av pensjonsforpliktelsene og pensjonsmidlene (korridor).

SKATT

Skatter kostnadsføres når de påløper, det vil si at skattekostnaden er knyttet til det regnskapsmessige resultat før skatt. Netto utsatt skattefordel er beregnet med 28% på grunnlag av de midletidige forskjeller som eksisterer mellom regnskapsmessige og skattemessige verdier. Skatteøkende og skattereduserende midlertidige forskjeller, som reverserer eller kan reversere i samme periode, er utlignet og nettoført.

Ved bruk av egenkapitalmetoden i tilknyttet selskaper, er resultatandelen allerede fratrukket skatt.

52

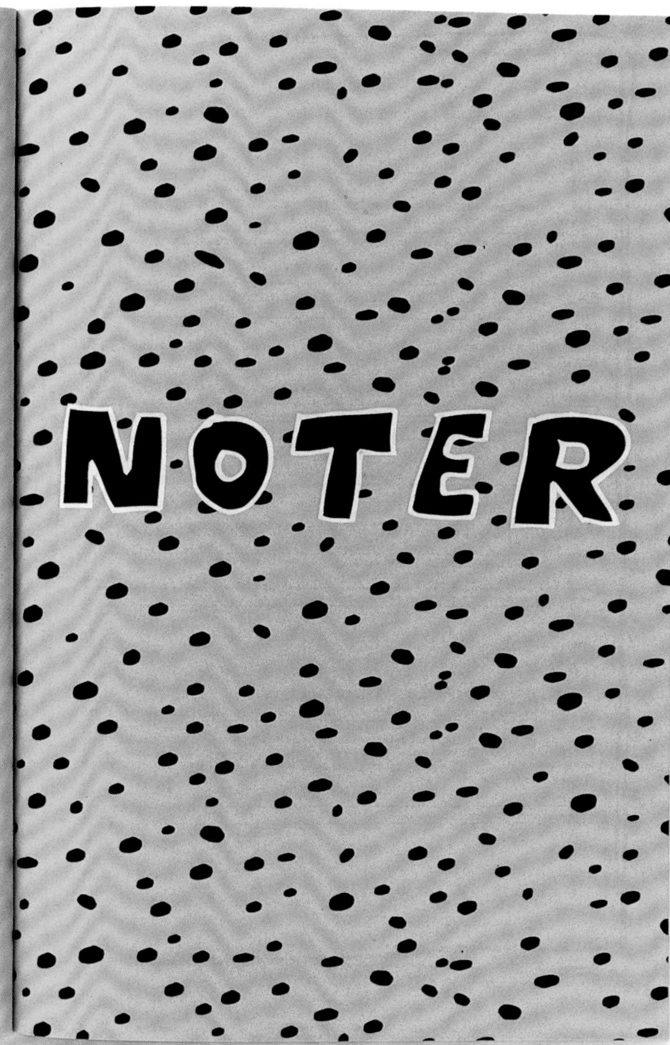

NOTER

NETTO PENSJONSKOSTNADER	2004	2003
Pensjonsopptjening	5 162	4 412
Amortisering gevinst	687	330
= Nåverdien av periodens pensjonsopptjening	5 849	4 742
Rentekostnad av pensjonsforpliktelsen	2 189	1 801
Avkastning på pensjonsmidlene	-1 834	-1 588
Netto pensjonskostnader	6 204	4 955
Arbeidsgiveravgift	192	978
Totale pensjonskostnader	6 396	5 933

Herav: overfinansiert 5.548
underfinanisert 11.134

Bankens netto pensjonsforpliktelse er ført opp som langsiktig gjeld i balansen

NETTO PENSJONSFORPLIKTELSER	2004	2003
Opptjente forsikrede pensjonsrettigheter	46 991	35 865
Opptjente ikke forsikrede pensjonsrettigheter	0	0
Pensjonsmidler	-28 347	-24 811
Beregnet pensjonforpliktelse	18 644	11 054
Utsatt forpliktelse / estimatavvik	-13 519	-8 265
Arbeidsgiveravgift av netto forpliktelse	461	799
Netto pensjonsforpliktelse	5 586	3 588

7 ANDRE DRIFTSKOSTNADER

	2004	2003
Driftskostnader faste eiendommer	2 132	2 956
Husleie	5 853	6 102
Lovpålagt revisjon (inkl. mva.)	645	707
Annet honorar til revisor (inkl. mva)	1 266	1 741
Diverse	19 579	17 051
Andre driftskostnader	29 475	28 557

56

NOTER

8 TAP PÅ UTLÅN OG GARANTIER

	2004	2003
Periodens endring i spesifiserte tapsavsetninger, uten kap. ikke innt.f. renter	-5 312	-11 288
Periodens endring i uspesifiserte tapsavsetninger	6 000	16 000
Konstaterte tap i perioden med spesifisert avsetninger	6 668	17 580
Konstaterte tap i perioden uten spesifisert tapsavsetninger	11 997	16 309
Inngått på tidligere konstaterte tap	-4 352	-849
Tap på utlån og garantier	15 001	37 752

	2004	2003
Påløpte, ikke inntektsførte renter på balanseført utlån per 1.1	1 110	3 597
Periodens inntektsføring av tidligere perioders renter på utlån, samt påløpte ikke inntektsførte renter på utlån som har gått ut av balansen	-1 081	-3 595
+ Periodens påløpte, ikke inntektsførte renter	33	1 108
= Påløpte, ikke inntektsførte renter på balanseført utlån per 31.12	62	1 110

	Brutto utlån		Garantier		Trekkfasilitet	
	2004	2003	2004	2003	2004	2003
Personkunder/Andre	10 562 855	7 762 928	128 849	8 218	3 592 164	1 853 992
Jordbruk, industri, bygg og anlegg	748 293	874 455	135 926	209 461	285 293	156 034
Varehandel, hotell/restaurant, transport, sosial/privat tjenesteyting og forretningsmessig tjenesteyting	1 516 350	1 261 678	86 626	94 541	506 070	467 726
Eiendomsdrift	4 744 699	4 161 041	242 668	304 733	1 080 262	628 708
Sum	17 572 197	14 060 102	594 069	616 953	5 463 789	3 106 460

	Misligholdte engasjementer		Tapsutsatte engasjementer		Spesifiserte tapsavsetninger	
	2004	2003	2004	2003	2004	2003
Personkunder/Andre	24 479	65 968	21 582	14 945	4 607	2 848
Jordbruk, industri, bygg og anlegg	48	35 968	2 889	38 013	10 931	14 100
Varehandel, hotell/restaurant, transport, sosial/privat tjenesteyting og forretningsmessig tjenesteyting	19 674	73 209	17 128	22 836	98	5 048
Eiendomsdrift		42			601	601
Sum	44 201	175 187	41 599	75 794	16 237	22 597

Trekkfasilitet er kassekreditter, tilleggskreditter og byggelånbevilgninger. Bankens avsetning til uspesifiserte tap i 2004 og 2003 utgjør henholdsvis kr 67,5 mill. og kr 61,5 mill. Disse er ikke fordelt etter næring og er ikke tilordnet de enkelte risikogrupper.

57

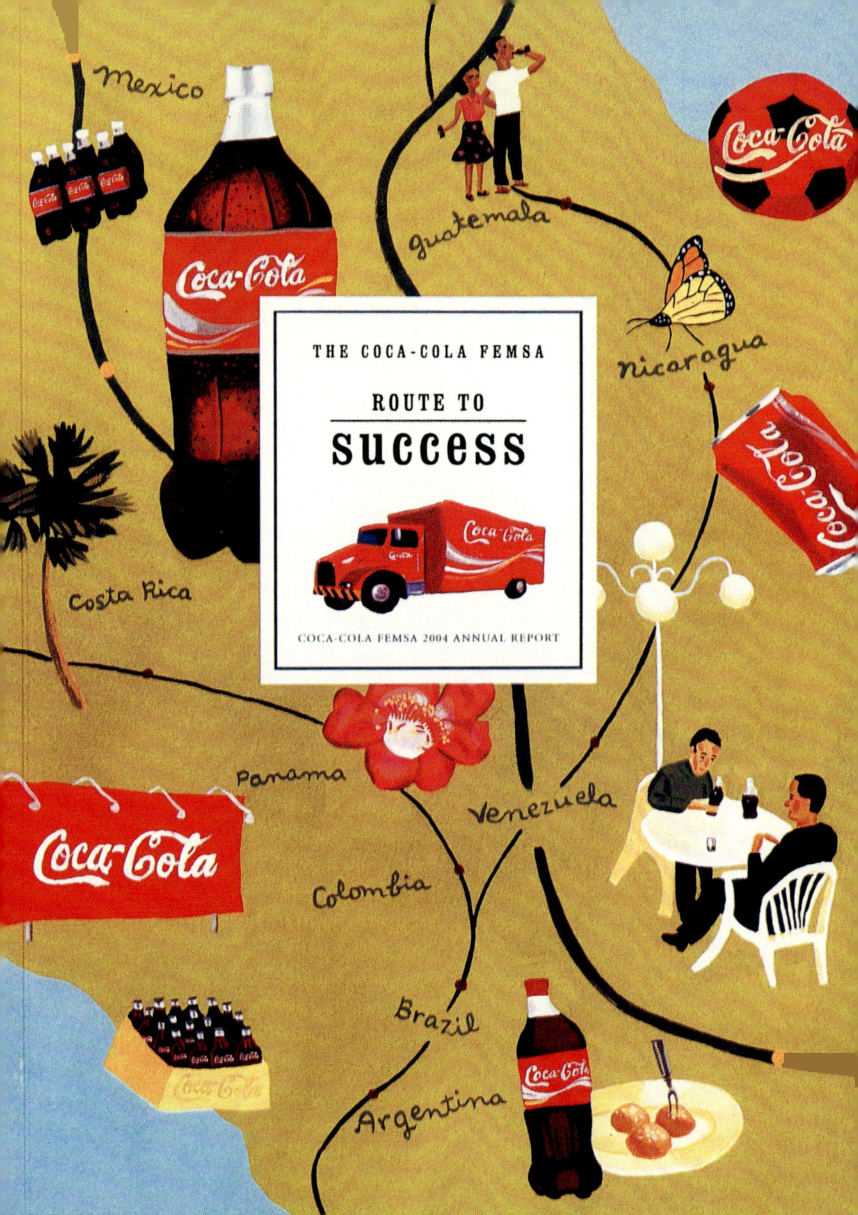

Mexico
Coca-Cola
Guatemala
Coca-Cola
THE COCA-COLA FEMSA
ROUTE TO
SUCCESS
Coca-Cola
COCA-COLA FEMSA 2004 ANNUAL REPORT
Nicaragua
Coca-Cola
Costa Rica
Panama
Venezuela
Coca-Cola
Colombia
Brazil
Coca-Cola
Argentina

Art Directors: Meow Vatanatumrak, Rachel Radtke, Robin Zvonek
Designer: Meow Vatanatumrak
Illustrator: Juliette Borda
Writer: Peter Warrick
Printer: Quantum Color Graphics, IL
Paper: cover: Fox River Coronado Stipple 100#C
text: Mohawk Superfine White Eggshell 100#T
French Paper 100#Text
Page count: 84 page body plus 6 page cover, gatefold
Print Run: 10,000
Size: 7.75" x 11.25"
Client: Coca-Cola Femsa

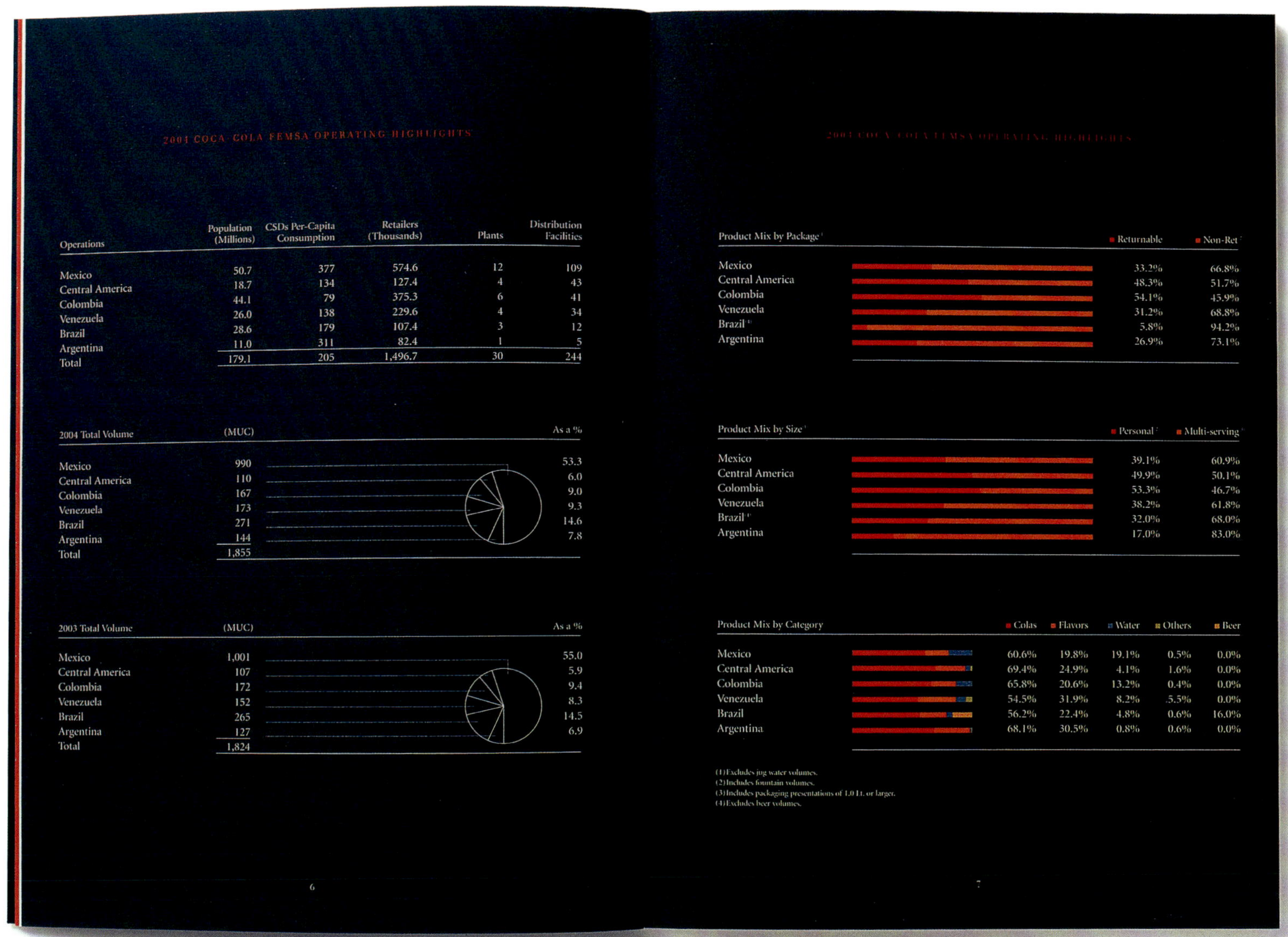

2004 COCA-COLA FEMSA OPERATING HIGHLIGHTS

Operations	Population (Millions)	CSDs Per-Capita Consumption	Retailers (Thousands)	Plants	Distribution Facilities
Mexico	50.7	377	574.6	12	109
Central America	18.7	134	127.4	4	43
Colombia	44.1	79	375.3	6	41
Venezuela	26.0	138	229.6	4	34
Brazil	28.6	179	107.4	3	12
Argentina	11.0	311	82.4	1	5
Total	179.1	205	1,496.7	30	244

2004 Total Volume	(MUC)	As a %
Mexico	990	53.3
Central America	110	6.0
Colombia	167	9.0
Venezuela	173	9.3
Brazil	271	14.6
Argentina	144	7.8
Total	1,855	

2003 Total Volume	(MUC)	As a %
Mexico	1,001	55.0
Central America	107	5.9
Colombia	172	9.4
Venezuela	152	8.3
Brazil	265	14.5
Argentina	127	6.9
Total	1,824	

6

2004 COCA-COLA FEMSA OPERATING HIGHLIGHTS

Product Mix by Package [1]	Returnable	Non-Ret [2]
Mexico	33.2%	66.8%
Central America	48.3%	51.7%
Colombia	54.1%	45.9%
Venezuela	31.2%	68.8%
Brazil [4]	5.8%	94.2%
Argentina	26.9%	73.1%

Product Mix by Size [1]	Personal [2]	Multi-serving [3]
Mexico	39.1%	60.9%
Central America	49.9%	50.1%
Colombia	53.3%	46.7%
Venezuela	38.2%	61.8%
Brazil [4]	32.0%	68.0%
Argentina	17.0%	83.0%

Product Mix by Category	Colas	Flavors	Water	Others	Beer
Mexico	60.6%	19.8%	19.1%	0.5%	0.0%
Central America	69.4%	24.9%	4.1%	1.6%	0.0%
Colombia	65.8%	20.6%	13.2%	0.4%	0.0%
Venezuela	54.5%	31.9%	8.2%	.5.5%	0.0%
Brazil	56.2%	22.4%	4.8%	0.6%	16.0%
Argentina	68.1%	30.5%	0.8%	0.6%	0.0%

(1) Excludes jug water volumes.
(2) Includes fountain volumes.
(3) Includes packaging presentations of 1.0 Lt. or larger.
(4) Excludes beer volumes.

7

Q&A with Paragraphs Design

What was the client's directive?

Coca-Cola Femsa acquired Panamco and became the 2nd largest Coca-Cola distributor in the world. The goal of the 2004 AR was strictly informational. The objective was to explain the acquisition, the business plan and how it would prove to be an intelligent, profitable business decision.

How did you define the problem?

The challenge was that each of the nine countries falling under the Coca-Cola Femsa corporate umbrella had very different cultures, business opportunities, challenges and issues. We needed to convey how the corporate best practices and business strategies would apply in every country, bringing the corporation together from a marketing, manufacturing and distribution sales process.

What was the approach?

We created the theme, "Route to Success," to take the reader through the process – how Coca-Cola Femsa was going to approach each country and what their process would be to unify the company and increase revenue. We chose illustration for our visual story as it was the best approach to give each country its own story yet tie the entire corporation together. We were able to highlight strong products within each region and explain what Coca-Cola Femsa would do to build the respective brands. We used the visuals to create human interest with cultural and regional callouts.

Were you happy with the result? What could have been better?

The results were phenomenal. The book won extensive awards including Best of International, Best Designed, Awards of Excellence, AR 100 and more. From a content and design standpoint it scored extremely high (10s out of 10s) in many different competitions including AR100, ARC Awards, Mercury Awards, Graphic Design USA, LACP, NAIC and more.

What was the client's response?

The client loved the book and used the illustrations as gifts for each of the countries and customers. The investment community clearly understood the direction the company was taking.

How involved was the CEO in your meetings, presentations, etc.?

The CEO is involved in the initial meetings when we conduct a

Q&A from a copy and theme standpoint. He is involved again in the concept selection phase. After that, it's his photo and a final review before printing.

Do you feel that designers are becoming more involved in copywriting?

Yes, we have been in business for 20 years and more than half of those years we wrote about 30 – 50% of the copy. We now write more than 80%. Writing the copy, conceptualizing the theme and writing the headlines accounts for 100% of our AR work.

How do you define success in Annual Report design?

The success of an AR is clearly, "Did the Annual Report clearly convey the message we wanted the reader to get?" If so, it was successful. If we as a design firm had fun in the process, if our clients had fun, if we created the best possible product with high imp act, if the design was never compromised and if all partners worked well as a team – then it was spectacularly successful.

How important are awards to your client?

A great book and an enjoyable process is the core reward. The awards are gravy. Being recognized by the design community, the business community, the communications and marketing community and the investment community tell us we are doing our job right. Awards tell us our approach and thinking outside the box are worth the extra effort, understood and appreciated. They give clients satisfaction that their support of our ideas and sticking to the core idea pays off. Winning awards encourage our clients to think with us in the process and not be afraid to take a chance in communicating their message. Awards prove differentiation pays off. They confirm our client's selection of us as a firm and help forge stronger ties as a successful partnership.

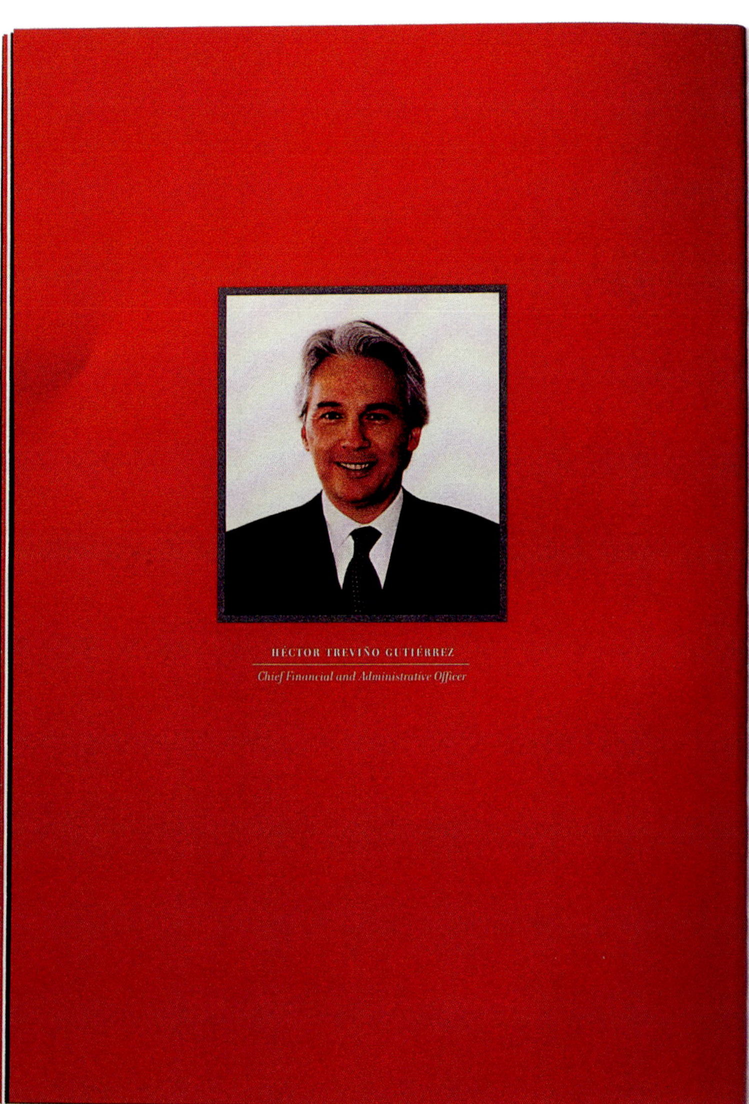

CFO'S LETTER TO SHAREHOLDERS

AN EXCITING GROWTH STORY

Dear Shareholders: Our geographic diversification is now an important part of our growth story. In 2004 our Central and South American operations represented more than 30 percent of our total cash-flow generation. In fact, the year-over-year profitability improvement of our Central and South American territories compensated for our Mexican territories' lower profitability. As a result, we posted solid consolidated results for the year:

- *Consolidated sales volumes reached almost 1.9 billion unit cases.*
- *Total revenues were Ps. 46.5 billion.*
- *Consolidated operating income totaled Ps. 7.7 billion, and operating margin was 16.6 percent.*
- *Consolidated net income was Ps. 5.4 billion, resulting in earnings per share of Ps. 2.93 (U.S.$2.63 per ADR).*
- *Total net debt at year-end 2004 was approximately U.S.$1.9 billion.*

During the year, we reduced our company's net debt by approximately U.S.$360 million. We further capitalized on the relatively low interest-rate environment and opportunities in the Mexican financial markets to eliminate our re-financing risk, reduce our foreign-currency exposure, and improve our debt-maturity profile.

9

The results were phenomenal, and the book also won awards in numerous major competitions.

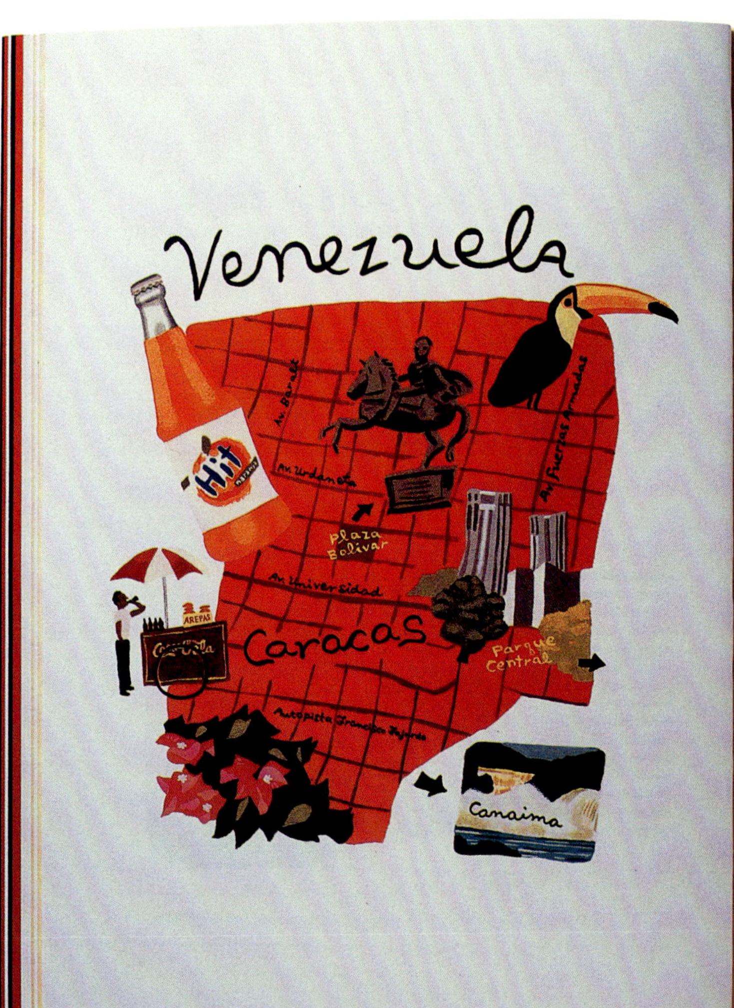

VENEZUELA

WE'RE ADAPTING

our strategies and best practices to suit Venezuela's marketplace environment

We are tailoring our commercial strategies and operating practices to capitalize on Venezuela's market opportunities. On the operations front, we are adapting lessons learned from Mexico and Argentina to improve our efficiency and productivity more rapidly. Since May 2003, we have converted five manufacturing plants into distribution facilities, streamlining our total number of plants from nine to four. We have used the company's scale to negotiate more favorable terms with our suppliers for myriad items—from manufacturing equipment, to raw materials for our bottles and cases, to replacement parts for our delivery trucks. Also, we have dramatically improved our dialogue with our employees and the unions, so that they can more clearly understand the challenges we face. We expect these initiatives will enable us to enhance our productivity going forward.

BRAND COCA-COLA SALES VOLUME (MUC)

02	03	04
78.4	86.5	94.2

375

MM Pesos

EBIT generation

Like Argentina, we leveraged Venezuela's economic recovery to post strong volume growth across practically every product and package category. We took advantage of the country's changing consumption patterns to roll out 2.25-liter and 3.1-liter non-returnable presentations of the value-protection brand *Grapette*. This should enable us to establish a broader base of price-conscious consumers. Additionally, our focus on increasing the visibility of our core brands is furthering our planned recovery of the *Hit* brand, which has shown volume growth of more than 20 percent over the last two years. In 2004 our volume of flavored carbonated soft drinks increased more than 24 percent, and our volumes of brand *Coca-Cola* rose more than 8 percent.

DID YOU KNOW?

We offer our beverages to 26 million consumers, a similar-sized market to the one we serve in Brazil.

FINANCIAL SECTION

SEVEN-YEAR SUMMARY

Millions of constant Mexican Pesos (Ps.) as of December 31, 2004, except income per share

	2004	2003(1)	2002	2001	2000	1999	1998
INCOME STATEMENT							
Total revenues	46,499	38,121	19,586	18,597	17,840	15,939	15,064
Cost of sales	23,964	19,367	9,098	8,630	8,675	8,294	8,191
Gross profit	22,535	18,754	10,488	9,967	9,165	7,645	6,873
Operating expenses(2)	14,839	11,655	5,581	5,594	5,653	5,034	4,646
Intangible amortization	–	–	41	113	121	131	142
Income from operations	7,696	7,099	4,866	4,260	3,391	2,480	2,085
Integral cost of financing	798	2,582	(584)	141	655	384	503
Other expenses, net	408	260	638	94	113	78	259
Income taxes and employee profit sharing	1,063	1,776	2,012	1,587	1,128	901	549
Net income for the year	5,427	2,481	2,800	2,438	1,495	1,117	774
Majority net income	5,404	2,463	2,800	2,438	1,495	1,117	774
Minority net income	23	18	–	–	–	–	–
RATIOS TO REVENUES (%)							
Gross margin (profit/net sales)	48.7	49.5	54.0	54.0	51.6	48.1	45.9
Operating margin	16.6	18.6	24.8	22.9	19.0	15.6	13.8
Net income	11.7	6.5	14.3	13.1	8.4	7.0	5.1
CASH FLOW							
Gross cash flow (EBITDA)(3)	10,020	8,863	5,967	5,449	4,754	3,696	3,061
Capital expenditures(4)	1,929	2,007	1,481	909	1,016	1,521	1,691
BALANCE SHEET							
Current assets	9,050	8,719	8,782	6,689	3,413	1,864	1,429
Property, plant and equipment, net	18,672	19,133	7,773	7,381	7,708	8,145	8,461
Investments in shares	418	518	136	152	169	165	135
Deferred tax and other assets, net	2,812	2,827	928	591	499	464	439
Intangible assets, net	36,114	35,471	283	1,014	1,717	1,947	2,413
Total Assets	67,066	66,668	17,902	15,827	13,506	12,585	12,877
Liabilities							
Short-term bank loans	3,272	3,132	10	16	18	30	1,540
Long-term bank loans and notes payable	21,716	27,456	3,467	3,226	3,540	3,770	4,422
Interest payable	314	395	79	73	80	87	107
Other current liabilities	7,101	6,675	2,728	2,628	2,204	2,517	1,426
Other long-term liabilities	4,554	4,716	1,037	932	1,188	283	206
Total Liabilities	36,957	42,374	7,321	6,875	7,030	6,687	7,701
Stockholders' Equity	30,109	24,294	10,581	8,952	6,476	5,898	5,176
Majority interest	29,400	24,120	10,581	8,952	6,476	5,898	5,176
Minority interest	709	174	–	–	–	–	–
FINANCIAL RATIOS (%)							
Current	0.85	0.85	3.12	2.46	1.48	0.71	0.46
Leverage	1.23	1.74	0.77	0.85	1.09	1.13	1.49
Capitalization	0.42	0.57	0.26	0.28	0.36	0.39	0.62
Coverage	4.42	6.45	67.05	91.93	19.14	8.03	4.88
DATA PER SHARE(5)							
Book Value	15.922	13.063	7.425	5.994	4.545	4.139	3.632
Majority net income	2.927	1.445	1.965	1.711	1.050	0.784	0.543
Dividends paid(6)	0.292	–	0.449	0.244	0.199	0.161	0.160
Headcount(7)	56,238	56,871	14,457	14,542	15,054	15,273	15,003

(1) Information considers full-year of KOF's original territories and eight months of our new territories acquired from Panamco.
(2) 1998 figure includes the fixed-asset adjustment from the write-down in the value of computer equipment and information systems.
(3) Income from operations plus non-cash charges.
(4) Includes investments in property, plant and equipment, returnable bottles and cases and other assets, net of retirements of property, plant and equipment.
(5) Based on 1,425 million shares until 2002, 2003 was computed using 1,846.4 million shares and the net income per share with 1,704.3 million and 2004 using 1,846.5 million and the net income per share with 1,846.4 million.
(6) Dividends paid during the year based on the prior year's net income.
(7) Includes third-party headcount.

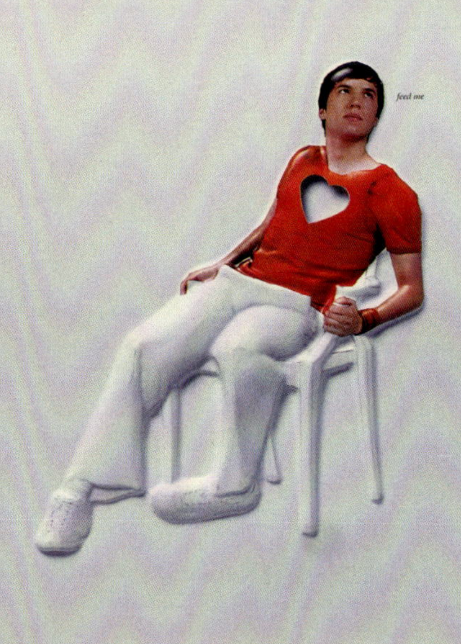
feed me

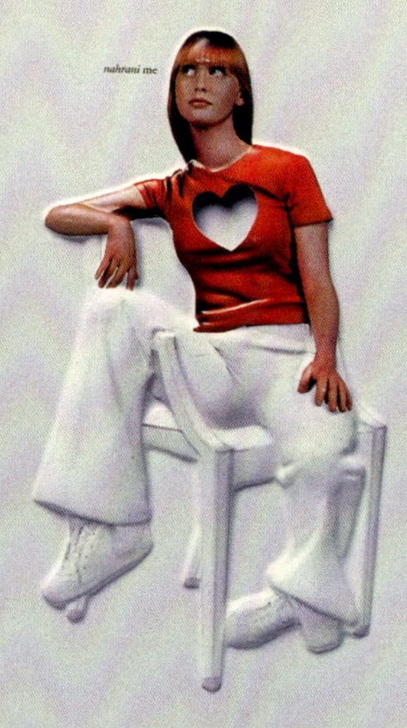
nahrani me

Art Directors, Designers: Davor Bruketa, Nikola Zinic Photographers: Marin Topic, Domagoj Kunic Printer: IBL, MIT d.o.o. Paper: Agripina Page count: 146 Print run: 3,000 Size: 225 x 265 mm Number of images: 10 Client: Podravka d.d., largest food company based in Central, Eastern and South-Eastern Europe

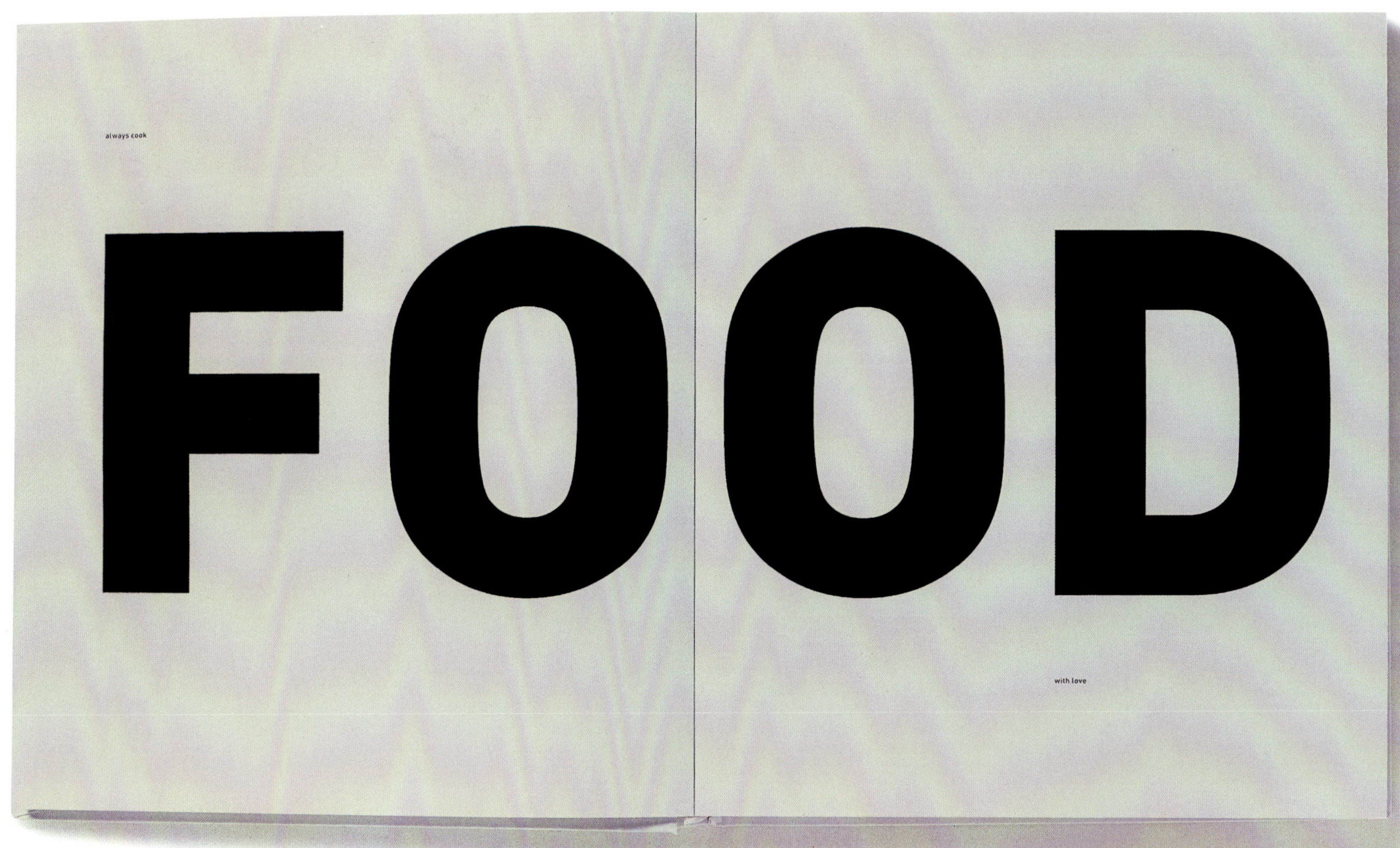

Q&A with Bruketa&Zinic

What was the client's directive?
To create an Annual Report that would reflect the company values, misson and vision.
How did you define the problem?
Annual Reports are a very conservative category, with rather strict rules when it comes to financial reports. The problem is how to obey the rules and make it a serious company stock market report, at the same time communicating values of the company in a new and creative way.
What was the approach?
We've enriched the standard structure of the Annual Report with some unexpected things.
Which disciplines or people helped you with the project?
The chefs - Podravka is a food company. Also IBL printing company did a terrific job.
Were you happy with the result? What could have been better?
Some of the things didn't quite turn out as we expected from the technical point of view.
What was the client's response?
They seem to be very pleased.
How involved was the CEO in your meetings and presentations?
We worked with corporate communications director Sasa Blazekovic. Darko Marinac, CEO, approved the project and created the space for creative solution of the task.
Do you feel that designers are becoming more involved in copywriting?
We've always written texts, which is normal, since our job is communication. It seems more and more people see their jobs in a much broader sense.
How do you define success in Annual Report design?
When a financial analyst decides to take it home and put it in his private library.
How important are awards to your client?
They are happy about them, of course. The recognition in a way confirms and rewards the efforts of everyone involved. Of course, they also push everyone forward, to try and do an even better job next time around.

Success is when a financial analyst puts your Annual Report in his private library.

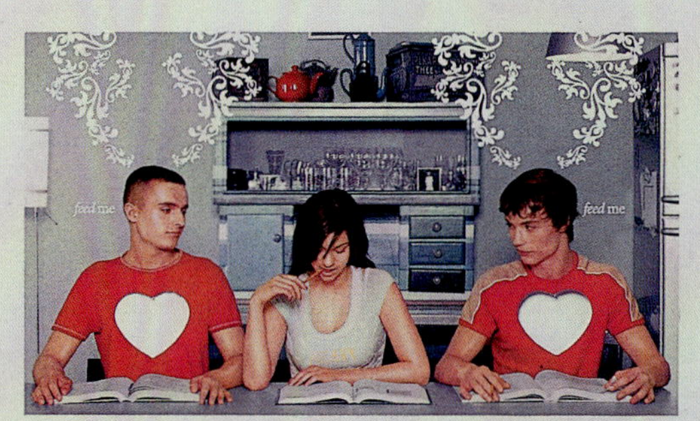

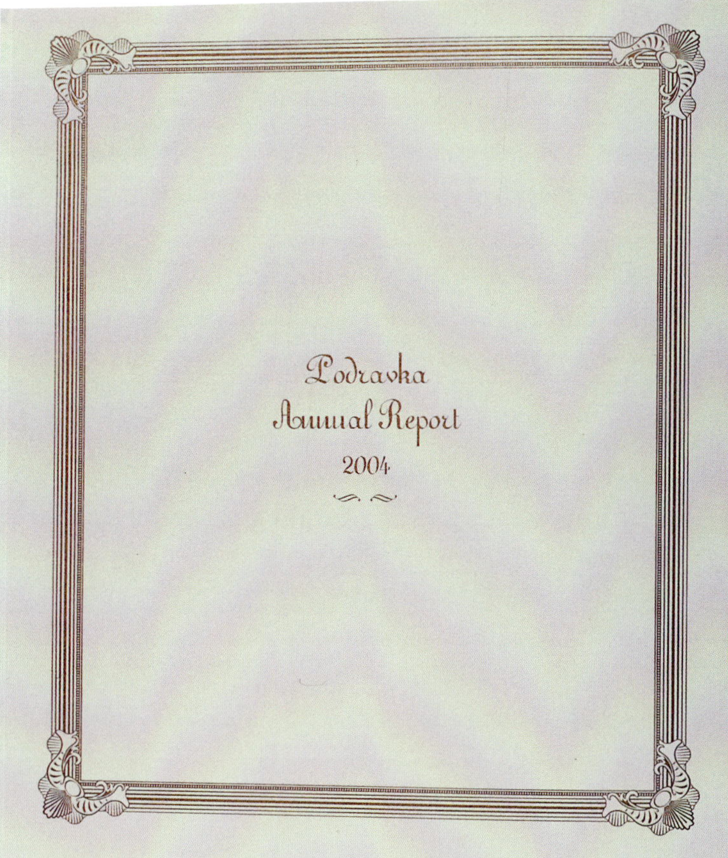

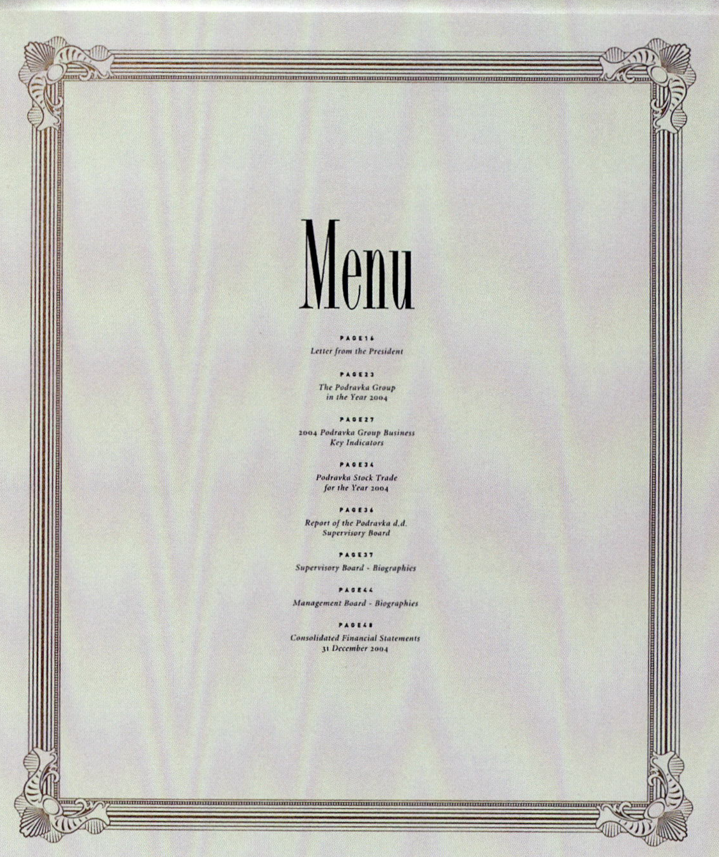

Menu

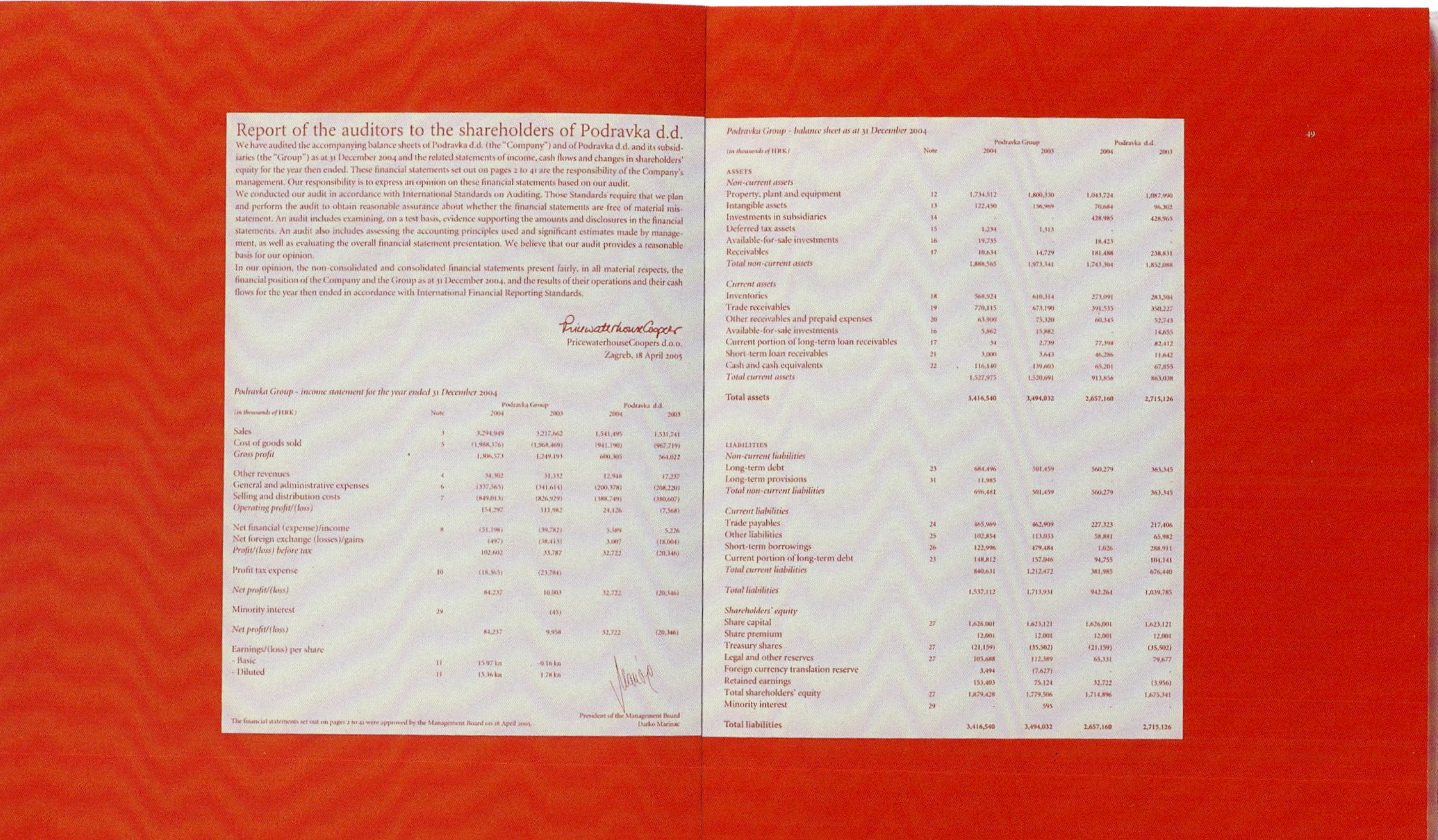

Report of the auditors to the shareholders of Podravka d.d.

We have audited the accompanying balance sheets of Podravka d.d. (the "Company") and of Podravka d.d. and its subsidiaries (the "Group") as at 31 December 2004 and the related statements of income, cash flows and changes in shareholders' equity for the year then ended. These financial statements set out on pages 2 to 41 are the responsibility of the Company's management. Our responsibility is to express an opinion on these financial statements based on our audit.

We conducted our audit in accordance with International Standards on Auditing. Those Standards require that we plan and perform the audit to obtain reasonable assurance about whether the financial statements are free of material misstatement. An audit includes examining, on a test basis, evidence supporting the amounts and disclosures in the financial statements. An audit also includes assessing the accounting principles used and significant estimates made by management, as well as evaluating the overall financial statement presentation. We believe that our audit provides a reasonable basis for our opinion.

In our opinion, the non-consolidated and consolidated financial statements present fairly, in all material respects, the financial position of the Company and the Group as at 31 December 2004, and the results of their operations and their cash flows for the year then ended in accordance with International Financial Reporting Standards.

PricewaterhouseCoopers
PricewaterhouseCoopers d.o.o.
Zagreb, 18 April 2005

Podravka Group - income statement for the year ended 31 December 2004

(in thousands of HRK)	Note	Podravka Group 2004	Podravka Group 2003	Podravka d.d. 2004	Podravka d.d. 2003
Sales	3	3,294,949	3,217,662	1,541,495	1,531,741
Cost of goods sold	5	(1,988,376)	(1,968,469)	(941,190)	(967,719)
Gross profit		1,306,573	1,249,193	600,305	564,022
Other revenues	4	34,302	31,332	12,948	17,237
General and administrative expenses	6	(337,565)	(341,614)	(200,378)	(208,220)
Selling and distribution costs	7	(849,013)	(826,929)	(388,749)	(380,607)
Operating profit/(loss)		154,297	111,982	24,126	(7,568)
Net financial (expense)/income	8	(51,198)	(39,782)	5,589	5,226
Net foreign exchange (losses)/gains		(497)	(38,413)	3,007	(18,004)
Profit/(loss) before tax		102,602	33,787	32,722	(20,346)
Profit tax expense	10	(18,365)	(23,784)		
Net profit/(loss)		84,237	10,003	32,722	(20,346)
Minority interest	29		(45)		
Net profit/(loss)		84,237	9,958	32,722	(20,346)
Earnings/(loss) per share					
- Basic	11	15.97 kn	-0.16 kn		
- Diluted	11	15.36 kn	1.78 kn		

The financial statements set out on pages 2 to 41 were approved by the Management Board on 18 April 2005.

President of the Management Board
Darko Marinac

Podravka Group - balance sheet as at 31 December 2004

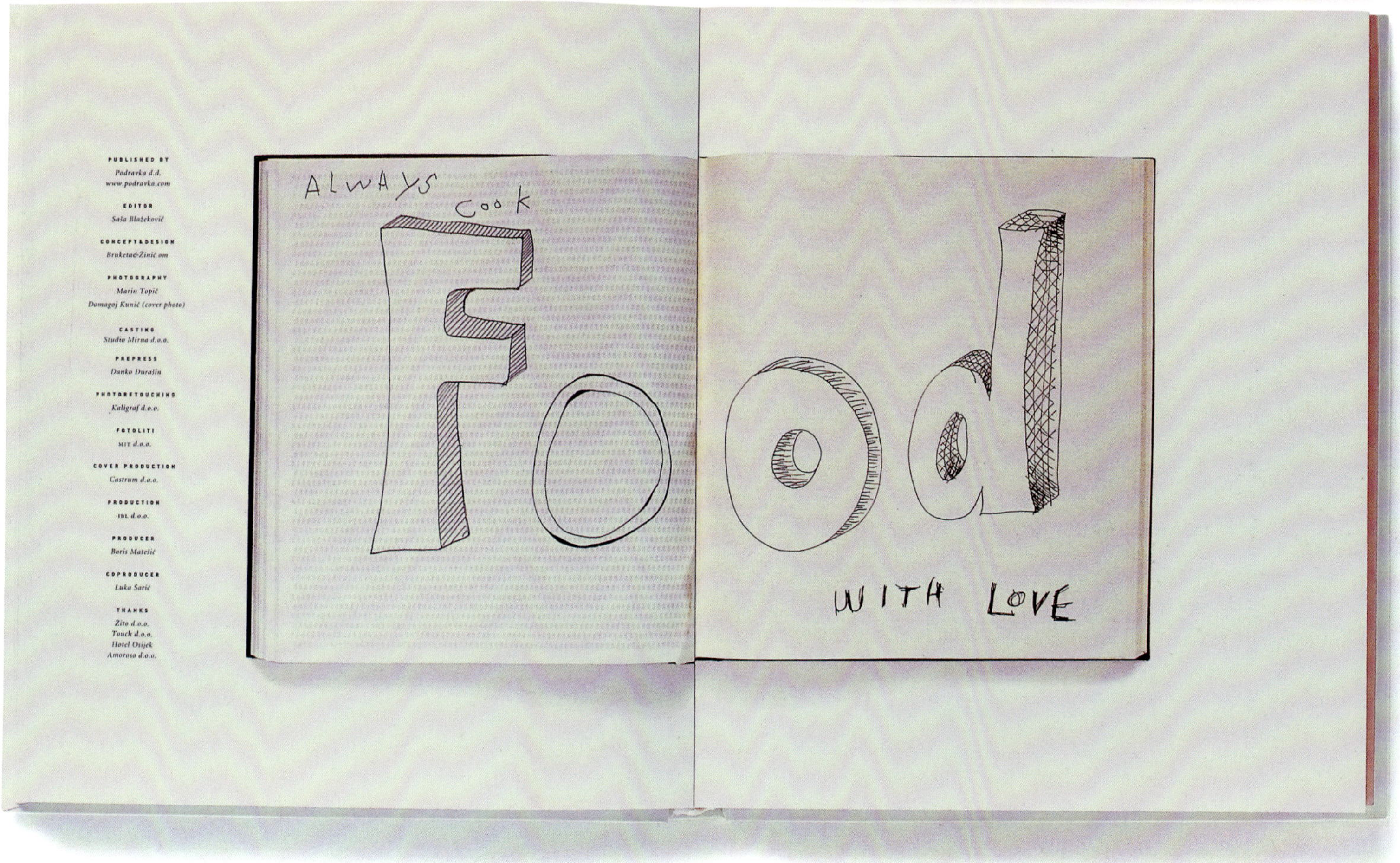

(in thousands of HRK)	Note	Podravka Group 2004	Podravka Group 2003	Podravka d.d. 2004	Podravka d.d. 2003
ASSETS					
Non-current assets					
Property, plant and equipment	12	1,734,512	1,800,330	1,043,724	1,087,990
Intangible assets	13	122,450	156,969	70,684	96,302
Investments in subsidiaries	14	-	-	428,985	428,965
Deferred tax assets	15	1,234	1,313	-	-
Available-for-sale investments	16	19,735	-	18,423	-
Receivables	17	10,634	14,729	181,488	238,831
Total non-current assets		1,888,565	1,973,341	1,743,304	1,852,088
Current assets					
Inventories	18	568,924	610,314	273,091	283,504
Trade receivables	19	770,115	673,190	391,535	350,227
Other receivables and prepaid expenses	20	63,900	75,320	60,345	52,743
Available-for-sale investments	16	5,862	15,882	-	14,655
Current portion of long-term loan receivables	17	34	2,739	77,398	82,412
Short-term loan receivables	21	3,000	3,643	46,286	11,642
Cash and cash equivalents	22	116,140	139,603	65,201	67,855
Total current assets		1,527,975	1,520,691	913,856	863,038
Total assets		3,416,540	3,494,032	2,657,160	2,715,126
LIABILITIES					
Non-current liabilities					
Long-term debt	23	684,496	501,459	560,279	363,345
Long-term provisions	31	11,985	-	-	-
Total non-current liabilities		696,481	501,459	560,279	363,345
Current liabilities					
Trade payables	24	465,969	462,909	227,323	217,406
Other liabilities	25	102,854	113,033	58,881	65,982
Short-term borrowings	26	122,996	479,484	1,026	288,911
Current portion of long-term debt	23	148,812	157,046	94,755	104,141
Total current liabilities		840,631	1,212,472	381,985	676,440
Total liabilities		1,537,112	1,713,931	942,264	1,039,785
Shareholders' equity					
Share capital	27	1,626,001	1,623,121	1,626,001	1,623,121
Share premium		12,001	12,001	12,001	12,001
Treasury shares	27	(21,159)	(35,502)	(21,159)	(35,502)
Legal and other reserves	27	105,688	112,389	65,331	79,677
Foreign currency translation reserve		3,494	(7,627)	-	-
Retained earnings		153,403	75,124	32,722	(3,956)
Total shareholders' equity	27	1,879,428	1,779,506	1,714,896	1,675,341
Minority interest	29	-	595	-	-
Total liabilities		3,416,540	3,494,032	2,657,160	2,715,126

PUBLISHED BY
Podravka d.d.
www.podravka.com

EDITOR
Saša Blažeković

CONCEPT&DESIGN
Bruketa&Žinić om

PHOTOGRAPHY
Marin Topić
Domagoj Kunić (cover photo)

CASTING
Studio Mirna d.o.o.

PREPRESS
Danko Durašin

PHOTORETOUCHING
Kaligraf d.o.o.

FOTOLITI
MIT *d.o.o.*

COVER PRODUCTION
Castrum d.o.o.

PRODUCTION
IRL *d.o.o.*

PRODUCER
Boris Matešić

COPRODUCER
Luka Šarić

THANKS
Žito d.o.o.
Touch d.o.o.
Hotel Osijek
Amoroso d.o.o.

ALWAYS cook
Food
WITH LOVE

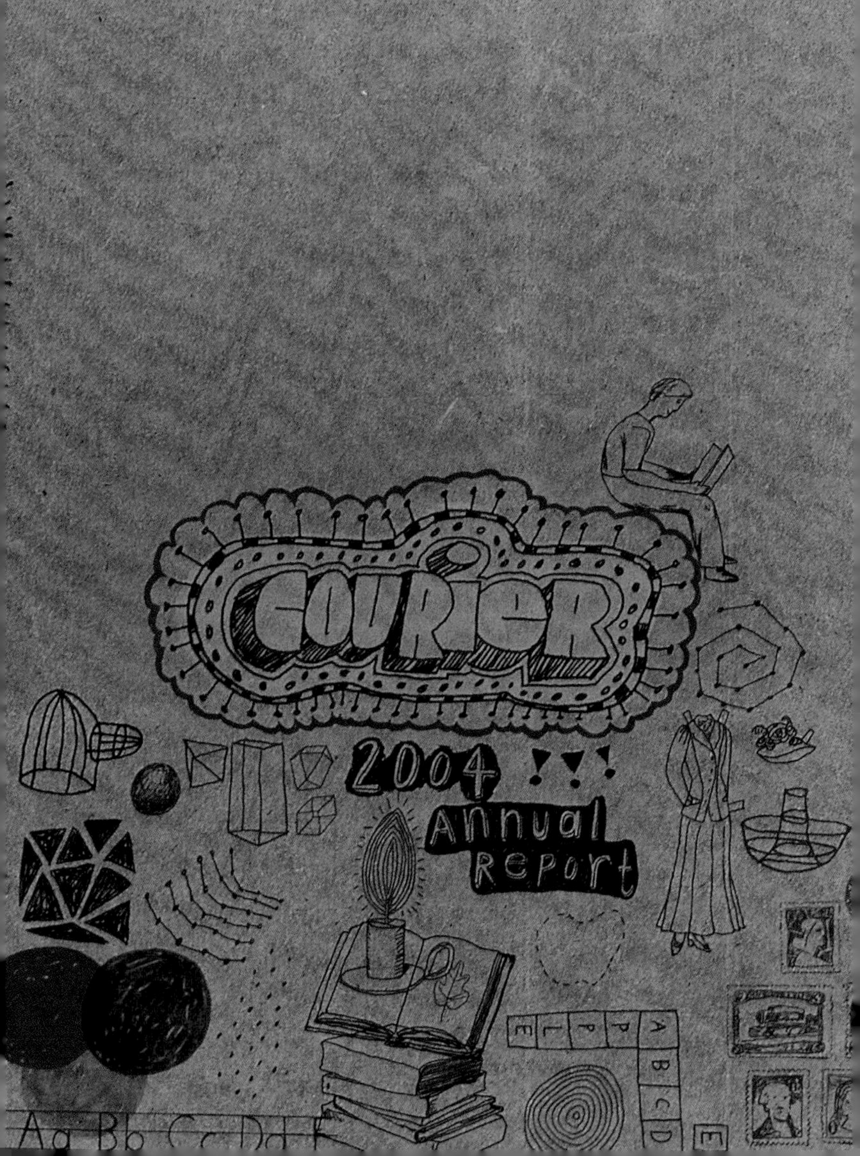
Courier
2004
Annual Report
A P P L E
A B C D E
Aa Bb Cc Dd

Art Director: Robert Krivicich,
Designers: Aaron Haesaert, Lucas Roy
Illustrators: Ben Schwab, Jeffrey Decoster
Photographer: Michael Weymouth
Writer: John Temple
Printer: Kirkwood Printing
Paper: McCoy Matte, Mohawk Options & Vellum
Page count: 72 +cover
Print run: 10,000
Size: 6.25" x 9"
Number of images: 16
Client: Courier Corp.

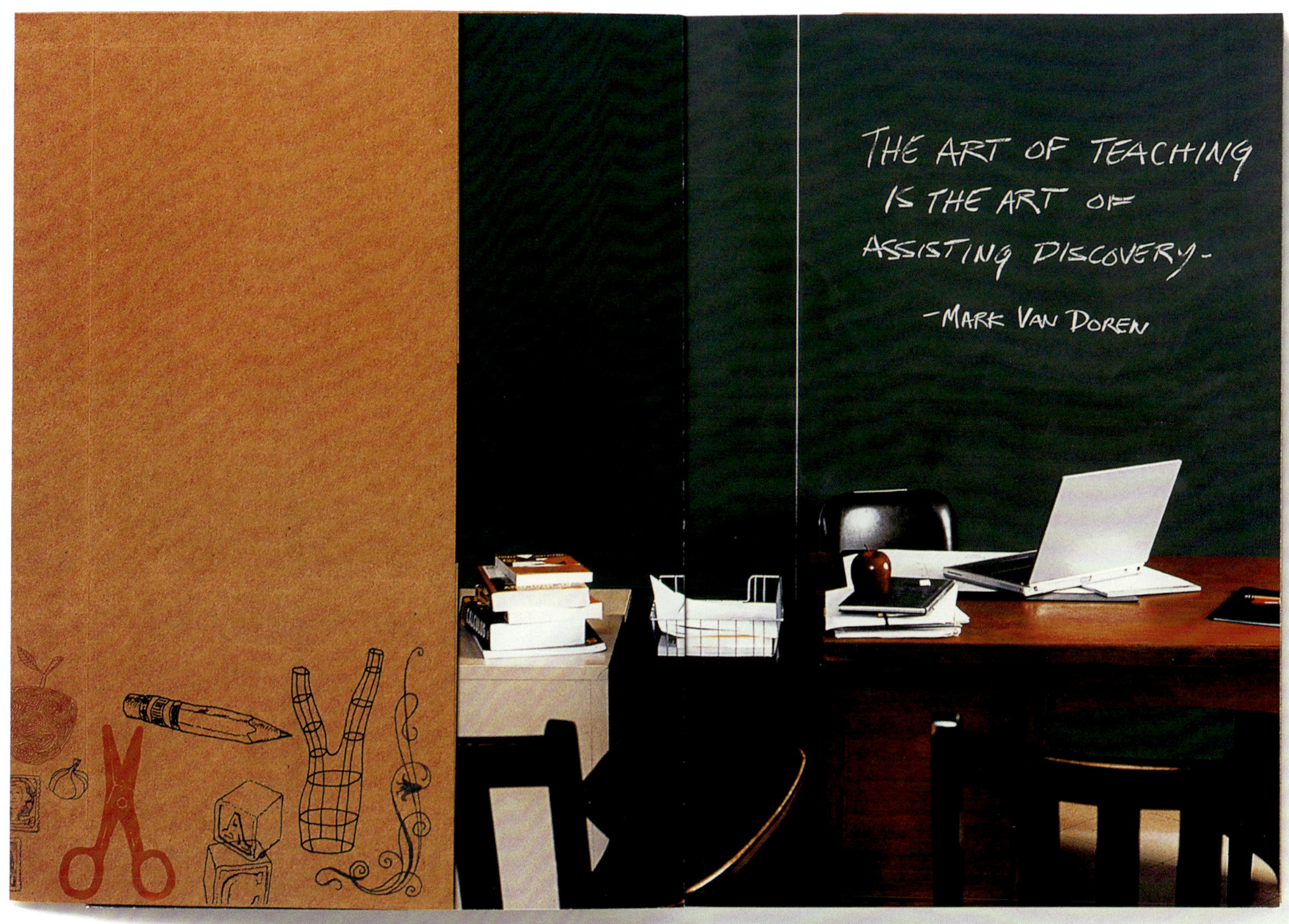

Q&A with Weymouth Design

What was the client's directive?

For Courier's 2004 Annual Report, the directive was to articulate the company's position within the growing educational market due to a recent demand for quality four-color, content-rich textbooks.

How did you define the problem?

There was only one direction to pursue, and that was to help Courier define their role within the educational market.

What was the approach?

The approach was to create a nostalgic feeling for school days, starting with a kraft paper book wrap, which was covered with doodles and artwork.

This direction led us to explore additional educational elements — photographic, typographic, and symbolic — telling a rich and visually eclectic story.

Which disciplines or people helped you with the project?

It always requires great talent to improve ideas and make them sing. Photography, illustration, and typography all played a role in refining the details in the annual. And quality printing was critical, bringing the book to life by replicating what the designer, photographer, and illustrator had in mind.

Were you happy with the result? What could have been better?

We were very happy with the result, as was the client. A few things could have been better, but they are all minutia.

How involved was the CEO in your meetings and presentations?

He was always involved and really enjoys the process. He pushes us; every year he almost expects us to go even further with the annual.

Do you feel that designers are becoming more involved in copywriting?

Yes, it is very important for a designer to be able to write, at least rough copy. It helps everyone involved, including the copywriter, to understand what the concept is and the appropriate tone.

How do you define success in Annual Report design?

We think it is achieved by telling an interesting story that people will read. We've seen people who know nothing about Courier pick up the annual purely out of curiosity, and start to flip through the entire book looking at the images, reading the copy and folding out the pages. If we can engage and entertain the audience, not just for nano-seconds but enough to actually get them to stay and read, even participate — we think that defines a successful report.

How important are awards to your client?

They are somewhat important, but not critical.

Every year, the CEO pushes us even further with the Annual.

6

REA:

High marks from students and teachers

PREPARE

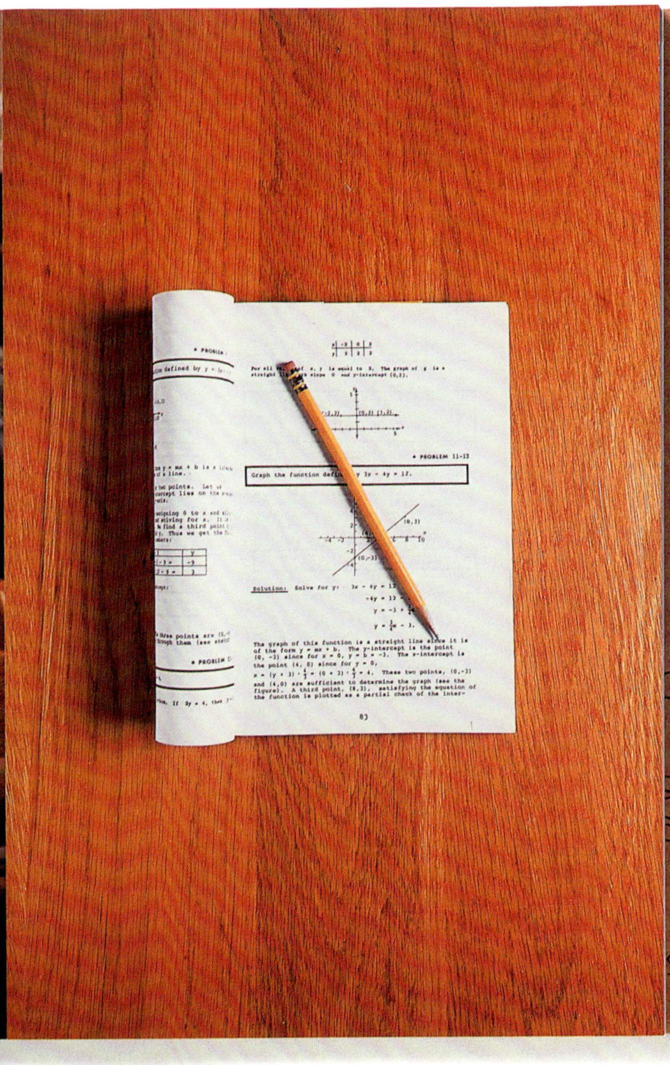

10

Book manufacturing:

Four-color phenomenon

PRODUCE

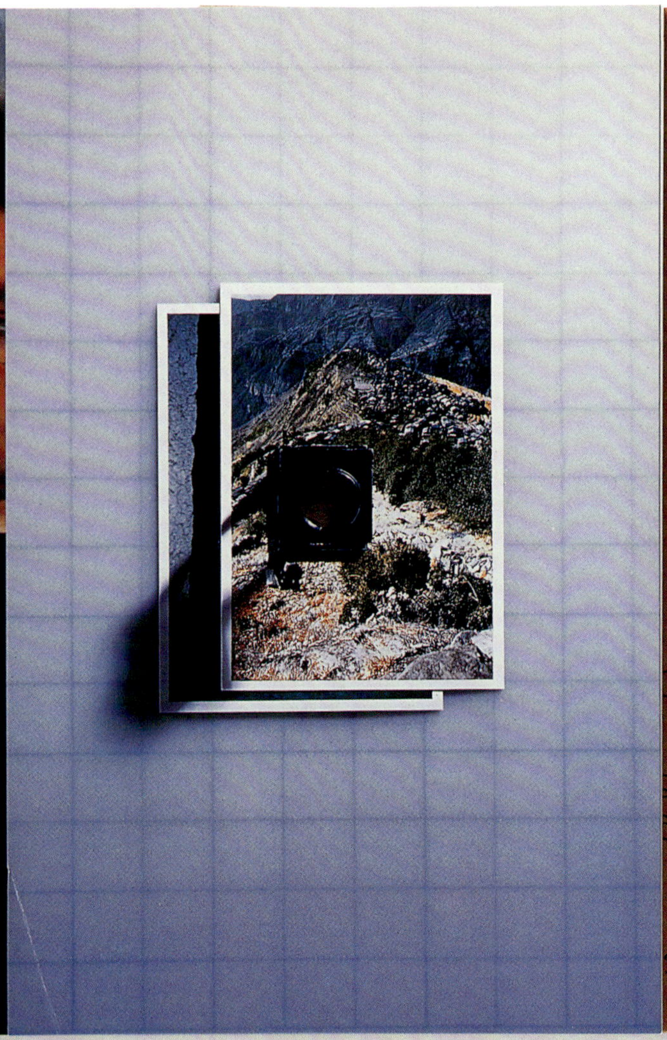

12

SECOND PERIOD:

DEAR SHAREHOLDERS, CUSTOMERS, EMPLOYEES and FRIENDS:

13

LETTER TO SHAREHOLDERS

Fiscal 2004 was another very good year for Courier. We set new sales and income records, with education sales driving increases in both of our operating segments. Our new four-color press, whose purchase raised a few eyebrows in the industry last year, proved to be a big hit with customers and led our book manufacturing segment to significant gains in textbook business. Our new specialty publishing acquisition, Research & Education Association (REA), quickly proved its merits as a complement to Dover Publications, strengthening our presence among students and teachers and sparking fresh thinking on our entire publishing lineup. We maintained our excellent cash position despite the cost of our investments in REA and the new press. And we outperformed the S&P 500 in total shareholder return for the fifth year in a row.

We didn't do everything we set out to do. We continued to encounter soft market conditions in specialty trade, which reduced sales growth in book manufacturing and at Dover as well. Fortunately, there was good news on both fronts by the end of the year. In book manufacturing, specialty trade sales finally turned positive in the fourth quarter, while long-term prospects in education led us to plan for more capacity in 2005 and beyond. And in publishing, both Dover and REA began taking steps to realize the combined growth opportunities that are now open to them.

MILESTONES

— We had our eighth straight year of earnings growth, as income from continuing operations rose to $20.5 million or $2.50 per diluted share, up 5% from $19.3 million or $2.37 per diluted share in fiscal 2003.
— Sales from continuing operations rose to a record $211 million from $202 million, an increase of 5% over last year.
— We finished the year with $24 million in cash, well positioned for future strategic moves.
— We had a three-for-two stock split and a double-digit dividend increase, enabling us to beat the S&P 500 in total shareholder return for the fifth straight year and the seventh out of the last eight.
— We continued to invest in new systems and equipment, realizing impressive results from our Man Roland press, which delighted customers and approached 100% utilization in less than six months.

16

2004 ANNUAL REPORT

segment as a whole is under new leadership with the promotion of Eric Zimmerman to the new position of Courier Vice President for Publishing. Eric, Paul, and Carl have exciting plans for the future of our publishing segment, and I am confident they will take it to a new level of sustained growth.

GOALS

Every year has its challenges and opportunities. This year we seized opportunities in education to grow beyond the limits we saw in our other markets. We expect more opportunities in the coming year, and we are ready to seize them, too.

Having started fiscal 2005 by successfully cheering the Boston Red Sox to a World Series victory, I have equal confidence in our Courier team. We have the people and the technology to drive greater growth in both of our businesses. And we have the focus, knowledge and will to do everything we set out to do. With that, here are our goals for 2005:

— Grow revenues and earnings to new records.
— Continue to build share in the education market.
— Bring our publishing brands to new markets and audiences.
— Deliver the best service ever.

As always, I am deeply grateful to everyone who has made our success possible. To our customers, employees, investors and friends—it's an honor and a thrill to serve you. I look forward to an excellent year and our next meeting.

James F. Conway III

James F. Conway III
Chairman, President and Chief Executive Officer

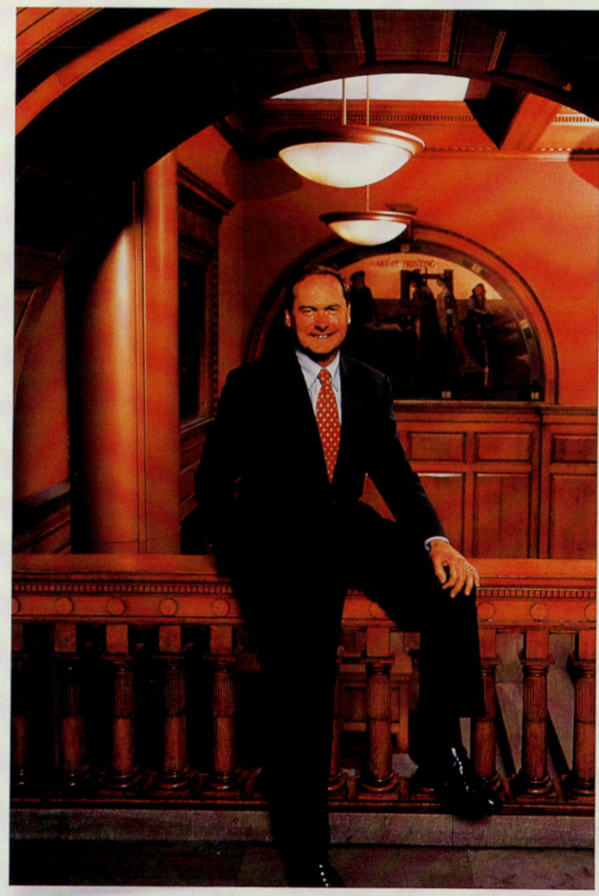

PLATE NO. 1

18

THIRD PERIOD:

CATCHING
the WAVE

BOOK MANUFACTURING

Rising textbook demand was key to the growth of Courier's book manufacturing business in 2004. It also proved the value of focusing on a balanced portfolio of primary markets where we can get to know our customers well, anticipate their needs, and plan for future growth.

20

2004 ANNUAL REPORT

Over the years Courier has steadfastly pursued a policy of disciplined investment in capacity and efficiency. In 2003, at a time when many competitors were cutting back on capital outlays, we committed to our single largest equipment investment ever with the purchase of a state-of-the-art four-color press from Man Roland for our Kendallville, Indiana plant. The wisdom of this move was demonstrated

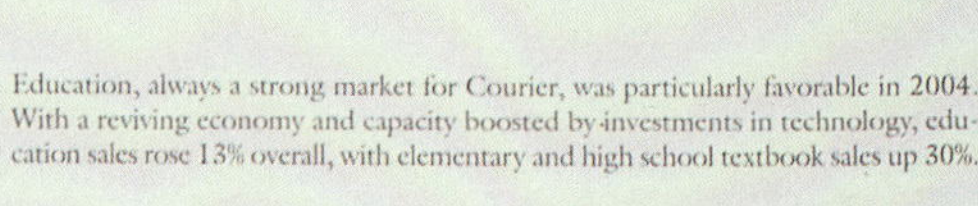

Education, always a strong market for Courier, was particularly favorable in 2004. With a reviving economy and capacity boosted by investments in technology, education sales rose 13% overall, with elementary and high school textbook sales up 30%.

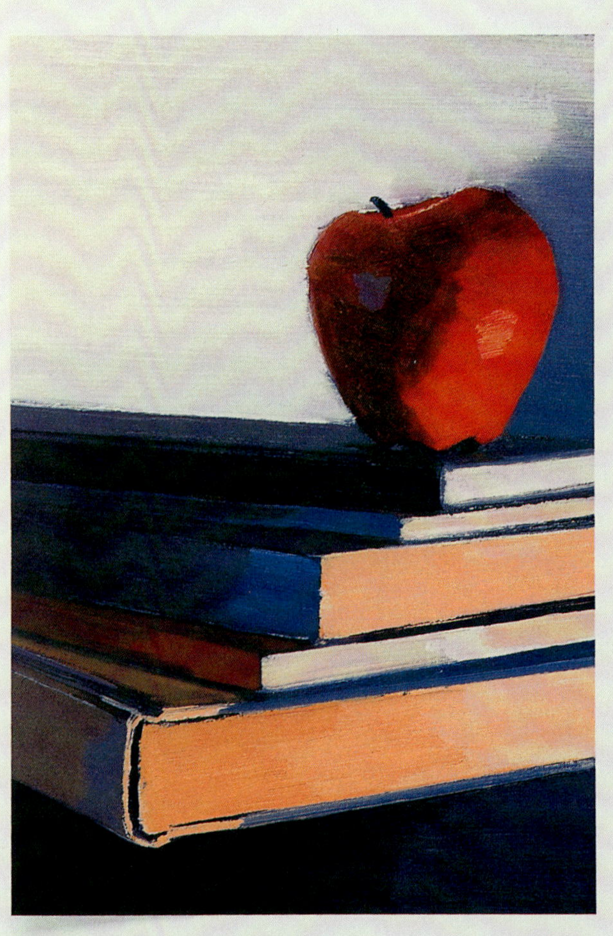

PLATE NO. 2

Stock-Based Compensation Pursuant to SFAS No. 123, "Accounting for Stock-Based Compensation," as amended by SFAS No. 148, the Company applies the recognition and measurement principles of APB Opinion No. 25, "Accounting for Stock Issued to Employees" and related interpretations. Accordingly, because the number of shares is fixed and the exercise price of the stock options equals the market price of the underlying stock on the date of grant, no compensation expense has been recognized. Had compensation cost for stock options and for grants under the ESPP been determined under the provisions of SFAS No. 123, the Company's net income would have been as follows:

	2004	2003	2002
Net income as reported	$ 20,540,000	$ 20,120,000	$ 16,175,000
Deduct: Stock-based compensation expense determined under SFAS No. 123, net of related tax effects	(1,306,000)	(965,000)	(637,000)
Pro forma net income	$ 19,234,000	$ 19,155,000	$ 15,538,000
Net income per share as reported:			
Basic	$ 2.58	$ 2.56	$ 2.09
Diluted	2.50	2.48	2.02
Pro forma net income per share:			
Basic	$ 2.42	$ 2.44	$ 2.01
Diluted	2.34	2.36	1.94

For purposes of pro forma disclosures, the fair value of each option grant was estimated on the date of grant using the Black-Scholes option-pricing model (see Note F).

B. Inventories

Inventories are valued at the lower of cost or market. Cost is determined using the last-in, first-out (LIFO) method for approximately 37% and 44% of the Company's inventories at September 25, 2004 and September 27, 2003, respectively. Other inventories, primarily in the specialty publishing segment, are determined on a first-in, first-out (FIFO) basis. REA's inventory of $1.3 million at September 25, 2004 is included in finished goods. Inventories consisted of the following at September 25, 2004 and September 27, 2003:

	2004	2003
Raw materials	$ 3,338,000	$ 1,704,000
Work in process	5,317,000	3,833,000
Finished goods	16,453,000	15,144,000
Total	$ 25,108,000	$ 20,681,000

On a FIFO basis, reported year-end inventories would have been higher by $5.5 million in both fiscal 2004 and 2003.

C. Income Taxes

The provision for income taxes from continuing operations differs from that computed using the statutory federal income tax rates for the following reasons:

	2004	2003	2002
Federal taxes at statutory rate	$ 11,043,000	$ 10,334,000	$ 8,457,000
State taxes, net of federal tax benefit	837,000	701,000	366,000
Tax benefit of export related income	(882,000)	(823,000)	(868,000)
Other	13,000	42,000	52,000
Total	$ 11,011,000	$ 10,254,000	$ 8,007,000

The provision for income taxes from continuing operations consisted of the following:

	2004	2003	2002
Currently payable:			
Federal	$ 7,325,000	$ 8,238,000	$ 5,776,000
State	1,215,000	1,078,000	700,000
	8,540,000	9,316,000	6,476,000
Deferred:			
Federal	2,398,000	870,000	1,507,000
State	73,000	68,000	24,000
	2,471,000	938,000	1,531,000
Total	$ 11,011,000	$ 10,254,000	$ 8,007,000

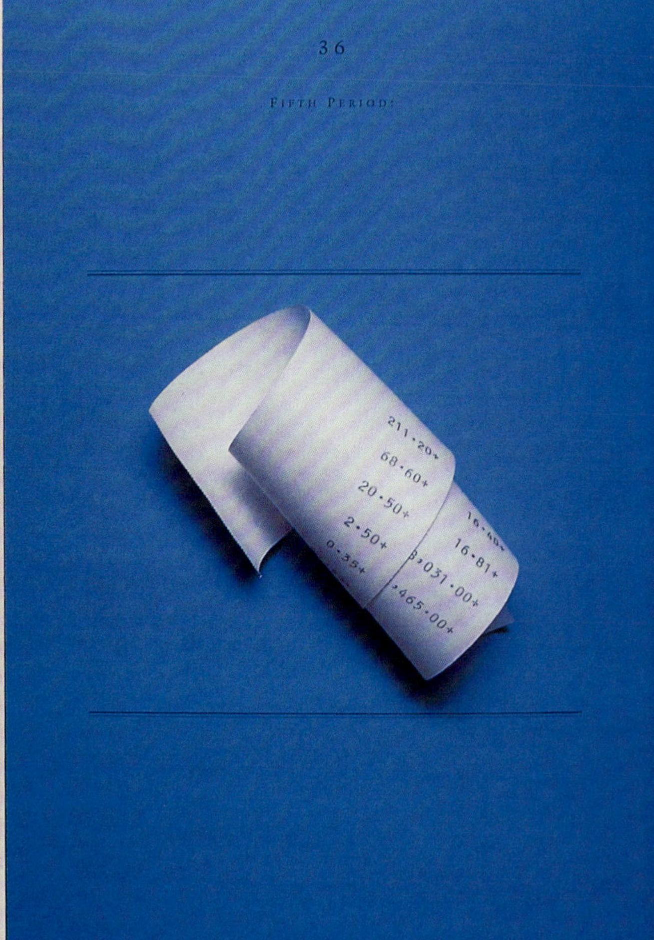

2004 Annual Review

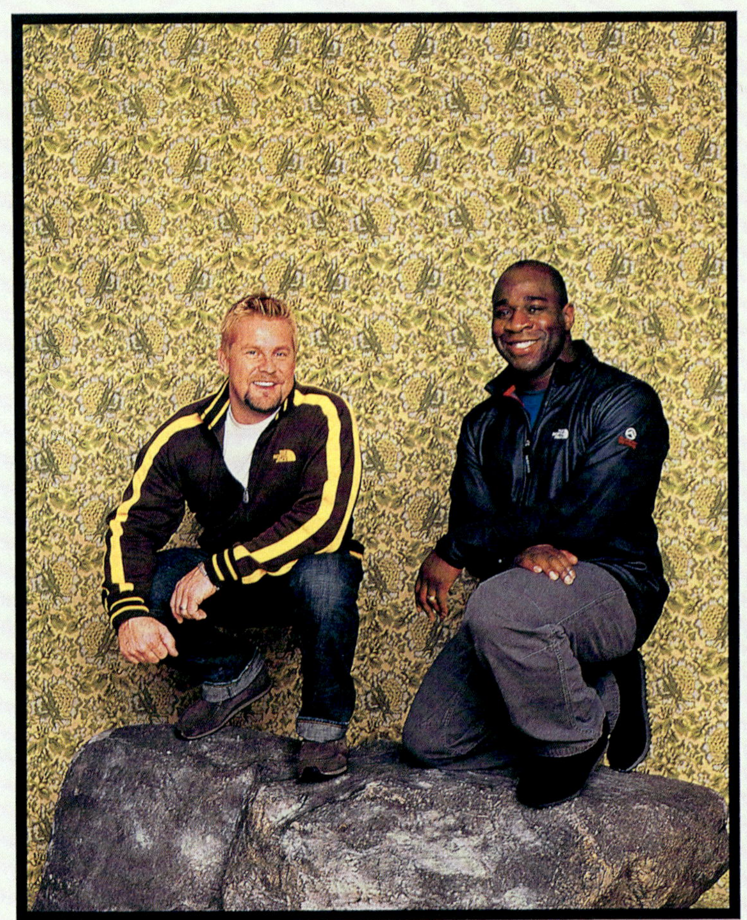

LIVING THE BRAND *VF Corporation 2004 Annual Report*

Art Director: David Schimmel
Designer: David Schimmel, Chris Kiorbey, financials
Photographer: Daniela Stallinger, Vincent Ricardel,
Writers: Walter Thomas, Cindy Knoebel
Printer: Hemlock, BC
Paper: Mohawk options, Mohawk opaque, financials
Page count: 108 +cover
Print run: 60,000
Size: 6" x 9"
Number of images: 27
Client: VF Corporation

VF IS ABOUT PEOPLE. Our people. And our consumers. In fact, one of the reasons we're so successful is because we're a reflection of our consumers. Like them, we're dreamers, rebels, adventurers, teachers and inventors. From our stockrooms to our boardroom, we live our brands.

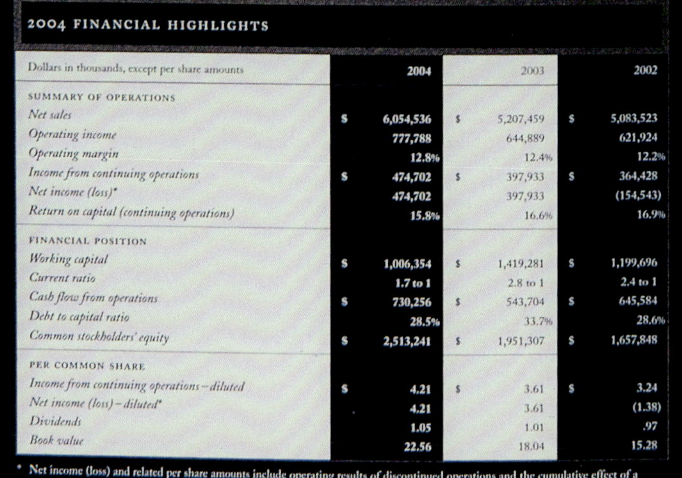

2004 FINANCIAL HIGHLIGHTS

Dollars in thousands, except per share amounts	2004	2003	2002
SUMMARY OF OPERATIONS			
Net sales	$ 6,054,536	$ 5,207,459	$ 5,083,523
Operating income	777,788	644,889	621,924
Operating margin	12.8%	12.4%	12.2%
Income from continuing operations	$ 474,702	$ 397,933	$ 364,428
*Net income (loss)**	474,702	397,933	(154,543)
Return on capital (continuing operations)	15.8%	16.6%	16.9%
FINANCIAL POSITION			
Working capital	$ 1,006,354	$ 1,419,281	$ 1,199,696
Current ratio	1.7 to 1	2.8 to 1	2.4 to 1
Cash flow from operations	$ 730,256	$ 543,704	$ 645,584
Debt to capital ratio	28.5%	33.7%	28.6%
Common stockholders' equity	$ 2,513,241	$ 1,951,307	$ 1,657,848
PER COMMON SHARE			
Income from continuing operations – diluted	$ 4.21	$ 3.61	$ 3.24
*Net income (loss) – diluted**	4.21	3.61	(1.38)
Dividends	1.05	1.01	.97
Book value	22.56	18.04	15.28

* Net income (loss) and related per share amounts include operating results of discontinued operations and the cumulative effect of a change in accounting policy in 2002. See details in the accompanying consolidated financial statements.

01

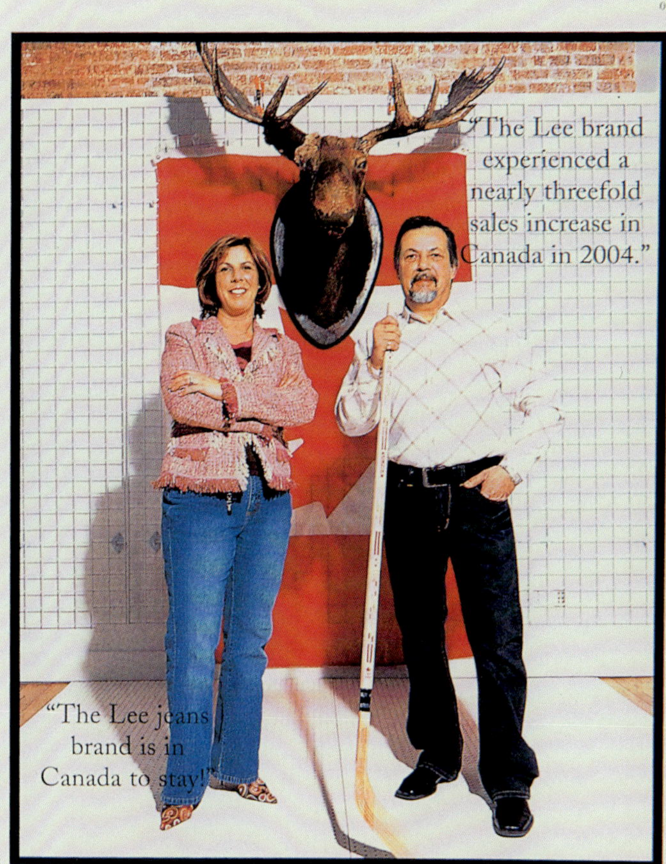

BARBARA NARDINI-ZITELLA *Sales Account Executive, Wrangler & Lee Brands Canada*
A Banner Year: 2004 was definitely the most energizing year in my 25-year career. The success of Lee in Canada has been overwhelming and I'm very proud to have been part of it. BRIAN WILLIAMS *VP, Wrangler & Lee Brands Canada & Puerto Rico*
2005 and Beyond: We have aggressive plans to fuel growth with exciting initiatives for the retail community and great products for consumers.

Q&A with And Partners

What was the client's directive?

To prominently feature employees and highlight the initial success and future promise of VF's aggressive growth plan.

How did you define the problem?

How can we recognize employees, explain VF's growth plan and also showcase the company's 55+ global lifestyle brands in a single, compelling and cohesive story?

What was the approach?

We dressed more than 40 employees in their respective brands, photographed them straight on, usually in pairs, in interesting brand-related contexts designed to connect with consumers. We then allowed them describe in their own words the role they proudly played in VF's growth plan and some of the results they achieved.

Which disciplines or people helped you with the project?

Writer(s), photographer(s), designers and an account manager.

Were you happy with the result? What could have been better?

We were happy, and more importantly, so was the client.

What was the client's response?

The client's response was overwhelmingly positive. The Annual Report played well internally because the employees photographed represented a variety of levels, and people loved seeing themselves and their colleagues in the book. The external message was equally strong, because it showed that real people were working really hard to produce tangible financial results. "Living the Brand" also succeeded in showing that a lot of popular consumer brands are now part of the VF family.

How involved was the CEO in your meetings, presentations, etc.?

The CEO provided initial strategic input and direction and then allowed everyone to do what they do best as far as creative development and implementation were concerned. He reviewed and blessed the outcome before it went on press. Day-to-day, And Partners worked closely with the head of Investor Relations, who was responsible for the Annual Report.

Do you feel that designers are becoming more involved in copywriting?

We have always believed that clients get the best results when design and copy are developed in tandem. An Annual Report depends heavily on text and messages told in words, so it would be impossible to design one without getting involved in the copy.

Typically we take a pass at composing the main messages, then depend on the copywriter to develop the themes further in the perfect words.

How do you define success in Annual Report design?

Being hired again the following year.

How important are awards to your client?

This client was not focused on awards when And Partners started working with them. Now they've gotten so many, they're always asking, "What have we won?" Everyone appreciates some recognition for good work.

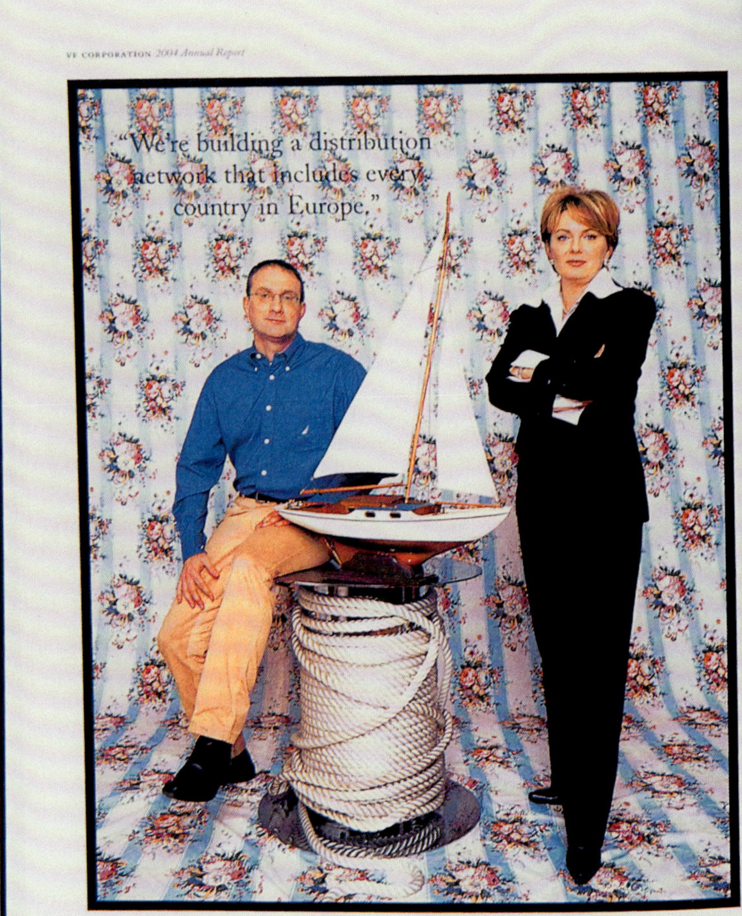

PAOLO DE MARCO *VP, General Manager, Nautica Europe* *Immediate Goal:* To create a motivated and efficient team to bring success in Europe for this great American brand. *Lifelong Goal:* Never stop learning. PATRICIA CANAVAN *VP, International Licensing, Nautica Apparel* *Formula for Growth:* Individual brand initiatives can be maximized when linked to VF's corporate strategy. *East Meets Quest:* The brand distribution model we implemented in China doubled our licensed business there in 2004. *What's Next:* Launching in India.

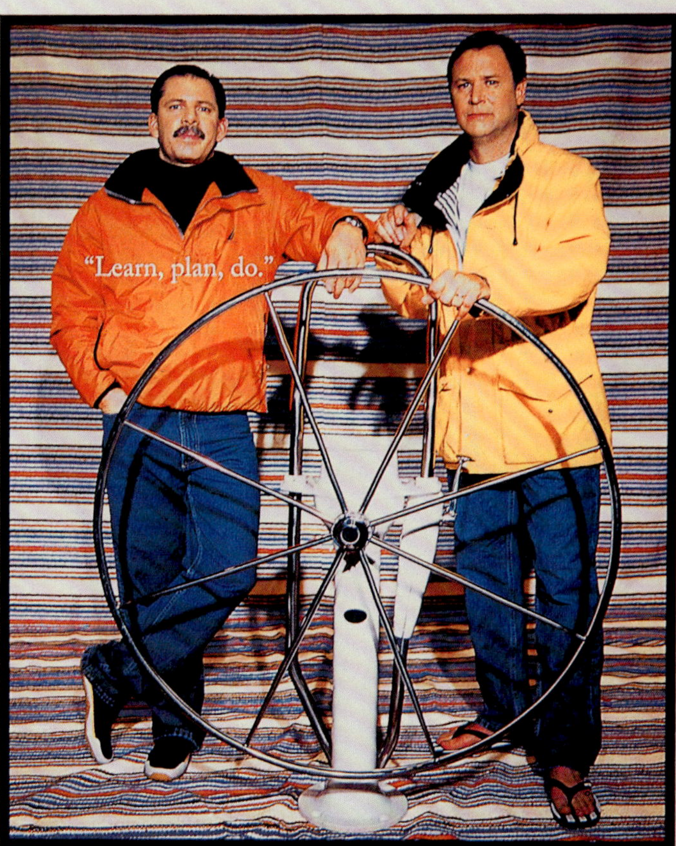

CHRIS FUENTES (L.) *VP, Marketing, Nautica* *Aspect of Company Culture He Most Admires:* Its quiet strength and determination. *Aspect of Himself He Most Admires:* My passion for winning as a team. CHRISTOPHER HEYN *President, Nautica International, Nautica Jeans Company, Nautica Children's Company* *Chris At a Glance:* High energy, passionate and compassionate. *Competitive Edge:* Maintaining a self-sharpening environment, staying ahead of the creative process and continuing to grow the brand. *Method to His Madness:* Identify the problem, create the solution and demand the resolution.

Success is being hired again the following year.

VF CORPORATION *2004 Annual Report*

BERNA GOLDSTEIN *Director of Merchandising, Bestform & Curvation, VF Intimates* *How Berna Sees Her Job:* A merchandiser is really the hub of a wheel. *How Berna Thinks:* "What if" instead of business as usual. *Upward Curve:* Not only did we expand our assortment for the *Curvation*® brand, we were also able to raise our retail price points. RAY NADEAU *VP, General Manager, Bestform & Curvation, VF Intimates* *A Typical Ray Day:* Focusing on the priorities that drive growth. *A Ray of Understanding:* My strength is knowing our consumer and retailer needs, and finding "white space" opportunities.

15

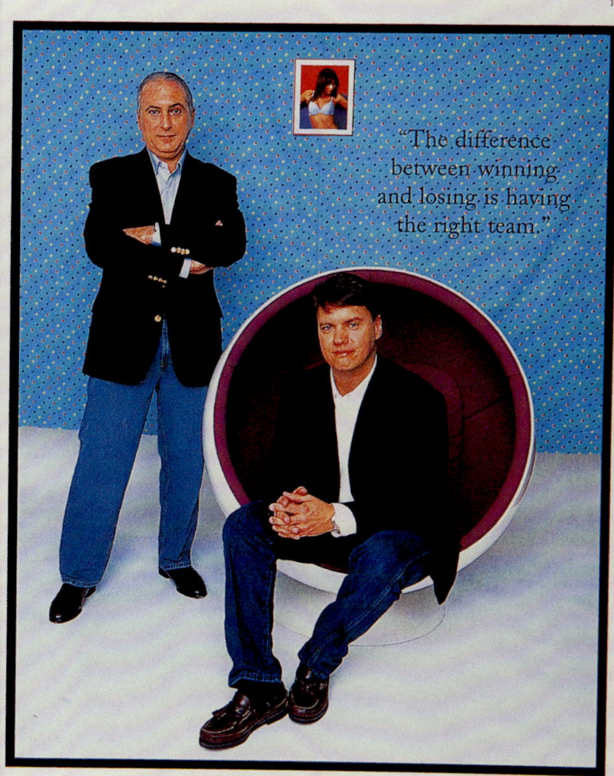

ART DECESARO (L) *VP, General Manager, Vassarette, VF Intimates* *Personal Compulsion:* Staying Number One. *Method:* By thinking outside of the box in both product innovation and marketing. *Outside the Box Idea:* Our introduction and sponsorship of the first female NASCAR race driver in the truck series. MILES BOHANNAN *Director of Marketing, Vassarette, VF Intimates* *Part of the Job:* Staying at the top of my game despite competitive pressure. *Top Two Qualities:* Open-mindedness and tenacity. *Keeping Growth on Track:* We initiated a focused direct mail piece aimed at Hispanic consumers.

TO OUR STOCKHOLDERS:

Last year at this time, we talked about our expectations for another record year in 2004, and projected a 5% increase in both sales and earnings. I'm pleased to report that we had a banner year, substantially exceeding those projections. In 2004 sales jumped 16%, topping the $6 billion mark for the first time in VF's history. Earnings increased 17% to a record $4.21 per share. Sales benefited from growth across most of our core businesses, plus the addition of three terrific new brands: *Vans*®, *Napapijri*® and *Kipling*®.

27

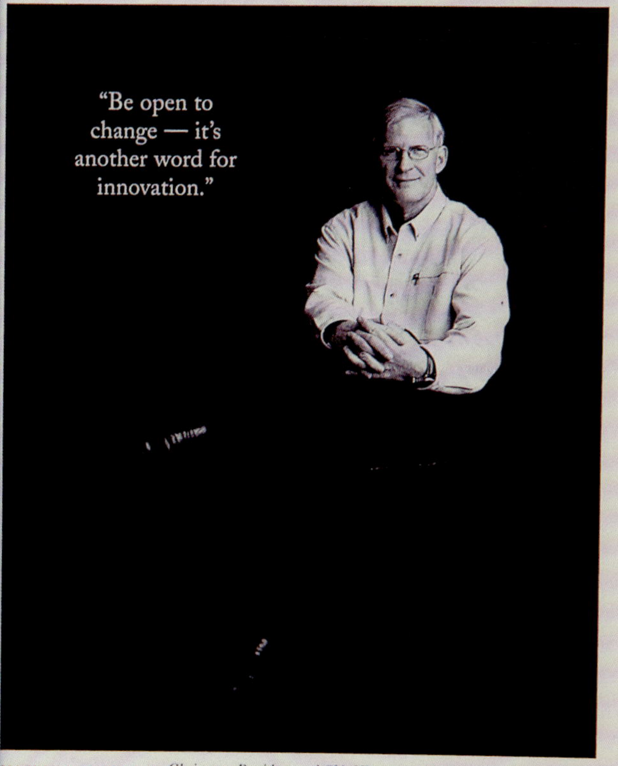

MACKEY J. MCDONALD *Chairman, President and Chief Executive Officer*

Despite this acquisition activity, we ended the year with our balance sheet in great shape and with very strong cash flow. Debt as a percentage of total capital was 28%, and cash flow from operations reached $730 million.

We paid out 25% of our earnings in dividends and increased the dividends paid to shareholders for the 32nd consecutive year. All of this resulted in a good year for our stockholders: VF's share price rose 28% in 2004 versus an increase of 9% for the S&P 500.

2004 marked the first year of our Company's ambitious new growth plan, which was the result of many months of hard work and analysis by scores of people both within and outside VF. Following several years of restructuring, business divestitures and relatively flat sales performance, it was time to take a new and more aggressive approach toward stimulating top line growth. That approach is already paying off, and we expect to continue the momentum this year.

In the course of developing this plan, we created and launched a new Vision Statement that heralds our commitment to growth and serves as a rallying point for all our associates and businesses. To wit: *VF will grow by building leading lifestyle brands that excite consumers around the world.* That says a lot in just a few words, but first and foremost, it states our commitment to growth. Our industry is consolidating and so are our customers. We intend to be an active participant in this process by adding brands and capabilities that will ensure that we remain vital to our customers and our consumers. The focus of our growth will be lifestyle brands — brands that through their products and positioning make a powerful statement about the aspirations, activities and interests of consumers. We also recognize that in order to grow, our brands must excite consumers through product innovation, quality, functionality and value. In short, consumers get excited about a brand when it makes them feel better about the lives they lead. And of course, as a global company, we're always looking to build great brands that have a truly global reach.

The strategic foundation of our growth plan consists of five key drivers. Our intense focus on these drivers resulted in a number of significant accomplishments in 2004.

Build New Growing Lifestyle Brands Our goal is to generate 8% sales growth annually, through growth in our core categories as well as through the addition of new lifestyle brands. In 2004 we saw a 9% sales gain in our Intimates coalition. Sales in our Imagewear coalition grew 6%, while Jeanswear coalition sales were about even with prior year levels. These businesses provide us with a powerful foundation: not only do they comprise leading brands and businesses in their categories, they are very stable and profitable, generating tremendous cash flow that is essential to increasing shareholder value. As we look to grow our category-driven brands, it will be in the context of extending them into additional product categories, new consumer segments and new geographic areas.

The biggest area of growth for us in 2004 was our Outdoor coalition, which achieved a sales gain of 73%. *The North Face*® brand had a stellar year, with sales up 38%. It was also an exceptionally busy year on the acquisition front for our Outdoor team, with the addition of three companies that had total annualized sales of $489 million at the time of purchase. Based in Southern California, *Vans*® is an authentic action sports shoe brand. *Napapijri*® is a premium European outdoor apparel brand, and *Kipling*® is a fun and fashionable brand of bags and accessories for women. Each acquisition fulfills all of our primary acquisition criteria:

- A strong brand with room to grow
- Adds a new category or consumer
- Strengthens our product or channel presence
- Has global reach
- Enjoys distinctive brand positioning
- Has the potential to reach our financial targets
- Is quickly accretive to earnings

Sportswear contributed $605 million to sales in 2004, reflecting a full year's contribution from the acquisition of Nautica in mid-2003. The *Nautica*® brand is performing above our expectations, and we're extremely pleased with the results we're seeing from our work to reposition the brand and improve our product offerings.

Expand our Share with Winning Customers Our big customers are getting bigger, and we need to partner with them in a different way in order to continue to grow our share of their business. In 2004 we added the talent and resources to spearhead the creation of a new customer team organization that is leveraging and coordinating our efforts across VF's brands and coalitions. We're also investing more to analyze our customers' businesses to help us identify new opportunities for mutual growth.

Stretch our Brands & Customers to New Geographies The focus internationally is, first and foremost, to build our brands into truly

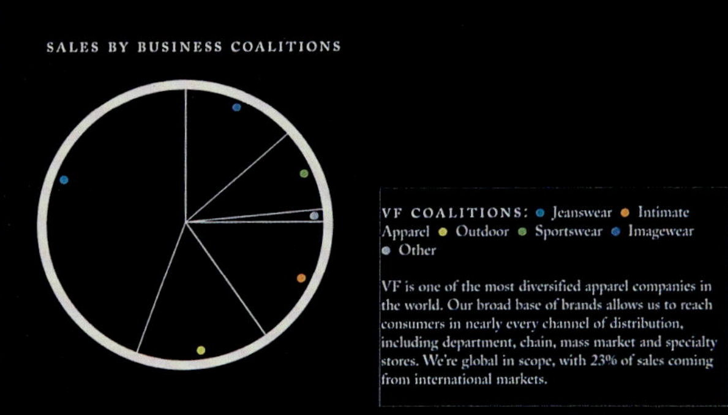

IMAGEWEAR A leader in both uniforms and licensed apparel, our Imagewear coalition performed solidly in 2004, with higher sales and record profits.

The coalition has been re-energized by its new "customer first" approach, which has led to a broad based reorganization into six customer-focused sectors: Industrial, Service, Protective, Public Safety, Affinity and Retail. Each sector is supported by a team that is dedicated to growing the business, an approach that has already started to pay off in the form of more innovative products, superior service and — most importantly — a tighter connection between our brands and consumers. We also are excited about our January 2005 acquisition of a licensee of the Harley-Davidson Motor Company, Inc., which extends our leadership in that business. We're delighted to be partners with one of the world's great lifestyle brands.

Lee Sport
Chase Authentics®
CSA
Red Kap
Bulwark
Penn State Textile
NFL Red®
NFL White®
Horace Small
VF Imagewear
Lee
Wrangler Hero
Chef Designs
E. Magrath
Byron Nelson
NBA
Harley-Davidson®
NCAA Blue Disc®

Our licensed apparel business had an extraordinary year, led by the Super Bowl, the Playoffs and the World Series. We're proud of our relationships with major sports, including the National Football League, Major League Baseball and NASCAR, which has enabled us to grow significantly by giving sports fans the products and quality they want. These high profile events require enormous service capabilities to turn out and deliver huge quantities of products featuring winning teams within hours of each event. For example, for the World Series, we delivered over two million units within 72 hours. In keeping with our Customer First initiative, we've organized our licensed business around each major customer to drive the right solution for their distinctive fan and consumer base. It's working — with licensed apparel sales growing at a double-digit rate for the past three years.

As the economy stabilized, so did our uniform business. In fact, our flagship *Red Kap*® brand had its strongest year since 2000. The industry continues to consolidate, but our position has never been stronger. *Horace Small*®, a leader in the public safety arena, has teamed with *The North Face*® brand to provide products such as *The Force*™ jacket. Made with the latest in fabric and construction technology, *The Force*™ jacket is designed with a layered approach, making it suitable for every public service activity, including those taking place in extremely cold conditions. The two brands are furthering their partnership this year with their support of "Cops on Top," a mountaineering program that honors officers who have lost their lives in the line of duty. And our *Bulwark*® brand, a leader in secondary protective apparel, continues to drive innovation for safer, more comfortable products. The service sector remains a bright spot in the employment picture, and we're participating via our *Penn State Textile*™ and *Chef Designs*® *Essentials with Style*™ brands, both leaders in their fields. At the same time, we're expanding our base of large corporate and government accounts, providing them with a one-stop shop for all their global uniform and apparel needs. In fact, VF Imagewear is the largest supplier of non-military apparel to U.S. government agencies, including U.S. Customs and Border Protection and the Transportation Security Administration.

Two new golf apparel brands for us are *E. Magrath*® and *Byron Nelson*®. Both are well-known within the golf industry and will help to extend our reach in corporate image apparel.

From the boardroom to the factory floor — and from the gridiron to the speedway — VF Imagewear has you covered.

CHANNELS OF DISTRIBUTION

BRANDS *Licensed Brands	United States Image	United States Retail
Lee Sport		●
*Chase Authentics**		●
CSA		●
Red Kap	●	
Bulwark	●	
Penn State Textile		●
*NFL Red**		●
*NFL White**		●
Horace Small		●
VF Imagewear		●
Lee		●
Wrangler Hero		●
Chef Designs		●
E. Magrath		●
Byron Nelson		●
NBA		●
*Harley-Davidson**		●
*NCAA Blue Disc**		●

VF CORPORATION *2004 Annual Report*

45

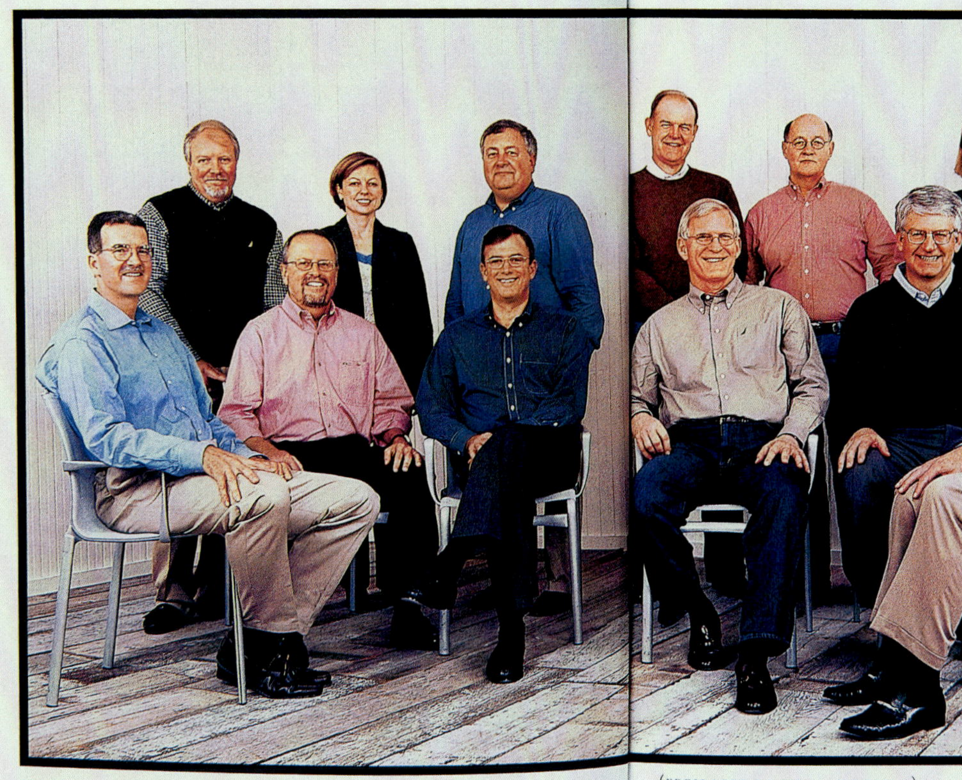

OPERATING COMMITTEE: (FROM LEFT TO RIGHT, SEATED) ROBERT K. SHEARER *VP, Finance and Global Processes and Chief Financial Officer* JOHN P. SCHAMBERGER *VP and Chairman, Cross Coalition Management* ERIC C. WISEMAN *VP and Chairman, Outdoor and Sportswear Coalitions* MACKEY J. MCDONALD *Chairman, President and Chief Executive Officer* GEORGE N. DERHOFER *VP and Chairman, Intimate Apparel and Imagewear Coalitions* MICHAEL T. GANNAWAY *VP, Customer Management*

(FROM LEFT TO RIGHT, STANDING) BOYD A. ROGERS *VP, Global Supply Chain and Technology* SUSAN LARSON WILLIAMS *VP, Human Resources* BRADLEY W. BATTEN *VP, Controller* TERRY L. LAY *VP and Chairman, Jeanswear Coalition* FRANK C. PICKARD III *VP, Treasurer* CANDACE S. CUMMINGS *VP, Administration, General Counsel and Secretary* FRANKLIN T. TERKELSEN *VP, Mergers and Acquisitions*

VF CORPORATION *2004 Annual Report*

CONSOLIDATED STATEMENTS OF COMMON STOCKHOLDERS' EQUITY

In thousands	Common Stock	Additional Paid-in Capital	Accumulated Other Comprehensive Income (Loss)	Retained Earnings
Balance, December 2001	$ 109,998	$ 884,638	$ (103,040)	$ 1,221,200
Net loss	–	–	–	(154,543)
Cash dividends:				
Common Stock	–	–	–	(106,018)
Series B Redeemable Preferred Stock	–	–	–	(2,755)
Tax benefit from Preferred Stock dividends	–	–	–	12
Redemption of Preferred Stock	–	–	–	(5,780)
Conversion of Preferred Stock	182	–	–	3,332
Purchase of treasury shares	(3,000)	–	–	(121,623)
Stock compensation plans, net	1,345	45,494	–	(381)
Common Stock held in trust for deferred compensation plans	–	–	–	(112)
Foreign currency translation	–	–	25,441	–
Minimum pension liability adjustment	–	–	(126,841)	–
Derivative financial instruments	–	–	(9,461)	–
Unrealized losses on marketable securities	–	–	(240)	–
Balance, December 2002	108,525	930,132	(214,141)	833,332
Net income	–	–	–	397,933
Cash dividends:				
Common Stock	–	–	–	(109,020)
Series B Redeemable Preferred Stock	–	–	–	(2,238)
Conversion of Preferred Stock	358	–	–	6,556
Purchase of treasury shares	(1,680)	–	–	(59,720)
Stock compensation plans, net	943	34,858	–	(333)
Common Stock held in trust for deferred compensation plans	24	–	–	1,092
Foreign currency translation	–	–	48,843	–
Minimum pension liability adjustment	–	–	(32,356)	–
Derivative financial instruments	–	–	819	–
Unrealized gains on marketable securities	–	–	7,380	–
Balance, December 2003	108,170	964,990	(189,455)	1,067,602
Net income	–	–	–	**474,702**
Cash dividends:				
Common Stock	–	–	–	**(115,900)**
Series B Redeemable Preferred Stock	–	–	–	**(1,831)**
Conversion of Preferred Stock	**205**	–	–	**3,729**
Stock compensation plans, net	**3,026**	**122,651**	–	**(273)**
Common Stock held in trust for deferred compensation plans	**(13)**	–	–	**(746)**
Foreign currency translation	–	–	**30,069**	–
Minimum pension liability adjustment	–	–	**41,712**	–
Derivative financial instruments	–	–	**(691)**	–
Unrealized gains on marketable securities	–	–	**5,294**	–
Balance, December 2004	**$ 111,388**	**$ 1,087,641**	**$ (113,071)**	**$ 1,427,283**

See notes to consolidated financial statements.

NOTES TO CONSOLIDATED FINANCIAL STATEMENTS DECEMBER 2004

NOTE A – SIGNIFICANT ACCOUNTING POLICIES

Description of Business: VF Corporation ("VF") is a multinational consumer apparel company based in the United States ("U.S."). VF, through its subsidiaries, designs and manufactures or sources from independent contractors a variety of apparel for all ages. VF has significant market shares in jeanswear, sportswear, intimate apparel and outdoor apparel marketed primarily under VF-owned brand names. VF is also a leader in occupational apparel and in daypacks, backpacks and technical outdoor equipment.

VF markets these products to a broad customer base of specialty, department and discount stores throughout the world. VF's ten largest customers, all U.S.-based retailers, accounted for 38% of consolidated 2004 sales and 29% of total accounts receivable at the end of 2004. Sales are made on an unsecured basis under customary terms that may vary by channel of distribution or by geographic region. VF continuously monitors the creditworthiness of its customers and has established internal policies regarding customer credit limits. The breadth of product offerings, combined with the large number and geographic diversity of its customers, limits VF's concentration of risks.

Fiscal Year and Basis of Presentation: VF operates and reports using a 52/53 week fiscal year ending on the Saturday closest to December 31 of each year. All references to "2004", "2003" and "2002" relate to the fiscal years ended on January 1, 2005 (52 weeks), January 3, 2004 (52 weeks) and January 4, 2003 (53 weeks), respectively. For presentation purposes herein, all fiscal years are presented as ended in December.

The financial position, results of operations and cash flows of two businesses that were disposed of during 2002 have been presented as discontinued operations for all periods. See Note C.

Principles of Consolidation: The consolidated financial statements include the accounts of VF and its wholly-owned and majority-owned subsidiaries, after elimination of intercompany transactions and profits. Minority ownership interests are not significant. Investments in 50%-owned joint ventures, in which VF does not exercise control, are accounted for using the equity method of accounting.

You are holding the 2004 annual report to stockholders of AMB Property Corporation.

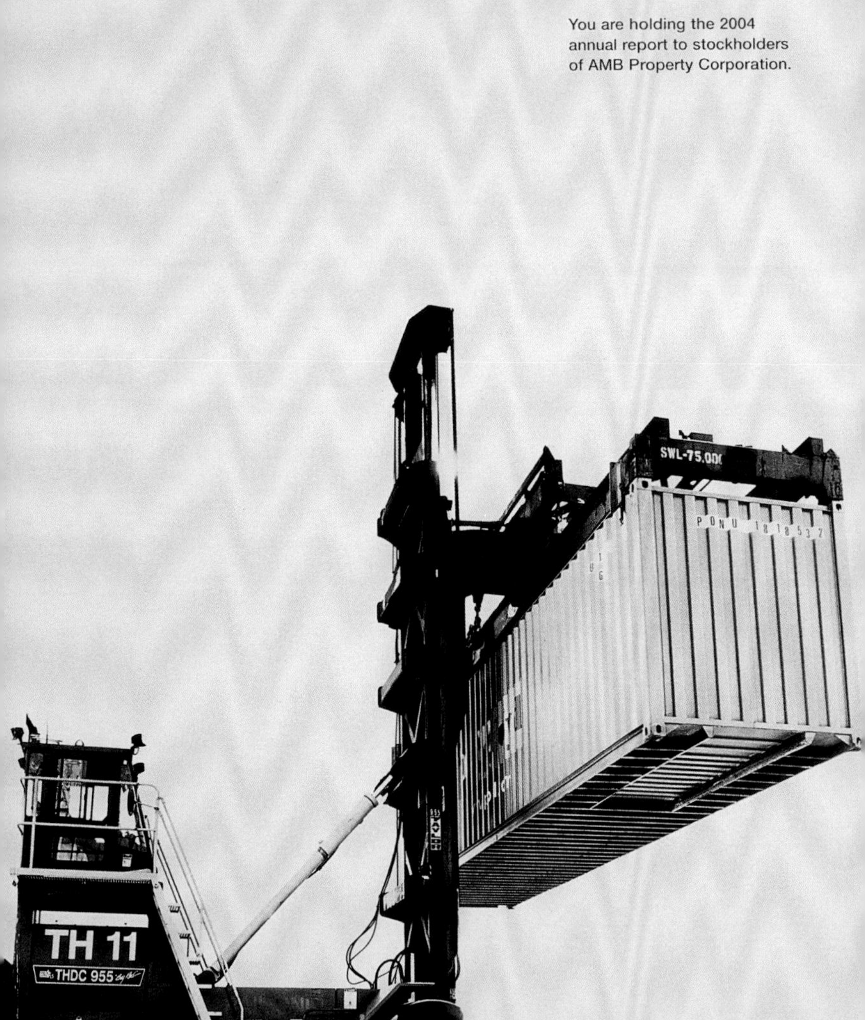

Art Director: Ted Bluey
Photographers: Christopher Griffith, Randy Yau

Writer: Rob Price
Printer: Cenveo SF
Page count: 70 +covers

Number of images:8
Print run: 22,000
Size: 8.5" x 11"

Paper: Sappi Hannoart Silk 100#C, Sappi Hannoart Silk 100#T

Mohawk Superfine Ultra White Eggshell 80#T
Client: AMB

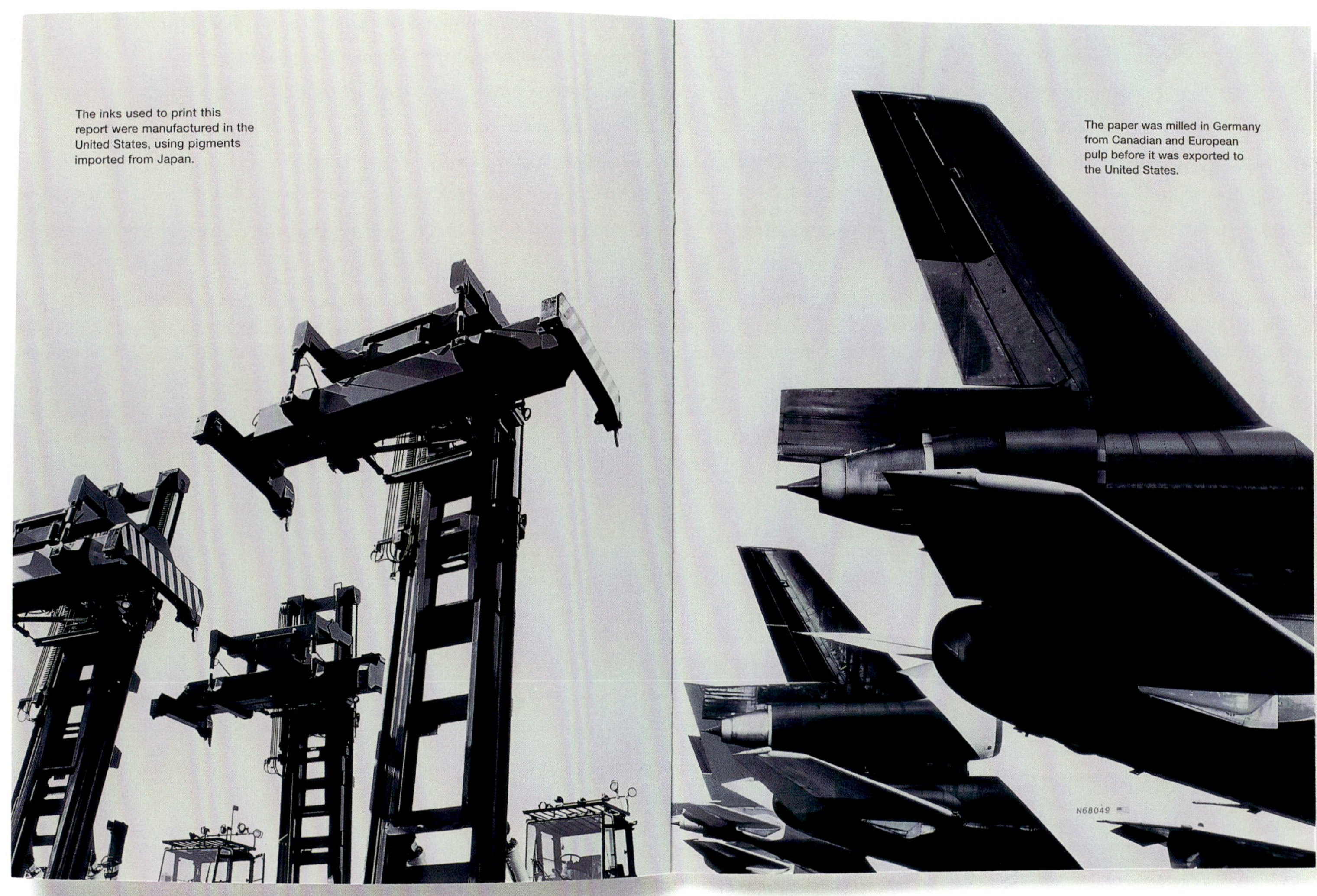

Q&A with Eleven Inc.

What was the client's directive?

AMB (which builds and operates distribution facilities in major transportation hubs) was in the process of aggressively expanding its global footprint. The client wanted the 2004 Annual Report to clearly articulate this aspect of the business, and AMB's growing significance in the global supply chain.

How did you define the problem?

The global supply chain is a business abstraction so complex that few people truly understand it. To help AMB shareholders appreciate the vast potential their company is tapping as it develops new properties abroad, we felt our job was to make the complexity of global trade easier to grasp—to put it into context.

What was the approach?

We used the Annual Report itself to illustrate the complexity of global trade—how this deceptively simple object was, itself, a microcosm of the global supply chain: ink pigments shipped from Japan, wood pulp from Canada, paper milling in Germany, printing in California, distribution from New Jersey, etc. Our point was that most products today are composed of piece-parts that come together from far-flung locales, and that each movement of goods represents a business opportunity for AMB.

Which disciplines or people helped you with the project?

The photographer and the writer were key to the success of this year's report. The graphic design of the book was really just an exercise in restraint; we wanted the story to be told very simply, and for the imagery to support the message. AMB's head of research also played an key role in crafting the market-specific analyses contained in the book.

Were you happy with the result? What could have been better?

Overall, we were very happy with the result. We had a few photographic surprises that happened while shooting. And, what we learned is that shooting the machinery of trade is not something

The graphic design was an exercise in restraint; we wanted the story to be told very simply.

Avcorp Industries, Inc.

Design Firm: SamataMason
Creative Director: Dave Mason

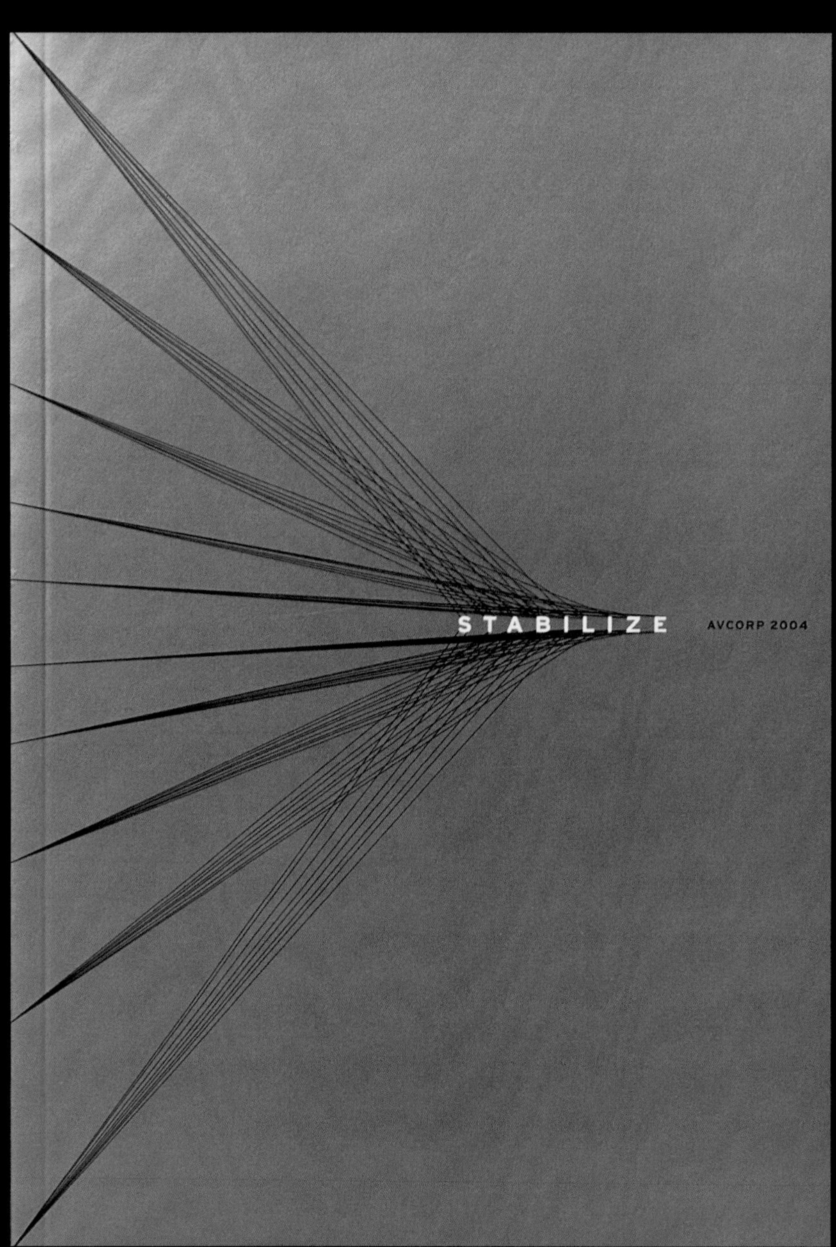

Designers: Pamela Lee, Keith Leinweber
Photographer: Victor Penner

Writers: Paul Kalil, Michael Schotz, Dave Mason
Printer: Blanchette Press

Paper: Luna gloss cover 80lb, text 100lb, Synergy Smooth text 70lb

Page count: 60 +4 page cover
Print run: 4,000

Size: 6" x 9"
Number of images: 8
Client: Avcorp Industries, Inc.

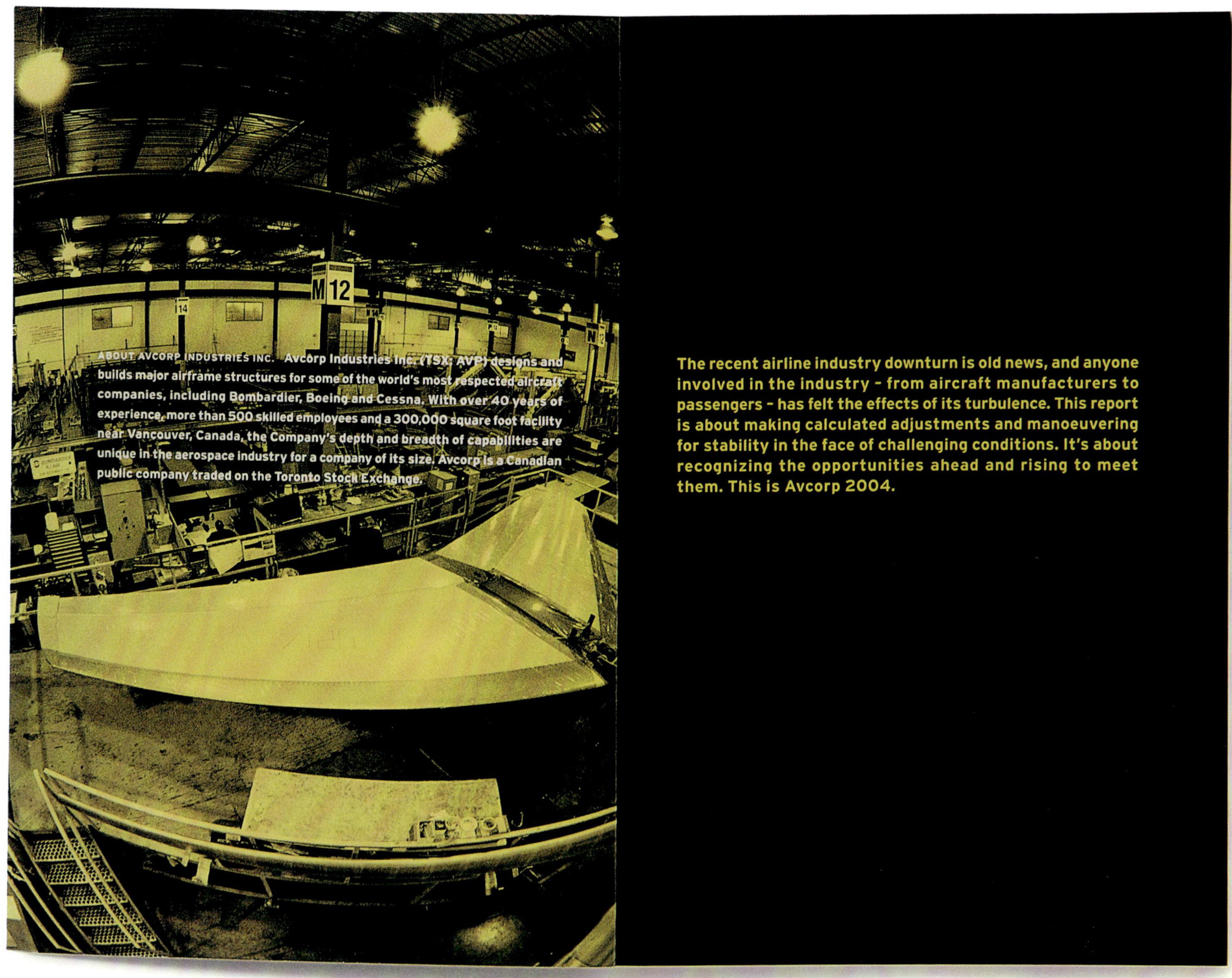

Q&A with SamataMason

What was the client's directive?
To communicate the efforts of the company's management to stabilize the company after a most difficult time in its development.
What was the approach?
We used the language of the client's industry, aeronautical engineering aviation, and key external evidence relating to the resurgence of the aviation and air travel industries to support the key message.
Which disciplines or people helped you with the project?
Victor John Penner, photographer. Blanchette Press, printer.
What was the client's response?
Very happy. They received positive feedback from many recipients.
How involved was the CEO in your meetings and presentations?
The CEO, CFO and key client team members were instrumental in helping define the report's central communication challenges.
Do you feel that designers are becoming more involved in copywriting?
Absolutely.
How do you define success in Annual Report design?
Happy client. Happy recipients. Happy us.
How important are awards to your client?
They're happy for us, but positive stakeholder response is the true measure for them.

The photographer and printer were brought into the creative development process.

SELECTED FINANCIAL DATA

Three-Year Results for Continuing Operations

unaudited, prepared in accordance with Canadian GAAP,
expressed in thousands of Canadian dollars except per share amounts

DECEMBER 31	2004	2003	2002[1,2]
OPERATIONS			
Revenues	$ 67,907	$ 55,272	$ 73,575
EBITDA[3,4]	(3,306)	1,748	(1,674)
Operating (loss) before tax	(6,257)	(3,740)	(4,389)
Net (loss)	(7,656)	(5,134)	(8,667)
Basic (loss) per share	(0.17)	(0.21)	(0.53)
Diluted (loss) per share	(0.17)	(0.21)	(0.53)
FINANCIAL POSITION			
Net capital expenditures	1,332	311	1,379
Total assets	43,417	44,448	54,978
Bank indebtedness and long-term debt[5]	20,039	17,791	31,858
Shareholders' equity	8,471	13,807	10,703
Ratio: debt/equity	2.37	1.29	2.98
Ratio: current assets/current liabilities	0.81	0.86	0.38
Shares outstanding at period end	46,370	42,108	18,697
Book value per share	0.18	0.33	0.57

[1] As restated for changes in accounting policies
[2] 15-month period from October 1, 2001 to December 31, 2002
[3] EBITDA = earnings before interest, taxes, depreciation and amortization
[4] EBITDA is not a recognized term under GAAP
[5] Includes EDC long-term debt reclassified to current debt (note 13)

4 >

Chairman's Letter to Shareholders

Dear Shareholder,

The year 2004 was a disappointing one for Avcorp Industries. In the third quarter of last year, the Board recognized changes needed to be made if the Company was to balance new business with a return to profitability. While it is easy to point to external circumstances such as 9/11, a rising Canadian dollar, the woes of the airline industry, the rising cost of fuel, changes in the regional jet market and offshore manufacturing, those excuses wear thin with time and only partially explain Avcorp's challenges.

During the third quarter of 2004 and again in the first quarter of 2005, the major shareholders led a funding initiative which saw an additional $9.4 million raised by the Company. Approximately $1 million in annual costs were eliminated from the head office and administrative overhead over the past 12 months, while at the same time achieving a 20% growth in revenue.

As part of the financing, I committed to assist the Company with its growth and restructuring, and become more actively involved. As a substantial investor who has been with the Company for over 11 years, I speak for everyone when I express extreme disappointment over the erosion of shareholder value during this period.

Everyone, from our customers, to the management team, our suppliers, as well as our valued employees (some of whom have been with us for over 30 years) have been more than patient during this process.

We must now deliver!

Avcorp has some of the most committed and skilled employees in the aerospace sector and their assistance and cooperation will be needed to achieve further productivity gains and expense reductions during 2005 and beyond to remain competitive.

I am confident the Company will begin to see the results of its past effort this year and will earn back the confidence and support of our many stakeholders.

MICHAEL SCHOLZ
CHAIRMAN

5 >

Revenue by Customer

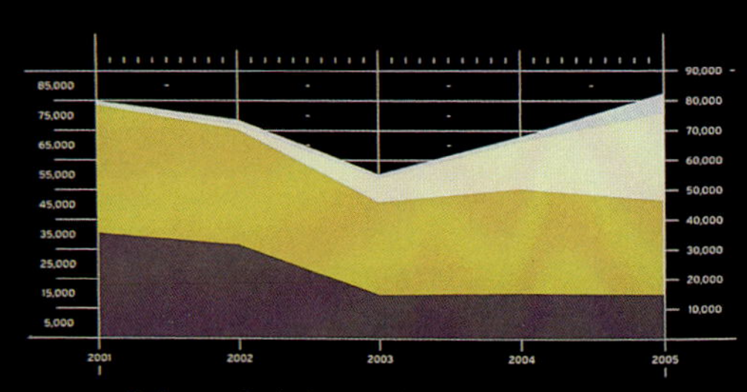

6 >

President's Letter to Shareholders

Dear Shareholder,

It is with some trepidation that I write this, my first letter to you as President. Anyone who has followed Avcorp for any period of time knows that, of all the stakeholders in the Company, it is the shareholder who has suffered most over the years. Although we incurred a $7,656,000 loss in 2004, I believe we have returned the Company to stability for the first time since the turbulence triggered by 9/11.

First and foremost, we have rebuilt the organization to address the weaknesses exposed by the industry turbulence and our own internal audit process during AS9100 quality system registration.

Secondly, we have more than doubled our sales to Cessna over 2003 (which were five times that of 2002), adding significantly to a revenue base previously dominated by Bombardier and Boeing. Some might say we have been too successful in this, since much of the new Cessna work is high on the learning curve and initially requires investment ($5,524,000 in 2004 alone). It is important to note that the long-term result of this new business will be a growth in profitability.

Last, but not least, our team is much stronger today than it has ever been, partly because we must be counted among the strong if the last three years did not kill us, but also because we have continued to hire the best people and invest heavily in training. Across the organization, from project management to shop floor, we have greater depth and capability in all areas.

The biggest challenge of 2004 was the performance of our Cessna Citation CJ3 program. Costs for the first few units built came in well above plan, a situation compounded by a rise in the Canadian dollar which further reduced margins. With the support of Cessna, we have taken major steps to lower costs and we continue these efforts as we drive the program to profitability.

7 >

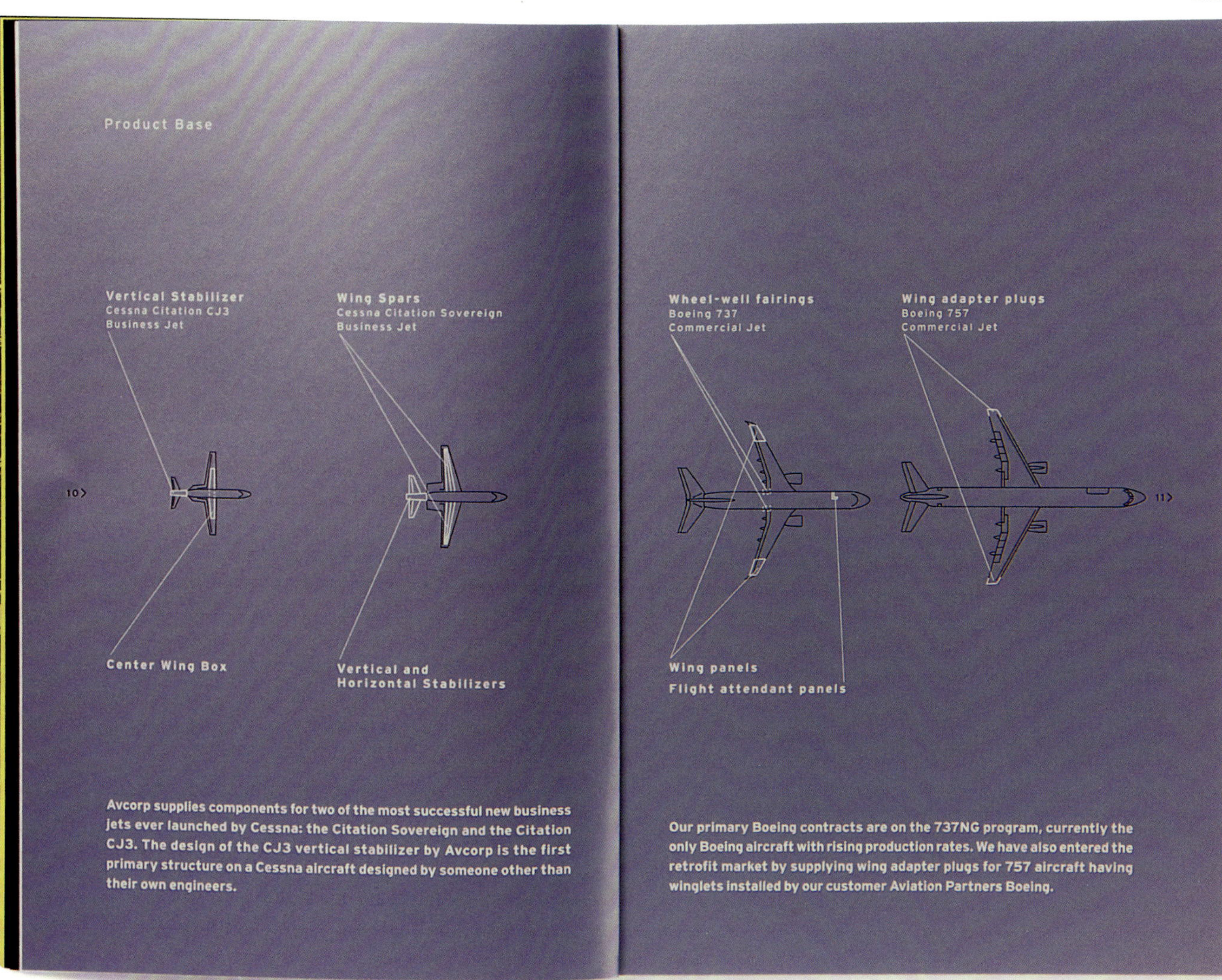

05. INVENTORIES

	DEC 31, 2004	DEC 31, 2003
Raw materials	$ 4,215	$ 2,598
Programs and contracts in progress (note 2)	8,780	6,955
Finished products	252	644
	13,247	10,197

06. DEVELOPMENT COSTS

Development costs represent hard and soft tooling, and proto-type design costs incurred for various customer programs.

	DEC 31, 2004	DEC 31, 2003
Opening balance	$ 4,163	$ 3,409
Additions	345	839
Amortization	(287)	(85)
	4,221	4,163

07. PROPERTY, PLANT AND EQUIPMENT

	DEC 31, 2004			DEC 31, 2003		
	COST	ACCUMULATED DEPRECIATION	NET	COST	ACCUMULATED DEPRECIATION	NET
Computer hardware and software	$ 3,598	$ 1,369	$ 2,229	$ 2,441	$ 1,096	$ 1,345
Machinery and equipment	27,362	13,384	13,978	26,541	11,675	14,866
	30,960	14,753	16,207	28,982	12,771	16,211

44>

Included in machinery and equipment are assets held under capital leases at a cost of $Nil (2003: $7,060,000) and accumulated depreciation of $Nil (2003: $2,531,000). Included in computer hardware and software are assets held under capital lease with a net book value of $640,000 (2003: $Nil), with depreciation charged of $Nil (2003: $Nil).

On July 17, 2003, the Company sold its land and building having a net carrying amount of $13,494,000 for gross proceeds of $16,000,000, representing $1,500,000 as a rent credit and $14,500,000 for the property. Net proceeds after fees were $14,206,000.

Concurrently, the Company entered into a 15-year leaseback agreement with the purchaser of the property. The $712,000 gain arising on disposal of the property was recorded as a deferred gain and is being amortized to income over the life of the lease. The rent credit from the purchaser of the property is a conditional prepaid rent towards rent in the sixth year of the lease (note 9).

08. INVESTMENT

On June 17, 2002, the Company acquired 5,264 Series D Preferred Stock of Eclipse Aviation Corporation for $1,527,000.

On December 31, 2004, the Company wrote down its investment by $768,000 to its estimated net realizable value of $759,000.

09. OTHER ASSETS

	DEC 31, 2004	DEC 31, 2003
Other receivable	$ 218	$ 680
Employee loan	-	50
Prepaid rent (note 7)	1,500	1,500
	1,718	2,230

Other receivable is an amount due from a customer special order which will be recovered during fiscal 2006.

During 2000, the Company advanced $150,000 to an officer and director, which was repayable on March 15, 2005. During the year ended December 31, 2004, the $50,000 balance of this loan was forgiven.

10. BANK INDEBTEDNESS

During the year ended December 31, 2003, the Company repaid its $6,033,000 line of credit. Interest was charged at bank's prime rate plus 2% up until the time of repayment.

45>

On January 9, 2004, the Company secured a $10,000,000 operating line of credit with a Canadian chartered bank having interest at prime plus 0.25% on the first $5,000,000 utilized and prime plus 1.00% on the second $5,000,000 utilized. This facility is due on demand.

As a condition of obtaining this operating line of credit, the following security has been provided:

- general security agreement registered in British Columbia providing a first charge over substantially all assets of the Company;
- general assignment of book debts registered in British Columbia;
- section 427 security over inventory registered with the Bank of Canada;
- postponement and subordination agreement from certain shareholders;
- postponement and subordination agreement with the holder of the $5,000,000 convertible debenture;
- irrevocable and unconditional guarantee of $4,000,000 by a Canadian financial institution; in consideration of the Canadian financial institution entering into and performing its obligations under this guarantee, the Company agreed to pay, on a monthly basis, a guarantee fee of 3% of the $4,000,000 unconditional guarantee calculated on a daily basis;
- $3,500,000 limited guarantee provided jointly and severally by certain shareholders (note 24); and
- evidence of fire and all risk insurance with the Bank as first loss payee.

SEVEROČESKÉ DOLY a.s.

annual report 2004

Art Director: Dusan Michelfeit, B.I.G. Prague
Designer: Klara Kvizova, Petr Krejzek, ReDesign
Photographer: Adam Holy
Writer: Dusan Michelfeit
Printer: REAL Tisk
Paper: Agrippina proofset
Page count: 76 +cover
Print run: 1,200
Size: 230x270 mm
Number of images: 15
Client: Severoceske Doly

Q&A with B.I.G.Prague

What was the client's directive?

There was no client's directive. The idea and creative brief was completely set by B.I.G. Prague (there is the long term confidence–our agency has produced AR for the company for 8 years).

How did you define the problem?

The question was how to introduce Severoceske doly – the leading mine company in CR, in an interesting, unusual, and attractive way.

What was the approach?

We offered the client the idea of the using professional slang, to present the equipment in combination with the picture of everyday life with the same name. The client accepted it and was involved and cooperative.

Which disciplines or people helped you with the project?

Ideas, creative briefs, texts, design structure and translations were done within the B.I.G. Prague consulting and production team. Photos and graphic design were created by ReDesign (B.I.G. Prague cooperated with them for 10 years).

Were you happy with the result? What could have been better?

We hope that we can be happy. Of course anything can be better than it is. In this case we were concerned with the colour shade – is it too strong, too provocative...?

What was the client's response?

Some doubts at the beginning were satisfied when the AR was complete. Many thanks were also given after Czech Top 100 best AR Awards, in which the AR was named top 10 in both content (information and communication value) and design.

How involved was the CEO in your meetings and presentations?

The CEO as never involved in person, but other responsible top management people were very cooperative.

Do you feel that designers are becoming more involved in copywriting?

Generally we do not see such a trend. In our case we use a very strong creative team that creates ideas, headlines, slogans, and preselects photos. There is also an everyday communication between the designer´s team and the photographer.

How do you define success in Annual Report design?

Simple but interesting idea, theme ("creative scenario"), attractive photos, illustrations (supported by expressive slogans), professional creative layout (suitable combination of design), and material (print techniques, binding). But I would still agree with the Czech proverb: "Sometimes, less means more" (If there is no idea, no excellent designer – then no complicated techniques, expensive materials, colors and pictures will help). AR should address the user, to encourage pleasant feeling and expression, to bring something new and surprising...

How important are awards to your client?

Very important – AR is the most representative material of the company towards its shareholders, partners etc. here and in abroad.

Sometimes, less means more.

Severočeské doly a.s. is the largest brown coal mining company in the Czech Republic. The company was established on 1 January 1994 by the merger of Doly Bílina and Doly Nástup Tušimice. The company operates in the North Bohemian brown coal basin. Its core businesses are the extraction, preparation, and sale of brown coal and related materials. The company's domestic market share in 2004 was 44.9%. Its largest customer is the electricity company ČEZ. The majority shareholder is the National Property Fund of the Czech Republic. Severočeské doly a.s. is a stable, successful corporation, a major participant in the development of both its sector and the region, with a traditional corporate culture, known and appreciated for being open and fair towards its business partners, the public, its employees, and its shareholders.

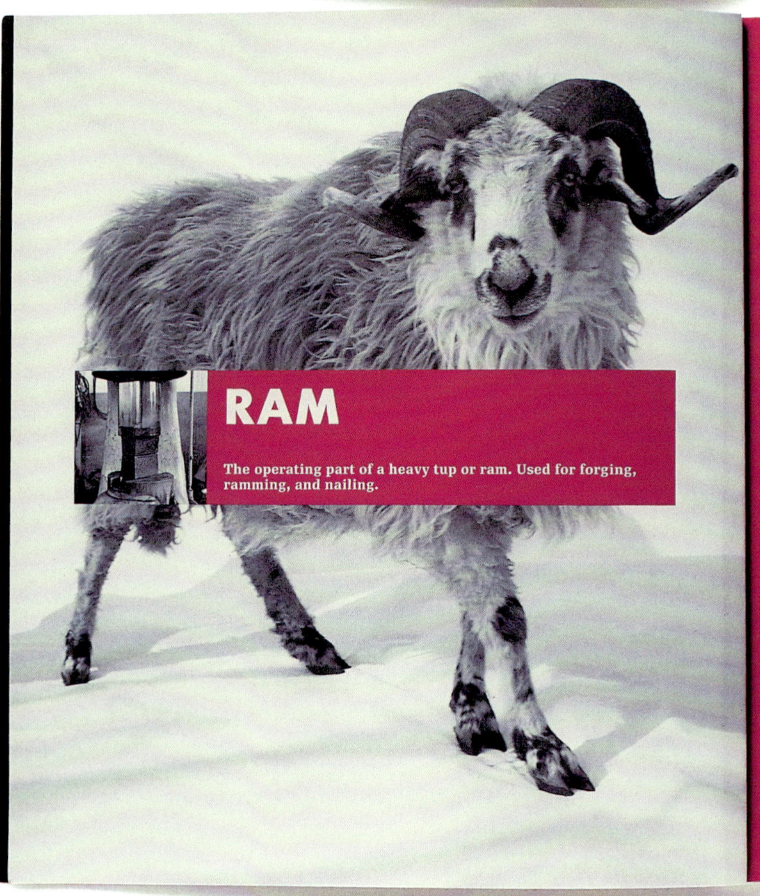

04
05

Key Figures

Indicator	Unit of measure	2004	2003	2002	2001	2000
Market share	%	44.9	45.2	43.8	44.4	44.0
Gross amount of coal extracted	tonnes thousands	22,023	23,440	21,812	23,095	22,872
Amount of coal sold	tonnes thousands	21,753	22,739	21,387	22,563	22,115
Revenues from operating activities	CZK millions	7,801	7,954	7,610	7,999	7,918
Operating costs	CZK millions	6,645	6,898	8,630	7,726	8,345
Value added	CZK millions	4,279	4,477	3,876	4,792	4,335
Operating profit	CZK millions	1,439	1,307	685	1,008	518
Financial profit	CZK millions	390	457	549	502	477
Net earnings	CZK millions	1,365	1,294	963	1,113	827
Fixed assets	CZK millions	17,040	17,556	16,854	14,938	13,915
Equity	CZK millions	16,339	17,065	16,468	15,850	14,745
Liabilities	CZK millions	5,932	6,034	5,809	6,576	5,535
Statutory reserves	CZK millions	4,034	3,972	3,858	3,893	3,552
Capital investment	CZK millions	1,255	1,084	1,370	1,549	2,040
Environmental expenditure	CZK millions	572.7	565.6	505.2	432.4	492.7
Depreciation level	%	61.8	59.8	57.7	55.8	59.1
Average number of employees	persons	3,724	3,934	4,154	5,510	5,800
Average monthly wage	CZK	20,892	19,596	18,360	16,438	15,361
Closing PSE share price at 31 December	CZK	1,480.0	935.0	433.9	286.6	244.1
P/E		9.76	6.50	4.05	2.32	2.62
Dividend per share	CZK	240	234.75	60	40	20

Other Capital Interests at 31 December 2004

Company	Number of shares	Shareholding at nominal value (CZK'000)	Share in registered capital (%)
Equity investments in associates			
Výzkumný ústav pro hnědé uhlí a.s.	27,399	27,399	38.97
SHD - KOMES a.s.	168,235	168,235	46.33
Coal Energy, a.s.	1	10,000	20.00
ENETECH a.s.	56	10,500	50.00
Other investment securities and participating interests			
Sokolovská uhelná, a.s.	1	1	0.00
Total other capital interests		**216,135**	

The company's stake in Výzkumný ústav pro hnědé uhlí (the Brown Coal Research Institute) allows it to participate in the management and supervision of the activities of the Institute, which is a key institution for applied research in fields crucial to the development of the brown coal industry.

The stake in SHD - KOMES is an instrument of control over one of the largest suppliers of materials consumed by Severočeské doly's operations. At the same time, the stake is a long-term investment in SHD - KOMES's fixed tangible assets that are useful in the commercial, service and tourism sectors.

In April 2004, Severočeské doly sold a 34.22% stake in the registered capital of Teplárna Ústí nad Labem.

In 2002, a project was implemented with ČEZ, Mostecká uhelná společnost, Sokolovská uhelná, and CARBOUNION BOHEMIA to establish the joint venture Coal Energy. This company started operating as an exporter of electricity generated at conventional Czech coal power stations in a move intended to eliminate the negative impact of putting Temelín Nuclear Power Station into service.

The main incentive behind the investment into ENETECH was to acquire a stake in a company with important mining technology know-how.

Personnel and Social Policies

The aim of the company's personnel and social strategy is to ensure the development of skilled, highly motivated employees, who are the cornerstone of success as the company seeks to meet its targets. The incentive programme focuses on employee bonuses, financial and non-financial employee benefits, and employee training. The social programme concentrates on promoting safety and health at work. The basic document for the company's personnel and social policy is the collective agreement concluded for the period from 2004 to 2006.

Number of Employees

At the end of 2004, the company had a headcount of 3,685 employees, i.e. 97 employees fewer than at year-end 2003, continuing the downward trend of previous years. By reducing its number of employees, the company was responding to influences from the energy market, in particular the startup of Temelín Nuclear Power Station and the need to increase the efficiency of production, ensuring a rise in labour productivity. In 2001-2003, the company released 1,084 employees to subsidiaries. In 2004,

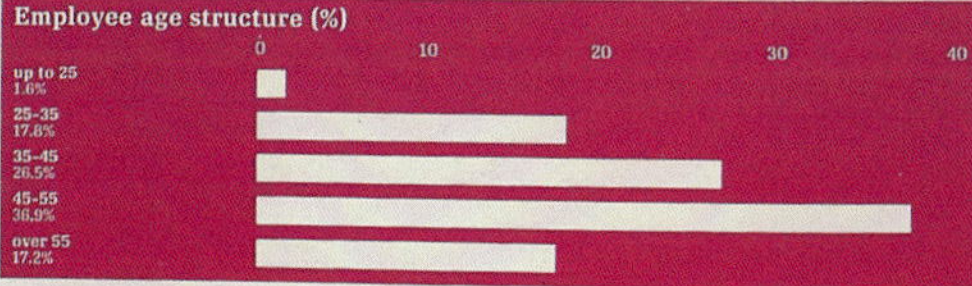

32
33

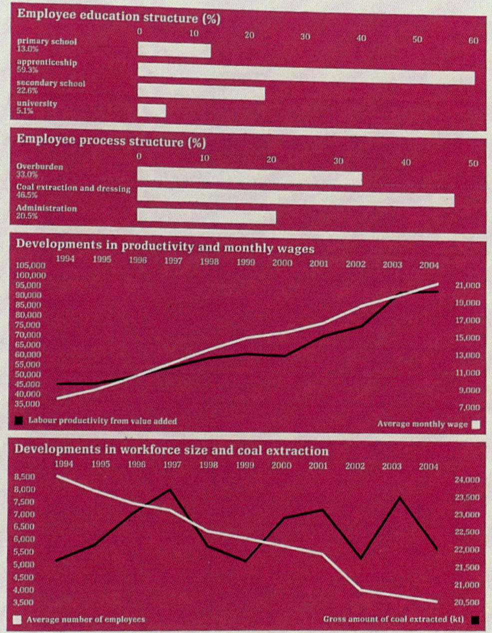

the company implemented the next stage of a plan to reduce the number of white-collar workers, as laid down in the project 'Optimization of the Organizational Structure'.

Wages and Labour Productivity

The average monthly wage at the company in 2004 was CZK 20,892 per employee (year-on-year growth of 6.6%). The rise in average earnings was achieved by increasing the tariff-based wages of employees by 5.5% and raising the supplementary wage. The company fulfilled all its obligations under the col-

Consolidated Financial Statements in Accordance with IFRS

Consolidated Balance Sheets at December 31, 2004 and 2003 (in CZK million)

	Note	2004	2003
ASSETS			
Property, plant and equipment:			
Plant in service		28,483	28,052
Less accumulated provision for depreciation		(17,216)	(16,318)
Net plant in service	4	**11,267**	**11,734**
Construction work in progress		684	518
Total property, plant and equipment		**11,951**	**12,252**
Other non-current assets:			
Investments	5	6,544	6,819
Investments in associates	6	304	789
Deferred tax assets	12	449	140
Intangible assets, net		84	105
Total other non-current assets		**7,381**	**7,853**
Current assets:			
Cash and cash equivalents	8	233	258
Investments	5	4,078	4,373
Accounts receivable, net	7	939	957
Materials and supplies, net		164	141
Other current assets		31	28
Total current assets		**5,445**	**5,757**
Total assets		**24,777**	**25,862**
LIABILITIES AND SHAREHOLDERS' EQUITY			
Shareholders' equity:			
Share capital	11	9,081	9,000
Net unrealized gains on available-for-sale assets		54	49
Retained earnings	11	5,646	7,569
Total shareholders' equity		**14,781**	**16,618**
Minority interests		**3**	**3**
Non-current liabilities:			
Provision for decommissioning, reclamation and mining damages	3	8,792	7,783
Deferred tax liability	12	44	53
Total non-current liabilities		**8,836**	**7,836**
Current liabilities:			
Accounts payable	9	665	814
Income tax payable		207	298
Accrued and other liabilities	10	285	293
Total current liabilities		**1,157**	**1,405**
Total liabilities and shareholders' equity		**24,777**	**25,862**

The accompanying notes are an integral part of these financial statements.

54
55

Consolidated Statements of Income for the Years Ended December 31, 2004 and 2003 (in CZK million)

	Note	2004	2003
Revenues:			
Sales of coal		7,361	7,520
Other sales		592	594
Total revenues		**7,953**	**8,114**
Expenses:			
Repairs, maintenance and other services		(1,620)	(1,517)
Personnel	13	(1,752)	(1,721)
Depreciation and amortization		(1,478)	(1,573)
Spare parts and other materials		(892)	(834)
Energy		(629)	(674)
Other operating expenses, net		(970)	283
Total expenses		**(7,341)**	**(6,026)**
Operating income		**612**	**2,088**
Other income/(expenses):			
Income from associates	6	28	60
Interest income		394	397
Interest on provisions	3	(420)	(414)
Other financial expenses, net		(363)	(16)
Total other income/(expenses)		**(361)**	**27**
Profit before income taxes		**251**	**2,115**
Income taxes	12	**(72)**	**(704)**
Profit after income taxes		**179**	**1,411**
Minority interests		–	–
Net profit from ordinary activities		**179**	**1,411**
Net profit per share (CZK per share) (Note 11)			
Basic		20	157
Diluted		20	157
Average number of shares outstanding (shares) (Note 11)			
Basic		9,000,055	8,999,958
Diluted		9,006,898	8,999,958

The accompanying notes are an integral part of these financial statements.

Consolidated Statements of Shareholders' Equity for the Years Ended December 31, 2004 and 2003 (in CZK million)

	Note	Number of shares	Share capital	Net unrealized gains/(losses)	Retained earnings	Total equity
Balance at December 31, 2002		**8,997,530**	**9,000**	**106**	**6,698**	**15,804**
Dividends paid		–	–	–	(540)	(540)
Capital contribution	11	2,525	–	–	–	–
Net loss on available-for-sale investments		–	–	(57)	–	(57)
Net profit		–	–	–	1,411	1,411
Balance at December 31, 2003		**9,000,055**	**9,000**	**49**	**7,569**	**16,618**
Dividends paid		–	–	–	(2,113)	(2,113)
Capital contribution	11	–	81	–	11	92
Net gain on available-for-sale investments		–	–	5	–	5
Net profit		–	–	–	179	179
Balance at December 31, 2004		**9,000,055**	**9,081**	**54**	**5,646**	**14,781**

The accompanying notes are an integral part of these financial statements.

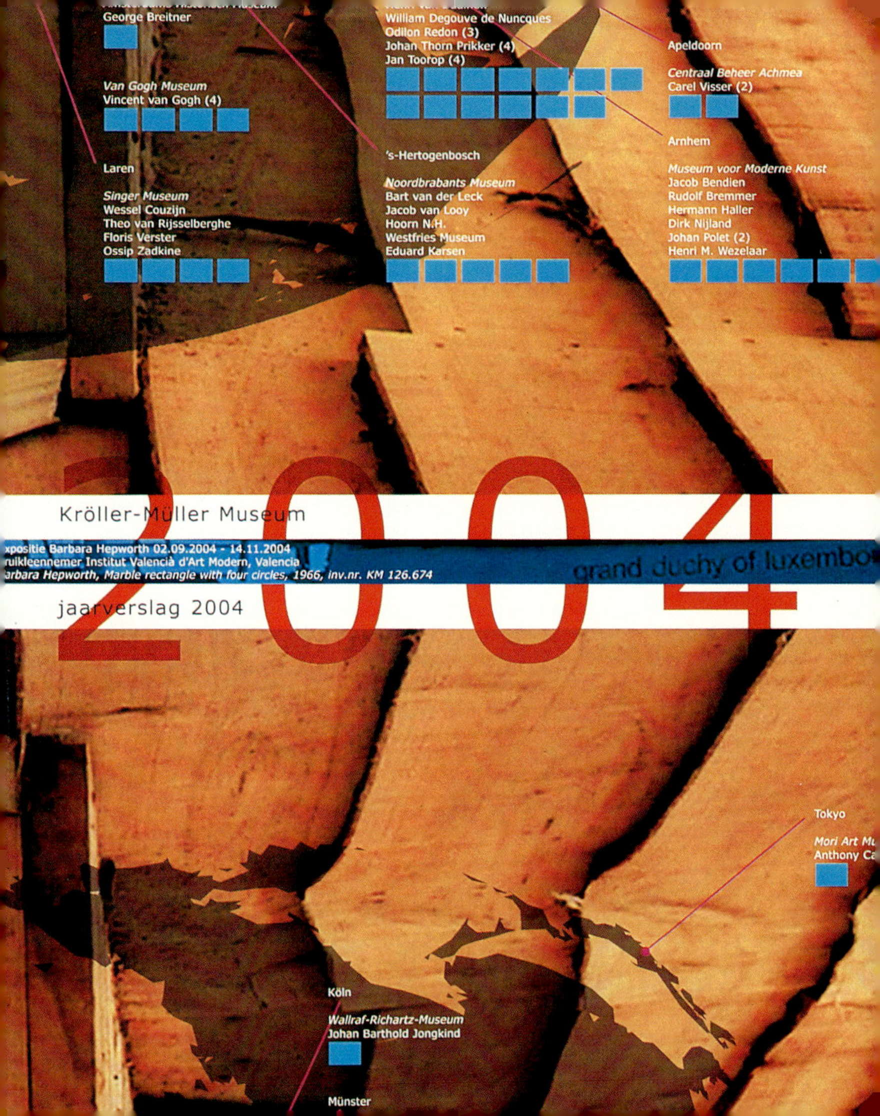

George Breitner

Van Gogh Museum
Vincent van Gogh (4)

Laren

Singer Museum
Wessel Couzijn
Theo van Rijsselberghe
Floris Verster
Ossip Zadkine

William Degouve de Nuncques
Odilon Redon (3)
Johan Thorn Prikker (4)
Jan Toorop (4)

's-Hertogenbosch

Noordbrabants Museum
Bart van der Leck
Jacob van Looy

Hoorn N.H.

Westfries Museum
Eduard Karsen

Apeldoorn

Centraal Beheer Achmea
Carel Visser (2)

Arnhem

Museum voor Moderne Kunst
Jacob Bendien
Rudolf Bremmer
Hermann Haller
Dirk Nijland
Johan Polet (2)
Henri M. Wezelaar

Kröller-Müller Museum

2004

xpositie Barbara Hepworth 02.09.2004 - 14.11.2004
ruikleennemer Institut Valencià d'Art Modern, Valencia
arbara Hepworth, Marble rectangle with four circles, 1966, inv.nr. KM 126.674

grand duchy of luxembo

jaarverslag 2004

Tokyo

Mori Art Mu
Anthony Ca

Köln

Wallraf-Richartz-Museum
Johan Barthold Jongkind

Münster

Designer: Alex Scholing
Photographers: Walter Herfst, Cary Markerink, Bob Goedewagen, Rik Klein Gotink
Writer: Wanda Vermeulen
Printer: Thoben offset Nijmegen
Page Count: 112
Number of images: 300
Print run: 500
Size: 20x26 cm
Paper: Hello Satin
Client: Kröller-Müller Museum

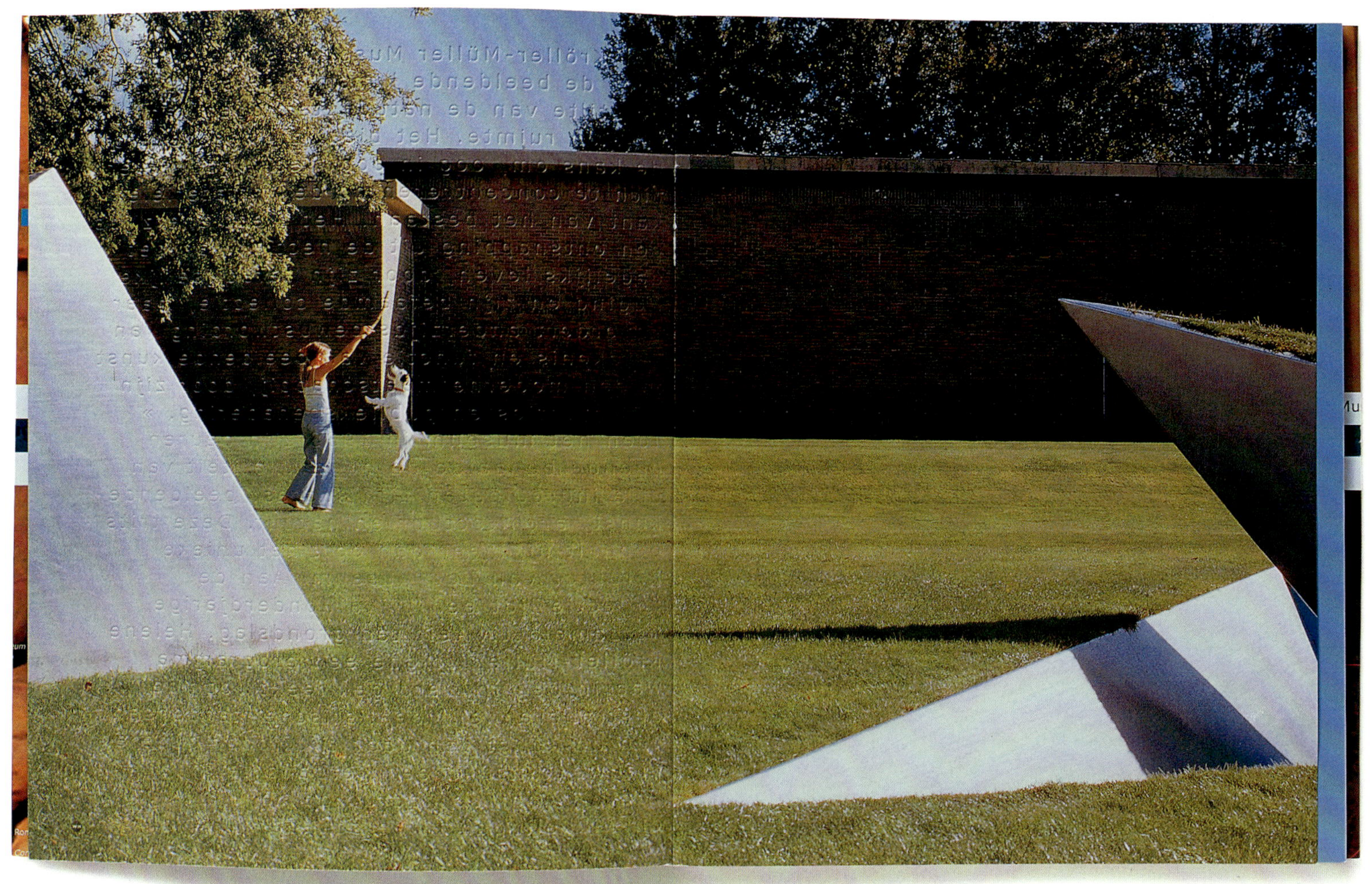

Q&A with Eat

What was the client's directive?

Until recently, an Annual Report was no more than one of many formal obligations the Kröller-Müller Museum (KMM) had to deal with. However, the communication people at the museum felt it had more potential than that. It was decided that, for the first time, the Annual Report would be utilized as a communication tool. The museum's directive: show the many aspects of the KMM, both in front of as well as behind the scenes, in a conclusive way. A clear and easy-to-read book with plenty of pictures to showcase both the atmosphere of the museum and all of its many varied operations.

How did you define the problem?

Museums in general, and the KMM in particular, are quite a lot more than what is seen by the general public. A company like KMM relies heavily on public appreciation, not just from visitors or the art world, but equally from a variety of other audiences like tax payers, government agencies, funds and sponsors, tour operators, local authorities, benefactors, artists and scientists, applicants, schools and universities, financial institutes and many others. An Annual Report is probably the only communication tool general enough and thorough enough to communicate with all of these parties at once. Apart from that, an Annual Report always gets a special kind of attention from the outside world that no other publication will ever get, which means it poses an opportunity to really showcase the value of an organization.

What was the approach?

The Annual Report had to talk to many people on many different levels and our approach was simple: show and tell as much as you can about what you do as a museum and present it in a way that allows access on more than one level. The result: a kaleidoscope of photographic accounts of special events, interviews with visitors, an illustrated monthly report of everything that mattered during the year, a separate catalogue of all acquisitions, a geographical overview of all art lendings, key figure sound bites, large atmospheric images, and organizational data, all presented in crystal clear form in an invitingly large typeface and bundled in an intriguing way. And, of course, it's a museum, so tone of voice should be serious and neutral without being unexpressive.

Which disciplines or people helped you with the project?

During the year, various photographers were commissioned to cover the many special events at the museum. The museum's communication department itself delivered all other content, including research, interviews, data and stories. The editorial concept was developed during brainstorms between the design firm and client.

Were you happy with the result? What could have been better?

A few minor production glitches aside, we were happy with the result. The AR turned out to be not only a valuable public relations asset for the KMM, but also for ourselves as the responsible design firm.

What was the client's response?

The KMM was, and still is, extremely happy with the result. They received tremendous, positive response, which is quite special; previously they didn't get any reaction at all on their Annual Reports. They are proud to give their ARs away; it's almost considered a present.

How involved was the CEO in your meetings and presentations?

The CEO was present during the initial brainstorms and briefings. After the first presentations the CEO took a step back, but was always available when needed.

Do you feel that designers are becoming more involved in copywriting?

We can only talk for ourselves here. We at Eat like to see every job in its entirety, which means not just the design part of it. We don't really think design, we think finished products and desired effects, and copy is as important in that as anything. So yes, we do like copy and we do like to be involved in it, though we rarely write ourselves. We also feel that many designers are mainly interested in text in the visual sense, not in what it actually says.

How do you define success in Annual Report design?

We think an Annual Report is successful when it proves beyond doubt that you stand out as an organization, both on and off stage, and that the quality of the output of your company is not incidental, but the natural result of a solid and reliable organization and process. The design of the Annual Report has to facilitate all this, and above that, communicate all the immaterial qualities of the company: vision, inspiration and energy.

How important are awards to your client?

Again, KMM relies heavily on public appreciation, so awards are very important, especially creative awards because they give body to their cultural image.

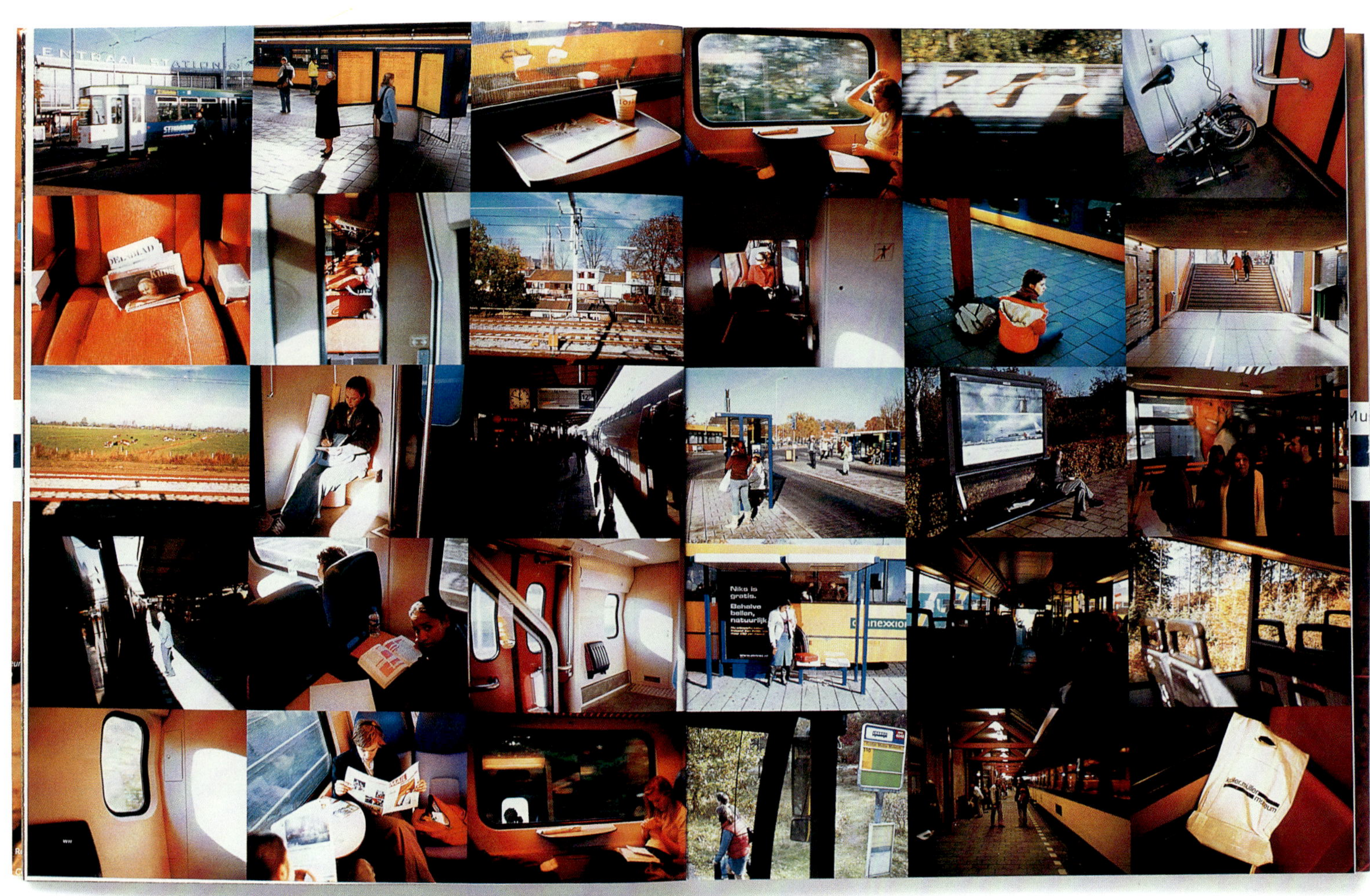

The Annual Report also has to communicate the immaterial qualities of the company, such as vision, inspiration and energy.

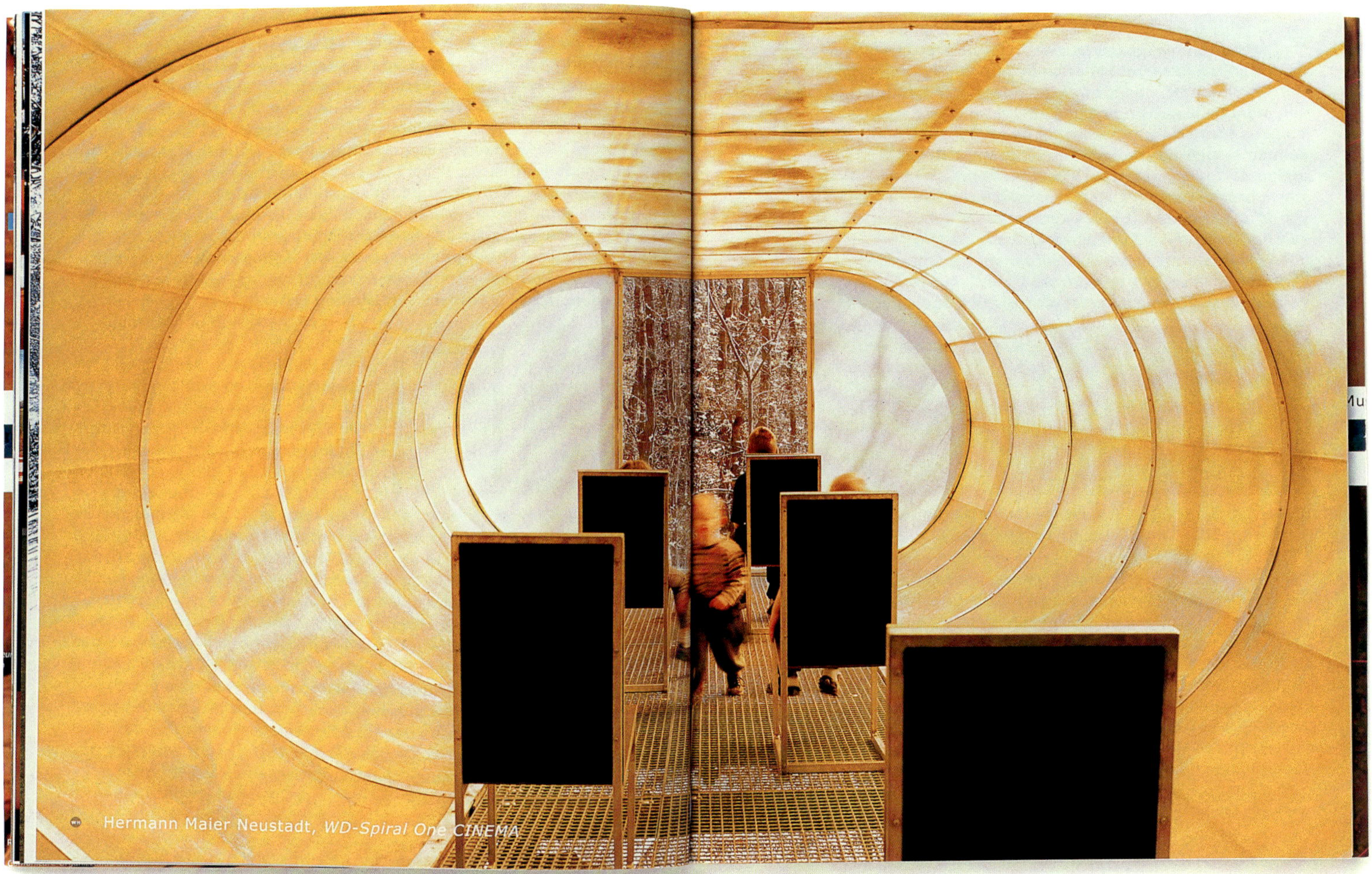

Hermann Maier Neustadt, *WD-Spiral One CINEMA*

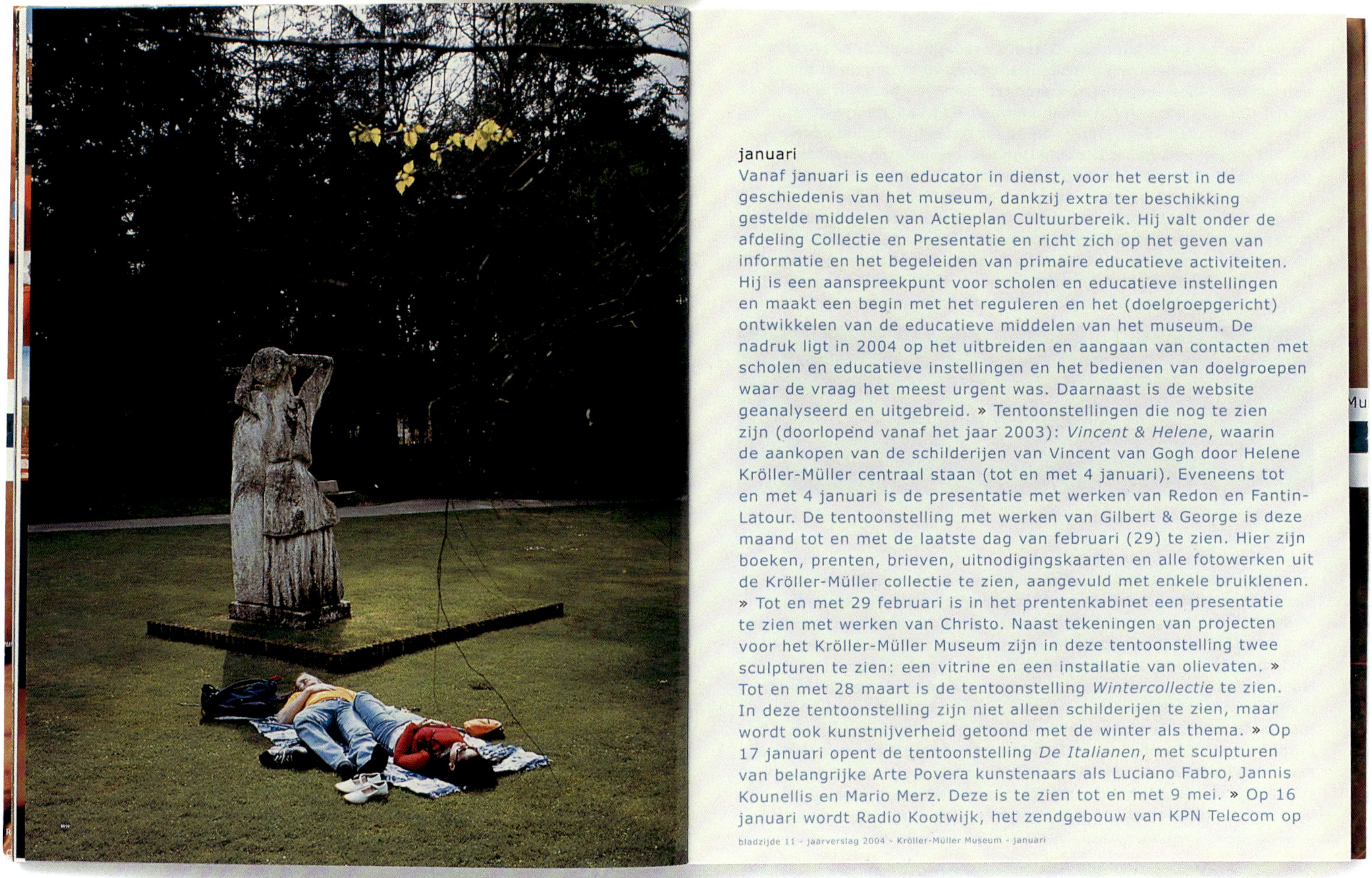

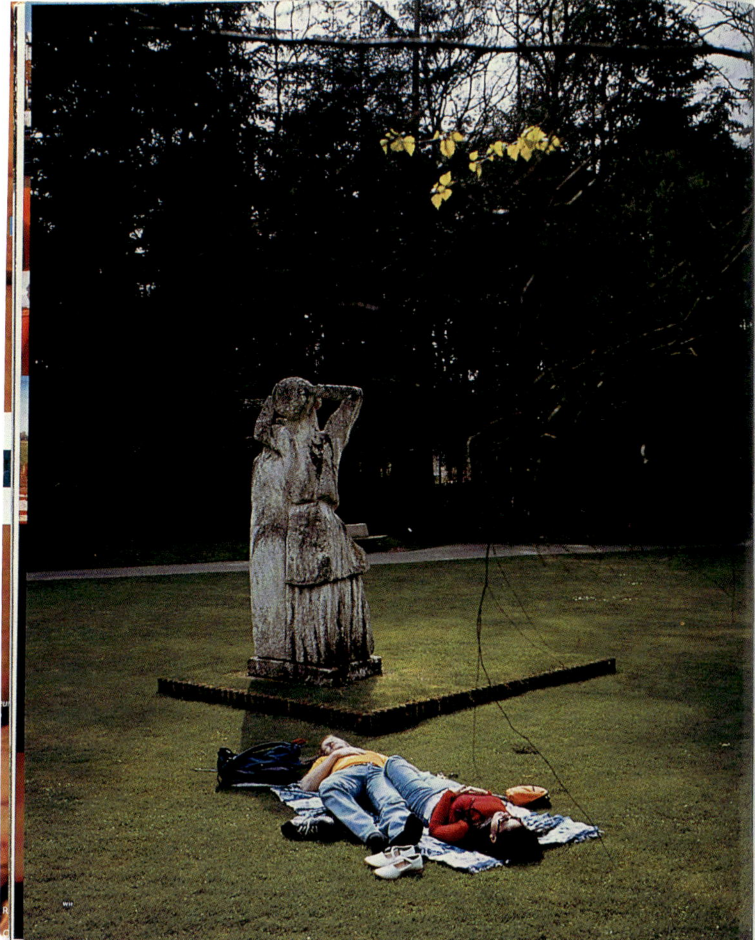

januari

Vanaf januari is een educator in dienst, voor het eerst in de geschiedenis van het museum, dankzij extra ter beschikking gestelde middelen van Actieplan Cultuurbereik. Hij valt onder de afdeling Collectie en Presentatie en richt zich op het geven van informatie en het begeleiden van primaire educatieve activiteiten. Hij is een aanspreekpunt voor scholen en educatieve instellingen en maakt een begin met het reguleren en het (doelgroepgericht) ontwikkelen van de educatieve middelen van het museum. De nadruk ligt in 2004 op het uitbreiden en aangaan van contacten met scholen en educatieve instellingen en het bedienen van doelgroepen waar de vraag het meest urgent was. Daarnaast is de website geanalyseerd en uitgebreid. » Tentoonstellingen die nog te zien zijn (doorlopend vanaf het jaar 2003): *Vincent & Helene*, waarin de aankopen van de schilderijen van Vincent van Gogh door Helene Kröller-Müller centraal staan (tot en met 4 januari). Eveneens tot en met 4 januari is de presentatie met werken van Redon en Fantin-Latour. De tentoonstelling met werken van Gilbert & George is deze maand tot en met de laatste dag van februari (29) te zien. Hier zijn boeken, prenten, brieven, uitnodigingskaarten en alle fotowerken uit de Kröller-Müller collectie te zien, aangevuld met enkele bruiklenen. » Tot en met 29 februari is in het prentenkabinet een presentatie te zien met werken van Christo. Naast tekeningen van projecten voor het Kröller-Müller Museum zijn in deze tentoonstelling twee sculpturen te zien: een vitrine en een installatie van olievaten. » Tot en met 28 maart is de tentoonstelling *Wintercollectie* te zien. In deze tentoonstelling zijn niet alleen schilderijen te zien, maar wordt ook kunstnijverheid getoond met de winter als thema. » Op 17 januari opent de tentoonstelling *De Italianen*, met sculpturen van belangrijke Arte Povera kunstenaars als Luciano Fabro, Jannis Kounellis en Mario Merz. Deze is te zien tot en met 9 mei. » Op 16 januari wordt Radio Kootwijk, het zendgebouw van KPN Telecom op

bladzijde 11 - jaarverslag 2004 - Kröller-Müller Museum - januari

het archief verregaand te ontsluiten. In april 2003 wordt begonnen met volledige digitalisering van het historisch fotomateriaal. De foto's worden gescand met een hoge (afdruk-)kwaliteit en geregistreerd in TMS. Daarnaast zijn voorzieningen getroffen zodat de originele foto's in optimale conditie bewaard worden. Het project van de afdeling wetenschappelijk onderzoek wordt deze maand afgerond. » Een projectmedewerker dient een subsidieaanvraag in bij de Mondriaan Stichting voor een onderzoek naar *Nederlandse toegepaste kunst uit de Kröller-Müller collectie, 1900-1940, in relatie tot de voormalige woonhuizen van de familie Kröller* (werktitel). Deze aanvraag is gehonoreerd met 45.000 euro. In de tweede helft van het verslagjaar is het conceptplan nader uitgewerkt en een begin gemaakt met het onderzoek. Het project heeft een

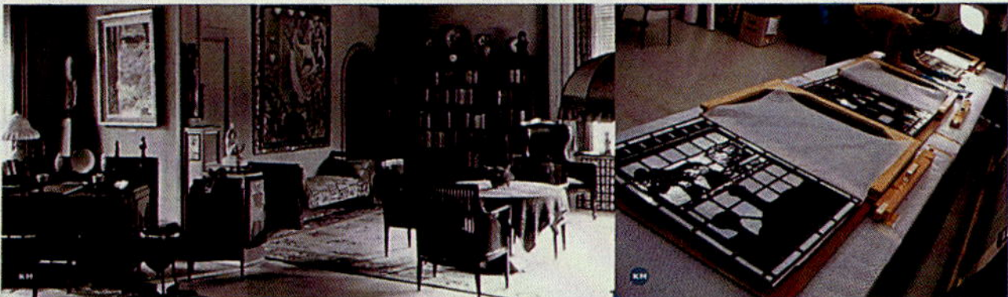

de salon van Helene Kröller-Müller ca. 1935 » onderzoek *Het mijnbedrijf* van Bart van der Leck

planning van zomer 2004 tot zomer 2006. » Het hoofd Collectie en Presentatie en de beeldenrestaurator bezoeken het atelier van kunstenaar Ger van Elk in Amsterdam, wat belangrijke informatie over werk in de collectie oplevert. Eveneens wordt het atelier van Adam Colton bezocht, waaruit een bruikleen voor de tuin voortkomt (zie december). Het fotorestauratie-atelier C.C. von Waldthausen wordt bezocht ter verkenning van een mogelijke samenwerking. » Er wordt begonnen met de voorbereidingen en restauratie van het glas-in-lood raam van Bart van der Leck voor de reizende tentoonstelling *Van Gogh to Mondrian* in de VS (zie ook mei). Het raam is volledig op conditie onderzocht, gereinigd en losse glasschilfers zijn onder de microscoop geconsolideerd. Ook de meubels die zijn opgenomen

in deze tentoonstelling zijn op conditie gecontroleerd en waar nodig geconsolideerd. Voor zowel het glas-in-lood als de meubels zijn speciale reiskisten ontworpen en gerealiseerd. » Deze maand wordt de totale koelcapaciteit van het museum met 300 KW uitgebreid door het bijplaatsen van een zevende koelmachine. Dit project is gestart in november 2003. «

april

Deze maand starten drie nieuwe tentoonstellingen. Op 3 april is dat *Twee broers*. Het museum toont nieuw werk van de Leidse kunstenaars en broers Pieter (1940) en Thom (1950) Geraedts. De tentoonstelling is te zien tot en met 6 juni 2004.

| Pieter Geraedts toont nieuwe werken van krantenpulp,

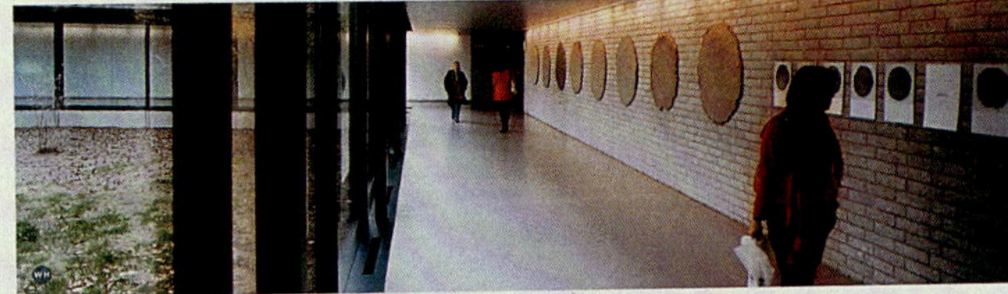

tentoonstelling *Twee broers*

gecombineerd met oudere werken van zijn hand uit de verzameling van het Kröller-Müller Museum. Zijn werk behelst een jarenlange uiteenzetting met de Leegte, als de ultieme tegenpool van het Bestaan. Hij is steeds op weg naar het laatst mogelijke werk, het ultiem maakbare kunstwerk. Hij wil zo onpersoonlijk en ongewild mogelijke kunstwerken maken. Hij wil het liefst als de natuur werken en niet naar de natuur. Een utopie? Pieter vindt houvast bij Spinoza: 'want het is immers duidelijk dat de Natuur geen enkel doel nastreeft en dat alle doeleinden niet anders zijn dan menselijke verzinselen'. » Thom Geraedts laat wandwerken (constellaties) zien van karton en lichte materialen en toont zijn vijf in zeer kleine oplages uitgegeven kranten. Hij laat eveneens een filmpje zien, dat de

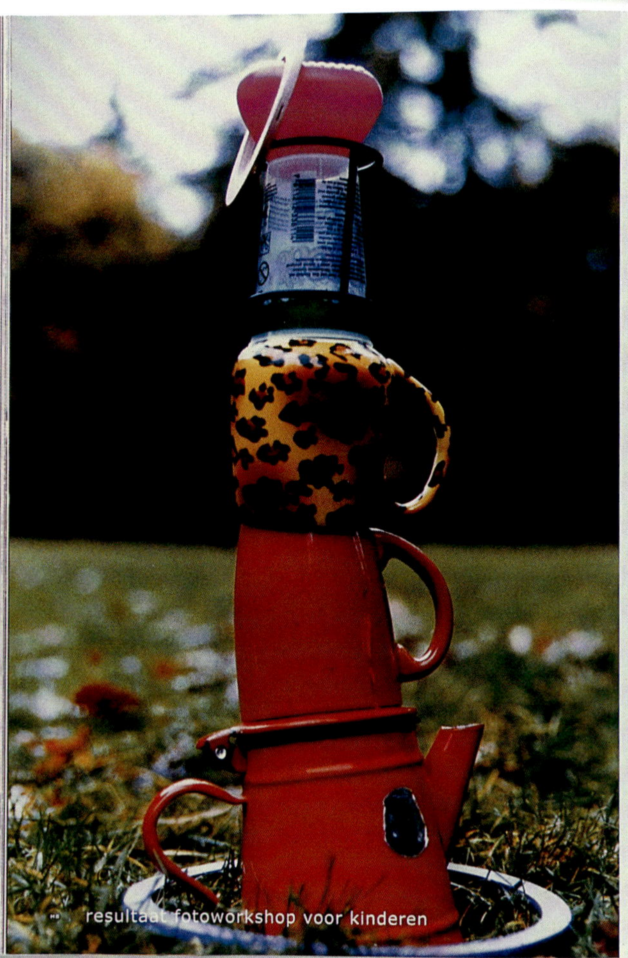

resultaat fotoworkshop voor kinderen

Sponsor Loterij BankGiro Loterij

ABN AMRO Bank

Daimler Chrysler

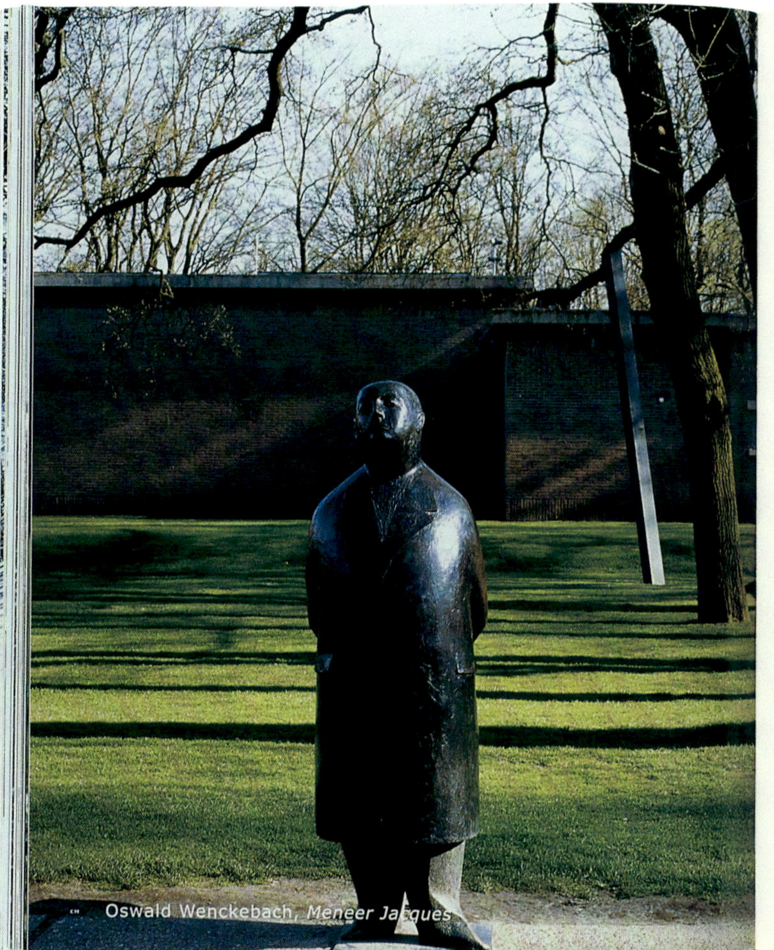

Oswald Wenckebach, *Meneer Jacques*

een vergelijkbare manier. Ik vind het ook bijzonder dat het hier rustig is. Als je naar het Van Gogh Museum gaat dan sta je in de rij met 2000 Amerikaanse toeristen. Hier hangt een totaal andere sfeer. Het is meer laid-back, ook door die combinatie van natuur en omgeving. » Ik mis hier weinig, misschien zoek je dat wat je hier niet vindt automatisch bij andere musea. Van hedendaagse kunst verwacht ik weinig, het grijpt je of het grijpt je niet. Het is aan of uit, liefde of haat. Soms vraag je je af wat iets in een museum doet, soms vind ik het ook helemaal prachtig. Dat vind ik hier ook terug, hetzelfde gevoel en dezelfde verhouding. » Een museumbezoek werkt niet vormend voor mij, ik zoek niet iets educatiefs. Ik hoef niets te leren over hoe ik kunst moet waarderen, dat doe ik wel op mijn eigen manier. Ik ben wel nieuwsgierig naar achtergronden van kunstwerken of kunstenaars. Het Kröller-Müller Museum zet voor mij wel in een stap in het proces, draagt bij aan het geheel. » Communicatie is tenslotte ook belangrijk. Ik ben hier nu ook omdat ik een recensie heb gelezen over de tentoonstelling *De favorieten van Helene*. Dat blijft hangen. En ik las ook iets over bijzondere rondleidingen in het Jachthuis St. Hubertus.'

'Mijn dag kan niet meer kapot na dit bezoek'

Bouwien Kuitert (66 jaar gepensioneerd groepsleidster gehandicapten) en Greet Jager (65 jaar AOW'er), Assen

BK:'Ik ben hier voor de derde keer, kom hier met grote tussenpozen. Greet is hier voor de eerste keer. We komen voor een dag hier, uit Assen en met het openbaar vervoer, bus en trein. We bezoeken veel musea in het noorden, zoals het Groninger museum, het grafisch museum, Drents museum, Stripmuseum, het Armando museum in Amersfoort maar ook in Amsterdam, het Stedelijk en Van Gogh Museum. » We zijn vandaag hier omdat we allebei iets hadden gelezen over het museum, in Kunst en Kitsch en een uitgebreid artikel in het Algemeen Dagblad. » We komen ook wel voor het park, maar vandaag was eigenlijk te koud. We komen deze zomer terug om daar van te genieten. Eigenlijk wilden we ook nog naar

bladzijde 79 - jaarverslag 2004 - Kröller-Müller Museum - de bezoeker aan het woord

Balans per 31 december 2004

activa 31 december 2004 (euro)		
vaste activa		
materiele vaste activa		
overige vaste activa	1.003.493	
som der vaste activa		1.003.493
vlottende activa		
voorraden	582.866	
vorderingen		
debiteuren	116.581	
overige vorderingen en vooruitbetaalde kosten	2.164.171	
	2.863.618	
liquide middelen	1.126.957	
som der vlottende activa		3.990.575
		4.994.068

bladzijde 104 - jaarverslag 2004 - Kröller-Müller Museum - balans

Exploitatierekening over 2004 (euro)

passiva 31 december 2004 (euro)		
eigen vermogen		
stichtingsvermogen	729.131	
reserve investeringsbijdrage	67.502	
		796.633
fonds kunstaankopen		1.339.352
voorzieningen		
voorziening pre-pensioen	1.078.532	
voorziening vut-regeling	14.279	
pensioenverplichtingen	21.613	
		1.114.424
kortlopende schulden		
crediteuren	359.884	
belastingen en premies sociale verzekeringen	127.802	
overige schulden	1.255.973	
		1.743.659
		4.994.068

bladzijde 105 - jaarverslag 2004 - Kröller-Müller Museum - balans

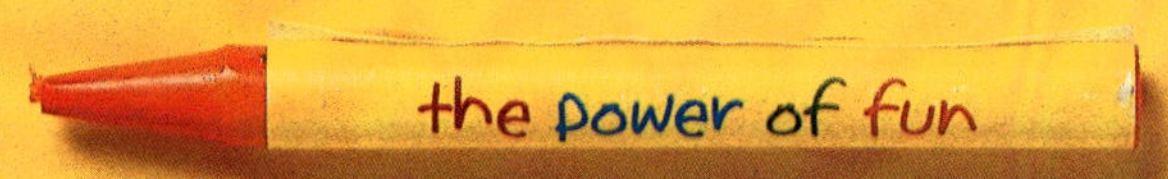

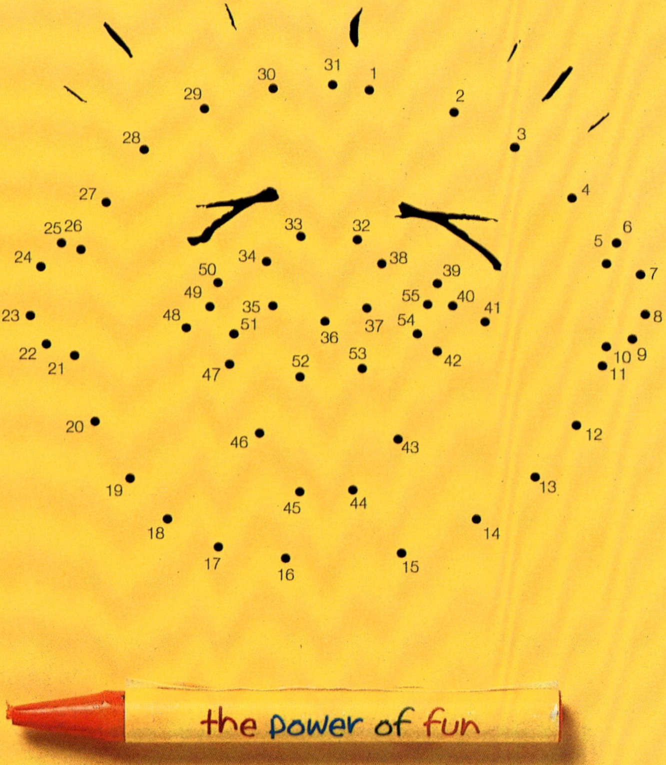

camp quality annual report 2004

laughter is the best medicine

ACN 052 097 720

Creative Director: Olivia Swinn and Michael Pennington
Designer: Sabine Steiner
Printer: Penfold Buscombe
Paper: Precision Offset
Page count: 36 +cover
Print run: 5,000
Size: 8.2677" x 11.6929"
Number of images: 18
Client: Camp Quality

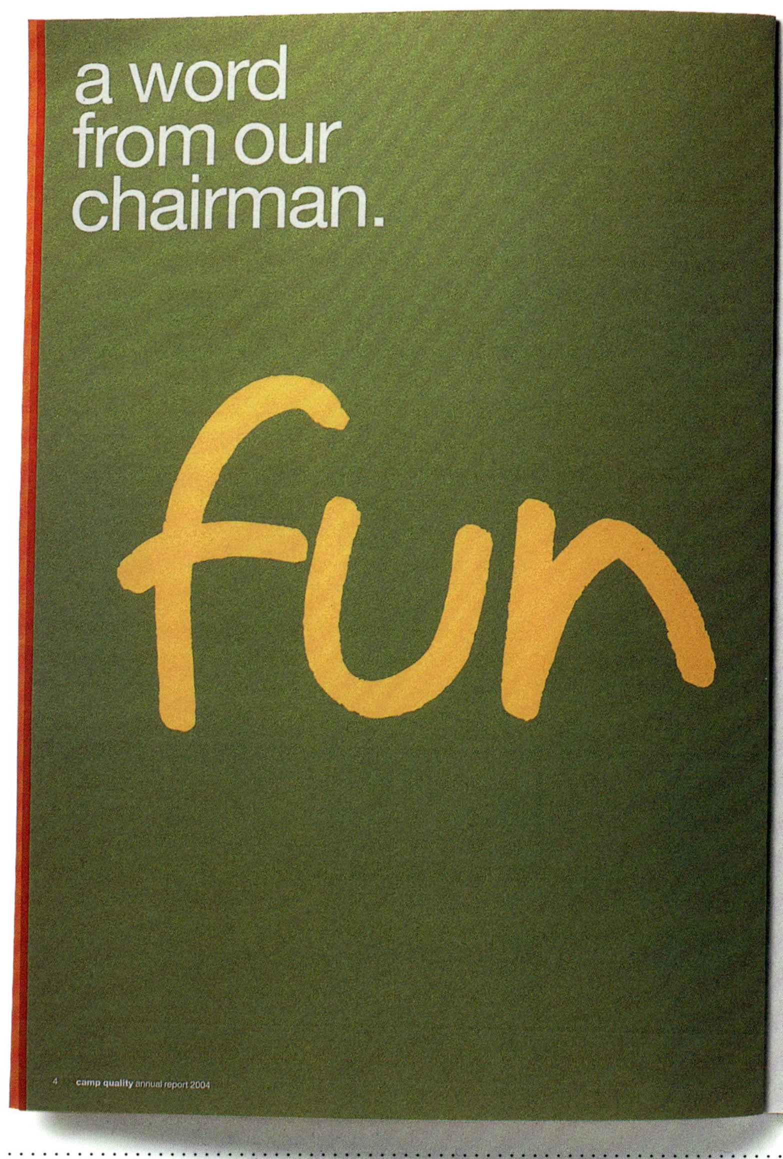

It gives me great pleasure to provide you with a copy of the 2003/04 Camp Quality Annual Report.

As you can see, everyone at Camp Quality passionately believes that the caring of sick children goes beyond medication and technology and that the power of fun plays a crucial role in supporting these children and their families in tackling the challenges that cancer brings.

Our unrelenting optimism, consultation with our stakeholders and strong corporate governance has maintained our focus and delivered some key targets in the following areas.

Financially: our culture of accountability and transparency along with strong business planning has helped us achieve budget and increase the stability of our long term future.

Programs: the introduction of several new programs based on the needs of our families. Overall our programs grew by 10% on the previous year.

Training: the implementation of manuals, programs and evaluations to address, deliver and monitor our processes and ensure high quality child protection training for our volunteers.

In moving forward the National Board will focus its resources and energies in the following manner.

1) Ensure that the number one priority for all our people is to maintain a passionate focus on caring for our sick children and their families.

2) Continue to enhance a culture of transparency and maintain our position of being at the forefront of Australian charities in terms of good governance.

3) Continue to enhance the skills and competencies of our staff and volunteers.

4) Complete a strategic and business plan for 2005/06 based on stakeholders feedback.

5) Continue to diversify our programs based on family needs as well as create a new puppet program to co-exist with our highly successful educational program in schools.

6) Work with other not for profits to reduce duplication, maximise resources and improve support to our children and their families.

On behalf of the Board I would like to thank all our families, staff, volunteers, sponsors and donors for their support and for living our culture of fun therapy.

J. Foote
John Foote
Chairman

camp quality annual report 2004 5

Q&A with DesignworksEnterpriseIG

What was the client's directive?

To design an Annual Report that reflected Camp Quality's brand space – "laughter is the best medicine" - and to make the Annual Report fun and interactive for stakeholders.

How did you define the problem?

How could we make the report reflect the childlike focus of the business as well as be relevant to an adult audience? And how could we underpin the audiences involved with Camp Quality in a way that was more engaging?

What was the approach?

We created a puzzle book that contained puzzles that adults could enjoy solving with personal letters to Camp Quality from key audiences, from the kids themselves to their families and sponsors.

Which disciplines or people helped you with the project?

Everything was done in house: concept, design, and copywriting.

Were you happy with the result? What could have been better?

We were happy with the result as several organizations receiving the report cancelled their Christmas parties and donated to Camp Quality instead. We were happy with the design, but hope to better it next year by being even more conceptual and whole hearted.

What was the client's response?

The client was delighted with it and even more so when it won a gold award in New York for a non profit organization.

How involved was the CEO in your meetings and presentations?

The CEO was involved in all key meetings.

How involved are designers with writing?

As an organization we believe very strongly that design is empty without great writing. Gone are the days when designers put lorem ipsom in as headlines. We employ 2 full time writers in our NZ offices who are intensely involved in all projects. In Sydney we are still

Several organizations receiving the report cancelled their Christmas parties and instead donated to Camp Quality.

looking to recruit a full time writer, however as designers we find it critical to good work to either work on our own copy or to bring in a freelance writer.

How would you define the success of an Annual Report?

A successful AR is one that is a true brand touchstone.

How important are awards to your clients?

Awards are a very good tool for us with our clients in that they create a lot of kudos for them, within their organization. They would not slavishly do something that went against their brand in order to win an award. However, winning a really prestigious or renowned award means that they are competing on a world stage with some of the best companies in the world. For down under clients that is desirable. For us as designers the recognition and enthusiasm for awards means that often we can push for engaging solutions.

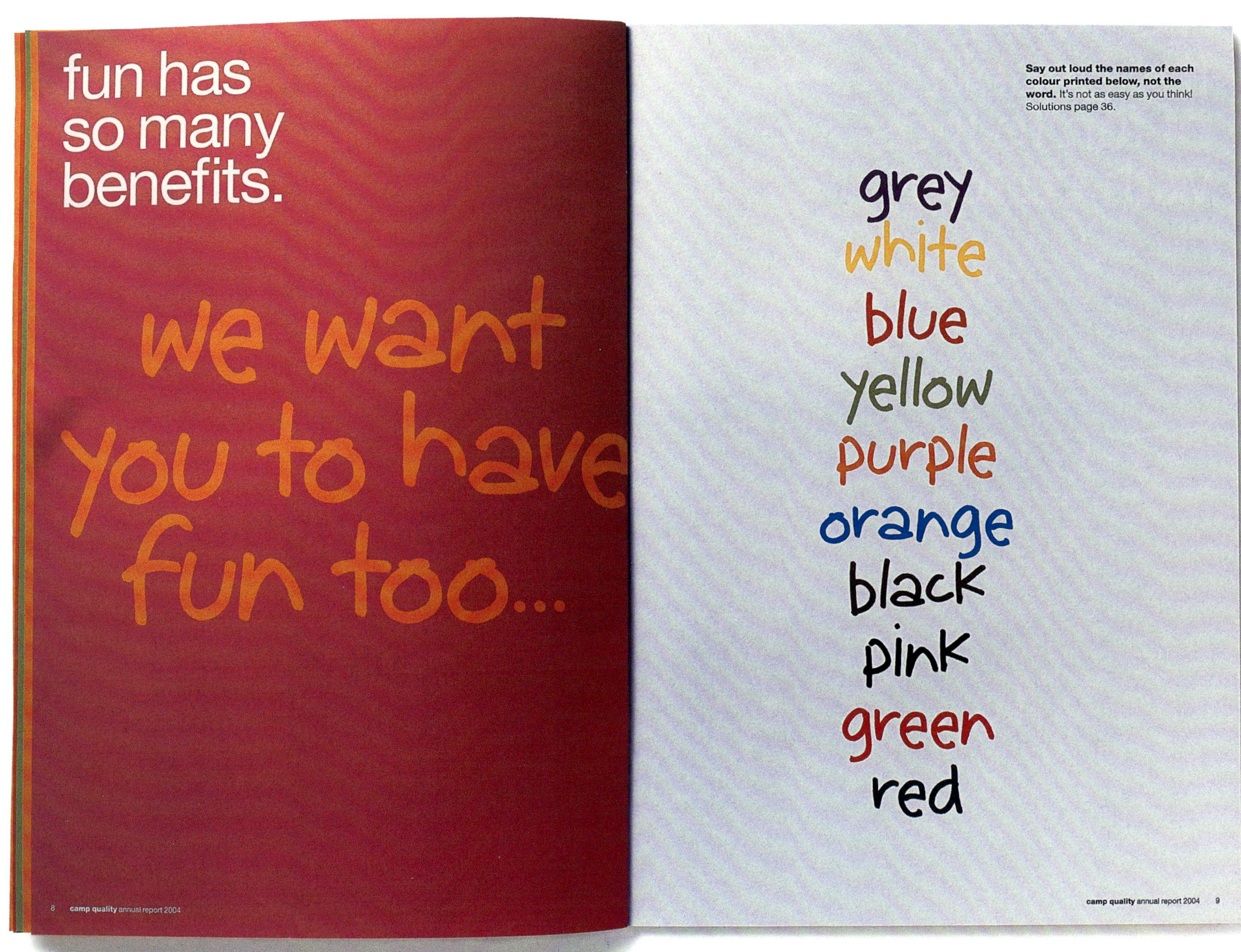

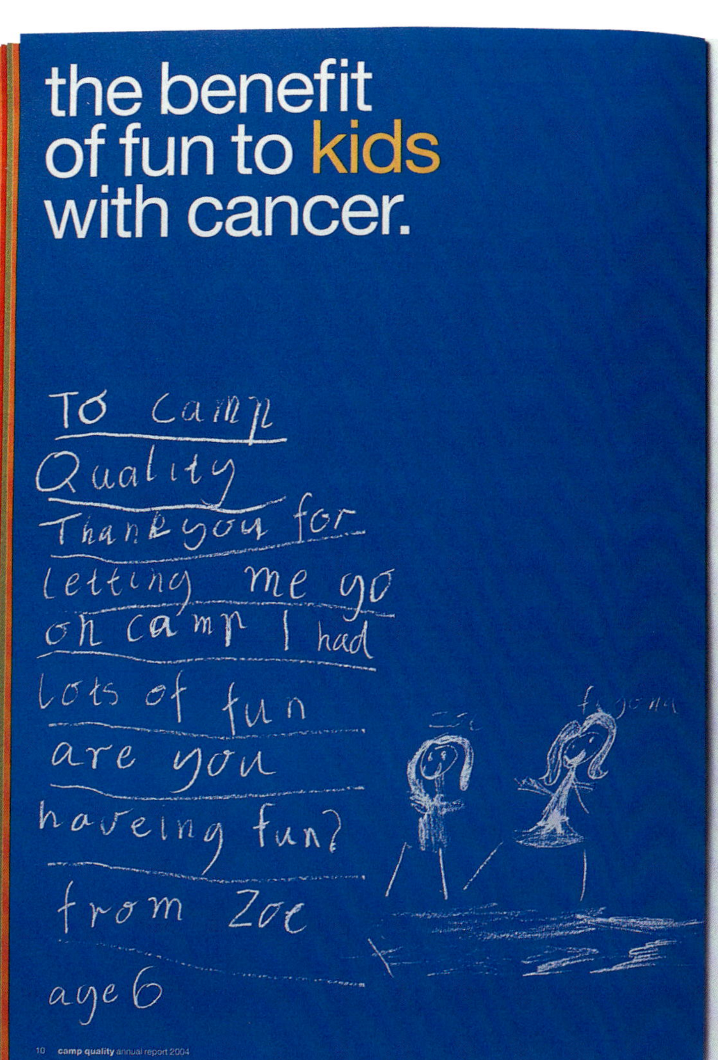

How many triangles can you find in this illustration? Count triangles of all sizes and orientations. Solutions page 36.

facts & figures for year end 2004.

Extract of audited financial statements

Statement of financial performance for the year ended 30 June 2004

	2004 $	2003 $
Revenue from ordinary activities	8,426,709	7,230,877
Employee benefits expense	(2,125,966)	(1,990,558)
Travel and motor vehicle expenses	(146,162)	(126,954)
Depreciation and amortisation expenses	(235,828)	(283,292)
Fundraising expenses	(981,487)	(771,169)
Advertising and promotion*	(306,261)	(1,160,725)
Direct Camping Program	(866,409)	(991,787)
Property expenses	(248,520)	(259,472)
Family programs and activities	(411,860)	(268,278)
Other program expenses	(137,019)	(337,930)
Contribution - Childrens Cancer Centre Foundation Trust	(200,000)	-
Telephone, postage, printing and stationery	(302,287)	(214,873)
Other expenses from ordinary activities	(447,530)	(136,526)
Profit from ordinary activities	**2,017,380**	**689,313**
Total changes in equity other than those resulting from transactions with owners as owners	**2,017,380**	**689,313**

*Advertising and promotion includes in-kind support valued at $193,840 (2003: $1,122,740).

Statement of financial position as at 30 June 2004

	2004 $	2003 $
Current assets		
Cash assets	2,685,553	1,734,641
Receivables	198,359	135,599
Other	182,583	171,631
Total current assets	**3,066,495**	**2,041,871**
Non-current assets		
Investments	10,624,370	9,165,664
Property, plant and equipment	2,413,350	2,471,746
Total non-current assets	**13,037,720**	**11,637,410**
Total assets	**16,104,215**	**13,679,281**
Current liabilities		
Payables	337,208	68,134
Provisions	171,676	114,750
Other	347,830	251,011
Total current liabilities	**856,714**	**433,895**
Non-current liabilities		
Provisions	32,758	48,022
Total non-current liabilities	**32,758**	**48,022**
Total liabilities	**889,472**	**481,917**
Net assets	**15,214,743**	**13,197,364**
Equity		
Reserves	5,092,284	4,188,094
Retained profits	10,122,459	9,009,270
Total equity	**15,214,743**	**13,197,364**

Statement of cash flows for the year ended 30 June 2004

	2004 $	2003 $
Cash flow from operating activities		
Receipts from supporters	6,583,248	5,257,834
Payments to suppliers and employees	(5,260,051)	(5,104,012)
Dividends and distributions received	538,893	203,343
Interest received	149,582	202,551
Net cash provided by operating activities	**2,011,672**	**559,716**
Cash flow from investing activities		
Proceeds from sale of property, plant and equipment	629,463	555,059
Proceeds from sale of investments	1,984,221	3,914,352
Payment for property, plant and equipment	(821,199)	(771,521)
Payment for investments	(2,853,245)	(4,265,000)
Net cash used in investing activities	**(1,060,760)**	**(567,110)**
Net increase/(decrease) in cash held	950,912	(7,394)
Cash at beginning of financial year	1,734,641	1,742,035
Cash at end of financial year	**2,685,553**	**1,734,641**

A complete set of financial statements and independent Audit Report can be provided to members upon request.

Violating a press law prohibiting
the publication of material considered
defamatory and offensive to religion

Promoting democracy

Speaking out in support of
women's rights and challenging
conservative religious beliefs

Subversive actions against
the state and collusion
with the political opposition
outside the country

Reporting on corruption
in the ruling party and
on planned attacks against the
political opposition; accused
of being a "media terrorist"

Arguing against terrorism
by the state and separatists;
speaking out for political and
ethnic pluralism and against child
soldiers and suicide bombings

Running counter to
the conservative dictates
of the Republic

Being an independent journalist

These are our crimes

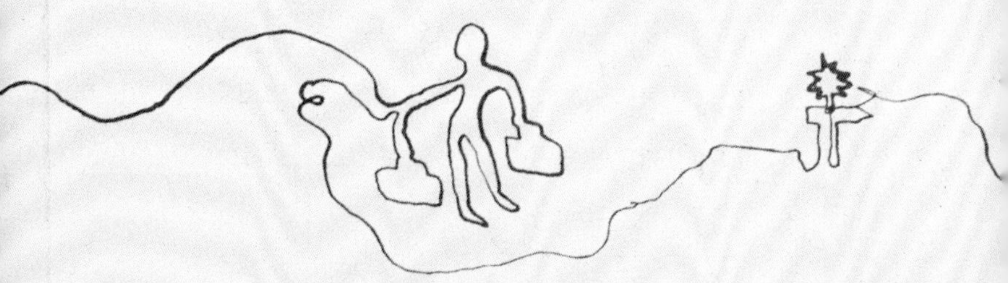

PEN CANADA
2004 05 ANNUAL REPORT

Designers: Gary Beelik, Jim Ryce Illustrator: Ben Weeks Photographer: Gary Mulcahey Writer/Researcher: David Cozaz Editor: Alison Gordon Printer: Somerset Graphics Co. Ltd. Page count: 78 + cover Number of images: 8 Print run: 2,000 Size: 5"x7" Paper: SMART Papers, Pegasus, White, 80lb text and cover, Smooth Client: PEN Canada

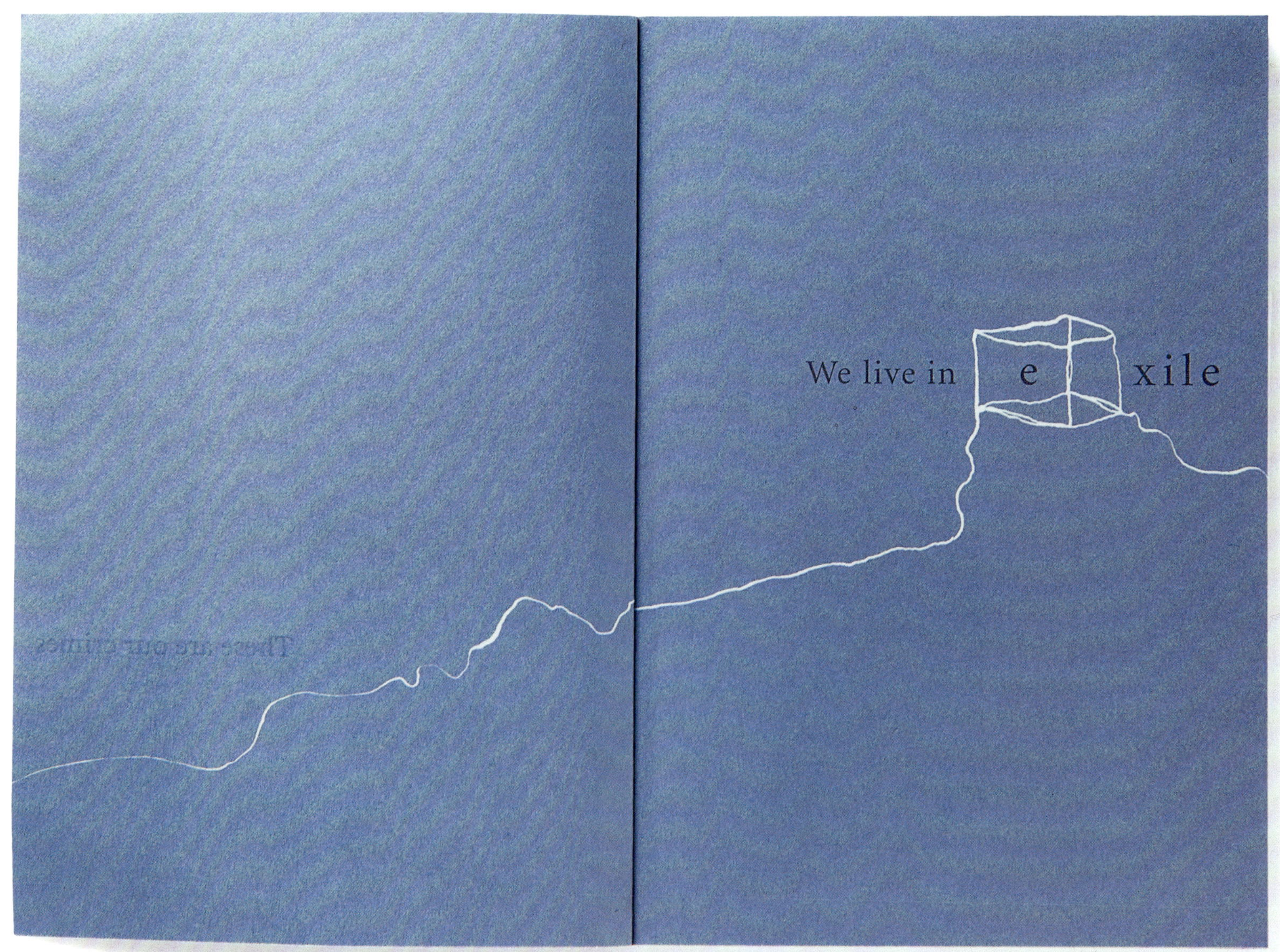

Q&A with Soapbox Design

What was the client's directive?

PEN Canada is a not-for-profit organization that Soapbox has worked with for the past 7 years. All of the design work is 100% pro-bono. The trade-off for this donation of time is the freedom to be completely creative. Over the course of our relationship, we have built a considerable amount of trust and understanding of what PEN does. Because of this trust, we are able to make concise recommendations for themes for each year's report. Our concepts are based on the accumulation of all other work done together over the course of the year. This year, one of the main issues that PEN has focused much of its efforts on were the many exiles that PEN has worked with. Once a prisoner has been freed from incarceration, they face the reality that they may not be safe in their homeland any more. We wanted to deal with the issue of "now what...?". The client agreed and the concept was born.

How did you define the problem?

With each report, the most important thing is to try and give the reader a clear idea of what it is that PEN Canada does on behalf of their honorary members. Telling the stories of these exiled writers and journalists who are now living in Canada was a very powerful way to communicate some of this incredible work.

What was the approach?

Our approach was to capture in photography the personality of the exiles that are now living in Canada... thanks to the help of PEN Canada. Along with the photographs, we told the stories of these amazing people. We felt it was important to help readers understand that these people were being persecuted, harassed and jailed for their beliefs. We hoped that when people read the stories, they would realize that these journalists are just doing what people in Canada do everyday. They offer opinions and commentary on social and political issues. The only difference is, we are free to express ourselves and have our own opinions without fear of punishment. The illustrations were then placed over the photographs to help illustrate their stories and journey. It reflects their journey from their "crimes" in their homeland to their "freedom" living in Canada. All the illustrations are linked to one another from page to page as these exiles are to each other through PEN's enormous help.

Which disciplines or people helped you with the project?

This year we were able to work with a great photographer, Gary Mulcahey, and a great illustrator, Ben Weeks. Both donated all their time and materials to the project. We also had help from Unisource Canada and Smart Papers who donated all the paper for the past 4 years. Somerset Graphics, the printer, has provided a great discount on the print fees to make this whole project work within the budget of $2,000.00 CDN inclusively.

Were you happy with the result? What could have been better?

We were pleased with the end result. Each of our suppliers worked with us as a team to make this project a complete success.

What was the client's response?

Our client felt that we had created a beautiful report and is always extremely grateful for the work that we do. Even though we gave them a complete description and mock-ups of our concepts, they are always surprised with the completed work on their behalf.

How involved was the CEO in your meetings, presentations, etc.?

First, we run the idea by the Executive Director of PEN and get approvals. The next step is to present a layout of all top-level creative. At this point, the client gives us the creative freedom to create, design, photograph, art direct and produce the report on their behalf. PEN supplies the writer and editor from their pool of industry supporters.

Do you feel that designers are becoming more involved in copywriting?

At Soapbox, we are involved with writing at concept or top level, then we leave the rest to the professionals.

How do you define success in Annual Report design?

Success at Soapbox is defined by providing a clear concept that is based on solid creative ideas that communicate the client's message.

How important are awards to your client?

Not important.

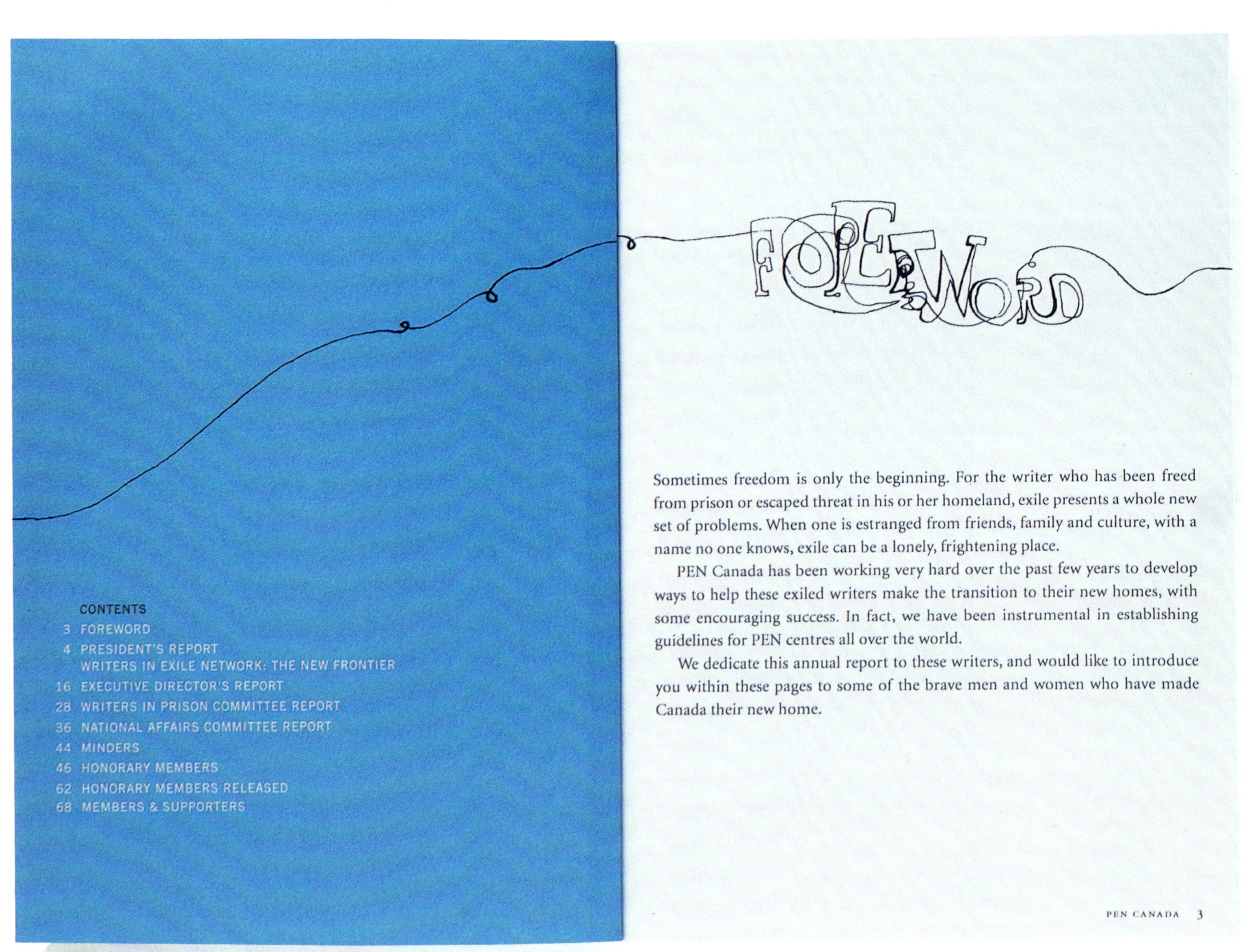

The artists and printers involved donated time and materials to make this project work within the budget.

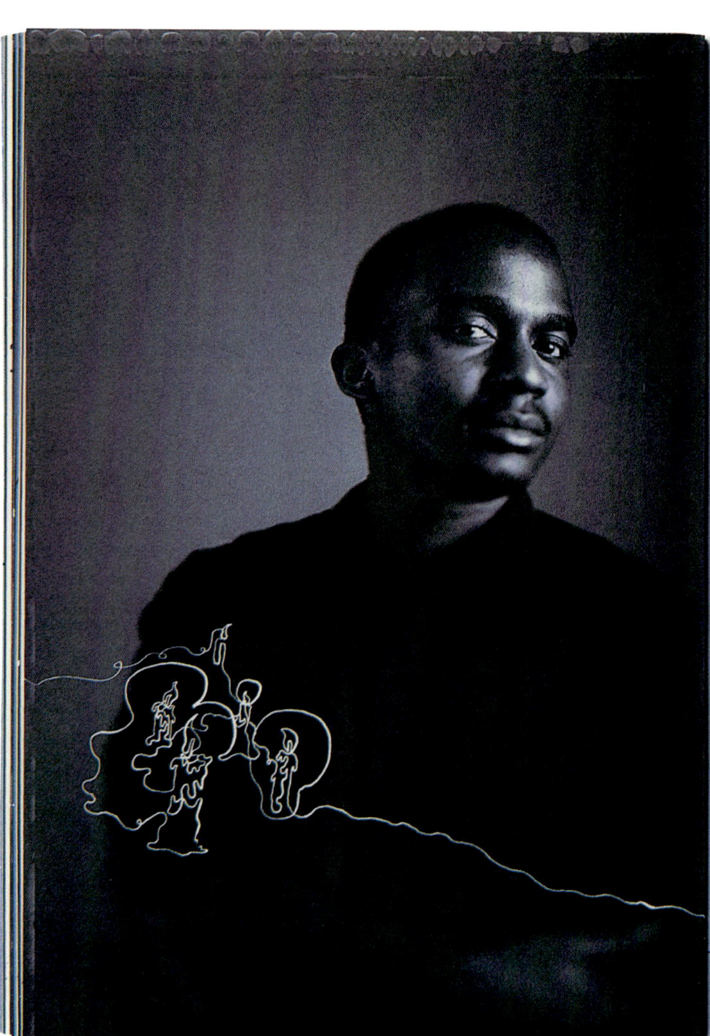

THOMAS MADONDORO

COUNTRY ZIMBABWE
OCCUPATION JOURNALIST
LIVING IN EXILE SINCE 2004

THESE ARE MY CRIMES
FOR REPORTING ON CORRUPTION IN THE RULING ZANU-PF PARTY AND ON PLANNED ATTACKS AGAINST THE POLITICAL OPPOSITION; ACCUSED OF BEING A "MEDIA TERRORIST"

Lord Acton's axiom, "power tends to corrupt; absolute power corrupts absolutely," may be perfectly applied to Zimbabwe president Robert Mugabe. Once a leader in the guerrilla movement in the former Rhodesia that led to the creation of an independent state in the 1970s, Mugabe has transformed himself from a rebel with a populist cause to a dictator who is intolerant of dissent.

Thomas Madondoro knows this very well. The journalist observed Mugabe's ruling ZANU-PF party with a critical eye, for both the private and public media. Madondoro began as a business reporter for the now-defunct *Daily News* and the *Herald*. He then joined the government's Information Centre, interpreting and circulating domestic economic policy for an international audience. Nevertheless, Madondoro never had the freedom to conduct analysis and write his articles independently. Realizing that he was just a tool for state propaganda, he resigned and returned to the private media.

Working for the *Financial Gazette*, Madondoro used his government contacts as well as the confidential information to which he had been privy, to write critical articles. He highlighted economic malfeasance, repression of opposition figures as well as state espionage of foreign diplomats. In August 2004, Madondoro's troubles began when he received threatening phone calls and youth militias followed him, calling him a "media terrorist." As Madondoro continued with his reporting, more threats followed. While investigating a story in rural Zimbabwe, he was detained and tortured by armed supporters of Mugabe. He left the country soon after.

PEN CANADA 41

WRITERS IN EXILE: A BRIEF HISTORY

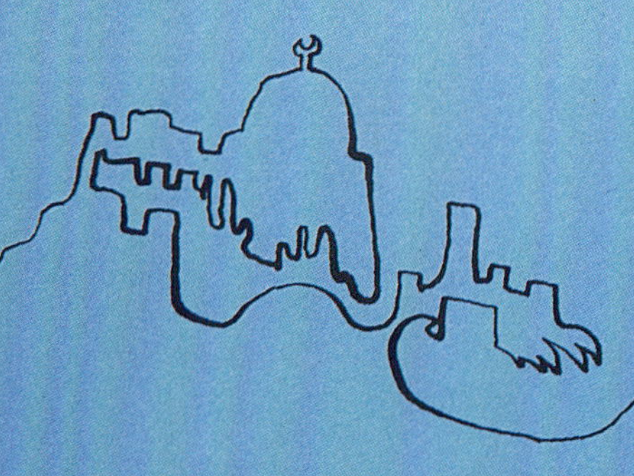

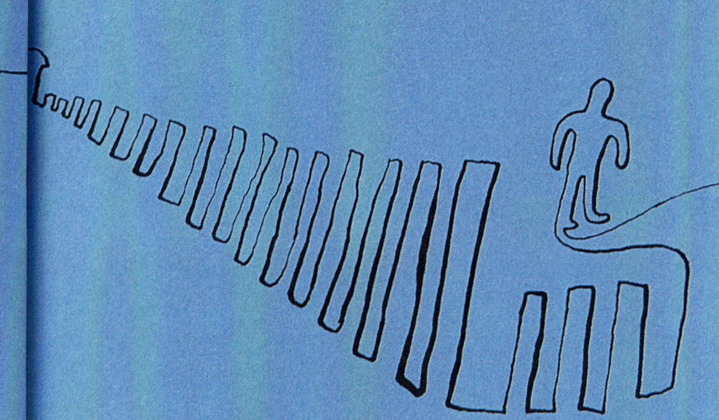

PEN Canada began working with exiled writers not as policy, but by necessity. In 1989, Chinese poet Duo Duo found himself exiled in Toronto after the Tiananmen massacre. Two years later journalist Martha Kumsa arrived from Ethiopia after spending nearly ten years in jail. In both these cases, PEN Canada staff and members did their best to help them establish new lives here, but had neither the resources nor the structure to do it. They cobbled together support systems as best they could, while beginning to search for ways to do it better.

The situation changed when writer and PEN Canada member John Fraser became Master of Massey College at the University of Toronto in 1994. As a close friend of Duo Duo, Fraser had seen first-hand the alienation of an exiled writer living alone in a strange city. Because Massey is a small residential college, he believed that establishing a position there for exiled writers could make their initial resettlement in Canada much easier.

Together with former PEN Canada president Graeme Gibson, Fraser approached the board of directors with his idea. The board agreed, and the PEN Canada Writers in Exile Network was born.

22 PEN CANADA

"As a child of Egyptian immigrants, growing up was a very difficult thing. I always felt like I didn't quite fit in. Sesame Street was my place of refuge. It was a happy place. I remember feeling that it was okay to be different, that on Sesame Street it didn't matter if you were blue or if you were green or if you were yellow."

– teacher and lifelong Sesame Street fan

2004 Annual Report

Art Director: Dave Mason
Designer: Beth May
Photographers: Victor John Penner, Albert Normandin
Writer: Gail David
Printer: Blanchette Press
Paper: Pegasus BW Vellum cover 80lb, Sterling Ultra Gloss cover 80lb, text 100lb, Pegasus Vellum text 80lb
Page count: 64 +cover
Print Run: 7,500
Size: 7.5" x 10", 32 images
Client: Sesame Workshop

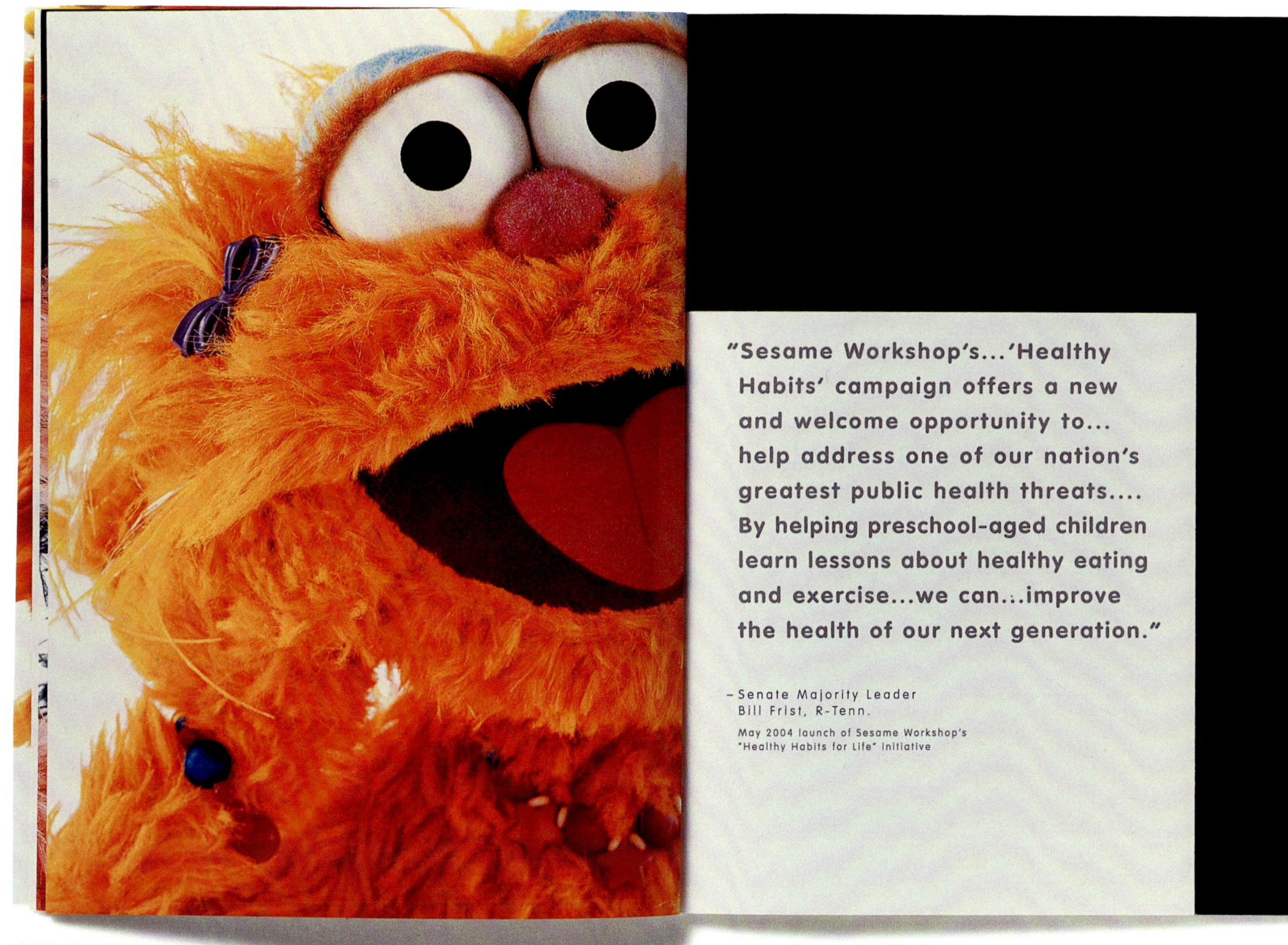

Q&A with SamataMason

What was the client's directive?

The client's desire was to communicate the international efforts of the organization and its co-production partners, and to demonstrate its effectiveness at addressing complex and far-reaching issues, one child at a time, millions of times every day.

What was the approach?

We built the book around the idea that Sesame Workshop has always had (and continues to have) a profound impact on the lives of those it touches, and that mass media still comes down to reaching and connecting with an individual.

Which disciplines or people helped you with the project?

We worked very closely with the team at Sesame Workshop to craft the messaging and gather materials to support it.

Were you happy with the result?

Yes. The report hit the mark on every point.

What was the client's response?

They were very happy with the book. Extremely positive feedback.

How involved was the CEO in your meetings, presentations, etc.?

The CEO, COO and other key executives and team members were very involved in providing insights and guidance to help shape the report's messaging challenges.

Do you feel that designers are becoming more involved in copywriting?

Absolutely.

How do you define success in Annual Report design?

Happy client. Happy recipients. Happy us.

How important are awards to your client?

That varies from client to client. Sesame Workshop has been very appreciative of the recognition.

Ultimately, mass media still comes down to connecting with an individual.

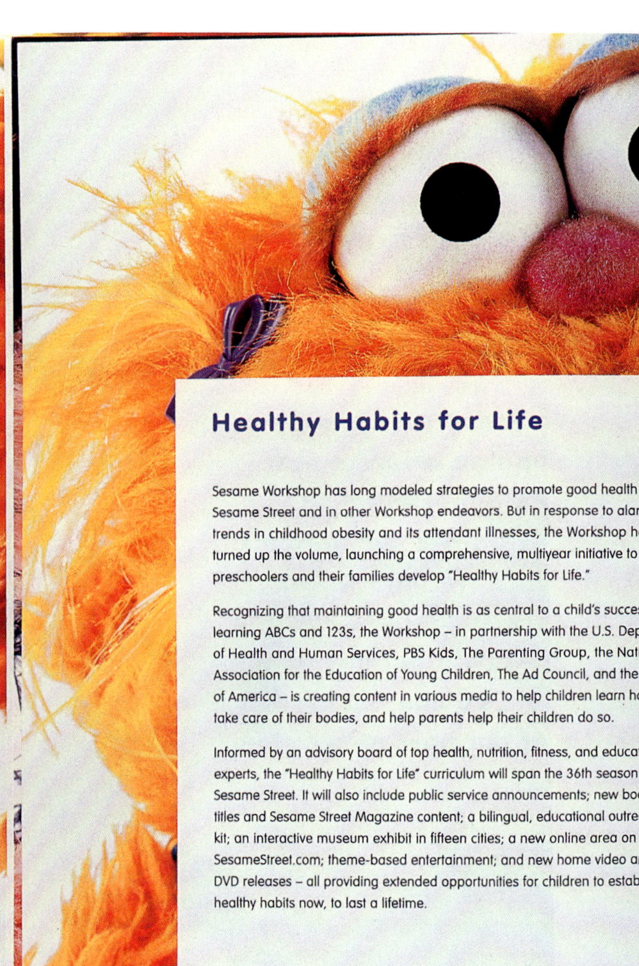

Healthy Habits for Life

Sesame Workshop has long modeled strategies to promote good health on Sesame Street and in other Workshop endeavors. But in response to alarming trends in childhood obesity and its attendant illnesses, the Workshop has turned up the volume, launching a comprehensive, multiyear initiative to help preschoolers and their families develop "Healthy Habits for Life."

Recognizing that maintaining good health is as central to a child's success as learning ABCs and 123s, the Workshop – in partnership with the U.S. Department of Health and Human Services, PBS Kids, The Parenting Group, the National Association for the Education of Young Children, The Ad Council, and the YMCA of America – is creating content in various media to help children learn how to take care of their bodies, and help parents help their children do so.

Informed by an advisory board of top health, nutrition, fitness, and education experts, the "Healthy Habits for Life" curriculum will span the 36th season of Sesame Street. It will also include public service announcements; new book titles and Sesame Street Magazine content; a bilingual, educational outreach kit; an interactive museum exhibit in fifteen cities; a new online area on SesameStreet.com; theme-based entertainment; and new home video and DVD releases – all providing extended opportunities for children to establish healthy habits now, to last a lifetime.

< Zoe SESAME STREET USA

15,000,000

children have been orphaned by HIV/AIDS, as of 2003.

Nowhere is this epidemic more devastating to children than in sub-Saharan Africa, home to 80% of those orphaned by the disease.

UNICEF Report: "Childhood Under Threat: The State of the World's Children 2005"

17,600,000

children under age 5 worldwide are estimated to be overweight.

In the United States, the prevalence of obese children aged 6 to 11 years has doubled since the 1960s.

World Health Organization: Global Strategy on Diet, Physical Activity and Health, 2003

20,000,000

children have been forced by conflict or human rights violations to leave their homes in the last decade.

UNICEF Report: "Childhood Under Threat: The State of the World's Children 2005"

65,000,000

of the world's primary-school-age girls do not attend school.

Implementation of the United Nations Millennium Declaration, Report of the Secretary-General, 2004

"...through education we can make measurable differences here and around the world, now and for generations to come."

the 6-year-old Iraqi girl who, in the midst of war, writes to tell us that she and her younger brother love and want to be friends with the characters on Alam Simsim, our Egyptian production broadcast via satellite to Iraq and 21 other Arab nations. Each is an example of progress – one child at a time.

I think we can all agree that education changes the course of history, that through education we can make measurable differences here and around the world, now and for generations to come. This was the conviction and idealism that sparked the creation of Sesame Street and the Workshop in the late 1960s, and even now with the world a different place, continues to sustain us. Despite all the changes of the last four decades, our vision, our values, our focus on helping children learn have remained constant. One child at a time, millions of children the world over.

Gary E. Knell
President and Chief Executive Officer

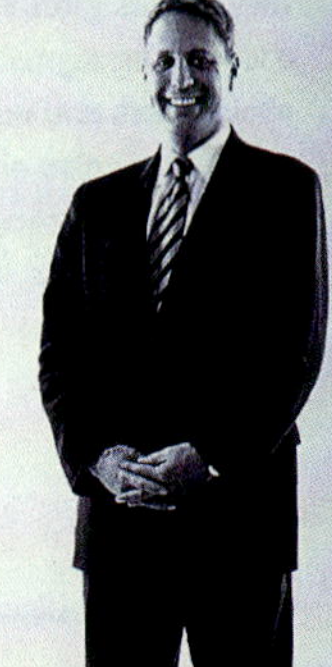

For more than 35 years, Sesame Workshop has been helping children learn, grow and reach their highest potential. From Brooklyn to Kabul, we connect with millions of children and effect change where it matters most.

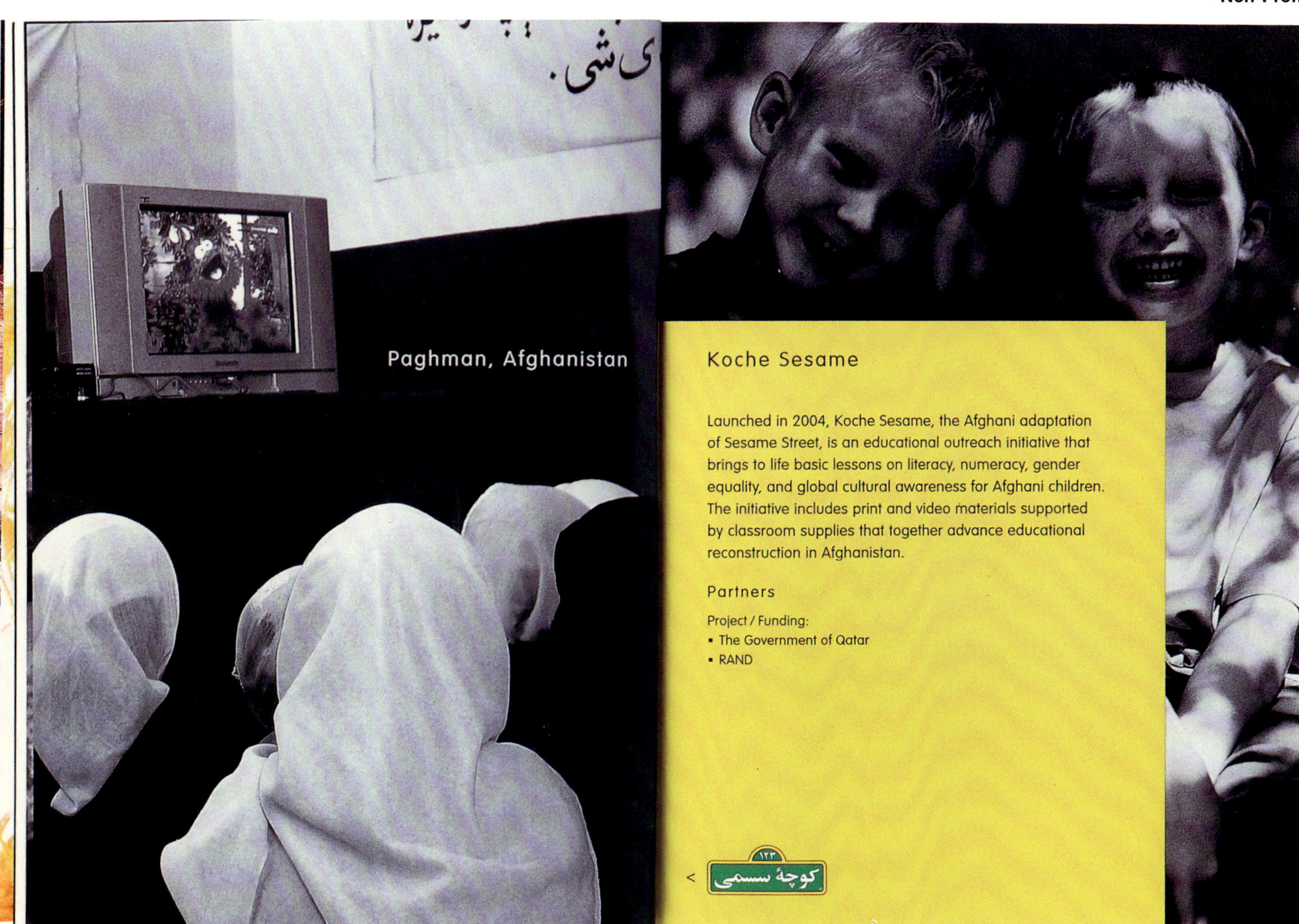
Paghman, Afghanistan

Koche Sesame

Launched in 2004, Koche Sesame, the Afghani adaptation of Sesame Street, is an educational outreach initiative that brings to life basic lessons on literacy, numeracy, gender equality, and global cultural awareness for Afghani children. The initiative includes print and video materials supported by classroom supplies that together advance educational reconstruction in Afghanistan.

Partners

Project / Funding:
- The Government of Qatar
- RAND

Consolidated Statement of Activities
For the years ended June 30 (000s omitted)

	'04	'03
Revenues		
Program Support	$ 23,960	$ 24,962
Program Sales and Royalties	6,809	10,900
Publishing and Licensing	66,043	57,185
Total Operating Revenues	96,812	93,047
Expenses		
Program Production	34,939	32,490
Publishing, Product Licensing, Development, and Distribution	19,327	17,365
Interactive Media	2,616	4,047
Corporate Affairs, Education, and Development	15,652	13,145
General and Administrative	19,169	19,798
Amortization	6,945	7,361
Total Operating Expenses	98,648	94,206
Operating Loss	(1,836)	(1,159)
Net Investment Income	9,124	4,123
Equity Earnings	–	967
Interest Expense	(1,217)	(3,023)
Other Nonoperating (Losses) Income	(3)	67,235
Increase (Decrease) in Net Assets	$ 6,068	$ 68,143

Consolidated Statement of Financial Position
For the years ended June 30 (000s omitted)

	'04	'03
Assets		
Cash and Short-Term Investments	$ 16,824	$ 3,147
Receivables		
Programs and Product Licenses and Contracts in Support of Programs, Net of Allowance for Doubtful Accounts	21,269	20,328
Grants	2,975	5,522
	24,244	25,850
Programs in Process	6,693	10,718
Marketable Securities	152,325	150,312
Intangible Assets	113,585	120,530
Fixed Assets	9,298	8,619
Other Assets	2,320	3,878
Total Assets	$ 325,289	$ 323,054
Liabilities and Net Assets		
Accounts Payable and Accrued Expenses	$ 24,134	$ 27,550
Deferred Program and Product License Revenues	18,434	18,465
Deferred Rent Payable	5,080	5,466
Debt Payable	60,000	60,000
Total Liabilities	107,648	111,481
Net Assets		
Unrestricted	217,143	207,412
Temporarily Restricted	498	4,161
Total Net Assets	217,641	211,573
Total Liabilities and Net Assets	$ 325,289	$ 323,054

Legal Aid Foundation of Los Angeles

Design Firm: Kuhlmann Leavitt, Inc.
Creative Director: Deanna Kuhlmann-Leavitt

THESE FACES
IN THE MIRRORS
ARE BUT
THE SHADOWS
AND PHANTOMS
OF MYSELF.

Henry Wadsworth Longfellow

Legal Aid Foundation of Los Angeles 2004 Annual Report

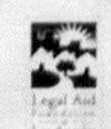

http://www.lafla.org

Art Director: Deanna Kuhlmann-Leavitt
Designer: Thomas Twellman
Photographer: Everard Williams, Jr.
Writers: Gary Phillips, Kathleen Sheldon
Printer: Reproxdigital
Paper: Neenah, Eames Painting Collection, Canvas Finish,
White 80lb text and cover
Page count: 28 page plus 8 page gatefold wrap
Print Run: 2,500
Size: 5.625" x 11.25"
Number of images: 11
Client: LAFLA, Legal Aid Foundation, Los Angeles

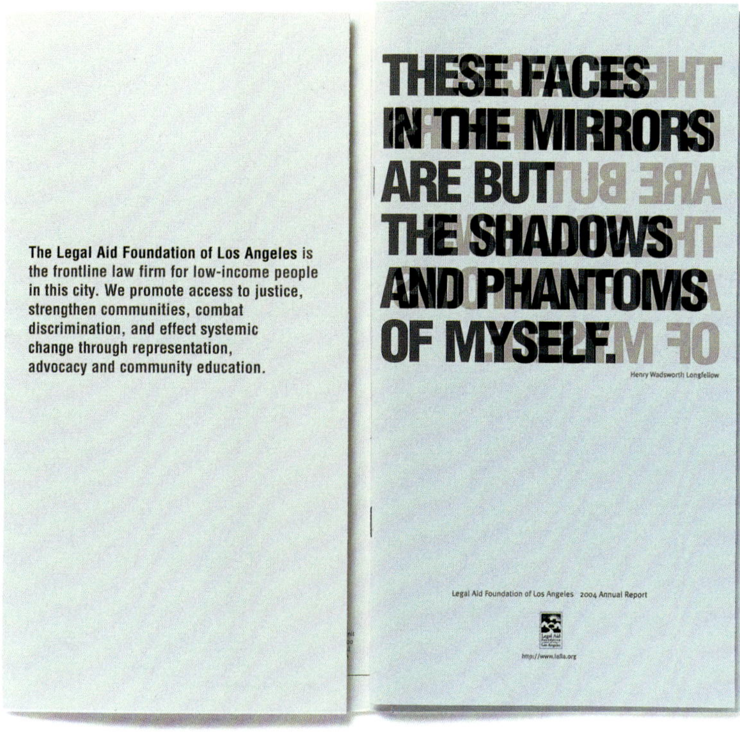

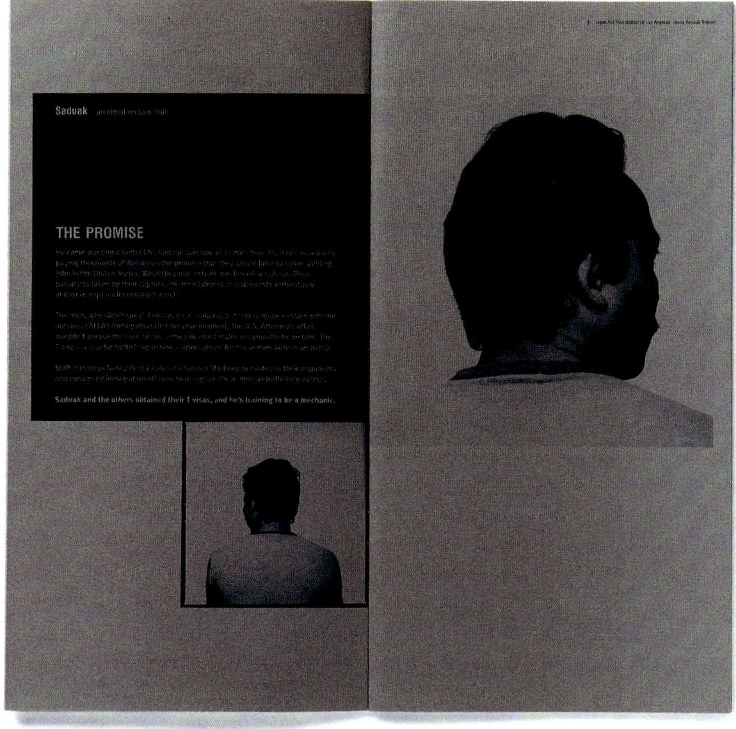

Q&A with Kuhlmann Leavitt, Inc.

What was the client's directive?
Tell the stories of five LAFLA clients assisted during 2004.

How did you define the problem?
Present each story distinctly from the next but in such a way that together they tell a bigger LAFLA story.

What was the approach?
Working with photographer Everard Williams, Jr., each client was photographed from the side, front and back. This approach gave us maximum flexibility in solving the above problem. Alternating photo placement, image size and page color allowed each story to stand on its own yet work together to tell a cohesive larger story.

Which disciplines or people helped you with the project?
LAFLA wrote the report and KLI sourced the cover statement. KLI worked with Everard Williams on the portraits and Reproxdigital on maximizing our print dollars without compromising quality.

Were you happy with the result?
We are very pleased.

What was the client's response?
For fourteen years they have been both pleased and supportive and this year was no exception.

How involved was the CEO in your meetings, presentations, etc.?
Our relationship with LAFLA is a collaborative process amongst the Foundation's Executive Director, LAFLA editors, Everard and Kuhlmann Leavitt, Inc. Like most of our clients, they understand, support and foster good design and know that this is best achieved through a participatory process.

Do you feel that designers are becoming more involved in copywriting?
Definitely. Designers must be more involved because the text and graphic messages are intertwined and inseparble.

How do you define success in Annual Report design?
You know you are on your way when you find smart clients that allow you to do great work so that at the end of the day everyone is satisfied and proud of the effort.

How important are awards to your client?
They are delighted to win awards ("Sweet!" to be more precise), but do not expect us to enter design competitions.

For fourteen years they have been pleased and supportive. This year was no exception.

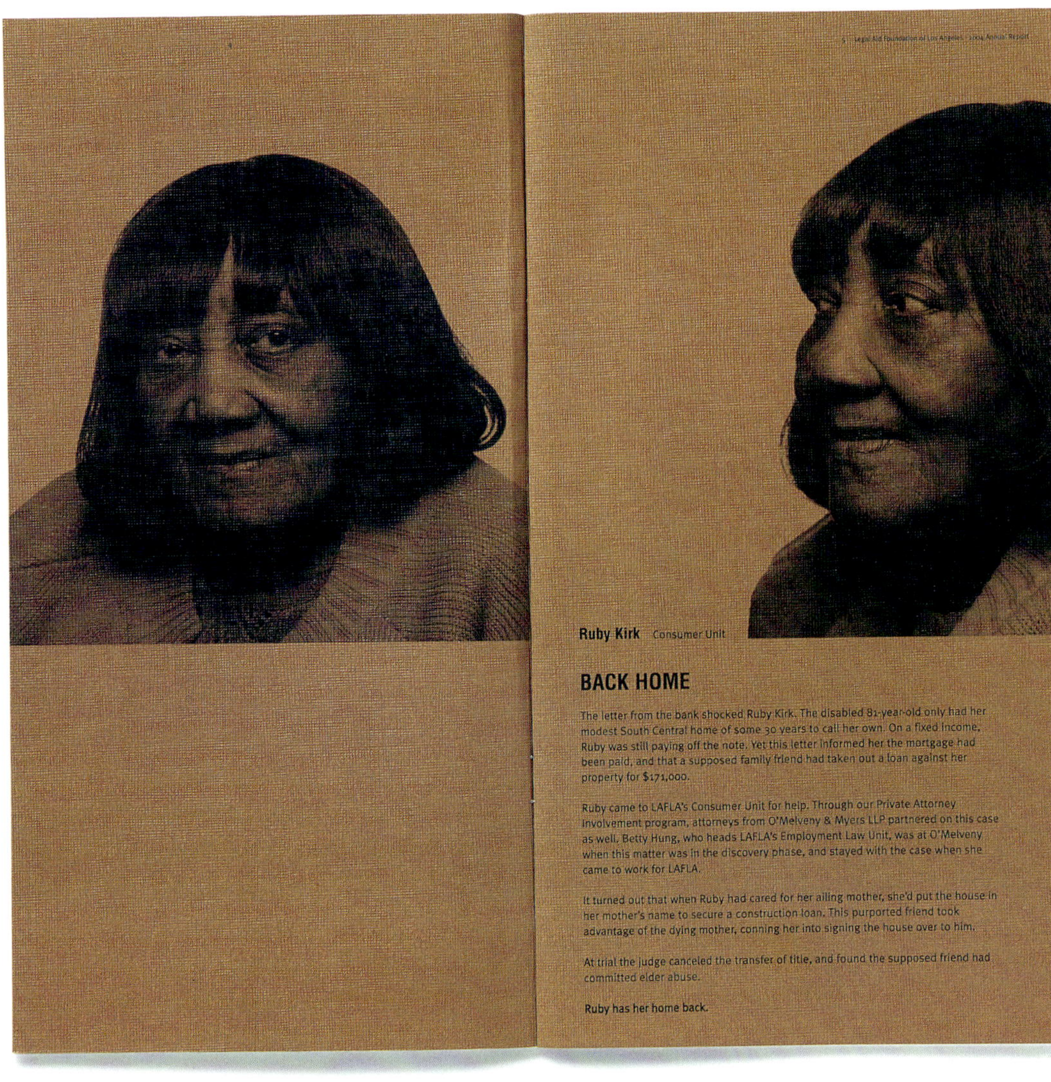

Legal Aid Foundation of Los Angeles 2004 Annual Report

Ruby Kirk Consumer Unit

BACK HOME

The letter from the bank shocked Ruby Kirk. The disabled 81-year-old only had her modest South Central home of some 30 years to call her own. On a fixed income, Ruby was still paying off the note. Yet this letter informed her the mortgage had been paid, and that a supposed family friend had taken out a loan against her property for $171,000.

Ruby came to LAFLA's Consumer Unit for help. Through our Private Attorney Involvement program, attorneys from O'Melveny & Myers LLP partnered on this case as well. Betty Hung, who heads LAFLA's Employment Law Unit, was at O'Melveny when this matter was in the discovery phase, and stayed with the case when she came to work for LAFLA.

It turned out that when Ruby had cared for her ailing mother, she'd put the house in her mother's name to secure a construction loan. This purported friend took advantage of the dying mother, conning her into signing the house over to him.

At trial the judge canceled the transfer of title, and found the supposed friend had committed elder abuse.

Ruby has her home back.

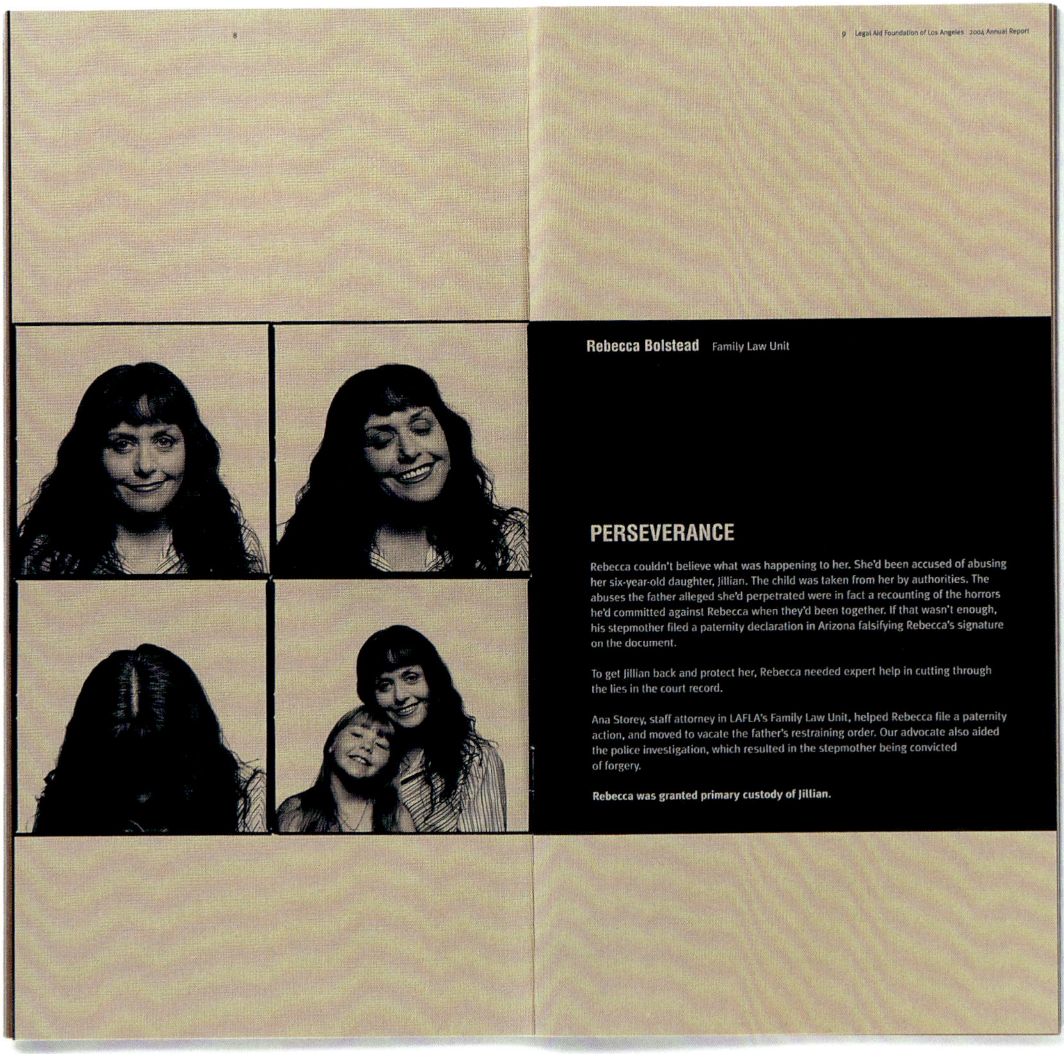

8

9 Legal Aid Foundation of Los Angeles 2004 Annual Report

Rebecca Bolstead Family Law Unit

PERSEVERANCE

Rebecca couldn't believe what was happening to her. She'd been accused of abusing her six-year-old daughter, Jillian. The child was taken from her by authorities. The abuses the father alleged she'd perpetrated were in fact a recounting of the horrors he'd committed against Rebecca when they'd been together. If that wasn't enough, his stepmother filed a paternity declaration in Arizona falsifying Rebecca's signature on the document.

To get Jillian back and protect her, Rebecca needed expert help in cutting through the lies in the court record.

Ana Storey, staff attorney in LAFLA's Family Law Unit, helped Rebecca file a paternity action, and moved to vacate the father's restraining order. Our advocate also aided the police investigation, which resulted in the stepmother being convicted of forgery.

Rebecca was granted primary custody of Jillian.

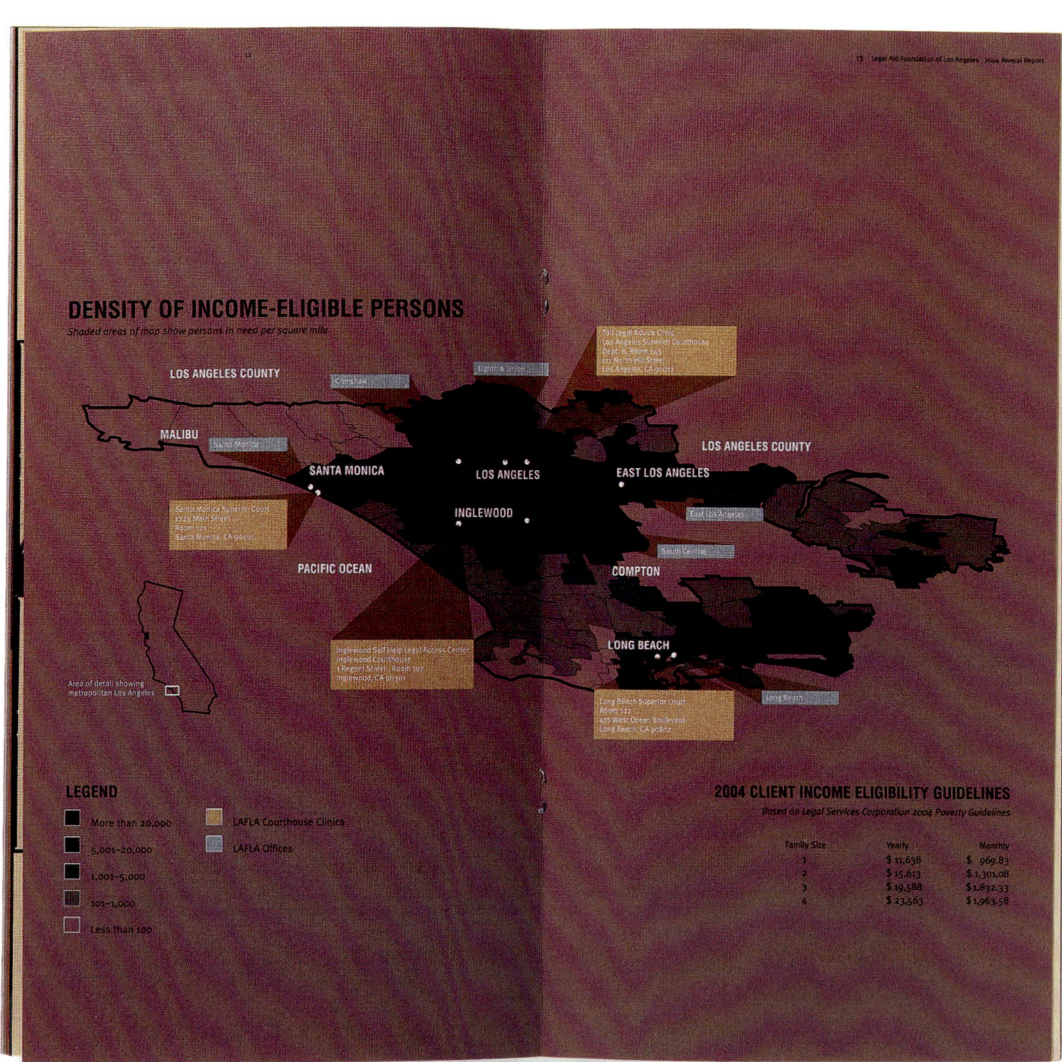

Family Size	Yearly	Monthly
1	$ 11,638	$ 969.83
2	$ 15,613	$ 1,301.08
3	$ 19,588	$ 1,632.33
4	$ 23,563	$ 1,963.58

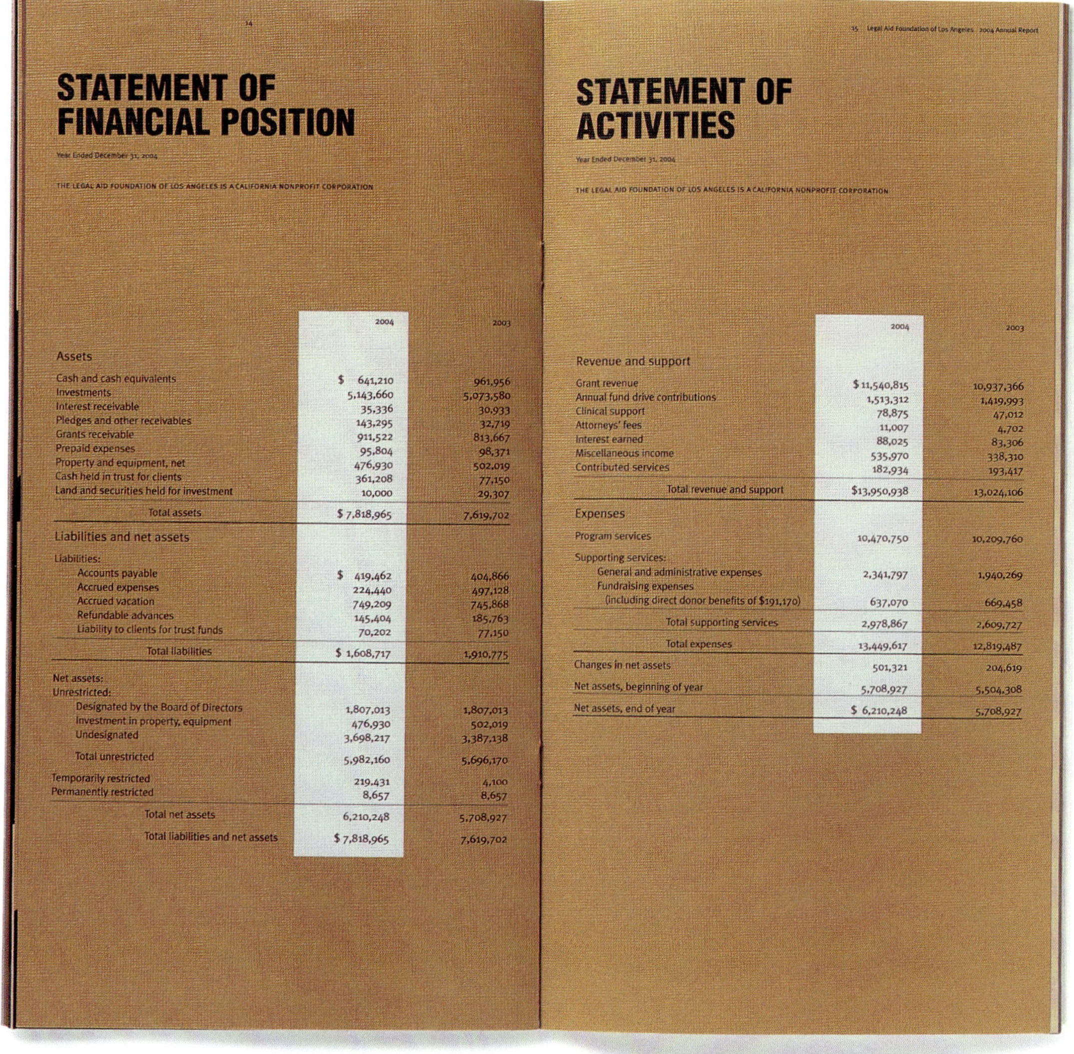

STATEMENT OF FINANCIAL POSITION

Year Ended December 31, 2004

THE LEGAL AID FOUNDATION OF LOS ANGELES IS A CALIFORNIA NONPROFIT CORPORATION

	2004	2003
Assets		
Cash and cash equivalents	$ 641,210	961,956
Investments	5,143,660	5,073,580
Interest receivable	35,336	30,933
Pledges and other receivables	143,295	32,719
Grants receivable	911,522	813,667
Prepaid expenses	95,804	98,371
Property and equipment, net	476,930	502,019
Cash held in trust for clients	361,208	77,150
Land and securities held for investment	10,000	29,307
Total assets	$ 7,818,965	7,619,702
Liabilities and net assets		
Liabilities:		
Accounts payable	$ 419,462	404,866
Accrued expenses	224,440	497,128
Accrued vacation	749,209	745,868
Refundable advances	145,404	185,763
Liability to clients for trust funds	70,202	77,150
Total liabilities	$ 1,608,717	1,910,775
Net assets:		
Unrestricted:		
Designated by the Board of Directors	1,807,013	1,807,013
Investment in property, equipment	476,930	502,019
Undesignated	3,698,217	3,387,138
Total unrestricted	5,982,160	5,696,170
Temporarily restricted	219,431	4,100
Permanently restricted	8,657	8,657
Total net assets	6,210,248	5,708,927
Total liabilities and net assets	$ 7,818,965	7,619,702

STATEMENT OF ACTIVITIES

Year Ended December 31, 2004

THE LEGAL AID FOUNDATION OF LOS ANGELES IS A CALIFORNIA NONPROFIT CORPORATION

	2004	2003
Revenue and support		
Grant revenue	$ 11,540,815	10,937,366
Annual fund drive contributions	1,513,312	1,419,993
Clinical support	78,875	47,012
Attorneys' fees	11,007	4,702
Interest earned	88,025	83,306
Miscellaneous income	535,970	338,310
Contributed services	182,934	193,417
Total revenue and support	$13,950,938	13,024,106
Expenses		
Program services	10,470,750	10,209,760
Supporting services:		
General and administrative expenses	2,341,797	1,940,269
Fundraising expenses (including direct donor benefits of $191,170)	637,070	669,458
Total supporting services	2,978,867	2,609,727
Total expenses	13,449,617	12,819,487
Changes in net assets	501,321	204,619
Net assets, beginning of year	5,708,927	5,504,308
Net assets, end of year	$ 6,210,248	5,708,927

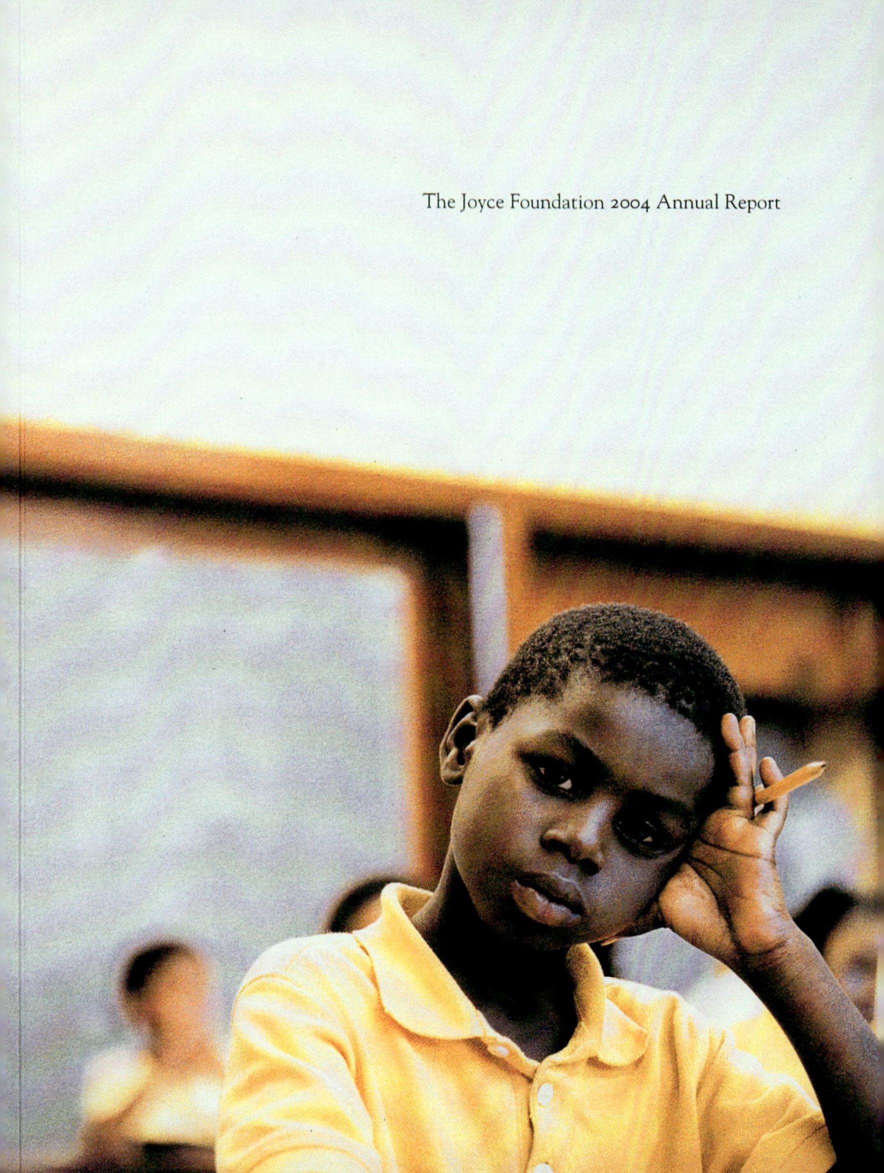
The Joyce Foundation 2004 Annual Report

Art Director: Kym Abrams
Designer: Melissa DePasquale
Illustrator: Charlie Simokaitis
Writer: Mary O'Connell
Printer: Active Graphics
Paper: 100# Mohawk Options cover, True White, Vellum, 100# Mohawk Options text, True White, Vellum, 80# Mohawk Vellum text, Warm White
Page count: 88 +4 cover
Print run: 3,500
Size: 8"x 11"
Number of images: 35
Client: The Joyce Foundation

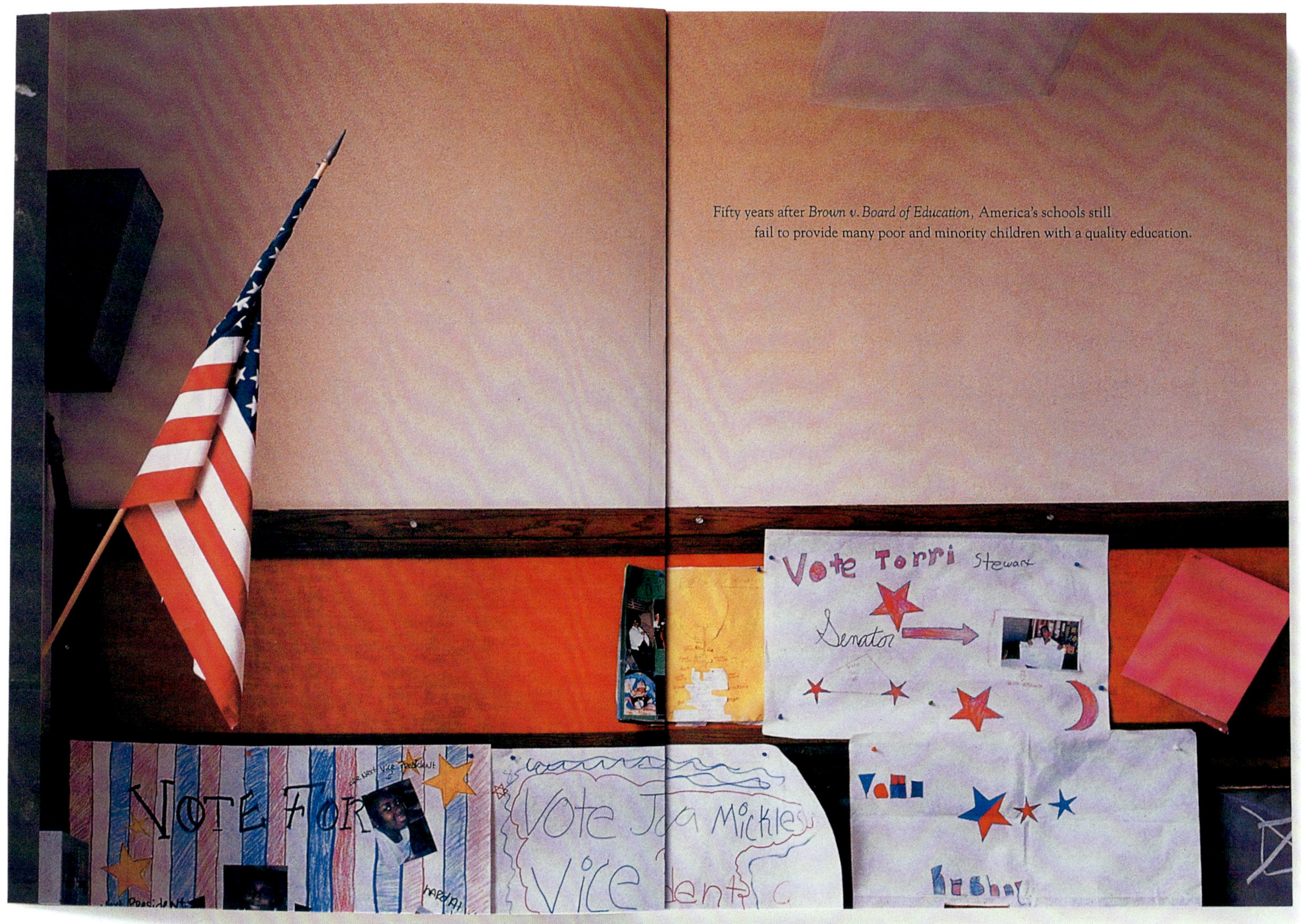

Q&A with Kym Abrams Design

What was the client's directive?

To put a human face on the issues of teacher quality.

How did you define the problem?

We allowed the photography to walk the reader through the book. The copy and photography work side by side to tell a dramatic story. The key messages and tone of the book are revealed in the cover and the first few spreads.

What was the approach?

To tell the story of two new teachers over the course of their first year teaching in a challenged community.

Which disciplines or people helped you with the project?

The process was extremely collaborative (we scheduled quarterly check-ins on the progress of our work). The client, the program officer, the CEO, the photographer, the printer, the designer, and the creative director all worked together—often in the same room.

Were you happy with the result?

We were delighted with the result.

What was the client's response?

They were pleased that "the collaboration worked so well: that we pushed hard on all fronts (concept, design, photography, editorial, production) to get the best result." Even more important than this, they felt the report "tells such an important story about what we need to do to bring out the best talents of all our children: getting them first-rate teachers."

How involved was the CEO in your meetings, presentations, etc.?

We were fortunate to have the vision of the CEO in setting a very high expectation for the book and supporting us and the photographer throughout the yearlong process. The CEO was part of the selection of the photographer and of the final images in the book.

Do you feel that designers are becoming more involved in copywriting?

The line between design and copy is more and more blurred. Our greatest successes result in a collaborative approach with the writers we work with and this project is no exception.

How do you define success in Annual Report design?

Getting people to read the content and understand our clients' work.

How important are awards to your client?

They make our clients feel good, but our clients feel that the design, more importantly, can help them tell their story.

The process was extremely collaborative.

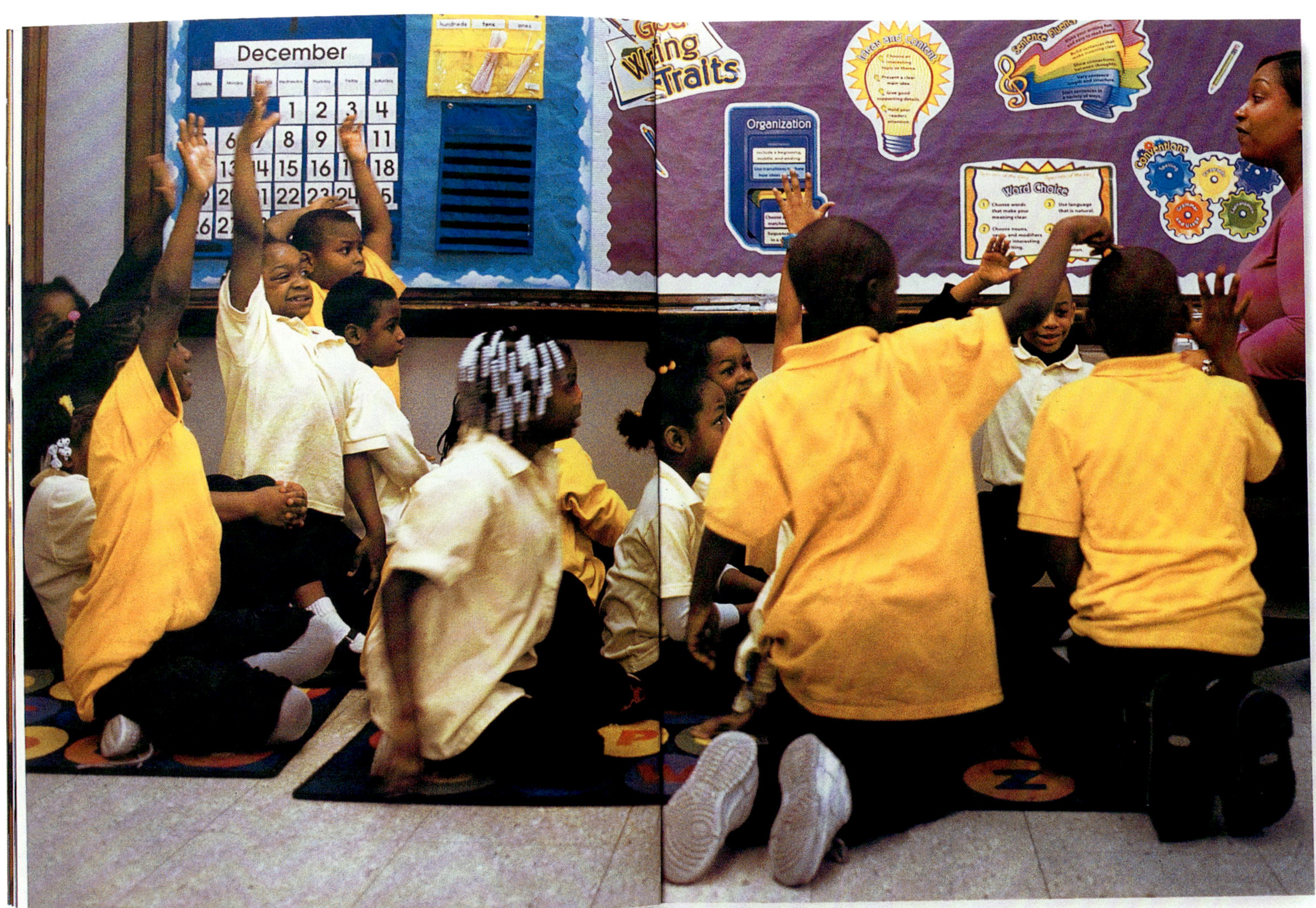

At first it was hard to get them to sit still for fifteen minutes of silent reading. Now, sometimes we go forty.

Sixth grade is a time of dramatic, if uneven, growth in maturity, which affects achievement. "Some days a student will throw a tantrum, then make some extremely generous gesture to a classmate. It can change by the hour!" George shakes his head: "Inside these adolescent bodies trying to be tough, I can still see the kids inside, and that makes me smile."

LaKimbra is smiling because, although she too has doubts, she also sees progress. She spent an afternoon recently having students read to her one-on-one. "One boy, at the beginning of the year, he wasn't reading at all. Today he opened the book, and the story he'd been having a hard time with, now he can read it!" Other kids are also reading better. "One of my goals was to have my kids be readers, be confident, be able to attack a text. It made me feel good to see the progress they've made."

If maturity is the big sixth-grade drama, sheer energy is what makes second graders a challenge. "My kids are so extreme," LaKimbra marvels. "When they're frustrated that they can't learn something—telling time, for example—I think, my God, will we ever get over this hump? But when they get it, they are so excited." Understanding both sides improves her teaching. "Before, I would think, am I teaching this wrong? Now I understand, they may be frustrated now, but they'll get it eventually, and when they do, they'll be proud of themselves."

Other supports have also helped her become a better teacher. Her AUSL mentor; professional development to identify the best strategies and materials; and New Teachers Network sessions, where first- and second-year teachers share ideas, all have been important, she says.

LaKimbra is "99 percent sure" she'll come back to Doolittle. Having settled into the school environment, she hopes that next year, "things that surprised me won't be a surprise. I'll know the dynamics of the school."

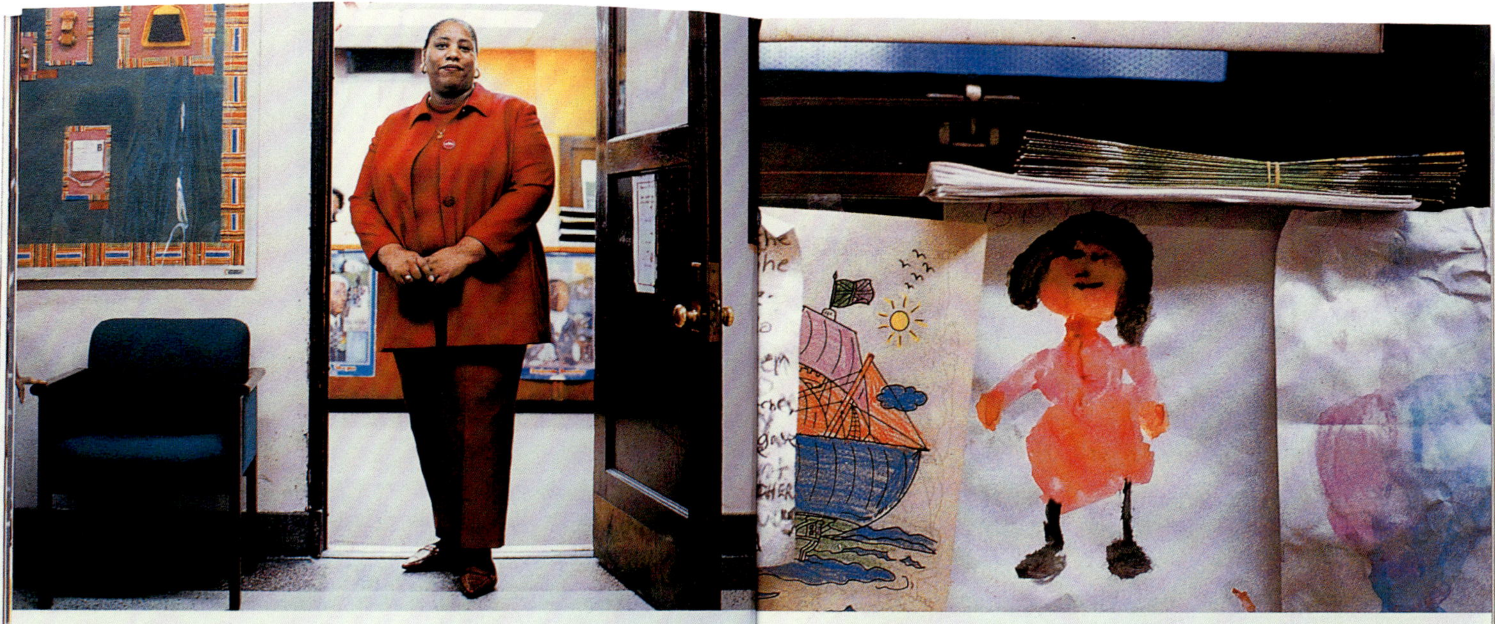

PRINCIPAL LEADERSHIP Good teachers are attracted to schools with strong principals; they avoid schools with weak or dysfunctional leadership. Good principals create conditions in which talented teachers thrive. But, like teaching, being a principal is a demanding job, one that requires a strong educational vision, managerial ability, leadership, stamina, resiliency, diplomatic skills, and a sense of humor all rolled into one. Joyce grants support work to establish sound criteria for choosing principals, build a pipeline of strong candidates, attract them to schools where the need is greatest, provide coaching and other support to help them do the job well, and give them the power and autonomy to attract and keep first-rate teachers.

EARLY CHILDHOOD EDUCATION Also critical in determining student achievement is exposure to the excitement of learning in early childhood. High-quality early care and education can reinforce children's natural curiosity and help them develop socially, emotionally, and cognitively—all essential for school readiness. But too few low-income children have access to such programs. Joyce grants support state-level efforts to enhance the educational possibilities of community-based child care, by improving training and standards for child care workers, working with community groups to offer flexible preschool programs in community settings, and pursuing other strategies for integrating early care and education.

INNOVATIONS With a long history of supporting educational innovation, Joyce continues to explore other strategies for closing the achievement gap, especially policy-oriented efforts to expand the supply of high-quality charter schools and small schools in Chicago, Cleveland, and Milwaukee.

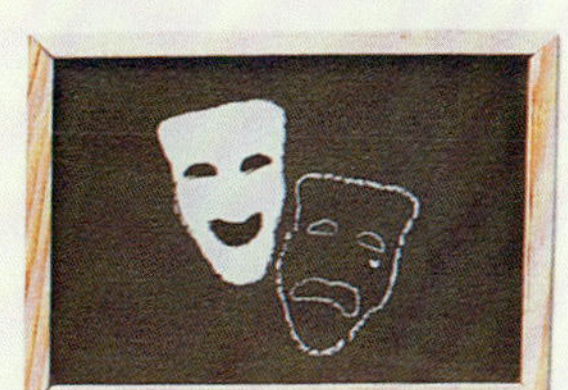

CULTURE

Chicago drew the attention of art lovers around the world in summer 2004 with the opening of Millennium Park. The city's latest lakefront attraction includes not only the traditional greenspace and recreation, but dramatic sculptures and fountains, a Frank Gehry-designed bandshell for outdoor concerts, and a mid-sized theatre for music and dance. Critics raved, and Chicagoans loved it: they came out in huge numbers on the opening weekend, not only to explore the park, but also to enjoy performances by arts groups as diverse, and extraordinary, as the city itself.

And that's the point about Chicago: its cultural life is rich, both downtown and in the ethnically diverse neighborhoods. Joyce funding has worked to connect the two.

Grants have supported the Latino Theater Festival at the top-drawer Goodman Theatre; staging by the Ravinia Festival of the Zulu opera, "Princess Magogo"; a performance series at the Museum of Contemporary Arts featuring outstanding performers, many of color, who attract a young and diverse audience; and a collaboration between the Adler Planetarium and the Mexican Fine Arts Center Museum to bring the wonders of astronomy to Chicagoans whose primary language is Spanish.

At the same time, Joyce has also supported smaller arts groups that bring arts programming, and a vibrant presence, to the city's neighborhoods: groups such as the Black Ensemble Theatre, Muntu Dance Theatre, Teatro Vista, and Congo Square. More communities will have a chance to make arts part of their future as the Foundation announced in early 2005 a grant to the Local Initiatives Support Corporation to incorporate arts into neighborhood development plans of three Chicago communities.

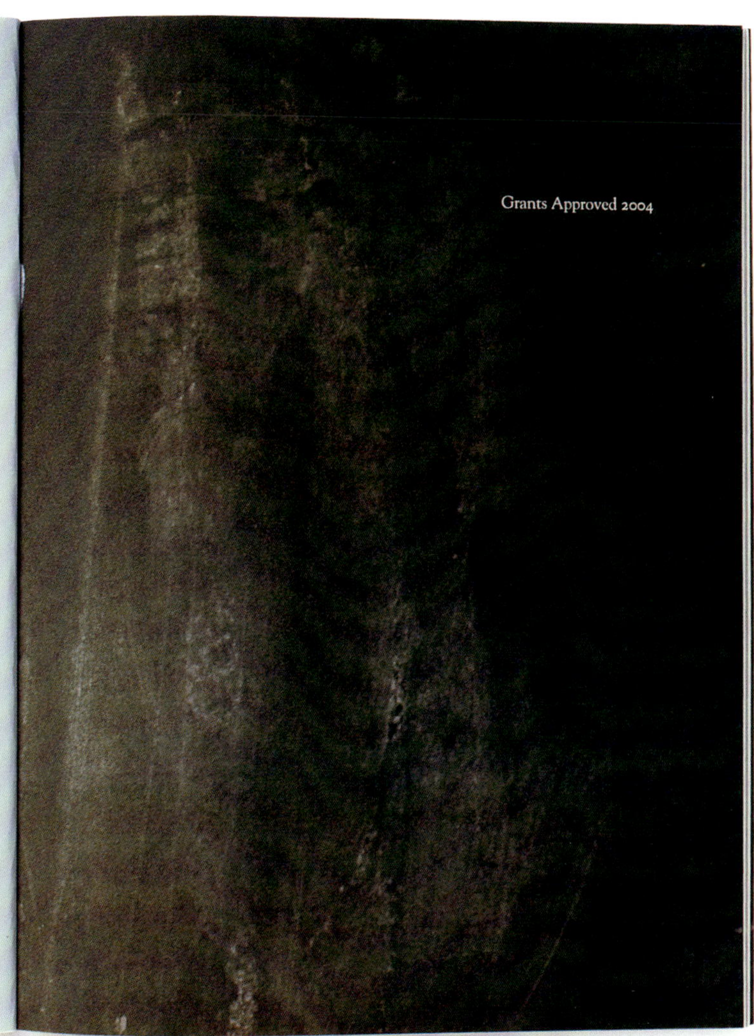

[illegible]

[illegible]

Creative Directors: Adam Brodsley, Eric Heiman
Designer: Adam Brodsley
Writer: Carol Miller
Printer: Blanchette Press
Page Count: 80
Number of images: 70
Print Run: 5,000
Size: 6" x 9"
Paper: Appleton Coated Utopia 2 Matte 80# text
Dege Parkhang Hand-made cover (good luck getting this one).
Client: The Bridge Fund

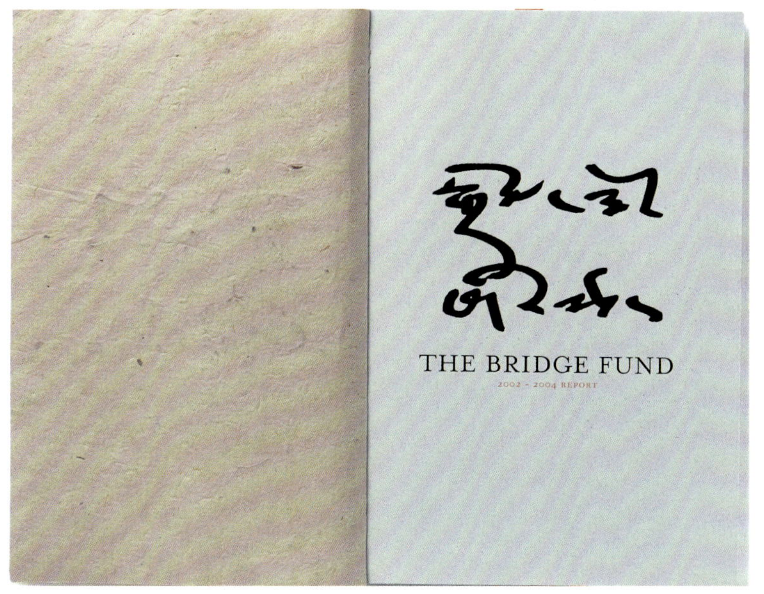

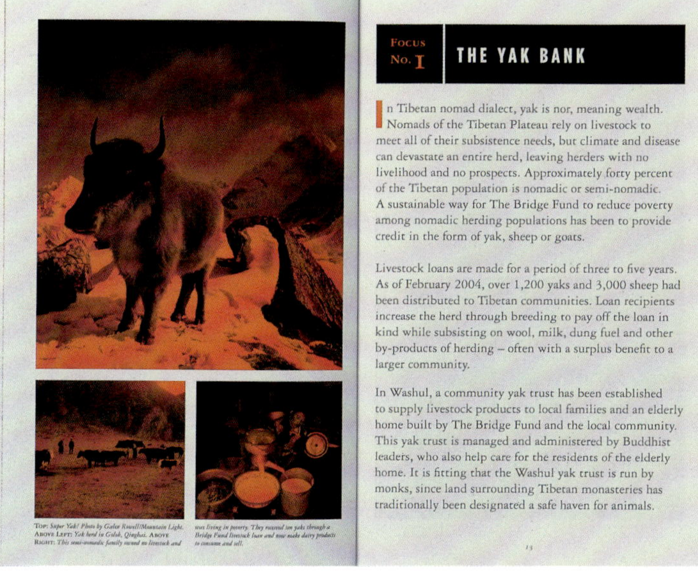

FOCUS No. I

THE YAK BANK

In Tibetan nomad dialect, yak is nor, meaning wealth. Nomads of the Tibetan Plateau rely on livestock to meet all of their subsistence needs, but climate and disease can devastate an entire herd, leaving herders with no livelihood and no prospects. Approximately forty percent of the Tibetan population is nomadic or semi-nomadic. A sustainable way for The Bridge Fund to reduce poverty among nomadic herding populations has been to provide credit in the form of yak, sheep or goats.

Livestock loans are made for a period of three to five years. As of February 2004, over 1,200 yaks and 3,000 sheep had been distributed to Tibetan communities. Loan recipients increase the herd through breeding to pay off the loan in kind while subsisting on wool, milk, dung fuel and other by-products of herding – often with a surplus benefit to a larger community.

In Washul, a community yak trust has been established to supply livestock products to local families and an elderly home built by The Bridge Fund and the local community. This yak trust is managed and administered by Buddhist leaders, who also help care for the residents of the elderly home. It is fitting that the Washul yak trust is run by monks, since land surrounding Tibetan monasteries has traditionally been designated a safe haven for animals.

Q&A with Volume Design Inc.

What was the client's directive?

The Bridge Fund, founded in 1996, had never had an annual or document to show the amazing work they accomplished over the nearly 10 years of their programs. The directive: design our Annual Report. The Bridge Fund's mission is to promote sustainable economic development, cultural heritage preservation and environmental conservation on the Tibetan plateau. Their priority is to assist the most disadvantaged Tibetan communities with a focus on nomadic and semi-nomadic populations that are most vulnerable to economic and social transitions. The Bridge Fund emphasizes self-reliance and promotes the development of regionally-based, Tibetan-run institutions and organizations.

How did you define the problem?

The annual served as a tangible document to show the meaningful work of The Bridge Fund beyond its financial data. By telling a few select stories of their projects and showing images of the people involved we could show donors and supporters that their work is having a real impact in Tibet. How could the experience of reading this annual draw people in?

What was the approach?

The book should be an interaction with the reader. The whole concept is based on the Buddhist Terma – hidden teachings meant to be revealed when the time is right. In this case what was hidden in between perforated pages was all the color photography associated with their work. Only the 2 color exterior text pages were visible upon first glance. This creates a memorable experience for the readers as they read the piece. Even the annual itself is a project to support the people. This is done by having the covers specially created with handmade Tibetan paper and a woodblock-printed logo by one of the oldest printing houses in the land. They also had handcarved, yak horn letter openers for each book to cut apart the pages. The book starts with an overview of the region, and proceeds to tell several engaging stories of different projects (ever hear of a Yak Bank?). After the stories come descriptions of each area of work paired with a virtue. For example, their healthcare projects are paired with the virtue compassion and its translation in Tibetan script. Finally come the financials. The annual closes with an image of butter lamps being lit – a traditional method of making devotional offerings of light.

Which disciplines or people helped you with the project?

Because no not-for-profit can justify spending money on marketing that should be going directly to their programs, there are many people that made this project possible and that should be acknowledged: the printer, Blanchette Press, working for a greatly reduced cost, paper donated by Appleton Coated(and not feeling threatened by the Tibetan papermaking operation infringing on their business), the Tibetans for making the letter openers and the paper more or less the right size, and the client for believing us when we said, "Trust us, it'll be great!"

Were you happy with the result? What could have been better?

It can always be better. It was an arduous process. What started out as the 2002-2003 Annual became the 2002-2004 Annual. That pretty much sums it up.

What was the client's response?

Everyone loves it (even the Dalai Lama).

How involved was the CEO in your meetings, presentations, etc.?

Always involved.

Do you feel that designers are becoming more involved in copywriting?

I hope so. This is part of design and/or telling a story. Or are we just stylists?

How do you define success in Annual Report design?

The intended audience is emotionally connected/affected. They get behind the cause.

How important are awards to your client?

More exposure= more exposure.

Even the Annual itself is a project for the people.

Covering 2.5 million square kilometers, the Tibetan Plateau is comparable in size to Western Europe and makes up one fifth of the total area of China. The Tibetan population, estimated between 5.5 and 6 million, is overwhelmingly rural and occupies some of the world's most remote territory. Its harsh climate, geographic isolation, high altitude, vast and rugged mountain terrain and lack of infrastructure make Tibet one of the poorest and most underdeveloped regions of China.

Many Tibetan communities lack the resources to fully participate in and benefit from the reforms that are driving economic growth in other parts of China. A significant percentage of rurally based Tibetans live without adequate access to education, healthcare and the resources to improve their economic status. Nomadic and semi-nomadic populations, as well as those with locally based subsistence economies, are most vulnerable to rapid economic and social changes.

As the stories that follow illustrate, livestock loans, quality of life improvements, education and training opportunities and support for local non-government organizations (NGOs) are a few of the ways in which The Bridge Fund is helping rural Tibetans sustain their families, preserve their communities and meet their own economic, social, cultural and environmental needs and challenges in the face of growth and change.

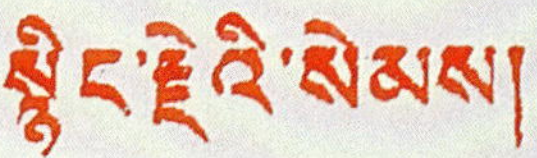

8

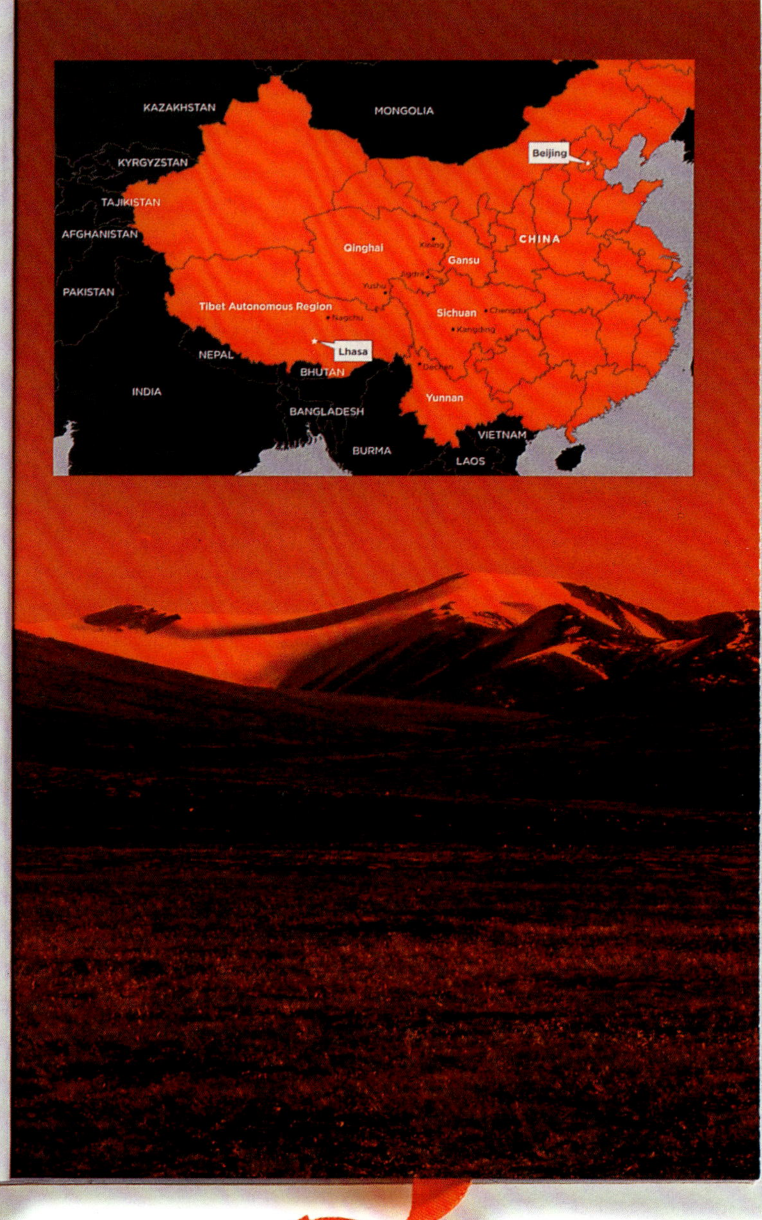

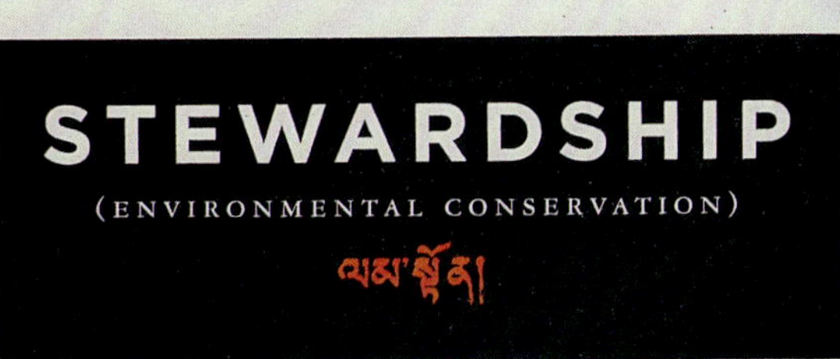

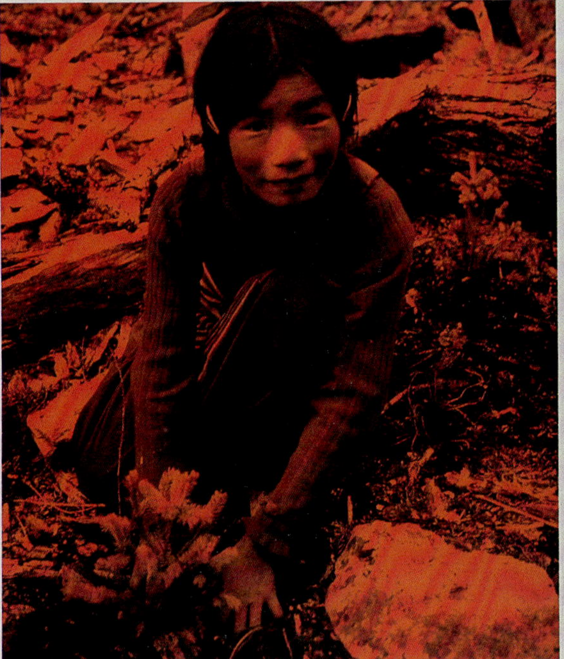

Young woman in Lendo planting fir trees to restore the local forest.

The fragile ecology of the Tibetan Plateau requires long-term resource protection and management planning. The Plateau is made up of several distinct biomes, ranging from forests to grasslands, desert to tundra. It is also the headwaters environment for many of Asia's major rivers. Environmental conditions in the upper watersheds of the Plateau affect all of Asia, and directly impact Southeast Asia's water and climatic systems downstream.

Protection and preservation of the Tibetan Plateau's wildlife and lands is also essential to all of Asia. Home to rare animal, bird and plant species, including the snow leopard, wild yak, blue sheep, red and musk deer, chiru (Tibetan antelope), red panda, black neck crane, ibis bill and numerous others, endangered species on the Plateau are a special natural treasure of the region.

The Bridge Fund works with Tibetan communities to assist locally driven, village-based environmental conservation projects as well as overarching initiatives that contribute to the conservation of wildlife and lands.

THE BRIDGE FUND PROMOTES GREATER PROTECTION OF THREATENED BIODIVERSITY, WILDLIFE AND RANGELAND ECOSYSTEMS THROUGH THE FOLLOWING INITIATIVES:

Environmental education materials for nomadic communities in the Changtang, including 20,000 Tibetan-language posters and calendars

Joint support for small-scale conservation activities in the Changtang with World Wildlife Fund

Eco-tourism training and planning workshops

Grant to China Exploration and Research Society (CERS), Hong Kong based NGO focused on cultural preservation and environmental conservation, to support Tibetan wildlife protection playing card project

Juniper re-forestation project on Chokpori Hill in Lhasa

Fencing and maintenance of re-forestation project in Litang County

Training and support for re-vegetation and household income generation program in Aba Prefecture

2002 FINANCIAL INFORMATION

TBF Europe $101,762 — 6%
U.S. Operating Expenses $458,500 — 27%
Fiduciary Management $97,545 — 6%
Tibetan Program $1,019,136 — 61%

2002 ANNUAL EXPENDITURES
Total Budget $1,676,943

Environment $4,878 — 1%
Community Development $174,954 — 15%
Education & Culture $361,505 — 35%
Tibetan Staff G&A $202,917 — 20%
Health $50,076 — 5%
Small Business Development $247,883 — 24%

2002 GRANTS BY SECTOR FOR TIBETAN PROGRAM

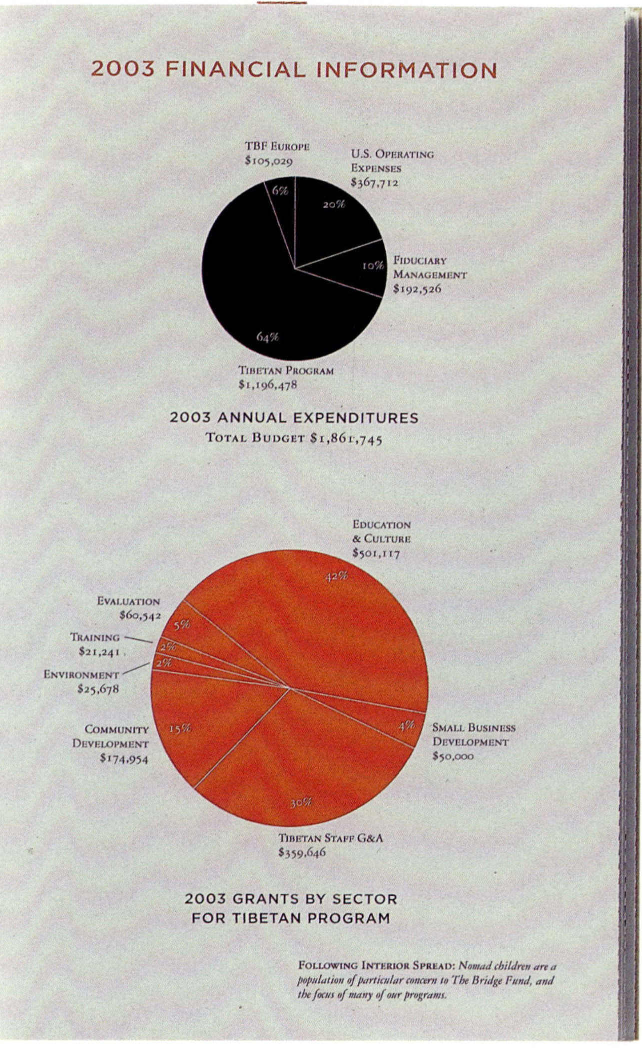

Following Interior Spread: *Nomad children are a population of particular concern to The Bridge Fund, and the focus of many of our programs.*

The George Gund Foundation

Design Firm: Nesnadny+Schwartz
Creative Director: Mark Schwartz

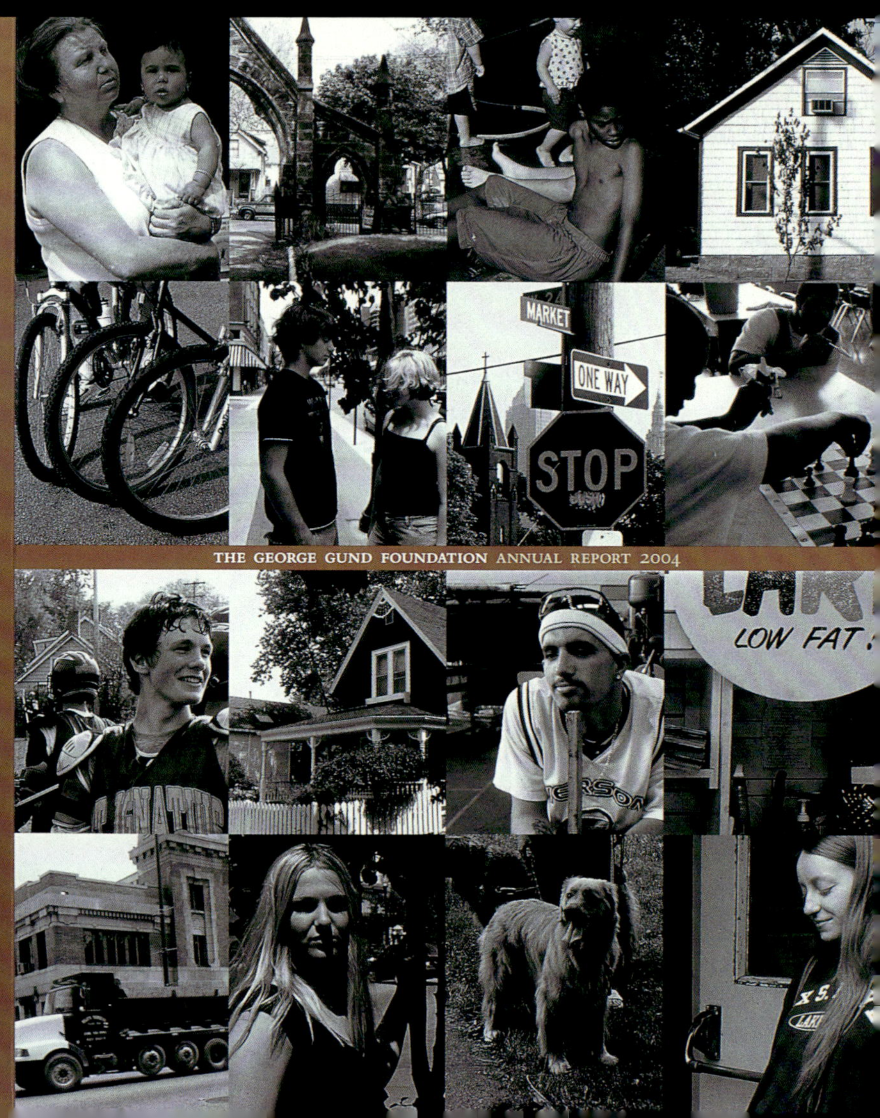

Designer: Michelle Moehler
Photographer: Thomas Roma
Writers: Geoffrey Gund, David Abbott, Deena Epstein
Printer: Fortran Graphics
Paper: Job Parilux, 100# Silk cover, Job Parilux, 100# Silk text, French Construction 70# Whitewash text
Page count: 52 +cover
Print run: 3,500
Size: 9" x 11.25"
Number of Images: 29
Client: The George Gund Foundation

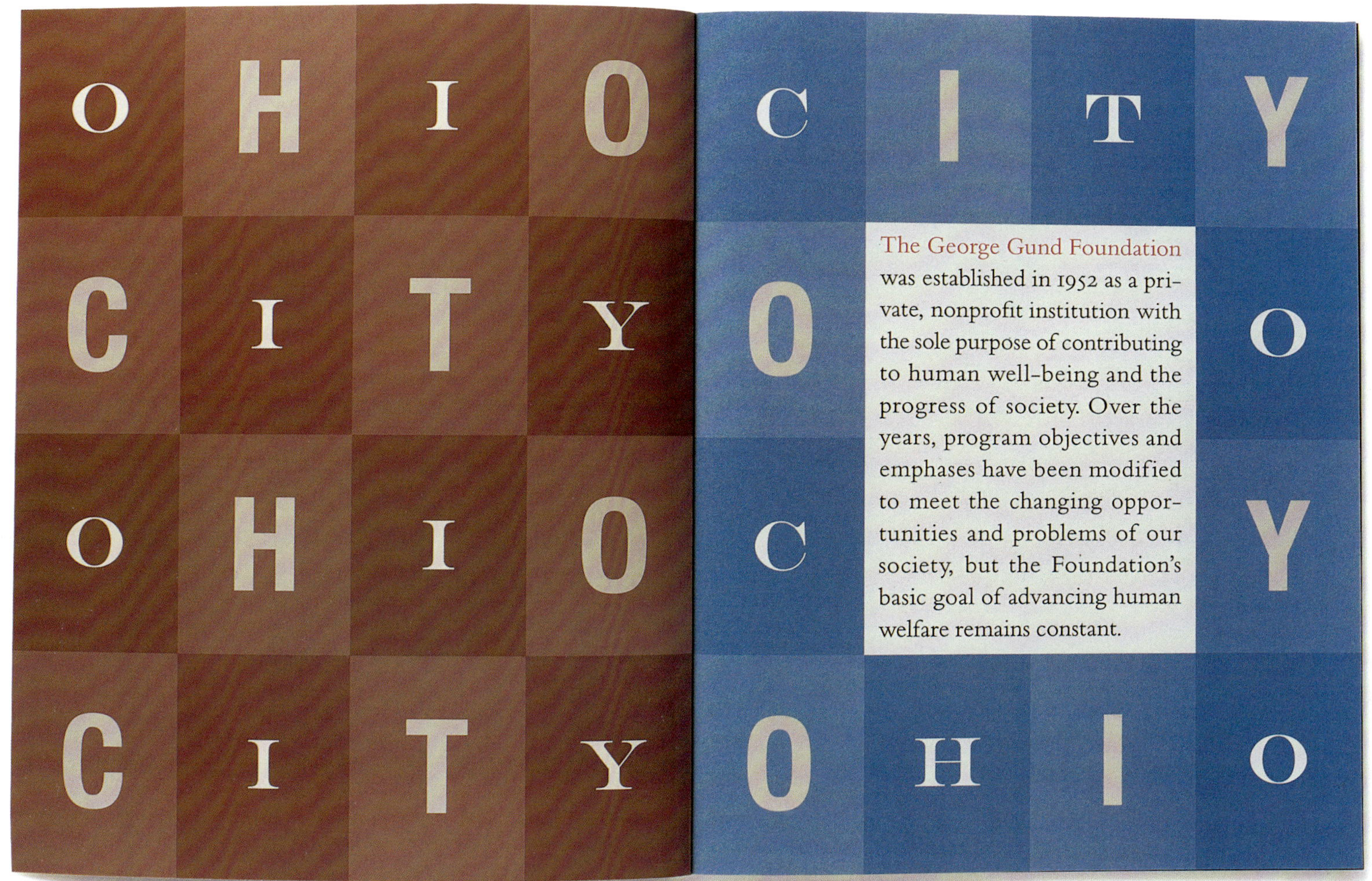

Q&A with Nesnadny+Schwartz

What was the client's directive?

The George Gund Foundation required an Annual Report that would effectively showcase its commitments for the 2004 year. Additionally, the piece had to describe Gund's grant making initiatives to its various constituents.

How did you define the problem?

We never really viewed this project or their needs as a "problem," but more of an "opportunity." The challenge is finding a way of expressing the Foundation's objectives and initiatives in a unique and provocative way – something more than just a list of names.

What was the approach?

The 2004 report focused on Ohio City, an area of Cleveland that represents many of the Foundation's interests and concerns.

Which disciplines or people helped you with the project?

Nesnadny + Schwartz has a long-standing devotion to incorporating fine arts with corporate and institutional communications. With the incredible imagery of Ohio City, a black and white fine arts photographer seemed the perfect choice. Fine art photographer Thomas Roma was commissioned to create a powerful photo essay, reflecting the Foundation's devotion to improving the lives of others.

Were you happy with the result? What could have been better?

We were very pleased with the results.

What was the client's response?

The client was very happy.

How involved was the CEO in your meetings, presentations, etc.?

The Executive Director, David Abbott, was directly involved with the initial concept, theme selection and subsequent design and photography presentations.

Do you feel that designers are becoming more involved in copywriting?

Yes.

How do you define success in Annual Report design?

When a piece is effective in reaching the target audience and communicating something to them that they did not expect. The use of nontraditional printing techniques and materials also makes a report more of a keepsake.

How important are awards to your client?

Awards serve as confirmation that a piece is an interesting and engaging communication tool but should never be the goal.

A successful report effectively reaches its target audience and communicates something unexpected.

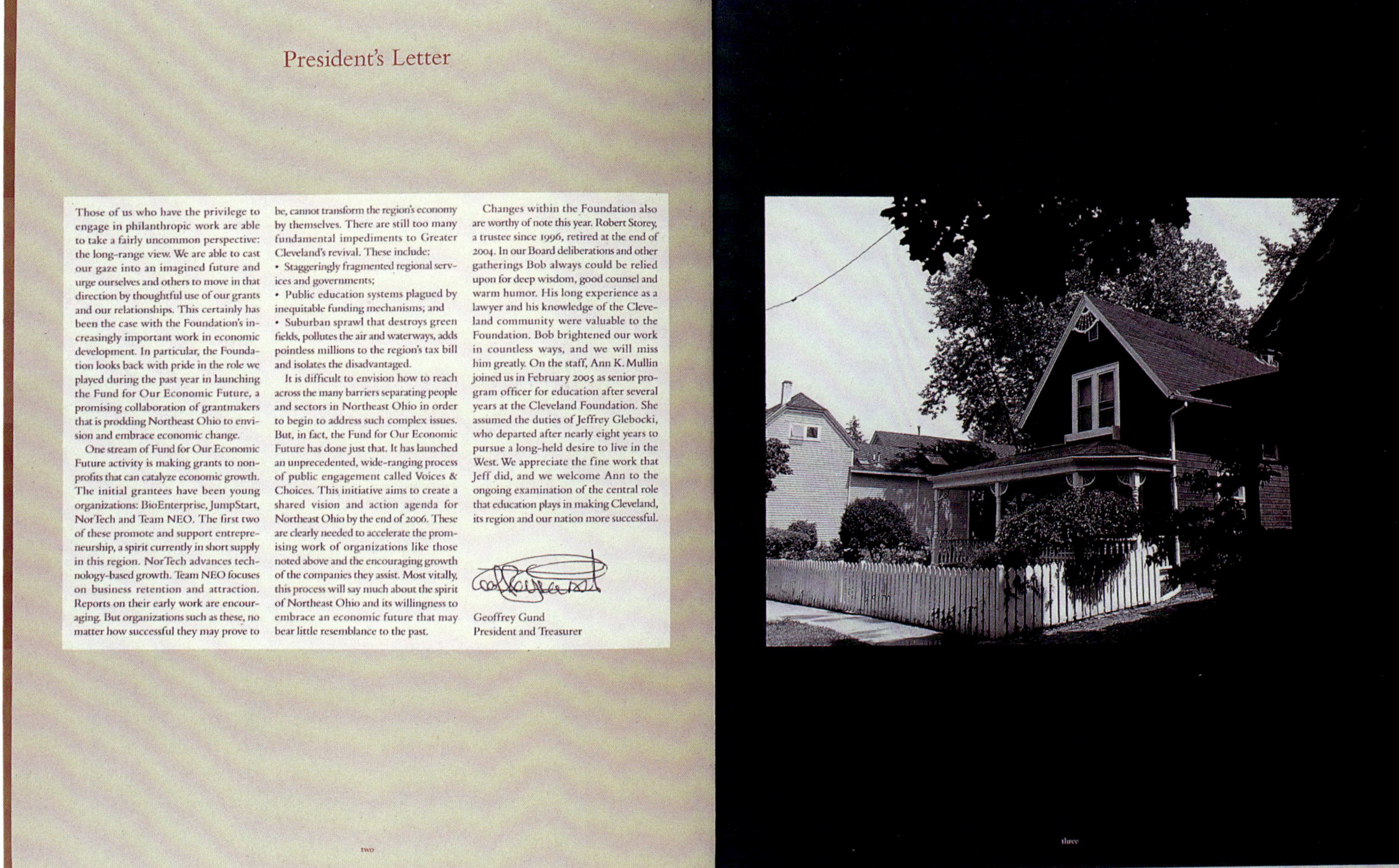

President's Letter

Those of us who have the privilege to engage in philanthropic work are able to take a fairly uncommon perspective: the long-range view. We are able to cast our gaze into an imagined future and urge ourselves and others to move in that direction by thoughtful use of our grants and our relationships. This certainly has been the case with the Foundation's increasingly important work in economic development. In particular, the Foundation looks back with pride in the role we played during the past year in launching the Fund for Our Economic Future, a promising collaboration of grantmakers that is prodding Northeast Ohio to envision and embrace economic change.

One stream of Fund for Our Economic Future activity is making grants to nonprofits that can catalyze economic growth. The initial grantees have been young organizations: BioEnterprise, JumpStart, NorTech and Team NEO. The first two of these promote and support entrepreneurship, a spirit currently in short supply in this region. NorTech advances technology-based growth. Team NEO focuses on business retention and attraction. Reports on their early work are encouraging. But organizations such as these, no matter how successful they may prove to be, cannot transform the region's economy by themselves. There are still too many fundamental impediments to Greater Cleveland's revival. These include:

- Staggeringly fragmented regional services and governments;
- Public education systems plagued by inequitable funding mechanisms; and
- Suburban sprawl that destroys green fields, pollutes the air and waterways, adds pointless millions to the region's tax bill and isolates the disadvantaged.

It is difficult to envision how to reach across the many barriers separating people and sectors in Northeast Ohio in order to begin to address such complex issues. But, in fact, the Fund for Our Economic Future has done just that. It has launched an unprecedented, wide-ranging process of public engagement called Voices & Choices. This initiative aims to create a shared vision and action agenda for Northeast Ohio by the end of 2006. These are clearly needed to accelerate the promising work of organizations like those noted above and the encouraging growth of the companies they assist. Most vitally, this process will say much about the spirit of Northeast Ohio and its willingness to embrace an economic future that may bear little resemblance to the past.

Changes within the Foundation also are worthy of note this year. Robert Storey, a trustee since 1996, retired at the end of 2004. In our Board deliberations and other gatherings Bob always could be relied upon for deep wisdom, good counsel and warm humor. His long experience as a lawyer and his knowledge of the Cleveland community were valuable to the Foundation. Bob brightened our work in countless ways, and we will miss him greatly. On the staff, Ann K. Mullin joined us in February 2005 as senior program officer for education after several years at the Cleveland Foundation. She assumed the duties of Jeffrey Glebocki, who departed after nearly eight years to pursue a long-held desire to live in the West. We appreciate the fine work that Jeff did, and we welcome Ann to the ongoing examination of the central role that education plays in making Cleveland, its region and our nation more successful.

Geoffrey Gund
President and Treasurer

two

three

Nontraditional printing techniques and materials make a report more like a keepsake.

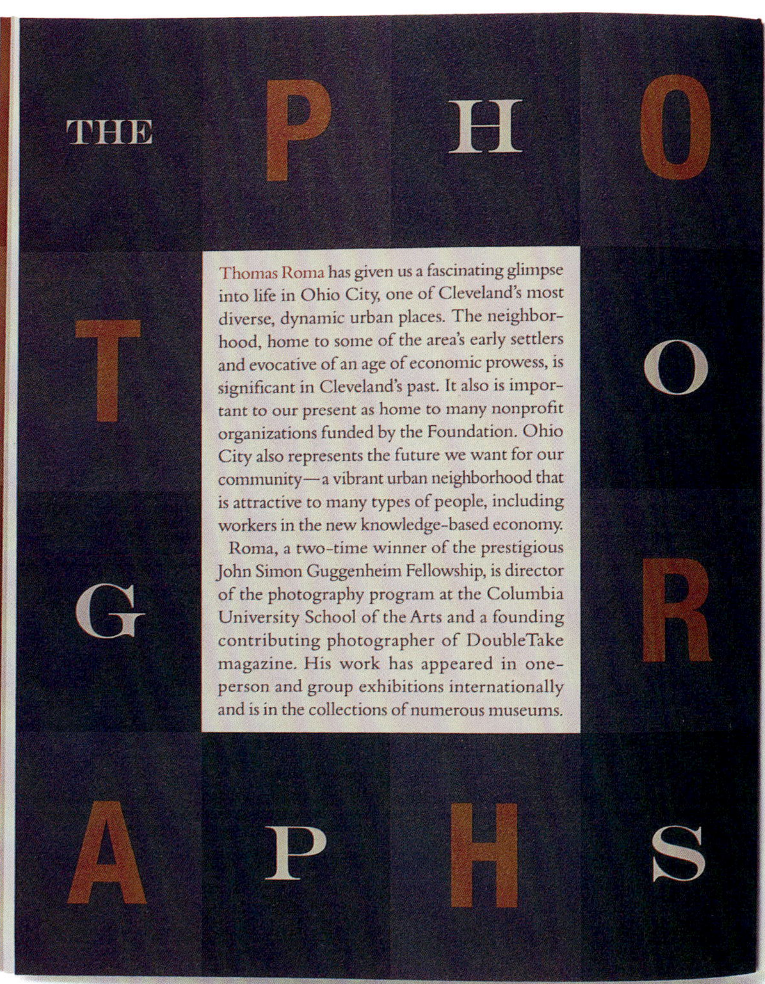

THE PHOTOGRAPHS

Thomas Roma has given us a fascinating glimpse into life in Ohio City, one of Cleveland's most diverse, dynamic urban places. The neighborhood, home to some of the area's early settlers and evocative of an age of economic prowess, is significant in Cleveland's past. It also is important to our present as home to many nonprofit organizations funded by the Foundation. Ohio City also represents the future we want for our community—a vibrant urban neighborhood that is attractive to many types of people, including workers in the new knowledge-based economy.

Roma, a two-time winner of the prestigious John Simon Guggenheim Fellowship, is director of the photography program at the Columbia University School of the Arts and a founding contributing photographer of DoubleTake magazine. His work has appeared in one-person and group exhibitions internationally and is in the collections of numerous museums.

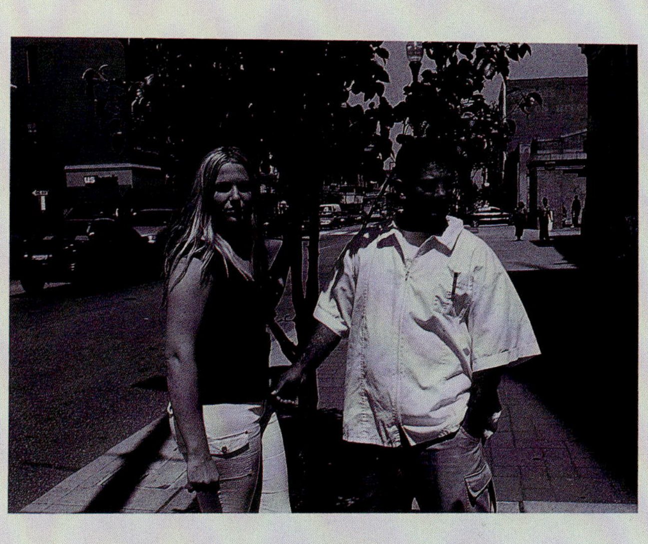

seven

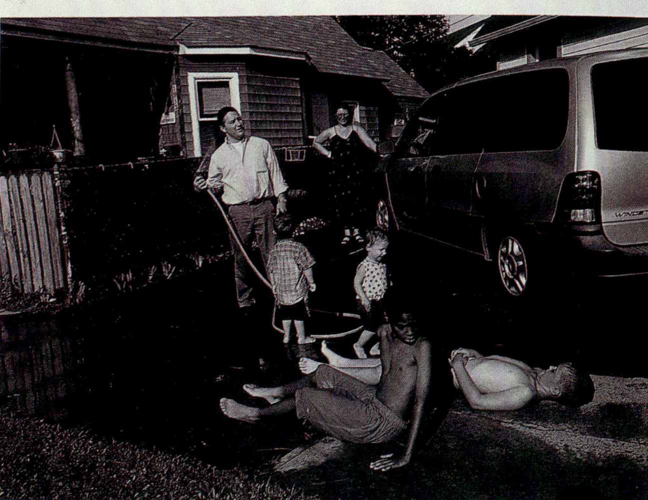

four

Executive Director's Letter

The photographic essay in this annual report depicts Cleveland's Ohio City neighborhood through the singular lens of Thomas Roma. Ohio City is one of the city's most diverse places, and it exuberantly bursts with sights and flavors. It challenges any effort to embrace it within one set of photos

We commissioned Roma's essay because Ohio City represents so many of the Foundation's interests and concerns. Over many years the Foundation has supported scores of organizations, in every one of our program areas, located there. The organizations and their work are themselves worthy of our support, but their presence in a single place suggests the greater importance of Ohio City.

It is a place of history. Once a separate municipality, Ohio City is one of Cleveland's most interesting neighborhoods because its dense Victorian housing and narrow streets evoke an era when Cleveland's economic brawn was virtually unmatched.

It is a place overflowing with social concern. Few neighborhoods are home to so many nonprofit organizations devoted to improving the lives of others. Human services, community development, the environment, arts, education—all of these have their advocates in Ohio City, serving the full diversity of people who live in the neighborhood and beyond.

It is a neighborhood that attracts new urbanists. The devastation of suburban sprawl has taken as severe a toll on Ohio City as other city districts, but three decades ago Ohio City also saw the first stirrings of reinvestment. That trend continues, with all of the complexity and the hope that accompany it.

Each of these characteristics makes Ohio City important—not merely to its residents, but also to the city as a whole and, indeed, to the larger region. Understanding that importance is especially vital to the expanding appreciation of regionalism. Ohio City's features—its density, diversity, historic character, proximity to downtown—make it an appealing home for people who have the ability to live anywhere. Many of those people are the entrepreneurs, the knowledge economy workers, the innovators who will drive much of our region's standing in the global marketplace. Northeast Ohio must pay special attention to its places that appeal to such people. The best of those places are authentic urban neighborhoods. Bland sprawl does not attract the inventive people we require; indeed, it repels them.

Special urban spaces—and there are many—need to be nurtured for the sake of the region's economic competitiveness. This means that the entire region has a stake in the success of neighborhoods like Ohio City. But our deeply fragmented political and governmental structures in Northeast Ohio nearly bar us from seeing that, let alone committing regional resources to it. Doing so in a way that does not exclude long-time residents and those with fewer choices than the new economy's workers is one of the real challenges of life in a vibrant urban setting. Yet, this too is as much a regional issue as it is a neighborhood concern. The demands of equity and justice cannot be confined to a single neighborhood. The very reasons why so many disadvantaged people reside in the central city are regional—suburban sprawl across a welter of political jurisdictions, exclusionary zoning, the near total absence of meaningful regional planning and so forth. Ways must be found to discuss and address these issues on a regional basis for the sake of the city, of the region, of us all.

Ohio City is just one of the extraordinary locations in this region's urban centers that merit renewed attention and investment. They embody much of our worthwhile past, and, if we take a closer look, we will realize that they also can be a key to our future.

David Abbott

David T. Abbott
Executive Director

five

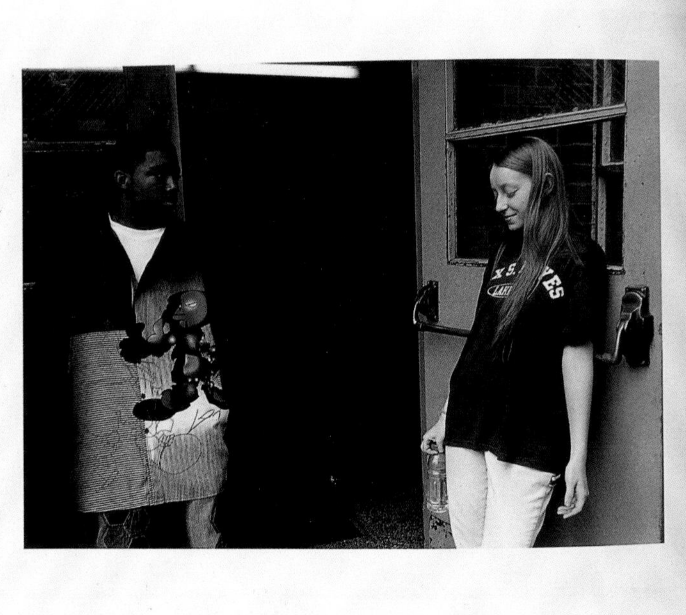

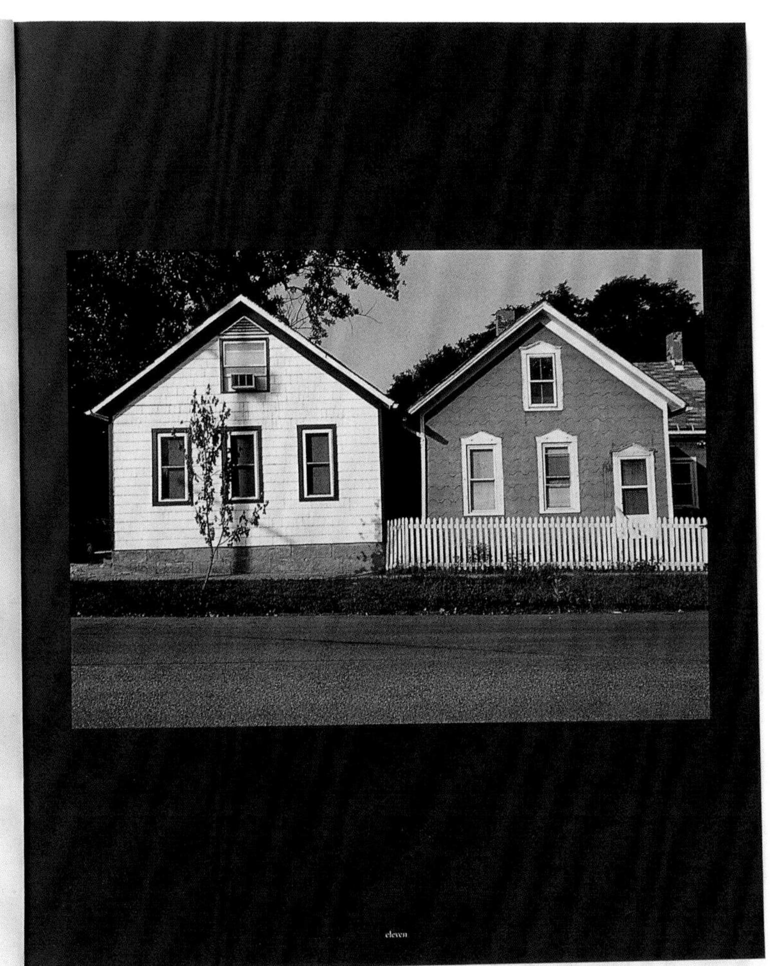

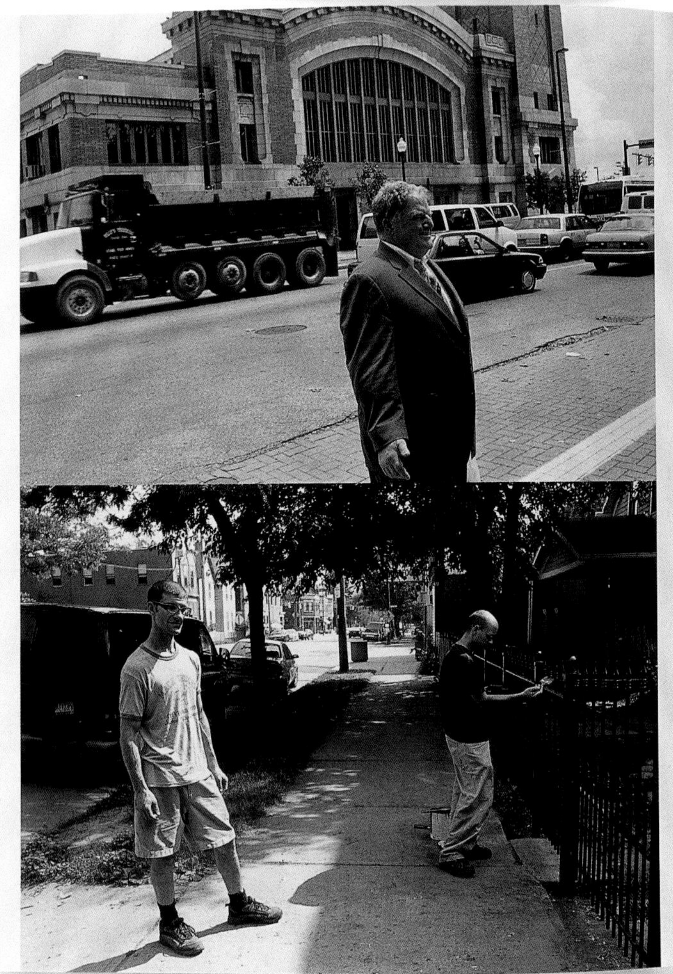

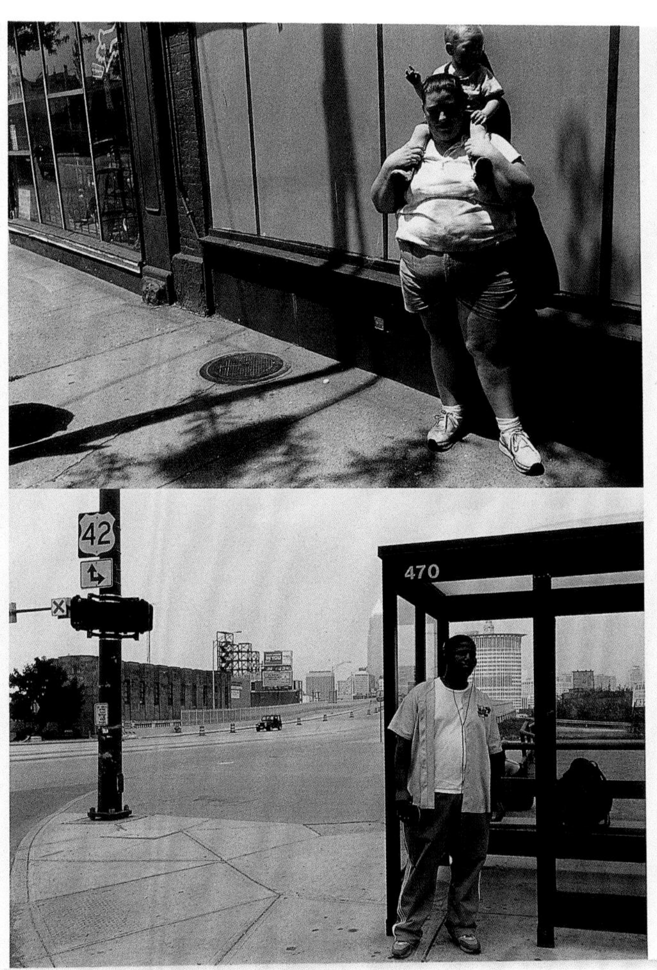
42
470

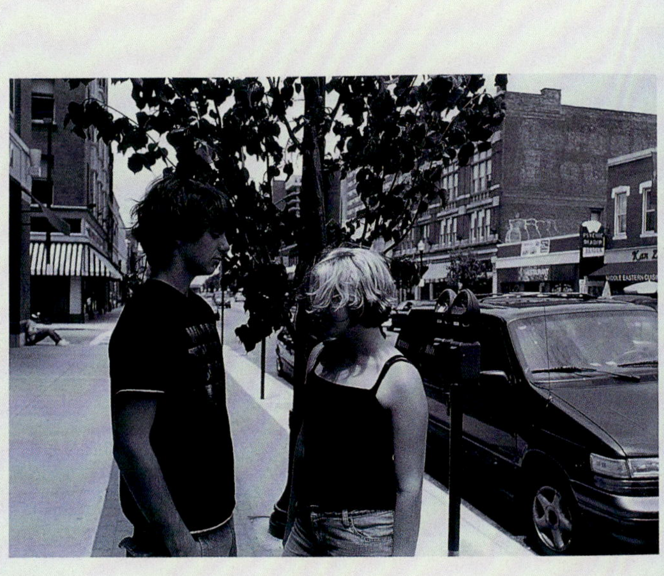

twenty-eight

OUR COMMITMENTS

2004

EDUCATION
$3,074,500 (67 grants)

ECONOMIC DEVELOPMENT & COMMUNITY REVITALIZATION
$4,741,500 (44 grants)
$350,000 (1 program-related investment)

ARTS
$2,097,895 (73 grants)

HUMAN SERVICES
$5,504,830 (96 grants)

ENVIRONMENT
$3,374,872 (72 grants)

SPECIAL PROJECTS
$9,042,950 (34 grants)

GRAND TOTAL
$28,186,547
(386 grants and 1 program-related investment)

TOTAL SINCE INCEPTION OF THE FOUNDATION IN 1952
$437,325,981

Condensed Financial Statements

Statements of Financial Position

December 31	2004	2003
ASSETS		
Cash and cash equivalents	$ 18,557,143	$ 76,672,916
Receivables	1,026,727	1,692,294
Marketable and U.S. Government securities	465,480,729	371,486,183
Other assets	286,508	310,018
Total assets	$ 485,351,107	$ 450,161,411
LIABILITIES		
Accounts payable and accrued expenses	$ 374,684	$ 446,267
Grants payable	12,581,710	5,585,800
Deferred federal excise tax	2,351,607	1,666,254
Total liabilities	15,308,001	7,698,321
NET ASSETS		
Income fund	(11,379,092)	(2,756,181)
Principal fund	481,422,198	445,219,271
Total net assets	470,043,106	442,463,090
Total liabilities and net assets	$ 485,351,107	$ 450,161,411

The accompanying notes are an integral part of the financial statements.

Statements of Activities

For the Years Ended December 31	2004	2003
INCOME FUND		
Revenues		
Dividend income	$ 5,940,373	$ 5,342,554
Interest income	3,918,997	4,582,642
Recovery of prior years' grants	42,773	—
	9,902,143	9,925,196
Expenses		
Grants authorized	27,818,047	17,712,771
Administrative expenses	3,657,382	3,673,630
Federal income tax	489,046	92,982
	31,964,475	21,479,383
Decrease in net assets in income fund before transfer	(22,062,332)	(11,554,187)
Transfer from principal fund	13,439,421	11,813,670
Increase (decrease) in net assets in income fund	(8,622,911)	259,483
Income fund net assets – beginning	(2,756,181)	(3,015,664)
Income fund net assets – ending	$ (11,379,092)	$ (2,756,181)
PRINCIPAL FUND		
Revenues and unrealized gains and losses:		
Net realized gains on securities	$ 15,918,494	$ 1,781,626
Net unrealized gains on securities	34,412,096	62,199,025
Federal excise tax on unrealized gains	(688,242)	(621,990)
Increase in net assets in principal fund before transfers	49,642,348	63,358,661
Transfers to income fund	(13,439,421)	(11,813,670)
Increase in net assets in principal fund	36,202,927	51,544,991
Principal fund net assets – beginning	445,219,271	393,674,280
Principal fund net assets – ending	$ 481,422,198	$ 445,219,271

The accompanying notes are an integral part of the financial statements.

Statements of Cash Flows

For the Years Ended December 31	2004	2003
CASH FLOWS FROM OPERATING ACTIVITIES		
Increase in net assets	$ 27,580,016	$ 51,804,474
Adjustments to reconcile increase in net assets to net cash used in operating activities:		
Depreciation and amortization	70,157	65,973
Net realized gains on securities	(15,918,494)	(1,781,626)
Net unrealized gains on securities	(34,412,096)	(62,199,025)
Deferred federal excise tax	685,353	618,476
Changes in assets and liabilities:		
Receivables	665,567	142,546
Other assets	(2,313)	(1,388)
Accounts payable and accrued expenses	(71,583)	289,118
Grants payable	6,995,910	(1,365,700)
Net cash used in operating activities	(14,407,483)	(12,427,152)
CASH FLOWS FROM INVESTING ACTIVITIES		
Proceeds from sale of securities	178,237,635	131,636,391
Purchase of investments	(221,901,591)	(123,337,828)
Purchase of equipment and improvements	(44,334)	(68,132)
Net cash provided by (used in) investing activities	(43,708,290)	8,230,431
Net decrease in cash and cash equivalents	(58,115,773)	(4,196,721)
Cash and cash equivalents – beginning	76,672,916	80,869,637
Cash and cash equivalents – ending	$ 18,557,143	$ 76,672,916
SUPPLEMENTAL DISCLOSURE OF CASH FLOW INFORMATION		
Cash paid during the year:		
Income taxes, excise	$ —	$ —
Interest	$ —	$ —

The accompanying notes are an integral part of the financial statements.

Notes to Financial Statements

December 31, 2004 and 2003

NOTE 1: SUMMARY OF SIGNIFICANT ACCOUNTING POLICIES

Nature of operations The George Gund Foundation ("the Foundation") is a private foundation which makes grants to educational, community service and philanthropic organizations, basically in Greater Cleveland.

Basis of accounting The Foundation's financial statements are presented on the accrual basis of accounting. Accordingly, revenues are recorded when earned, and expenses are recognized when incurred. The Foundation has only unrestricted net assets.

Use of estimates The preparation of financial statements in conformity with generally accepted accounting principles requires management to make estimates and assumptions that affect the reported amounts of assets and liabilities and disclosure of contingent assets and liabilities at the date of the financial statements and the reported amounts of revenues and expenses during the reporting period. Actual results could differ from those estimates.

Cash and cash equivalents Cash and cash equivalents consist of highly-liquid investments with maturity dates of three months or less which are readily convertible into cash.

Investments Marketable and U.S. securities are reported at their market value. Securities traded on a national securities exchange are valued at the last reported trading price on the last business day of the year. Realized gains or losses are determined by comparison of asset cost to net proceeds received. Unrealized gains or losses are determined by comparison of asset cost to market values at the end of the year. Presenting the fair value of program-related investments is impractical since the purpose of these investments is to provide low interest loans to nonprofit organizations to assist them in their specific projects.

Distress Centres of Toronto

Design Firm: GJP
Creative Director: Dave Watson

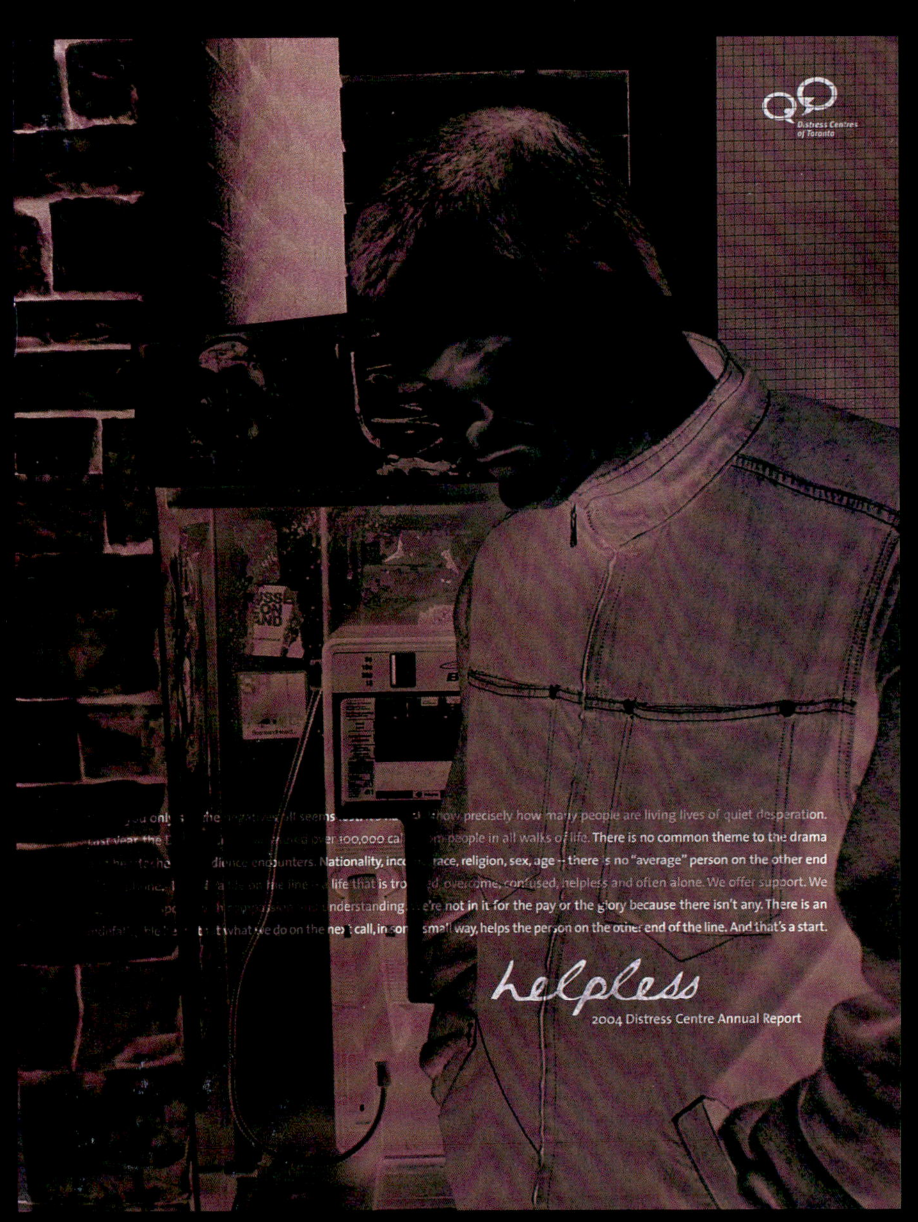

Designers: Dave Watson, Chris Duchaine Photographer: Russell Monk	Writer: Trevor Schonfeld Printer: Bowne Paper: BXL Clear	Polyester cover, Mohawk Superfine and Interior Page count: 20 +cover	Print run: 750 Size: 8.75" x 11.75" Number of Images: 11	Client: Distress Centres of Toronto

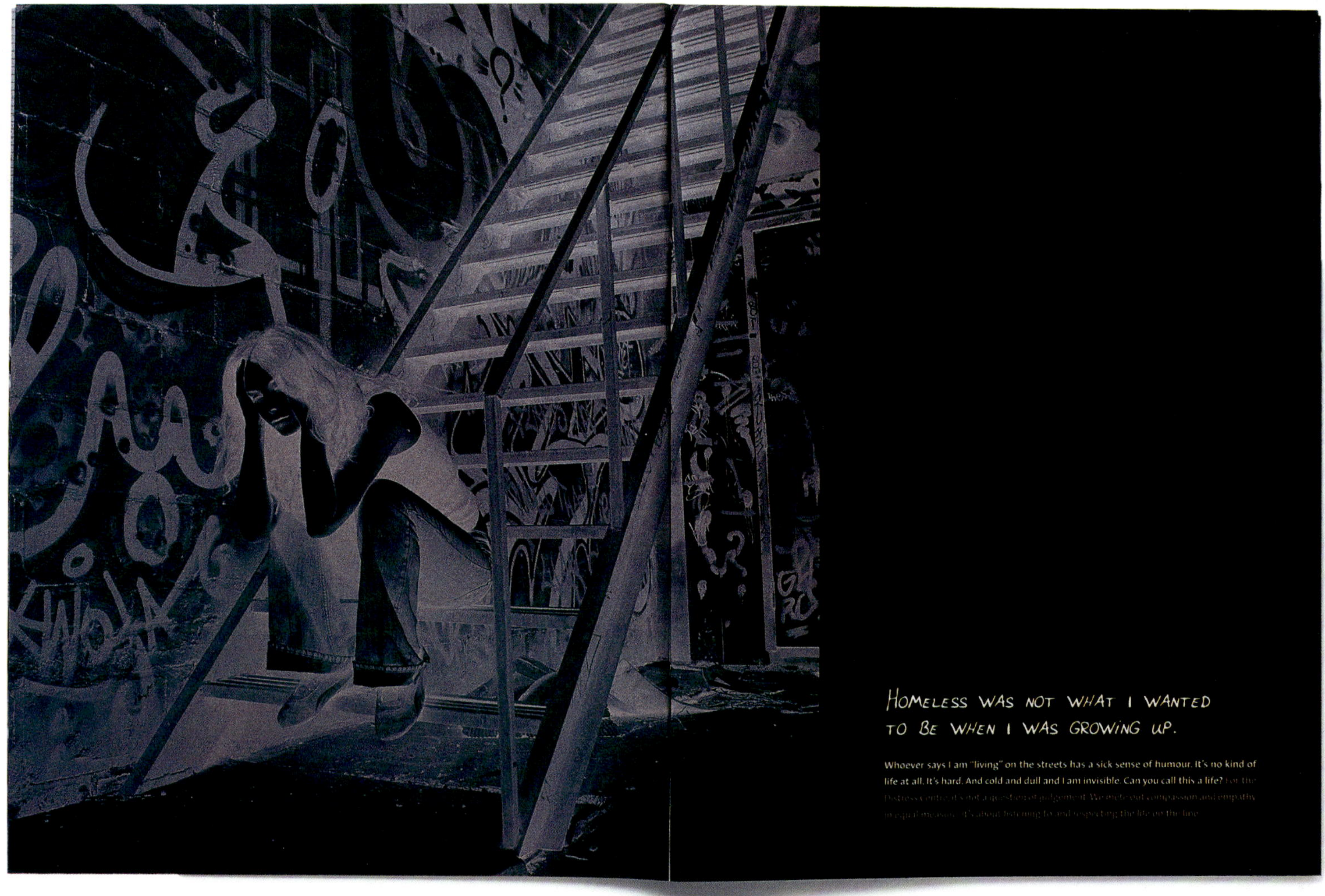

Q&A with GJP

What was the client's directive?

The directive from Distress Centre for this year's annual was simple: Highlight a cross-section of the different types of calls DC receives on a daily basis.

How did you define the problem?

The largest problem we faced was to ensure that we didn't portray challenges the callers face through "rose colored glasses." When a person in distress calls the DC, it is a step in the right direction. It is not the complete solution. Often times the DC volunteer will just be a good listener.

What was the approach?

The concept behind using photo-negative images came from one of the testimonials we heard - when you are at the end of your rope, your world seems flipped upside down. So we used the photo-negative imagery to tell the "helpless" side of the story. When you reach the centre spread in the report, you see an image that is half negative and half positive, with the DC hotline phone number reversed out. From this "turning point," the remainder of the images are then turned into photo-positives and the storytellers are revealed. This was a visual metaphor for the healing process.

Which disciplines or people helped you with the project?

This project was a true form of collaboration between designer, writer, photographer and printer. Each person brought so many different ideas to the table to bring this story to life.

Were you happy with the result? What could have been better?

Overall, we were very happy with the results. The printer was a major player on the team and brought the piece to an entirely different level. From printing the ink on the inside of the clear cover so that it wouldn't scratch to the double hits of the metallic inks, they went above and beyond the call of duty. As with any project there would be a few things that I would change, but that is normal with any designer, I would imagine.

What was the client's response?

The CEO of the Distress Centre is a dream client. When we first presented the idea for this year's annual the CEO began to cry…with joy. It was something I will never forget. It helped remind all of us

The CEO's tears of joy helped remind all of us why we got into this business.

why we got into this business in the first place.

How involved was the CEO in your meetings, presentations, etc.?

Throughout the project the CEO offered helpful suggestions on the different distress stories we created. We often would look to her to make sure the stories, the portrayals and the tone of the copy were authentic.

Do you feel that designers are becoming more involved in copywriting?

Yes, during this project the writer and designer would bounce lines back and forth trying to communicate as much human emotion as possible. Often times a designer will write a line to show the writer what is in his or her head, and then ask them to build on that.

How do you define success in Annual Report design?

We define success if the reader does more than a casual "flip-through." Today, it is becoming increasingly more difficult to tell the important stories behind the Company – behind the results. I'm sure it's a common problem for all great annual report designs. To get to the heart of the story behind the year's performance. Making the organization feel like they are "top of mind" is always something to strive for.

How important are awards to your client?

Our client is always happy to hear when we win awards for their projects because it helps justify the late nights and weekends we spent working on it. However, the most important thing for the DC is to drive awareness. Their annual is the single largest communication devise they have, and are always wanted to make the most of it.

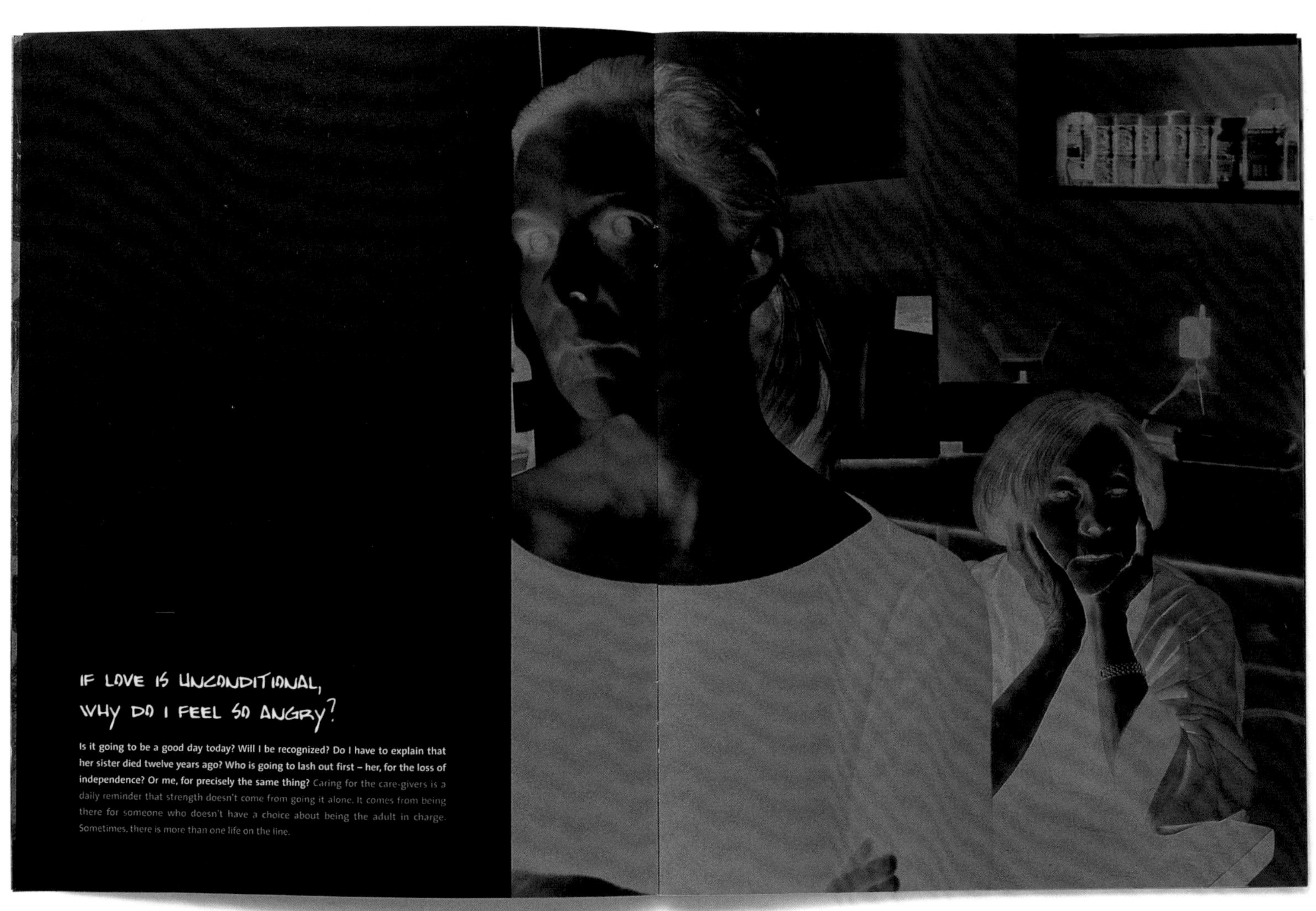

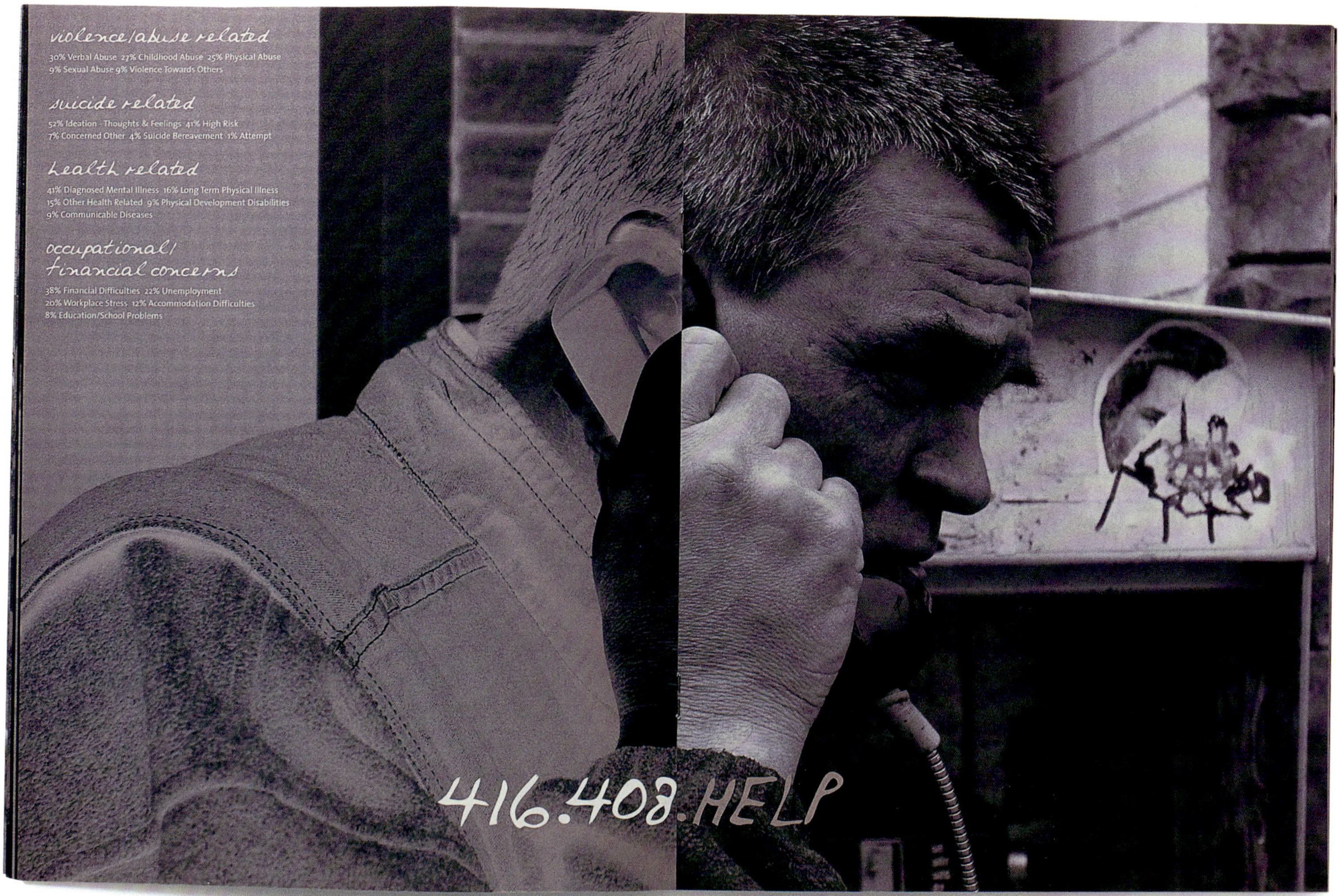

violence/abuse related

30% Verbal Abuse 27% Childhood Abuse 25% Physical Abuse 9% Sexual Abuse 9% Violence Towards Others

suicide related

52% Ideation - Thoughts & Feelings 41% High Risk 7% Concerned Other 4% Suicide Bereavement 1% Attempt

health related

41% Diagnosed Mental Illness 16% Long Term Physical Illness 15% Other Health Related 9% Physical Development Disabilities 9% Communicable Diseases

occupational/ financial concerns

38% Financial Difficulties 22% Unemployment 20% Workplace Stress 12% Accommodation Difficulties 8% Education/School Problems

416.408.HELP

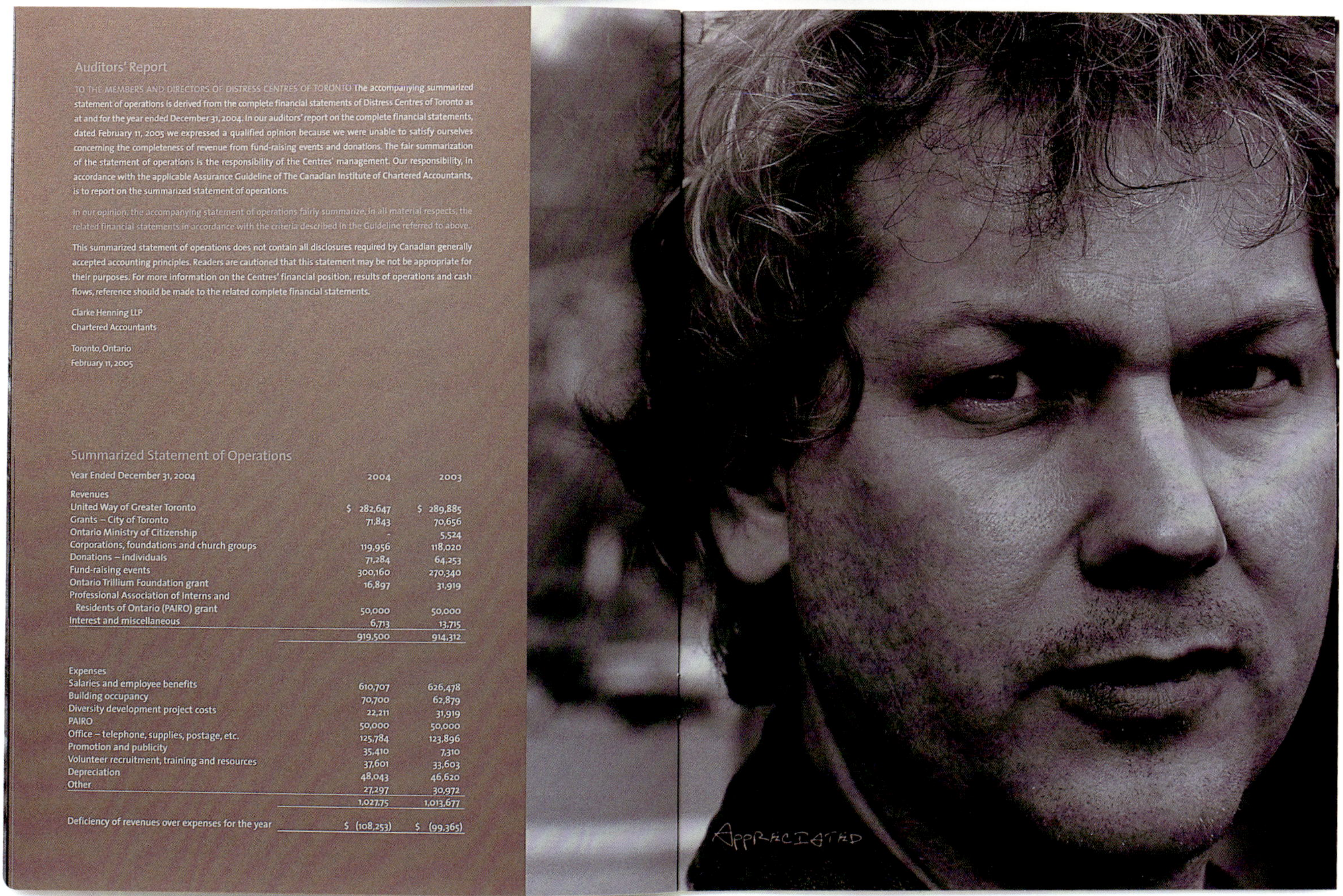

Auditors' Report

TO THE MEMBERS AND DIRECTORS OF DISTRESS CENTRES OF TORONTO The accompanying summarized statement of operations is derived from the complete financial statements of Distress Centres of Toronto as at and for the year ended December 31, 2004. In our auditors' report on the complete financial statements, dated February 11, 2005 we expressed a qualified opinion because we were unable to satisfy ourselves concerning the completeness of revenue from fund-raising events and donations. The fair summarization of the statement of operations is the responsibility of the Centres' management. Our responsibility, in accordance with the applicable Assurance Guideline of The Canadian Institute of Chartered Accountants, is to report on the summarized statement of operations.

In our opinion, the accompanying statement of operations fairly summarize, in all material respects, the related financial statements in accordance with the criteria described in the Guideline referred to above.

This summarized statement of operations does not contain all disclosures required by Canadian generally accepted accounting principles. Readers are cautioned that this statement may be not be appropriate for their purposes. For more information on the Centres' financial position, results of operations and cash flows, reference should be made to the related complete financial statements.

Clarke Henning LLP
Chartered Accountants

Toronto, Ontario
February 11, 2005

Summarized Statement of Operations

Year Ended December 31, 2004	2004	2003
Revenues		
United Way of Greater Toronto	$ 282,647	$ 289,885
Grants – City of Toronto	71,843	70,656
Ontario Ministry of Citizenship	-	5,524
Corporations, foundations and church groups	119,956	118,020
Donations – individuals	71,284	64,253
Fund-raising events	300,160	270,340
Ontario Trillium Foundation grant	16,897	31,919
Professional Association of Interns and Residents of Ontario (PAIRO) grant	50,000	50,000
Interest and miscellaneous	6,713	13,715
	919,500	914,312
Expenses		
Salaries and employee benefits	610,707	626,478
Building occupancy	70,700	62,879
Diversity development project costs	22,211	31,919
PAIRO	50,000	50,000
Office – telephone, supplies, postage, etc.	125,784	123,896
Promotion and publicity	35,410	7,310
Volunteer recruitment, training and resources	37,601	33,603
Depreciation	48,043	46,620
Other	27,297	30,972
	1,027,75	1,013,677
Deficiency of revenues over expenses for the year	$ (108,253)	$ (99,365)

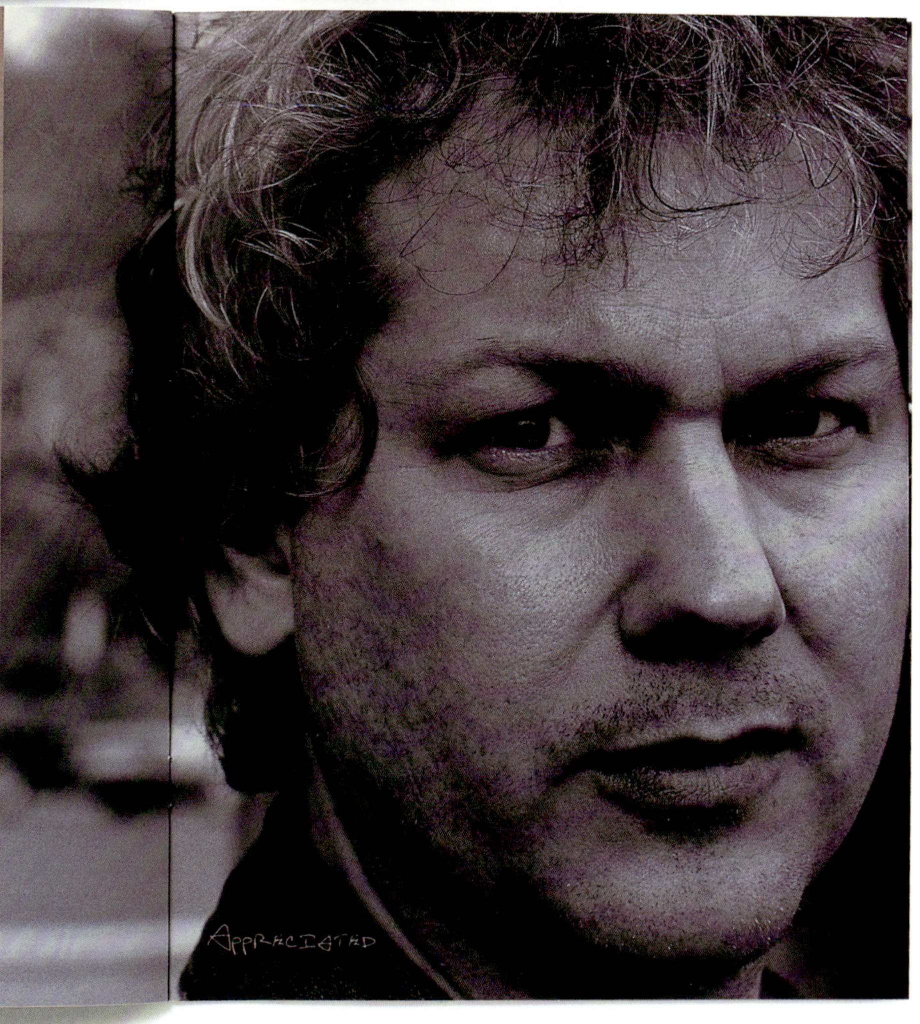

ANNUAL REPORT FOR 2004

THE JAMES IRVINE FOUNDATION

EXPANDING OPPORTUNITY FOR THE PEOPLE OF CALIFORNIA

Pentagram Design Partner: Kit Hinrichs Art Director: Belle How	Designer: Jessica Siegel Illustrator: Nicholas Wilton Printer: Lithographix	Paper: Cougar Opaque cover 100# cover, Cougar Opaque text 80#	Page count: 48 Print Run: 5,000 Size: 9" x 12"	Number of images: 11 photos Client: The James Irvine Foundation

ABOUT JAMES IRVINE

A native Californian, James Irvine devoted most of his life to his business interests in San Francisco and the development of his 110,000-acre ranch in Orange County, which he inherited from his father in 1886.

Mr. Irvine believed that significant community responsibility came with his ownership of the ranch, and his philanthropic activities culminated with the formation in 1937 of The James Irvine Foundation. He directed that Foundation grants promote the general welfare of the people of California, and by the time of his death in 1947, the Foundation had begun to make grants to educational and cultural institutions and other nonprofit organizations. Since its founding in 1937, the Foundation has made grants totaling more than $850 million for the people of California.

ABOUT THE COVER

Katia Vang is a second-generation Californian of Hmong descent and a nursing student at California State University, Fresno. Ms. Vang is also a volunteer at Stone Soup Fresno, a community center that serves the large and growing Southeast Asian refugee population in the San Joaquin Valley. She is pictured in traditional Hmong costume, standing before a tapestry that depicts the story of the Hmong fleeing their native country of Laos following the Vietnam War.

In 2004, with a grant from Irvine, Stone Soup Fresno developed Project Common Thread, a program designed to preserve and promote the cultural arts of the Hmong and foster cross-cultural awareness in the San Joaquin Valley. As part of Project Common Thread, Ms. Vang helped to establish a Hmong girls choir, which has been well received in the community, and she continues to teach traditional songs that capture the history and culture of the Hmong people.

TABLE OF CONTENTS

THE JAMES IRVINE FOUNDATION

The mission of The James Irvine Foundation is to expand opportunity for the people of California to participate in a vibrant, successful, and inclusive society. In pursuit of this mission, the Foundation is guided by the following goals: advance the educational and economic prospects of low-income Californians to create and share in the state's prosperity; engage a broad cross section of Californians in the civic and cultural life of their communities and the state; enhance mutual understanding and communication among diverse racial, ethnic, and socioeconomic groups; and enrich the state's intellectual and creative environment.

ADVANCE

ENGAGE

ENHANCE

ENRICH

Q&A with Pentagram Design

What was the client's directive?
The main objective is to communicate the Foundation's goals and methods for providing opportunity to the people of California.
How did you define the problem?
The design problem was to describe the Foundation's objectives in a compelling way.
What was the approach? To feature case studies of three specific yet diverse programs, with photographs of some of the actual grantees from three unique regions who benefit from the work of the Foundation.
Which disciplines or people helped you with the project?
In addition to the Pentagram team, the photographer, John Blaustein, traveled across California to photograph grantees.
How involved was the CEO in your meetings and presentations?
Very. He attended all presentations, wrote the president's letter, and reviewed all materials closely.
Do you feel that designers are becoming more involved in copywriting?
I think that designers help define the overall focus and tone of the work, which ultimately influences the copywriting.
How do you define success in annual report design?
One way in which an annual can be deemed successful is when it generates a positive conversation within its intended audience.
How important are awards to your client?
Anything that helps expand awareness for the Foundation is always well received.

An annual may be deemed successful if it generates positive conversation within its intended audience.

ALLIANCE FOR EDUCATION

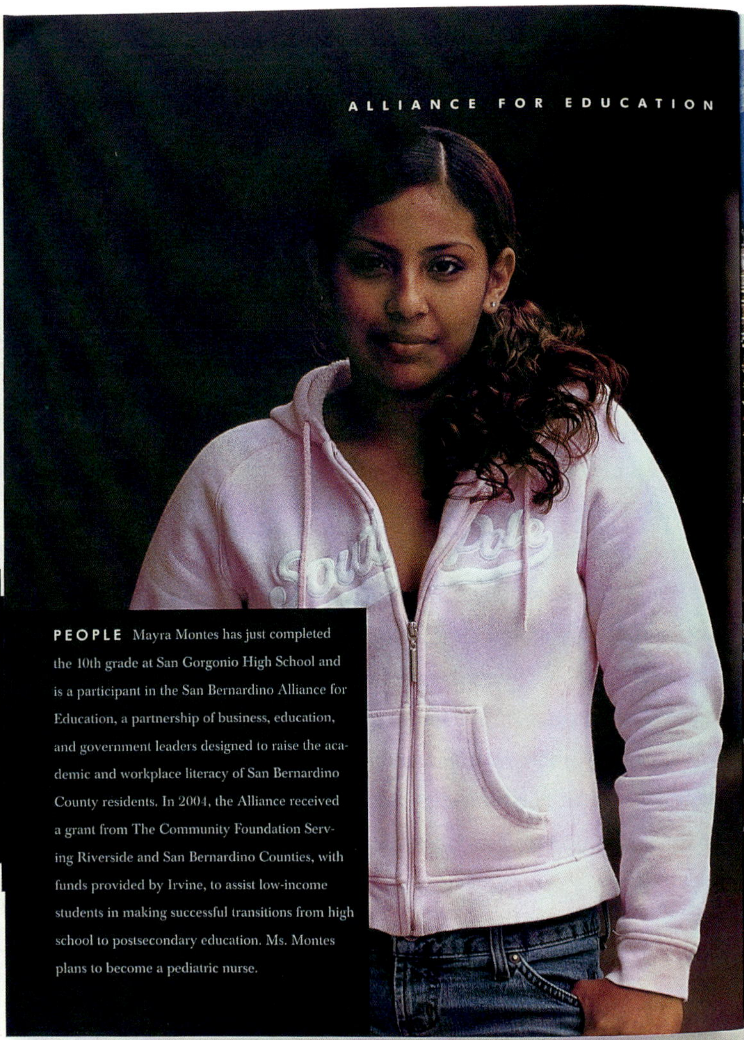

PEOPLE Mayra Montes has just completed the 10th grade at San Gorgonio High School and is a participant in the San Bernardino Alliance for Education, a partnership of business, education, and government leaders designed to raise the academic and workplace literacy of San Bernardino County residents. In 2004, the Alliance received a grant from The Community Foundation Serving Riverside and San Bernardino Counties, with funds provided by Irvine, to assist low-income students in making successful transitions from high school to postsecondary education. Ms. Montes plans to become a pediatric nurse.

THE INLAND EMPIRE

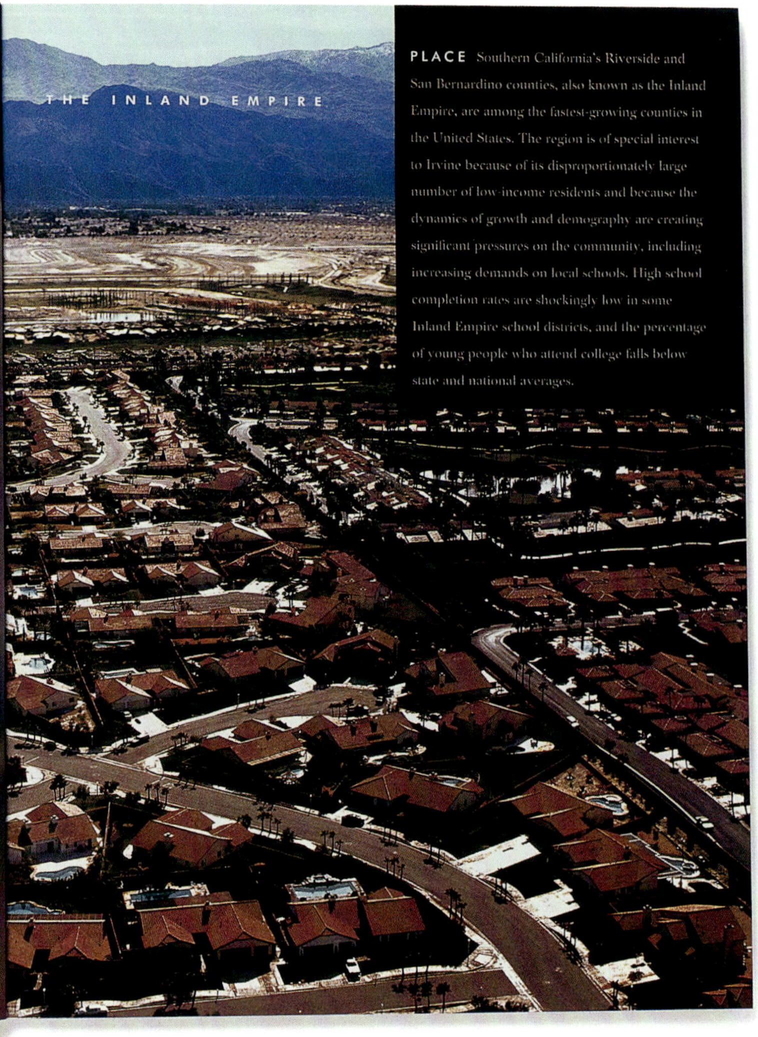

PLACE Southern California's Riverside and San Bernardino counties, also known as the Inland Empire, are among the fastest-growing counties in the United States. The region is of special interest to Irvine because of its disproportionately large number of low-income residents and because the dynamics of growth and demography are creating significant pressures on the community, including increasing demands on local schools. High school completion rates are shockingly low in some Inland Empire school districts, and the percentage of young people who attend college falls below state and national averages.

FROM THE PRESIDENT AND CHIEF EXECUTIVE OFFICER

James Irvine's mandate in creating the Foundation carries as much resonance today as it did in 1937. What emerges from reading his Indenture of Trust, which provides the governing direction for the Foundation, is that he cared about improving people's lives, especially those who faced difficult prospects. He also had great affection for California, which provided the land upon which he created his wealth. People and place were important concepts for our founder and remain at the center of how this Foundation approaches its work today.

The refocused mission that emerged from our recent strategic planning work – to expand opportunity for the people of California to participate in a vibrant, successful, and inclusive society – flows directly from our founder's wishes. Our three core grantmaking programs – Arts, California Perspectives, and Youth – bring this mission to life in an integrated way that builds upon Irvine's unique history and competencies as a statewide funder.

"Our goal in this year's report is to provide readers with a clear and tangible picture of how our institution positions itself to carry out James Irvine's vision in view of our long history, our enduring values, and our finite resources."

In 2004, we completed the first full year of grantmaking reflecting our new directions, and to demonstrate an ongoing commitment to our founder's core principles, this annual report focuses on three P's: purpose, people, and place.

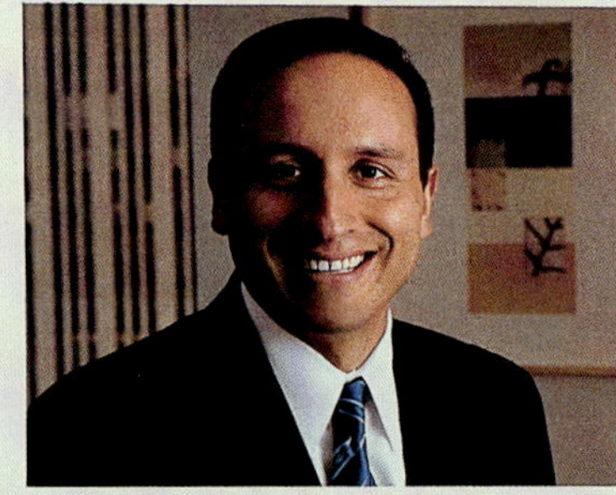

In the pages that follow, we outline the core purpose for each of our programs. Along with those statements of purpose, we profile some of the people and organizations we are privileged to support, and highlight a sampling of the places in California where we do our work. Our goal in this year's report is to provide readers with a clear and tangible picture of how our institution positions itself to carry out James Irvine's vision in view of our long history, our enduring values, and our finite resources.

For The Jame Irvine Foundation, 2004 established the platform for the future. We will build upon this platform in the years ahead in ways that honor the rich legacy of those who preceded us, that demonstrate our understanding of an ever-shifting external environment in California, and that reflect the values and principles that led James Irvine to create this philanthropic enterprise.

Sincerely,

James E. Canales
President and Chief Executive Officer
July 2005

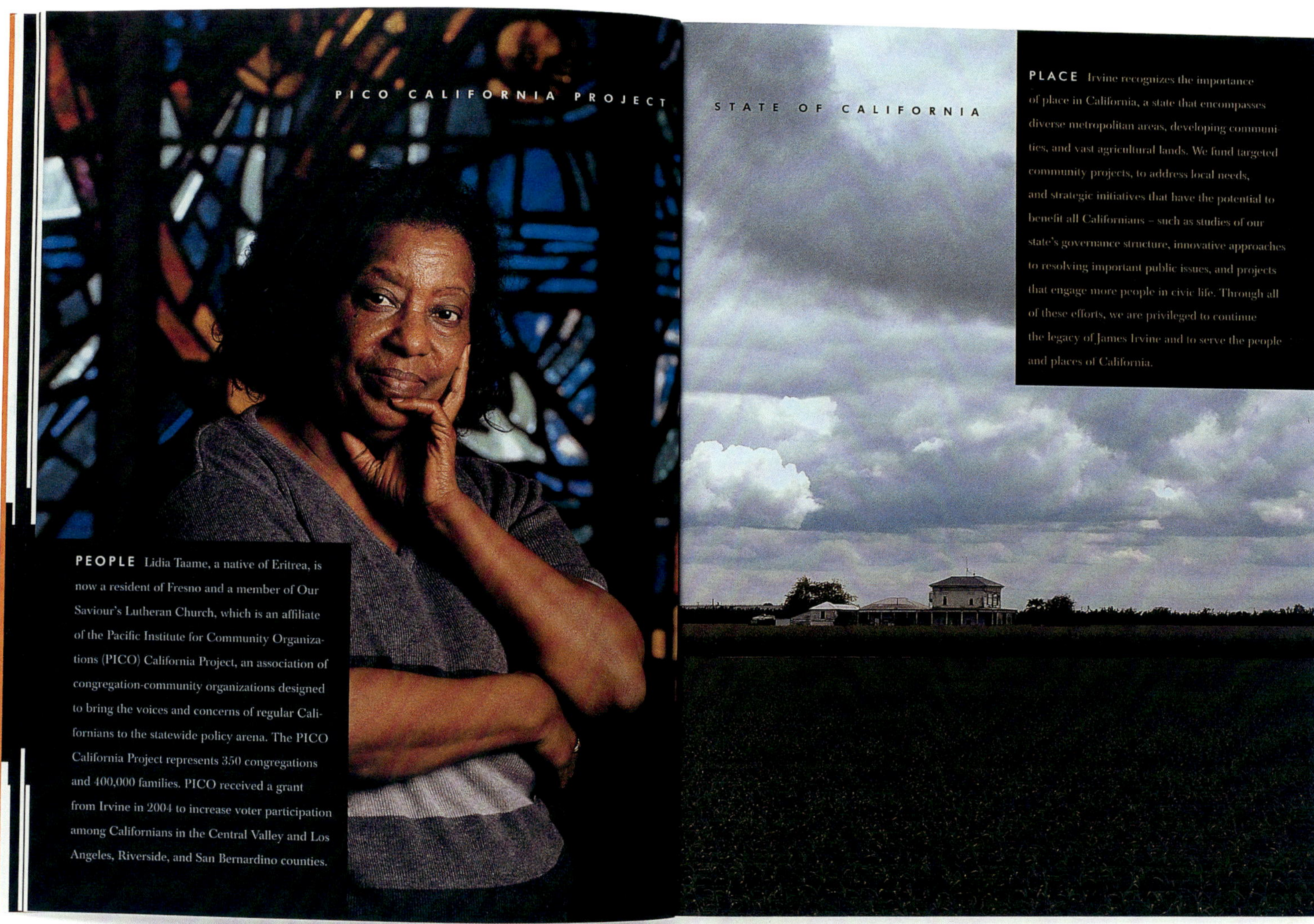

THE JAMES IRVINE FOUNDATION
STATEMENTS OF ACTIVITIES AND CHANGES IN NET ASSETS

Years ended December 31, 2004 and 2003

	2004	2003
Investment Income:		
Interest	$ 13,656,815	$ 14,903,140
Dividends	18,681,944	13,621,673
Operating loss from alternative investments	(2,430,569)	(4,392,321)
Fee income	214,010	226,412
Investment income before net realized and unrealized gains on investments	30,122,200	24,358,904
Net realized and unrealized gains on investments	216,404,531	273,091,409
Total investment income	246,526,731	297,450,313
Investment Expenses	6,201,289	6,097,415
Net Investment Gain Before Federal Excise Taxes	240,325,442	291,352,898
Federal Excise Taxes	2,834,165	546,766
Net Investment Gain	237,491,277	290,806,132
Expenses:		
Grants approved by the Board of Directors	53,773,804	50,530,557
Conditional grant activity and other–net	(1,235,997)	921,686
Grant expense – net	52,537,807	51,452,243
Program administration expenses	5,641,696	6,438,298
Total expenses	58,179,503	57,890,541
Change in Net Assets – Unrestricted	179,311,774	232,915,591
Net Assets – Unrestricted:		
Beginning of year	1,321,181,259	1,088,265,668
End of year	$ 1,500,493,033	$ 1,321,181,259

See notes to financial statements.

THE JAMES IRVINE FOUNDATION
STATEMENTS OF CASH FLOWS

Years ended December 31, 2004 and 2003

	2004	2003
Cash Flows from Operating Activities:		
Change in net assets – unrestricted	$ 179,311,774	$ 232,915,591
Adjustments to reconcile change in net assets–unrestricted to net cash and cash equivalents used in operating activities:		
Depreciation and amortization	497,990	554,673
Property and equipment write-offs	4,481	96,328
Net realized and unrealized gains on investments	(216,404,531)	(273,091,409)
Operating loss from alternative investments	2,430,569	4,392,321
Changes in operating assets and liabilities:		
Interest and dividends receivable	333,739	669,080
Prepaid excise taxes and other	27,833	(312,006)
Accounts payable and other accrued liabilities	505,775	(2,308,920)
Grants payable	2,534,129	(4,376,271)
Net cash and cash equivalents used in operating activities	(30,758,241)	(41,460,613)
Cash Flows from Investing Activities:		
Purchases of investments	(987,143,809)	(833,345,305)
Proceeds from sales, maturities, and distributions from investments	1,016,175,394	886,980,467
Purchases of property and equipment	(415,480)	(45,869)
Principal repayments from Program Related Investment Fund loan recipients	-	718,615
Net cash and cash equivalents provided by investing activities	28,616,105	54,307,908
(Decrease) Increase in Cash and Cash Equivalents	(2,142,136)	12,847,295
Cash and Cash Equivalents – Beginning of year	37,544,017	24,696,722
Cash and Cash Equivalents – End of year	$ 35,401,881	$ 37,544,017
Supplemental Disclosure of Cash Flow Information – Federal excise taxes paid	$ 2,520,000	$ 700,519

See notes to financial statements.

Society of Graphic Designers of Canada

Design Firm: SamataMason
Creative Director: Dave Mason & Pamela Lee

... as we move from the information age into the age of ideas... designers, with their ability for whole-brain thinking and their talents for creation and iteration, are becoming among the most influential shapers of the future.

Designers: Pamela Lee, Dave Mason, Keith Leinweber

Photographer: Victor John Penner
Printer: Blanchette Press

Paper: Euro Art Silk cover 80lb, Euro Art Silk text 80lb, Venetian text 70lb

Page count: 212 +4 (cover)
Print run: 2,000
Size: 5" x 6.625"

Number of Images: 16
Client: Society of Graphic Designers of Canada

I think that good clients (smart business people) appreciate honesty and quality, and if you deliver that, then you'll always have work coming through the door.

Q&A with SamataMason

What was the client's directive?
To deliver a message that the GDC is a truly national organization that helps define and promote professional practice among its members.
What was the approach?
We focused on the connectivity evidenced through the "voice" of the GDC - the comments, conversations and rants of nationwide members and other interested individuals expressed through the organization's online forum.
Which disciplines or people helped you with the project?
Victor John Penner, photographer. Blanchette Press, printers.
Were you happy with the result?
Absolutely.
What was the client's response?
Happy, after receiving positive feedback from a variety of recipients.
How involved was the CEO in your meetings and presentations?
We worked closely with Matt Warburton, Past President, and Peggy Cady, President, to define the communication issues.
Do you feel that designers are becoming more involved in copywriting?
Absolutely.
How do you define success in Annual Report design?
Happy client. Happy recipients. Happy us.
How important are awards to your client?
Well, since these clients are designers themselves, my guess is, pretty important.

Success for us: a happy client, happy recipients, happy us.

WE CONNECT

Design, including that for the web, is not about pushing elements around on a page, bending or shaping the line length, changing colours and then just pouring it into a new bucket such as a poster, billboard or cellphone. It begins at the beginning with content creation.

WE CONNECT!

YOU folks are the GDC! YOU are how the change gets put into effect!

WE CONNECT!

I just hope they have the sense to avoid spec work.

Creativity. Ethics. Copyright. Typography. Colour. Accreditation. Printing. Education. Signage. Clients. Usability. Spec work. Fees for services. Paper. Technology. Photography. Competition. Contracts. RFPs. Process. Accounting. Interns. Awards. Advertising. Taxation. Communication. The issues that face graphic designers are varied and complex.

There is no greater evidence of the power of connection than the GDC Listserv. Designers from every corner of Canada—and from outside its borders—connect through this vehicle to ask and answer questions, engage in meaningful debate, and address the issues that shape our profession. Through their actions, they form a community whose boundaries are defined only by the growing scope of common interests, and by an uncommon commitment to dialogue and communication.

The GDC connects.

SUMMARY

It has certainly been a demanding and invigorating year. Many thanks to those on the National Executive, the National Council, our Committee Chairs and our staff member for the time they have devoted to GDC and for the work accomplished by all. Thanks also to Craig Medwyduk MGDC, VP Education until October 2004, for getting our National Scholarship Awards program off to a great start.

We have made measurable, significant accomplishments, creating structural building blocks for accreditation. We have increased the profession's visibility in Canada and internationally, and we have strengthened the foundations of the GDC.

The GDC's responsiveness to the needs of Members and Chapters fosters the strength of the organization and the development of the profession. As we move toward the Society's 50th year, we must keep our lines of communication open, and our focus on our major goals and on planning for the future. I urge National Council, Committee Chairs and Board Members to continue their active involvement in this process—and, to keep up their open dialogue with members. Working together, we can make the changes that will support designers, improve standards, and enhance the design profession in the coming years.

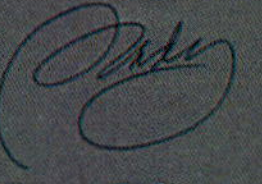

Peggy Cady MGDC
NATIONAL PRESIDENT 2004-06

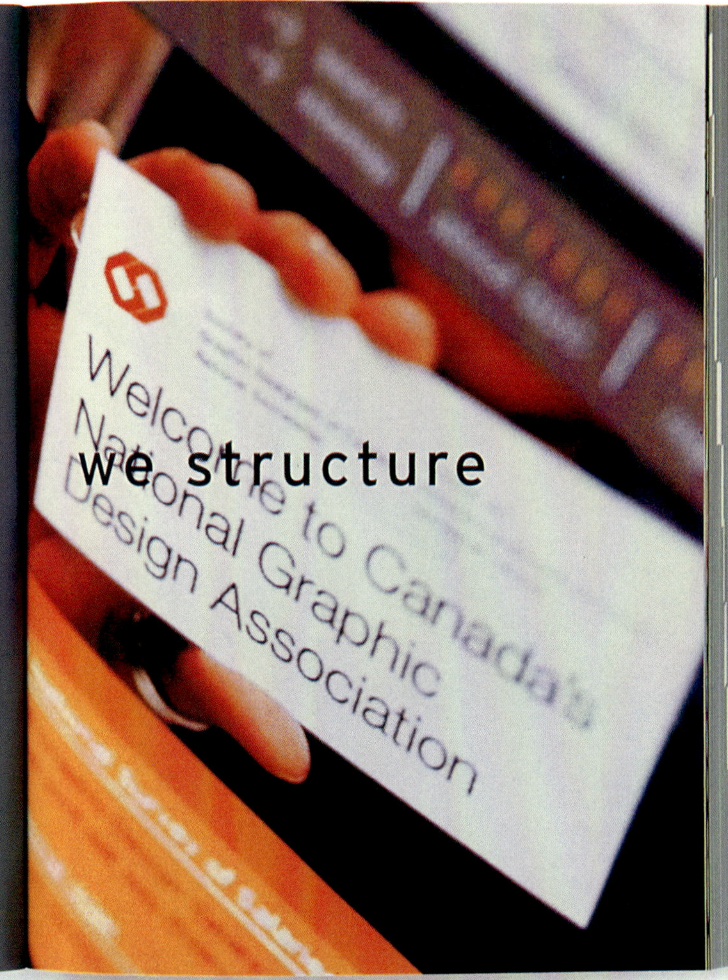

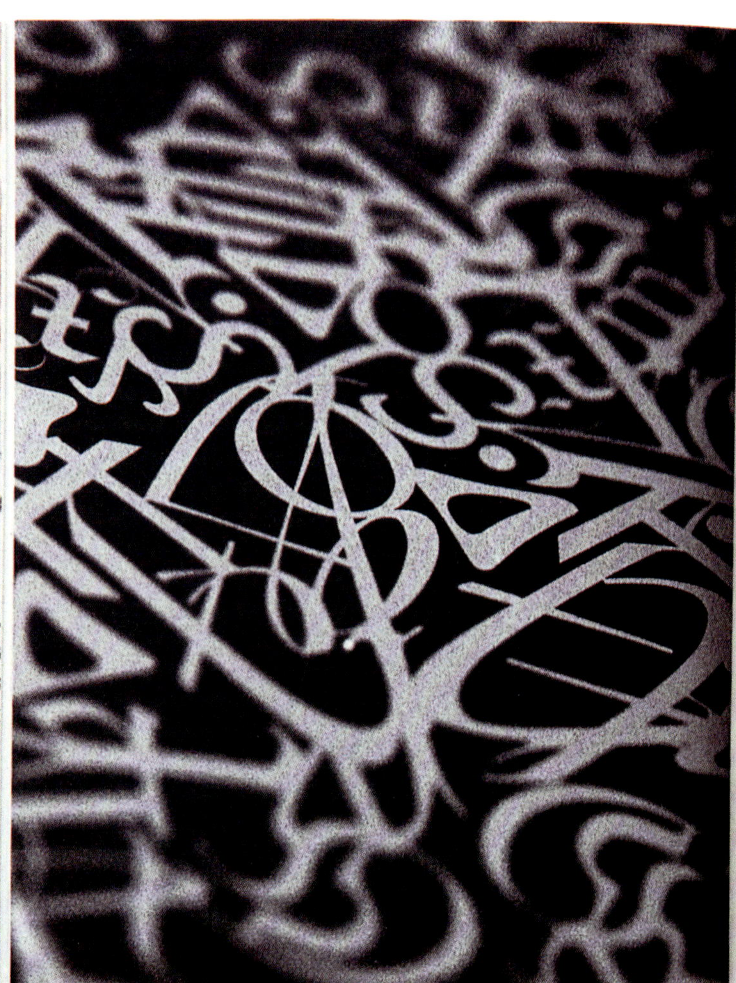

Treasurer's Report

2004 HIGHLIGHTS
RETURN TO A BALANCED BUDGET

Increased revenues and tightly-controlled expenditures created a small surplus of earnings in 2004, the first since 2000.

On January 1, 2004, the national portion of the membership dues for FGDC and MGDC members increased from $100 to $175 per annum, and the national dues for LGDC members increased from $90 to $135. These new rates of dues were the primary reason the 2004 revenues increased to $144,340 (over 130% of the 2003 revenue of $109,931).

The increased national dues allowed a modest (14%) increase in spending over the previous year. Website development was the largest increase in discretionary expenditures, resulting in improved functionality for board members at both National and Chapter levels as well as for the members of the Society, and improved information and access for our clients and the general public.

REVENUE AND EXPENSES 2004,
COMPARED TO BUDGET PROJECTIONS 2004, AND AUDITED 2003

The 2004 audited financial statements do not categorize items as clearly as the Executive would prefer, so the following table is a reconfiguration of the data to assist understanding from a budgeting and management point of view.

YEAR ENDING DECEMBER 31,	AUDITED 2004	BUDGETED 2004	AUDITED 2003
REVENUE			
Dues:			
National membership dues	$ 83,650	$ 85,106	$ 50,833
Chapter membership dues	55,160	55,290	48,460
Unidentified receipts	1,871	—	3,255
	140,681	140,396	102,548
Dues transfers to Chapters	(50,608)	(55,290)	(46,445)
Dues transfers to Chapters for prior years	(950)	—	—
Applied Arts subscriptions for Chapters	(5,858)	—	—
Unidentified disbursements to Chapters	—	—	(2,015)
	83,265	85,106	54,088
Sponsorship revenue	—	—	5,221
Scholarship revenue	2,000	3,000	1,000
Donations received	1,000	—	500
Miscellaneous revenue	658	758	662
Net national revenue	$ 86,923	$ 88,864	$ 61,471

YEAR ENDING DECEMBER 31,	AUDITED 2004	BUDGETED 2004	AUDITED 2003
EXPENDITURES			
Icograda membership fees	3,462	3,800	3,599
Wages	27,604	27,500	25,000
Rent	2,171	2,219	2,519
PROFESSIONAL:			
Auditing and accounting fees	4,454	7,781	7,781
Legal fees	941	—	943
	5,395	7,781	8,724
Bank charges	1,553	1,398	1,398
Insurance	517	274	274
OFFICE:			
General	1,548	3,873	4,812
Postage and courier	4,853	3,538	3,701
	6,401	7,411	8,486
PHONE:			
General	2,843	2,400	2,400
Executive teleconferences	1,296	1,476	1,476
	4,139	3,876	3,876
Annual General Meeting	13,303	13,500	15,585
WEBSITE:			
Hosting, Listserv, traffic, domain names	1,666	725	1,739
Development	10,550	10,550	—
Maintenance: service contract	3,675	3,675	—
	15,891	14,950	1,739
Advertising and promotion	—	—	310
Scholarship awards	2,000	3,000	2,500
Net expenditures	$ 82,436	$ 85,709	$ 72,271
Excess (deficiency) of revenue after expenditures	$ 4,487	$ 3,154	$ (10,800)

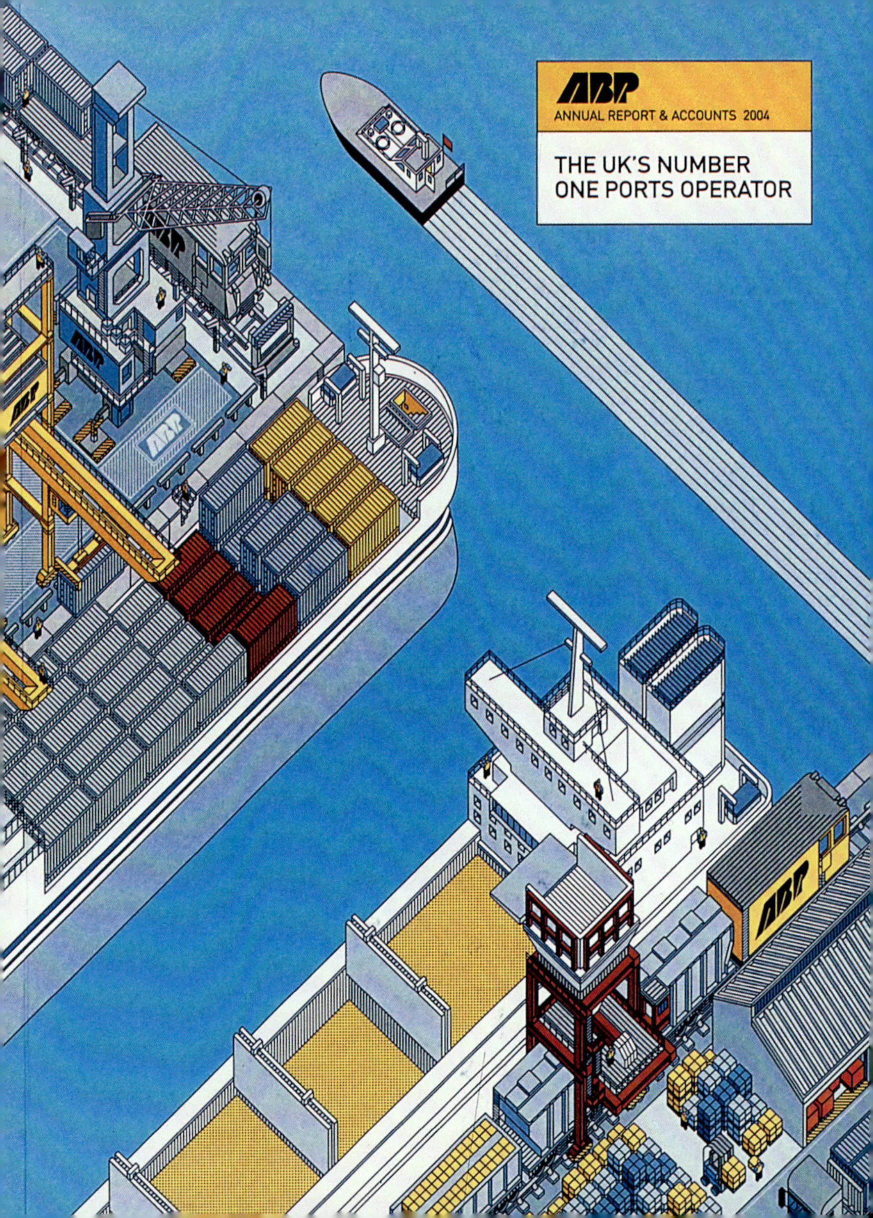
ABP
ANNUAL REPORT & ACCOUNTS 2004
THE UK'S NUMBER ONE PORTS OPERATOR

Creative Directors: Alan Dye, Nick Finney, Ben Stott
Designer: Daniel Lock
Illustrator: Johnny Kelly
Photographer: Ed Reeve
Printer: St. Ives Westerham Press
Paper: cover, Challenger Offset 250 gsm, text, Challenger Offset 110 gsm
Page count: 101
Print run: 19,000
Size: A4 +6 (cover)
Number of Images: 30
Client: Associated British Ports

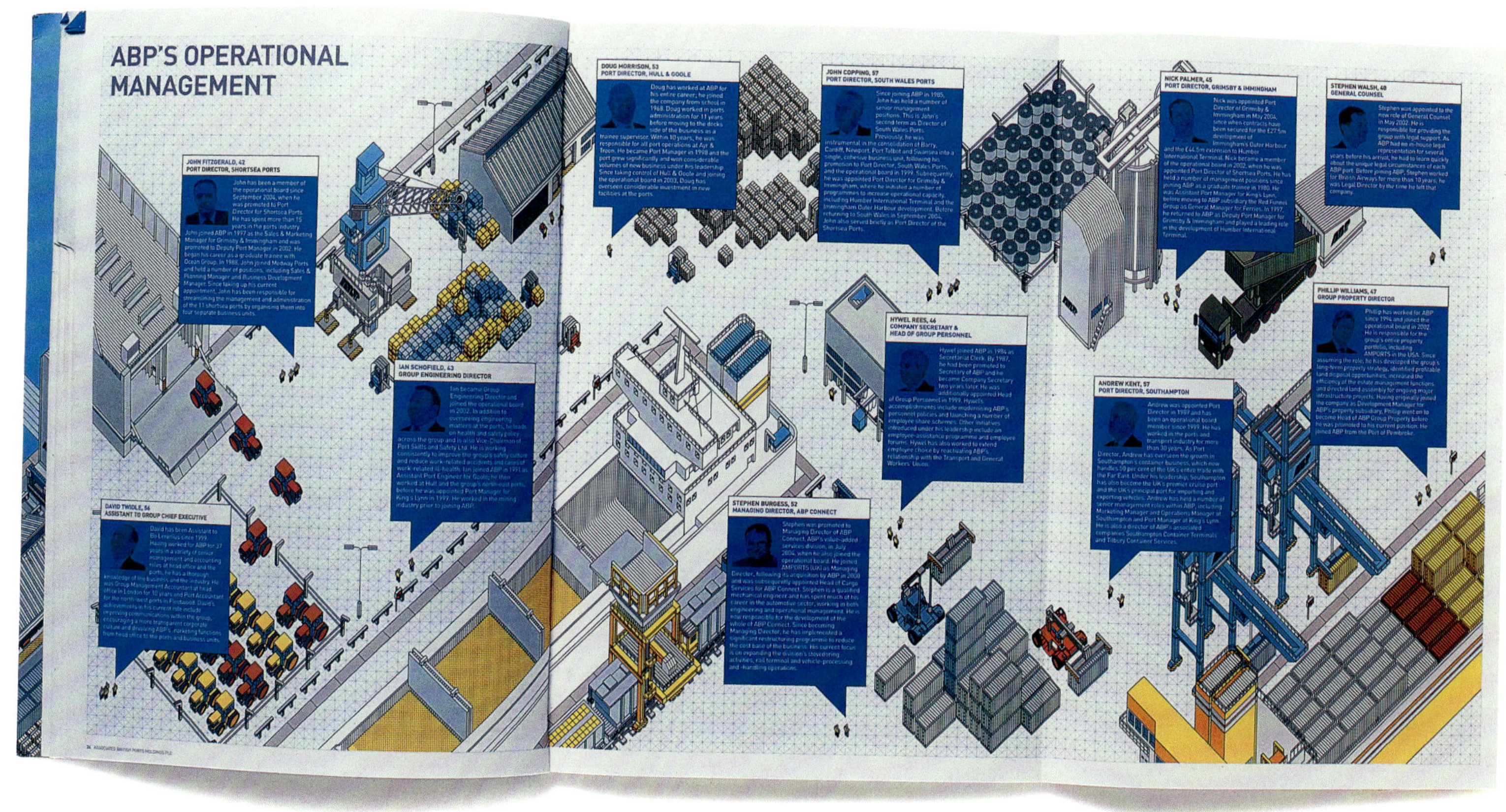

Q&A with NB Studio

What was the client's directive?

ABP is a FTSE 250 company and is currently the number one ports operator in the UK. The Authority handles millions of tons of cargo from coal and agribulks to ferry and cruise passengers.

Our brief was to design a clearly articulated Annual Report confirming ABP's strategy and growth. In particular, detail the company's competitive position and its combination of projects both large and small that have created huge growth opportunities.

How did you define the problem?

One of the main problems was how to show ABP's business as dynamic and exciting when a port is essentially a pretty grim, un-photogenic and dull place. Then there was the other issue, which was how to turn a dry and text heavy document into an interesting, engaging and beautiful Annual Report!

What was the approach?

We decided to take an illustrative approach showing ABP from a different angle. Using Axometric illustrations we created a typical port scene conveying the complexity of ABP's business activities and sites. This type of illustration allowed for a lot of detail, enabling us to capture the daily comings and goings and present it as an absorbing miniature world.The same style was employed throughout the document to convey bar and pie charts, maps and operational projects all backed up by tight typography and layout.

Which disciplines or people helped you with the project?

Project management was undertaken by The Merchant Group and typset by Bettina Brux.

Were you happy with the result?

Our original design included no photography; we had the BOD and management team drawn in our illustrative style. We unfortunately had to change to photographic portraits later, which was a shame.

What was the client's response?

They absolutely loved it! This type of approach was a real departure for them and from previous Annual Reports. Some client feedback included, "It does all the 'tricks' it is meant to do, but it is also an exquisite work of art…"

How involved was the CEO in your meetings, presentations, etc.?

We had regular meetings with members of the board to present our designs, which was incredibly helpful and insightful in understanding the message the company wanted to get across.

Do you feel that designers are becoming more involved in copywriting?

We do the occasional bit of copywriting, but generally we think that it is best left to the professionals.

How do you define success in Annual Report design?

I heard that city analysts, the people that actually use Annual Reports, normally skip straight to the back of the report just to look at the results, as that is the most important information to them. If you can create a design that is so visually interesting and engaging that [it] makes them pick your report up first out of the huge pile they have on their desk and spend some time looking through it, then you have won! It is up to the companies' results to do the rest.

How important are awards to your client?

I think the full page devoted to ABP's recent awards at the back of their Corporate and Social Responsibility report demonstrates their enthusiasm for them!

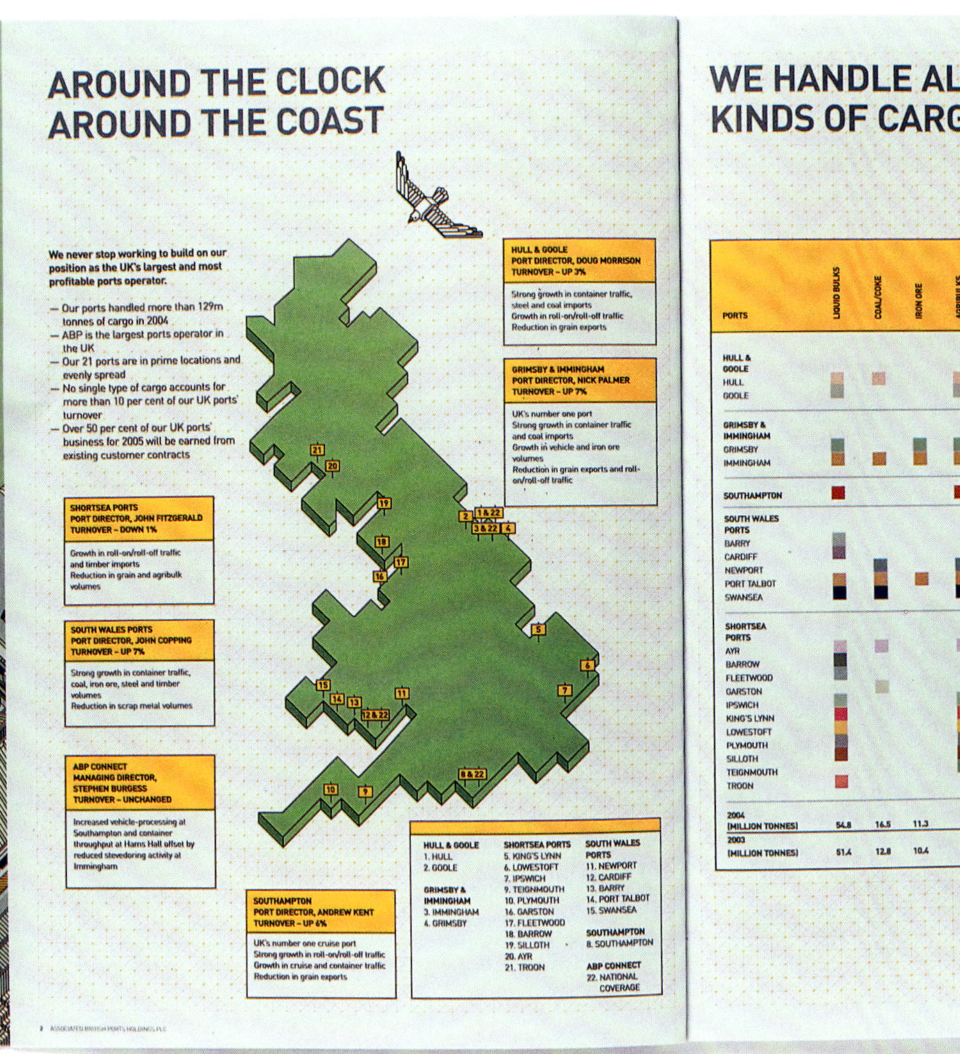

WE HANDLE ALL KINDS OF CARGO

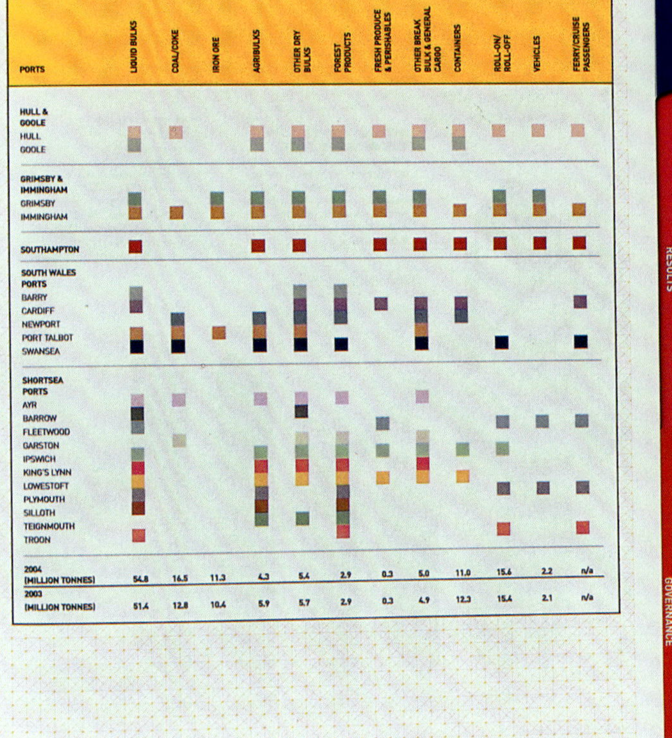

WE'RE STICKING TO THE STRATEGY THAT WE LAUNCHED IN 2000. OUR GROWTH TELLS YOU WHY

Our track record speaks for itself. Since the beginning of 2000, we have delivered on our promise of a more focused business and more consistent growth.

FOCUSING ON OUR CORE UK PORTS & TRANSPORT BUSINESS
By getting back to basics, we have been able to target investment and resources at the heart of our business, maximising its growth potential. Since the beginning of 2000, we have won over 80 new long-term contracts and invested in excess of £155m in new revenue-earning projects.

INSTILLING RIGOROUS CAPITAL EXPENDITURE DISCIPLINES
Nothing gets approved without meeting our hurdle rate of 15 per cent – any revenue-earning investment has to meet our internal rate of return criteria. As for maintenance capital expenditure, we aim to keep this at or below our rate of depreciation.

DEVELOPING VALUE-ADDED SERVICES
The launch of ABP Connect in 2001 has enabled us to maximise the potential of our port network by offering customers additional services such as cargo-handling, warehousing and vehicle-processing. ABP Connect has grown turnover by 48.2 per cent since its inception.

HARNESSING TALENT FOR THE FUTURE
The composition of our main board and the operating board is very different to early 2000. In addition, over 75 per cent of our senior managers have changed jobs at least once during the past five years. As much as possible, we have promoted from within and rewarded talent with early responsibility to create a dynamic team to lead the business into the future.

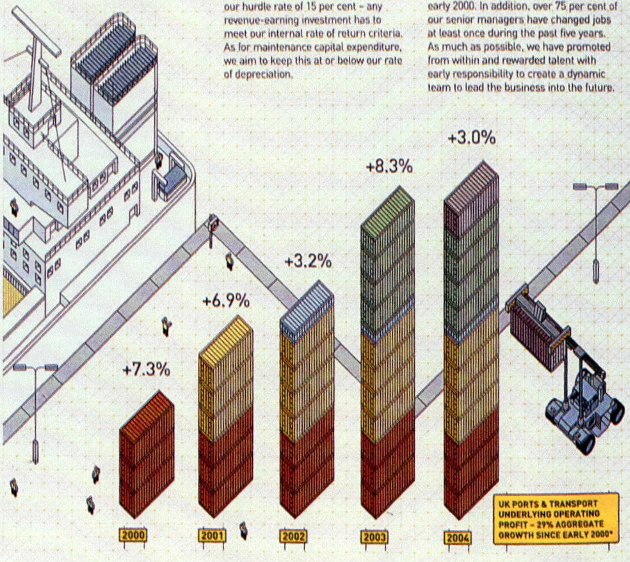

* Continuing operations before goodwill amortisation and exceptional items under FRS 17

SINCE 2000, WE'VE DELIVERED A TOTAL SHAREHOLDER RETURN IN EXCESS OF 100 PER CENT

DISPOSING OF NON-CORE ASSETS
Over £103m received from disposals with the sale of Red Funnel Group in 2000 and AMPORTS Aviation division in 2002.

SELLING £200M OF LAND NOT NEEDED FOR PORT OPERATIONS
Our target of £200m – set at the beginning of 2000 – has been exceeded. We have now extended this by a further £50m.

RETURNING VALUE TO SHAREHOLDERS
Share repurchase programmes totalling £220m were completed in 2001. In 2004, a new £100m programme was announced following the government's decision not to proceed with our application to build Dibden Terminal. This was extended by £30m following the sale of some of our property interests in Cardiff. The programme has recently been further extended by £75m to £205m.

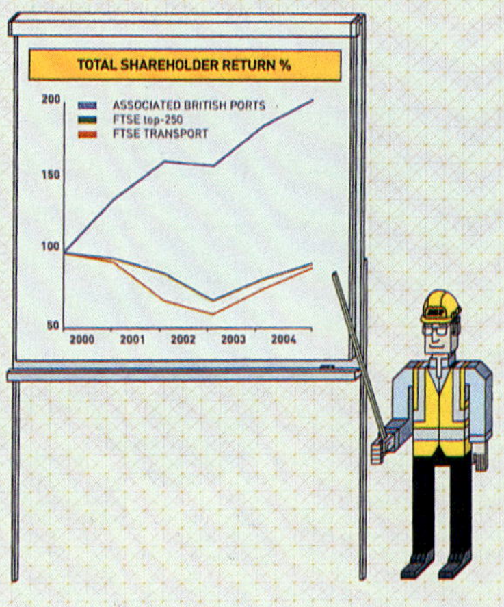

PERFORMANCE
RESULTS
GOVERNANCE

A CLOSE LOOK AT OUR PERFORMANCE

ABP

39% GROWTH IN DIVIDEND PER SHARE OVER THE LAST 5 YEARS

UNDERLYING EARNINGS PER SHARE*	DIVIDEND PER SHARE
+6%	+5%

*Before goodwill amortisation and exceptional items

CONTENTS

PERFORMANCE
RESULTS
GOVERNANCE

GROUP CHIEF EXECUTIVE'S REVIEW

Bo Lerenius
Group Chief Executive

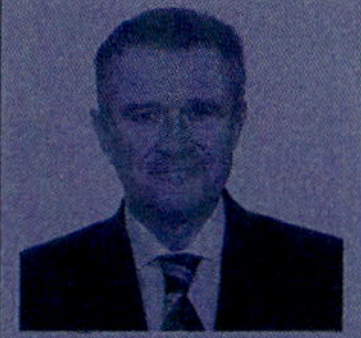

Since introducing our low-risk growth strategy, we have added more than 80 new major customer contracts.

Our core UK ports and transport business continued to grow in 2004. We signed 17 new contracts with major customers during the year, taking the total number of significant contract wins since the beginning of 2000 to more than 80.

We only build new facilities for customers once they have signed medium- to long-term contracts that will give us a return of 15 per cent or more on our investment, with between 10 and 11 per cent of this normally guaranteed by the customer. This low-risk growth strategy has enabled us to outgrow the UK-listed ports sector in terms of underlying operating profit over the past five years.

Looking forward, we plan to invest more than £400m in our UK ports over the next 10 years. The government's decision to refuse our application to develop Dibden Terminal, a deep-sea container port at Southampton, was disappointing. Nonetheless, we will continue to develop the Port of Southampton, but clearly not at the rate that we could have achieved had the Dibden Terminal application been approved.

The major growth projects in the near future are focused on the Humber Estuary, where our investments could exceed £200m. We are building a roll-on/roll-off facility for DFDS Tor Line to enable it to accommodate bigger ships and have signed agreements with several customers to develop a further terminal for coal imports. Both facilities are located at the Port of Immingham and will become operational in 2006. At Hull, final contractual discussions are taking place with customers for the shortsea container terminal that we aim to build. In January, the government informed us that it was minded to approve the development and we expect the final decision in the first half of 2005. We are also evaluating the possibility of another major development at Hull.

As we see plenty of investment opportunities to grow our existing ports network, we do not expect to make any acquisitions in the near future. Getting a return of 15 per cent or more from organic growth is a more efficient use of capital than buying – and integrating – a competitor. Investing in our core business represents a better use of shareholders' money.

The Department for Transport introduced security legislation during the year that required new security measures at all of our UK ports. This led to cost increases in some areas, which we have passed on to customers.

Our operating expenses benefited from the cost-reduction programme of 2003. However, profit growth was slowed by the departure from Immingham of Cobelfret, one of ABP Connect's biggest customers. This is the first time in five years that a major customer has moved its business away from ABP. To mitigate the impact of this departure, we secured a new customer, Ferryways NV, from January 2005 for part of the roll-on/roll-off facility that Cobelfret used, restructured ABP Connect and offered early retirement to employees throughout the UK to reduce the cost base. The cost-reduction measures will deliver an ongoing annual cost saving of at least £4.5m from 2005. This, coupled with the replacement business that the group has already secured, will offset the loss of Cobelfret's business from the beginning of 2005. If we could now add a second roll-on/roll-off customer to fill the remaining capacity at Immingham, ABP Connect would be in a stronger position than when it had the Cobelfret contract; however, this may take some time due to the intensity of competition in the sector.

17 NEW CONTRACTS WON IN 2004

We have continued to improve our much smaller business in the USA by applying our UK strategy as far as the more volatile local market will allow. Our aim is to fill the spare capacity within our six facilities while minimising non-revenue-earning capital investment. We have made progress in securing longer customer contracts and we also now have a much greater spread of business compared to five years ago. The numbers remain small compared to our UK ports and transport business, but are growing satisfactorily. Vehicle volumes are double what they were when we acquired the business in 1998.

We said that we would address the low level of gearing that we had maintained on the group balance sheet if the government rejected our application to develop Dibden Terminal. Following the negative decision on Dibden and the sale of surplus property interests in Cardiff Bay, we chose to return the spare cash to shareholders through a £130m share buyback programme, which was launched initially in April 2004. Once it is complete, we will buy back a further £75m over the following three years, as we expect to continue to generate more money than we need to maintain and develop the business. This should return the group's gearing to its previously stated range of between 50 and 70 per cent.

By the end of 2004, we had exceeded the £200m target that we set in 2000 for the disposal of non-core property and land. We intend to sell a further £50m of non-core assets over the next few years, subject to planning consents. There will be further disposals in the future, but on a relatively modest scale.

Personnel movements resulted in a number of management changes during the year. We promote from within as much as possible. To invigorate our business, which is important for its long-term health, we ensure that managers change positions periodically and have exposure to different elements of the group. Over 75 per cent of the delegates at our senior management conference in 2004 had changed jobs at least once during the previous five years. We reward talent with early responsibility, which is why a younger and more dynamic management team has emerged since 2000 to lead the business into the future.

I am pleased to report that there have been fewer injuries to our employees over the course of the year and that none has been serious. Our annual accident incident rate improved from 17.7 per thousand employees in 2003 to 14.0 per thousand employees in 2004.

Fatalities are the worst thing that can happen in our business and we naturally do everything we can to prevent them. Our safety systems and risk assessment processes are, I believe, second to none and I visit the ports on a regular basis throughout the year to review our safety practices. In addition to the two fatalities reported in 2003, we suffered one death involving a third-party employee on our facilities during 2004; in two cases no action has been taken against the group and the remaining incident has led to the Health and Safety Executive commencing proceedings against us under the Health and Safety at Work Act.

We are extremely conscious of the environment, as our business activities have an environmental impact. I believe that we have become more socially responsible in our business practices and provide more transparency on our operations and dealings with stakeholders. I was delighted when the group received one of the prestigious Investor Relations magazine awards in 2004 for excellence in shareholder communications, as these awards reflect the views of the very demanding analyst and investor communities.

Given our strong strategic position, I am confident about the future. Our business is in excellent shape. Our 21 UK ports have a good geographical spread and handle around one quarter of all trade in and out of the UK. We have many high-quality, long-term contracts, but no dominant customers and no trade accounts for more than 10 per cent of our UK ports revenue. With more than 50 per cent of our budgeted UK ports business for 2005 coming from customer contracts, earnings visibility is very good. As our latest repurchase of shares demonstrates, we continue to generate more cash than we need to grow our core UK ports and transport business.

Thank you for your continued support.

Bo Lerenius

BO LERENIUS
GROUP CHIEF EXECUTIVE
16 FEBRUARY 2005

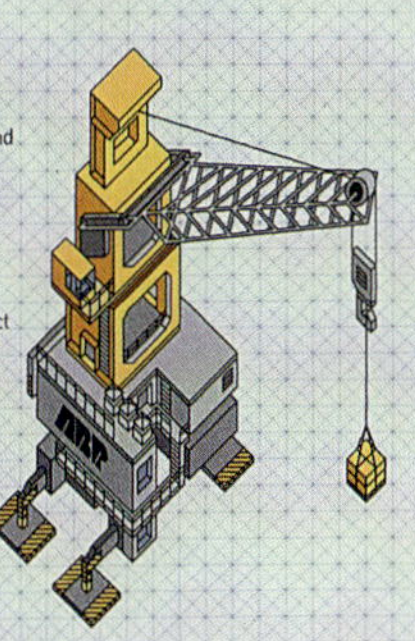

PERFORMANCE
RESULTS
GOVERNANCE

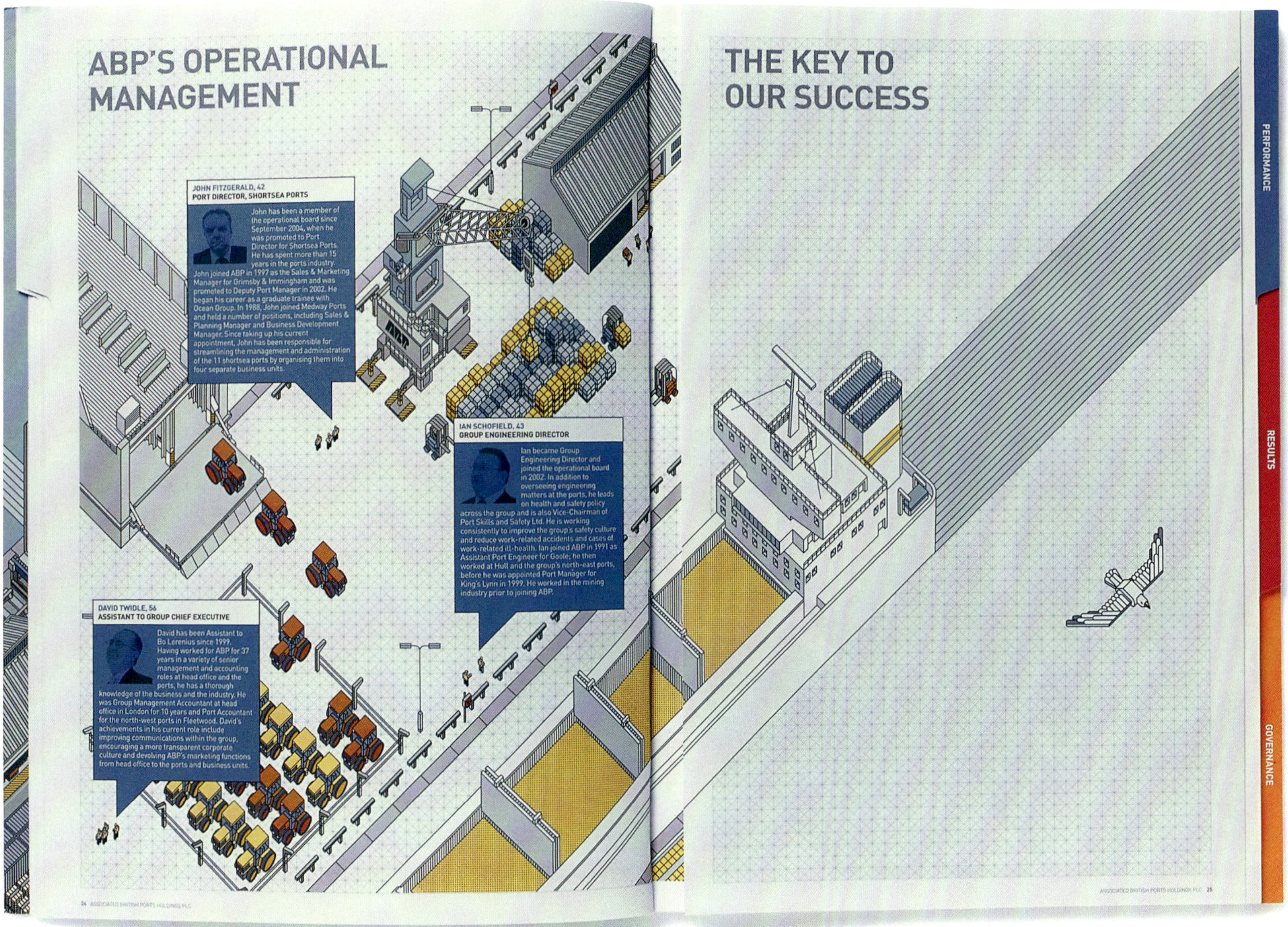

ABP'S OPERATIONAL MANAGEMENT

JOHN FITZGERALD, 42
PORT DIRECTOR, SHORTSEA PORTS

John has been a member of the operational board since September 2004, when he was promoted to Port Director for Shortsea Ports. He has spent more than 15 years in the ports industry. John joined ABP in 1997 as the Sales & Marketing Manager for Grimsby & Immingham and was promoted to Deputy Port Manager in 2002. He began his career as a graduate trainee with Ocean Group. In 1988, John joined Medway Ports and held a number of positions, including Sales & Planning Manager and Business Development Manager. Since taking up his current appointment, John has been responsible for streamlining the management and administration of the 11 shortsea ports by organising them into four separate business units.

IAN SCHOFIELD, 43
GROUP ENGINEERING DIRECTOR

Ian became Group Engineering Director and joined the operational board in 2002. In addition to overseeing engineering matters at the ports, he leads on health and safety policy across the group and is also Vice-Chairman of Port Skills and Safety Ltd. He is working consistently to improve the group's safety culture and reduce work-related accidents and cases of work-related ill-health. Ian joined ABP in 1991 as Assistant Port Engineer for Goole; he then worked at Hull and the group's north-east ports, before he was appointed Port Manager for King's Lynn in 1999. He worked in the mining industry prior to joining ABP.

DAVID TWIDLE, 56
ASSISTANT TO GROUP CHIEF EXECUTIVE

David has been Assistant to Bo Lerenius since 1999. Having worked for ABP for 37 years in a variety of senior management and accounting roles at head office and the ports, he has a thorough knowledge of the business and the industry. He was Group Management Accountant at head office in London for 10 years and Port Accountant for the north-west ports in Fleetwood. David's achievements in his current role include improving communications within the group, encouraging a more transparent corporate culture and devolving ABP's marketing functions from head office to the ports and business units.

THE KEY TO OUR SUCCESS

PERFORMANCE
RESULTS
GOVERNANCE

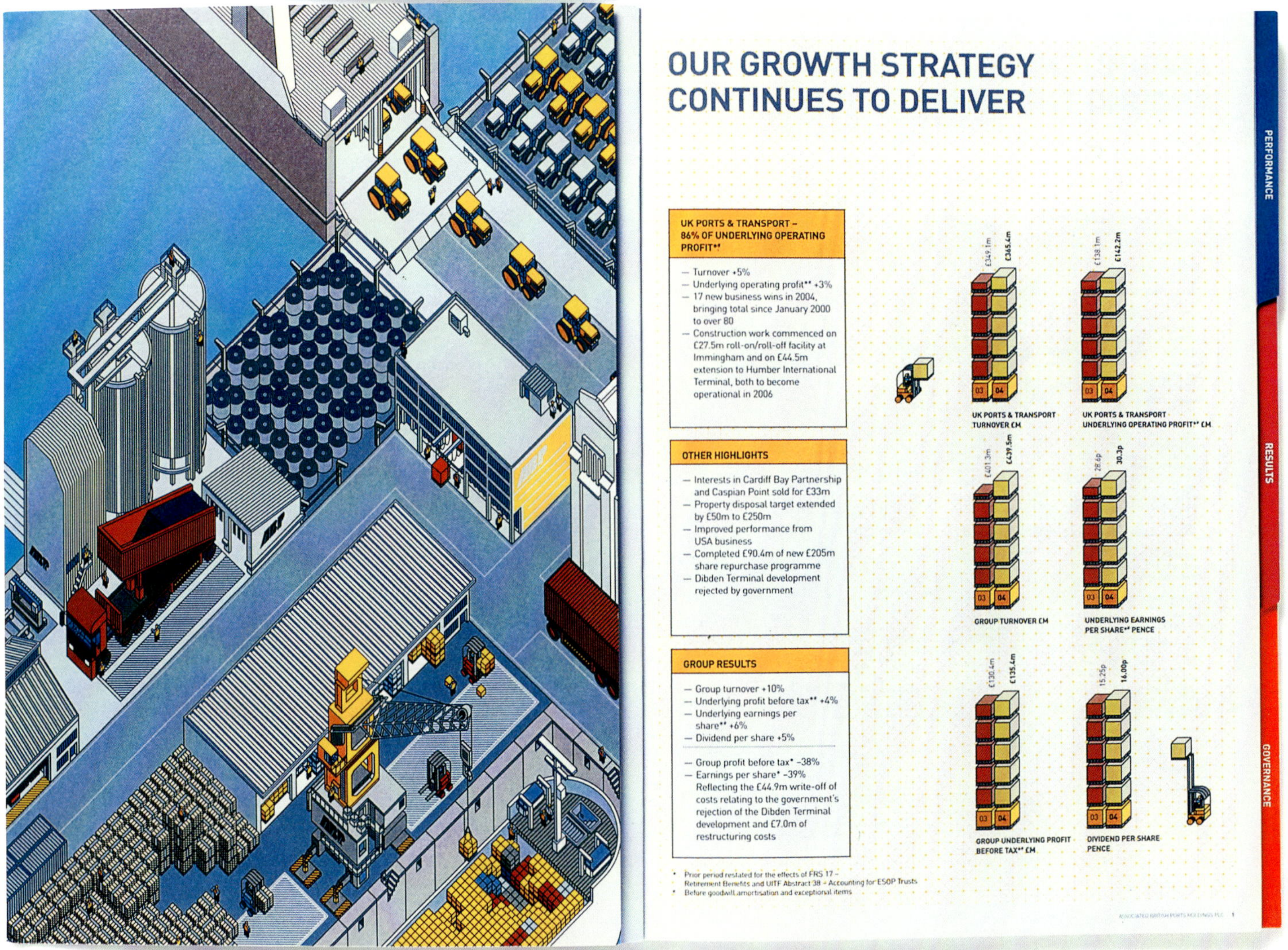

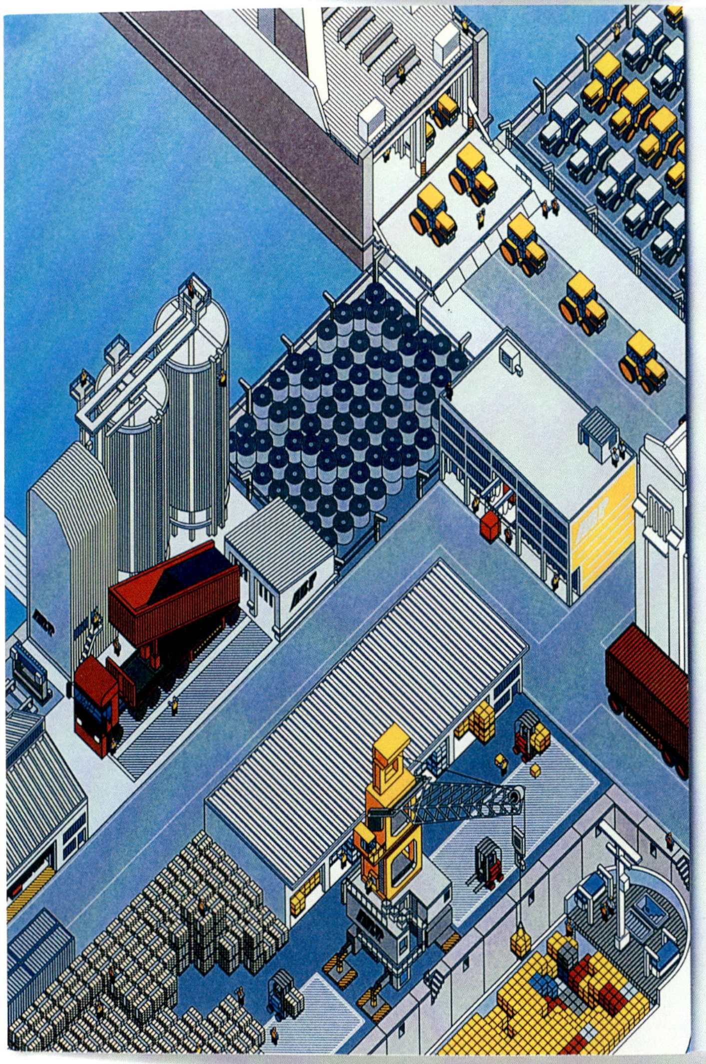

OUR GROWTH STRATEGY CONTINUES TO DELIVER

UK PORTS & TRANSPORT – 86% OF UNDERLYING OPERATING PROFIT**

- Turnover +5%
- Underlying operating profit** +3%
- 17 new business wins in 2004, bringing total since January 2000 to over 80
- Construction work commenced on £27.5m roll-on/roll-off facility at Immingham and on £44.5m extension to Humber International Terminal, both to become operational in 2006

OTHER HIGHLIGHTS

- Interests in Cardiff Bay Partnership and Caspian Point sold for £33m
- Property disposal target extended by £50m to £250m
- Improved performance from USA business
- Completed £90.4m of new £205m share repurchase programme
- Dibden Terminal development rejected by government

GROUP RESULTS

- Group turnover +10%
- Underlying profit before tax** +4%
- Underlying earnings per share** +6%
- Dividend per share +5%

- Group profit before tax* –38%
- Earnings per share* –39%

Reflecting the £44.9m write-off of costs relating to the government's rejection of the Dibden Terminal development and £7.0m of restructuring costs

£349.1m £365.4m
03 04
UK PORTS & TRANSPORT TURNOVER £M

£138.1m £142.2m
03 04
UK PORTS & TRANSPORT UNDERLYING OPERATING PROFIT** £M

£401.3m £439.5m
03 04
GROUP TURNOVER £M

28.6p 30.3p
03 04
UNDERLYING EARNINGS PER SHARE** PENCE

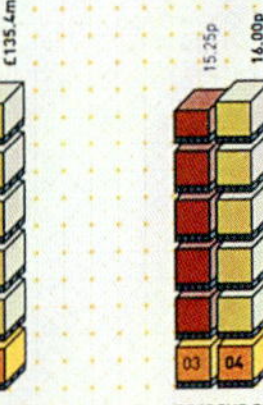

GROUP UNDERLYING PROFIT BEFORE TAX** £M

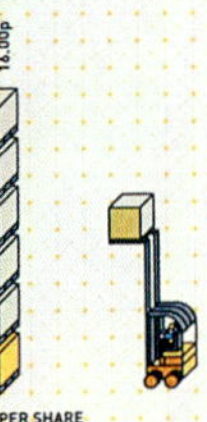

DIVIDEND PER SHARE PENCE

* Prior period restated for the effects of FRS 17 – Retirement Benefits and UITF Abstract 38 – Accounting for ESOP Trusts
** Before goodwill amortisation and exceptional items

PERFORMANCE
RESULTS
GOVERNANCE

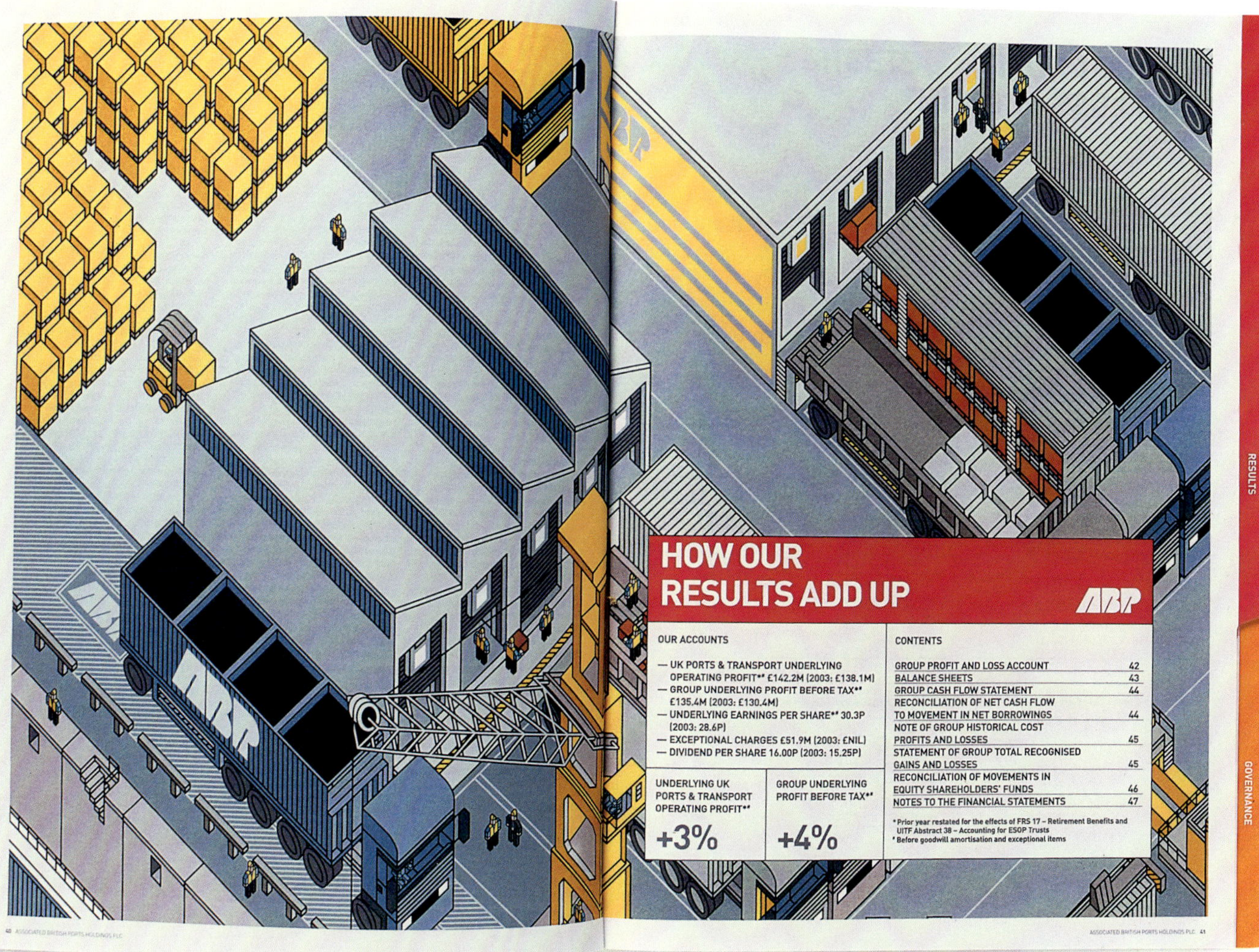

NOTES TO THE FINANCIAL STATEMENTS

23. PROVISIONS FOR LIABILITIES AND CHARGES (CONTINUED)

DEFERRED TAXATION

	GROUP 2004 £M	GROUP 2003* £M
Excess of capital allowances over depreciation	61.5	63.0
Other	(0.3)	(0.6)
	61.2	62.4

RESTRUCTURING

The restructuring provision relates to the voluntary early retirement benefit scheme, together with the restructuring of ABP Connect (see note 3).

ONEROUS CONTRACTS

The provision for onerous contracts represents amounts provided in relation to property leases where the unavoidable costs under the lease exceed the economic benefit. In determining the provision, cash flows have been discounted on a pre-tax basis.

OTHER

Other provisions primarily relate to obligations from commitments entered into as part of the development of Dibden Terminal (see note 3).

24. DEFERRED INCOME

Movements on capital investment grants are set out below:	GROUP 2004 £M	GROUP 2003 £M
Balance not yet credited to profit and loss account at 1 January	10.6	8.7
Grants receivable	0.5	2.5
	11.1	11.2
Credited to profit and loss account	(0.7)	(0.6)
BALANCE NOT YET CREDITED TO PROFIT AND LOSS ACCOUNT AT 31 DECEMBER	10.4	10.6

25. RETIREMENT BENEFITS

A. DESCRIPTION OF PLANS

The group participates in a number of pension schemes, principally in the UK. The major scheme is a funded defined benefits scheme – The Associated British Ports Group Pension Scheme. The defined benefits section of this scheme was closed to new members with effect from 1 April 2002. New members joining this scheme from 1 April 2002 are offered membership of a defined contributions section, which at 31 December 2004 constituted less than 0.6 per cent of the total asset value. The assets of the group's pension schemes are held in trust funds independent of its finances. Other schemes comprise defined contribution plans and unfunded retirement benefit arrangements in respect of former employees.

B. SUMMARY

(i) Profit and loss account

The total pension costs included in the profit and loss account for the group, which are disclosed in note 7 to the accounts, are derived as follows:

	2004 £M	2003* £M
Defined benefits scheme and unfunded retirement benefit arrangements (note 25c)	6.4	7.2
Defined contribution scheme	0.6	0.4
Cost of pension benefits in other group schemes	0.7	0.9
Operating profit charge	7.7	8.5
Net credit to finance income	(5.3)	(3.3)
PROFIT AND LOSS CHARGE	2.4	5.2

* Prior year restated for the effects of FRS 17 – Retirement Benefits and UITF Abstract 38 – Accounting for ESOP Trusts (note 35)

60 ASSOCIATED BRITISH PORTS HOLDINGS PLC

25. RETIREMENT BENEFITS (CONTINUED)

(ii) Balance sheet

The pension asset and unfunded retirement benefit liabilities (net of deferred tax liability) at 31 December were:

	2004 £M	2003* £M
Pension asset	24.3	26.3
Unfunded retirement benefit liabilities	(2.2)	(2.2)
NET PENSIONS ASSET	22.1	24.1

C. DEFINED BENEFITS SCHEME AND UNFUNDED RETIREMENT BENEFIT ARRANGEMENTS

The latest formal valuation of The Associated British Ports Group Pension Scheme was carried out as at 31 December 2003. The valuation of the liabilities detailed below has been derived by projecting forward the position as at 31 December 2003 and has been performed by an independent actuary, Hewitt, Bacon & Woodrow. FRS 17 gives the present value of pension liabilities by discounting pension commitments (including an allowance for salary growth), using a AA corporate bond yield.

The value of unfunded retirement benefit arrangements has also been assessed by the actuary Hewitt, Bacon & Woodrow, using the same assumptions as those used to calculate The Associated British Ports Group Pension Scheme liabilities.

(i) Assumptions

The major financial assumptions used by the actuary under FRS 17 as at 31 December were as follows:

	2004 %	2003 %	2002 %
Inflation	2.75	2.50	2.35
Rate of increase in pensionable salaries	4.25	4.00	3.85
Rate of increase for pensions in payment	2.75	2.50	2.35
Rate of increase for deferred pensions	2.75	2.50	2.35
Discount rate	5.30	5.40	5.50

(ii) Profit and loss account

The amount charged to operating profit and the amount credited to finance income during the year were as follows:

	2004 £M	2003* £M
OPERATING PROFIT		
Current service cost	(6.4)	(7.2)
Past service cost	–	–
Total charge to operating profit	(6.4)	(7.2)
FINANCE INCOME		
Expected returns on pension scheme assets	25.4	22.6
Interest on pension scheme liabilities	(19.9)	(19.1)
Interest on unfunded retirement benefit liabilities	(0.2)	(0.2)
Net credit to finance income	5.3	3.3
NET PENSION CHARGE	(1.1)	(3.9)

* Prior year restated for the effects of FRS 17 – Retirement Benefits and UITF Abstract 38 – Accounting for ESOP Trusts (note 35)

RESULTS

GOVERNANCE

ASSOCIATED BRITISH PORTS HOLDINGS PLC 61

is*

PRICEWATERHOUSECOOPERS

Annual Review 2004 Australia

Creative Director: Olifvia Swinn
Designer: Adam Trunk
Photographer: Tim Bauer

Printer: Penfold Buscombe
Paper: Beckett Radiance
Page count: 88 +cover

Print Run: 3,500
Size: 8.2677" x 11.6929"
Number of Images: 32

Client: PricewaterhouseCoopers

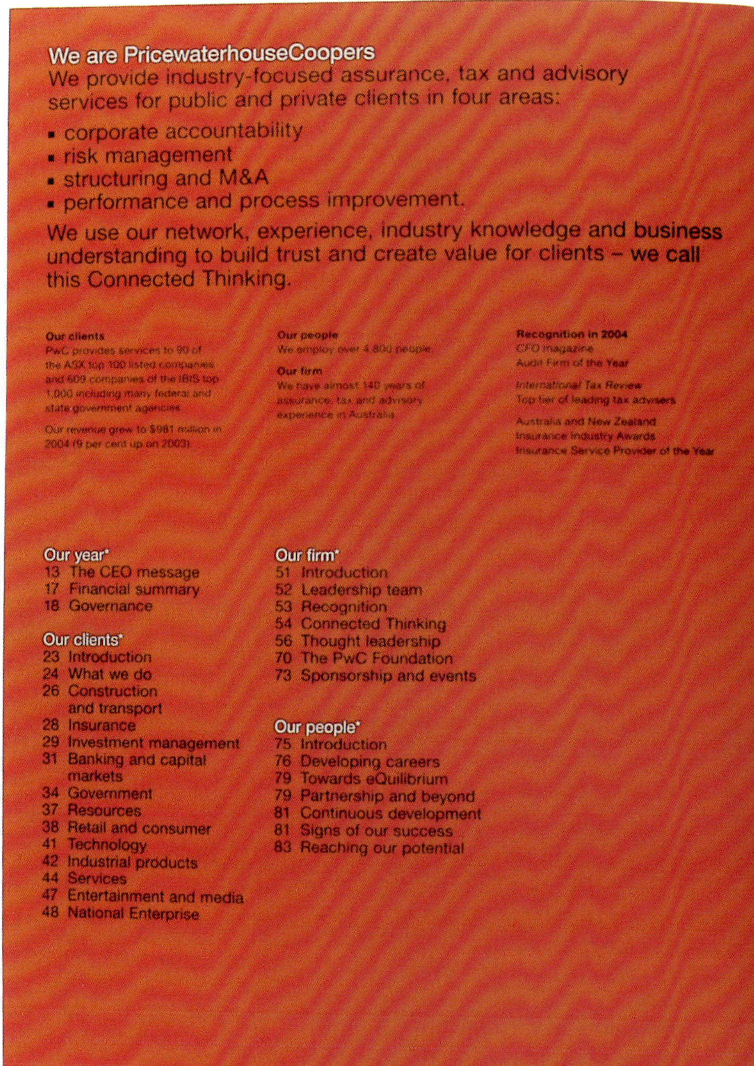

We are PricewaterhouseCoopers
We provide industry-focused assurance, tax and advisory services for public and private clients in four areas:

- corporate accountability
- risk management
- structuring and M&A
- performance and process improvement.

We use our network, experience, industry knowledge and business understanding to build trust and create value for clients – we call this Connected Thinking.

Our clients
PwC provides services to 90 of the ASX top 100 listed companies and 609 companies of the IBIS top 1,000 including many federal and state government agencies.

Our revenue grew to $981 million in 2004 (9 per cent up on 2003).

Our people
We employ over 4,800 people.

Our firm
We have almost 140 years of assurance, tax and advisory experience in Australia.

Recognition in 2004
CFO magazine
Audit Firm of the Year

International Tax Review
Top tier of leading tax advisers

Australia and New Zealand Insurance Industry Awards
Insurance Service Provider of the Year

PricewaterhouseCoopers is*
aware that it takes more than rhetoric and good intentions to fulfil our mission to be the professional services firm of our time. We constantly remind ourselves that it requires the highest standards of work and behaviour in everything we do. It is a mission requiring unceasing dedication, hard work, investment in our people and an unfailing commitment to our clients. We know that trust is not given automatically but must always be earned. And in fulfilment of that trust, we do not shirk our responsibility to help shape and promote confidence in the Australian market and regulatory environment. In these and many other ways we try our hardest to ensure that our firm...

Annual Review 2004 1

Q&A with DesignworksEnterpriseIG

What was the client's directive?

To create an Annual Report that documents their past year's performance and achievements using their brand positioning, "Connected Thinking," and create a report that reinforces PwC's positioning as the number one financial services firm in the Australian market.

How did you define the problem?

How does one of the top four global accounting firms break clear of the opposition? How does a global brand have relevance and context in the local market? "We have 100 pages of information to document... it has to be informative, engaging and compelling."

What was the approach?

PricewaterhouseCoopers is the leading financial professional services firm in Australia. The is* report showcases the industry expertise, thought leadership and business understanding needed to build trust and create value for clients. As a testament to the people who work at PwC, the report starts and finishes with themed black and white portraits of employees, supported by their own philosophies. The report is divided into three sections: Clients, People and Firm. Throughout the report the reader finds factual industry case studies to provide evidence of industry specialisation, and an inspirational section dedicated to thought leadership, which is headed-up by editorial images of influential people from the past, such as Einstein, Picasso and Muhammad Ali.

Which disciplines or people helped you with the project?

Apart from the editorial content, a large part of the visual equity of the PwC palette is the reliance on great photography, so a synergistic relationship with the photographer, stylist, and producers is very important. The high quality print production would not have been possible without a dedicated team of art workers and a print specialist managing all the presswork. And of course the open-mindedness of the client and the unwavering tenacity of our Account Director made the report more successful.

Were you happy with the result? What could have been better?

We were constantly challenging the client to take a more creative approach to the Annual Report as well as making it informative. From an A-Class portraiture photographer to images of inspirational heroes throughout history to recommending the most expensive stock and print production, the client continually gave us the mandate to create the best report we could and it gave us great satisfaction to see the end result. As far as what could be better... the "Clients" section is a little too long and a little too text heavy. Typically as creatives we would like the report to be more visually appealing, but the client has to cover off all areas of their business and supporting evidence via case studies. So it was an agreeable compromise.

What was the client's response?

The client was very happy with the result. It gave them a great platform to engage staff via the portraiture, and it also gave them international kudos for winning a silver and gold award in New York.

How involved was the CEO in your meetings and presentations?

The main point of contact throughout the process was the writer/editor (who was an employee of PwC). Although the CEO was not present in the creative meetings, he was consistently involved at integral sign off stages of the Annual Report.

How involved are designers with writing?

As an organisation we believe very strongly that design is empty without great writing. Gone are the days when designers put lorem ipsom in as headlines. We employ 2 fulltime writers in our NZ offices who are intensely involved in all projects. In Sydney we are still looking to recruit a fulltime writer, however as designers we find it critical to good work to either work on our own copy or to bring in a freelance writer.

How would you define the success of an Annual Report?

The success of an AR is one that is a true brand touchstone.

How important are awards to your clients?

Awards are a very good tool for us with our clients in that they create a lot of kudos for them within their organisation. I don't think they would slavishly do something that went against their brand to win an award but winning really prestigious or renowned awards means that they are competing on a world stage with some of the best companies in the world and for down under clients that is desirable. For us as designers the recognition and enthusiasm for awards means that often we can push more lateral and engaging solutions.

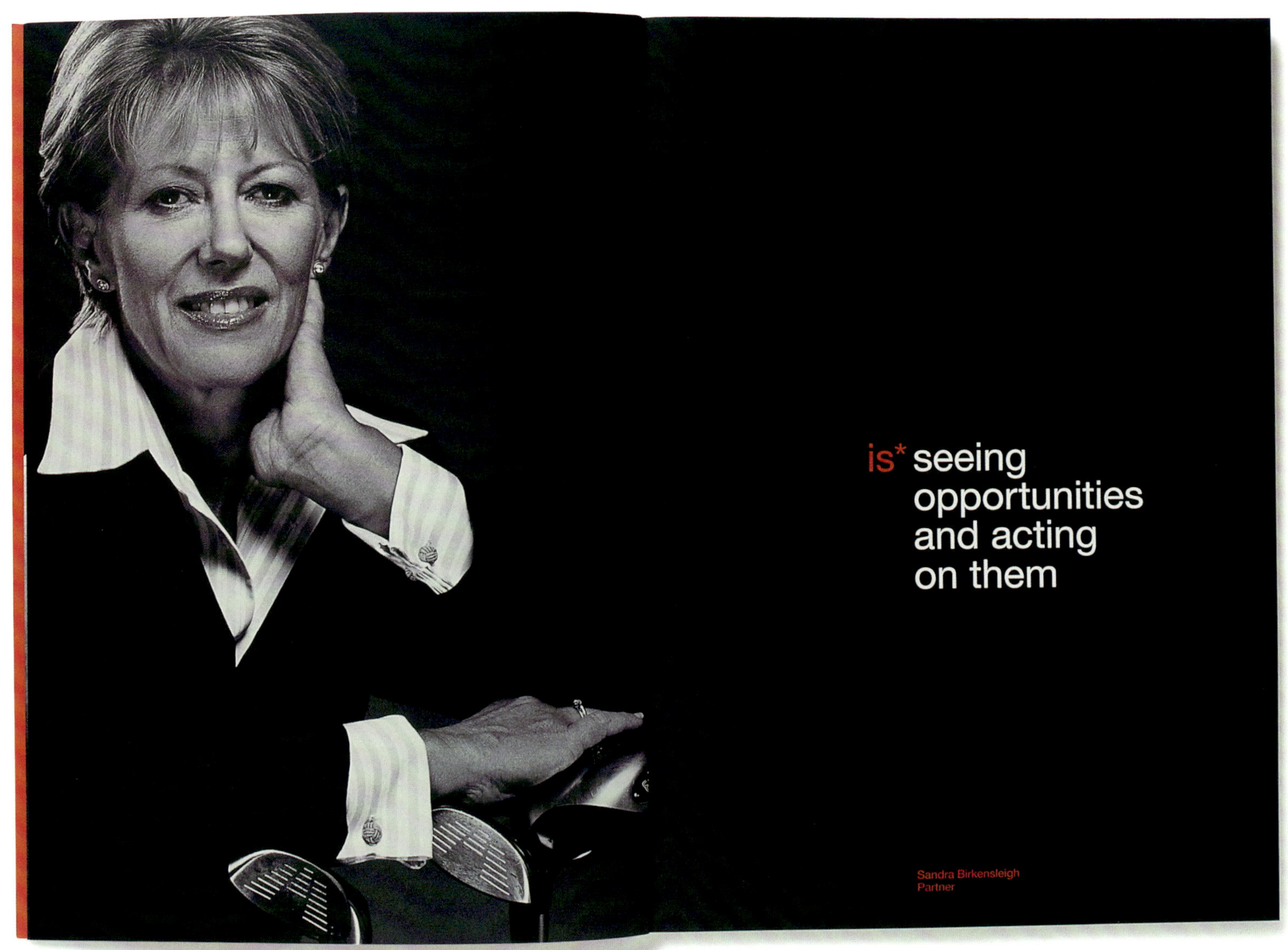

As designers we find it is critical to work on our own copy or bring in a freelance writer.

is* the ceo message

Another negative consequence of over-regulation is a risk-averse business culture. Instead of enhancing Australia's reputation as a 'smart nation', focused on innovation and other performance-enhancing opportunities, this ever-increasing volume of governance obligations could stagnate our business culture.

For these reasons we are actively supportive of current moves to investigate and report on ways to improve the existing stock of regulations, reform the regulatory process, and rationalise overlapping regulations between the three tiers of government in Australia.

Building on success

Finally, I cannot miss the opportunity to mention some of the firm's many pleasing achievements for 2004, during which we worked hard to assist business in the development of more robust and transparent corporate reporting models, while retaining its focus on core activities.

The firm's work on foreign exchange losses at the National Australia Bank was truly brand defining. The report has been widely recognised as being an easy-to-read analysis of an extremely complex matter. It is also the first investigative report of its type to tackle the important issue of the culture of an organistion. The PwC team worked closely with the Australian Prudential Regulation Authority (APRA) whose subsequent report was, I believe, a significant affirmation of the work of the PwC team.

Our work advising Macquarie Communications Infrastructure Group on its successful $3 billion UK acquisition of ntl:Broadcast – one of the case studies detailed in this Annual Review – was an example of the breadth and depth of our cross-border networks, skills and industry knowledge.

In addition to our extensive advisory work among the country's major companies and institutions, we also worked with many dynamic medium-sized Australian companies to help them achieve their goals. The diversity of this work is a reflection of the diversity of the Australian business world itself, ranging from advising Super Cheap Auto on its IPO, to helping Warrnambool Cheese and Butter Factory achieve its growth objectives.

We are also proud to have deepened our connections within the communities in which we operate. The PwC Foundation that we launched in 2002 is now an integral part of the PwC culture, and making significant contributions to causes about which our people are passionate. These include relief for the victims of the recent Asian tsunami, helping disadvantaged young people, reducing poverty, and addressing pressing health and environmental issues.

The firm's appointment as the official professional services adviser and sponsor to the Melbourne 2006 Commonwealth Games is a further gratifying mark of our community standing.

Our performance in 2004 in all of these ways is wholly due to the efforts of our people and the support of our clients. So I would like to thank our people for their hard work and commitment to our clients.

Our efforts were recognised in 2004 when, for the third time in four years, the firm was awarded *CFO* magazine's Audit Firm of the Year accolade. For the fourth year running we were also awarded the highest recognition in *International Tax Review's* Leading Tax Advisers survey.

Late in the year, I announced that Rob Ward, our national managing partner and formerly leader of our Assurance practice, would move to New York as deputy leader of our global Assurance business.

As well as the recognition implicit in this appointment of the outstanding quality of our local Assurance practice, Rob's appointment both highlights and confirms the global connections and resources that make our firm truly unique. These strengths were further underlined recently when I also announced the appointment of Paul Koenig, our tax and legal services leader, to the Eurofirm's tax and legal leadership team and to the German firm's tax leadership team. Paul will remain a partner of the Australian firm and his appointments in Europe will further strengthen our ties with PwC's global network.

Both these moves are reminders that the phrase 'Connected Thinking' is much more than a market positioning statement for PwC. It truly represents what is most distinctive in our approach.

We begin 2005 with a great sense of excitement and expectation. We are proud of the recognised vibrancy and dynamism of the firm, of our record of always reaching out for the best thinking, stretching for the highest standards, and leveraging our global resources to build value for our clients.

I trust that the 2004 PwC annual review provides you with some useful insights into our firm, the business issues affecting our industry and our clients, and the work through which we aim to be the professional services firm of our time.

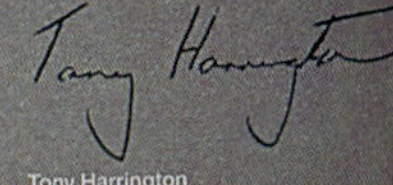

Tony Harrington

is* our financial summary

Total revenue for calendar 2004 was $981 million, representing an increase of 9 per cent on the previous year and confirming that PricewaterhouseCoopers comfortably maintains its position as the leading professional services firm in Australia.

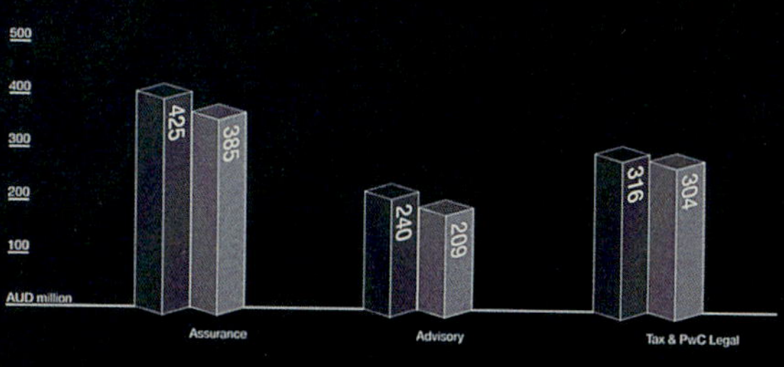

Revenue by line of service

2004 2003

Revenue by line of service*

	2004	2003	Growth
Assurance	424,725	385,429	10.2%
Advisory	239,894	208,694	15.0%
Tax & Legal**	316,046	304,216	3.9%
Totals	980,665	898,339	9.2%

Revenue by market segment

	2004	2003	Growth
Assurance – Institutional	190,006	187,626	1.3%
Advisory – Institutional	292,489	244,119	19.8%
Total Institutional	482,495	431,745	11.8%
Total National Enterprise	498,170	466,594	6.8%
Totals	980,665	898,339	9.2%

*These figures are consistent with PricewaterhouseCoopers' global reporting
**Legal refers to PwC Legal, an associated PwC firm

Clients by industry

	2004	Share of business
Consumer and Industrial Products	233,912	24%
Consumer Goods and Retail		
Industrial Products		
Financial Services	252,925	26%
Banking and Capital Markets		
Insurance and Investment Management		
Resources, Services and Government	343,526	35%
Government		
Resources		
Services		
Construction and Transport		
Technology, Information, Communications & Entertainment	150,302	15%
Technology		
Entertainment and Media		
Totals	980,665	100%

is* thought leadership

Maintaining profitable growth is the challenge for major banks

Australia's major banks seem assured of strong profits for the immediate future as many factors that have underpinned their record growth remain largely unchanged: the buoyant economy, consumer confidence, low interest rates and effective management.

"Whether profits can keep increasing at the same rate is a key question," says PwC Banking and Capital Markets Leader Rahoul Chowdry. "The challenge for the Big Four will be to fine tune operations, which over recent years have become increasingly efficient, without taking undue risks as they pursue growth."

PwC's analysis confirms that average profits of the Big Four rose almost 6 per cent in 2004. Their combined total profits, which reached $10.54 billion in 2002 before slipping back to $10.5 billion in 2003, surged to $11.1 billion in 2004.

The 2004 result reflected improvements across most key measures tracked in PwC's six-monthly analysis. Growth in net interest income was 7.2 per cent. Non-interest income grew by about 11 per cent. Bad debts dipped below 0.5 per cent, making the asset quality of Australian banks among the best in the world.

Similarly, the 'super regional' banks, Suncorp and St. George Bank, also benefited from market conditions and experienced very strong financial results. Market share growth from non-traditional business lines and further geographic expansion pushed up profits. The combined earnings of the two financial services providers grew by $1.5 billion or 25 per cent on the previous year.

While costs rose 10 per cent, partly because of acquisitions and restructuring, banks also invested in additional staff, opened new branches, refurbished old ones and spent money on customer management software. They increased spending in these areas to attract customers and offset the steady decline in interest income over the past five years.

"Banks are looking for a point of difference and customer service is currently one of the most important," says Chowdry. "Competition for business will remain fierce."

Growth in domestic credit averaged a record 14 per cent over the year to September, underpinning the booming home loan market. Housing loan portfolios were up 20 per cent during the year; however, they grew at only 7 per cent in the second half, indicating the beginning of the much-publicised slowdown.

Business credit growth picked up in 2004, averaging 8 per cent and banks will rely more heavily on business lending as growth in other areas, particularly home lending, declines.

"The banks are being pushed into riskier home loan products as their balance sheet growth slows," says Chowdry. "Business banking is seen by many as the next growth area. Maintaining an appropriate balance between risk and reward in both areas will be particularly important."

Non-interest income grew marginally from 44 per cent of income to 45 per cent over the year and banks will continue their efforts to increase earnings in this area. Fee income from managed funds and other investment products rose, and results from insurance were good. Wealth management is likely to continue to be a source of growth for the banks, particularly if stock markets continue their recent good performance.

As the slowdown in top-line growth continues, there will be a renewed focus on making back-office processes more efficient and on smarter use of technology, particularly as new global and local regulatory changes will increase costs in the short term.

These include the move to international financial reporting standards from 1 January 2005 and SEC registrants' obligation to comply with more stringent governance standards under the Sarbanes-Oxley legislation. Additionally, the Australian Prudential Regulation Authority has mandated that banks must meet the Basel II Accord's capital adequacy and risk management standards from 2007.

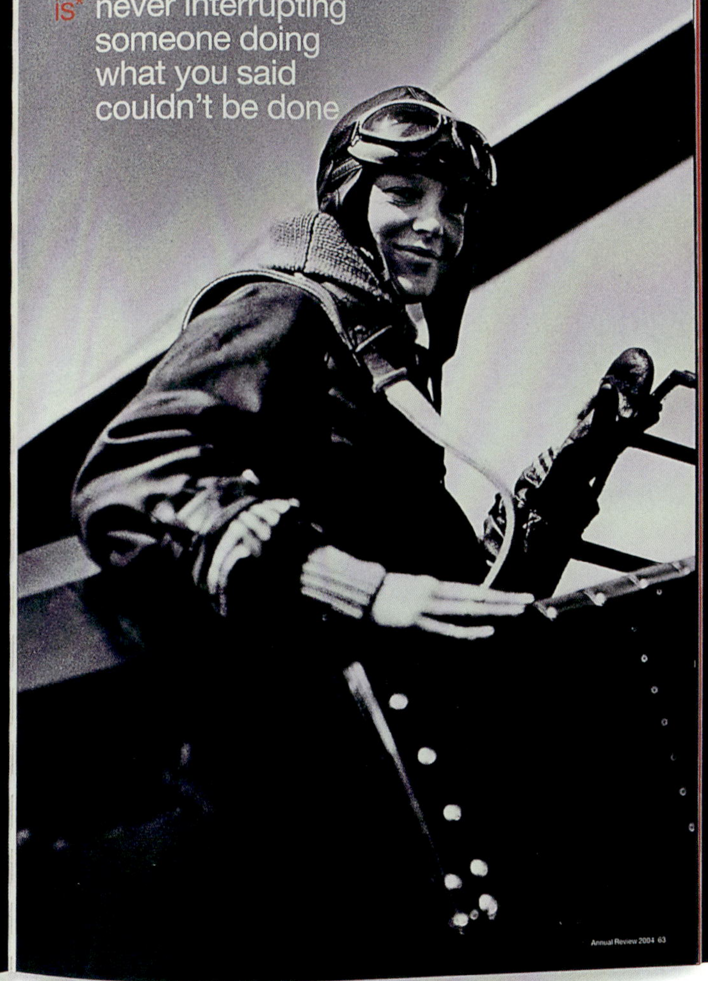

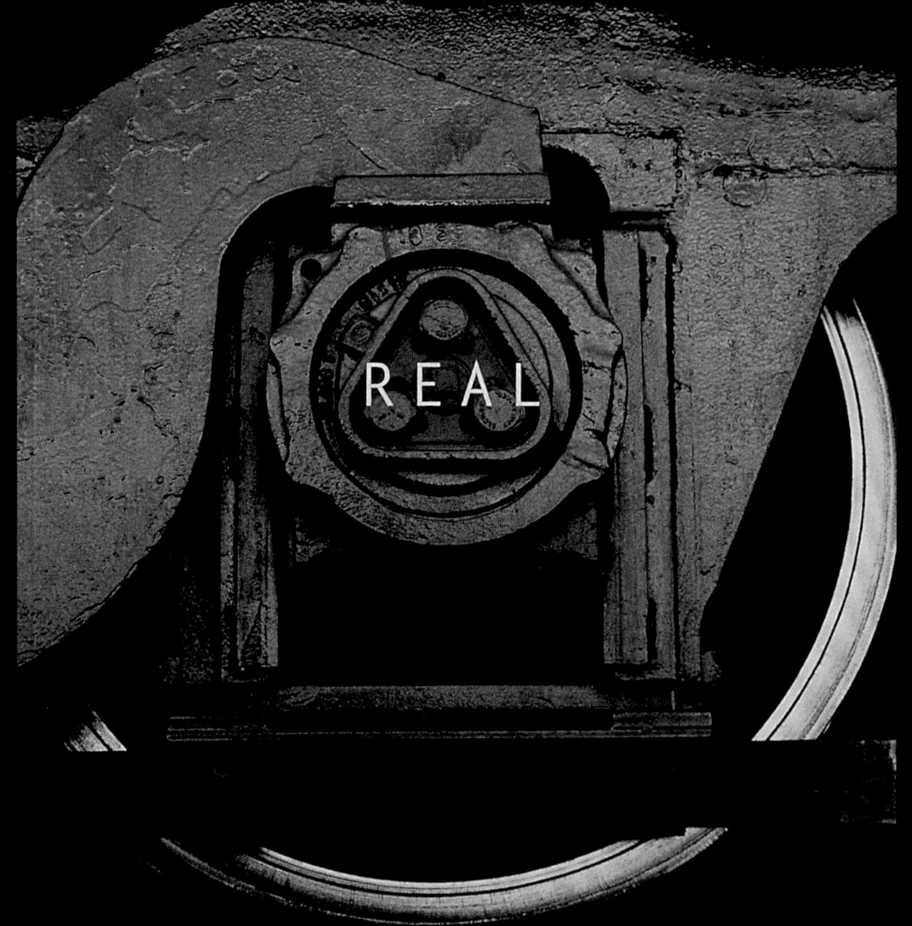
REAL

Creative Director: David Kohler
Designer: Eunice Woo
Photographer: Todd Boebel, Charlie Westerman
Printer: Digital Color Concepts
Paper: 100lb Scheufelen Consort Royal Brilliance Blue White
Page count: 132 +4 (cover)
Print run: 33,000
Size: 8" x 10"
Number of images: 6
Client: GATX Corporation

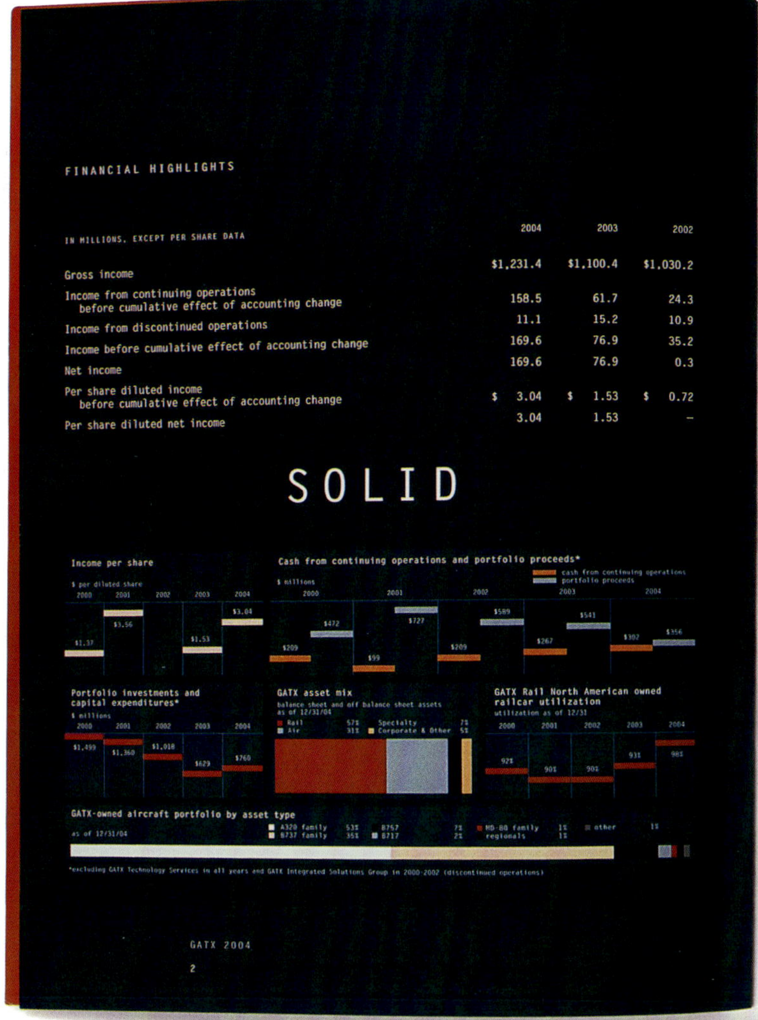
FINANCIAL HIGHLIGHTS

IN MILLIONS, EXCEPT PER SHARE DATA	2004	2003	2002
Gross income	$1,231.4	$1,100.4	$1,030.2
Income from continuing operations before cumulative effect of accounting change	158.5	61.7	24.3
Income from discontinued operations	11.1	15.2	10.9
Income before cumulative effect of accounting change	169.6	76.9	35.2
Net income	169.6	76.9	0.3
Per share diluted income before cumulative effect of accounting change	$ 3.04	$ 1.53	$ 0.72
Per share diluted net income	3.04	1.53	–

SOLID

GATX 2004
2

DEAR SHAREHOLDERS

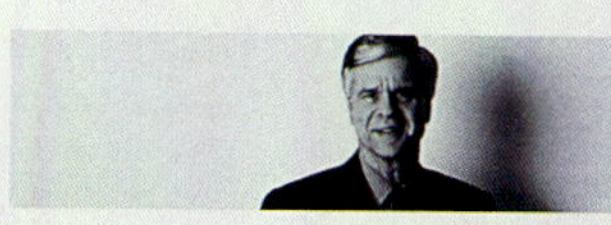
RONALD H. ZECH, CHAIRMAN AND CEO

I am pleased with the progress GATX made in 2004 and proud of what our people accomplished. After three very challenging years, 2004 felt like the beginning of a return to normalcy with an increased focus on growth.

In 2004, the rail industry improved significantly as order backlogs trended up at railcar manufacturers, and shipments and carloadings on North American railroads increased in all our key markets. With the strengthening rail market, we increased utilization of the rail fleet from 93% to 98% during the year. To meet demand, we took more than 1,300 railcars from inventory and put them into active service. And with a stronger market, we made significant new fleet investments, acquiring 6,200 cars, both new and in the secondary market, and increased our investment in our locomotive fleet. We also saw a rise in lease renewal rates for the first time in several years and expect that positive trend to continue in 2005. Our European units made progress in operating profitability and also enhanced their business models. In 2005, we will build on our momentum by continuing to maximize the value of our existing railcars, improve efficiency in maintenance, and profitably grow the fleet.

In spite of significant growth in global revenue passenger miles, the air market remained volatile in 2004, and airlines, particularly North American air carriers, continued to struggle. Through this turbulence, our Air group continued to maintain high fleet utilization and managed 50 aircraft transitions with little downtime. Lease rates, particularly on the newer, narrowbody aircraft that make up a significant portion of our fleet, returned to levels not seen since prior to 9/11. While this is certainly a positive note, risks in this business remain, and our Air group continues its diligence in monitoring and managing both our and our partners' fleets. In 2005, we will continue to pursue new management and partnership opportunities and focus on maintaining a high level of fleet utilization while increasing lease rates and profitability.

Our Specialty portfolio again contributed nicely to our bottom line in 2004 – and we expect it to do so for many years to come. The largest segment of our Specialty portfolio is our shipping and marine joint ventures, which performed particularly well as worldwide demand for dry bulk items and chemicals increased, driving cargo rates and vessel demand higher. The Specialty portfolio quality improved dramatically in 2004, and we had another solid year from remarketing income. We will continue to pursue new investments in shipping and marine and other targeted assets in 2005.

The results at American Steamship Company (ASC), our Great Lakes shipping operation, also reflected the healthier North American economy and high demand for iron ore and other core industrial materials. ASC has improved efficiency and utilization, and, in 2005, we expect ASC to further capitalize on a strong shipping market.

As the positive momentum clearly began to take hold in 2004, I took time to reflect on the progress we have made in recent years and on management transition.

3

Q&A with Addison

What was the client's directive?

To show the strength, value and expertise of GATX Corporation as a leasing partner.

How did you define the problem?

Unlike other financial institutions, GATX owns physical assets that retain value.

What was the approach?

We showcased the physical assets of the company and used them as a metaphor to position GATX as Strong, Solid, Lasting, Experienced and Flexible. Striking black-and-white photography, rich in detail, lent a deep sense of genuineness, precision and value.

Which disciplines or people helped you with the project?

Design, photography, writing.

Were you happy with the result?

Yes, we were very happy with the results.

What was the client's response?

The Annual Report and the theme Real became the platform for all corporate communications within GATX.

How involved was the CEO in your meetings, presentations, etc.?

The project was lead by the CFO and the Director of Investor Relations.

Do you feel that designers are becomi ng more involved in copywriting?

Yes, Addison wrote the headlines and theme for this year's book.

How do you define success in Annual Report design?

When an Annual Report delivers a cohesive message from the front cover to the last page.

How important are awards to your client?

They weren't important until they started winning them.

This Annual Report and its theme became the basis for all corporate communications within GATX.

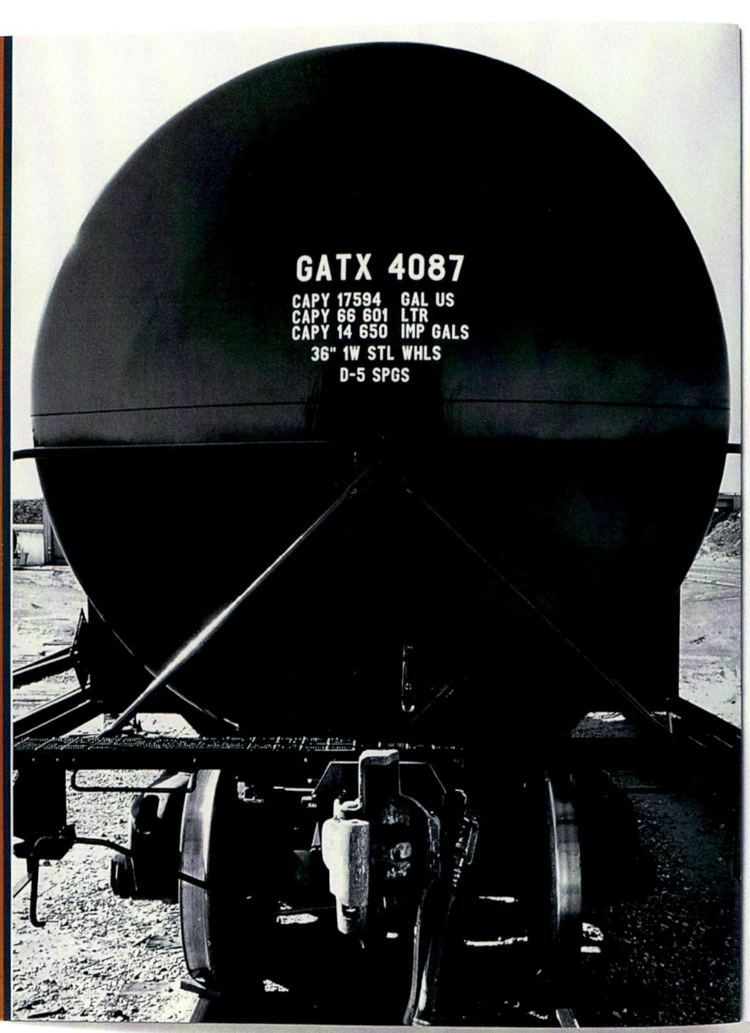

OUR FLEET OF SPECIALIZED TANK CARS SERVES THE TRANSPORTATION REQUIREMENTS OF THE CHEMICAL, FOOD, AND PETROLEUM INDUSTRIES IN NORTH AMERICA.

STRONG

Miles of railcars along the tracks; commercial aircraft traversing the globe; ships churning across the sea and the Great Lakes — the assets of GATX support the economic infrastructure of North America and the world. These assets are also the foundation upon which GATX Corporation was built. GATX was founded in 1898 to lease railcars to shippers and railroads. In 2004, with owned and managed fleets of approximately 168,000 railcars, 874 locomotives, 229 commercial aircraft, and a growing fleet of marine vessels, GATX has a leading presence in the transportation leasing industry.

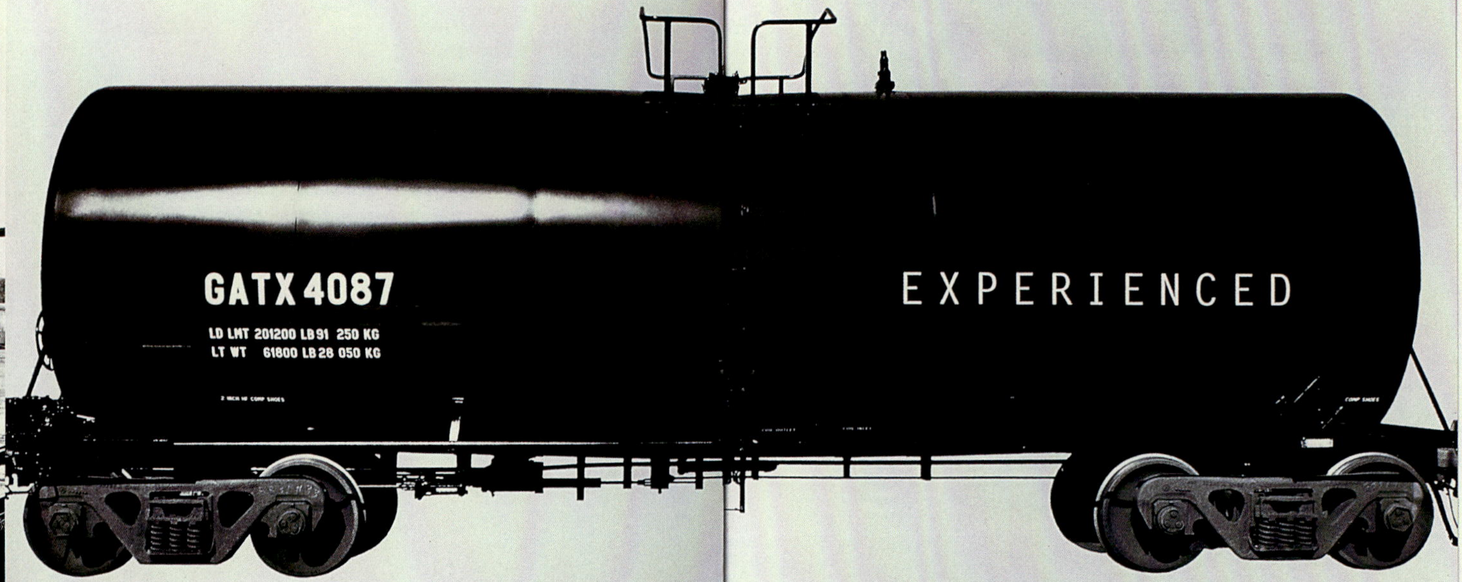

EXPERIENCED

WE KNOW OUR ASSETS INSIDE AND OUT, AND WE WORK WITH OUR CUSTOMERS TO FIND THE RIGHT SOLUTIONS TO MEET THEIR PARTICULAR NEEDS.

At GATX, our day-to-day business appears simple: buy a railcar or aircraft, lease it to a customer. But these assets are vital to the economy and our lives — whether it's a tank car carrying chemicals to support manufacturing, an inland vessel moving iron ore across the Great Lakes for a revitalized steel industry, or people in an aircraft flying home for the weekend — a great deal of skill, experience, and expertise stands behind each asset. With 106 years of rail leasing expertise, 37 years in commercial aircraft, and more than 30 years in shipping, GATX knows and understands each individual asset and each market those assets serve.

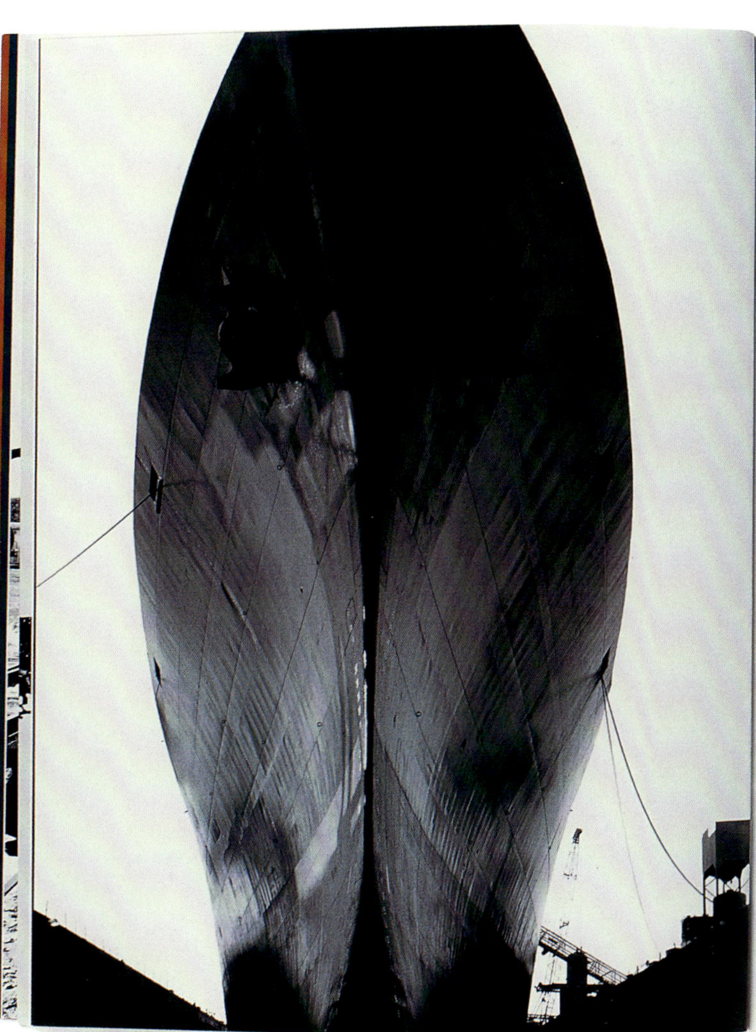

WITH A BROAD MARKET FOR OUR ASSETS, WE CAN RE-LEASE OR REMARKET – OR EVEN MODIFY OR RECONFIGURE – THE ASSETS FOR NEW CUSTOMERS OR THE CHANGING NEEDS OF OUR EXISTING CUSTOMERS.

FLEXIBLE

What appears simple can be complex – but by knowing our assets, we take that complexity and turn it into flexibility to meet our customers' needs. With more than 60 different types of tank cars, numerous freight cars, locomotives, and aircraft configurations, and a diverse pool of marine assets, GATX employs engineers and technical experts to customize our assets for our customers' particular requirements.

Beyond the physical configuration, GATX also works with the customer to find the appropriate asset financing solution. And we have taken these skills abroad, with a growing rail presence in Europe and air assets leased throughout the world. In adapting our assets to the changing needs of the market, GATX provides the flexibility and customization necessary to keep our customers moving.

15

NOTES TO CONSOLIDATED FINANCIAL STATEMENTS — (Continued)

CONSOLIDATED QUARTERLY FINANCIAL DATA
(unaudited)

	First Quarter(c)	Second Quarter	Third Quarter	Fourth Quarter	Total
		In millions, except per share data			
2004					
Gross Income	$257.8	$283.0	$325.3	$365.3	$1,231.4
Ownership costs and operating expenses from continuing operations(a)	191.9	214.2	217.8	225.1	849.0
Income from continuing operations	19.7	19.7	48.2	70.9	158.5
Income (loss) from discontinued operations	3.2	15.1	(7.5)	.3	11.1
Net income	$ 22.9	$ 34.8	$ 40.7	$ 71.2	$ 169.6
Per Share Data:(b)					
Basic:					
Income from continuing operations	$ .40	$ .40	$ .98	$ 1.43	$ 3.21
Income (loss) from discontinued operations	.06	.31	(.16)	.01	.23
Total	$ .46	$ .71	$ .82	$ 1.44	$ 3.44
Diluted:(d)					
Income from continuing operations	$ .38	$ .38	$ .85	$ 1.23	$ 2.86
Income (loss) from discontinued operations	.06	.28	(.12)	.01	.18
Total	$ .44	$ .66	$ .73	$ 1.24	$ 3.04
2003					
Gross Income	$251.9	$282.2	$290.4	$275.9	$1,100.4
Ownership costs and operating expenses from continuing operations(a)	191.5	210.1	208.9	207.2	817.7
Income from continuing operations	.3	18.1	21.3	22.0	61.7
Income from discontinued operations	1.5	6.7	1.4	5.6	15.2
Net income	$ 1.8	$ 24.8	$ 22.7	$ 27.6	$ 76.9
Per Share Data:(b)					
Basic:					
Income from continuing operations	$ .01	$ .37	$ .43	$ .45	$ 1.26
Income from discontinued operations	.03	.14	.03	.11	.31
Total	$ .04	$ .51	$ .46	$ .56	$ 1.57
Diluted:(d)					
Income from continuing operations	$ .01	$ .37	$ .42	$ .42	$ 1.24
Income from discontinued operations	.03	.13	.03	.10	.29
Total	$ .04	$ .50	$ .45	$ .52	$ 1.53

(a) Operating expenses include maintenance expense, marine operating expenses, and other operating expenses.

(b) Quarterly earnings per share results may not be additive, as per share amounts are computed independently for each quarter and the full year is based on the respective weighted average common shares and common stock equivalents outstanding.

(c) Financial data for the Technology segment has been segregated as discontinued operations for all periods presented. As a result, amounts have been restated from Form 10-Q filed with the SEC for the quarterly period ended March 31, 2004.

(d) Amounts shown as diluted earnings per share in the first, second and third quarters of 2004 and the third and fourth quarters of 2003 have been restated from amounts previously reported to reflect the impact of EITF 04-8. See Note 2 to the consolidated financial statements.

Note: Certain amounts have been reclassified to conform to the current presentation.

98

Item 9. *Changes in and Disagreements with Accountants on Accounting and Financial Disclosure*

None.

Item 9A. *Controls and Procedures*

Management's Report Regarding the Effectiveness of Disclosure Controls and Procedures

The Company's management, with the participation of its principal executive and principal financial officers, have conducted an evaluation of the Company's disclosure controls and procedures (as defined in Rules 13a-15(e) and 15d-15(e) of the Securities Exchange Act of 1934 (the "Exchange Act")). Based on such evaluation, the Company's Chief Executive Officer and Chief Financial Officer have concluded that as of the end of the period covered by this annual report, the Company's disclosure controls and procedures were effective.

Management's Report Regarding the Effectiveness of Internal Control and Procedures

The Company's management is responsible for establishing and maintaining adequate internal control over financial reporting as defined in Rules 13a-15(f) and 15d-15(f) of the Exchange Act for the Company. The Company's internal control over financial reporting is designed to provide reasonable assurance regarding the reliability of financial reporting and the preparation of financial statements for external purposes in accordance with generally accepted accounting principles. The Company's internal control over financial reporting includes those policies and procedures that:

(i) pertain to the maintenance of records that, in reasonable detail, accurately and fairly reflect the transactions and dispositions of the assets of the Company;

(ii) provide reasonable assurance that transactions are recorded as necessary to permit preparation of financial statements in accordance with generally accepted accounting principles, and that receipts and expenditures of the Company are being made only in accordance with authorizations of management and directors of the Company; and

(iii) provide reasonable assurance regarding prevention or timely detection of unauthorized acquisition, use or disposition of the Company's assets that could have a material effect on the financial statements.

Because of its inherent limitations, internal control over a financial reporting may not prevent or detect misstatements. In addition, projections of any evaluation of effectiveness to future periods are subject to the risk that controls may become inadequate as a result of changes in conditions, or that the degree of compliance with the applicable policies and procedures may deteriorate.

The Company's management, with the participation of its principal executive and principal financial officers, has conducted an evaluation of the Company's internal control over financial reporting as of the end of the period covered by this annual report based on the framework in Internal Control-Integrated Framework issued by the Committee of Sponsoring Organizations of the Treadway Commission. Such evaluation included reviewing the documentation of the Company's internal controls, evaluating the design effectiveness of the internal controls and testing their operating effectiveness.

Based on such evaluation, the Company's management has concluded that as of the end of the period covered by this annual report, the Company's internal control over financial reporting was effective.

Ernst & Young LLP, the independent registered public accounting firm that audited the financial statements included in this annual report has issued an attestation report on the management's assessment of the Company's internal control over financial reporting. That report appears below.

99

“We ride with you.”

HARLEY-DAVIDSON
MOTOR
COMPANY

HARLEY-DAVIDSON, INC. 2004 ANNUAL REPORT

Art Director: Jason Jones
Designers: Adam Dines, Ron Berkheimer

Photographer: Charlie Simokaitis
Writer: Bob Klein

Printer: Litho Inc, MN
Page count: 80 +4
Number of images: 24

Print run: 404,000
Size: 8" x 10"
Paper: 80# Utopia 2

Dull text, 70# Mohawk Opaque Smooth
Client: Harley-Davidson

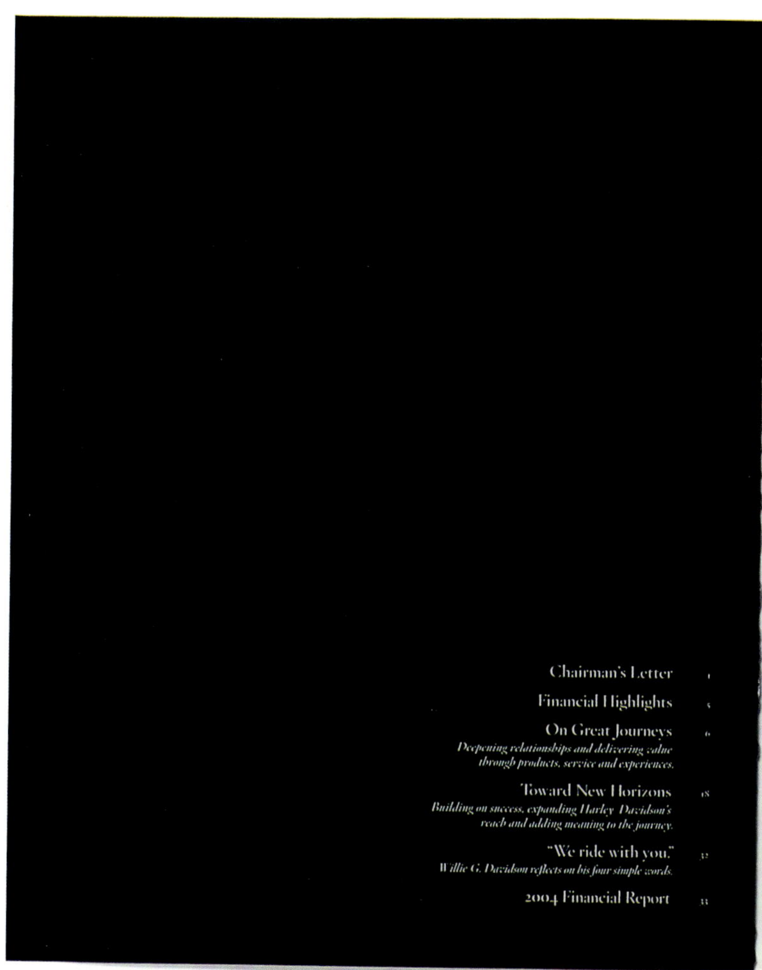

Dear Fellow Shareholders,

The first time I walked through the front door at 3700 West Juneau Avenue as a Harley-Davidson employee back in 1975, one thing was highly apparent.

At the time, Harley-Davidson had four V-Twin motorcycles in its model line. The newest of the bunch was going on five years old and I was the person who had just been tapped as the Company's vice president of engineering, with the mission of jump-starting product development.

However, the thing that was so apparent wasn't the volume of work ahead, ample though it was. It was the deep sense of awareness that all our employees had for the central importance of both the motorcycles and the whole motorcycling experience in the lives of our customers.

Harley-Davidson® motorcycles were truly "more than a machine," to borrow an advertising phrase from that era. And the people who worked at Harley-Davidson were so deeply attuned to this everlasting relationship between rider, motorcycle and experience because many were riders themselves.

Today, we have another phrase for it: "we ride with you." First given voice by Willie G. Davidson at Harley-Davidson's 95th Anniversary celebration, "we ride with you" expresses the relationship, both literal and emotional, between Harley-Davidson, its customers and all of the Company's stakeholders.

HARLEY-DAVIDSON 2004 ANNUAL REPORT 1

Q&A with VSA Partners

What was the client's directive?

Our assignment was to thoroughly and clearly communicate to Harley-Davidson investors and stakeholders about the Company's 2004 fiscal year performance and overall brand accomplishments.

How did you define the problem?

Life at Harley-Davidson is about great journeys, a series of touchpoints that produce inspired moments for riders and results for shareholders. Harley-Davidson is a company with an incessant desire and drive to go new places, dedicated to keeping products and experiences relevant to new times and ever changing customer desires. They do this by staying close to their customers.

What was the approach?

At Harley-Davidson, motorcycles are "more than a machine." Harley has a deep sense of awareness for the central importance of both the motorcycles and the whole motorcycling experience in the lives of its customers. They connect with riders by being riders. "We ride with you" says it all.

Which disciplines or people helped you with the project?

Writer: Bob Klein, Harley-Davidson Manager, Corporate Communication. Photographer: Charlie Simokaitis.

Were you happy with the result? What could have been better?

Yes. More pages.

What was the client's response?

Harley is Harley, yet Harley is humble. The Motor Company has always been very appreciative of our collaborative effort and ability to inspire new ideas that have challenged and helped grow their brand.

How involved was the CEO in your meetings and presentations?

Jeffrey L. Bleustein was Harley-Davidson's active CEO when the 2004 Annual Report rolled off the press. His involvement was crucial to the strategic and thematic development of the AR's overall framework and messaging. His continued and valued interest was apparent right up to the press date.

Do you feel that designers are becoming more involved in copywriting?

Content is King and design follows. In order for one to effectively communicate design, one must first understand the content. With that in mind, if called upon, I believe most designers can… and often do, play an important role when it comes to copywriting.

How do you define success in Annual Report design?

Holding a relationship with a client that has lasted 16 years. And clearly communicating the essence of the company you represent in a way that captivates the shareholder's imagination.

How important are awards to your client?

They very much enjoy seeing our collaborative work come to fruition in the form of awards and acclaim.

Content is King, and design follows.

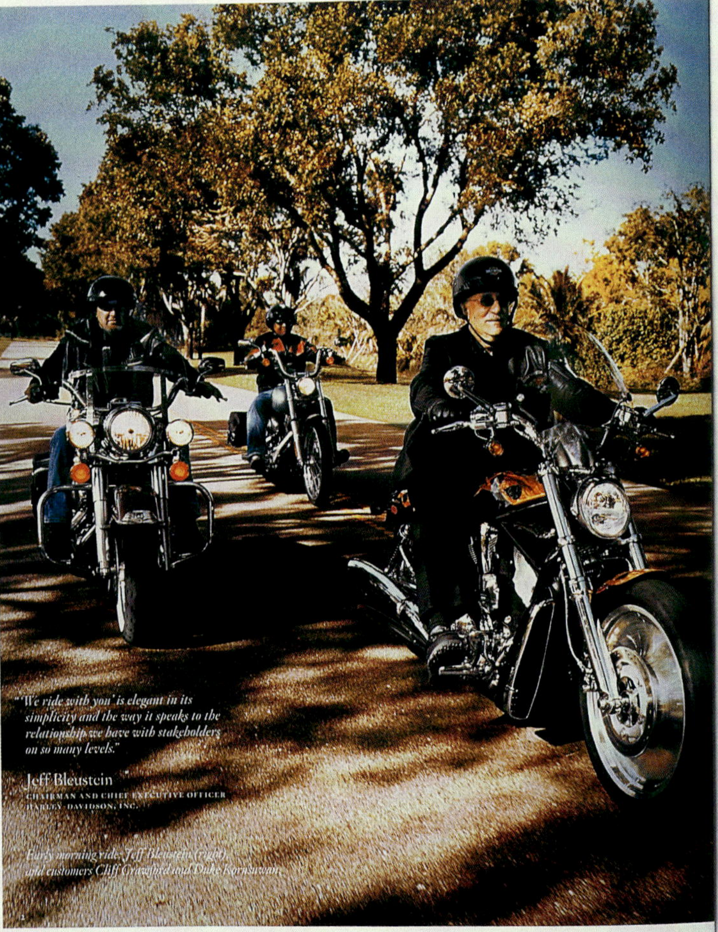

Early morning ride: Jeff Bleustein (right) and customers Cliff Crawford and Duke Kornsuwan

In the literal sense, we ride with customers at rallies and events, and out on the open road.

Beyond the literal idea that we'd rather be out there riding motorcycles than sitting in a meeting, "we ride with you" reflects our entire approach to business. It means that we do what we say we're going to do. It means that employees have opportunities for professional growth as the Company grows. When we work with suppliers to help them operate more efficiently, it means that we also help Harley-Davidson achieve its cost and supply goals. In short, "we ride with you" means that when we succeed, so do you, as customers, investors or any of our stakeholders.

Speaking of success, in 2004, Harley-Davidson, Inc. recorded its 19th consecutive year of record revenue and earnings. Consolidated revenue for the Company was $5.02 billion, an 8.5% increase over 2003, while net income was $889.8 million, a 16.9% increase over the prior year. Diluted earnings per share rose to $3.00, a 20% increase over 2003. The Company shipped 317,289 Harley-Davidson motorcycles in 2004, a 9.0% increase over 2003.

U.S. retail sales of Harley-Davidson motorcycles for 2004 grew 7.1% and the Company maintained its market share lead at 49.5% of the heavyweight motorcycle (651+cc) market. International retail sales of Harley-Davidson motorcycles grew 1.5% in 2004, compared to the prior year.

Parts & Accessories (P&A) revenue increased 9.7% to $781.6 million in 2004. Revenue from General Merchandise, which includes MotorClothes® apparel and collectibles, totaled $223.7 million, a 5.8% increase from the prior year.

Harley-Davidson Financial Services, Inc. (HDFS) recorded solid gains again in 2004. Operating income of $188.6 million increased 12.3% compared to 2003, reflecting both the quality of HDFS' product offerings and its ongoing ability to be responsive to customers' motorcycle financing and insurance needs. In 2004, HDFS made retail loans totaling $2.1 billion on more than 135,000 motorcycles, improving its share of loans for new Harley-Davidson motorcycles sold in the U.S. to 40%, compared to 38% the prior year.

Buell motorcycles had its XB12 motorcycle products in the market for the full year in 2004 and introduced the new CityX™ to strong reviews in July. Buell® XB motorcycle retail sales were up 19% on a worldwide basis, led by Europe, where Buell XB sales were up 46%.

Harley-Davidson's performance in 2004 continued to reward investors handsomely. The price of Harley-Davidson stock appreciated 27.8% and closed at $60.75 at year-end. We more than doubled the dividend payout to $119 million in 2004, including two quarterly dividend increases of 25% each. We also repurchased 10.6 million shares of Harley-Davidson stock in 2004 and the Board of Directors authorized the repurchase of an additional 20 million shares going forward.

Propelling that performance is a range of new products and initiatives that speak to our constant drive to innovate and to grow demand.

We brought eight new motorcycle models—six Harley-Davidson and two Buell models—to market in 2004, to a warm reception by customers, motorcycle magazines and dealers around the globe.

P&A introduced 1,137 new accessories in its ever-expanding array of ways for customers to customize their personal motorcycles. New riding gear and fashion apparel from the Harley-Davidson MotorClothes line underscored the positioning of General Merchandise as the fashion and function leader in motorcycling apparel.

Rider's Edge®—The Harley-Davidson Academy of Motorcycling had another great year. In 2004, 18,427 people took the Rider's Edge New Rider Course, up 30% from 2003. We believe that Rider's Edge will continue as a strong enabler for introducing customers to motorcycling and our products.

In early 2004, we articulated our belief that for the foreseeable future there is an underlying core growth rate for Harley-Davidson motorcycle sales, estimated to be in the range of 7% to 9% per year. At that time, we also expressed the view that we could sustain a mid-teens earnings growth rate, based on the 7% to 9% growth in motorcycle sales, ongoing productivity improvements in all areas of the business, as well as earnings contributions from Parts & Accessories, General Merchandise and Financial Services—all of which are experiencing the benefits of our growing base of customers.

Our 2004 results reaffirm that these performance expectations are appropriate and for 2005, we have established a goal to ship 339,000 Harley-Davidson motorcycles to dealers and distributors worldwide.

Narrowing the gap between supply and demand has been a key part of the Company's Strategic Plan for Sustainable Growth and was a major reason for the Company's capacity expansion over much of the past ten years. It has resulted in better product availability and has had the effect of beginning to normalize retail pricing. This, along with the ability of Harley-Davidson dealers to provide the close attention to customer needs that buyers of premium motorcycles expect, will all increase customer satisfaction and demand.

Consumer demand—how we create it and how we satisfy it—is the common thread in our 19-year record of performance. Going forward, we continue to ramp up product development. We are hard at work to bring exciting new products to market and to add new dimensions to the total ownership experience.

This 2004 annual report explores a sample of our approaches to preserving strong relationships with the current Harley-Davidson family and to attracting new members to that family. In it, you will hear from some of the leaders who are helping to do just that.

Whether it's ratcheting up our product development efforts, exploring new ways to provide even more great experiences for customers

or gearing up to sell our American-made motorcycles in additional markets abroad, Harley-Davidson is a company with an incessant desire and drive to go to new places—but always in a distinctly Harley-Davidson way.

As we've said many times, our employees are our most important resource and are our only sustainable long-term competitive advantage. Harley-Davidson remains a leader in providing the tools and learning opportunities that serve to develop skills and nurture talent throughout the organization, including our Union partners represented by the Paper, Allied-Industrial, Chemical and Energy Workers International Union and by the International Association of Machinists and Aerospace Workers.

I'm especially proud to report that Harley-Davidson received a prestigious Catalyst Award in 2004 for our efforts to expand the role of women in the organization, promote workplace diversity, and ensure the visibility and optimization of talent across the organization. Not only are these practices the right thing to do; they also make powerful business sense. We believe that the better our employees reflect an increasingly diverse base of customers, the more successful we will be as a company.

Harley-Davidson made *Fortune* magazine's annual "100 Best Companies to Work For" list—for the seventh time in eight years—based largely on *Fortune's* research, including employee responses to surveys. We also were deeply honored to receive a Freedom Award from the National Committee for Employer Support of the Guard and Reserve, a Department of Defense agency, in recognition of our support of employees who serve in our nation's Armed Forces.

At a leadership level, Harley-Davidson enhanced its capabilities in several areas in 2004. In November, the Company elected NAVTEQ President and CEO Judson Green to the Board of Directors. Prior to assuming the leadership of NAVTEQ in 2000, Judson was Chairman of Walt Disney Attractions, the theme park and resort segment of The Walt Disney Company, and also had served as Chief Financial Officer of The Walt Disney Company. His background makes him exceptionally well-suited to contribute in key ways to our focus on delighting customers and exceeding their expectations.

At the senior leadership level in manufacturing, Roy Coleman accepted a new role as Vice President, Advanced Operations, focusing on Operational Excellence and Rod Copes was promoted to Vice President and General Manager, Powertrain Operations at Harley-Davidson's Pilgrim Road plant. Dave Bozeman was promoted to General Manager of the Capitol Drive Powertrain Operations and Mike Heerhold was promoted to General Manager of the Company's Tomahawk Operations.

In business operations, Bill Dannehl was named Vice President, North American Sales and Dealer Services; Jon Flickinger was named President and Chief Operating Officer, Buell Motorcycle Company; John Hevey was named Vice President, Strategic Planning and New Business Development; and Lara Lee was promoted to Vice President, Destinations and Rider Services.

These moves and others throughout the Company recognize the talents and contributions of these leaders. But they also reflect Harley-Davidson's longstanding practice of building experienced leaders by providing broad growth and development opportunities.

I can think of no better example of how this leadership development process benefits investors than the Board of Directors' decision to elevate our Chief Financial Officer, Jim Ziemer, to succeed me as CEO upon my retirement from that post in April 2005, and to elect Jim to the Board. He brings to his new job a broad knowledge of the business and the enthusiastic support and trust of the entire organization. During his 35-year career with Harley-Davidson, Jim has been a key contributor to the Harley-Davidson team and I am confident he will continue to take the Company forward.

Over the 30 years that I have been a part of the Harley-Davidson family, the Company has prevailed through some trying times and has soared to heights that I could never have imagined.

As we close the 2004 chapter of the Company's epic journey, I want to thank all the members of the Harley-Davidson family for making this the great company that it is and for making 2004 another milestone. I am truly fortunate to have been at the Company during this period of time and I look forward, as continuing Chairman of the Board, to playing a role in an even brighter future.

As much as some things have changed since I first walked through the door at 3700 West Juneau Avenue in 1975, one thing hasn't. This is still a company run by people who love the product, who understand our customers and who share in a proud history. They are people who are engaged and ingrained in the experience of motorcycling and sharing it with others, and who are dedicated to keeping the products and experiences relevant to new times and changing customer desires. They are people who appreciate the importance of each Harley-Davidson stakeholder—whatever their relationship with the Company.

"We ride with you!"

Jeffrey L. Bleustein

CHAIRMAN AND CHIEF EXECUTIVE OFFICER
HARLEY-DAVIDSON, INC.

Selected Financial Data

(in thousands except per share amounts)	2004	2003	2002	2001	2000
Income statement data:					
Net revenue	$ 5,015,190	$ 4,624,274	$ 4,090,970	$ 3,406,786	$ 2,943,346
Cost of goods sold	3,115,655	2,958,708	2,673,129	2,253,815	1,979,572
Gross profit	1,899,535	1,665,566	1,417,841	1,152,971	963,774
Financial services income	305,262	279,459	211,500	181,545	140,135
Financial services expense	116,662	111,586	107,273	120,272	102,957
Operating income from financial services	188,600	167,873	104,227	61,273	37,178
Selling, administrative and engineering expense	726,644	684,175	639,366	551,743	485,980
Income from operations	1,361,491	1,149,264	882,702	662,501	514,972
Gain on sale of credit card business		—	—	—	18,915
Investment income, net	23,101	23,088	16,541	17,478	17,583
Other, net	(5,106)	(6,317)	(13,416)	(6,524)	(2,914)
Income before provision for income taxes	1,379,486	1,166,035	885,827	673,455	548,556
Provision for income taxes	489,720	405,107	305,610	235,709	200,843
Net income	$ 889,766	$ 760,928	$ 580,217	$ 437,746	$ 347,713
Weighted average common shares:					
Basic	295,008	302,271	302,297	302,506	302,691
Diluted	296,852	304,470	305,158	306,248	307,470
Earnings per common share:					
Basic	$ 3.02	$ 2.52	$ 1.92	$ 1.45	$ 1.15
Diluted	$ 3.00	$ 2.50	$ 1.90	$ 1.43	$ 1.13
Dividends paid	$ .405	$ .195	$ .135	$ .115	$ .098
Number of shareholders of record	86,329	84,987	79,420	75,235	70,942
Balance sheet data:					
Working capital	$ 2,093,576	$ 1,773,354	$ 1,076,534	$ 949,154	$ 799,521
Current finance receivables, net	1,207,124	1,001,990	855,771	656,421	530,859
Long-term finance receivables, net	905,176	735,859	589,809	379,335	234,091
Total assets	5,483,293	4,923,088	3,861,217	3,118,495	2,436,404
Current finance debt	495,441	324,305	382,579	217,051	89,509
Long-term finance debt	800,000	670,000	380,000	380,000	355,000
Total finance debt	1,295,441	994,305	762,579	597,051	444,509
Shareholders' equity	$ 3,218,471	$ 2,957,692	$ 2,232,915	$ 1,756,283	$ 1,405,655

HARLEY-DAVIDSON, INC.
Dividends per Share, 2002–2004

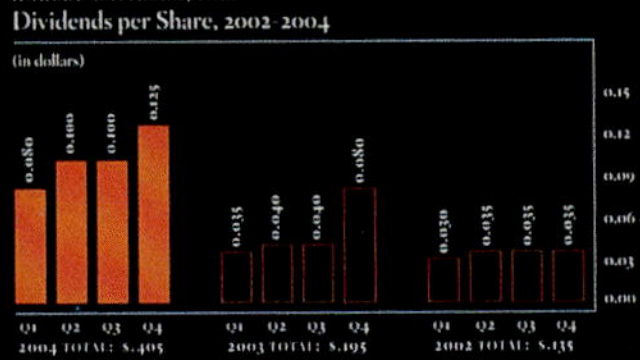

HARLEY-DAVIDSON, INC.
Common Stock Prices, 2002–2004

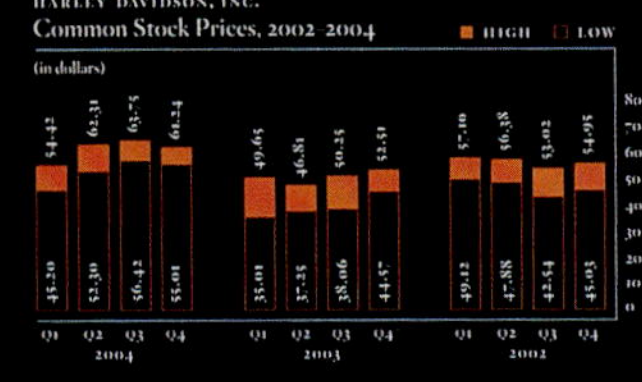

Success is a 16 year relationship based on our ability to clearly communicate the client's essence.

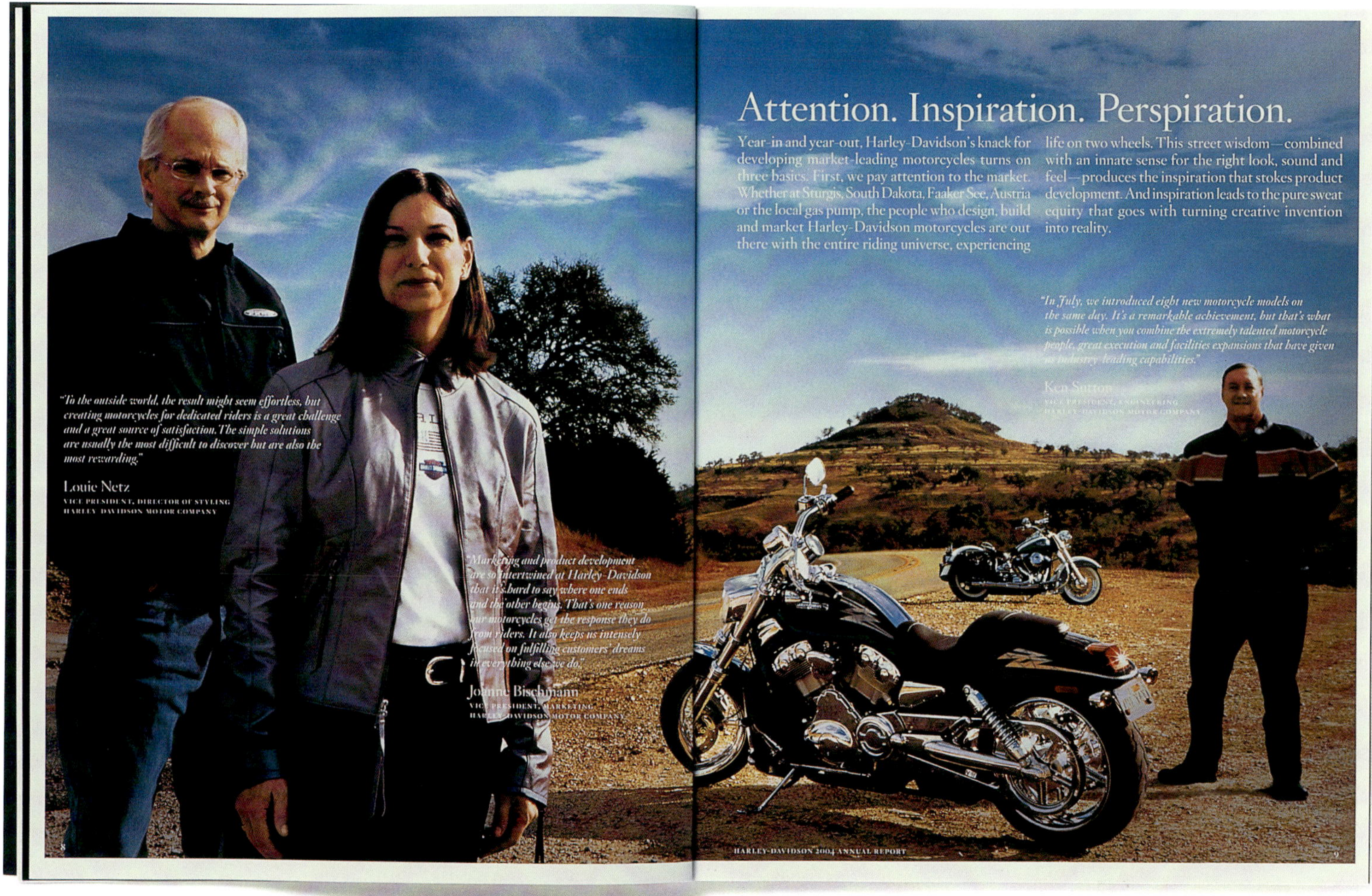

Attention. Inspiration. Perspiration.

Year-in and year-out, Harley-Davidson's knack for developing market-leading motorcycles turns on three basics. First, we pay attention to the market. Whether at Sturgis, South Dakota, Faaker See, Austria or the local gas pump, the people who design, build and market Harley-Davidson motorcycles are out there with the entire riding universe, experiencing life on two wheels. This street wisdom—combined with an innate sense for the right look, sound and feel—produces the inspiration that stokes product development. And inspiration leads to the pure sweat equity that goes with turning creative invention into reality.

"To the outside world, the result might seem effortless, but creating motorcycles for dedicated riders is a great challenge and a great source of satisfaction. The simple solutions are usually the most difficult to discover but are also the most rewarding."

Louie Netz
VICE PRESIDENT, DIRECTOR OF STYLING
HARLEY-DAVIDSON MOTOR COMPANY

"Marketing and product development are so intertwined at Harley-Davidson that it's hard to say where one ends and the other begins. That's one reason our motorcycles get the response they do from riders. It also keeps us intensely focused on fulfilling customers' dreams in everything else we do."

Joanne Bischmann
VICE PRESIDENT, MARKETING
HARLEY-DAVIDSON MOTOR COMPANY

"In July, we introduced eight new motorcycle models on the same day. It's a remarkable achievement, but that's what is possible when you combine the extremely talented motorcycle people, great execution and facilities expansions that have given us industry-leading capabilities."

Ken Sutton
VICE PRESIDENT, ENGINEERING
HARLEY-DAVIDSON MOTOR COMPANY

8 HARLEY-DAVIDSON 2004 ANNUAL REPORT 9

Life at Harley-Davidson is about great journeys, a series of touchpoints that produce inspired moments for riders and results for shareholders.

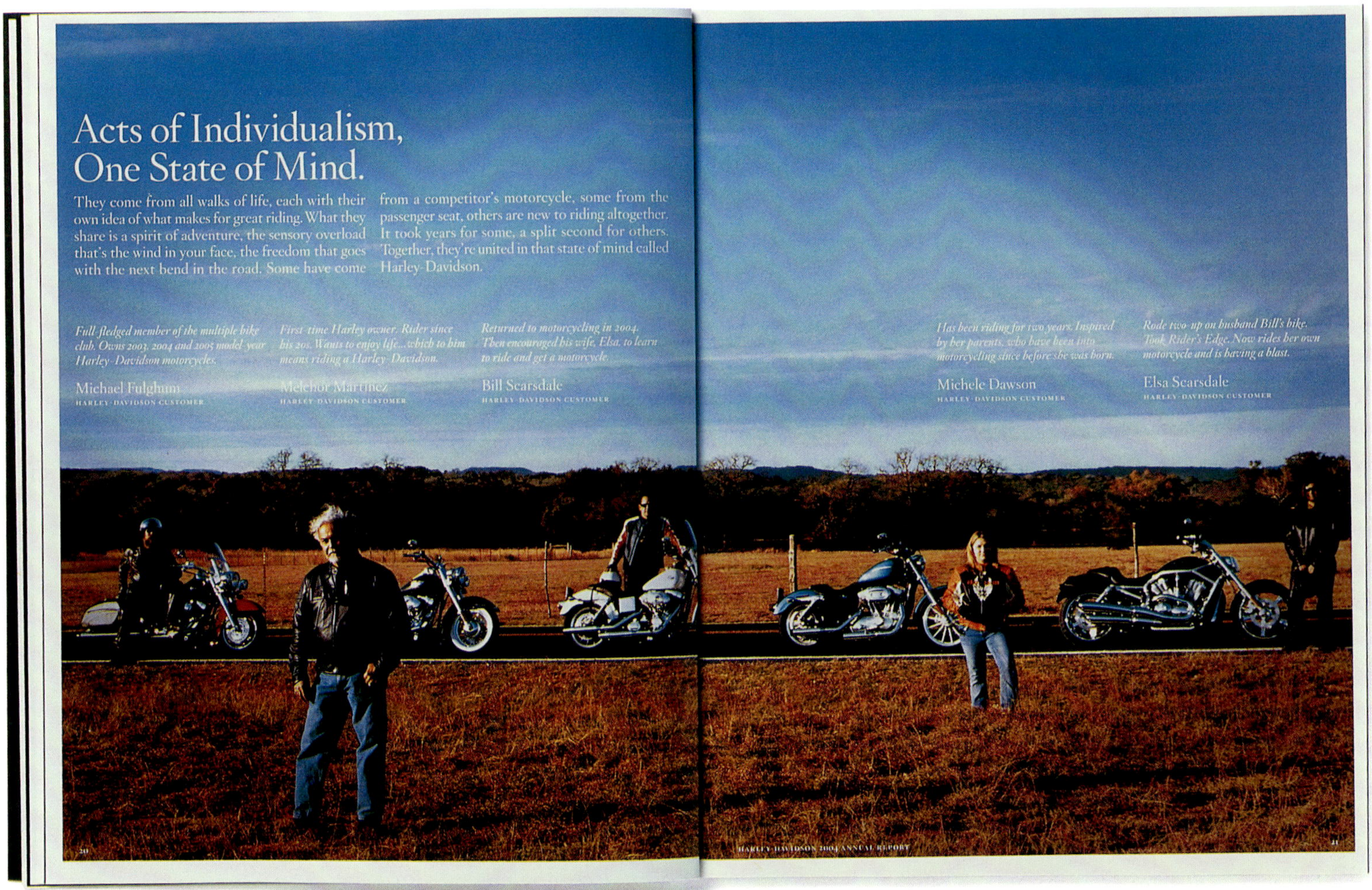

Acts of Individualism, One State of Mind.

They come from all walks of life, each with their own idea of what makes for great riding. What they share is a spirit of adventure, the sensory overload that's the wind in your face, the freedom that goes with the next bend in the road. Some have come from a competitor's motorcycle, some from the passenger seat, others are new to riding altogether. It took years for some, a split second for others. Together, they're united in that state of mind called Harley-Davidson.

Full-fledged member of the multiple bike club. Owns 2003, 2004 and 2005 model-year Harley-Davidson motorcycles.

Michael Fulgham
HARLEY-DAVIDSON CUSTOMER

First-time Harley owner. Rider since his 20s. Wants to enjoy life...which to him means riding a Harley-Davidson.

Melchor Martinez
HARLEY-DAVIDSON CUSTOMER

Returned to motorcycling in 2004. Then encouraged his wife, Elsa, to learn to ride and get a motorcycle.

Bill Scarsdale
HARLEY-DAVIDSON CUSTOMER

Has been riding for two years. Inspired by her parents, who have been into motorcycling since before she was born.

Michele Dawson
HARLEY-DAVIDSON CUSTOMER

Rode two-up on husband Bill's bike. Took Rider's Edge. Now rides her own motorcycle and is having a blast.

Elsa Scarsdale
HARLEY-DAVIDSON CUSTOMER

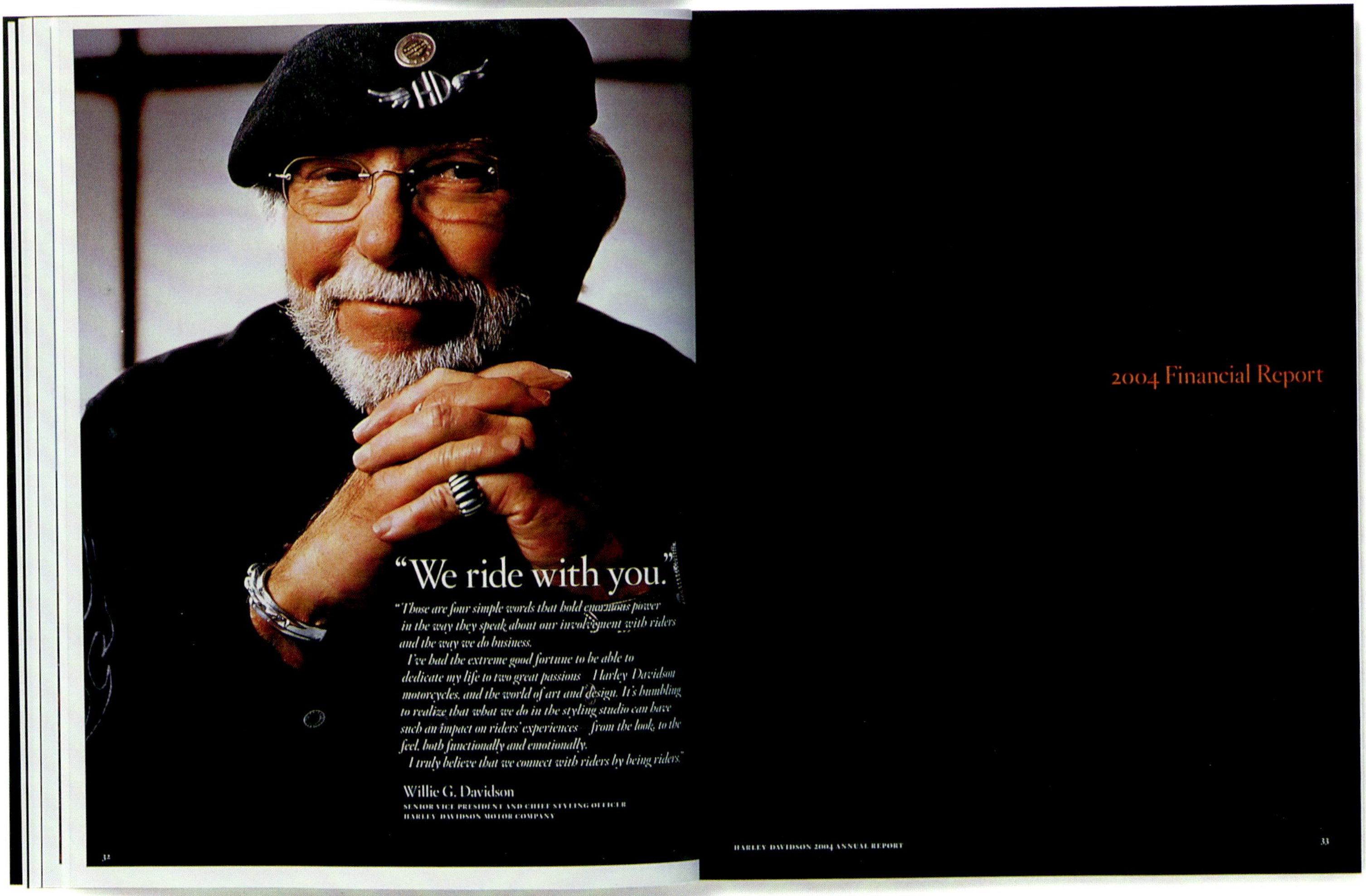

"We ride with you."

"Those are four simple words that hold enormous power in the way they speak about our involvement with riders and the way we do business.

I've had the extreme good fortune to be able to dedicate my life to two great passions – Harley-Davidson motorcycles, and the world of art and design. It's humbling to realize that what we do in the styling studio can have such an impact on riders' experiences – from the look, to the feel, both functionally and emotionally.

I truly believe that we connect with riders by being riders."

Willie G. Davidson
SENIOR VICE PRESIDENT AND CHIEF STYLING OFFICER
HARLEY-DAVIDSON MOTOR COMPANY

2004 Financial Report

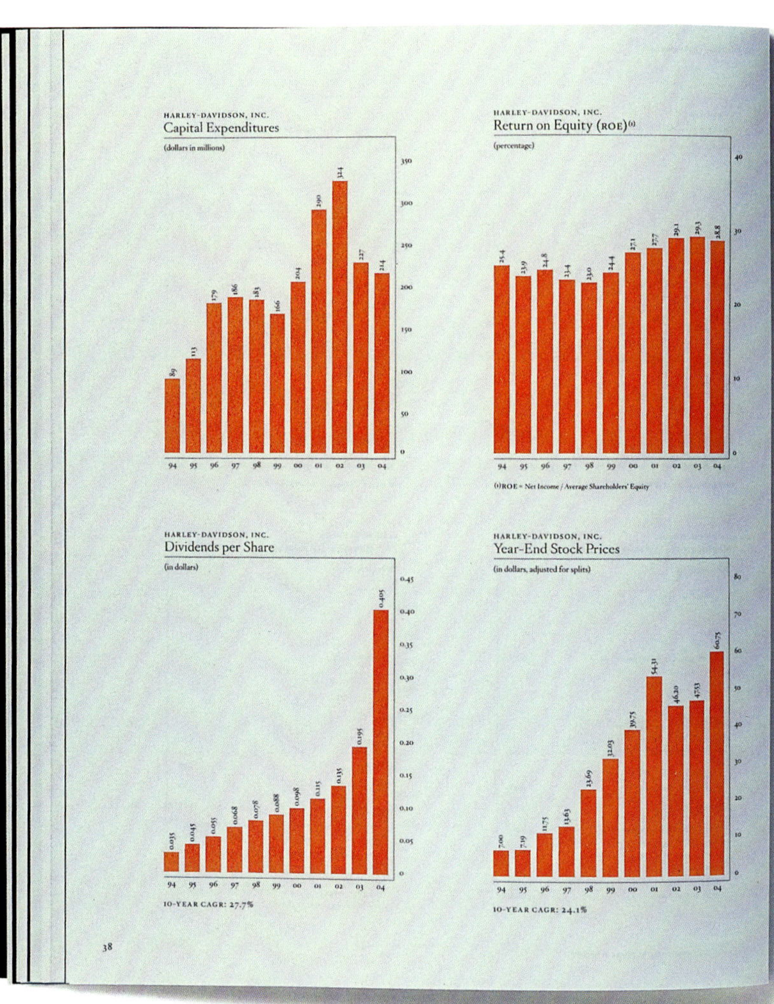

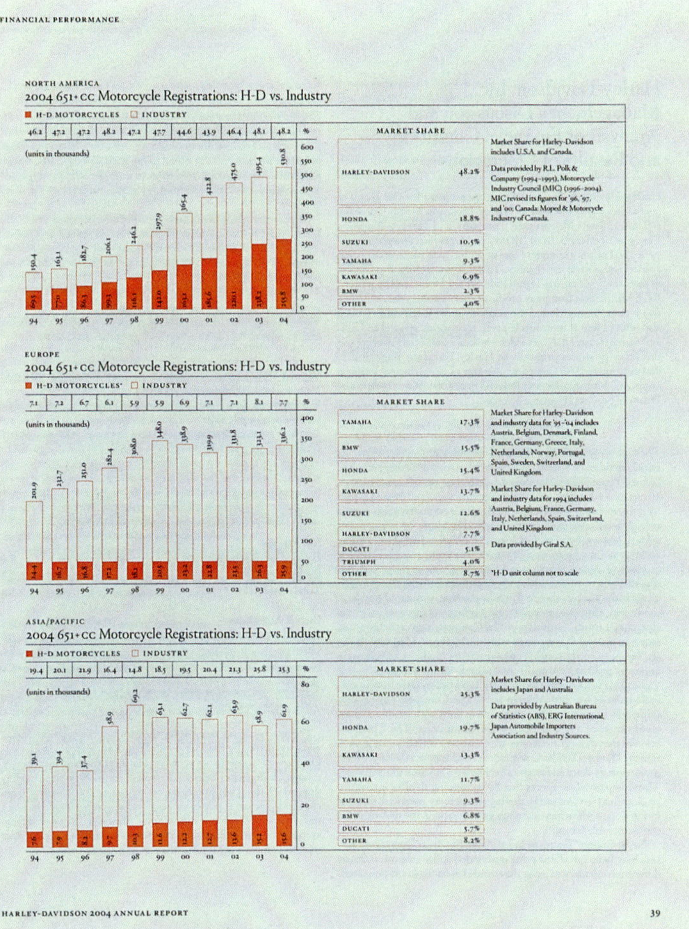

Consolidated Balance Sheets

(in thousands, except share amounts)

December 31,	2004	2003
ASSETS		
Current assets:		
Cash and cash equivalents	$ 275,159	$ 329,329
Marketable securities	1,336,909	993,331
Accounts receivable, net	121,333	112,406
Current portion of finance receivables, net	1,207,124	1,001,990
Inventories	226,893	207,726
Deferred income taxes	60,517	51,156
Prepaid expenses and other current assets	38,337	33,189
Total current assets	3,266,272	2,729,127
Finance receivables, net	905,176	735,859
Property, plant and equipment, net	1,024,665	1,046,310
Goodwill	59,456	53,678
Other assets	227,724	358,114
	$ 5,483,293	$4,923,088
LIABILITIES AND SHAREHOLDERS' EQUITY		
Current liabilities:		
Accounts payable	$ 244,202	$ 223,902
Accrued expenses and other liabilities	433,053	407,566
Current portion of finance debt	495,441	324,305
Total current liabilities	1,172,696	955,773
Finance debt	800,000	670,000
Other long-term liabilities	90,846	86,337
Postretirement healthcare benefits	149,848	127,444
Deferred income taxes	51,432	125,842
Commitments and contingencies (Note 6)		
Shareholders' equity:		
Series A Junior participating preferred stock, none issued	—	—
Common stock, 329,908,165 and 326,489,291 shares issued in 2004 and 2003, respectively	3,300	3,266
Additional paid-in capital	533,068	419,455
Retained earnings	3,844,571	3,074,037
Accumulated other comprehensive (loss) income	(12,096)	47,174
	4,368,843	3,543,932
Less:		
Treasury stock (35,597,360 and 24,978,798 shares in 2004 and 2003, respectively), at cost	(1,150,372)	(586,240)
Total shareholders' equity	3,218,471	2,957,692
	$ 5,483,293	$4,923,088

The accompanying notes are an integral part of the consolidated financial statements.

52

CONSOLIDATED STATEMENTS

Consolidated Statements of Cash Flows

(in thousands)

Years ended December 31,	2004	2003	2002
Cash flows from operating activities:			
Net income	$ 889,766	$ 760,928	$ 580,217
Adjustments to reconcile net income to net cash provided by operating activities:			
Depreciation	214,112	196,918	175,778
Provision for long-term employee benefits	62,806	76,422	57,124
Provision for finance credit losses	3,070	4,076	6,167
Gain on current year securitizations	(58,302)	(82,221)	(56,139)
Net change in wholesale finance receivables	(154,124)	(154,788)	(140,107)
Contributions to pension plans	—	(192,000)	(153,636)
Tax benefit from the exercise of stock options	51,476	13,805	14,452
Deferred income taxes	(41,513)	42,105	38,560
Other	27,301	16,051	7,057
Net changes in current assets and current liabilities	(24,866)	(18,644)	16,089
Total adjustments	79,960	(98,276)	(34,655)
Net cash provided by operating activities	969,726	662,652	545,562
Cash flows from investing activities:			
Capital expenditures	(213,550)	(227,230)	(323,866)
Finance receivables acquired or originated	(2,394,644)	(2,090,201)	(1,731,169)
Finance receivables collected	274,670	252,705	230,153
Proceeds from securitizations	1,847,895	1,724,060	1,246,262
Collection of retained securitization interests	125,732	118,113	89,970
Purchase of marketable securities	(1,091,326)	(1,538,548)	(1,508,285)
Sales and redemptions of marketable securities	742,284	1,145,000	1,253,719
Purchase of remaining interest in joint venture	(9,500)	—	—
Other, net	10,689	9,690	22,813
Net cash used in investing activities	(707,750)	(606,411)	(720,403)
Cash flows from financing activities:			
Proceeds from issuance of medium-term notes	—	399,953	—
Net increase (decrease) finance credit facilities and commercial paper	305,047	(175,835)	165,528
Dividends paid	(119,232)	(58,986)	(41,457)
Purchase of common stock for treasury	(564,132)	(103,880)	(56,814)
Issuance of common stock under employee stock option plans	62,171	19,378	12,679
Net cash (used) provided by financing activities	(316,146)	80,630	79,936
Net increase (decrease) in cash and cash equivalents	(54,170)	136,871	(94,905)
Cash and cash equivalents:			
At beginning of year	329,329	192,458	287,363
At end of year	$ 275,159	$ 329,329	$ 192,458

The accompanying notes are an integral part of the consolidated financial statements.

HARLEY-DAVIDSON 2004 ANNUAL REPORT 53

PINNACLE WEST CAPITAL CORPORATION

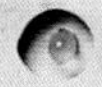

EVERY TIME
This Light Blinks…

··· 2004 ANNUAL REPORT ···

Art Directors: Mike Campbell,
Greg Fisher
Designer: GG Lemere
Printer: Prisma
Graphic Corporation
Page count: 90
Number of images: 0
Print run: 85,000
Size: 7.5" x 9.5"
Paper: cover, Mohawk
vellum 80#C, text,
Mohawk vellum 100#T,
Mohawk vellum 70#T
Client: Pinnacle
West Capital Corporation,
generates, sells, and
delivers electricity product

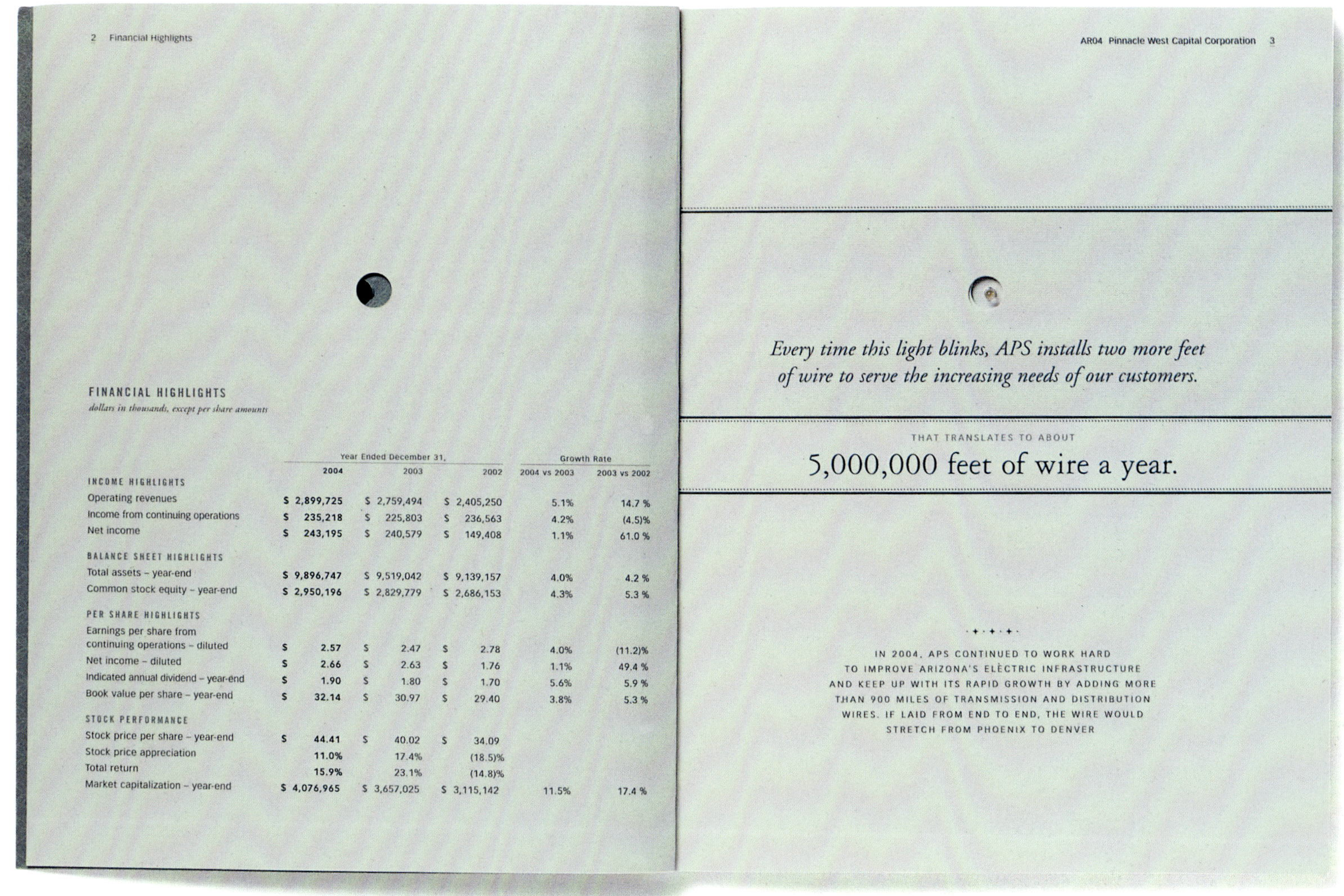

2 Financial Highlights

FINANCIAL HIGHLIGHTS

dollars in thousands, except per share amounts

	Year Ended December 31,			Growth Rate	
	2004	2003	2002	2004 vs 2003	2003 vs 2002
INCOME HIGHLIGHTS					
Operating revenues	$ 2,899,725	$ 2,759,494	$ 2,405,250	5.1%	14.7 %
Income from continuing operations	$ 235,218	$ 225,803	$ 236,563	4.2%	(4.5)%
Net income	$ 243,195	$ 240,579	$ 149,408	1.1%	61.0 %
BALANCE SHEET HIGHLIGHTS					
Total assets – year-end	$ 9,896,747	$ 9,519,042	$ 9,139,157	4.0%	4.2 %
Common stock equity – year-end	$ 2,950,196	$ 2,829,779	$ 2,686,153	4.3%	5.3 %
PER SHARE HIGHLIGHTS					
Earnings per share from continuing operations – diluted	$ 2.57	$ 2.47	$ 2.78	4.0%	(11.2)%
Net income – diluted	$ 2.66	$ 2.63	$ 1.76	1.1%	49.4 %
Indicated annual dividend – year-end	$ 1.90	$ 1.80	$ 1.70	5.6%	5.9 %
Book value per share – year-end	$ 32.14	$ 30.97	$ 29.40	3.8%	5.3 %
STOCK PERFORMANCE					
Stock price per share – year-end	$ 44.41	$ 40.02	$ 34.09		
Stock price appreciation	11.0%	17.4%	(18.5)%		
Total return	15.9%	23.1%	(14.8)%		
Market capitalization – year-end	$ 4,076,965	$ 3,657,025	$ 3,115,142	11.5%	17.4 %

AR04 Pinnacle West Capital Corporation 3

Every time this light blinks, APS installs two more feet of wire to serve the increasing needs of our customers.

THAT TRANSLATES TO ABOUT

5,000,000 feet of wire a year.

IN 2004, APS CONTINUED TO WORK HARD TO IMPROVE ARIZONA'S ELECTRIC INFRASTRUCTURE AND KEEP UP WITH ITS RAPID GROWTH BY ADDING MORE THAN 900 MILES OF TRANSMISSION AND DISTRIBUTION WIRES. IF LAID FROM END TO END, THE WIRE WOULD STRETCH FROM PHOENIX TO DENVER

Q&A with Campbell Fisher Design

What was the client's directive?

Pinnacle West Capital Corporation is a holding company for the largest electric utility in Arizona. The directive this year was to represent their accommodation of Arizona's relentless growth.

How did you define the problem?

Arizona's rapid expansion and Pinnacle West's capacity to accommodate this growth is a common concern for customers and shareholders alike.

What was the approach?

This annual takes a very direct approach by sharing the sheer numbers with the reader. The blinking light was used to illustrate that every time the light blinks, Arizona's power needs grow, and thusly, Pinnacle West is efficiently adapting to that growth.

Which disciplines or people helped you with the project?

Pinnacle West: CEO, VP of Communications, APS Advertising and Creative Services, Manager of Editorial Services. Campbell Fisher Design: Creative & Art Direction, Design, Production.

Were you happy with the result?

We were pleased with the result.

What was the client's response?

The client was excited by the fact that there was such high demand for this year's annual. They felt it clearly said their message of building infrastructure for unrelenting growth with the added benefit of the light bulb that made it more than just an informational document.

How involved was the CEO in your meetings and presentations?

Concepts were narrowed down and then presented to the CEO who ultimately chose the concept and design.

Do you feel that designers are becoming more involved in copywriting?

Yes, we work closely with the copywriter in order to create synergy between the Annual Report's financial message and the overall concept and design of the book.

How do you define success in Annual Report design?

When we can find the balance between achieving our client's goals while creating a piece that is conceptually and visually distinctive.

How important are awards to your client?

Their ultimate concern is the messaging and the relationship they are creating with their various audiences, but they always enjoy the recognition of awards.

Success for us is when we can achieve the client's goals, and also attain visual distinction.

3.7%
3.3%
3.1%
3.7%
4.1%
2004
2003
2002
2001
2000
1.3%
2004
2003
2002
2001
2000
APS
INDUSTRY NATIONAL AVERAGE

APS CUSTOMER GROWTH

Our accelerating customer growth continues at a pace three times the industry average.

Every time this light blinks, APS customers increase their peak energy demand by 130 watts.

THAT TRANSLATES TO ABOUT

350,000,000 watts a year.

IN 2005, THE PEAK ENERGY DEMAND OF OUR CUSTOMERS IS PROJECTED TO INCREASE 350 MILLION WATTS OVER 2004. THIS INCREASE REPRESENTS ENOUGH ENERGY TO SERVE THE EQUIVALENT OF 100,000 ARIZONA HOMES.

ACHIEVING EXCELLENCE

In 2004, the Palo Verde Nuclear Generating Station marked its 13th consecutive year as the nation's largest power producer of any kind.

ACCOMPLISHMENTS

- In 2004, our company reduced our number of preventable recordable injuries, breaking the previous record low and setting a new safety performance standard.
- In the last 20 years, our West Phoenix, Ocotillo and Yucca Power Plants have zero combined lost-time accidents.
- SunCor, our real estate development company, produced significant earnings again this year – contributing $45 million to the bottom line.
- For the third time in as many studies, we earned the top rating – AAA – from Innovest Strategic Value Advisors, for our environmental performance.
- In 2004, Innovest Strategic Advisors also ranked Pinnacle West as the top utility in its Intangible Value Assessment (IVA). The IVA is designed to uncover investment value potential by measuring companies in areas such as corporate governance, community outreach, labor relations and regulatory relations.

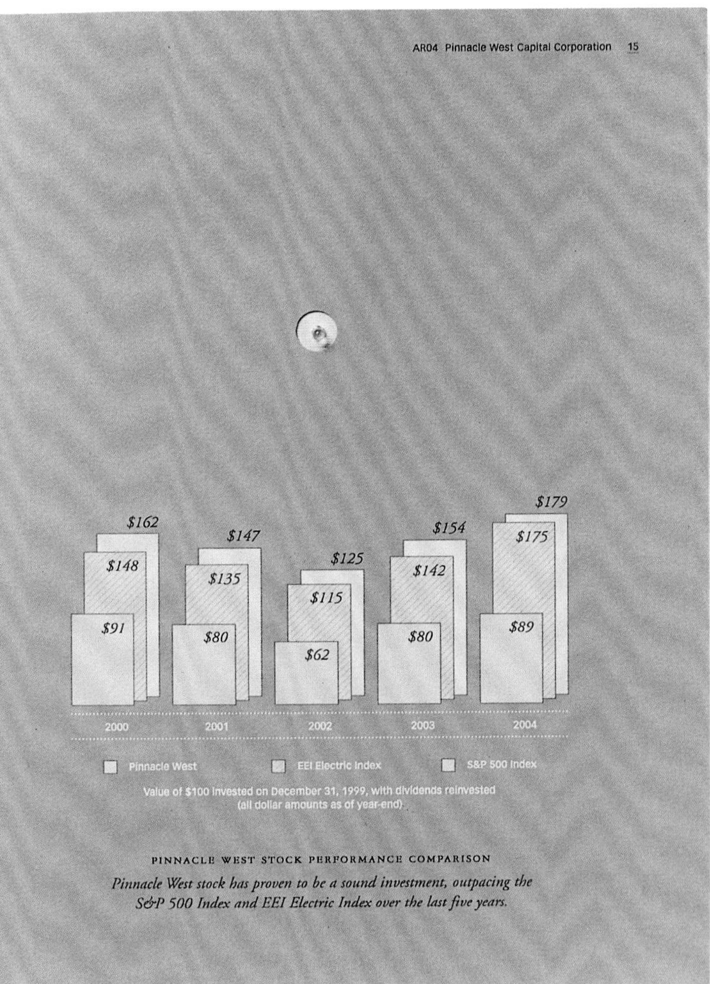

PINNACLE WEST STOCK PERFORMANCE COMPARISON

Pinnacle West stock has proven to be a sound investment, outpacing the S&P 500 Index and EEI Electric Index over the last five years.

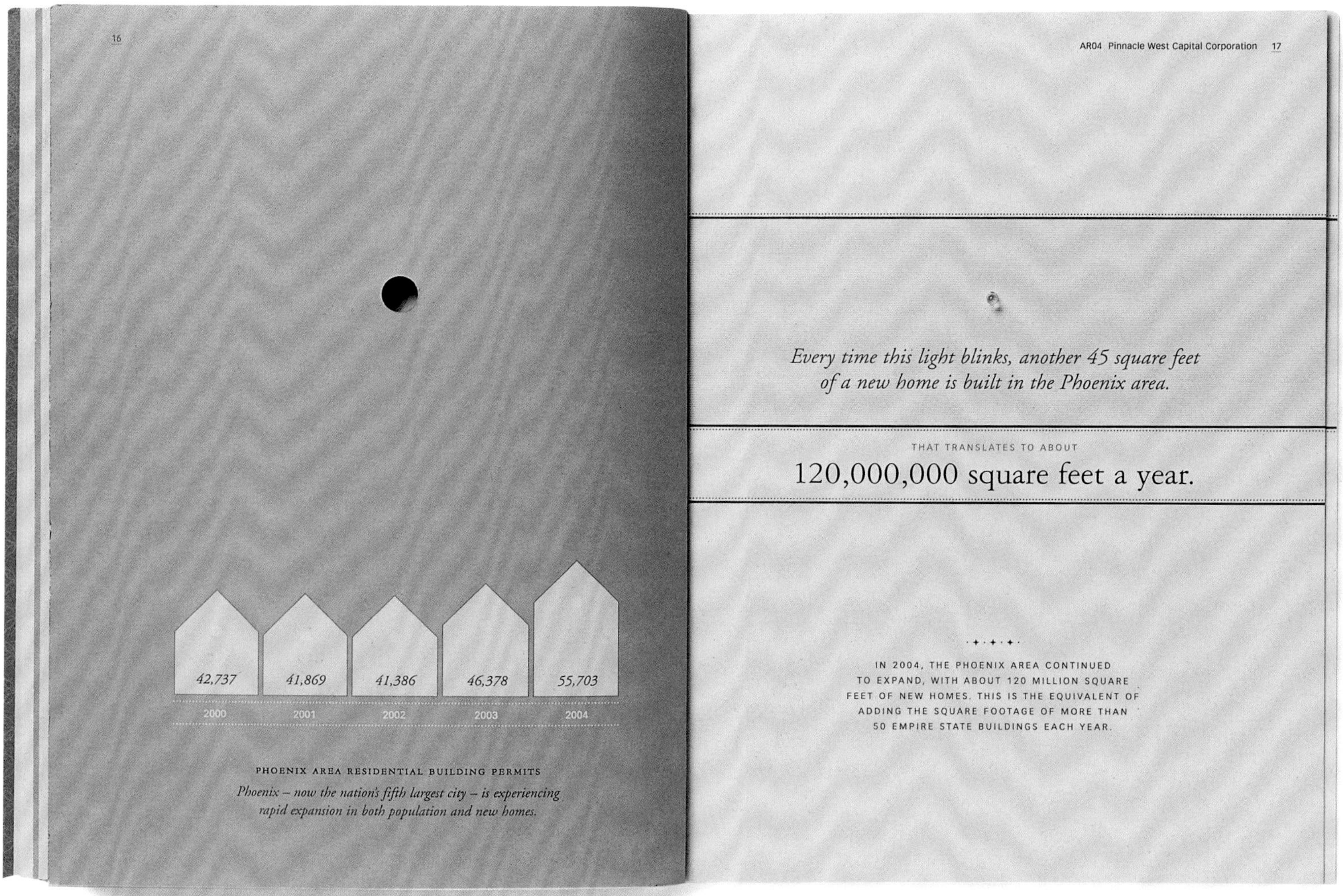

42,737 | 41,869 | 41,386 | 46,378 | 55,703
2000 | 2001 | 2002 | 2003 | 2004

PHOENIX AREA RESIDENTIAL BUILDING PERMITS

Phoenix – now the nation's fifth largest city – is experiencing rapid expansion in both population and new homes.

Every time this light blinks, another 45 square feet of a new home is built in the Phoenix area.

THAT TRANSLATES TO ABOUT

120,000,000 square feet a year.

IN 2004, THE PHOENIX AREA CONTINUED TO EXPAND, WITH ABOUT 120 MILLION SQUARE FEET OF NEW HOMES. THIS IS THE EQUIVALENT OF ADDING THE SQUARE FOOTAGE OF MORE THAN 50 EMPIRE STATE BUILDINGS EACH YEAR.

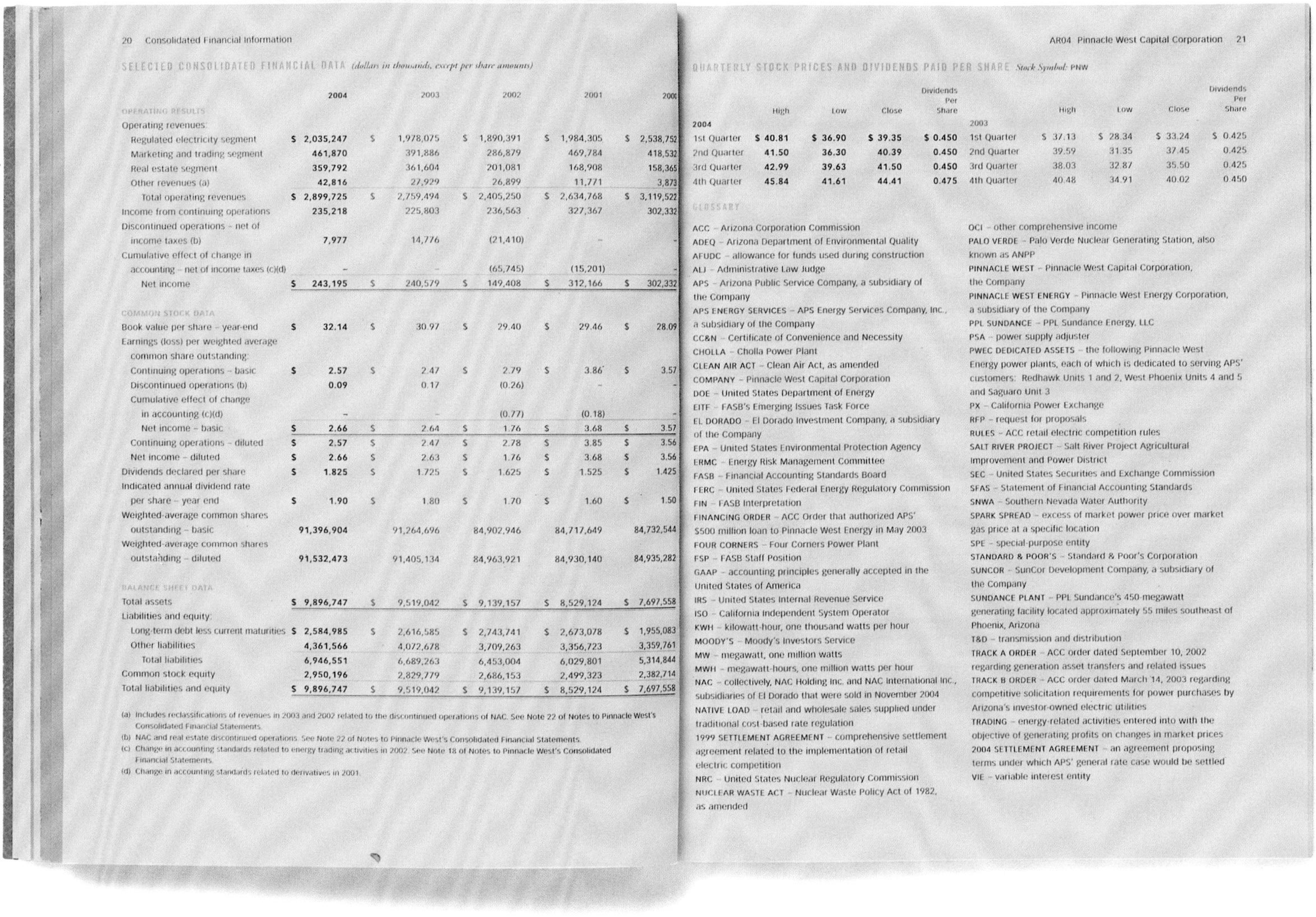

SELECTED CONSOLIDATED FINANCIAL DATA *(dollars in thousands, except per share amounts)*

	2004	2003	2002	2001	2000
OPERATING RESULTS					
Operating revenues:					
Regulated electricity segment	$ 2,035,247	$ 1,978,075	$ 1,890,391	$ 1,984,305	$ 2,538,752
Marketing and trading segment	461,870	391,886	286,879	469,784	418,532
Real estate segment	359,792	361,604	201,081	168,908	158,365
Other revenues (a)	42,816	27,929	26,899	11,771	3,873
Total operating revenues	$ 2,899,725	$ 2,759,494	$ 2,405,250	$ 2,634,768	$ 3,119,522
Income from continuing operations	235,218	225,803	236,563	327,367	302,332
Discontinued operations – net of income taxes (b)	7,977	14,776	(21,410)	–	–
Cumulative effect of change in accounting – net of income taxes (c)(d)	–	–	(65,745)	(15,201)	–
Net income	$ 243,195	$ 240,579	$ 149,408	$ 312,166	$ 302,332
COMMON STOCK DATA					
Book value per share – year-end	$ 32.14	$ 30.97	$ 29.40	$ 29.46	$ 28.09
Earnings (loss) per weighted average common share outstanding:					
Continuing operations – basic	$ 2.57	$ 2.47	$ 2.79	$ 3.86	$ 3.57
Discontinued operations (b)	0.09	0.17	(0.26)	–	–
Cumulative effect of change in accounting (c)(d)	–	–	(0.77)	(0.18)	–
Net income – basic	$ 2.66	$ 2.64	$ 1.76	$ 3.68	$ 3.57
Continuing operations – diluted	$ 2.57	$ 2.47	$ 2.78	$ 3.85	$ 3.56
Net income – diluted	$ 2.66	$ 2.63	$ 1.76	$ 3.68	$ 3.56
Dividends declared per share	$ 1.825	$ 1.725	$ 1.625	$ 1.525	$ 1.425
Indicated annual dividend rate per share – year end	$ 1.90	$ 1.80	$ 1.70	$ 1.60	$ 1.50
Weighted-average common shares outstanding – basic	91,396,904	91,264,696	84,902,946	84,717,649	84,732,544
Weighted-average common shares outstanding – diluted	91,532,473	91,405,134	84,963,921	84,930,140	84,935,282
BALANCE SHEET DATA					
Total assets	$ 9,896,747	$ 9,519,042	$ 9,139,157	$ 8,529,124	$ 7,697,558
Liabilities and equity:					
Long-term debt less current maturities	$ 2,584,985	$ 2,616,585	$ 2,743,741	$ 2,673,078	$ 1,955,083
Other liabilities	4,361,566	4,072,678	3,709,263	3,356,723	3,359,761
Total liabilities	6,946,551	6,689,263	6,453,004	6,029,801	5,314,844
Common stock equity	2,950,196	2,829,779	2,686,153	2,499,323	2,382,714
Total liabilities and equity	$ 9,896,747	$ 9,519,042	$ 9,139,157	$ 8,529,124	$ 7,697,558

(a) Includes reclassifications of revenues in 2003 and 2002 related to the discontinued operations of NAC. See Note 22 of Notes to Pinnacle West's Consolidated Financial Statements.
(b) NAC and real estate discontinued operations. See Note 22 of Notes to Pinnacle West's Consolidated Financial Statements.
(c) Change in accounting standards related to energy trading activities in 2002. See Note 18 of Notes to Pinnacle West's Consolidated Financial Statements.
(d) Change in accounting standards related to derivatives in 2001.

QUARTERLY STOCK PRICES AND DIVIDENDS PAID PER SHARE *Stock Symbol:* PNW

2004	High	Low	Close	Dividends Per Share
1st Quarter	$ 40.81	$ 36.90	$ 39.35	$ 0.450
2nd Quarter	41.50	36.30	40.39	0.450
3rd Quarter	42.99	39.63	41.50	0.450
4th Quarter	45.84	41.61	44.41	0.475

2003	High	Low	Close	Dividends Per Share
1st Quarter	$ 37.13	$ 28.34	$ 33.24	$ 0.425
2nd Quarter	39.59	31.35	37.45	0.425
3rd Quarter	38.03	32.87	35.50	0.425
4th Quarter	40.48	34.91	40.02	0.450

GLOSSARY

ACC – Arizona Corporation Commission
ADEQ – Arizona Department of Environmental Quality
AFUDC – allowance for funds used during construction
ALJ – Administrative Law Judge
APS – Arizona Public Service Company, a subsidiary of the Company
APS ENERGY SERVICES – APS Energy Services Company, Inc., a subsidiary of the Company
CC&N – Certificate of Convenience and Necessity
CHOLLA – Cholla Power Plant
CLEAN AIR ACT – Clean Air Act, as amended
COMPANY – Pinnacle West Capital Corporation
DOE – United States Department of Energy
EITF – FASB's Emerging Issues Task Force
EL DORADO – El Dorado Investment Company, a subsidiary of the Company
EPA – United States Environmental Protection Agency
ERMC – Energy Risk Management Committee
FASB – Financial Accounting Standards Board
FERC – United States Federal Energy Regulatory Commission
FIN – FASB Interpretation
FINANCING ORDER – ACC Order that authorized APS' $500 million loan to Pinnacle West Energy in May 2003
FOUR CORNERS – Four Corners Power Plant
FSP – FASB Staff Position
GAAP – accounting principles generally accepted in the United States of America
IRS – United States Internal Revenue Service
ISO – California Independent System Operator
KWH – kilowatt-hour, one thousand watts per hour
MOODY'S – Moody's Investors Service
MW – megawatt, one million watts
MWH – megawatt-hours, one million watts per hour
NAC – collectively, NAC Holding Inc. and NAC International Inc., subsidiaries of El Dorado that were sold in November 2004
NATIVE LOAD – retail and wholesale sales supplied under traditional cost-based rate regulation
1999 SETTLEMENT AGREEMENT – comprehensive settlement agreement related to the implementation of retail electric competition
NRC – United States Nuclear Regulatory Commission
NUCLEAR WASTE ACT – Nuclear Waste Policy Act of 1982, as amended
OCI – other comprehensive income
PALO VERDE – Palo Verde Nuclear Generating Station, also known as ANPP
PINNACLE WEST – Pinnacle West Capital Corporation, the Company
PINNACLE WEST ENERGY – Pinnacle West Energy Corporation, a subsidiary of the Company
PPL SUNDANCE – PPL Sundance Energy, LLC
PSA – power supply adjuster
PWEC DEDICATED ASSETS – the following Pinnacle West Energy power plants, each of which is dedicated to serving APS' customers: Redhawk Units 1 and 2, West Phoenix Units 4 and 5 and Saguaro Unit 3
PX – California Power Exchange
RFP – request for proposals
RULES – ACC retail electric competition rules
SALT RIVER PROJECT – Salt River Project Agricultural Improvement and Power District
SEC – United States Securities and Exchange Commission
SFAS – Statement of Financial Accounting Standards
SNWA – Southern Nevada Water Authority
SPARK SPREAD – excess of market power price over market gas price at a specific location
SPE – special-purpose entity
STANDARD & POOR'S – Standard & Poor's Corporation
SUNCOR – SunCor Development Company, a subsidiary of the Company
SUNDANCE PLANT – PPL Sundance's 450-megawatt generating facility located approximately 55 miles southeast of Phoenix, Arizona
T&D – transmission and distribution
TRACK A ORDER – ACC order dated September 10, 2002 regarding generation asset transfers and related issues
TRACK B ORDER – ACC order dated March 14, 2003 regarding competitive solicitation requirements for power purchases by Arizona's investor-owned electric utilities
TRADING – energy-related activities entered into with the objective of generating profits on changes in market prices
2004 SETTLEMENT AGREEMENT – an agreement proposing terms under which APS' general rate case would be settled
VIE – variable interest entity

Creative Directors Art Directors Designers Photographers Illustrators Writers

DesignFirms

Clients

DirectoryofDesignFirms

Addison
20 Exchange Place 18th Fl.
New York, NY 10005
USA
Tel 212.229.5000
Fax 212.929.3010

And Partners
158 West 27 Street 7th Fl.
New York, NY 10001
USA
Tel 212.414.4700
Fax 212.414.2915

B.I.G. Prague
Business Information
Group s.r.o. Opletalova
55 Prague, 110 00
Czech Republic
Tel +420 221 602 455
Fax +420 224 229 771

Bruketa&Zinic
Zavrtnica 17
Zagreb (Hrvatska) 10 000
Croatia
Tel +385 1 6064 000
Fax +385 1 6064 001

Campbell Fisher Design
3333 East Camelback Rd.
Suite 200
Phoenix, AZ 85018
USA
Tel 602.955.2707
Fax 602.955.2878

Clemenger BBDO
8 Kent Terrace
Wellington, New Zealand
Tel +64 4 802 3360
Fax +64 4 802 3318

DesignworksEnterpriseIG
1 Barrack Street, Level 1
Sydney NSW 2000
Australia
Tel +02 9299 8966
Fax +02 9262 6806

Eat
Gedempt Hamerkanaal
96 Amsterdam 1021kr
Netherlands
Tel +31 2049 40130

Eleven Inc.
445 Bush Street 8th Fl.
San Francisco, CA 94108
USA
Tel 415.707.1111

Fasett as
Lars Hertervigsgate 3
Stavanger 4006
Norway
Tel +47 51 84 48 00
Fax +47 51 84 48 01

GJP
154 Pearl Street
Toronto M5H 1E4
Canada
Tel 416.979.7999

KMS Team
Deroystr. 3-5
Munich Bavaria 80335
Germany
Tel +4989 490411 0
Fax +4989 490411 49

Kuhlmann Leavitt, Inc
7810 Forsyth Blvd, 2W
St. Louis, MO 63105
USA
Tel 314.725.6616

Kym Abrams Design
213 W. Institute Pl. Suite 608
Chicago, IL 60610
USA
Tel 312.654.1005

NB Studio
24 Store Street
London, London
WC1E 7Ba, UK
Tel +0207 580 9195
Fax +020 7580 9196

Nesnadny+Schwartz
10803 Magnolia Drive
Cleveland, OH 44106
USA
Tel 216.791.7721
Fax 216.791.9560

P22 type foundry
PO Box 770
Buffalo, NY 14213
USA
Tel 716.885.4490

Paragraphs Design
329 W18th Street, Suite 801
Chicago, IL 60616
USA
Tel 312.288.0200
Fax 312.828.9888

Pentagram
387 Tehama Street
San Francisco, CA 94103
USA
Tel 415.896.0499
Fax 415.541.9106

Pivot Design, Inc.
230 West Huron, 4th Fl.
Chicago, IL 60610
USA
Tel 312.787.7707

SamataMason
101 South First Street
Dundee, IL 60118
USA
Tel 847.428.8600
Fax 847.428.6564

Soapbox Design
Communications
187 King Street East 3rd Fl.
Toronto, Ontario M5A 1J5
Canada
Tel 416.920.2099
Fax 416.920.8178

Stoyan Design
2482 Newport Blvd. Suite 8
Costa Mesa, CA 92627
USA
Tel 949.631.6314
Fax 949.631.6611

Volume Design Inc
2130-B Harrison Street
San Francisco, CA 94110
USA
Tel 415.503.0800
Fax 415.503.0818

VSA Partners
1347 South State Street
Chicago, IL 60605
USA
Tel 312.427.6413

Weymouth Design
332 Congress Street 6th Fl.
Boston, MA 02210
USA
Tel 617.542.2647
Fax 617.451.6233

Graphis Annual Report Judges

2005

Dana Arnett
VSA Partners, Inc.
Chicago, Illinois.

Jill Howry
Howry Design Associates
Los Angeles

Tom Laidlaw
The Laidlaw Group
Boston, Massachusetts

Greg Samata
Samata Mason Inc.
West Dundee, Illinois

Mike Weymouth
Weymouth Design
Boston, Massachusettes

2006

Delphine Hirasuna
Hirasuna Editorial
San Francisco, California
Over the course of her career, Delphine Hirasuna has written more than 100 Annual Reports for industries ranging from forest products and banking to biotechnology and retail. Through Hirasuna Editorial, founded in 1985, she provides editorial supervision and copywriting services to corporations, Graphic Design firms and Advertising agencies throughout the US. Delphine is also the editor of the much-acclaimed @ *Issue Magazine*, sponsored by Sappi Fine Paper and Lithographix, and has previously served as editor of Fox River's *Neo* and *Apple Media Arts*. Her articles and essays on design have appeared in a number of design publications, including *Graphis*, *Communication Arts*, *Step*, and *Graphic Design America 3*.
Over the years, her projects have won dozens of national and international awards. In addition to her corporate consulting work, Delphine has co-authored several books on design and other subjects, including "TypeWise" and "Long May She Wave," with Kit Hinrichs of Pentagram. Her most recent book is "The Art of Gaman," on the arts and crafts of the Japanese American internment camps during World War II. A columnist for the two largest Japanese-American newspapers for many years and the author of a Japanese cookbook, she has been a popular guest lecturer. In 2002, she was named a laureate of the San Francisco Public Library. Prior to starting her own business, Delphine served as corporate publications manager at Potlatch Corporation, where she produced the company's award-winning Annual Report and corporate magazine. Previously, she spent ten years at Transamerica Corporation and its subsidiary, Transamerica Airlines, producing their publications. Her early career began in financial public relations and journalism, working for Ruder & Finn, the *San Francisco Chronicle Features Syndicate* and the *Lodi News-Sentinel*.

John Klotnia
Opto Design
New York, New York
John Klotnia is a co-founder of Opto Design in New York City. Opto specializes in Annual Report design, brand identity, editorial and web development for a variety of clients such as Alexandria Real Estate Equities, Inc., The New York Times Company, Rizzoli Publishing, Business-Week, New York Public Radio, Studio 360, Booz Allen Hamilton and New York University. Born in Homewood, Illinois, John received his BFA in Graphic Design from the University of Illinois, Urbana-Champaign, in 1987. In that same year, he moved to New York and joined Bonnell Design Associates. Then in 1989, John accepted a design position at Pentagram NY, where he quickly rose to become an Associate Partner working with Woody Pirtle. While there, he produced Annual Reports for United Technologies, The Rockefeller Foundation, Texaco and Nine West. In 1999, John, along with his good friend and colleague, Ron Louie, a former Pentagram designer himself and design director for New York Times Digital, opened shop in the West Village and formed Opto Design. For his design, John has been recognized by the AIGA, *Graphis*, Mead Paper, *Communication Arts*, ASME, AR100 and his work is in the permanent collection of the Library of Congress. John lives in Park Slope with his wife, Laura, and two sons, Aaron and William.

Steve Frykholm
Herman Miller
Zeeland, Michigan
After teaching in Nigeria with the US Peace Corps, Steve attended and graduated from Cranbrook Academy of Art. Furniture icon Herman Miller, Inc. then hired him to be its first internal graphic designer. For 35 years he has been largely responsible for Herman Miller's image and graphic identity, its posters, Annual Reports, and other collateral literature.

Not only has Steve received Herman Miller's highest recognition for an employee, The Carl F. Frost Award, but he has also received recognition from professional peers. His work has been published and exhibited, and he's received Gold and Silver medals, Triad awards, and Certificates of Excellence from AIGA, N.Y. Art Directors Club, American Center for Design, Mead Annual Report Show, *Communication Arts*, *Graphis*, *Creativity*, *Print*, and *ID*.

Steve and his wife, Nancy Phillips, an interior architectural designer and equestrian, live in rural Michigan where she rides dressage and he spreads manure and photographs wild flowers.

Douglas J. Oliver
Douglas Oliver Design Office
Santa Monica, California
Douglas J. Oliver is President and Chief Creative Officer of Douglas Oliver Design Office, located in Santa Monica, California. His work has been recognized by all of the major design institutions, garnering awards from *Communication Arts Design Annual*, *Graphis Annual Reports*, *The AR 100*, *Critique Magazine's* "The Big Crit," American Institute of Graphic Arts, New York Art Director's Club, The Los Angeles Art Director's Club, and The Western Art Director's Club. His work is also part of the Permanent Design Collection of the Library of Congress.

The consistent excellence of Doug's design of Annual Reports also made him a perenial favorite in the prestigious Mead Annual Report Show. His Annuals were chosen among the best for 15 consecutive years, until the Mead Show came to an end in 2001.

He began his professional career in Los Angeles, working with the legendary James Cross and the late Robert Miles Runyan, who is often called the "father of the modern Annual Report." In 1983, Doug opened his own studio to design for Fortune 500 companies, major universities, institutions and foundations across the US, Europe and Japan.

Over the years, Doug has remained active in the larger design community. In 1998, he served as Chair of The Annual Report Design Conference held at the World Trade Center in New York City. More recently, he returned to his alma mater, the University of Kansas, as a Hallmark Symposium speaker. He has also maintained close ties with Art Center, serving as an alumni board member, teacher, guest speaker and consultant. In 2004, Doug was one of a handful of graphic designers included in Art Center's "Design Impact," which detailed the contributions of Art Center alumni over the past 75 years.

Gilmar Wendt
SAS
London, England
Born in Berlin to an East-German father and a West-German mother, Gilmar Wendt studied Graphic Design with Hans Peter Willberg and Olaf Leu in Mainz, Germany, before joining Groothuis+Malsy in Bremen. At G+M he designed over 100 books and jackets, and was responsible for the multi award-winning books of the DuMont Literatur Publishing House. He quickly progressed from designer to Art Director as G+M became one of the top ten creative agencies in Germany.

In 1999 he followed his girlfriend Christine to London and joined SAS. SAS has been going for 16 years, helping its various blue-chip clients communicate more effectively with their investors, business customers and employees. Gilmar became SAS's Creative Director in 2003, Christine's husband in 2004, and a shareholding partner in 2005.

His Annual Report clients include Ericsson, MFI furniture Group, BBA, Lonmin, ScottishPower and Sainsburys.Gilmar has won numerous industry awards. Some of them are TDC, ADC New York and Germany, *Graphis Annual Reports*, *The Black Book*, British Design and Art Direction (D&AD), *Design Week*, Red-Dot and Best German Books.

Gilmar regularly gives workshops and lectures at colleges. He is a Fellow and council member of the International Society of Typographic Designers and a member of D&AD.

Graphis Professional Books
Available at your local bookstore or
www.graphis.com

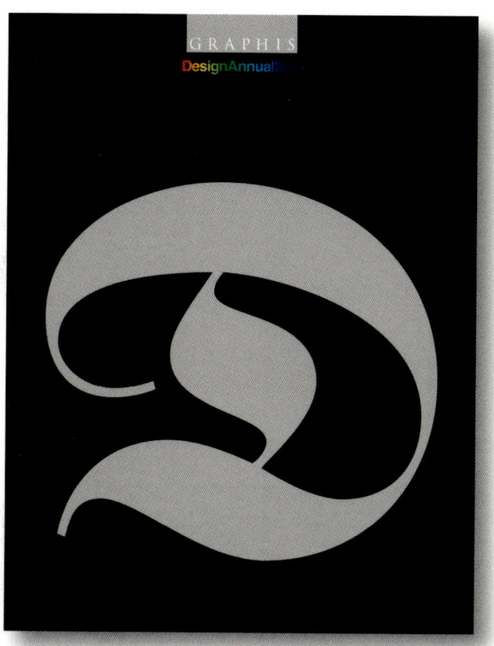
GRAPHIS
DesignAnnual

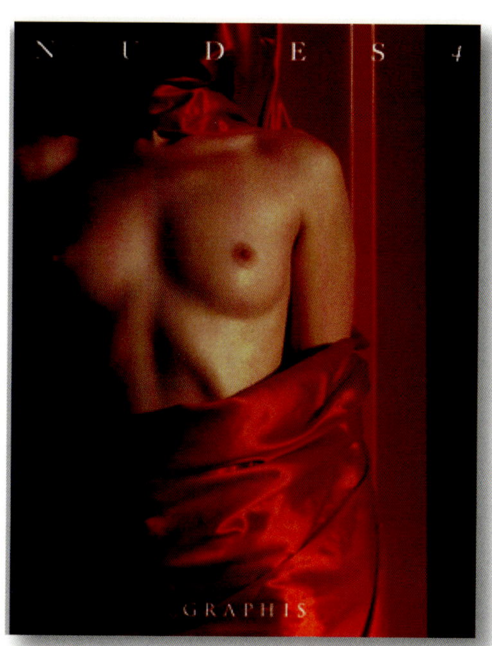
N U D E S 4
GRAPHIS

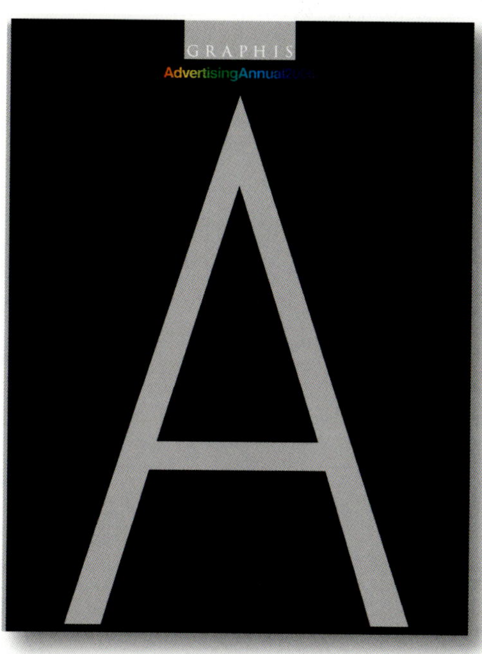
GRAPHIS
AdvertisingAnnual

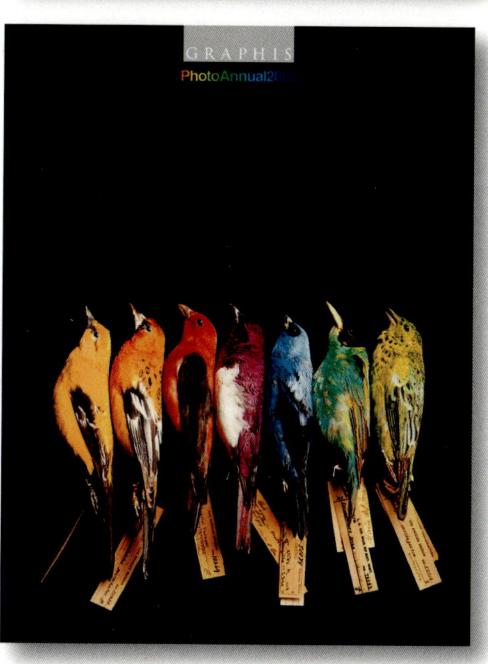
GRAPHIS
PhotoAnnual

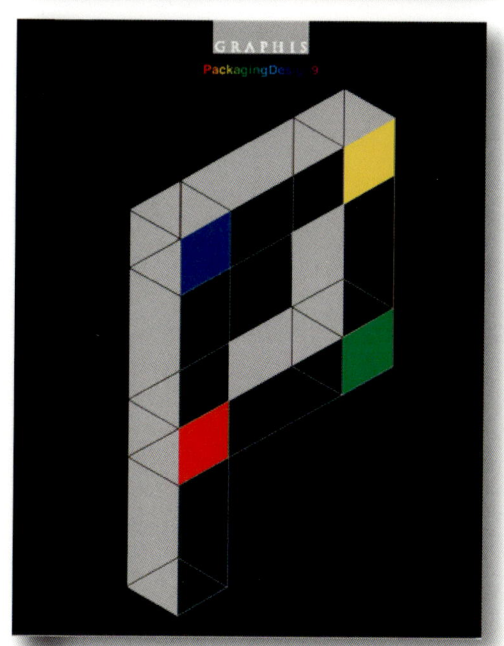
GRAPHIS

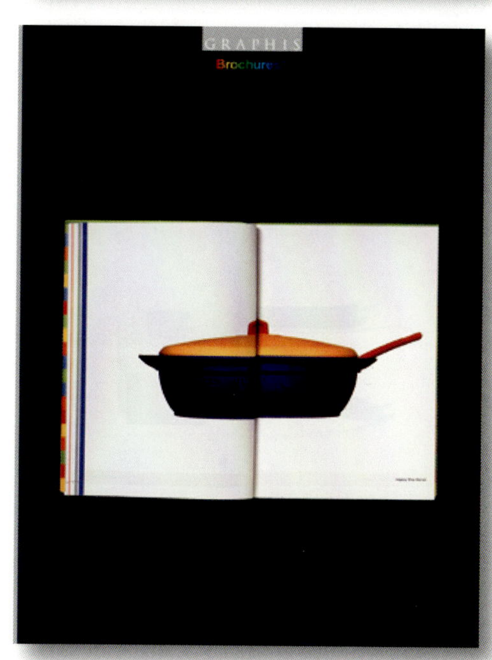
GRAPHIS

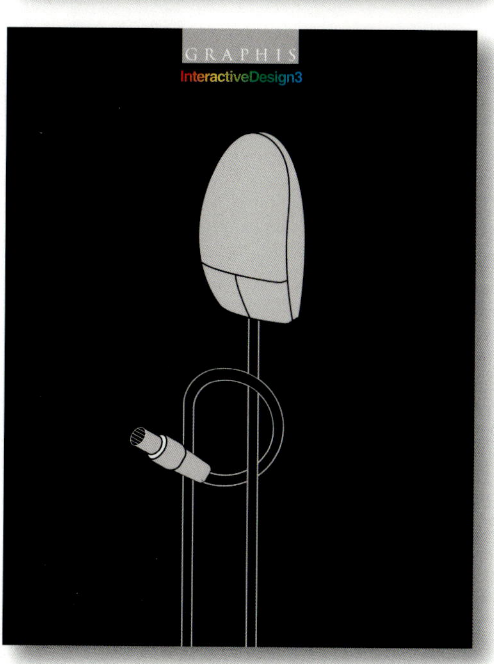
GRAPHIS
InteractiveDesign3

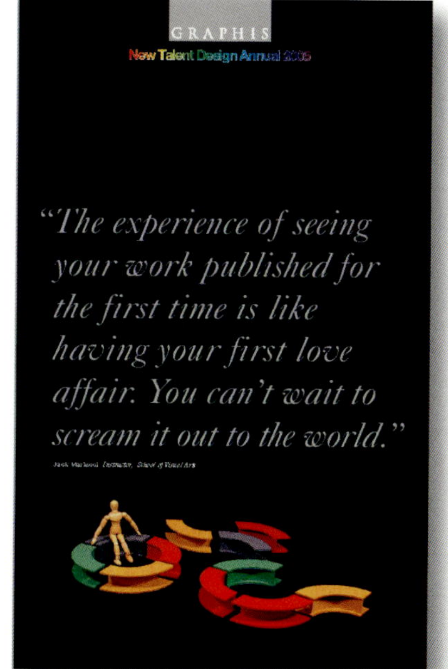
GRAPHIS
New Talent Design Annual
"The experience of seeing your work published for the first time is like having your first love affair. You can't wait to scream it out to the world."

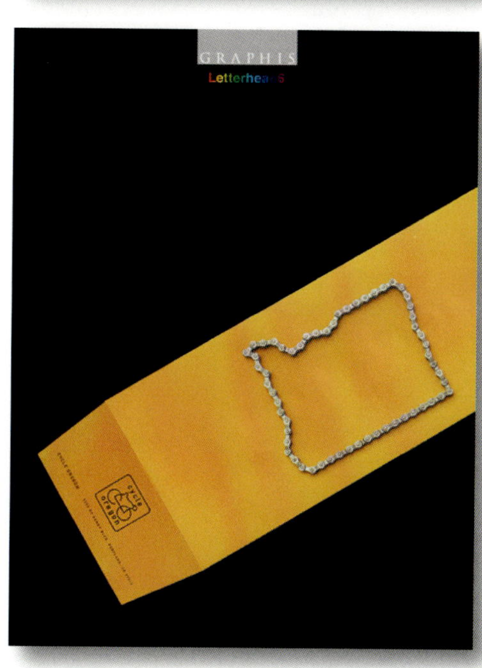
GRAPHIS

Graphis

Advertising

Graphis

Photography

Graphis

THE BEST IN THE AMERICAS

Design&Art

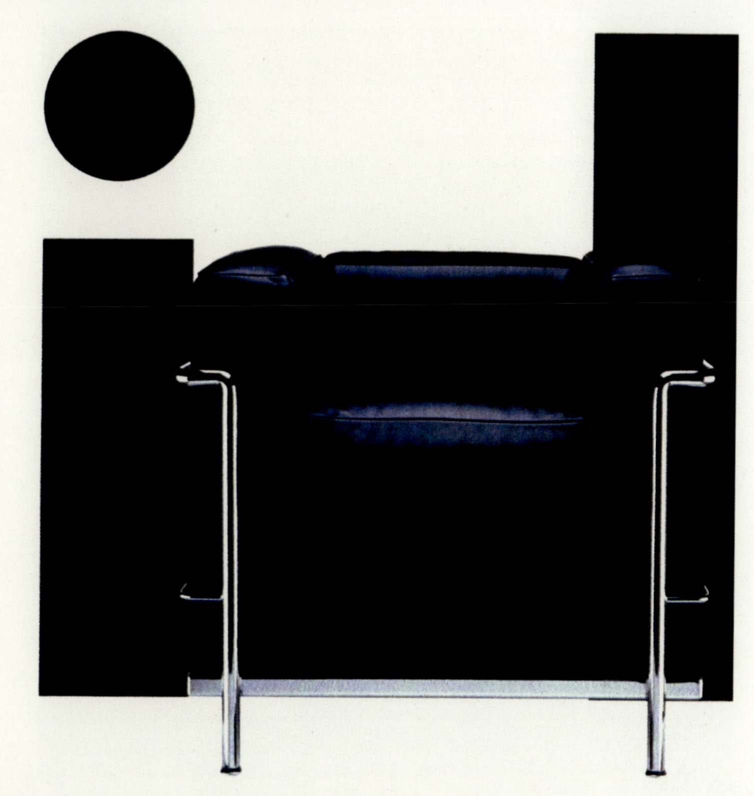